THE
AMERICAN
PAST—*Conflicting*
Interpretations of
the Great Issues

VOLUME **I**

VOLUME **I**

Edited by **Sidney Fine** and **Gerald S. Brown**

The University of Michigan

THE
AMERICAN
PAST–*Conflicting*
Interpretations of
the Great Issues

Fourth Edition

Macmillan Publishing Co., Inc.
NEW YORK

Copyright © 1976, Macmillan Publishing Co., Inc.

Printed in the United States of America

Earlier editions © 1961 and copyright © 1965 and 1970 by Macmillan Publishing Co., Inc.

Macmillan Publishing Co., Inc.
866 Third Avenue, New York, New York 10022

Collier Macmillan Canada, Ltd.

Library of Congress Cataloging in Publication Data

Fine, Sidney, (date)   ed.
  The American past.

    1. United States—History—Addresses, essays,
lectures. 2. United States—History—Philosophy—
Addresses, essays, lectures. I. Brown, Gerald Saxon,
ed. II. Title.
E178.6.F523 1976   973   75–2200
ISBN 0–02–337531–0 (v. 1)

Printing: 1 2 3 4 5 6 7 8   Year: 6 7 8 9 0 1

To Jean and Dorothy

Preface

The editors have been gratified at the reception accorded the previous editions of *The American Past* by both teachers and students. This fourth edition, like its predecessors, has three main features: It brings into sharp focus the major issues of the American past; it presents conflicting interpretations of these issues; and it draws for its selections upon historical literature that is often relatively inaccessible to the college student. The literature presented here is taken from the professional historical journals, from periodicals of a more general nature, and from monographs and other works. Each of the items selected, in the editors' view, makes a distinct, individual contribution to our knowledge of a controversial historical problem.

For each of the great issues selected, two historians present either directly conflicting interpretations or interpretations that illuminate the whole problem from complementary, but essentially different, approaches or emphases. Each historian is represented by a substantial piece of writing within the limits of which he or she could, so to speak, move around and develop an interpretation in some depth and with the degree of sophistication that characterizes the mature writing of history. The editors have deliberately avoided the snippets and shreds and the *mélange* of primary and secondary materials that so often typify volumes of this kind. It is hoped that it is history with style and meaning that is presented here.

Selections in Volume I, edited by Gerald S. Brown, pertain to the period before 1865; selections in Volume II, edited by Sidney Fine, pertain to the years since then. The two volumes are designed to supplement the textbook and the lectures in the survey course in American history. Each pair of selections is preceded by a brief introduction that places the two interpretations in their historical and historiographical setting and points up the nature of the conflict between them.

A quarter of the selections in this edition are new. In the years since the third edition was published, the writing of American history has gone on apace, and the present edition reflects some of the directions this writing has taken. The events since the publication of the previous edition have made Americans more conscious of and sensitive to the nature of their historical past; the new material in this edition reveals how American historians have attempted to make this past meaningful and relevant. The dialectical approach that characterized the earlier editions has been continued, but it is hoped that the dialectic has been sharpened.

S. F.

G. S. B.

Contents

I *The Puritan State and Puritan Society:*
Perry Miller Versus the Revisionists   *1*

"The Puritan State and Puritan Society"
—*Perry Miller*   *7*
from *Errand into the Wilderness*

"American Puritan Studies in the 1960's"
—*Michael McGiffert*   *19*
from *William and Mary Quarterly*

II *Democracy in Colonial America: Fact or*
Fiction?   *45*

"Middle-Class Democracy and the Revolution in
Massachusetts, 1691–1780"
—*Robert E. Brown*   *47*
from *Middle-Class Democracy and the Revolution in*
Massachusetts, 1691–1780

"Historians and the Problem of Early American
Democracy"
—*J. R. Pole*   *54*
from *American Historical Review*

III *The British Empire Before the American Revolution: English Whigs Versus American Whigs*   ·75

"The Fulfilment of Legislative Power"
—*Jack Richon Pole*   78
from *Political Representation in England and the Origins of the American Republic*

"The Role of the Lower Houses of Assembly in Eighteenth-Century Politics"
—*Jack P. Greene*   88
from *Journal of Southern History*

IV *The Relevance of Mr. Jefferson: To the Kennedy–Johnson Era; To the Nixon Era*   109

"The Relevance of Mr. Jefferson"
—*Dumas Malone*   112
from *Virginia Quarterly Review*

"Presidential Leadership and National Unity: The Jefferson Example
—*Dumas Malone*   124
from *Journal of Southern History*

V *1776 and 1976: New Directions or Conservative Continuations?*   137

"Republicanism and Radicalism in the American Revolution: An Old-Fashioned Interpretation"
—*Cecelia M. Kenyon*   140
from *William and Mary Quarterly*

"Revolution and the Political Integration of the Enslaved and Disenfranchised"
—*Gordon S. Wood*   165
from the *American Enterprise Institute's Distinguished Lecture Series on the American Bicentennial*

VI *The Confederation Period: Federalist (Radical) Versus Nationalist (Conservative)*   *179*

"The Confederation Period: Perspectives and
Significance"
—*Merrill Jensen*   *181*
from *The New Nation; A History of the United States During
the Confederation Period, 1781–1789*

"The Confederation Period and the American Historian"
—*Richard B. Morris*   *192*
from *William and Mary Quarterly*

VII *The Constitution: Economic Determinism
or Eighteenth-Century Political Theory?*   *209*

"An Economic Interpretation of the Constitution of the
United States"
—*Charles A. Beard*   *212*
from *An Economic Interpretation of the Constitution of the
United States*

" 'That Politics May Be Reduced to a Science': David
Hume, James Madison, and the Tenth 'Federalist' "
—*Douglass Adair*   *228*
from *Huntington Library Quarterly*

VIII *Alexander Hamilton: Realist or Idealist?*   *243*

"The Controversial Mr. Hamilton"
—*Saul K. Padover*   *245*
from *The Mind of Alexander Hamilton*

"Alexander Hamilton: Rousseau of the Right"
—*Cecelia M. Kenyon*   *265*
from *Political Science Quarterly*

IX *The War of 1812: The Issues Versus the Consequences*   *281*

"This Unnatural War"
—*Bradford Perkins*
from *Prologue to War*   *284*

"Dissent in the War of 1812"
—*Samuel Eliot Morison*
from *Dissent in Three American Wars*   *299*

X *The American West as Symbol and Myth: Poetic Inspiration or Pragmatic Perspective?*   *313*

"The Agricultural West in Literature"
—*Henry Nash Smith*
from *Virgin Land: The American West as Symbol and Myth*   *316*

"The Frontier West as Image of American Society, 1776–1860"
—*Rush Welter*
from *Pacific Northwest Quarterly*   *349*

XI *Slavery: The Tannenbaum–Elkins Interpretation Versus More Recent Research*   *361*

"Interpretations of Slavery: The Slave Status in the Americas"
—*Arnold A. Sio*
from *Comparative Studies in Society and History*   *365*

"Slavery in Brazil and the United States: An Essay in Comparative History"
—*Carl N. Degler*
from *American Historical Review*   *384*

XII *The Middle Period in American History: The Age of Jackson Versus the Age of Egalitarianism*   413

"The Jacksonians, 1829–1841"
—*Bray Hammond*   416
from *Banks and Politics in America from the Revolution to the Civil War*

"Jacksonian Democracy: Concept or Fiction?"
—*Lee Benson*   441
from *The Concept of Jacksonian Democracy: New York as a Test Case*

XIII *John C. Calhoun: Philosopher of Liberty or Marx of the Master Class?*   451

"A Footnote on John C. Calhoun"
—*Ralph Henry Gabriel*   454
from *The Course of American Democratic Thought*

"John C. Calhoun: The Marx of the Master Class"
—*Richard Hofstadter*   460
from *The American Political Tradition*

XIV *Manifest Destiny: A Mystique or an Extension of the Area of Freedom?*   481

"Build Thee More Stately Mansions"
—*Bernard DeVoto*   483
from *The Year of Decision: 1846*

"Extension of the Area of Freedom"
—*Albert K. Weinberg*   507
from *Manifest Destiny: A Study of Nationalist Expansionism in American History*

XV The Thrust of Abraham Lincoln: Toward the American Nation or Toward the American Dream?

533

"The Nationalism of Abraham Lincoln"
—*James A. Rawley*
from *Civil War History*

536

"Watchman, What of the Night?"
—*G. S. Boritt*
from "Lincoln and the Economics of the American Dream"
from a forthcoming book

551

XVI The American Civil War: The Last Capitalist Revolution Versus the Slave South

563

"The American Civil War: The Last Capitalist Revolution"
—*Barrington Moore, Jr.*
from *Social Origins of Dictatorship and Democracy: Lord and Peasant in the Modern World*

567

"The Slave South: An Interpretation"
—*Eugene D. Genovese*
from *The Political Economy of Slavery: Studies in the Economy and Society of the Slave South*

600

THE
AMERICAN
PAST—*Conflicting*
Interpretations of
the Great Issues

VOLUME I

The Puritan State and Puritan Society: Perry Miller Versus the Revisionists

Introduction The interpretation of the Puritan State and Puritan Society, like the interpretation of history in general, has an evolutionary and changeful character. In the 1920's and 1930's H. L. Mencken in a popular sense and James Truslow Adams in a scholarly sense—and, to a degree, following the judgment of a descendant of Puritan stock of an earlier generation, Charles Francis Adams—viewed the rule of the Puritan Oligarchy in a most unsympathetic manner. Adams wrote: "As a period it was singularly barren and almost inconceivably somber."[1] *Puritan* and *Puritanism* became pejorative terms. In later critiques Kenneth Ballard Murdock, Samuel Eliot Morison, and Perry Miller struck a new tone. Morison wrote: "Now all my studies of early New England go to prove that there was no 'glacial' period; that interest in literature and scholarship grew rather than diminished during the entire course of the seventeenth century; that the dominant Puritan clergy, far from being indifferent to culture and hostile to science as the Adams school briskly asserted, did everything possible to stimulate, promote, and even produce intellectual activity. Moreover, it was largely the clergy who persuaded a poor and struggling people to set up schools and a college which continued to serve the community in later generations."[2] Perry Miller himself, writing in 1956 and referring to his own work and that of his "senior" colleagues Murdock and Morison, stated, with the true confidence and humility of the scholar: "I suppose the saddest comment I can make upon the whole enterprise is that, after three decades of endeavor, though we have shaken a few complacencies, we have not arrived at the comprehensive understanding we presumptuously proposed. Hence the exaltation I feel at seeing young scholars—notably Edmund S. Morgan and Bernard Bailyn—coming so grandly along."[3]

Perry Miller is a magisterial figure in the scholarly effort to fix the place of the Puritans and the Puritan Way in our historical literature. His studies are full and broad across the whole field. He is represented below by his "piece"[4] (Miller's own language) "The Puritan State and Puritan Society," originally written as a preface for a section of an earlier work, *The Puritans* (1938), which he and Thomas H. Johnson edited. Because in its present form the accompanying texts of *The Puritans* are omitted, Miller states, ". . . I have rewritten the concluding paragraphs in order to indicate briefly the evolutionary thesis that was implicit in the extracts themselves."

Here is a key interpretative passage of Miller's "piece":

There was, it is true, a strong element of individualism in the Puritan creed; every man had to work out his own salvation, each soul had to face

---

[1] Charles Francis Adams, *Massachusetts: Its Historians and Its History* (1893), p. 64.
[2] Samuel Eliot Morison, *The Intellectual Life of Colonial New England* (1956), p. vi.
[3] Perry Miller, *Errand into the Wilderness* (1964), pp. viii–ix.   [4] *Ibid.*, pp. ix–x.

his maker alone. But at the same time, the Puritan philosophy demanded that in society all men, at least all regenerate men, be marshaled into one united array. The lone horseman, the single trapper, the solitary hunter was not a figure of the Puritan frontier; Puritans moved in groups and towns, settled in whole communities, and maintained firm government over all units. Neither were the individualistic business man, the shopkeeper who seized every opportunity to enlarge his profits, the speculator who contrived to gain wealth at the expense of his fellows, neither were these typical figures of the original Puritan society. Puritan opinion was at the opposite pole from Jefferson's feeling that the best government governs as little as possible. The theorists of New England thought of society as a unit, bound together by inviolable ties; they thought of it not as an aggregation of individuals but as an organism, functioning for a definite purpose, with all parts subordinate to the whole, all members contributing a definite share, every person occupying a particular status. "Society in all sorts of humane affaires is better than Solitariness," said John Cotton. The society of early New England was decidedly "regimented." Puritans did not think that the state was merely an umpire, standing on the side lines of a contest, limited to checking egregious fouls but otherwise allowing men free play according to their abilities and the breaks of the game. They would have expected laissez faire to result in a reign of rapine and horror. The state to them was an active instrument of leadership, discipline, and wherever necessary, of coercion; it legislated over any or all aspects of human behavior, it not merely regulated misconduct but undertook to inspire and direct all conduct. The commanders were not to trim their policies by the desires of the people, but to drive ahead upon the predetermined course; the people were all to turn out as they were ordered, and together they were to crowd sail to the full capacity of the vessel. The officers were above the common men, as the quarter-deck is above the forecastle. There was no idea of the equality of all men.

Michael McGiffert, in the essay reprinted here states his case clearly: "It is the intent of this paper to give an account, with some commentary, of trends in the study of seventeenth century New England Puritanism, focusing on the scholarship of the 1960's and paying particular regard to the work that has been done since the death of Perry Miller in 1963." McGiffert finds that historians of Puritanism and the Puritans in the 1960's have three major criticisms of Miller's work: that Miller perceived, on the great scale, a monolithic character in seventeenth century Puritanism, whereas Puritanism was strikingly pluralistic; that Miller adopted ". . . a version of the idea of declension" (defined in a footnote favorable to Miller by one of McGiffert's correspondents as "changing and adapting . . . not necessarily declining") which in reality was only ". . . the distressed clerical fancy of the later Mathers and their woeful colleagues"; and finally that Miller's definition of Puritanism is defective.

In a final assessment McGiffert concludes: "At present Puritan and New England historiography is remarkable more for vitality than for coherence. This may signify an impending change of paradigm, yet, as Kuhn points out paradigm revolutions cannot occur unless and until an alternative paradigm is available to replace the outworn one—and that is very far from the present case in Puritan studies. Nor is it probable that the revolution will happen soon: the distintegration of Miller's hegemony has not gone far enough for reintegration to be, at this point, either meaningful or plausible. For the present one must be content to observe so many good scholars, some established, some rising all to borrow an avuncular phrase from Perry Miller '. . . coming so grandly along'."

Professor McGiffert has asked me to include this addendum to my Introduction and I gladly comply.

Contributions to Puritan studies in the 1970's have gone far toward fulfilling the promise of the previous decade. The investigation of Puritan typology, for example, has been especially fruitful, as Sacvan Bercovitch's edition of essays, Typology and Early American Literature *(1972), demonstrates. Inquiries into the mystical and mythical dimensions of Puritan piety are being vigorously pursued, and interest in the theology of the covenant and of conversion continues to be active. Recent studies have also deepened our appreciation of the millennial ardor that fired the founders of New England. (For a stimulating interpretation of Puritan millennialism see J. F. Maclear, "New England and the Fifth Monarchy,"* William and Mary Quarterly, *XXXII [1975], containing copious bibliographical references.) Current literary scholarship—slighted in my article for lack of space—confirms the assertion that "that field is a rich one" (see, for example, the impressive bibliography in Bercovitch, ed.,* The American Puritan Imagination: Essays in Revaluation *[1974]), while its quality belies my worry lest the field's "fertility be impaired by over-cultivation."*

The following monographs, all but one of them published in the early 1970's, furnish convincing evidence of the remarkable durability and variety of Puritan studies: T. H. Breen, The Character of the Good Ruler: Puritan Political Ideas in New England, 1630–1730 *(1970); Stephen Foster,* Their Solitary Way: The Puritan Social Ethic in the First Century of Settlement in New England *(1971); David D. Hall,* The Faithful Shepherd: A History of the New England Ministry in the Seventeenth Century *(1972); E. Brooks Holifield,* The Covenant Sealed: The Development of Puritan Sacramental Theology in Old and New England, 1570–1720 *(1974); James W. Jones,* The Shattered Synthesis: New England Puritanism before the Great Awakening *(1973); Robert Middlekauff,* The Mathers: Three Generations of Puritan Intellectuals, 1596–1728 *(1971); Robert G. Pope,* The Half-Way Covenant: Church Membership in Puritan New England *(1969); Darrett B. Rutman,* American Puritanism: Faith and Practice *(1970); Larzer Ziff,* Puritanism in America: New Culture in a New World *(1973). See also the long essay by Sacvan Bercovitch, "Horologicals to Chronometricals: The Rhetoric of the Jeremiad," in Eric Rothstein, ed.,* Literary Monographs, III (University of Wisconsin Press, 1970). Most of these writings are the products of* *younger men, and it is interesting to note that several of them (Breen, Foster, Hall, Holifield, Middlekauff, Pope) took their doctoral degrees at Yale University where they came under the influence and inspiration of Edmund S. Morgan, Sydney E. Ahlstrom, and other senior scholars.*

In addition to improving our understanding of Puritan thought—and feeling—challenging, refining, or amending the masterwork of Perry Miller—much of this new scholarship consciously addresses the problem of relating ideas to actions in the context of seventeenth-century New England. In describing Puritanism as a "culture," for example, Larzer Ziff undertakes "to synthesize the special concerns of intellectual, social, and economic history into a single account. . . ." Similarly, observing that "two schools of thought have grown up, one devoted to New England as a Puritan idea, *the other devoted to the study of New England as a* society, *each tending to be oblivious of the other," Darrett Rutman introduces his* American Puritanism *as an attempt "to bridge the gap between these schools." These efforts at synthesis have been greatly advanced—indeed, have been necessitated—by the publication in the 1970s of several important studies in the social history of early New England, written by scholars who apply the techniques of intensive demographic and quantitative analysis to particular communities and to institutions such as the family. Some of this work was cited in my article, but most of it had not yet appeared in book form when the article was written.*

Nineteen-seventy was the banner year, when the emergence of the new "school" of social history was signaled by the publication of four major studies: John Demos, A Little Commonwealth: Family Life in Plymouth Colony; *Philip J. Greven, Jr.,* Four Generations: Population, Land, and Family in Colonial Andover, Massachusetts; *Kenneth A. Lockridge,* A New England Town, The First Hundred Years: Dedham, Massachusetts, 1636–1736; *and Michael Zuckerman,* Peaceable Kingdoms: New England Towns in the Eighteenth Century. *To these titles should be added Paul Boyer and Stephen Nissenbaum,* Salem Possessed: The Social Origins of Witchcraft *(1974).*

These and other pioneering studies, including a large number of articles in scholarly journals, are providing the "detailed, sophisticated history of colonial society" that, as Bernard Bailyn noted in 1954, was not available to Miller. To my embarrassment they make clear that my 1970 assessment of their tendencies—"the social historians seem to be discovering that life in New England was from the outset more democratic, more diverse, and more fluid than one would be led to conclude from the prescriptions of Winthrop's Arbella *sermon"—was not only misleading but vacuous. More competent appraisals will be found in Richard S. Dunn, "The Social History of Early New England,"* American Quarterly, *XXIV (1972), 661–679; Rhys Isaac, "Order and Growth, Authority and*

Meaning in Colonial New England," American Historical Review, *LXXVI (1971), 728–737; John M. Murrin, review essay in* History and Theory, *XI (1972), 266–275; and John J. Waters, "From Democracy to Demography: Recent Historiography on the New England Towns," in Alden T. Vaughan and George A. Billias, eds.,* Perspectives on Early American History *(1973), 229–249.*

Although I stand happily corrected in regard to the bearings of the social historiography of early New England, in other respects I would not modify the main emphases of "Puritan Studies in the 1960's" were I to bring the article up to date. Subject to speculation is the question whether the next few years may complete the "paradigm revolution" that the 1960's initiated. The great business of that revolution is still to bring intellectual history, social history, and literary history into synthesis. Yet much remains to be done before a fresh synthesis can be accomplished, especially along the lines of social history where the work to date, while it has generated much new knowledge, is fragmentary and the findings are by no means wholly consistent.

Institute of Early American History and Culture   MICHAEL MCGIFFERT
Williamsburg, Virginia
September 1974

The Puritan State
and Puritan Society
——*Perry Miller*

[A short two decades ago, the effort to expound Puritan political doctrine put upon the conscientious historian an obligation to make painfully clear that it was not at all "liberal." There was then an obstinate holdover from the myth constructed by patriotic orators of the nineteenth century, by filial pietists who were determined to find in the Puritans prophets of the American Constitution and of the Bill of Rights. Hence it was natural for students of the sources to insist upon the authoritarian, the totalitarian elements in a complex and sophisticated philosophy.

With the change that has supposedly come over the ruling temper of the nation, the temptation becomes exactly contrary: to dwell upon the inherent individualism, the respect for private conscience, the implications of revolution, nurtured by the Puritan doctrine.

From neither resistance to the *Zeitgeist* will come more than a partial apprehension of the reality. This article was originally written as preface to a chapter of selections of political utterances in *The Puritans*, which Thomas H. Johnson and I edited in 1938. That volume, having served its purpose, is now out of print, but students have asked me to salvage this discourse. Since it is now unsupported by accompanying texts, I have rewritten the concluding paragraps in order to indicate, briefly, the evolutionary thesis that was implicit in the extracts themselves.]

It has often been said that the end of the seventeenth and the beginning of the eighteenth century mark the first real break with the Middle Ages in the history of European thought. Even though the Renaissance and Reformation transformed many aspects of the Western intellect, still it was not until the time of Newton that the modern scientific era began; only then could men commence to regard life in this world as something more than preparation for life beyond the grave. Certainly if the eighteenth century inaugurated the modern epoch in natural sciences, so also did it in the political and social sciences. For the first time since the fall of the Roman Empire religion could be separated from politics, doctrinal ortho-

Reprinted by permission of the publishers from Perry Miller, *Errand into the Wilderness*, Cambridge, Mass.: The Belknap Press of Harvard University Press, pp. 141–152. Copyright, 1956, by the President and Fellows of Harvard College.

doxy divorced from loyalty to the state, and the citizens of a nation be permitted to worship in diverse churches and to believe different creeds without endangering the public peace. Various factors contributed to effecting this revolution; the triumph of scientific method and of rationalism made impossible the older belief that government was of divine origin; the rise of capitalism, of the middle class, and eventually of democracy, necessitated new conceptions of the role of the state. Social leadership in England and America was assumed by a group of gentlemen who were, by and large, deists or skeptics, and to them all religious issues had become supremely boring. At the same time the churches themselves, particularly the newer evangelical denominations, were swinging round to a theology that made religious belief the subjective experience of individual men, entirely unrelated to any particular poltical philosophy or social theory.

In order to understand Puritanism we must go behind these eighteenth-century developments to an age when the unity of religion and politics was so axiomatic that very few men would even have grasped the idea that church and state could be distinct. For the Puritan mind it was not possible to segregate a man's spiritual life from his communal life. Massachusetts was settled for religious reasons, but as John Winthrop announced, religious reasons included "a due forme of Government both ciuill and ecclesiasticall," and the civil was quite as important in his eyes as the ecclesiastical. Only in recent years has it become possible for us to view the political aspects of Puritanism with something like comprehension and justice. For two centuries our social thinking has been dominated by ideas that were generated in the course of a sweeping revolt against everything for which the Puritans stood; the political beliefs of the Puritans were forgotten, or, if remembered at all, either deplored or condemned as unfortunate remnants of medievalism. Puritanism has been viewed mainly as a religious and ethical movement. But of late years the standards of the eighteenth century have for the first time come under serious criticism and in many quarters are showing the strain. In few circumstances the social philosophy of Puritanism takes on a new interest, and quite possibly becomes for us the most instructive and valuable portion of the Puritan heritage.

The Puritan theory of the state began with the hypothesis of original sin. Had Adam transmitted undiminished to his descendants the image of God in which he had been created, no government would ever have been necessary among men; they would all then have done justice to each other without the supervision of a judge, they would have respected each other's rights without the intervention of a policeman. But the Bible said —and experience proved—that since the Fall, without the policeman, the judge, the jail, the law, and the magistrate, men will rob, murder, and fight among themselves; without a coercive state to restrain evil impulses and administer punishments, no life will be safe, no property secure, no honor observed. Therefore, upon Adam's apostasy, God Himself instituted governments among men. He left the particular form to be determined by circumstance—this was one important human art on which the Puritans said the Bible was *not* an absolute and imperious lawgiver but He enacted that all men should be under some sort of corporate rule, that they should all submit to the sway of their superiors, that no man should live apart from his fellows, that the government should have full power to enforce obedience and to inflict every punishment that the crimes of men deserved.

There was, it is true, a strong element of individualism in the Puritan creed; every man had to work out his own salvation, each soul had to face his maker alone. But at the same time, the Puritan philosophy demanded that in society all men, at least all regenerate men, be marshaled into one united array. The lone horseman, the single trapper, the solitary hunter was not a figure of the Puritan frontier; Puritans moved in groups and towns, settled in whole communities, and maintained firm government over all units. Neither were the individualistic business man, the shopkeeper who seized every opportunity to enlarge his profits, the speculator who contrived to gain wealth at the expense of his fellows, neither were these typical figures of the original Puritan society. Puritan opinion was at the opposite pole from Jefferson's feeling that the best government governs as little as possible. The theorists of New England thought of society as a unit, bound together by inviolable ties; they thought of it not as an aggregation of individuals but as an organism, functioning for a definite purpose, with all parts subordinate to the whole, all members contributing a definite share, every person occupying a particular status. "Society in all sorts of humane affaires is better than Solitariness," said John Cotton. The society of early New England was decidedly "regimented." Puritans did not think that the state was merely an umpire, standing on the side lines of a contest, limited to checking egregious fouls but otherwise allowing men free play according to their abilities and the breaks of the game. They would have expected *laissez faire* to result in a reign of rapine and horror. The state to them was an active instrument of leadership, discipline, and, wherever necessary, of coercion; it legislated over any or all aspects of human behavior, it not merely regulated misconduct but undertook to inspire and direct all conduct. The commanders were not to trim their policies by the desires of the people, but to drive ahead upon the predetermined course; the people were all to turn out as they were ordered, and together they were to crowd sail to the full capacity of the vessel. The officers were above the common men, as the quarter-deck is above the forecastle. There was no idea of the equality of all men. There was no questioning that men who would not serve the purposes of the society should be whipped into line. The objectives were clear and unmistakable; any one's disinclination to dedicate himself to them was obviously so much recalcitrancy and depravity. The government of Massachusetts, and of Connecticut as well, was a dictatorship, and never pretended to be anything else; it was a dictatorship, not of a single tyrant, or of an economic class, or of a political faction, but of the holy and regenerate. Those who did not hold with the ideals entertained by the righteous, or who believed God had preached other principles, or who desired that in religious belief, morality, and ecclesiastical preferences all men should be left at liberty to do as they wished—such persons had every liberty, as Nathaniel Ward said, to stay away from New England. If they did come, they were expected to keep their opinions to themselves; if they discussed them in public or attempted to act upon them, they were exiled; if they persisted in returning, they were cast out again; if they still came back, as did four Quakers, they were hanged on Boston Common. And from the Puritan point of view, it was good riddance.

These views of the nature and function of the state were not peculiar to the Puritans of New England; they were the heritage of the past, the ideals, if not always the actuality, of the previous centuries. That government was established by God in order to save depraved men from their own depravity had been orthodox Christian teaching for centuries; that men should be arranged in serried ranks, inferiors obeying superiors, was the essence of feudalism; that men should live a social life, that profit-making should be restrained within the limits of the "just price," that the welfare of the whole took precedence over any individual advantage, was the doctrine of the medieval church, and of the Church of England in the early seventeenth century. Furthermore, in addition to these general principles, there were two or three more doctrines in the New England philosophy which also were common to the age and the background: all the world at that moment believed with them that the church was to be maintained and protected by the civil authority, and a certain part of the world was contending that government must be limited by fundamental law and that it takes its origin from the consent of the people.

Every respectable state in the Western world assumed that it could allow only one church to exist within its borders, that every citizen should be compelled to attend it and conform to its requirements, and that all inhabitants should pay taxes for its support. When the Puritans came to New England the idea had not yet dawned that a government could safely permit several creeds to exist side by side within the confines of a single nation. They had not been fighting in England for any milk-and-water toleration, and had they been offered such religious freedom as dissenters now enjoy in Great Britain they would have scorned to accept the terms. Only a hypocrite, a person who did not really believe what he professed, would be content to practice his religion under those conditions. The Puritans were assured that they alone knew the exact truth, as it was contained in the written word of God, and they were fighting to enthrone it in England and to extirpate utterly and mercilessly all other pretended versions of Christianity. When they could not succeed at home, they came to America, where they could establish a society in which the one and only truth should reign forever. There is nothing so idle as to praise the Puritans for being in any sense conscious or deliberate pioneers of religious liberty—unless, indeed, it is still more idle to berate them because in America they persecuted dissenters for their beliefs after themselves had undergone persecution for differing with the bishops. To allow no dissent from the truth was exactly the reason they had come to America. They maintained here precisely what they had maintained in England, and if they exiled, fined, jailed, whipped, or hanged those who disagreed with them in New England, they would have done the same thing in England could they have secured the power. It is almost pathetic to trace the puzzlement of New England leaders at the end of the seventeenth century, when the idea of toleration was becoming more and more respectable in European thought. They could hardly understand what was happening in the world, and they could not for a long time be persuaded that they had any reason to be ashamed of their record of so many Quakers whipped, blasphemers punished by the amputation of ears, Antinomians exiled, Anabaptists fined, or witches executed. By all the lights which had prevailed in Europe at the time the Puritans had left, these were achievements to which any government could point with pride. In 1681 a congregation of Anabaptists, who led a stormy and precarious existence for several years in Charlestown, published an attack upon the government of Massachusetts Bay; they justified themselves by appealing to the example of the first settlers, claiming that like themselves the founders had been nonconformists and had fled to New England to establish a refuge for persecuted consciences. When Samuel Willard, minister of the Third Church in Boston, read this, he could hardly believe his eyes; he hastened to assure the authors that they did not know what they were talking about:

> I perceive they are mistaken in the design of our first Planters, whose business was not Toleration; but were professed Enemies of it, and could leave the World professing they *died no Libertines*. Their business was to settle, and (as much as in them lay) secure Religion to Posterity, according to that way which they believed was of God.

For the pamphlet in which Willard penned these lines Increase Mather wrote an approving preface. Forty years later, he and his son Cotton participated in the ordination of a Baptist minister in Boston, and he then preached on the need for harmony between differing sects. But by that time much water had gone under the bridge, the old charter had been revoked, there was danger that the Church of England might be made the established church of the colonies, theology had come to be of less importance in men's minds than morality, the tone of the eighteenth century was beginning to influence opinion—even in Boston. Increase was old and weary. Puritanism, in the true sense of the word, was dead.

Of course, the whole Puritan philosophy of church and state rested upon the assumption that the Word of God was clear and explicit, that the divines had interpreted it correctly, and that no one who was not either a knave or fool could deny their demonstrations. *Ergo*, it seemed plain, those who did deny them should be punished for being obstinate. John Cotton said that offenders should not be disciplined for their wrong opinions, but for persisting in them; he said that Roger Williams was turned out of Massachusetts not for his conscience but for sinning against his own conscience. Roger Williams and John Cotton debated the question of "persecution" through several hundred pages; after they had finished, I think it is very doubtful whether Cotton had even begun to see his adversary's point. And still today it is hard to make clear the exact grounds upon which Roger Williams became the great apostle of religious liberty. Williams was not, like Thomas Jefferson, a man to whom theology and divine grace had become stuff and nonsense; on the contrary he was pious with a fervor and passion that went beyond most of his contemporaries. So exalted was his conception of the spiritual life that he could not bear to have it polluted with earthly considerations. He did not believe that any man could determine the precise intention of Scripture with such dreadful certainty as the New England clergy claimed to possess. Furthermore, it seemed to him that even if their version were true, submission to truth itself was worth nothing at all when forced upon men by the sword. Williams evolved from an orthodox Puritan into the champion of religious liberty because he came to see spiritual truth as so rare, so elevated, so supernal a loveliness that it could not be chained to a worldly establishment and a vested interest. He was a libertarian because he contemned the world, and he wanted to separate church and state so that the church would not be contaminated by the state; Thomas Jefferson loved the world and was dubious about the spirit, and he sought to separate church and state so that the state would not be contaminated by the church. But John Cotton believed that the state and church were partners in furthering the cause of truth; he knew that the truth was clear, definite, reasonable, and undeniable; he expected all good men to live by it voluntarily, and he was sure that all men who did not do so were obviously bad men. Bad men were criminals, whether their offense was theft or a belief in the "inner light," and they should be punished. Moses and Aaron, the priest and the statesman, were equally the vice-regents of God, and the notion that one could contaminate the other was utter insanity.

The two other ideas derived from the background of the age, rule by fundamental law and the social compact, were also special tenets of English Puritanism. For three decades before the settlement of Massachusetts the Puritan party in England had been working hand in glove with the Parliament against the King. The absolutist Stuarts were allied with the bishops, and the Puritan agitator and the Parliamentary leader made common cause against them both. As a result of this combination, the Puritan theorists had taken over the essentials of the Parliamentary conception of society, the contention that the power of the ruler should be exercised in accordance with established fundamental law, and that the government should owe its existence to a compact of the governed. Because these ideas were strategically invaluable in England, they became ingrained in the Puritan consciousness; they were carried to the New England wilderness and were preached from every pulpit in the land.

The Puritans did not see any conflict between them and their religious intentions. In New England the fundamental law was the Bible. The magistrates were to have full power to rule men for the specific purposes to which the society was dedicated; but they as well as their subordinates were tied to the specific purposes, and could not go beyond the prescribed limits. The Bible was clear and definite on the form of the church, on the code of punishments for crimes, on the general purposes of social existence; its specifications were binding on all, magistrates, ministers, and citizens. Consequently, the Puritans did not find it difficult to conclude that in those matters upon which the Bible left men free to follow their own discretion, the society itself should establish basic rules. The New England leaders and the people frequently disagreed about what these rules were, or how detailed they should be made, but neither side ever doubted that the community must abide by whatever laws had been enacted, either by God or by the state. The government of New England was, as I have said, a dictatorship, but the dictators were not absolute and irresponsible. John Cotton was the clerical spokesman for the Massachusetts rulers, but he stoutly demanded "that all power that is on earth be limited."

The belief that government originated in the consent of the governed was equally congenial to the Puritan creed. The theology is often enough described as deterministic, because it held that men were predestined to Heaven or Hell; but we are always in danger of forgetting that the life of the Puritan was completely voluntaristic. The natural man was indeed bound in slavery to sin and unable to make exertions toward his own salvation; but the man into whose soul grace had been infused was liberated from that bondage and made free to undertake the responsibilities and obligations of virtue and decency. The holy society was erected upon the belief that the right sort of men could of their own free will and choice carry through the creation and administration of the right sort of community. The churches of New England were made up of "saints," who came into the church because they wanted membership, not because they were born in it, or were forced into it, or joined because of policy and convention. Though every resident was obliged to attend and to pay taxes for the support of the churches, no one became an actual member who did not signify his strong desire to be one. The saints were expected to act positively because they had in them a spirit of God that made them capable of every exertion. No doubt the Puritans maintained that government originated in the consent of the people because that theory was an implement for chastening the absolutism of the Stuarts; but they maintained it also because they did not believe that any society, civil or ecclesiastical, into which men did not enter of themselves was worthy of the name.

Consequently, the social theory of Puritanism, based upon the law of God, was posited also upon the voluntary submission of the citizens. As men exist in nature, said Thomas Hooker, no one person has any power over another; "there must of necessity be a mutuall ingagement, each of the other, by their free consent, before by any rule of God they have any right or power, or can exercise either, each towards the other." This truth appears, he argues, from all relations among men, that of husband and wife, master and servant; there must be a compact drawn up and sealed between them.

> From *mutuall acts* of consenting and ingaging each of other, there is an impression of *ingagement* results, as a *relative bond,* betwixt the contractours and confederatours, wherein the *formalis ratio,* or *specificall nature* of the covenant lieth, in all the former instances especially *that of* corporations. So that however it is true, the rule bindes such to the duties of their places and relations, yet it is certain, it requires that they should *first freely ingage* themselves in such covenants, and *then* be carefull to fullfill such duties. A man is allowed freely to make choice of his wife, and she of her husband, before they need or should perform the duties of husband and wife one towards another.

The rules and regulations of society, the objectives and the duties, are erected by God; but in a healthy state the citizens must first agree to abide by those regulations, must first create the society by willing consent and active participation.

These ideas, of a uniform church supported by the civil authority, of rule by explicit law, of the derivation of the state from the consent of the people, were transported to the wilderness because they were the stock ideas of the time and place. What the New England Puritans added of their own was the unique fashion in which they combined them into one coherent and rounded theory. The classic expression of this theory is the speech on liberty delivered by John Winthrop to the General Court in 1645. In that year Winthrop was serving as lieutenant governor, and as such was a justice of the peace; a squabble broke out in the town of Hingham over the election of a militia officer; Winthrop intervened, committing one faction for contempt of court when they would not give bond to appear peaceably before the legislature and let the affair be adjudicated. Some of the citizens were enraged, and the lower house of the General Court impeached Winthrop for exceeding his commission and going beyond the basic law of the land. He was tried and acquitted; thereupon he pronounced his magnificent oration, setting before the people the unified theory of the Puritan commonwealth.

As he expounds it, the political doctrine becomes part and parcel of the theological, and the cord that binds all ideas together is the covenant. Winthrop argues that individuals, in a natural state, before grace has been given them, are at absolute liberty to do anything they can, to lie, steal, murder; obviously he is certain that natural men, being what they are, will do exactly these things unless prevented. But when men become regenerate they are then at "liberty" to do only what God commands. And God commands certain things for the group as a whole as well as for each individual. Regenerate men, therefore, by the very fact of being regenerate, come together, form churches and a state upon explicit agreements, in which they all promise to live with one another according to the laws and for the purposes of God. Thus the government is brought into being by the act of the people; but the people do not create just any sort of government, but the one kind of government which God has outlined. The governors are elected by the people, but elected into an office which has been established by God. God engenders the society by acting through the people, as in nature He secures His effects by guiding secondary causes; the collective will of regenerate men, bound together by the social compact, projects and continues the will of God into the state. As John Davenport expressed it, "In regular actings of the creature, God is the first Agent; there are not two several and distinct actings, one of God, another of the People: but in one and the same action, God, by the Peoples suffrages, makes such an one Governour, or Magistrate, and not another." So, when men have made a covenant with God they have thereby promised Him, in the very terms of that agreement, to compact among themselves in order to form a holy state in which His discipline will be practiced. As one of the ministers phrased it:

> Where the Lord sets himselfe over a people, he frames them unto a willing and voluntary subjection unto him, that they desire nothing more then to be under his government . . . . When the Lord is in Covenant with a people, they follow him not forcedly, but as farre as they are sanctified by grace, they submit willingly to his regiment.

When men have entered these covenants, first with God, then with each other in the church and again in the state, they have thrice committed themselves to the rule of law and the control of authority. Winthrop can thus insist that though the government of Massachusetts is bound by fundamental law, and though it takes its rise from the people, and though the people elect the officials, still the people's liberty in Massachusetts consists in a "liberty to that only which is good, just and honest." By entering the covenant with God, and the covenant with each other, the citizens renounce all natural liberty, surrender the right to seek for anything that they themselves might lust after, and retain only the freedom that "is maintained and exercised in a way of subjection to authority."

The theory furnishes an excellent illustration of the intellectual ideal toward which all Puritan thought aspired; in the realm of government as of nature, the Puritan thinker strove to harmonize the determination of God with the exertion of men, the edicts of revelation with the counsels of reason and experience. On one side, this account exhibits the creation of society as flowing from the promptings and coaction of God; on the other side it attributes the origination to the teachings of nature and necessity. The social compact may be engineered by God, but it is also an eminently reasonable method of bringing a state into being. Delimitation of the ruler's power by basic law may be a divine ordinance to restrain the innate sinfulness of men, but it is also a very natural device to avoid oppression and despotism; the constitution may be promulgated to men from on high, but it is in fact very much the sort which, had they been left to their own devices, they might have contrived in the interests of efficiency and practicality. Men might conceivably have come upon the erection of governments through explicit compacts, in which they incorporated certain inviolable regulations and a guarantee of rights, quite as much by their own intelligence as by divine instruction. As always in Puritan thought, there was no intention to discredit either source, but rather to integrate the divine and the natural, revelation and reason, into a single inspiration. "Power of Civil Rule, by men orderly chosen, is Gods Ordinance," said John Devenport, even if "It is from the Light and Law of Nature," because "the Law of Nature is God's Law." The Puritan state was thus from one point of view purely and simply a "theocracy"; God was the sovereign; His fiats were law and His wishes took precedence over all other considerations; the magistrates and ministers were His viceroys. But from another point of view, the Puritan state was built upon reason and the law of nature; it was set up by the covenant of the people, the scope of its power was determined by the compact, and the magistrates and ministers were the commissioned servants of the people.

As this theory stands on paper it is, like so many edifices of the Puritan mind, almost perfect. When it was realized in practice, however, there were at least two difficulties that soon became apparent. For one, not all the people, even in New England, were regenerate; in fact, the provable elect were a minority, probably no more than one-fifth of the total population. But this did not dismay the original theorists, for they had never thought that mere numerical majorities proved anything. Consequently, though the social compact furnished the theoretical basis of society in New England, nevertheless it was confined to the special few; the election of officers and the passing of laws was given to those only who could demonstrate their justification and sanctification. The congregational system, with its membership limited to those who had proved before the church that they possessed the signs of grace, offered a ready machinery for winnowing the wheat from the chaff. Therefore, under the first charter the suffrage in Massachusetts was limited to the church members. In Connecticut the franchise was not officially restrained in this fashion, but other means served as well to keep the electorate pure and orthodox. The "citizens," as they were called, elected delegates to the General Court, chose judges, and passed laws. The others, the "inhabitants," had equality before the law, property rights, police protection; they were taxed no more than the citizens or submitted to no indignities, but they were allowed no voice in the government or in the choice of ministers, and only by the mere force of numbers gained any influence in town meetings.

The restriction of the franchise to church membership seemed to solve the first difficulty confronted by the Puritan theorists. But in time it only brought them face to face with the second and more serious problem: the whole structure of theory which Winthrop outlined in his speech, and which the sermons of the 1660's and 1670's reiterated, fell apart the moment the "citizens" were no longer really and ardently holy. Just as soon as the early zeal began to die down, and the distinction between the citizens and the inhabitants became difficult to discern, then the purely naturalistic, rational, practical aspect of the political theory became detached from the theological, began to stand alone and by itself. As the religious inspiration waned, there remained no reason why all the people should not be held partners to the social compact; the idea that God worked His ends through the covenant of the people grew vague and obscure, while the notion that all the people made the covenant for their own reasons and created the state for their own purposes took on more and more definite outlines. As toleration was forced upon the colonies by royal command, or became more estimable as religious passions abated, the necessity for the social bond being considered a commitment of the nation to the will of God disappeared. Instead, men perceived the charms and usefulness of claiming that the compact had been an agreement of the people, not to God's terms, but to their own terms. The divine ordinance and the spirit of God, which were supposed to have presided over the political process, vanished, leaving a government founded on the self-evident truths of the law of nature, brought into being by social compact, instituted not for the glory of God, but to secure men's "inalienable rights" of life, liberty, and the pursuit of happiness. Except that, until Jefferson rewrote the phrase, the sacred trinity of interests which government could not tamper with were more candidly summarized as life, liberty—and property.

After the new charter of 1691—which Increase Mather negotiated and which for him was a diplomatic triumph, but which nevertheless was an imposition upon Massachusetts from the outside—leaders of the colony made various efforts to accommodate the original conception of social purpose to the constitutional requirements of the document. I have elsewhere described their flounderings (*The New England Mind: From Colony to Province*, 1953), and the literature of the eighteenth century clearly yields up the evolution of a political philosophy which, by the time of the revolution, was entirely perfected (see Alice M. Baldwin, *The New England Clergy and the American Revolution*, Durham, North Carolina, 1928). Historians now agree that the first clear break with the seventeenth-century complex was John Wise's *Vindication of the Government of the New England Churches* in 1717. Though actually this book had little or no effect on colonial thinking, and does not appear to have been cited even in the revolutionary debates, still it was far ahead of its own time in proclaiming that a contractual system of government, with inalienable rights preserved in society from the original state of nature, was the dictate of aboriginal reason, that it could be said to have only subsequently obtained "the Royal Approbation" of the Creator. The transformation of the doctrine of the founders into a weapon for burgeoning nationalism was virtually completed in 1750 when Jonathan Mayhew, preaching on the anniversary of the day on which the Puritans had decapitated Charles I, delivered "A Discourse Concerning Unlimited Subjection." To this enlightened Puritan it now appeared that the purposes of society are not at all those of the deity but of the subjects. The advantage to be derived from corporate existence is no longer the salvation but the well-being of the citizen. The power even of the Puritan God— and therefore, naturally, that of an English King—is bound by the terms of compact. New England's errand into the wilderness—having set out from the federal theology—had now developed into an assurance that God Himself would respect the laws we have agreed upon. As for King George, if he imposes a tax to which we do not ourselves consent, and if we thereupon resist him, "even to the dethroning him," we are not criminals: we have only taken "a reasonable way" of vindicating our natural rights.

In 1750 Mayhew's boldness still dismayed most of his contemporaries, as did also his theological liberalism, but it was only a matter of time before the community caught up with at least his political argument. Hence he is the most obvious link between Puritan and revolutionary ideas. However, in the excitement of embracing Mayhew's radicalism, few at the time of the war had the leisure or inclination to look back to

Winthrop or to inquire how they had managed to travel the tortuous road from his doctrine of federal liberty to their constitutionalism. There ceased to survive even the faintest memory of an era when the social contract had incorporated absolute subjection to the ontological realities of the good, just, and honest—those anterior verities which existed from eternity, long before any peoples anywhere were gathered into societies and which no mere convention of the citizens could alter or redefine.

American Puritan Studies in the 1960's
—*Michael McGiffert**

It is the intent of this paper to give an account, with some commentary, of trends in the study of seventeenth-century New England Puritanism, focusing on the scholarship of the 1960's and paying particular regard to the work that has been done since the death of Perry Miller in 1963. The restriction to New England and to the seventeenth century is regrettable but necessary in view of the expanse of scholarship to be surveyed, for the field of Puritan studies is remarkable both for the productivity of accomplished scholars and for the promising enterprises of younger men and women. It cannot be said today, as James Truslow Adams stated nearly forty years ago, that "it is almost as difficult to get a new crop from [New England history] as from the worn-out soil of a New England farm."[1] So spoke Adams in 1930, the same year in which

From Michael McGiffert, "American Puritan Studies in the 1960's" in the *William and Mary Quarterly*, XXVII (1970), 36–67. Reprinted by permission of the author.
* An earlier version of this article was read at the Twenty-third Conference on Early American History, Clemson University, Oct. 5, 1968. Mr. McGiffert wishes to thank the following for their advice and assistance: John K. Nelson, Jesper Rosenmeier, Arthur Cushman McGiffert, Jr., and Robert A. Skotheim. With a few exceptions this article does not include works published since the spring of 1969.

[1] *Nation*, CXXXI (1930), 20. The growing popularity of Puritan studies can be gauged from the recent publication of three readers on Puritanism: David D. Hall, ed., *Puritanism in Seventeenth-Century Massachusetts* (New York, 1968); Sydney V. James, ed., *The New England Puritans* (New York, 1968); Michael McGiffert, ed., *Puritanism and the American Experience* (Reading, Mass., 1969). Another indication is the increasing availability of Puritan writings in microfilm and print. See, for example, Thomas Hooker, *Redemption: The Three Sermons*, ed. Everett H. Emerson (Gainesville, 1956); David D. Hall, ed., *The Antinomian Controversy, 1636–1638: A Documentary History* (Middletown, Conn., 1968); John Norton, *The Answer*, trans. Douglas Horton (Cambridge, Mass., 1958); Larzer Ziff, ed., *John Cotton on the Churches of New England* (Cambridge, Mass., 1968); William Ames, *The Marrow of Theology*, ed. and trans. John D. Eusden (Boston, 1968); A. W. Plumstead, ed., *The Wall and the Garden: Selected Massachusetts Election Sermons, 1670–1775* (Min-

Samuel Eliot Morison noted that, *mirabile dictu,* three biographies of Anne Hutchinson had come to his hands for review, one of them "clothed in a lovely jazzy jacket showing a flapper Anne hitting the trail to Rhode Island, with lightning playing all about." [2] Another sign of the times was Miller's review, a year later, of Herbert W. Schneider's *The Puritan Mind*—a review that the cognoscenti could read in the light of Miller's own undertaking: "Its defects are those of a pioneer, or almost pioneer, work: a tendency to too easy generalizations, to accepting a few outstanding documents as typical statements of a complex movement, to neglecting sources and influences which place an intellectual development in its true light. We shall not be able to achieve what the writer of the jacket blurb has called 'a spiritual Baedecker of New England's capital' until the intellectual edifices have been more precisely located." [3] These three statements—by Adams, Morison, and Miller—suggest the distance we have come. In both abundance and ability Puritan studies, since Miller and largely because of his tremendous labors, go far toward bearing out Sydney E. Ahlstrom's observation that "Puritanism has become the area of American historical work where the greatest sophistication has been achieved; hence it continues to attract keen historians who are doing impressive work—and in diverse ways." [4] Especially noteworthy are fresh studies in Puritan thought, a growing interest in the

neapolis, 1968); Bernard Bailyn, ed., *The Apologia of Robert Keayne* (New York, 1964); Edmund S. Morgan, ed., *The Founding of Massachusetts: Historians and the Sources* (Indianapolis, 1964); Edmund S. Morgan, ed., *Puritan Political Ideas, 1558–1775* (Indianapolis, 1965); Edmund S. Morgan, ed., *The Diary of Michael Wigglesworth, 1653–1657* (New York 1965); and the republication of Perry Miller, ed., *The Complete Writings of Roger Williams* (New York, 1963), esp. VII. Volumes in the forthcoming Garrett Press reprint series include *Mourt's Relation,* Peter Bulkeley's *The Gospel-Covenant,* John Cotton's *A Discourse about Civil Government, A Treatise of the Covenant,* and *The Powering Out of the Seven Vials,* Increase Mather's *Ichabod,* Samuel Sewall's *Phaenomena quaedam Apocalyptica,* Thomas Shepard's *Three Valuable Pieces,* and several of Cotton Mather's works.

2 Helen Augur, *An American Jezebel: The Life of Anne Hutchinson* (New York, 1930), reviewed by Samuel Eliot Morison, *New England Quarterly,* III (1930), 359.

3 Herbert W. Schneider, *The Puritan Mind* (New York, 1930), reviewed by Perry Miller, *New Eng. Qtly.,* IV (1931), 343.

4 Sydney E. Ahlstrom to McGiffert, June 25, 1968. Compare Edmund S. Morgan, "The Historians of Early New England," in Ray Allen Billington, ed., *The Reinterpretation of Early American History: Essays in Honor of John Edwin Pomfret* (San Marino, Calif., 1966), 41: "The historiography of early New England has reached in the past forty years a level of sophistication unmatched in the study of any other part of American history."

This is the place to acknowledge with gratitude the courtesy of the scholars who responded to the following queries, addressed to them by mail during the spring and summer 1968:

(1) Please describe your own work and the major conclusions to which it has led or seems to be leading.

(2) Please indicate the relation, if any, of your investigations and conclusions to those of the late Perry Miller.

(3) In what direction(s), in your judgment, is the interpretation of Puritanism currently moving? In what direction(s) ought it to move?

(4) Please identify other scholars whose work bears significantly on the matter at hand, including such as have not yet published extensively or at all.

Of the nearly 80 persons to whom this request for information was sent, replies were received from 46. The most helpful came from Sydney E. Ahlstrom, Sacvan Bercovitch, B. Katherine Brown, John M. Bumsted, Conrad Cherry, John S. Coolidge, Cedric Cowing, Richard Crowder, Thomas M. Davis, Richard S. Dunn, Everett H. Emerson, Eugene R.

religious psychology of the Puritans, and intensive inquiries into the organization and operation of New England society.

Because this new work takes many of its cues from Miller's writings, though it parts company from him at important points, it may be well to recall briefly the main outlines of Miller's discussion of the nature and early history of the "New England Mind." His Puritans were resolute and articulate Englishmen, of Independent Non-Separatist persuasion, who, arriving in New England in force in the 1630's, endeavored to complete the Reformation by setting up a "city upon a hill" for Christendom, including old England, to admire and perchance to emulate. Fired by a vision of the redemptive community, they were bent on proving that Christians could live together lovingly in godly relations. What gave these ventures distinction was, above all else, the intellectual muscularity of their commitment. Stressing the "majesty and coherence" [5] of Puritan thought, Miller agreed with Moses Coit Tyler that Puritan New England was primarily "a thinking community," [6] and he attempted to string its early history "upon the thread of an idea." [7] These first New Englanders made much of the idea of covenant; by it they made intelligible and tried to order the relations of man to God, providentially and soteriologically, and man to man, communally. They were preoccupied with post-Genevan problems of moral obligation, assurance of salvation, and divine transcendence; the covenant helped them with "the task of bringing God to time and to reason, of justifying His ways to man in conceptions meaningful to the intellect, of caging and confining the transcendent Force . . . by the laws of ethics . . . without losing the sense of the hidden God. . . ." [8] Institutionally, the covenant defined the ends and means of the Puritan enterprise. It provided disciplinary sanctions for the Bible Commonwealth, and, implemented in John Winthrop's "due form of government," it licensed the effort to construct a regime of the "visible saints" who, though a small minority, grasped power in both church and state.

Miller discerned in Puritan New England "an ideal laboratory" for the study of intellectual change. The area, he wrote, "was relatively isolated, the people were comparatively homogeneous, and the forces of history played upon it in ways that can more satisfactorily be traced than

Fingerhut, Stephen Foster, Joy Gilsdorf, Philip J. Greven, Jr., Michael G. Hall, George D. Langdon, Jr., David Levin, Mason I. Lowance, Jr., Charles S. McCoy, William G. McLoughlin, Robert Middlekauff, Edmund S. Morgan, John F. H. New, Robert G. Pope, Sumner Chilton Powell, Richard Reinitz, Darrett B. Rutman, Robert F. Scholz, Clifford K. Shipton, Kenneth Silverman, Keith L. Sprunger, Jonathan Sullivan, Douglas H. Taylor, G. B. Warden, Ola Elizabeth Winslow, Gene Wise, and Larzer Ziff. These scholars have generously granted permission to use their observations in this paper, without the benefit of which it could not have been written. I hope I have dealt fairly with their views.

[5] Perry Miller, *Orthodoxy in Massachusetts, 1630–1650* (Boston, 1959), xx.

[6] Quoted in Robert Allen Skotheim, "The Writing of American Histories of Ideas: Two Traditions in the XXth Century," *Journal of the History of Ideas*, XXV (1964), 257.

[7] Miller, *Orthodoxy in Massachusetts*, xii.

[8] Perry Miller, "The Marrow of Puritan Divinity," *Errand into the Wilderness* (Cambridge, Mass., 1956), 56.

in more complex societies." [9] In this "laboratory" the Puritans worked out not, as they intended, the sublime drama of salvation but the lesser though historically more instructive process of cultural adaptation. Miller's imagination was caught by a perception of "the uniqueness of the American experience"; [10] he found the sources of that experience, as well as of American ways of perceiving it, in the transforming of English Puritanism into something identifiably American: his later books were studies of "the accommodation to the American landscape of an imported and highly articulated system of ideas" [11] which his earlier books described. In Samuel Danforth's compelling metaphor, the Puritans ran an errand into a wilderness; but the wilderness claimed them, even as they tamed it, and redefined the errand in distinctively American terms. Losing both the European audience and the sense of the urgency of the original mission, the children of the founders came to feel at home in their new world, and while their society expanded and splintered, their sensibilities shrank to the compass of provincial New England. To say, therefore, that the Puritan undertaking failed is to say, ironically and precisely, that the Puritans became Americans: they learned to make do, more or less amiably, with their "mess of American pottage." [12]

I

Granting that this summary does far less than common justice to Miller's scholarship, it may be remarked that his argument has lately come under some rather searching criticism. Intellectual historians are finding that he "did not always have the right answers." [13] Historians of religion are reinterpreting the relations of American Puritanism, in its origins and evolution, to the larger movements of the Reformation: Social and institutional historians are recovering the details of a New England way of life which some of them take pains to distinguish from a New England way of thought. Much of the new work is avowedly, sometimes contentiously, revisionist, and it tends to be highly specialized. "We are in a period of disintegration," writes Richard Reinitz, "following upon Miller's great synthetic work." [14]

One sign of disintegration is the enthusiasm with which students of Puritanism and New England declare themselves to be "pluralists" and announce that the early culture of the region was highly "pluralistic."

9 Perry Miller, The New England Mind: From Colony to Province (Cambridge, Mass., 1953), x. Hereafter cited as New England Mind, II.
10 Miller, Errand, ix.
11 New England Mind, II, x. See Ahlstrom to McGiffert, June 25, 1968: "I would venture to say that it is the paradigmatic nature of the Puritan experience that makes this entire scholarly enterprise so valuable an illustration of the way in which historical study itself is a vital aspect of America's moral and intellectual life."
12 Nicholas Noyes, New England's Duty and Interest (Boston, 1968), 76.
13 Robert G. Pope to McGiffert, June 6, 1968.
14 Reinitz to McGiffert, May 12, 1968. "I wish I could say," Reinitz continues, "that I thought we were engaged in the checking of Miller's hypotheses, but I fear that the anxiety for originality may be leading to more destructive than constructive activity."

This assertion is often pitched against the monistic implications of Miller's decision in the first volume of *The New England Mind* to treat the literature of Puritanism "as though it were the product of a single intelligence. . ."; [15] the damning catchword is "monolithic." Thus Everett H. Emerson avers that "we now recognize Puritanism as much less unified than Miller made it out to be." [16] Similarly, John M. Bumsted holds that "there is no such animal as 'New England' or 'American' Puritanism as a monolithic intellectual, religious, or ecclesiastical entity"; Sydney Ahlstrom refers to "the Puritan 'Mind'" and "Massachusetts 'Orthodoxy'" as "fallacious concretions"; Kenneth Silverman sees only heterodoxy in Massachusetts—"a welter of uncertainty among Puritans themselves regarding practically every religious, political, literary, and social notion entertained" in seventeenth-century New England.[17] Such statements abound; [18] only very rarely will a writer risk asserting that there existed a "striking unanimity of opinion not only among the body of settlers but also among [the] secular and theological leadership" of early Massachusetts.[19] Recent studies in Puritan literature and biographies of New England worthies contribute, more or less advertently, to this disassembling of the New England Way, given the particularistic instinct of literary scholars and the biographic press toward individualization of experience and character.[20]

The report of pluralism is so spirited and so common that it is prob-

[15] Perry Miller, *The New England Mind: The Seventeenth Century* (New York, 1939), vii. Hereafter cited as *New England Mind*, I.

[16] Emerson to McGiffert, May 13, 1968. Emerson refers specifically to Miller's treatment of Calvin and the covenant theology.

[17] John M. Bumsted, The Pilgrims' Progress: The Ecclesiastical History of the Old Colony, 1620–1775 (unpubl. Ph.D. diss., Brown University, 1965), 303–304; Ahlstrom, *Church History*, XXXII (1963), 107; Silverman to McGiffert, July 22, 1968.

[18] See, for example, Bernard Bailyn, *William and Mary Quarterly*, 3d Ser., XXI (1964), 127; George Drake, *Church Hist.*, XXXV (1966), 117; C. C. Goen, *Church Hist.*, XXXVII (1968), 221; Norman S. Grabo, *Wm. and Mary Qtly.*, 3d Ser., XIX (1962), 479; David Kobrin, "The Expansion of the Visible Church in New England: 1629–1650," *Church Hist.*, XXXVI (1967), 207; Kenneth A. Lockridge, "The History of a Puritan Church, 1637–1736," *New Eng. Qtly.*, XL (1967), 399–400; William W. MacDonald, *New Eng. Qtly.*, XL (1967), 621; Clifford K. Shipton, *New Eng. Qtly.*, XL (1967), 127; Richard C. Simmons, *Journal of American Studies*, I (1967), 285; Leo F. Solt, *Wm. and Mary Qtly.*, 3d Ser., XIX (1962), 300–302; Larzer Ziff, *American Literature*, XXXV (1963), 371. The pluralist thesis is strongly asserted in Darrett B. Rutman, *Winthrop's Boston* (Chapel Hill, 1965); Darrett B. Rutman, "The Mirror of Puritan Authority," in George A. Billias, ed., *Selected Essays: Law and Authority in Colonial America* (Barre, Mass., 1965), 149–167; and Clifford K. Shipton, "The Locus of Authority in Colonial Massachusetts," *ibid.*, 136–148. The earliest call for a pluralist approach appears to have come from Edmund S. Morgan, "New England Puritanism: Another Approach," *Wm. and Mary Qtly.*, 3d Ser., XVIII (1961), 236; see also Edmund S. Morgan, *American Historical Review*, LXXI (1966), 664.

[19] B. Richard Burg, "The Ideology of Richard Mather and Its Relationship to English Puritanism Prior to 1660," *Journal of Church and State*, IX (1967), 364. Reference to the "monolithic" structure of seventeenth-century New England society and thought has been common among historians who treat the eighteenth century and find it useful, as Miller did, to set the fragmentation of the latter period over against the comparative unity and simplicity of the former. See Richard L. Bushman, *From Puritan to Yankee: Character and the Social Order in Connecticut, 1690–1765* (Cambridge, Mass., 1967), ix, 16, 72, 107; and Rutman's review, *Journal of American History*, LIV (1967), 631–632.

[20] This paper does not attempt to discuss recent literary studies: that field is a rich one—though there may be cause to fear lest its fertility be impaired by over-cultivation.

ably idle to demur that Miller's treatment of the Puritans belied, to a fair degree, his "monolithic" titles. Though his excited encounter with Puritan ideas led him to assert that "the first three generations in New England paid almost unbroken allegiance to a unified body of thought," [21] thus furnishing "a coherence," as he put it, "with which I could coherently begin" to study "the innermost propulsion of the United States," [22] it is also true that he was keenly aware of the ambiguities and complexities of his subject.[23] To cite an obvious and crucial instance, Miller demolished the notion that the ministers of the Bay were of one mind in prosecuting Anne Hutchinson. He knew how to relish Thomas Shepard's grim little note, "Mr. Cotton: repents not: but is hid only," [24] and he saw through the false front of consensus that the clergy later erected around the recollection of the Antinomian crisis. It would be hard to decide whether Miller's achievement consisted more in his mastery of the grand pattern of Puritan thought or in his deft dissection of its inner tensions and nuances. Either way, he found great diversity within the Puritan coherence. His more outspoken critics, for their part, deny the coherence itself—and their declarations of extreme pluralism bespeak the dishevelled state of Puritan studies in the post-Miller period. "Dissensus" becomes the rule among both scholars and Puritans.[25]

Associated with the assault on the "monolith" is an argument against reading New England's history as a kind of "Brown's Descent" or "willy-nilly slide"—to lift a title from Robert Frost—down the hard slope of the hill on which the Puritan citadel was originally set. Thus Miller is sometimes taxed with adopting a version of the idea of declension that was, in reality, a figment of the distressed clerical fancy of the later Mathers and their woeful colleagues.[26] Though this is not the place to try to untangle Miller's vigorously complicated feelings toward Puritans and Puritanism, it may be remarked that, when not overborne by nausea at the thought of the abominable Cotton Mather, he stood clear of the ministerial myth

To keep up with the work that is being done, check *Early American Literature*, edited by Everett H. Emerson and published at the University of Massachusetts. Since 1958, when Morgan published his brilliant study of John Winthrop, useful biographical work has appeared on William Ames, John Cotton, John Eliot, Anne Hutchinson, Cotton Mather, Samuel Sewall, Edward Taylor, Michael Wigglesworth, Roger Williams, and the generations of the Winthrops.

[21] *New England Mind*, I, vii.   [22] Miller, *Errand*, viii.

[23] Alan Heimert states that *New England Mind*, II, depicts "a society that is not monolithic, but compulsively fragmenting and equipped with a panoply of ideas. The discussions of the Half-Way Covenant, the charter controversy, and 'toleration' proceed from an awareness of social and intellectual divisions that had theretofore eluded the eyes of discerning political or economic historians." Alan Heimert, "Perry Miller: An Appreciation," *Harvard Review*, II (1964), 33–34.

[24] Perry Miller, "The Autobiography of Thomas Shepard," Massachusetts Colonial Society, *Publications*, XXVII (Boston, 1932), 386n.

[25] See Morgan, "Historians of Early New England," in Billington, ed., *Reinterpretation of Early American History*, 57: "The discovery of variety is perhaps the salient feature of post-Miller studies."

[26] On the issue of "declension" see Rutman, *Winthrop's Boston, passim;* Rutman, "Mirror of Puritan Authority," in Billias, ed., *Selected Essays,* 164; Morgan, "New England

of the Glory Departing; [27] he would probably not be charged otherwise had he not chosen to entitle an important essay "Declension in a Bible Commonwealth." Was there really, he asked of the Reforming Synod, "so awful a deterioration"?—and replied with Thomas Hutchinson that "'we have no evidence of any extraordinary degeneracy,'" except, perhaps, among the clergy themselves in point of status and morale. The "mass of the people" was not degenerate; New England folk went right on earning a night's repose by a day's work, "clearing the land, attending sermons (and taking notes), searching their souls, praying for grace, and humbling themselves for their unworthiness." These were the fundamental social facts of the period in which New England moved from colony to province. If, however, "as we measure facts, New England was not declining, it was certainly changing," and changing in ways its Elishas could interpret only as deterioration. The "orthodox colonies," Miller wrote, had been founded on a code of "medieval" authority and order; "the code resisted change, and therefore changes became declensions. . . ." [28] Hence the jeremiads were to be explained psychologically, in terms of the trauma of the clergy, as releases or rituals that, ironically, enable the saints to go on sinning (their energies freed, as Miller dryly notes, "to continue working with the forces of change") [29] and the ministers to go on ministering.

Miller thus read the jeremiads as effusions of tormented men who could not appreciate the joke that time and place and their own belief had played on them.[30] Their sermons were baffled, sometimes self-serving,

---

Puritanism," *Wm. and Mary Qtly.,* 3d Ser., XVIII (1961), 237–242; Rutman, "Another Approach to New England Puritanism Assayed," *Wm. and Mary Qtly.,* XIX (1962), 408–441; Morgan's further statement, *Wm. and Mary Qtly.,* 3d Ser., XIX (1962), 642–644; Robert G. Pope, The Half-Way Covenant: Church Membership in the Holy Commonwealths, 1658–1690 (unpubl. Ph.D. diss., Yale University, 1967); and Lewis M. Robinson, A History of the Half-Way Covenant (unpubl. Ph.D. diss., University of Illinois, 1963). Cotton Mather played a key part in Miller's account. See David Levin, ed., *Bonifacius: An Essay upon the Good by Cotton Mather* (Cambridge, Mass., 1966), x–xi; and David Levin, "The Hazing of Cotton Mather: The Creation of a Biographical Personality," *New Eng. Qtly.,* XXXVI (1963), 147–171. Highly illuminating are Gene Wise's observations on Mather's role as exemplar and victim in Miller's "ironic paradigm" of Puritan history: "Implicit Irony in Recent American Historiography: Perry Miller's New England," *Jour. of Hist. of Ideas,* XXIX (1968), 597n, 598. Among the scholars who are reexamining Increase and Cotton Mather are, in addition to Levin, Michael G. Hall, Mason I. Lowance, Jr., Robert Middlehauff, Kenneth Silverman, and Peter H. Smith. Their work may yield some surprises. For example, Silverman writes to McGiffert, July 22, 1968, "We have long missed the great amount of humor in [Cotton] Mather, and in Puritan writing generally, as also the scatology."
[27] Warden to McGiffert, July 15, 1968: "I think Miller's major point was that Puritanism was changing and adapting (the essential meaning of the word 'declension') not necessarily declining, except from an absolutist standpoint which neither he nor the Puritans shared." Pope makes a similar point writing to McGiffert, June 6, 1968.
[28] New England Mind, II, 47–48.
[29] Miller, "Declension in a Bible Commonwealth," *Nature's Nation,* 48.
[30] Miller, "'Preparation for Salvation' in Seventeenth-Century New England," *ibid.,* 50: "Whether the colonies had in fact so woefully fallen off need not concern us. The point is that the ministers, and in all probability most of the people, believed that the case was desperate, and the staggering tabulation of sins, crimes, and offenses published by the Synod of 1679 furnished sufficient documentation."

always ambiguous outcries: in them the New England mind flapped loose like Michael Wigglesworth's neighbor's stable door. No longer did the ruling tenets of the founders account satisfactorily for New England's experience. Puritanism's paradoxes, as Edmund S. Morgan remarks, had deepened into contradictions,[31] and even the concept of covenant had become dysfunctional. Thus, referring to the social complexity of 1700, Miller wrote that "if you started, as did New Englanders, from such a conception of unity as prevailed under the old charter (a period enhanced by the jeremiads into a veritable golden age), what happened between 1698 and 1701 would seem a convergence of devilish and disruptive forces beyond the ability of man to subdue." [32] The "if" operates ironically in this sentence, and, indeed, Miller's handling of the jeremiad is prevailingly ironic. Emphasizing this, Gene Wise notes that whereas the progressive historian Thomas J. Wertenbaker takes the jeremiads literally, Miller sees them as "strategic." According to Wise, Wertenbaker "reads *The Necessity of Reformation* on its face as a sociological report on decay in Puritan morality," but Miller understands that the jeremiad "was not sociological investigation, it was purgation by incantation." [33] Declension is thus too simple a category for the complex changes which Miller traced—and that is exactly the ironic point of his exposure, as subtle as it is devastating, of the treasonous simplicities of the jeremiads.

Finally among these general considerations—and crucially for the field that is here called Puritan studies—there remains a recalcitrant problem of definition. Miller was satisfied, at least for anthological purposes, to let Puritanism mean "that point of view, that philosophy of life, that code of values, which was carried to New England by the first settlers in the early seventeenth century" [34]—a description commodious enough to embrace Roger Williams as well as John Cotton, Anne Hutchinson as well as John Wilson, and a host of unregenerate sorts as well as the godly few. But if definition implies both a boundary, however vague, and an essence, somehow distinctive, Miller's is plainly defective, as witness the dissatisfaction of other scholars who have, in their turn, tried their hands at defining Puritanism. Ralph Barton Perry, for example, tends to equate Puritanism with Calvinism, so that Huguenots, Scotch-Irish Presbyterians, and German and Dutch Reformed communicants are, for his purposes, converted into "Puritans." Alan Simpson and Sydney E. Ahlstrom admit the Quakers into the Puritan fold, and Ahlstrom insists that the religious thought of early Virginia was molded by Puritan influences. Herbert W. Schneider shuts out the Quakers, together with the banished followers of Williams and Mistress Hutchinson, but lets in

---

31 Edmund S. Morgan, "Perry Miller and the Historians," *Harvard Rev.*, II (1964), 56.
32 *New England Mind*, II, 242.
33 Wise, "Implicit Irony," *Jour. of Hist. of Ideas*, 595. *New England Mind*, II, 34.
34 Perry Miller and Thomas H. Johnson, eds., *The Puritans* (New York, 1938), I

the Plymouth Separatists. Edmund S. Morgan formerly appeared to rule out Separatists like Williams on the ground that they would not or could not suffer sufficiently from "the Puritan dilemma," but in his recent study of Williams, a book whose theme is again the problem of the Puritan ethic, Morgan makes a point of Williams's essential Puritanism. Perhaps the largest concept of Puritanism is the one once sought by Kenneth B. Murdock: "The literary student needs a definition generous enough to include John Robinson, Nathaniel Ward, Bradford, and Winthrop, as well as Baxter, Bunyan, Milton, and Marvell, and comprehensive enough to cover Plymouth Separatists as well as Massachusetts Independents, Congregationalists, Baptists, and Seekers—all the sects which, taken together, make up Puritanism as a school of thought. . . ." [35] Given such variety of definition, one is inclined to conclude that it is a particular glory of Puritan studies to have maintained, against the temptation to become precisionistic (which is to say, puritanical), a certan accommodating ineffability.

More broadly understood, the problem of definition touches the nature of Puritanism (how intellectual?), the structure of Puritan experience (monolithic?), and the American history of the Puritan movement (declension?). In discussing the assumptions on which they believe Miller's work rests, and in pursuing their independent researches, historians begin to exhibit a sharpened sensitivity to the interpenetration of these themes and issues, and to their implications for both the craft and the philosophy of history. To take one example only: if, as Paul K. Conkin points out, "Puritanism is defined in a narrow doctrinal way, then much of New England, or even American, intellectual history is a story of the decline and fall of Puritan or Calvinist doctrine." That fall is marked by burgeoning heresies, imperfectly absorbed or exorcised, by unexpected shifts of sentiment and language, by breakings-in of alien ideas, by slippages of thought toward some new magnetic north of the mind, by hair-splittings that are magnified into deep fractures of the theological system—so that in retrospect the old body of intellect takes on a deceptive appearance of simplicity and telic control; it comes to seem "a formal abstraction, an overly coherent model of orthodoxy," in other words, a doctrinal monolith. But if, to pursue Conkin's insight, Puritanism is seen as "a collection of basic attitudes rather than as a specific and static ideology, the spectacle of Puritan decline becomes the more complex

[35] Ralph Barton Perry, *Puritanism and Democracy* (New York, 1944), 62–81; Alan Simpson, *Puritanism in Old and New England* (Chicago, 1955), 1ff.; Sydney E. Ahlstrom, "Thomas Hooker—Puritanism and Democratic Citizenship," *Church Hist.*, XXXII (1963), 420; Herbert W. Schneider, "The Puritan Tradition," in F. Ernest Johnson, ed., *Wellsprings of the American Spirit* (New York, 1948), 3–4; Edmund S. Morgan, *The Puritan Dilemma: The Story of John Winthrop* (Boston, 1958); Edmund S. Morgan, *Roger Williams: The Church and the State* (New York, 1967); Kenneth B. Murdock, "The Puritan Tradition," in Norman Foerster, ed., *The Reinterpretation of American Literature* (New York, 1928), 88.

study of varied Puritan development."[36] Historians are becoming increasingly alert to the ways in which their rather arbitrary decisions about what to study powerfully, if subtly, affect the sense they make of it. One's interest in Puritanism may be primarily intellectual or literary or homiletical or institutional or characterological: because each approach has its more or less peculiar conceptual and procedural imperatives, the initial definitional choice will make some, perhaps a considerable, difference in the interpretative outcome.

II

Miller's special subject was the New England mind, and the validity of his discussion of that mind depends on the accuracy of his treatment of its governing ideas and assumptions, foremost among them the notion of the covenant. Though few scholars dispute the thesis that seventeenth-century New England thought, monolithic or not, was focused in the concept of the covenant,[37] questions have arisen concerning Miller's interpretation of the role and significance of the concept which present a serious problem for his entire argument. To the degree that his comprehension of the covenant can be shown to be flawed, our understanding of the nature, dynamic, history, and legacy of American Puritanism will have to be corrected, and there are signs that the correction may have to be radical.

The covenant interested Miller particularly in its character as transaction or contract, voluntarily subscribed, with binding obligations on both sides. The Puritans' allegiance to the idea, so conceived, seemed to him a sign of waning piety,[38] and he pointed to the irony whereby the covenant, originally intended "to make a bit more plausible the mysteries of the Protestant creed," came to take "such mastery over the creed as in effect to pervert it. . . ."[39] The creed was initially and essentially Calvinistic; the covenant, developed against the threats of Arminians and Antinomians, marked an epochal departure from Calvinism. To Miller, Calvin's God was a "mailclad Seigneur," an inscrutable, capricious,

36 Paul K. Conkin, *Puritans and Pragmatists: Eight Eminent American Thinkers* (New York, 1968), 2–3.
37 Exceptions are duly noted. Keith L. Sprunger to McGiffert, July 14, 1968: "I do not fully accept his [Miller's] interpretation of the covenant in Puritanism nor his saying that the New Englanders were not authentic Calvinists. I believe that they were and that the covenant made very little difference in the overall thrust of Puritan theology. . . ." Silverman to McGiffert, July 22, 1968: "Miller's basic notion—which I take it is that the Covenant idiom is the deepest fact of Puritan life, and that the breakup of Puritan life can best be studied in a loss of Covenant imagery—I do now question. . . . I see only heterodoxy in the literature, and my sense of things is that the Covenant idiom was called into question from the beginning by some, and also remained persuasive to others at a later date than Miller suggests." Cf. Emerson's statement that "the Covenant metaphor is not often found in Hooker's works." Everett H. Emerson, "Thomas Hooker: The Puritan as Theologian," *Anglican Theological Review*, XLIX (1967), 10.
38 *New England Mind*, I, 396.   39 Miller, *Errand*, 49.

arbitrary Power Who had no need or respect for covenants.[40] This carica-ture[41] enabled Miller to dramatize the Puritans' flight to a juristic, even a businesslike, Deity Who was reasonable, consistent, and law-abiding. Enthralled by the notion of transaction—"an 'if I believe' necessitating a 'you have to save me'"[42]—the New England clergy saved themselves from Arminianism merely by insisting that their doctrine was not Arminian and by declaring, while they steadily enlarged man's part in the operations of grace, that God alone could fulfill the conditions of the covenant. Though Miller never denied—on the contrary, he strongly affirmed—the persistence in Puritanism of a deep sense of God's mystery and majesty, the stress of his account of the covenant fell on its anticipa-tions of the Enlightenment into which the posterity of Puritans would enter, with John Wise, when the "diverse attitudes which had somehow been awkwardly and unwittingly put together in the covenant theology" came apart.[43]

Miller's critics contend that he exaggerated the voluntaristic and ra-tionalistic bearings of the covenant in Puritan thought, thereby making the theological and, as it were, emotional distance from Geneva to Boston far greater than it actually was. While allowing for variations of em-phasis, they find that to the Puritans the idea signified less a treaty between God and man than a gift of God's free mercy to creatures who, of themselves, could do nothing either to deserve or to negotiate it. Thus David D. Hall writes that "the covenant theology can be rescued from the framework of The New England Mind. The alternative to Miller's theory is that the covenant theology grew out of the strain of Protestantism that made an experimental faith the basis of the Christian life. . . ."[44] Norman Pettit argues that Miller's "interpretation of covenant theology has tended to restrict the Puritan imagination and to distort certain con-

---

[40] Miller, "Marrow," Errand, 69; New England Mind, I, 397.
[41] Charles A. Barker, Amer. Hist. Rev., LXXIII (1968), 903; Everett H. Emerson, "Calvin and the Covenant Theology," Church Hist., XXV (1956), 136–144; Norman Pettit, The Heart Prepared: Grace and Conversion in Puritan Spiritual Life (New Haven, 1966), 40n; Charles S. McCoy to McGiffert, May 6, 1968. The sharpest criticism of Miller's view of Calvin comes from David D. Hall, The Puritans versus John Calvin: A Critique of Perry Miller, The New England Mind (unpubl. paper, American Historical Association, Toronto, Dec. 30, 1967): Miller's Calvin "is the stage figure Calvin constructed by nineteenth-century Protestants who were liberals in theology and who wished to paint Calvin in colors so dark that their rebellion against orthodoxy would seem justified. . . . It is ironic that Miller carried over into The New England Mind such a conception of Calvin, for it is the picture that his-torians like Vernon L. Parrington relied upon in their attacks upon the New England Puritans." Ibid., 7. The irony is compounded by Miller's sympathy—so far as an atheist could be sympathetic—with the neo-Calvinism of Reinhold Niebuhr. An objection similar to Hall's is entered by Gerald J. Goodwin, "The Myth of 'Arminian-Calvinism' in Eigh-teenth-Century New England," New Eng. Qtly., XLI (1968), 216.
[42] Miller, "Marrow," Errand, 71.   [43] Ibid., 98.
[44] Hall, Puritans versus Calvin, 6. Commenting on Hall's paper, Stephen Foster entered a caveat for Miller's critics: "Of course, for every passage from an eminent divine emphasizing the justness and rationality of the Covenant, another can be adduced arguing just the opposite, but isn't that exactly Miller's point? He argued that the covenant theology seethed with latent tensions and paradoxes, that it was ambivalent. Stressing one half of the ambivalence, as many of Miller's critics have done, does not somehow disprove the other half." Stephen Foster, Perry Miller and the New England Mind: A Commentary

cepts"; it "both negates the significance of the interior life and diminishes the range of Puritan religious thought." In particular, Pettit finds it "hard to see . . . how covenant theology was intended to supply a bargaining basis for man's relationship with God."[45] Richard L. Greaves poses the key question: was the covenant "essentially a pact or a testament, a contract or a promise?"[46] As pact it imposed an ethical obligation to meet its conditions—to prepare for salvation, to keep the faith, to strive for godliness—and it presupposed some degree of ability on man's part, God helping, to do these things; as promise it expressed man's infinite dependence on grace. These different senses of the covenant are often difficult to disentangle; insofar as they are distinguishable they can be traced to Continental sources, the covenant-as-pact principally to the Rhineland, the covenant-as-promise principally to Geneva. Each found lodging in English Puritanism; each was carried to New England; elements of each were mingled in the preaching of every American exponent of the Federal Theology. As Miller stated, "Puritanism looked upon itself as the synthesis of piety and reason, and the federal Puritans looked upon the covenant theology as the perfection of that synthesis."[47] If, however, Miller's critics are right, Puritans approved the covenant for reasons primarily of the heart. It claimed their minds because it spoke directly to their deepest spiritual hungerings for direction, assurance, and acceptance —because, as Leonard Trinterud has argued, "it could so readily and simply give intellectual expression to . . . the lush, warm flow of mystical piety and devotion" that welled from the medieval folk-soul of England and made Puritanism preeminently a religion of the broken yet uplifted heart.[48]

(unpubl. paper, American Historical Association, Toronto, Dec. 30, 1967), 5. The "ambivalence" of the covenant in the Old Testament iis shown by Delbert R. Hillers, *Covenant: The History of a Biblical Idea* (Baltimore, 1969).

[45] Pettit, *Heart Prepared*, 219–220.

[46] Richard L. Greaves, "John Bunyan and Covenant Thought in the Seventeenth Century," *Church Hist.*, XXXVI (1967), 158. For a sharp definitional distinction between covenant (unconditional selfless commitment) and contract (conditional, self-interested transaction) see H. Richard Niebuhr, "The Idea of Covenant and American Democracy," *Church Hist.*, XXIII (June, 1954), 126–135. Niebuhr finds the two mixed in Puritanism, while noting the historical "tendency of the covenant idea to degenerate into the limited contract idea. . . ."

[47] *New England Mind*, I, 373.

[48] Leonard Trinterud, "The Origins of Puritanism," *Church Hist.*, XX (1951), 50. See also, C. Conrad Cherry, "The Puritan Notion of the Covenant in Jonathan Edwards' Doctrine of Faith," *Church Hist.*, XXXIV (1965), 328–341; Emerson, "Calvin and Covenant Theology," *Church Hist.*, XXV (1956), 136–144. William W. McKee, The Idea of Covenant in Early English Puritanism (1580–1643) (unpubl. Ph.D. diss., Yale University, 1948); Jens G. Moller, "The Beginnings of Puritan Covenant Theology," *Journal of Ecclesiastical History*, XIV (1963), 46–67; Norman Pettit, *Heart Prepared*, 220; C. J. Sommerville, "Conversion versus the Early Puritan Covenant of Grace," *Journal of Presbyterian History*, XLIV (1966), 178–197; John von Rohr, "Covenant and Assurance in Early English Puritanism," *Church Hist.*, XXXIV (1965), 195–203; William G. Wilcox, New England Covenant Theology: Its English Precursors and Early American Exponents (unpubl. Ph.D. diss., Duke University, 1959); James Rodney Fulcher, Puritan Piety in Early New England (unpubl. Ph.D. diss., Princeton University, 1963); John D. Eusden, "Natural Law and Covenant Theology in New England, 1620–1670," *Natural Law Forum*, V (1960), 1–30.

In 1955 Simpson charged that Miller had "told us too much about the Puritan mind and not enough about the Puritan's feelings," [49] and a year later James F. Maclear observed that the "mystical element" in New England Puritanism had been "almost entirely neglected" by historians whose interest "centered largely on the rational aspects of Puritan theological science rather than on its expression in religious life and faith." Maclear counted the costs of this neglect. By discounting the warmth of piety, it "seriously distorted" the picture of Puritanism. By failing to appreciate Anne Hutchinson's "enthusiasm" as an authentic, if vagrant, expression of the Puritan spirit, it made the Antinomian Controversy an "enigma" and an "alien intrusion"; likewise it concealed the deep inner affinities between Puritanism and Quakerism. It tempted the historian to treat Puritan thought as static and rigid, and it "created the greatest confusion with regard to the relation of American to English Puritanism." Consequently, Maclear called for "a radically different approach," to begin "with a full recognition of the emotional, the experiental, and ultimately the mystical element in the synthesis which stood at the center of Puritan evangelical religion." [50]

Maclear's argument was directed implicitly, as was Simpson's explicitly, against Miller's concept and treatment of the New England Mind. Though Miller acknowledged the thrust of Puritan passion and its power to make Puritans "reel and stagger" [51] as well as to mount revolutions and build Zions in wildernesses, he confined his analysis, for the most part, to the intellectual contrivances by which passion was expressed or disciplined; he was more interested in the "articulated philosophy" than

---

[49] Simpson, *Puritanism*, 21. See also Gordon Stevens Wakefield, *Puritan Devotion: Its Place in the Development of Christian Piety* (London, 1957), 2; Sacvan Bercovitch, "Typology in Puritan New England: The Williams-Cotton Controversy Reassessed," *American Quarterly*, XIX (1967), 189; Norman S. Grabo, *Edward Taylor* (New Haven, 1961), 41; Norman S. Grabo, "The Veiled Vision: The Role of Aesthetics in Early American Intellectual History," *Wm. and Mary Qtly.*, 3d Ser., XIX (1962), 498–500, 504–505, 508–509; and Frederick B. Tolles, *Amer. Lit.*, XXXIX (1967), 401.

[50] James F. Maclear, "The Heart of New England Rent: The Mystical Element in Early Puritan History," *Mississippi Valley Historical Review*, XLII (1956), 621–622. Maclear took many of his cues from the growing literature on the piety of English Puritanism which now includes the following studies: Jerald C. Brauer, Francis Rous, Puritan Mystic, 1579–1659: An Introduction to the Study of the Mystical Element in Puritanism (unpubl. Ph.D. diss., University of Chicago, 1948); Horton Davies, *The Worship of the English Puritans* (London, 1948); William Haller, *The Rise of Puritanism* (New York, 1938); Winthrop S. Hudson, "Mystical Religion in the Puritan Commonwealth," *Journal of Religion*, XXVIII (1948), 51–56; George A. Johnson, "From Seeker to Finder: A Study in Seventeenth-Century Spiritualism before the Quakers," *Church Hist.*, XVII (1948), 299–315; Rufus M. Jones, *Mysticism and Democracy in the English Commonwealth* (Cambridge, Mass., 1932); U. Milo Kaufmann, *The Pilgrim's Progress and Traditions in Puritan Meditation* (New Haven, 1966); M. M. Knappen, ed., *Two Elizabethan Puritan Diaries* (Chicago, 1933); Geoffrey F. Nuttall, *The Holy Spirit in Puritan Faith and Experience* (London, 1947); Geoffrey F. Nuttall, *Studies in Christian Enthusiasm* (Wallingford, Pa., 1948); Wakefield, *Puritan Devotion;* Cynthia Griffin Wolff, "Literary Reflections of the Puritan Character," *Jour. of Hist. of Ideas*, XXIX (1968), 13–32.

[51] Miller, *Errand*, 190.

in its "emotional propulsion" [52]—more in the contents of the Puritan head
than in the urges of the Puritan heart. His choice of documents reflected
this preference: he based his readings of Puritanism on "what was said
and done publicly," [53] while the "private" materials, recording the groans
from the closet where the Puritan wrestled in anguish with his dark
angels, went comparatively unheeded. The "mind" Miller wrote about
was consequently more doctrinal than devotional, more polemical than
prayerful. Alan Heimert has rightly observed that Miller's definition of
"mind" comprehended "*both* the depth of feeling *and* the forms of
thought in which such depths found expression." [54] There remains, however, an impression that Miller overstated the rigorous intellectuality of
Puritanism, perhaps because, as Robert F. Scholz suggests, he was working "with a rationalistic-idealistic model of the human mind" (as distinguished, for example, from an existential model) which led him to
stress "basic systems or configurations of ideas (like the Federal Theology) . . ." [55] and betrayed him into formalism. Linking this problem
of intellectualism to the problem of the monolith, Douglas H. Taylor
comments that "many scholars assume a thing called Puritanism, turn
it into a category, evaluate responses to the thing, and I think in the
process overrate the *theological* impact of 'the thing' on American
thought." [56]

From the reexamination of Puritan piety by such post-Miller scholars
as Pettit, Hall, Norman Grabo, James Rodney Fulcher, and Daniel B.
Shea, Jr., comes a freshened sense of the inwardness of the Puritan
spirit.[57] One can also detect a growing suspicion that the Puritans were
theologically far less coherent than Miller made them out to be. Not only

[52] *New England Mind*, I, 67. Robert Middlekauff reverses the relationship between piety
and intellect, making the former a function of the latter, in his valuable essay, "Piety and
Intellect in Puritanism," *Wm. and Mary Qtly.*, 3d Ser., XXII (1965), 458–470.
[53] *New England Mind*, II, x.
[54] Heimert, "Miller: An Appreciation," *Harvard Rev.*, II (1964), 340.
[55] Scholz to McGiffert, June 25, 1968. Nowhere in Miller's writings will one find a
rigorous definition of "mind." On this problem see Richard Reinitz, "Perry Miller and
Recent American Historiography," *Bulletin of the British Association for American Studies*,
VIII (1964), 27–35; Robert A. Skotheim, *American Intellectual Histories and Historians*
(Princeton, 1966), 193–195; and Robert Polk Thomson, *Wm. and Mary Qtly.*, 3d Ser., XXIII
(1966), 646.
[56] Taylor to McGiffert, Aug. 30, 1968.
[57] Fulcher, Puritan Piety in Early New England; Grabo, Taylor; Hall, ed., *Antinomian
Controversy*; Pettit, *Heart Prepared*; Daniel B. Shea, Jr., *Spiritual Autobiography in Early
America* (Princeton, 1968). Fulcher defends the thesis that "the dynamics of the [Puritan]
movement must be accounted for in terms of its piety." Hall attributes the severity of the
Antinomian affair to the "spiritual depression" that occurred in the Bay in 1635–1636 when
the "revival" that had begun in 1633 collapsed into "a mood of acute religious anxiety,"
accompanied in some quarters by anticlericalism. Hall, Puritans versus Calvin, 13–18. For
a counter-suggestion see John F. H. New, Vision Become a Book: The New England Mind
(unpubl. paper, American Historical Association, Toronto, Dec. 30, 1967): "Miller's omni-
present setting was Augustinian piety. One may doubt whether Puritanism's main impulse
was piety and whether it was Augustinian." *Ibid.*, 8–9.

was their preaching, like that of their mentor, William Ames,[58] primarily concerned with religious experience, but they often displayed, like Ames or William Perkins or Richard Sibbes, "a minimum of concern for the rigors of dogma." [59] It is notoriously said that the Puritans were Arminians in their pulpits but Calvinists in their closets. It might be more accurate to say that in their pulpits they were moralists and in their closets pietists. For example, one who struggles through the unpublished diary in which Thomas Shepard recorded his spiritual agitations, anxieties, and occasional delights may be surprised to find that twice in a stretch of four years, and each time at considerable length, this capable theologian and evangelist found it needful to rehearse the reasoning by which the most basic tenet of the Reformation—the doctrine of justification by faith— was drawn out of Scripture. Shepard's performance is labored, causing the reader to wonder why he made such rough going of a logic which all Puritans are supposed to have had by heart. At another level it might be worth asking whether the jumble of heresies laid to Anne Hutchinson's charge reveals the Puritans' theological ingenuity or, perhaps, their theological confusion. Possibly, after all, Winthrop was not so far out when he observed that except for some few adepts no man could sound the bottom of the Antinomian Controversy.[60] In a word, there is at least a possibility, Miller to the contrary notwithstanding, that the original New Englanders were catch-as-catch-can theologians and that it was not so much their allegiance to the federal creed or their Ramean logic but, in Simpson's words, the "stretched passion" [61] that best defines them. This emphasis on Puritan emotionality is reinforced by scholars who have

---

[58] Miller's discovery of Ames (and, through Ames, of Petrus Ramus) has been improved by Eusden's edition of *The Marrow of Theology;* Douglas Horton, trans., *William Ames by Mathew Nethunus, Hugo Visscher, and Karl Reuter* (Cambridge, Mass., 1965); Walter J. Ong, *Ramus, Method, and the Decay of Dialogue* (Cambridge, Mass., 1958); and the writings of Keith L. Sprunger: The Learned Doctor Ames (unpubl. Ph.D. diss., University of Illinois, 1963), "Ames, Ramus, and the Method of Puritan Theology," *Harvard Theological Review,* LIX (1966), 133–151, and "Technometria: A Prologue to Puritan Theology," *Jour. of Hist. of Ideas,* XXIX (1968), 115, 122. It is misleading, however, to argue as does Douglas Horton in his edition of Norton's *The Answer* that Ames would "rule the theological mind of New England with unruffled serenity for a hundred years" after the planting of the Bay colony. (p. xvii)
[59] On Sibbes, see Pettit, *Heart Prepared,* 67. And see Pettit's essay, "Lydia's Conversion," Cambridge Historical Society, *Proceedings,* XL (Cambridge, Eng., 1964–1966), 59–83, wherein special emphasis is placed on the "movement in Puritanism toward experiential immediacy. . . ." (p. 66) Daniel J. Boorstin may prove to have been substantially correct in asserting that Winthrop and his coadjutors were "less interested in theology itself, than in the application of theology to everyday life," and that, in this sense at least, "although the Puritans in the New World made the Calvinist theology their point of departure, they made it precisely that and nothing else." Daniel J. Boorstin, *The Americans: The Colonial Experience* (New York, 1958), 5–6. See also Emil Oberholzer, Jr., *Delinquent Saints: Disciplinary Action in the Early Congregational Churches of Massachusetts* (New York, 1956), 6–7: "Theology was not unimportant to [the Puritan] . . . but theology was not allowed to stand in the way of morality. . . . The Puritan used his head to systematize his theology, but this, too, was subordinate to faith, and for the Puritan faith was not the acceptance of a system of doctrine (*fides*) but trust in God (*fiducia*). . . ." See also *ibid.,* 28–29.
[60] James K. Hosmer, ed., *Winthrop's Journal* (New York, 1908), I, 216–217.
[61] Simpson, *Puritanism,* 21.

34 – Michael McGiffert

called attention to the Puritans' expectation of the imminent Eschaton. John Cotton believed that Christ would come again in 1655, and with his colleagues, if Joy Bourne Gilsdorf is correct, intended the enterprise of the Bay "to be a penultimate and hopefully short-lived anticipation of the millenial Kingdom"—a Kingdom "envisaged as an apocalyptic vindication of the New England Way." [62] Spiritual fervor was undoubtedly intensified by the chiliasm of New Englanders who beyond their desire to conduct a reformist flank-attack on old England—beyond all considerations of earthly consequence whatever—regarded their new world as the beginning of the world's end.

Miller has also been challenged on another point of his reconstruction of Puritan thought, namely, his pioneering treatment of the Puritans' interpretation of Scripture, with particular regard to the method of exegesis known as typology. Typology, it will be recalled, is the art of finding in the persons and events of the Old Testament prefigurations of Christ and the coming Kingdom. Thus Joseph in the pit and Jonah in the whale adumbrate Christ's descent into hell, and, if the typological reference were extended to the whole history of redemption, the Atlantic voyaging of the 1630's might be called antitypical to the Mosaic crossing of the Red Sea. Miller's account of typology hinges on Roger Williams; [63] restoring Williams to the Reformation, Miller argued that what made him peculiar among Puritans was essentially his exploiting of a typological hermeneutics that orthodox clergymen, like the Continental reformers before them, did not trust. This was "the open secret of [Williams's] radicalism," including his advocacy of religious liberty: "Roger Williams and a 'typologist.' John Cotton and his colleagues were 'federalists.'" [64] The latter, it is true, "did not entirely condemn typology"; they "recognized

---

[62] Gilsdorf to McGiffert, Sept. 3, 1968. See Joy Bourne Gilsdorf, The Puritan Apocalypse: New England Eschatology in the Seventeenth Century (unpubl. Ph.D. diss., Yale University, 1964). On Cotton's anticipation of Christ's return see Jesper Rosenmeier, "VERITAS: The Sealing of the Promise," Harvard Library Bulletin, XVI (1968), 33–35; Jesper Rosenmeier, The Teacher and the Witness: John Cotton and Roger Williams," Wm. and Mary Qtly., 3d Ser., XXV (1968), 411ff.; Jesper Rosenmeier, Image of Christ: The Typology of John Cotton (unpubl. Ph.D. diss., Harvard University, 1965), 16, 167–168, 191–192. On the millenarian strain in Johnson's Wonder-Working Providence, see Sacvan Bercovitch, "The Historiography of Johnson's Wonder-Working Providence," Essex Institute Historical Collections, CIV (1968), 157ff.

[63] And on Jonathan Edwards, for strong objections have been raised to Miller's interpretation of Edwards's typologizing, as presented in the introduction to Images or Shadows of Divine Things by Jonathan Edwards (New Haven, 1948). See Mason I. Lowance, Jr., Images and Shadows of Divine Things: Puritan Typology in New England from 1660 to 1750 (unpubl. Ph.D. diss., Emory University, 1967), and Thomas M. Davis, The Traditions of Puritan Typology (unpubl. Ph.D. diss., University of Missouri, 1968).

[64] Miller, ed., Williams's Writings, VII, 10. See also Perry Miller, Roger Williams: His Contribution to the American Tradition (Indianapolis, 1953), 33–38. The extravagance of Miller's prose in the preface to Williams's Writings, VII, may indicate intellectual strain. Williams's "fervent typological passion" is said to be "fantastic" and "bizarre," "wild and impressionistic," and Williams's addiction to typology is attributed to "the peculiar maggot in his brain. . . ." Yet though "strangely ill," he is better off than the medieval theologians who suffered "a kind of typological craze" that thrust them into "a mystagogic maze in which, it seemed to the Reformers, the Scriptures were being strangled." Miller's argu-

that it, if used with extreme caution, might have its uses," and Cotton himself "experimented with it to the very limit of safety," [65] yet Puritan divines found typology on the whole both distasteful and dangerous because it opened the door to subjective, visionary misreadings of the Word. Williams's controversy with Massachusetts thus pitted an ardent typologist against theologians who were mainly antitypological, while his particular quarrel with Cotton matched two kinds of typologists.

Recent studies endorse Miller's efforts to recapture Williams from the modernists while correcting his views of typology. They maintain convincingly that typology was not inconsistent with the federal theology, that Puritans of all sorts engaged in typological exercises, that typology was freely employed by the Continental reformers. Protestant thinkers valued typology primarily for its service in establishing symbolically the continuity of the *Heilsgeschichte:* like the theory of the covenant it set forth the ongoing, governing, redeeming purpose of God in history. And since the climax of history was to occur in Massachusetts, the Bay ministers found typology peculiarly attractive: Boston would be the conclusive antitype of Israel. "Not only was typology an essential part of their method of reading the history of God's redemptive Providence," remarks Mason I. Lowance, Jr., "it was also a rich source for affirming the Divine role of New England in the fulfillment of God's universal plan." [66]

As for the Williams-Cotton affair, scholars are inclined to deemphasize the importance of typology. Leroy Moore holds that the "key to Williams' thought . . . is not typology but unqualified allegiance to divine sovereignty": Williams was simply a better Calvinist than his federal opponents.[67] Jesper Rosenmeier stresses Williams's daring notion of the Incarnation: "Where Cotton and the Bay Puritans viewed the history of redemption as an essentially unchanged covenant of grace, Williams interpreted Christ's incarnation as the historical moment when God had

ment is usually least effective when his language is most flamboyant—when, as Loren Baritz remarks, he apparently attempted to "achieve drama through rhetoric." See *New Eng. Qtly.,* XXXIX (1966), 96. See also Peter Gay, *A Loss of Mastery: Puritan Historians in Colonial New England* (Berkeley, 1966), 142.

[65] Miller, *Williams,* 37.

[66] Samuel Mather, *The Figures or Types of the Old Testament,* ed. Mason I. Lowance, Jr. (New York, 1969), v. Cf. Davis, Traditions of Puritan Typology, 281: for Calvin, "typology is the single most important method for interpreting the Scriptures. . . ." On typology, in addition to the writings cited n. 63 above, see Mason I. Lowance, Jr., "Typology and the New England Way: Cotton Mather and the Exegesis of Biblical Types," *Early American Literature,* IV (1969), 15–37; Rosenmeier, The Image of Christ; Rosenmeier, "VERITAS," *Harvard Lib. Bull.,* XVI (1968), 26–37; and Rosenmeier, "Teacher and Witness," *Wm. and Mary Qtly.,* 3d Ser., XXV (1968), 408–431; Richard M. Reinitz, "Symbolism and Freedom: The Use of Biblical Typology as an Argument for Religious Toleration in Seventeenth-Century England and America (unpubl. Ph.D. diss., University of Rochester, 1967); Edmund S. Morgan, "Miller's Williams," *New Eng. Qtly.,* XXXVIII (1965), 513–523; Morgan, *Roger Williams,* 90–93; Bercovitch, "Typology in Puritan New England," *Amer. Qtly.,* XIX (1967), 166–191, and Sacvan Bercovitch, "The Historiography of Johnson's *Wonder-Working Providence,*" *Essex Inst. Hist. Coll.,* CIV (1968), 138–161.

[67] Leroy Moore, "Religious Liberty: Roger Williams and the Revolutionary Era," *Church Hist.,* XXXIV (1965), 60. Moore agrees with Miller, however, that "the typological approach to the Bible was 'feared and detested' by the Bay Puritans and, therefore, became a very significant element in their disagreement with Williams."

changed the nature of His kingdom radically." [68] Reinitz contends that Williams merely *used* typology: "Although typology was a useful tool for him, his feelings about the relations of church and state were derived from other sources," specifically from a concept of conscience that differed sharply from Cotton's.[69] If these writers are correct, whatever the mark of Williams's idiosyncracy may prove to have been, it will not be typology: the way in which Puritans read their Bibles will be reinterpreted as an expression of more basic intellectual and emotional stances.[70] More largely considered, typology can be expected to continue to merit the attention of intellectual historians, just as it commands the interest of literary scholars who know that the poems of an Edward Taylor cannot be explicated without a thorough knowledge of the types and antitypes.[71]

---

[68] Rosenmeier, Image of Christ, 415. Rosenmeier demonstrates Cotton's enthusiasm for typology, especially in Cotton's exegesis of Canticles. See *ibid.*, 106–109; and Rosenmeier, "Teacher and Witness," *Wm. and Mary Qtly.*, XXV (1968), 425–430. His dissertation has an interesting discussion of the place of typology in the Antinomian Controversy—a central place, if it is conceded to Rosenmeier that the theological nub of the conflict was the meaning of "the seal of the spirit," typologically interpreted. Rosenmeier, Image of Christ, 117–164. Suggestive also is Rosenmeier's observation that New England's growing conservatism and provincialism can be seen in the Puritans' changing sense of their role in the history of redemption: ". . . until 1630, the Puritan ministers interpreted the history of redemption as a dynamic unfolding process. Christ was *redeeming* the world, irresistibly propelling man and the entire creation toward the glory of his future kingdom. . . . However, in the sermons preached in New England after 1630 there is a growing shift of emphasis, evident especially after 1638, from Christ's *redeeming* the world to His having already *redeemed* it." Rosenmeier, "Teacher and Witness," *Wm. and Mary Qtly.*, XXV (1968), 424. A more conventional treatment, though not altogether in agreement with Miller, is Richard Etulain, "John Cotton and the Anne Hutchinson Controversy," *Rendezvous*, II (1967), 9–18.

[69] Reinitz, Symbolism and Freedom, 200. Cf. Darrett B. Rutman, *Wm. and Mary Qtly.*, 3d Ser., XXI (1964), 303. Rutman accepted Miller's contention that Williams was exceptional in his enthusiasm for typology but treated Williams's typologizing as merely a matter of polemical expediency. Nearer the root of Williams's dissent Rutman discerned "a literal acceptance" of the Book of Revelation.

[70] Among recent examinations of the Williams-Cotton contest, that of Bercovitch comes closest to Miller in emphasizing the central importance of typology. Bercovitch discovers a crucial distinction in modes of typologizing, Williams's having been "allegorical" where Cotton's was "historical." Bercovitch, "Typology in Puritan New England," *Amer. Qtly.*, XIX (1967), 175.

[71] On the general relation of typology to literature consult Ursula Brumm, *Die Religiöse Typologie in Amerikanische Denken* (Leiden, 1963), and A. C. Charity, *Events and Their Afterlife: The Dialectics of Christian Typology in the Bible and Dante* (Cambridge, Eng., 1966). More specialized studies include Victor Harris, "Allegory to Analogy in the Interpretation of Scripture," *Philological Quarterly*, LXV (1966), 1–23; Northrop Frye, "The Typology of *Paradise Regained*," *Modern Philology*, LIII (1956), 227–238; and William G. Madsen, "Earth the Shadow of Heaven: Typological Symbolism in *Paradise Lost*," *PMLA* (1960), 519–556. Students of Puritan types should be more familiar than most have shown themselves to be with the theological literature on the subject. See, for example, the essays by Gerhard von Rad, Rudolf Bultmann, and Walter Eichrodt, in Claus Westermann, ed., *Essays on Old Testament Hermeneutics* (Richmond, 1963); Jean Daniélou, *From Shadows to Reality: Studies in the Biblical Typology of the Fathers* (Westminster, Md., 1960); Leonhard Goppelt, *Typos: Die typologische Deutung des alten Testament in Neuen* (Guetsersloh, 1939); essays by G. W. H. Lampe and K. J. Woolcombe, in *Essays in Typology, Studies in Biblical Theology*, No. 22 (Naperville, Ill., 1957); Horace D. Hummel, "The Old Testament Basis of Typological Interpretation," *Biblical Research*, IX (1964), 38–50; R. A. Markus, "Presuppositions of the Typological Approach to Scripture," *Church Quarterly Review* CLVIII (1957), 442–451. Still useful is Milton Terry, *Biblical Hermeneutics* (New York, 1885), 683–684.

Miller's call,[72] twenty years ago, for a fuller study of typology than he was then prepared to make has been well answered, and the answering has been valuable in opening new perspectives on, and raising new questions about, Puritan faith and conviction.

III

While the reassessment of the Puritan mind and spirit proceeds, a number of scholars, among whom the leading figures are B. Katherine Brown, John M. Bumsted, John Demos, David H. Flaherty, Philip J. Greven, Jr., George D. Langdon, Jr., Kenneth A. Lockridge, Darrett B. Rutman, Richard C. Simmons, Robert E. Wall, Jr., and John J. Waters, have undertaken to recover the social and institutional history of early New England, more or less apart from the record of intellect and piety. Going out on the town and farm, into the shops and homes and fields and marketplaces and meeting-houses, they are attempting to report the life that New Englanders actually lived. Inspiration for this work, entailing an arduous exhumation of local documentary remains and some degree of quantitative analysis, comes chiefly from such non-Millerian sources as recent advances, especially European, in community studies, demography, and comparative institutional history.[73] To a significant degree the new social history is written without explicit reference to Miller's exposition of Puritan thought, though its bearing on the ideational aspect of Puritan studies is suggested by Mrs. Brown's query, "If his [Miller's] basic assumption concerning the structure of Massachusetts society was wrong, what happens to his theories of the intellectual side of American Puritanism?" [74] It being noted, for example, that the "mind" Miller wrote about was the mind of the articulate, educated few, the question reasonably follows whether the notions of this "speaking aristocracy" were faithfully reflected in the sentiments of the "silent democracy" either in the churches or among the far more silent crowd of the unregenerate who numbered by Miller's own figure (taken from James Truslow Adams) fully four-fifths of the people of Massachusetts. This question connects with several others in the historical sociology of New England. Bumsted writes that "the main outlines are clear of the framework of the Puritan intellectual position as revealed in the literary sources, and further work will only correct minor points. To this extent Miller can be said to be definitive. But a whole host of questions remain unanswered: did the writers of the time practice what they preached? What was the common man thinking (and doing)? What relationship exists between socio-economic factors

---

[72] Miller, ed., *Images or Shadows,* 141–142.
[73] The most thorough review of this material will be found in Philip J. Greven, Jr., "Historical Demography in Colonial America," *Wm. and Mary Qtly., 3d Ser.,* XXIV (1967), 438–454.
[74] B. Katherine Brown to McGiffert, June 24, 1968.

and ideas? Below the ideational level, what did New England really look like and how did it operate?" [75] Was there, such questions go to ask, an entity that can properly be called *Puritan* New England?

Back of questions like these moves a suspicion, sometimes voiced as an accusation, that "Puritan historiography in America has been too exclusively intellectual," [76] not to say intellectualistic. Those who believe this tend to find "Miller's noetic concerns largely irrelevant" [77]; they see his New Englanders as mere "walking doctrines and riding heresies," [78] and some of them are inclined to be exclamatory in celebrating their liberation from the "Millerite Establishment" and their own rising empire. In contrast to the kind of intellectual history, exemplified by the first volume of *The New England Mind,* in which ideas are studied for their own sake, largely independent of non-intellectual circumstance and abstracted from any context save that of the mind itself, the social historians often show as little interest in the life of the mind as Miller showed in his earlier books in social and economic factors.[79] It does not necessarily follow, however, that, to quote the warning of the scholar who has done more than any other to explore the relations of thought and experience in colonial New England, "great danger . . . lurks in the possibility, perhaps the likelihood, that institutional historians will try to operate outside the context of ideas," and that "it will set the study of New England Puritanism backward if students of institutions try to magnify their subject matter to the point where it excludes the intellectual framework in which New England institutions must properly be viewed." [80] No doubt it would be foolish to try to reconstruct the life of the mind—or, for that

---

[75] John M. Bumsted to McGiffert, May 17, 1968. Schlatter's statement that "all scholars agree that it was the Puritan leaders who shaped the culture of New England, whatever the rank and file may have wanted" seems less accurate now than it was when made. Richard Schlatter, "The Puritan Strain," in John Higham, ed., *The Reconstruction of American History* (New York, 1962), 26. See, for example, Darrett B. Rutman to McGiffert, May 13, 1968, and Rutman, "Mirror of Puritan Authority," in Billias ed., *Selected Essays,* 146–167; see also, Louis B. Wright, *Amer. Hist. Rev.,* LXXIII (1967), 587: ". . . the impact of dogmatic theology upon the population as a whole has been vastly exaggerated."

[76] Schlatter, "Puritan Strain," in Higham, ed., *Reconstruction of American History,* 44.

[77] Foster to McGiffert, July 3, 1968. This is Foster's observation, not necessarily his own position.

[78] Larzer Ziff, *New Eng. Qtly.,* XXXVI (1963), 401.

[79] Cf. Morgan, "Miller and Historians," *Harvard Rev.,* II (1964), 54: "Miller scarcely mentioned actions as they affected ideas. And yet by spelling out the ideas through which people of that time understood what they were doing, he rewrote their history. In occasional sentences, as in an unembellished line drawing, he was able, almost casually, to reconstruct social, political, and even economic history. Once one had the scheme to the thing clear, he seemed to say, it was scarcely worth the trouble to paint in the details of who did precisely what." See also, Heimert, "Miller: An Appreciation," *Harvard Rev.,* II (1964), 1–20.

[80] Morgan to McGiffert, May 21, 1968. "I think," Morgan writes in the same letter, "the most profitable direction for studies of Puritanism at the present time lies in the close analysis of institutions. Miller confined himself to the history of ideas and merely extrapolated occasional remarks about institutions as implications of the ideas with which he was dealing. It would be worthwhile for other scholars to study institutional history . . . in the light of the ideas." Morgan elaborates these points in "Historians of Early New England," in Billington, ed., *Reinterpretation of American History,* 58–60.

matter, the life of the body—from the seventeenth-century counterpart of the laundry list.[81] Yet, just as Miller, forty years ago in graduate school, had to escape the contexts that were then available to him, so the social historian at present, if he is to master his craft, *must* operate for the time being "outside the context of ideas." He must do so partly because the pattern of Puritan ideas has lately become a little hazy and partly because the relations of ideas and institutions are too complex and too little understood to justify designating the one as "context," the other as content, one as "framework," the other as furniture.[82] Moreover, as John Higham has suggested, the parting of social from intellectual history, one instance of which is the split in Puritan studies, frees the student of ideas from "overextended commitments" and produces what Higham supposes to be a healthy tension "between two different but equally revealing types of historical patterns: the arrangement of ideas into a working system, and the arrangement of people into a functioning society." [83] Eventually that tension may be resolved in a new synthesis in which the inner and outer worlds of New England, each world more fully and exactly known, will be put together again. Meanwhile, as the work goes forward on each side of the schism, the profession should seek ways of cultivating a company of scholars whose competence transcends our present categories and who can achieve a capacious and subtle understanding of what it is that, in Ola Elizabeth Winslow's nice phrase, "allows it [New England] to be almost a culture. . . ." [84]

In the second volume of *The New England Mind* Miller undertook to extract from the history of primitive New England "certain generalizations about the relations of thought or ideas to communal experience." [85] In so doing, as a sympathetic reviewer noted, he was obliged "to run far ahead of his interference" for he needed "a detailed, sophisticated history of colonial society" that did not exist. Therefore, though he "extemporized a social history subtler than any yet written," his treatment of the "com-

---

81 Cf. Foster to McGiffert, Aug. 16, 1968.

82 Skotheim properly makes the important point that in this respect as in others, "the trends in Puritan scholarship are not simply reactions to Miller," since "the same trends are seen throughout present scholarship in American intellectual history" generally. Skotheim to McGiffert, Sept. 13, 1968.

83 John Higham, "American Intellectual History: A Critical Approach," *Amer. Qtly.*, XIII (1961), 231.

84 Winslow to McGiffert, June 4, 1968. In addition to the other studies cited in these notes, the following cast light on the institutional history of Puritan New England: Emery Battis, *Saints and Sectaries: The Antinomian Controversey in the Massachusetts Bay Colony* (Chapel Hill, 1962)—it is worth noting that Battis anticipates the current main division in Puritan studies by his attempt to psychoanalyze Anne Hutchinson and by his sociological investigation of her supporters; Richard S. Dunn, *Puritans and Yankees: The Winthrop Dynasty of New England, 1630–1717* (Princeton, 1962); Kai T. Erikson, *Wayward Puritans: A Study in the Sociology of Deviance* (New York, 1966); Emil Oberholzer, Jr., "The Church in New England Society," in James Morton Smith, ed., *Seventeenth-Century America: Essays in Colonial History* (Chapel Hill, 1959), 143–165; and Ola Elizabeth Winslow, *Meetinghouse Hill, 1630–1783* (New York, 1952).

85 *New England Mind*, II, x.

munal experience" could not be "entirely successful."[86] Now the information that Miller did not have is being furnished, and the prospects for a synthetic treatment of behavior and thought are the brighter because the social historians tend to focus on matters of institutional practice, the ideology of which has been examined by historians of ideas. Suspecting that New England, even in its initial glory, did not perfectly conform to Winthrop's "medieval dream," the social historians are trying to measure the extent of popular participation and influence in local politics,[87] re-examining the institutional history of the churches and their relations to the New England governments,[88] and exploring approaches to the problem of calculating social mobility. These inquiries lead toward studies of land systems, wealth distribution, and population.[89] They also induce the historian to look freshly at English society and to reappraise the character

---

[86] Bernard Bailyn, *New Eng. Qtly.*, XXVII (1954), 116.

[87] See B. Katherine Brown, "Freemanship in Puritan Massachusetts," *Amer. Hist. Rev.*, LIX (1954), 865–883; B. Katherine Brown, "Puritan Democracy: A Case Study," *Miss. Valley Hist. Rev.*, L (1963), 377–396; B. Katherine Brown, "Puritan Democracy in Dedham, Massachusetts: Another Case Study," *Wm. and Mary Qtly.*, 3d Ser., XXIV (1967), 378–396. See also Donald W. Koch, "Income Distribution and Political Structure in Seventeenth-Century Salem, Massachusetts," *Essex Inst. Hist. Coll.*, CV (1969), 50–69; George D. Langdon, Jr., *Pilgrim Colony: A History of New Plymouth, 1620–1691* (New Haven, 1966); Kenneth A. Lockridge and Alan Kreider, "The Evolution of Massachusetts Town Government, 1640–1740," *Wm. and Mary Qtly.*, 3d Ser., XXIII (1966), 549–574; Richard C. Simmons, "Freemanship in Early Massachusetts: Some Suggestions and a Case Study," *Wm. and Mary Qtly.*, 3d Ser., XIX (1962),, 422–428; Richard C. Simmons, "Godliness, Property, and the Franchise in Puritan Massachusetts: An Interpretation," *Jour. of Amer. Hist.*, LV (1968), 495–511; Robert Emmet Wall, Jr., "A New Look at Cambridge," *Jour. of Amer. Hist.*, LII (1965), 599–605; John J. Waters, "Hingham, Massachusetts, 1631–1661: An East Anglian Oligarchy in the New World," *Journal of Social History*, I (1968), 351–370. A related study is that of Mary Jeanne Anderson Jones, *Congregational Commonwealth: Connecticut, 1636–1662* (Middletown, Conn., 1968).

[88] In addition to the writings cited in the previous note, see J. M. Bumsted, "A Well-Bounded Toleration: Church and State in the Plymouth Colony," *Jour. of Church and State*, X (1968), 265–279; Richard C. Simmons, "The Founding of the Third Church in Boston," *Wm. and Mary Qtly.*, 3d Ser., XXVI (1969), 241–252. Two recent articles stress the inclusivist tendencies of Non-Separatist Congregationalism. See Raymond P. Stearns and David D. Brawner, "New England Church 'Relations' and Continuity in Early Congregational History," American Antiquarian Society, *Proceedings*, LXXV (Worcester, 1965), 13–45; and Kobrin, "The Expansion of the Visible Church in New England," *Church Hist.*, XXXVI (1967), 189–209.

[89] John Demos, "Families in Colonial Bristol, Rhode Island: An Exercise in Historical Demography," *Wm. and Mary Qtly.*, 3d Ser., XXV (1968), 40–57, and John Demos, "Notes on Life in Plymouth Colony," *Wm. and Mary Qtly.*, 3d Ser., XXII (1965), 264–286. See the following by Philip J. Greven, Jr.: "Family Structure in Seventeenth-Century Andover, Massachusetts," *Wm. and Mary Qtly.*, 3d Ser., XXIII (1966), 234–256; Four Generations: A Study of Family Structure, Inheritance, and Mobility in Andover, Massachusetts, 1630–1750 (unpubl. Ph.D. diss., Harvard University, 1965); "Historical Demography," *Wm. and Mary Qtly.*, 3d Ser., XXIV (1965), 434–454, and "Old Patterns in the New World: The Distribution of Land in 17th Century Andover," *Essex Inst. Hist. Coll.*, CI (1966), 113–148. Kenneth A. Lockridge, "Land, Population and the Evolution of New England Society 1630–1790," *Past and Present*, XXXIX (1968), 62–80, and Kenneth A. Lockridge, "The Population of Dedham, Massachusetts, 1636–1736," *Economic History Review*, 2d Ser., XIX (1966), 318–344. Herbert A. Whitney, "Estimating Precensus Populations: A Method Suggested and Applied to the Towns of Rhode Island and Plymouth Colonies in 1689," *Annals of the Association of Amer. Geographers*, LIX (1965), 179–189. Cf. Greven, Jr., to McGiffert, July 25, 1968: ". . . I think that demographic work will be important for nearly every aspect of American life, including religious experience, but not a single person, as far as I know, has done anything so far which might confirm or deny my feelings and intuitions on the subject."

of early emigration to New England in order to identify behavioral and institutional continuities and discontinuities, accommodations to the American environment and resistances to accommodation. Lockridge puts the complex question, "How was rural America like rural England, and how, when, and in what ways was it becoming uniquely American?" Through the results to date are inconclusive, and though there is some disagreement on the utility of documents, as well as on the nature and interpretation of findings,[90] the social historians seem to be discovering that life in New England was from the outset more democratic, more diverse, and more fluid than one would be led to conclude from the prescriptions of Winthrop's *Arbella* sermon.[91]

---

[90] Kenneth A. Lockridge, Dedham 1636–1736: The Anatomy of a Puritan Utopia (unpubl. Ph.D. diss., Princeton University, 1965), 2. Holding that much in New England culture that has been thought to be peculiarly Puritan will be shown to have been commonly English, Rutman anticipates "significant breakthroughs in the area of social history which will . . . link New England firmly with old England." Rutman to McGiffert, May 13, 1968. Greven goes a step farther to suggest "an ironic interpretation of early American society: that it may, for a while at least, have been more 'traditional' in character than English society itself." Greven, "Historical Demography," *Wm. and Mary Qtly.*, 3d Ser., XXIV (1967), 453. These suppositions run counter to the views of Sumner Chilton Powell who found in Sudbury, Mass., evidence of "revolution in the systems of social and economic status." Sudbury's folk "made a staggering number of changes . . . in religion, in social organization, in local government, and in attitude and values generally. . . . Life in Sudbury was indeed a 'new' England." Sumner Chilton Powell, *Puritan Village: The Formation of a New England Town* (Middletown, Conn., 1963), 83, 140, 143. Waters's findings for early Hingham tend to support Greven's suggestion of early New England conservatism: "Hingham exemplifies the retention of old-world forms and values in the wilderness." Waters, "Hingham, Massachusetts," *Jour. of Soc. Hist.*, I (1968), 351–370. See also, H. Roy Merrens, "Historical Geography and Early American History," *Wm. and Mary Qtly.*, 3d Ser., XXII (1965), 529–548. On the perplexing question of the provenance of the New England Church Way, see Larzer Ziff, "The Salem Puritans in the 'Free Aire of a New World,'" *Huntington Library Quarterly*, XX (1957), 373–384, and Larzer Ziff, *The Career of John Cotton: Puritanism and the American Experience* (Princeton, 1962). This problem is also touched by Edmund S. Morgan, *Visible Saints: The History of a Puritan Idea* (New York, 1963), esp. 80–83; Everett H. Emerson, *John Cotton* (New Haven, 1965), Chap. IV; Keith L. Sprunger, "William Ames and the Settlement of Massachusetts Bay," *New Eng. Qtly.*, XXXIX (1966), 66–79; and Rutman, *Winthrop's Boston*, 283–285. For a lively, candid discussion of the aims and problems of the new social historians see *Occasional Papers in Old Colony Studies*, I (1969). Especially effective in relating changing values to changing social patterns is David H. Flaherty, Privacy in Colonial New England, 1630–1776 (unpubl. Ph.D. diss., Columbia University, 1967).

[91] On the issue of democracy in colonial New England see the exchange between B. Katherine Brown and Richard C. Simmons, Kenneth A. Lockridge, and Stephen Foster, *Wm. and Mary Qtly.*, 3d Ser., XXV (1968), 330–339. Stephen Foster, "The Massachusetts Franchise in the 17th Century," *Wm. and Mary Qtly.*, XXIV (1967), 621. The author argues that the lamentable condition of the records "makes it impossible to estimate the number of men actually legally empowered to vote and hold office in the Bay Colony under the Old Charter." On another problem of interpretation compare Rutman's assertion that "wills and inventories are our best evidence of the everyday life of the past," (Darrett B. Rutman, *Husbandmen of Plymouth: Farms and Villages in the Old Colony, 1620–1692* [Boston, 1967], 30) with Lockridge's observations on the grave risks of over-reliance on probate records. (Lockridge, *Wm. and Mary Qtly.*, 3d Ser., XXV [1967], 516–517.) Lockridge, "Evolution of New England Society," *Past and Present*, XXXIX (1968), 79–80. Greven, "Historical Demography," *Wm. and Mary Qtly.*, 3d Ser., XXIV (1967), 434–454, and David J. Rothman, "A Note on the Study of the Colonial Family," *Wm. and Mary Qtly.*, 3d Ser., XXIII (1966), 627–634, suggest the questions to which social historians do and should address themselves.

IV

To conclude: it is possible in the 1960's to speak of American Puritan studies as a field of scholarship, and to appraise its estate and activity, because Perry Miller, above all others, made the American Puritans studiable. He did this not only by the herculean labor of reading and explaining what the Puritans wrote but, more fundamentally, by constructing a model—in currently fashionable nomenclature, a paradigm—that, though modified or challenged in some particulars by later work, still gives the subject whatever definition and discipline it can rightly claim to possess. A paradigm is defined by a historian of science, Thomas S. Kuhn, as a system for acquiring, validating, organizing, and applying knowledge; it is an orderly way of scanning and making sense of some large body of data—for example, Copernican astronomy, Newtonian physics, Darwinian biology.[92] A paradigm embraces both the kinds of questions that are asked and the answers that are given, together with the methods by which answers are secured and the basic assumptions by which they are ordered; it generates and guides research by providing "model problems and solutions to a community of practitioners"[93] or believers. Paradigms cease to command commitment, according to Kuhn, when under repeated testing they fail to furnish systemically compatible answers to the questions they inspire. The anomalies that crop up in the normal course of research gradually induce a crisis of credibility in the paradigm. Ultimately the anomalies may become so numerous (though a single significant and highly resistant discrepancy may turn the trick), obstinate, and acute that the recognition of them as such precipitates a "paradigm revolution." Then, because the exceptions can no longer be persuasively said to prove the rule, the old rule must be revoked and a new one enacted which makes the "exceptions" normative.

A paradigm is a view of the "world," or of some aspect of it, from the "inside." It is the construct of assumptions, explanations, and expectations by which intellectual organization and meaning are imposed on experience. It may not be stretching a useful concept unduly, however, to make it refer also to the view from the "outside"—that is, to the interpretative patterning by which historians contrive to organize and make intelligible the flux of the past. Insofar as the outer or historical view differs from the inner or immediate view—as, in the nature of the case, it

92 The following discussion is based on Thomas S. Kuhn, *The Structure of Scientific Revolutions* (Chicago, 1962), and informed by Wise, "Implicit Irony," *Jour. of Hist. of Ideas,* XXIX (1968), and Murray G. Murphey, "On the Relation Between Science and Religion," *Amer. Qtly.,* XX (1968), 283ff.

93 Kuhn, *Scientific Revolutions,* x. As Morgan notes, "New England historiography has reached the critical point where it generates its own energy." Morgan, "Historians of Early New England," in Billington, ed., *Reinterpretation of Early American History,* 42.

always must to a greater or less degree—it takes the latter as part of the data from which to fashion, and on which to fix, the interpretative paradigm. Thus in American historiography we may plausibly speak of the "progressive paradigm" of Vernon Parrington and Charles Beard, the "consensus paradigm" of Daniel Boorstin and Louis Hartz, or, for that matter, Miller's paradigm of Puritanism. Such usage is the more permissible because historical paradigms (which are also, of course, expressions—more or less partial, self-conscious, and tendentious—of some aspect or aspects of the inner view of the contemporary world of the historian) appear to change through processes and for causes not radically dissimilar to those that operate in the changing of more general paradigms.

Five years after Miller's death, though there are signs of a deepening crisis of credibility, it is still too soon to calculate the life-span of his paradigm and quite impossible to predict the shape of the synthesis that may eventually bring clarity out of the present exuberant multiplicity of Puritan studies. Robert A. Skotheim remarks, and this paper confirms, that Miller's work is more admired than emulated,[94] but just how such profundity and breadth and power of scholarship could be "emulated" is not easy to see. The frequent assertion by some intellectual historians and many social historians that Puritanism was pluralistic indicates a degree of dissatisfaction with the reigning paradigm—yet reports of a paradigm revolution [95] seem premature. Definitions of Puritanism vary, but it is too facile to conclude that "there was no Puritan way, . . . merely actions, reactions, interactions." [96] Historiographers have begun to assess Miller's place in the traditions of American history, the evolution of American thought, and the making of American myth,[97] and one critic has boldly suggested that "Miller was primarily an artist" whose work, to be rightly appreciated, must be approached from the vantage point of art, not that of historical "science" [98]—but it is not yet clear how judgments on Miller's

[94] Robert A. Skotheim, *American Intellectual Histories and Historians,* 308.

[95] In effect, by Rutman in numerous reviews and especially in his *Winthrop's Boston.* But see Sacvan Bercovitch in *Early American Literature,* IV (1969), 51: ". . . to discard Miller's framework is to set back, not liberate the study of Puritanism . . . for all its imperfections, the framework is still viable, and . . . it will become part of the larger synthesis we look forward to at the end of the present splintering of interests."

[96] Rutman, *Winthrop's Boston,* 274.

[97] See Skotheim, "American Histories of Ideas," *Jour. of Hist. of Ideas,* XXV. (1964), 257–278, and Skotheim, *American Intellectual Histories and Historians,* 186–212, 307–309; Reinitz, "Miller and Recent American Historiography," *Bull. of Brit. Assoc. for Amer. Studies,* VIII (1964), 27–35; Wise, "Implicit Irony," *Jour. of Hist. of Ideas,* XXIX (1968); and Henry F. May, "The Recovery of American Religious History," *Amer. Hist. Rev.,* LXX (1964), 84–85. Reinitz and Wise find in Miller a chance to break away from the categories of both "progressive" and "consensus" history.

[98] David A. Hollinger, "Perry Miller and Philosophical History," *History and Theory,* VII (1968), 200. Hollinger's article is the most recent, extensive, and perceptive analysis of Miller's craft. For other insights, mostly fragmentary, consult Neil Harris, *Amer. Qtly.,* XIX (1967), 726, 729; Donald Fleming, "Perry Miller and Esoteric History," *Harvard Rev.,* II (1964), 25–29; Wise, "Implicit Irony," *Jour. of Hist. of Ideas,* XXIX (1968), 15–16, 18, 25; Heimert, "Miller: An Appreciation," *Harvard Rev.,* II (1964), 40ff.; Morgan, "Miller and the Historians," *Harvard Rev.,* II (1964), 55, 57; and Morgan, *Wm. and Mary Qtly.,* 3d Ser., XI (1954), 294.

scholarship will be affected by bringing it under these purviews. At present Puritan and New England historiography is remarkable more for vitality than for coherence. This may signify an impending change of paradigm, yet, as Kuhn points out, paradigm revolutions cannot occur unless and until an alternative paradigm is available to replace the old outworn one—and that is very far from the present case in Puritan studies. Nor is it probable that the revolution will happen soon: the disintegration of Miller's hegemony has not gone far enough for reintegration to be, at this point, either meaningful or plausible. For the present one must be content to observe so many good scholars, some established, some rising, all, to borrow an avuncular phrase from Perry Miller, "coming so grandly along." [99]

---

[99] Miller, *Errand,* ix.

▌▌ *Democracy in Colonial America: Fact or Fiction?*

Introduction Fifty years ago Carl Becker, with rare historical insight, posed a dual question concerning the interpretation of the American Revolution. He declared there were two problems involved: the problem of home rule and the problem of who should rule at home. The first problem concerned imperial relations; the second problem concerned the relations in civil society of Americans in America. The second problem has as its fundamental query the relationship of colonial democracy to the American Revolution.

Robert E. Brown, who has intensively studied the structure of society in colonial Massachusetts, has concluded that in that colony a middle-class democracy existed before the Revolution, and that the Revolution had the purpose of preserving a social order and not of changing it. He thus asserts that as far as Massachusetts is concerned, the majority ruled at home, and further believes that what was true in Massachusetts "was not fundamentally different from the other colonies and states." His recent study, in collaboration with his wife, of colonial Virginia leads to the conclusion: "Except for slavery and British influence, what now passes in this country as middle-class representative democracy was well-entrenched in the Old Dominion long before the American Revolution." (*Virginia 1705–1786: Democracy or Aristocracy* (1964), p. 308.) The real meaning of the Revolution, in Brown's view, is thus to be sought in the struggle for independence from Britain.

J. R. Pole, in the second piece of historical writing given here, characterizes Brown's interpretation as not subtle, but not absolute nonsense either. He feels that Brown's interpretation is simplistic and mechanical, that "it leaves unfulfilled the rather more complex task of perceiving the democratic elements in their proper places within a system conceived in another age, under a different inspiration." That different inspiration lay in the Whig philosophy of government known, understood, and admired in colonial America and in eighteenth-century England alike and firmly based in a deferential and ordered society with appropriate institutions for its operation. In a light vein, and glancing with wry humor at the concept that colonial America might have been democratic, Pole gibes: "If this was democracy, it was a democracy that wore its cockade firmly pinned into its periwig." Of the "politics of deference" Pole writes with warmth, with nostalgia, and with an appreciation of the antique without pejorative overtones: "Deference: it does not seem, in retrospect, a very secure cement to the union of social orders. Yet to those who live under its sway it can be almost irresistible. It was beginning to weaken no doubt, in [John] Adams own political lifetime. . . . But not easily, not all at once, not without a struggle.

"It was this which collapsed in ruins in the upheaval of Jacksonian democracy. And that, perhaps, is why the election of so ambiguous a leader was accompanied by such an amazing uproar."

46

Middle-Class Democracy and the Revolution in Massachusetts, 1691-1780

——Robert E. Brown

Introduction

For the past fifty years or more a thesis has been current in the teaching and writing of American history, political science, and literature that the society which produced the American Revolution and the federal Constitution was not a democratic society. There are differences of opinion as to just how undemocratic this society was, but in general the point is usually made that even though eighteenth-century America was more democratic than Europe, democracy as we know it did not arrive in this country until the time of Andrew Jackson.

This concept of an undemocratic society is based on two major assumptions: one, that property qualifications for voting eliminated a large portion of the free adult male population from participation in political affairs; the other, that inequitable representation heavily favored the older aristocratic commercial areas along the seacoast at the expense of the more recently settled inland agricultural areas. Hence it followed naturally that colonial political and economic life was dominated by the upper economic classes.

Writers who accept the thesis that colonial society was undemocratic have also generally followed the interpretation that the American Revolution was a "dual" revolution. On one hand, there was the conflict between Great Britain and her American colonies—what might be called the "War for Independence." But accompanying this, and of equal or perhaps greater significance, was a struggle within the colonies over which class would dominate economic and political life. According to this theory, the second phase of the conflict, which might well be designated the "American Revolution" to distinguish it from the "War of Independence," was primarily an effort by the unenfranchised and dissatisfied lower classes to gain economic, political, and social equality with their betters.

Both the "War of Independence" and the "American Revolution" suc-

From Robert E. Brown, *Middle-Class Democracy and the Revolution in Massachusetts, 1691–1780*, pp. V–VII, 401–408. Copyright 1955 by the American Historical Association, used with permission of Cornell University Press.

ceeded to a greater or lesser extent in their objectives, according to most writers. The first won political independence for the colonies from Great Britain, although economic independence was not achieved until the War of 1812. The second succeeded by the elimination of colonial ruling classes, or a reduction in their power, and by the elevation of the "common man" to a position of importance in society which he had not hitherto enjoyed. This was reflected in the elimination or diminution of such manifestations of aristocratic domination as property qualifications for voting, inequitable representation, established churches, and entail and primogeniture in the distribution of inheritances. Later, aristocratic upper classes staged a "counterrevolution" by putting over a conservative Constitution on the people, and it was not really until the time of Andrew Jackson that democracy came fully into its own.

In the following pages I have raised some questions about this accepted interpretation as it applies to one colony and state, Massachusetts from 1691 to 1780. Did an upper economic class control economic life in the colony? Were property qualifications for voting sufficiently high to exclude an important number of adult men from participation in politics? Is the "American Revolution" interpretation a valid one, and if not, what part did democracy play in the "War for Independence"? And did the Revolution result in social changes in the state of Massachusetts significant enough to justify the concept of an "internal revolt"?

In the process of gathering material for this work, I have also seen sufficient evidence to suggest the need for reconsideration of assumptions with regard to other colonies as well as to Massachusetts.

Some of the basic ideas in the following pages first made their appearance as a doctoral dissertation at the University of Wisconsin in 1946. Since then, additional research has added much new material, and much rewriting has changed the original organization materially. But most of the general thesis presented in the original dissertation withstood the test of additional research; in fact, much of it was greatly strengthened by new material. Naturally for a work of this scope there are sources which I did not consult, but I reached a point where additional sources were merely adding more weight to points already well documented. . . .

* * *

Conclusion

In Massachusetts, therefore, we find one of the unique "revolutions" in world history—a revolution to preserve a social order rather than to change it. It was not, as we have often assumed, a dual revolution in which Americans won their independence from the British on one hand, and in which unenfranchised and underprivileged lower classes wrested democratic rights from a privileged local aristocracy on the other.

To understand what happened, we must first have a clear picture of Massachusetts society. Economically speaking, it was a middle-class society in which property was easily acquired and in which a large portion of the people were property-owning farmers. There was undoubtedly more economic democracy for the common man then than there is now. A large permanent labor class was practically nonexistent; men could either acquire land and become farmers or work for themselves as skilled artisans. If we insist that Americans who came to this country brought their accustomed class or caste lines with them, we must do so in the face of all the evidence to the contrary. If there was anything that observers at the time agreed on, it was that American society was almost the exact opposite of European society. There was nothing approaching the spread between the rich and the poor that Europe had at that time or that we have at present; a much larger proportion of society owned property then than now. Yet today, many people, even including many laborers, look on American society as predominantly middle class, though the opportunity for almost universal ownership of property is far less now than it was before the Revolution.

Economic opportunity, or economic democracy, in turn contributed to political democracy. While it is true that property ownership was a prerequisite for province and town voting, it is also true that the amount of property required for the franchise was very small and that the great majority of men could easily meet the requirements. There were probably a few men who could not qualify for voting, but the number could not have been very large. We cannot condone the practice of excluding even those few, but we should try to place the unenfranchised in their proper perspective. It makes a tremendous difference in our understanding of colonial society whether 95 per cent of the men were disfranchised or only 5 per cent. Furthermore, representation was apportioned in such a way that the farmers, not a merchant aristocracy, had complete control of the legislature.

It is not enough to say that the people of Massachusetts perhaps had more democracy than the people of Europe, but that they still did not have what we call democracy today. Neither is it sufficient to say that the germs of democracy were present, or that democracy, as a growing process if not as a reality, could be found in colonial times. When Hutchinson said that anything that looked like a man was a voter and that policy in general was dictated by the lower classes, he was certainly using the term "democracy" as we mean it now. A Hutchinson might deplore the view that government existed for the benefit of the people and that the people were to decide when government had served its proper functions, but this is the democratic idea. He might also deplore the fact that the people not only elected their representatives but also told them how to vote, yet this, too, is democracy.

In many respects, the people of Massachusetts had a government more responsive to the popular will than we have at the present time. There were far more representatives in proportion to population than we now have, and the representatives were more responsible to their constituents for their actions than are legislators at present. If a man votes against his belief to please his constituents so that he can hold his elected position, we cannot demand much more of democracy.

The number of men who could vote in the colony must not be confused with the number who did vote. These are entirely different problems, for the fact that there was much indifference on election day did not mean that many men could not participate. If we are attempting to explain events in terms of class conflict or internal revolution, it is especially important that we do not confuse the unfranchised and the disinterested. It is one thing if a man wants the vote but cannot meet the property requirements; it is another if he has the vote but fails to use it. Neither should we confuse the issue by giving percentages of voters in terms of the entire population, for probably less than 20 per cent of the people in colonial times were adult men.

In addition to economics and politics, there were also other manifestations of democracy in colonial Massachusetts. The system of education was, for its day, undoubtedly the best provided for the common people anywhere, and the correct comparison is with other educational systems at the time, not with our own. Many democratic practices were used in the operation of the Congregational church, and again we should remember that some 98 per cent of the people were Congregationalists. Furthermore, the Congregational church was not established as it was in England. Men who belonged to other churches did not pay taxes to the Congregational church; education and political office were open to those who were not Congregationalists. Perhaps there was not the complete religious freedom—or religious indifference—that we now associate with a liberal society, but there was also little dissatisfaction with religion to contribute to internal conflict. Even the colonial militia was democratic in its organization and in the influence which it exerted on politics.

In brief, Massachusetts did not have a social order before the American Revolution which would breed sharp internal class conflicts. The evidence does not justify an interpretation of the Revolution in Massachusetts as an internal class conflict designed to achieve additional political, economic, and social democracy. Although democracy was important as a factor in the conflict, it was a democracy which had already arrived in the colony long before 1776.

If we turn to British-American relations, however, we do not need to search long to find areas of conflict. The British for many years had developed a mercantilist-imperialist colonial system that had not functioned as expected. The aim of the system, as men at the time frankly admitted, was the ultimate benefit of the mother country. They believed that colonies should be regulated, both economically and politically, to further the well-being of the parent state. British officials were fully aware of the shortcomings in colonial administration, but, until 1760, Britain was not in a favorable position to remedy these defects. British officials were also fully aware of the fact that colonial democracy was one of the chief obstacles to effective enforcement of British colonial policy.

These two ingredients—an effective middle-class democracy and British imperial policies which had been thwarted by this democracy—explain what happened in Massachusetts from 1760 to 1776. In order to make their colonial system effective, the British believed that they had to recover authority over colonial officials. This, in turn, called for a colonial revenue which would be administered by Parliament, especially to pay the salaries of colonial officials and thus remove them from under the dominating influence of colonial assemblies. But of course the assembly of Massachusetts was fully aware of the power which control of the purse conferred and was equally determined to retain this power over British officials.

Throughout the story runs another thread—the threat, or at least what the British considered the threat, of colonial independence. This gave an air of urgency to British measures. There was the frequently expressed fear that time was on the side of the colonists. A rapidly growing population, bolstered by a phenomenal birthrate due to economic opportunity and by immigrants attracted by economic and political democracy, posed the problem to the British of recovering authority before the colonies became too large. When the showdown came with the Tea Act and the Coercive Acts, there was no doubt whatever that the British intended to curtail colonial democracy as a necessary step toward recovery of British authority and the prevention of colonial independence. The result was the very thing the British had tried to prevent—American independence.

Obviously democracy played an important part in the events before 1776, not as a condition to be achieved but as a reality which interfered with British policies. If the British had been successful, there would undoubtedly have been much less democracy in Massachusetts—hence the interpretation that the Revolution was designed to *preserve* a social order rather than to change it. We search in vain for evidence of class conflict that was serious enough to justify revolution; we do not have to look far for copious quantities of proof that colonial society was democratic and that the colonists were attempting to prevent British innovations.

Furthermore, the results of the Revolution more than confirm the interpretation presented here. There is a logic to what happened after the Revolution—or perhaps it would be more accurate to say what did not happen—if we accept the fact that the people of Massachusetts were not conducting an internal revolution. We are not confronted with the contradiction, which most writers fail to resolve, of a social revolution which was presumably successful but which failed to achieve social change. Why would a people, who were supposedly demanding a more democratic government, adopt a constitution which restricted democracy even more than it had been restricted in colonial days? On the other hand, the Massachusetts Constitution of 1780 was a logical consequence of a middle-class society which believed in the protection of property because most men were property owners. The almost complete absence of social revolution in Massachusetts should stand as convincing evidence that internal social revolution was not one of the chief aims of the American Revolution as far as the people of Massachusetts were concerned.

It is not necessary to explain whatever conservatism existed in colonial times in terms of a limited electorate. There is implied in this approach an assumption that universal suffrage will result in increased liberalism, but this is not necessarily so. The elections of 1920, 1924, 1928, and even 1952, when women as well as men had the vote, should convince us that "the people" can and do vote for conservatism. If the people of Massachusetts believed that a man should own property to be a voter or that an official should be a Protestant to be elected to office, they might well vote for both propositions and not be out of character. And since most men in Massachusetts were Protestants and property owners, the fact that both property and religious qualifications found their way into the Constitution of 1780 should not be surprising.

We do not need a "conservative counterrevolution" or a thermidorean reaction to explain either the Massachusetts Constitution of 1780 or the adoption of the federal Constitution in 1788. If there was no "social revolution," there could hardly be a "conservative counterrevolution." Both constitutions must be explained in terms of a middle-class society in which most men could vote.

In recent years it has been frequently said that the British did not intend to tyrannize the colonies by the policies which they adopted. Colonists thought otherwise, however, and judging by the material presented in these chapters, one might suspect that many British policies looked like tyranny to them. Perhaps we of today would also consider as tyranny trials without juries, instructions by the king which were supposed to be law, taxation by a people who were considered foreigners, a declaration by the Parliament of these same "foreign people" that it had the power to legislate in all cases whatsoever, appointed governors who could dissolve assemblies or determine town meetings, and navigation acts regulating colonial trade in British interests. It would be interesting to speculate on the reaction of a modern oleomargarine manufacturer whose suit against the butter interests was to be tried in Wisconsin by a jury of Wisconsin dairy farmers presided over by a judge appointed by the governor of Wisconsin. This hypothetical case might seem exaggerated, but it is not too far removed from the attitude expressed by colonists toward their relations with the British. The fact is that colonists looked on British measures as tyrannical, and if we are going to explain colonial actions, we must consider the colonial point of view.

How should we rate in importance the various factors that entered into this British-American war? That, of course, is difficult to answer, but it is not so difficult to say that many items contributed and that some were probably more important to some individuals than to others.

There is no doubt that economic motives were fundamental. That Americans would oppose a mercantilist system which they considered inimical to their interests should not be surprising. After all, they looked on many British regulations as simply devices by which some segments of the Empire were favored at the expense of other segments. The tax program also had its economic side, for as many men said, a mother country which could collect a stamp tax could also tax a man's land, his cattle, or his home. Undoubtedly, too, the threat of monopoly contained in the Tea Act had its economic influence. In fact, a middle-class society would almost inevitably place great emphasis on property and its economic interests, a fact which is only too apparent in the sources. The importance of economic factors, however, did not lie in their contribution to class conflict as a cause of the American Revolution.

But economic elements were not the only forces making for revolution. Equally significant was the fact that Massachusetts had long been accustomed to democratic government and intended to maintain its accustomed system. Politics inevitably include economics, since economic subjects are some of the most important items in politics, but not all politics is economic. The very fact that people govern their own destinies is important in itself. As one old soldier of the Revolution put it, the British intended to govern the Americans and the Americans did not intend that they should. To a people accustomed to the democracy both of province and town affairs, the danger inherent in British imperial controls was far more than a mere threat. When the common people talked of dying for their liberties or pledging their lives and property for the defense of their liberties, they were not dealing in abstractions; and they would not have talked in this way if their society had been dominated by a merchant aristocracy.

Neither can religious democracy be ignored as a factor in the Revolution. We must remember that the people of Massachusetts were accustomed to a church organization which lived by democratic procedures and opposition to the Church of England. We must not forget, either, that many people at the time considered religion more important than politics. The threat that the British might impose the Church of England on them and enforce conformity was not a threat to be taken lightly. As many of them often said, religious and political freedom were inextricably connected and would rise or fall together. Little wonder, then, that the Congregational clergy supported the Revolution almost to a man.

This study of Massachusetts raises some rather serious questions about our interpretation of colonial society and the Revolution in other colonies. Were the other colonies as undemocratic as we have supposed them to be? Was their economic and social life dominated by a coastal aristocracy of planters in the South and merchants in the North? How was property distributed? Exactly how many men could meet the voting qualifications? Was representation restricted in such a way that conservative areas could dominate the legislature? These are questions for which we need well-documented answers before we interpret the colonial and revolutionary periods with any assurance of accuracy.

Evidence which has turned up in the course of this study suggests that Massachusetts was not fundamentally different from the other colonies and states. If so—and the idea is certainly worth extensive investigation—we might be forced to make some drastic revisions in our interpretation of American history before 1830. Perhaps we will find in America as a whole, as in Massachusetts, that American democracy as we know it goes far deeper than the election of 1828 and that the "common man" in this country had come into his own long before the era of Jacksonian Democracy.

Historians and the Problem of Early American Democracy
—J. R. Pole *

The earliest national period of United States history combines two themes. It is a period of revolution and also of constitution making. Charter governments, whether royal or proprietary, give way to new governments which claim to derive the whole of their authority from the American electorate. The Americans, though working from experience, build for the future. This fact is of cardinal importance for any attempt to understand their work or the state of mind in which it was undertaken.

The claim of the new government raises a problem that was not solved

From *American Historical Review*, LXVIII (April 1962), 626–646. Reprinted by permission of the author.

* Mr. Pole, Lecturer in American history at University College London and author of numerous articles, among them, "Representation and Authority in Virginia from the Revolution to Reform" (*Journal of Southern History*, XXIV [Feb. 1958]), is interested chiefly in early American history. This article was read in an earlier version at the April 1960 conference of the British Association for American Studies in Bristol.

by the mere exercise of effective, but revolutionary powers. Was their authority strictly compatible with the doctrine that governments derive their just powers from the consent of the governed? What was meant by "consent"? How was such consent obtained or certified?

The attempt to answer these questions leads the historian into a recon-struction of the character of these early institutions and an inquiry into the ideas by which they were governed. In the light of subsequent Ameri-can development, it has led historians to address themselves to the prob-lem of deciding whether or not these institutions were democratic. Whether or not we choose to adopt this particular definition, whether or not we regard it as a useful tool of analysis, the underlying problem is one that the historian cannot easily avoid. No history of the American Revolu-tion and of constitution making could be written without discussion of the doctrines on which the Americans based their resistance, the question of what meaning these doctrines bore for the different American partici-pants, and of the degree of participation, the attitude and purposes of different elements in American society.

There is a problem of the relationship of ideas to institutions; there is a previous problem of the ideas themselves. I do not think that the broad and undifferentiated use of the term "democracy" helps either to describe the institutions or to explain the ideas. I do not even think that our analysis of these matters will be much affected by the use of this concept. But the thesis has been advanced [1] that the American colonies were already full-fledged democracies before the American Revolution began, from which it follows that the cardinal principle of the Revolution was a defense of democratic institutions against royal or parliamentary tyranny. It is a thesis that has the advantage of an attractive simplicity, and it is one that can be supported by a good deal of evidence, especially if that evidence is read without much relation to the context of eighteenth-century political ideas. It also has the merit of providing the occasion, and in order that the argument should not go by default, the necessity of a more searching in-quiry into the realities.

To use the word "democracy" is to raise, but not I think to solve, a prob-lem of definition. And it is not an easy one. There is so little agreement about what is meant by "democracy," and the discussion has such a strong tendency to slide noiselessly from what we *do* mean to what we *ought* to mean, that for purposes of definition it seems to be applicable only in the broadest sense. And this sense has the effect of limiting, rather than of advancing, our understanding of the past.

But I must certainly admit that if I did think the word "democracy" in fact did justice to the problem, then I would have to accept it despite the risks involved. More than this: we ought to have some agreement as to

[1] Robert E. Brown, *Middle-Class Democracy and the Revolution in Massachusetts, 1691–1780* (Ithaca, N.Y., 1955), esp. 401–408.

what meaning it can be made to bear. It makes good sense in a purely comparative view to call the American colonies and early states democratic when contrasting them with the Prussia of Frederick II or the Habsburg Empire; they were in the same sense democratic compared with France or with England, with which they had so much in common. There might be less unintended irony in calling them part of the "free world" than in doing the same today with Spain, Formosa, or the Union of South Africa. In the broad strokes we use to differentiate between tyrannies and free states the term will serve as a starting point, but not as a conclusion. It is interesting, when one begins to look more closely at the structure of the complex societies of the eighteenth century, how rapidly these broad distinctions lose their value and cease to serve any analytical purpose. As R. R. Palmer has recently remarked, surveying the Western world before the French Revolution, "No one except a few disgruntled literary men supposed that he lived under a despotism." [2] When one considers how complex the machinery of administration, of justice, for the redress of grievances and, if any, of political representation must become in any ancient and intricately diversified society, it is easy to feel that the more democratic virtues of the American societies were related, more than anything else, to their relative simplicity and lack of economic and functional diversity. But a closer inspection, not only of the structure, but of the development, of colonial institutions reveals a tendency that puts the matter in another light; for these institutions were unmistakably molded in the shape of English institutions and were conforming themselves, both socially and politically, to the conventions of the period.

The alternative view, which I want to suggest, does not confine itself merely to rejecting the "democratic" interpretation by putting in its place a flat, antidemocratic account of the same set of institutions. What it does, I think, is to see the democratic elements in their proper perspective by adding a further dimension without which the rest is flat, incomplete, and, for all its turbulence, essentially lifeless. This is the dimension of what Cecelia Kenyon has called "institutional thought." [3]

To take this view, one has to free oneself from a tendency that has become very difficult to resist. I mean the strong, though wholly anachronistic tendency to suppose that when people who were accustomed to ways and ideas which have largely disappeared into the past felt grievances against their government, they must necessarily have wanted to express their dissatisfaction by applying the remedies of modern democracy; and, again, that when their demands were satisfied, the aspirations thus fulfilled must have been modern, democratic aspirations.

The idea that the great mass of the common people might actually have

[2] R. R. Palmer, *The Age of the Democratic Revolution* (Princeton, N.J., 1959), 51.
[3] Cecelia M. Kenyon, "Men of Little Faith: The Anti-Federalists on the Nature of Representative Government," *William and Mary Quarterly*, XII (Jan. 1955), 4.

given their consent to concepts of government that limited their own participation in ways completely at variance with the principles of modern democracy is one that lies completely outside the compass or comprehension of the "democratic" interpretation. That interpretation insists on the all-importance of certain democratic features of political life, backed by certain egalitarian features of social life having a strong influence on political institutions. What it misses is that these features belonged within a framework which—to polarize the issue at the risk of using another broad term—was known to the world as Whiggism. The institutions of representative government derived from the time when the Whig concept of representative government was being worked out in England and, both by extension and by original experience, in the American colonies (and when the foundations were laid for the Whig interpretation of history). Even where democratic elements were strong and dominant, the animating ideas belonged to a whole Whig world of both politics and society. More than this, the colonial and early national period in which they played so important a part was pervaded by a belief in and a sense of the propriety of social order guided and strengthened by principles of dignity on the one hand and deference on the other. It was, to use the term coined by Walter Bagehot in his account of Victorian England, a deferential society.[4]

There is, of course, nothing very new about the theory that early American society was relatively egalitarian and that this situation was reflected in political institutions and conduct. It was a view that became fashionable in the days of George Bancroft. But it has been reformulated, with formidable documentation, in Robert E. Brown's work on Massachusetts and in his attack on Charles Beard.[5] To regain our perspective it seems necessary for a moment to go back to Beard.

Beard, as we know, distinguished in his study of the Constitution between two leading types of propertied interest, basically those of land and commerce. Commercial property was supposed to have been strongly represented in the Constitutional Convention, landed property outside. The opposition in some of the state ratifying conventions was supposed to have arisen from the outraged interests of the landed classes.

Despite intense opposition in certain states, the Constitution was eventually ratified. But here Beard went further. He asserted that ratification was not a true expression of the will of the people. He based this argument on the prevalence of property qualifications for the suffrage, which meant that only a minority of freeholders and other owners of property could participate in the elections to the ratifying conventions, which in consequence were not truly representative. There are two elements in

---

[4] See also E. S. Griffith, *History of American City Government: Colonial Period* (New York, 1938), 191; Clifford K. Shipton, review of Brown, *Middle-Class Democracy, Political Science Quarterly*, LXXI (No. 2, 1956), 306–308.

[5] Robert E. Brown, *Charles Beard and the Constitution: A Critical Analysis of "An Economic Interpretation of the Constitution"* (Princeton, N.J., 1956).

Beard's hypothesis, as Brown has pointed out.[6] On the one hand, Beard advances the alleged clash between the mercantile and landed interests, with the mercantile coming out on top because of the power conferred by its economic advantages; on the other, he implies the existence of a connection between the landed opposition to ratification and the supposedly disfranchised masses, whose silence so damagingly detracts from the authority of the Constitution. It is not my purpose to discuss the question as to whether Beard's argument has stood the test of recent scrutiny. Another aspect, which may be called that of the moral consequences of Beard's work, deserves more consideration than it has received.

The Philadelphia Convention was described by Thomas Jefferson as "an assembly of demi-gods," a judgment to which posterity murmured "Amen." There are, however, marked disadvantages about being descended from demi-gods; they not only lack a sense of humor, but they set an appallingly high standard. What a relief it must have been, after the first shock of Beard's iconoclasm had died down, to find that they were only human after all! Beard had questioned the Constitution at two points. In the first place, by implying that it was the work of men motivated by private economic interests he made it possible to reconsider its wisdom and justice; but in the second place, when he denied that it had received the sanction of a genuine, popular ratification he made it possible —perhaps obligatory—to question the authority of the Constitution precisely because it did not owe its origin to the only recognized source of such authority in the whole science of government as understood in America: the consent of the governed.

To this problem, Brown's critique of Beard is directly relevant. He not only pursues Beard with a determination that recalls John Horace Round's pursuit of Edward Freeman, but in his work on Massachusetts, he makes a thorough and painstaking investigation of the institutions of that province, in which he reaches the conclusion that colonial Massachusetts was already so fully democratic that no case can be made for an interpretation of the American Revolution there in terms of an internal "class war." It is in this connection that Brown broadens his front to develop an attack on Carl Becker.[7] The Revolution was a war of secession, fought for the preservation of American democracy against the antidemocratic policy of the crown. Nothing more, and nothing less. The joint foundations of all this are the wide extent of the suffrage franchise and the wide distribution of middling quantities of property.

The consequences are obvious. If the states, and not only the states but the colonies, were ruled by the consent of the governed, then Beard's unenfranchised masses disappear, and the Constitution is restored to its

[6] *Ibid.*, 50–51, 53–55, 180–81, 194.   [7] Brown, *Middle-Class Democracy*, Chap. IV.

high place not only in the affection of the American people, but in their scale of approbation.

American history has been written not merely as the story of the people who went to, and lived in, America. It has been developed as the history of liberty. Innumerable books carry in their titles the message that colonial development was a progress toward liberty; since the Revolution, it has sometimes been possible to discern in accounts of American history a certain messianic quality, which some have felt to have been reflected periodically in American diplomacy. History written in this way frequently finds itself obliged to ask how a man, or a movement, stands in relation to the particular values for which American history is responsible. A recent study of Alexander Hamilton's place in the origins of political parties, for example, speaks of the need to determine Hamilton's "rightful place in our history." [8] It becomes important, not just to write a man's biography or to assess his contribution, but to place him correctly on the eternal curve upon which American political performances seem to be graded.

The writing of history thus becomes a matter, not only of finding out what actually happened, but of judging the past. It is a process that cuts both ways. For earlier generations of Americans were keenly—almost disconcertingly—aware of the example they were setting for their descendants. (There is a town meeting entry in Massachusetts, in 1766, which calls the attention of future generations to the sacrifices the townsmen were making for their liberties.[9]) They knew that they would be judged. They were not only building institutions, they were setting standards, for the future. This can become a nerve-racking business. As has been remarked in a different connection (by a writer in the *Times Literary Supplement*) the past and the present seem to watch each other warily as from opposite boxes at the opera, each suspecting the other of being about to commit a *faux pas*.[10]

The two great instruments of American nationhood were the Revolution, with its banner, the Declaration of Independence, and the Constitution. Baptism and confirmation. It would be hard to imagine a more important commitment, not only for the interpretation of the American experience, but one might almost say for the emotional stability of the interpreter, than to place his own values in their proper relation to these events, or if that cannot be done, then to place these events in their proper relation to his values.

---

[8] Joseph E. Charles, "Hamilton and Washington," *William and Mary Quarterly*, XII (Apr. 1955), 226. A further example in connection with Hamilton, whose career provokes this kind of judgment, is found in the title of Louis M. Hacker's *Alexander Hamilton in the American Tradition* (New York, 1957).

[9] Lucius R. Paige, *A History of Cambridge, Massachusetts, 1630–1877* (New York, 1883), 137.

[10] "Imaginative Historians: Telling the News about the Past," *Times Literary Supplement, Special Supplement on The American Imagination*, Nov. 6, 1959.

Accordingly, historians have brought the problem of values firmly into their assessment of history. They ask, "How democratic was early American society?" And they do not hesitate to reply, if their findings tell them so, that it was not democratic enough. Or, which is still more confusing, that it was struggling forward toward a fuller ideal of democracy. Accounts of this period repeatedly explain that such features of government as property qualifications for the suffrage and political office were still regarded as necessary at that time. "Still." These people had the right instincts; they were coming on nicely; but, unlike ourselves, they had not yet arrived.

There thus develops a tendency to adopt a completely anachronistic note of apology for the insufficiency of democratic principles in early American institutions.[11]

I would like here to anticipate the objection that I am advocating that moral judgments should be taken out of historical writing. Neither do I deny that major developments can and ought to be traced to their minor origins. Moral judgments about the past are not necessarily anachronistic. It is not, I think, unhistorical to believe that some of the acts of treachery and cruelty or of violent aggression which comprise so great a proportion of recorded human activity were morally wrong, or even to maintain that they influenced the course of events for the worse. But when judgments of moral value are applied to complex social systems, they expose the judge to a peculiar danger of self-deception, perhaps even of self-incrimination. The historian must not only be careful, he must also be highly self-critical, when he embarks on assessments of the moral shortcomings of the past.

The reading of values into historical analysis is particularly liable to deception when the values of the present are themselves made the basis for the selection of materials, which are then judged in the light of the values in question. This may happen when the importance of different institutions or opinions is estimated on the basis of our own opinion of the role they ought to have played in their own time.

Without doubt there is a place for such judgments. There is a place for criticism of the Hanoverian House of Commons—rather a large place. But when we discuss that body our task is not that of apologizing for the fact that the bright light of nineteenth-century democracy had not yet broken on such persons as Pitt or Burke or Shelburne or Fox. Our problem, as I understand it, is that of reconstructing the inner nature of political society in their age and of asking how far Parliament answered the needs of that society, and how far it did not. And that is a matter of what history

[11] Even Brown does so. In pointing out how few men were disfranchised in Massachusetts, he significantly remarks, "We cannot condone the practice of excluding those few," though he rightly adds that it makes a tremendous difference whether they were 95 per cent or 5 per cent. Brown, *Middle-Class Democracy*, 402.

was actually about, not what it ought to have been about. The historian has a responsibility to the past, but it is not that of deciding within what limits he can recommend it to the approbation of his readers.

The American Revolution was certainly a war for self-determination. But self-determination and democracy are not interchangeable terms, though they can be confused with a facility that has not been without its significance in American diplomacy. A society need not be democratic in order to achieve a high degree of internal unity when fighting for self-determination. Again, a measure of democracy, or a wider diffusion of political power, may well be brought about as an outcome of such a struggle. Such a development was in fact one of the most important consequences of the American Revolution.

It must be acknowledged that the sources of colonial history supply an impressive quantity of material that can be marshaled against my own views of this subject, though not enough as yet to weaken my conviction of the validity of historical evidence.

Much evidence of this sort comes from New England, and Massachusetts is rich in examples. In 1768 General Thomas Gage wrote to Viscount Hillsborough, "from what has been said, your lordship will conclude, that there is no government in Boston, there is in truth, very little at present, and the constitution of the province leans so much to democracy, that the governor has not the power to remedy the disorders which happen in it." [12] The next year Sir Francis Bernard wrote to Viscount Barrington,

> . . . for these 4 years past so uniform a system for bringing all power into the hands of the people has been prosecuted without interruption and with such success that all fear, reverence, respect and awe which before formed a tolerable balance against the power of the people, are annihilated, and the artificial weights being removed, the royal scale mounts up and kicks the beam. . . . It would be better that Mass. Bay should be a complete republic like Connecticut than to remain with so few ingredients of royalty as shall be insufficient to maintain the real royal character. [13]

In 1766 Thomas Hutchinson reported: "In the town of Boston a plebeian party always has and I fear always will command and for some months past they have governed the province." [14] Describing elections in 1772, Hutchinson told Hillsborough, "By the constitution forty pounds sterl.— which they say may be in clothes household furniture or any sort of property is a qualification and even into that there is scarce ever any

---

[12] *Correspondence of General Thomas Gage* . . . , ed. Clarence E. Carter (2 vols., New Haven, Conn., 1931, 1933), I, 205.
[13] Quoted by R. V. Harlow, *History of Legislative Methods before 1825* (New Haven, Conn., 1917), 39–40.
[14] Brown, *Middle-Class Democracy*, 57.

inquiry and anything with the appearance of a man is admitted without scrutiny." [15]

The franchise was certainly broad. Brown has shown that in many towns as many as 80 per cent of the adult male population, in some more than 90 per cent, were qualified by their property to vote in provincial elections.[16] Three towns appear in the nineties, three in the fifties, the rest in between. These findings tend to confirm and strengthen the impression that prevailed among contemporaries, that Massachusetts was a hotbed of "democratical" or "levelling" principles: the more so after Boston junta got control of the General Court.

These expressions raise two issues, one of definition, the other of interpretation.

The point of definition first: when the indignant officers of government described these provinces as "democratical," they were of course not talking about representative government with universal suffrage. They shared not only with their correspondents, but in the last analysis even with their political opponents, the assumption that the constitutions of the colonies, like that of Britain, were made up of mixed elements; they were mixed constitutions, in which the commons were represented in the assembly or commons house. In each constitution there were different orders, and the justification, the *raison d'être*, of such a constitution was that it gave security to each. When they said that the government was becoming "too democratical" or "leaned towards democracy" they meant that the popular element was too weighty for the proper balance of a mixed constitution. They used these expressions as terms of abuse. Not that that matters: we may be impressed by their indignation, but we are not obliged to share it. What is more important to the historian is that the leaders of these movements which took control of the assemblies were in general prepared to accept the same set of definitions.

This they demonstrated when they came to establish new constitutions. The theory of mixed government was maintained with as little adulteration as possible. The difference they had to face was that all the "orders" now drew their position in the government from some form of popular representation. Most of the new constitutions represented the adaptation of institutions which undeniably received their authority from the people, an authority conceived, if not in liberty, then certainly in a revolutionary situation, to the traditional and equally important theory of balanced government.

This does not dispose of the second point, that of interpretation. Suppose that, in this form of mixed government, the "democratical" arm actually gathers up a preponderance of political power. This, after all, was

---

[15] *Ibid.*, 291.   [16] *Ibid.*, 50.

what happened in the Revolution and had been happening long before. Does this give us a democracy? It is a question of crucial importance and one to which one school of thought returns an uncritically affirmative answer. Much of the power and internal influence within each colony was indeed concentrated in its assembly. This concentration reflected, or rather represented, the distribution of power and influence in the colony in general. If the domestic distribution of power tends toward oligarchy rather than democracy—to use the language of the time—then the power of that oligarchy will be exercised in, and through, the assembly itself: just as in the House of Commons. A difference of degree, not of kind. And in fact this most significant aspect of the domestic situation in the colonies applied with hardly less force in leveling Boston than in high-toned Virginia.

In Virginia one feels that an immigrant from England would at once have been at home.[17] There were many instances of hotly contested elections, of treating and corruption, of sharp practice by sheriffs. It would not be difficult, however, to adduce evidence of democratic tendencies in Virginia elections. Especially in the spring elections of 1776 there were many signs that the freeholders were taking their choice seriously, and several distinguished gentlemen were either turned out of their seats or given a nasty fright. But it is an unmistakable feature of Virginia elections that although the freeholders participated often quite fully, the contests were almost invariably between members of the gentry. To seek election to the House of Burgesses was to stake a distinct claim to social rank. Virginia elections were of course conducted viva voce under the friendly supervision of the local magnates. The comparatively broad base of politics in Virginia makes it all the more instructive to look into the real concentration of political power. There were two main areas: the House of Burgesses and the county courts (not taking account of the council and governor).

Effective power in the House of Burgesses was concentrated in a few hands. The house began to use the committee system in the late seventeenth century and had brought it to a high efficiency well before the middle of the eighteenth.[18] The famous Virginia ruling families of this era always occupied a large share of the key positions, enough to ensure their own domination. Before the Revolution, of some hundred members who regularly attended the house, only about twenty took an active part in proceedings. Three families, the Robinsons, the Randolphs, and the Lees, provided most of the leaders. A very recent study shows that of

---

[17] Charles S. Sydnor, *Gentlemen Freeholders* (Chapel Hill, N.C., 1952); David J. Mays, *Edmund Pendleton, 1721–1803* (2 vols., Cambridge, Mass., 1952); J. R. Pole, "Representation and Authority in Virginia from the Revolution to Reform," *Journal of Southern History*, XXIV (Feb. 1958), 16–50.

[18] Harlow, *Legislative Methods*, 10–11.

630 members between 1720 and 1776, only 110 belonged throughout the period to the "select few who dominated the proceedings of the house." [19]

These men, many of whom were linked by ties of family, had the characteristics of a strong social and political elite. They were large land-owners and generally were substantial slaveowners. Some were merchants. A few, such as Edmund Pendleton, had arrived by intellectual ability and hard work combined with legal training. But Pendleton had the patronage of a great family. All those with ambition were land speculators. This gave them an interest in western development, an interest which no doubt extended to the policy of making western areas attractive to the prospective settler. Probably for this reason they wanted to extend the suffrage, which they twice tried to do in the 1760's by reducing the amount of uncleared land required as a qualification. The crown disallowed these acts, though on other grounds. This reform was completed in the first election law after the Revolution. Despite the famous reforms pressed through by Jefferson, no concessions were made on matters of fundamental importance. It is a striking tribute to the tremendous security of their hold on the country that in the new state constitution there was no pro-vision for special qualifications for membership in the legislature. The qualifications of voters and of representatives for the time being remained as before. It is a silent piece of evidence, possibly, but one that speaks loudly of their eminent self-confidence.

Life in the counties was dominated by the county courts, which touched the interests of the common people far more closely than did the remote and occasional meetings of the legislature. The courts, which knew little of any doctrine of separation of powers, exercised all the main functions of both legislative and judicial administration. These included tax assess-ment, granting licenses, supervising highways, and authorizing construc-tions. They had nothing elective in their nature. Membership was by co-option. The courts made the important county nominations for con-firmation by the governor. And the county courts were made up of the leading men of the county, representing at the local level the material of which the House of Burgesses was composed at the central. They seem on the whole to have worked well enough. And it is likely that if they had in fact been elected by the freeholders, their membership would have been about the same. Assuredly they were not tyrannical; equally certainly they were not democratic. They were a good example of what is usually meant by oligarchy.

What happened in the American Revolution in Virginia was that the policies of the British government clashed with the interests of this

---

[19] Jack P. Greene, "Foundations of Political Power in the Virginia House of Burgesses, 1720–1766," *William and Mary Quarterly*, XVI (Oct. 1959), 485–506; quotation from p. 485.

ambitious, proud, self-assured, and highly competent provincial government. In arguing its case, both to the British authorities and to its own
people, this government appealed to the principles on which it claimed
to be founded, which were philosophically the same and historically comparable to those of Parliament itself. For historical reasons, the Virginia
Whigs were somewhat closer to the radical, or popular side, of the Whig
spectrum. But in Virginia as in other provinces, it was the principles
generally understood as Whig principles that were at stake, and it was
these principles which were affirmed and re-established in the new set of
domestic state constitutions.

From time to time, as the war went on, the upper classes felt tremors
of alarm in which they revealed something of their relationship to the
common people.

Thus John Augustine Washington, writing to Richard Henry Lee of
the difficulties of getting the militia to obey a marching order, and the
secret proceedings by which they bound themselves to stand by each other
in refusing to leave the state, remarked: "I fear we have among us some
designing dangerous characters who misrepresent to ignorant, uninformed
people, the situation of our affairs and the nature of the contest, making
them believe it is a war produced by the wantonness of the gentlemen,
and that the poor are very little, if any interested." [20] Another of Lee's
correspondents, on the need to arouse popular support, wrote: "The
spark of liberty is not yet extinct among our people, and if properly
fanned by the Gentlemen of Influence will, I make no doubt, burst out
again into a flame." [21]

These hints, these references which illuminate the assumptions of
political life, often reveal more than formal expositions of doctrine, or
even the official records.

These "Gentlemen of Influence," the ruling class, were prepared to
extend the suffrage when it suited their interest to do so in the 1760's, but
refused to take the same step when it would have opened the question of
political power, a generation later. The first demands for reform, in both
suffrage and distribution of representation, began to appear about the turn
of the century. And these demands were met with a prolonged and bitter
resistance, leading only to reluctant and unsatisfactory concessions even
in the famous constitutional convention of 1829–1830. The struggle was
carried on until a more substantial extension of political rights was at
last achieved in 1850. The forces that Virginia's political leadership so
long and so determinedly held at bay can, I think, without exaggeration,
be called the forces of democracy.

It is a very familiar fact about the early state constitutions that they were

---

[20] Quoted in Pole, "Representation and Authority in Virginia," 28.   [21] *Ibid.*, 28–29.

generally conservative in character, in that they retained much of the principles and structure of the governments of the colonies. The colonies were already self-governing in the main, and this self-government was administered by representative institutions. When one's attention is confined to these institutions, it can soon become rather difficult to see in what respect they were not, in a common-sense use of the word, democratic. After all, they were accessible to the people, they received petitions and redressed grievances, they possessed the inestimable right of free speech, and in the battles they fought, they were often engaged, in the interest of the colonies, against royal governors.

All these features were not merely consistent with, they were the formative elements of, the great Whig tradition of Parliament since the Glorious Revolution and before. They were, like so many other things, derivable from Locke. With certain exceptions, such as the difficulty of the Regulator rising in North Carolina, it would be true that colonial assemblies lay closer to the people than did the British House of Commons. For one thing, there were far more representatives per head of population in the colonies than in Britain. Parliament had 1 member to every 14,300 persons, the colonies approximately 1 to every 1,200.[22] And this meant that legislative methods and principles were more likely to be familiar to the ordinary colonist. To put it in contemporary terms, the colonies, on the whole, had a great many more constituencies like Middlesex or Westminster, except that they were mostly country and not town constituencies. It might be very close to the mark to press the analogy further and say that they had a great many constituencies that very much resembled Yorkshire—the Yorkshrire of Sir George Saville, the Yorkshire of Christopher Wyvill.

What does seem striking about these in many ways highly representative colonial assemblies is, as I suggested earlier, the determination and sureness of touch with which they assumed the characteristics of Parliament. These were characteristics originally designed to secure the liberty of the people's representatives: free speech in debate, freedom of members from arrest or molestation, and freedom of the assembly from abuse by breach of privilege. But there were all too many occasions on which it must have seemed that these safeguards were designed to secure the assemblies against abuse, in the form of free speech and fair comment, by their own constituents.[23]

The colonial assemblies became extraordinarily sensitive to the question of privilege. Strictly from an institutional viewpoint, they were deliberately building on the tradition of Parliament. But institutional studies always

---

[22] Mary P. Clarke, *Parliamentary Privilege in the American Colonies* (New Haven, Conn., 1943), 268.
[23] *Ibid.,* 127.

seem to tempt the historian to arrive at his answer the short way, by examining structure, without asking questions about development.

Much research has recently been done on what Palmer calls the "constituted bodies" [24] which held a strong and growing position in the Western world in the eighteenth century. They were numerous and differed greatly, one from another, and from one century to another—first of all the variety of political or judicial bodies: diets, estates, assemblies, parlements; then the professional associations or guilds; as well as religious orders, and those of the nobilities of Europe.

There seems strong reason for holding that the colonial assemblies were behaving in close conformity with the other bodies of this general type. At their best they were closer to local interests, but no less characteristically, they displayed a remarkable diligence in the adoption of parliamentary abuses. They would send their messengers far into the outlying country to bring to the bar of the house some individual who was to be humbled for having committed a breach of privilege, which very often meant some private action affecting the dignity or even the property of the sitting member. Criticism of the assemblies, either verbal or written, was a risky business. The freedom of the colonial press was very largely at the mercy of the assembly's sense of its own dignity, so much so that a recent investigator doubts whether the famous Zenger case, [25] which is supposed to have done so much toward the establishment of freedom of the press in the colonies, really had any general significance or immediate consequences. The fact is that restrictions on free press comment on assembly actions were not the policy of the crown but the policy of the assemblies.

Expulsions from colonial assemblies were frequent. And in case a parallel with the action of the Commons in the Wilkes case were needed to round off the picture, we may remark that colonial assemblies repeatedly excluded members who had been lawfully elected by their constituents. [26]

There was another feature in which these assemblies showed their affinity with the outlook of their times. In spite of the amount of choice open to the electors, there was a growing tendency for public office, both the elective and the appointive kinds, to become hereditary. It was of course very pronounced in Europe; it is surely no less significant when we see it at work in America. The same family names occur, from generation to generation, in similar positions. And this was no less true in New England than in Virginia or South Carolina or Maryland.

If this was democracy, it was a democracy that wore its cockade firmly pinned into its periwig.

---

[24] Palmer, *Democratic Revolution*, 27–44.

[25] Leonard W. Levy, "Did the Zenger Case Really Matter? Freedom of the Press in Colonial New York," *William and Mary Quarterly*, XVII (Jan. 1960), 35–50

[26] Clarke, *Parliamentary Privilege*, 194–96.

One of the most interesting consequences of the revolutionary situation was that it demanded of political leaders a declaration of their principles. Thus we get the famous Virginia Bill of Rights, the work of George Mason; the Declaration of Rights attached to the 1780 constitution of Massachusetts; and the constitutions themselves, with all that they reveal or imply of political ideas; and in the case of Massachusetts we can go even further, for there survive also, in the archives of that state in Boston, the returns of the town meetings which debated that constitution and in many cases recorded their vote, clause by clause.

This constitution, in fact, was submitted to the ratification of what counted then as the whole people—all the adult males in the state. The constitutional convention had been elected on the same basis. The constitution which was framed on this impressive foundation of popular sovereignty was certainly not a democratic instrument. It was an articulate, indeed a refined expression, of the Whig view of government—of government-in-society—as applied to the existing conditions in Massachusetts, and as interpreted by John Adams.

The property qualifications for the suffrage were, in round figures, about what they had been under the charter. In practice they proved to have very little effect by way of restricting participation in elections. The introduction of decidedly steeper qualifications for membership in the assembly meant that that body would be composed of the owners of the common, upward of one-hundred-acre family farm, and their mercantile equivalent. The pyramid narrowed again to the senate, and came to a point in the position of governor. These restrictions were new, but gave little offense to the general sense of political propriety; the suffrage qualifications were objected to in about one-fifth of the recorded town meeting debates.[27]

The house and senate represented different types of constituency, and the difference is one of the clues to institutional thought. The house represented the persons of the electorate living in corporate towns, which were entitled to representation according to a numerical scale of population; very small communities were excluded. The town remained the basic unit of representation. The senate, on the other hand, represented the property of the state arranged in districts corresponding to the counties; the number of members to which each county was entitled depended, not on population, but on the taxes it had paid into the state treasury. The result in

[27] The constitution of 1780 is discussed in: S. E. Morison, "The Struggle over the Adoption of the Constitution of Massachusetts, 1780," Massachusetts Historical Society *Proceedings*, L (Boston, 1916–17), 353–412; Robert J. Taylor, *Western Massachusetts in the Revolution* (Providence, R. I., 1954); J. R. Pole, "Suffrage and Representation in Massachusetts: A Statistical Note," *William and Mary Quarterly*, XIV (Oct. 1957), 560–92. The town meeting records are in Volumes CCLXXVI and CCLXXVII in the Massachusetts Department of Archives, the State House, Boston.

distribution of representatives in the senate was not actually much different from the apportionment that would have been obtained by population,[28] but the intention was there, and the plan conformed to the principles of political order by which the delegates were guided.[29]

New York, which established popular election of its governor, and North Carolina took the matter further by differentiating between the qualifications of voters for the senate and the house of representatives.

How then are we to explain the paradox of popular consent to a scheme of government which systematically excluded the common people from the more responsible positions of political power? The historian who wishes to adopt the word "democracy" as a definition must first satisfy himself that it can be applied to a carefully ordered hierarchy, under the aegis of which power and authority are related to a conscientiously designed scale of social and economic rank, both actual and prospective; if this test fails him, then he must ask himself whether he can call the system a democracy, on the ground that it was a form of government established with the consent of the governed. Those who wish to argue this line have the advantage of finding much serviceable material that can be adopted without the rigors, or the risks, of a historically-minded analysis. It is possible to concentrate all attention on those aspects of the system which we would now call democratic, to assert that these elements exerted a controlling influence and that all the rest was a sort of obsolescent window dressing. Such a view may not be particularly subtle, but on the other hand it is not absolute nonsense. It is, perhaps, the easiest view to arrive at through an extensive reading of local economic records in the light of a clear, but vastly simplified interpretation of the political process; but it leaves unfulfilled the rather more complex task of perceiving the democratic elements in their proper place within a system conceived in another age, under a different inspiration.

In the Whig philosophy of government the basic principle, preceding representative institutions, is the compact. The people already owned their property by natural right, and they are supposed to have come into the compact quite voluntarily to secure protection both to their property and to their persons. For these purposes government was formed. What was done in Massachusetts seems to have been a solemn attempt to re-enact the original compact in the new making of the state. It was even possible to deploy the theory of compact as an excuse for seizing other people's property: in 1782 the legislature of Virginia resolved that the estates of British subjects might be confiscated because they had not been

---

[28] As noted by Palmer, *Democratic Revolution*, 226

[29] It may be permissible to mention that Brown, in his study of this constitution, omits to note this provision for tax payment as the basis of county representation. In itself, this may seem a small clue, but the thread leads into another world of political ideas than that of modern democracy. Brown, *Middle-Class Democracy*, 393.

parties to the original contract of the people of that state.[30] And the Virginia constitution had not even been submitted for popular ratification!

Massachusetts and New Hampshire, in fact, were the only states in which popular ratification was sought for the revolutionary constitution. In a society whose moral cohesion was supplied by the sense of deference and dignity, it was possible for the broad mass of the people to consent to a scheme of government in which their own share would be limited. Some of them of course expected to graduate to the higher levels; government was not controlled by inherited rank.

This factor—the expectation of advancement—is an important feature of the American experience; it is one which is often used to excuse the injustice of exclusion from government by economic status. The *address* that the Massachusetts convention delegates drew up in 1780 to expound the principles on which they had acted makes the point that most of those excluded by the suffrage qualification could expect to rise sufficiently in their own property to reach the level of voters. The exclusion of the artisan and laborer from the assembly was, however, more likely to prove permanent.

It would be a mistake to suppose that the body of citizens included in the electoral system at one level or another, or expecting to gain their inclusion, was really the whole body. There are always farm laborers, journeymen, migrant workers, and one may suspect that the numbers excluded by law were larger than the terms of the *Address* suggest. But even if we are disposed to accept the high level of popular participation in elections as being weighty enough to determine our definitions, it is surely wise to pause even over the legal disfranchisement of one man in every four or five, and in some towns one man in three.

This constitutional scheme was derived from a mixture of experience, theory, and intention. It is the intention for the future which seems to call for scrutiny when we attempt a satisfactory definition of these institutions.

In the first place there is the deliberate disfranchisement of the small, perhaps the unfortunate, minority; the fact that the number is small is not more significant than that the exclusion is deliberate. In the second place, there is the installation of orders of government corresponding to orders of society; the fact that the lines are imprecise and that the results are uncertain is again not more significant than that the scale is deliberate.

It was a rule of Whig ideology that participation in matters of government was the legitimate concern only of those who possessed what was commonly called "a stake in society." In concrete terms this stake in society was one's property, for the protection of which, government had been

---

[30] Edmund Randolph to James Madison, Richmond, Dec. 27, 1782, Madison Papers, Manuscript Division, Library of Congress.

originally formed. As a means to that protection, he was entitled, under a government so formed, to a voice: to some form of representation.

But there is a further problem. To put it briefly, what is to happen if the expected general economic advancement does not take place? Accumulations of wealth were far from being unknown; what if the further accumulation of wealth and the advance of the economy were to leave an ever-increasing residue of the population outside the political limits set by these constitutions? It is unlikely that their framers were ignorant of such possibilities. The growth of Sheffield, Manchester, and Leeds was not unknown; London was not easy to overlook; the Americans had close ties with Liverpool and Bristol. The fact is that a future town proletariat would be specifically excluded by the arrangements that were being made.

The historian who insists that this system was a model of democracy may find that the advance of the economy, a tendency already affecting America in many ways, leaves him holding a very undemocratic-looking baby. In the Philadelphia Convention, James Madison bluntly predicted that in future times "the great majority" would be "not only without landed, but any other sort of, property"—a state in which they would either combine, to the peril of property and liberty, or become the tools of opulence and ambition, leading to "equal danger on the other side." [31] The objection became common when state constitutions were under reform. Opponents of suffrage extension in the constitutions of the 1820's, who included many of the recognized leaders of political life, had a better right than their opponents to claim to be the legitimate heirs of the Whig constitution makers of the revolutionary era.

The constitution of the two legislative houses was based on the view that society was formed for the protection of persons and their property and that these two elements required separate protection and separate representation. This was one of the leading political commonplaces of the day. It is implied by Montesquieu; Jefferson accepts it in his *Notes on Virginia*; Madison held the view throughout his career; Hamilton treated it as a point of common agreement.[32] It is worth adding that it lay behind the original conception of the United States Senate in the form envisaged by the Virginia plan, a form which was subverted when the Senate became the representative chamber of the states. The whole subject was, of course, familiar to John Adams, who went on thinking about it long after he had drawn up a draft for the constitution of his state in 1780.

---

[31] *Records of the Federal Convention*, ed. Max Farrand (4 vols., New Haven, Conn., 1927), II, 203–204.

[32] Charles de Secondat, Baron de Montesquieu, *Oeuvres complètes* (Paris, 1838), *De l'esprit des lois*, 267; James Madison, *Writings*, ed. Gaillard Hunt (9 vols., New York, 1910), V, 287; Hamilton's speech in *Debates and Proceedings of Convention of New York, at Poughkeepsie 1788* (Poughkeepsie, N. Y., 1905), 26.

John Adams, as he himself anticipated, has been a much-misunderstood man. But it is important that we should get him right. No American was more loyal to Whig principles, and none was more deeply read in political ideas.

Adams is often said to have been an admirer of aristocracy and of monarchy. His admiration for the British constitution was easy to treat as an admission of unrepublican principles. But he really believed in the British constitution as it ought to have been, and he prudently averted his gaze from what it was in his own day. If Adams had lived in England in the 1780's, he would have been an associator in Wyvill's parliamentary reform movement, rather than a Foxite Whig.

Adams was profoundly impressed with the advantages enjoyed by birth, wealth, superior education, and natural merit, and the tendency for these advantages to become an inherited perquisite of the families that enjoyed them. He was equally clear about the corrupting influence of this sort of power. For this reason he wanted to segregate the aristocracy in an upper chamber, a process which he called "a kind of ostracism." The strong executive in which he believed was intended as a check not on the commons so much as on the aristocracy.

He developed this view of the function of the upper chamber in his *Defence of the Constitutions of the United States* (1786–1787). It is not wholly consistent with the view given in the *Address* [33] attached to the draft Massachusetts constitution of 1780, in which the line taken was that persons and property require separate protection in different houses. This view is itself a reflection of more than one tradition. It reflects the traditional structure of the legislature—council and assembly, lords and commons; it reflects also the idea that the state is actually composed of different orders (a word of which John Adams was fond) and that these orders have in their own right specific interests which are entitled to specific recognition. They are entitled to it because it is the purpose of the state to secure and protect them: that in fact was why the state was supposed to have come into existence.

Adams once, in later years, wrote to Jefferson: "Your *aristoi* are the most difficult animals to manage in the whole theory and practice of government. They will not suffer themselves to be governed." [34] Yet in spite of his intense distrust of them, I think his attitude was two sided. I find it difficult to read his account of the role played in society by the aristocracy without feeling that there was to him, as there is to many others, something peculiarly distinguished and attractive about these higher circles, elevated by nature and sustained by society above the

---

[33] This, however, was the work of Samuel Adams. (William V. Wells, *The Life and Public Services of Samuel Adams* [3 vols., Boston, 1865], III, 89–97.)

[34] Quoted in Palmer, *Democratic Revolution*, 273, n. 52.

ordinary run of men. And had he not, after all, sons for whom he had some hopes? Some hopes, perhaps, for the family of Adams?

Governor Bernard had lamented the disappearance from prerevolutionary Massachusetts of those balancing factors, "Fear, reverence, respect and awe." Disappearance at least toward the royal authority. They did not disappear so easily from domestic life. There is nothing which reveals these deferential attitudes more fully than in respect to birth and family, given on trust. Adams therefore tells us much, not only of himself but of his times, when he draws attention to inequality of birth:

Let no man be surprised that this species of inequality is introduced here. Let the page in history be quoted, where any nation, ancient or modern, civilized or savage, is mentioned, among whom no difference was made, between the citizens, on account of their extraction. The truth is, that more influence is allowed to this advantage in free republics than in despotic governments, or would be allowed to it in simple monarchies, if severe laws had not been made from age to age to secure it. The children of illustrious families have generally greater advantages of education, and earlier opportunities to be acquainted with public characters, and informed of public affairs, than those of meaner ones, or even than those in middle life; and what is more than all, a habitual national veneration for their names, and the characters of their ancestors, described in history, or coming down by tradition, removes them farther from vulgar jealousy and popular envy, and secures them in some degree the favour, the affection, the respect of the public. Will any man pretend that the name of Andros, and that of Winthrop, are heard with the same sensations in any village of New England? Is not gratitude the sentiment that attends the latter? And disgust the feeling excited by the former? In the Massachusetts, then, there are persons descended from some of their ancient governors, counsellors, judges, whose fathers, grandfathers, and great-grandfathers, are mentioned in history with applause as benefactors to the country, while there are others who have no such advantage. May we go a step further,—Know thyself, is as useful a precept to nations as to men. Go into every village in New England, and you will find that the office of justice of the peace, and even the place of representative, which has ever depended only on the freest election of the people, have generally descended from generation to generation, in three or four families at most.[35]

Deference: it does not seem, in retrospect, a very secure cement to the union of social orders. Yet to those who live under its sway it can be almost irresistible.

---

[35] John Adams, *Defence of the Constitutions of the United States* . . . (3 vols., Philadelphia, 1797), I, 110–11.

It was beginning to weaken, no doubt, in Adams' own political lifetime. "The distinction of classes" Washington said to Brissot de Warville in 1788, "begins to disappear." But not easily, not all at once, not without a struggle.

It was this which collapsed in ruins in the upheaval of Jacksonian democracy. And that, perhaps, is why the election of so ambiguous a leader was accompanied by such an amazing uproar.

III The British Empire Before the American Revolution: English Whigs Versus American Whigs

Introduction In the 1760's American legislative power and political representation were the two lines of colonial development that came together under the pressure of British legislation of a repressive and coercive nature. "The good old cause"—the Whig creed—developing from the seventeenth-century struggle between Crown and Parliament was well known and heartily accepted in America before the Revolution. In this sense Jefferson was a loyal Whig, as was George III. "The American Whigs of the revolutionary era and their British contemporaries were fellow citizens of a Whig Republic." The central doctrine of the Whig creed, accepted on both sides of the Atlantic, ran to this effect: The supreme power in the state is the legislative power. But included in this power are more than parliaments and assemblies—in England Crown, Lords, and Commons, in America Governor, Council, and Assembly. This is mixed government. Further, mixed government involves the representative principle so that laws deriving from it may be lawful. This representative principle was certainly not what we today would understand as "one man, one vote." To Locke it was tacit consent; later it was called "virtual representation," i.e., representation of diverse interests and not individuals. The idea of virtual representation was very serviceable in defense of a mixed government's position against reformers at home and colonials overseas. However, in the latter case, as Pole remarks, the concept "died soon after being discovered."

Thus we have British Whigs and American Whigs both accepting legislative supremacy in its large sense, but more and more seeing its most English expression in the Commons and its most American expression in the Assemblies. So English Whigs in Commons and American Whigs in colonial Assemblies called out against each other. "John Adams of Massachusetts or James Madison of Virginia could have entered British politics, and Charles Grey, Charles Fox—even Lord North could have entered American politics with a great deal more chance of being understood than Sieyès or Robespierre could have done in England, and with a great deal more physical safety than Tom Paine experienced in France." J. R. Pole's account of the fulfillment of legislative power in the Anglo-American arena is a superb essay in comparative history. It sweeps across the centuries and passes and repasses the Atlantic with consummate confidence and acumen and withal grace and wit.

Jack P. Greene, in the second piece presented here, gives a firm chronological and critical account of the growth of legislative power of the Lower Houses of Assembly from the restoration of Charles II in England to the American Revolution. This essay complements rather than contradicts Pole's work. Greene shows the Lower Houses of Assembly in America as largely impotent vis a vis Parliament to 1689, forging ahead through struggle from 1689 to 1763, and, in the stress and crisis of the 1760's, emerging to a dominant place. But the British mood had changed as well, and the "fit of absence of mind" was replaced by inquiry and restraint. Imperial legislation of a penal character was enacted. The battle was joined. "At issue was the whole political structure forged by the lower houses over the previous century. In this context the American Revolution became in essence a war for political survival, a conflict involving not only individual rights as traditionally emphasized by historians of the event but assembly rights as well." Greene's work gives us chronology, exposition, and interpretation; Pole's work adds the coping stone of a high historical imagination.

The Fulfilment
of Legislative Power
——*Jack Richon Pole*

Two American revolutions converged in 1776 and ran in a mingled stream until the final achievement of Independence. The first of these, announced to the world by the Declaration of Independence and carried out by the ensuing war, would not have been possible without the character that colonial politics had taken from the second, inner revolution, which had developed according to an entirely different rhythm, in time far more gradual, and in temperament essentially civilian.

This civilian process was nothing less than the American fulfilment of the great Whig tradition, which had once, not inappropriately, been known as "the good old cause." The American Whigs of the revolutionary era and their British contemporaries were fellow-citizens of a Whig Republic. They not only spoke the same language and appealed to the same heritage but to an almost disarming extent they tended to approve and deprecate the same things. This very similarity accounts for some of the difficulty of interpreting the principles that were involved in the conflict; and it also tends to conceal the nature of the particular emphasis and quality that American experience had given to the leading Whig doctrine to have emerged from the English struggles of the seventeenth century.

Those struggles were pitched over the question of lawful power, which in its nature meant the authority to give laws; and Locke here made judicious use of Hooker to affirm the supreme authority of the legislative power. The argument supposed, as Locke stated, that all rightful government was in some way fiduciary, sanctioned by the consent of the people and containing an element of representation. The notion that every man in England was virtually present in Parliament to consent to the passing of laws and taxes never, of course, had much to do with the facts; the consent of all was a legal fiction. Yet it was a significant fiction, for it was the persistence of some such justification in the minds of lawyers that made them consider the laws lawful.

In England after the Restoration of the legislative power could never mean less than the Crown, Lords, and Commons in Parliament assembled. Yet the Stuart monarchs, at odds with their subjects as represented in

From Jack Richon Pole, *Political Representation in England and the Origins of the American Republic* (1966), pp. 503–513. Reprinted by permission of St. Martin's Press, Inc., New York, and The Macmillan Company of Canada Limited.

Parliament, showed a marked propensity for relying on foreign aid; an attitude that became more compromising when their foreign associations and private convictions connected them with the Roman Catholic religion. From the constitutional view it became curiously beside the point that many ordinary English people still shared that religion with their monarchs. Given the Protestantism of the major interests represented in Parliament, the effect was to give a particularly sharp edge to the claims made by Parliament as the spokesman of the estates of the realm against the Crown: it led to a deep implicit emphasis on the Englishness of Parliament. Even the later adoptive monarchy of the Whigs, first in the persons of William and Mary, then in the Hanoverians, was saddled with the implication of alien connections which might cut across the interests of England; and against which specific statutory precautions were held to be necessary. For the Whigs, as for the Tories, of the Convention Parliament it was enough that the legislative power be lodged in the constituted Houses of Parliament. There was no disposition to ask searching questions about the precise meaning of the representation* in those houses of the people outside.

In the American colonies, the tension between the Crown and the Parliament had an ironical reflection. Representative Assemblies had been called to assist in the work of government; and when issues arose on which royal or proprietary Governors, armed with instructions from England, clashed with the demands of those colonial interests which had attained representation in the Assemblies, then it was the British Governor who stood out as the representative of a kind of alien interest. In a system of divided powers the different branches show an almost unavoidable tendency to suspect slights on their own dignity and to develop a strong sense of institutional identity. The actual composition of the Assemblies combined with these factors, during recurrent clashes with the Governors, to build in colonial minds a deep and abiding feeling for the *Americanness* of the Assemblies.

American colonists absorbed the doctrine of legislative supremacy, but they also received the theory, as well as the institutional forms, of mixed government. The men who ran colonial affairs had good reasons to believe in it. For one thing, that form bore a flattering resemblance to the Aristotelian prescription for stability in the state; and for another, since both classical and English education taught them that the executive power, the nobility, and the commons or "democracy" were all permanent and necessary ingredients of society, and since mixed government on the Whig model meant a popular power that could check the prerogative while assuring representation to the commons, neither history nor contemporary politics could show them any better prescription for political liberty.

For a period of about fifty years, before the American Revolution, the forms and the theory of mixed government came under gruelling and cumulative pressure. During this time the Assemblies, by a variety of means but in ways that produced the same general result, came to absorb the largest share of that very legislative power which all regarded as supreme.

Each colonial Assembly made itself in the image of the British House of Commons. It quickly established control over that vital factor, its own composition, claiming as the Commons had done under James I the power to judge the credentials of its own members. In addition to electing their own speakers, the Assemblies also asserted the familiar privileges during the duration of their sessions—freedom of speech, freedom of members from arrest, and the articles of parliamentary privilege. Privileges in fact could be used in a high-handed way to restrain the liberty of the Press and even the liberty of citizens to criticise the Assembly or to impugn the honour of the members.

Colonial Assemblies were not normally the scenes of any single-minded unity of purpose or the agencies of any one movement. There is little reason to suppose that in their clashes with governors they felt themselves driving relentlessly on towards ultimate independence; nor were colonial politics perpetually dominated by such conflicts. There were, however, certain specific issues in whose determination lay a significant shift of real power. The most obvious was the question of governors' salaries, in which the northern colonies had won, by the middle of the 1730s, an ascendancy that was to prove enduring. The power claimed by the Assembly of Massachusetts to control the disbursement of funds raised by its own vote was a gain from which there would be no subsequent retreat. Massachusetts and Pennsylvania had enjoyed from early years the advantages of annual elections; in Virginia, the attempt of the House of Burgesses to place the Assembly on a septennial basis, though no more than a move to adopt British practices, stood forth as an unmistakable assertion of legislative power over constitutional matters and as such was disallowed by the Crown. When—as in 1767—the Crown intervened to prevent the formation of new constituencies it thereby limited the power of the Assembly to control its representative character and function. These issues, the regularity of elections and the representative base, were understood on both sides to involve the full meaning of constitutional authority. They were conflicts about real power; they were also conflicts about the location of rightful power—of power centred on consent. The Crown could not afford to yield to colonial Assemblies the whole of the ground on which, even by British theory, the right to govern was based.

The fact that the colonial governor came over armed with royal instructions which he was not obliged to reveal, or portions of which he could reveal as suited his own timing, and the further fact that his gestures summoned up the huge shadow of the British Crown, did not free him from the need to negotiate constantly to maintain his position. It was his natural policy to ally himself with groups whom he thought capable of controlling the legislature; some, notably Spotswood in Virginia, sought to build an extensive party in the Assembly; while all governors could be expected to deploy their powers of patronage to secure the loyalty of influential colonists. But even the strongest found fatal flaws in their armoury. Their financial weaknesses were due partly to the permanent refusal of British governments to put colonial salaries on the Civil List; and even where these questions were not paramount, governors could never get things done for long without winning the collaboration of the Assemblies; they were chronically weakened, in terms of the kind of influence which governments normally exerted in the period, by the simple fact that colonial government never developed the intricacy and complexity that might have given rise to extensive patronage and consequent power.

The most potent, though not the most pliable instrument available to the Governor was his Council. The Council usually combined both judicial and legislative with an element of executive power. In Pennsylvania it was a frail thing, almost withering after 1701, so that some people were left with the impression that the province had a unicameral government. In Massachusetts, under the Charter of 1691, the Council was elected by the Assembly, but even so it did not materially differ in style from that of Virginia or other provinces in which it was composed of men of acknowledged rank and wealth.

Colonial electors in general and on most occasions agreed as to the right of such men to hold commanding positions in government. Moreover the bicameral system had not been imposed on the colonies by British command; colonial bicameralism was an indigenous growth. The emergence of an upper chamber corresponded both to the needs of government and more particularly under that government to the needs of the high and mighty propertied interests of a profoundly property-conscious society. Since the possession of property was itself the chief manifestation of liberty the existence of an upper chamber, not only before the Revolution but subsequently as a direct result of it, was a natural and proper consequence of the determination of the colonists to defend their liberties.

At the end of the seventeenth century the Council stood as one of the strongest institutions in the colonies, fully equal to holding its own with the other branches of government. It would have been hard to predict that within some twenty-five years it would begin to lose its grip in face of the competition of the Assembly. Yet, in spite of that, the decline in the influence of the colonial Council was in turn an indigenous process, owing nothing to British example and resulting from a gradual, but on the whole deliberate, alteration in the choices of the leading colonists, and from changes in the character of their society. It is no less fascinating, for that reason, to observe the remarkable correspondence of this process with the relative decline of the House of Lords. This is not, of course, to say that the House of Lords lost its influence over British life and social values; it is rather to say that as the embodiment of an estate, as a branch of government, it became more and more homogeneous with the House of Commons. An almost identical trend was noted by Jefferson as a reason for criticism of the Virginia Senate soon after the Revolution; and Jefferson, a loyal Whig, was complaining that the two Houses ought to stand for separate interests!

Comparisons often prove more striking for the contrasts than the similarities they reveal, and the significance of these similar developments in British and American institutions lay in the enormous difference of pace. The House of Lords continued to fascinate the British mind—and some American minds, too—deep into the twentieth century; the name alone reverberated with a feudal grandeur that was wholly absent from the history and could have little effect on the ambitions of Americans thinking of their own Upper Houses. (Some of this sentiment clung to the United States Senate; but it had other interests to represent and other values to defend.) Moreover, and this difference was of overwhelming importance, the House of Lords was always more than the representation of the nobility: it consisted of the nobility in their persons; and if Americans, or British governments planning American institutions, had really meant to lay down the aristocratic principle as the basis for American politics, they should have conferred the right to a personal seat in the Upper House on all men above a certain definable status. To select a small minority for this distinction, especially when it ceased even to be a representative minority, was a policy that directed the ambitions of the remainder towards the honours and rewards of the elective chamber.

The decline of the Council—and the process was analogous if not actually parallel to that of the Lords—took place as the leading men came to appreciate that they could exert more influence in the elective Assemblies than in an appointive upper House. It was in their Assemblies that Americans found the legitimate, American expression of that great instrument of the Whig purposes—the legislative power. Some significance must also attach to the size of the Assemblies, which were much larger than the Councils. Precisely because the colonists looked on themselves as English, their Assemblies became in their minds the agencies of all rightful power over taxation and local government.

The consequences were of incalculable importance not only in bringing on the American Revolution of separation from Britain but in forming the character of the new state governments and eventually that of the American Constitution. In the final colonial phase, with the Council unable—or unwilling—to oppose the will of the Assembly, the colonial governor was reduced to a position not much above that of a rather strong negotiator in a foreign country. What had happened, after some half-century of gradual accretion of power by the popular House, was that notwithstanding the theory of mixed government to which nearly all still officially subscribed, the real and effective legislative power—that of making laws which would be obeyed—had been gathered up in a single branch, and that branch rested directly on the electorate. The rise of the representative arm of government had converged with the domestic drive towards legislative power.

The American Revolution was not brought about as a defence of a stable or static democratic form of government against the encroaching tyranny of Crown or Parliament. It was not fought in order to inaugurate sweeping advances towards more democratic forms of government. It developed, point by point, out of the policies of British administrations and the interpretations given by leading colonists to those policies. It was a struggle between British initiative and colonial resistance; but neither the timing nor the methods nor the strength of that resistance were mere accidents of response to British policies. It may truly be said that the final stages in the Americanisation of the colonial legislatures were forced by unwanted British measures—that the meeting of the streams of full legislative power and of American political representation was compelled by the structure of British dykes. But these were streams which sprang from American sources; and their confluence—and thus the American Revolution itself— were the culmination of some half-century's momentum. In that very significant sense the American Revolution was not a beginning but an end.

The old Assemblies, the new and revolutionary provincial Congresses, contained their fair and politically respectable proportion of members who would have been content to have averted that culmination. Many more were concerned to moderate its implications for domestic government. But whatever their preferences, the Americans could not escape (and many of them of course embraced) the consequences of having made an independent Confederation from the base provided by a long cycle of domestic development. The fact now was that the whole responsibility for government in the former colonies rested solely in American hands and that the whole was therefore based squarely on American representation.

Formerly the theory of mixed government had always provided that a portion—which in America had necessarily meant the major portion—of the general legislative power was to belong to the representative branch. In Britain that branch was the House of Commons; in the American colonies, the Assemblies. The merit of the colonial Council lay in the very fact that, not being subject to the electorate, it stood for certain more stable interests, could perform more specialist duties, and by its mere existence provided a check or balance to the popular House. The Council, however, did not govern by any hereditary right; it stood on shaky foundations, especially as the great weight of opinion in America was against such things as hereditary political power. The effect of the assumption of legislative power by the representative branch, carried forward into actual independent sovereignty, was to deprive the interests in the Councils of the last vestige of a claim to a place in government on any appointive or privileged basis. Councils were in truth very soon to be reconstituted under the name of Senates. But they could never be reconstituted on the former ground; the whole legislature, including the Governor—the whole of the old and venerable "legislative power"—was henceforth to be in some form representative; all future legislative chambers were to draw their powers and owe their membership to elections.

This turn of events meant that America had arrived by 1776, not as a matter of some pugnaciously abstract theorising but as a matter of plain, unavoidable fact, at a position which only the most violent Radicals would have affirmed in Britain. By 1797, driven almost to despair by the Pitt régime, seeing no hope of power for themselves, and therefore perhaps willing to risk the more, the parliamentary Whigs led by Fox and Grey began to make a similar assertion about the British Constitution. They began to declare that the fundamental principle of the Constitution was representation: the institutions, including even the Lords and the Crown, were merely instruments. That high-water mark of radicalism at least revealed the direction in which the tide would flow. It was not a point to which any of them, least of all Grey, would return when the twist of politics gave them the power to act.

So complete was the assumption of legislative power by the Assemblies that their immediate successors, the provincial conventions based on the same electorates, exercised their authority to form new, independent Constitutions for their states. Only in Massachusetts (and later in New Hampshire) were these instruments of government even submitted to the people for ratification. In Massachusetts, however, the force of the popular belief in the theory of compact took the unprecedented course of converting that theory into something closely resembling fact; and in the elections for the Constitutional Convention to meet in 1779–80, every adult man in the state was given the vote; a franchise whose extraordinary and fundamental nature was to be underlined by the ensuing Constitution, which actually narrowed the suffrage for Assembly elections.

The idea of the constituent power of the people took root. When the great Convention of Philadelphia came at last to consider the problem of ratification, the tactical acumen of the leaders of that body perceived the advantage of what the theory of compact already taught: that a constitution ratified by popular conventions would have the strongest possible case to call itself "the supreme law of the land." The subsequent state ratifying conventions were not in fact as universally based as had been that of Massachusetts; but the principle of the constituent power of the people (soon afterwards to be adopted in France) was, in intention, of the same origin.

Written Constitutions offered a welcome opportunity to affirm undying principles. One of the principles which had come down to the Americans, though somewhat tangled in the teachings of Montesquieu and the inferences to be drawn from the British Constitution, was that of the separation of powers. The powers which were supposed to be separated had a tendency to shift their identity from time to time. Once they had been mainly the executive and the deliberative branches of government; the separation of powers could at times mean little more than a prohibition against plural office-holding. It was a doctrine which gained much prestige in America from the dark lessons inculcated by British history in the eighteenth century; the corruption of the Commons by the Crown was a stark warning about the perils that could attend the merging of such powers. State constitutions tended to affirm the principle of separation while reposing most of the power in the elective Assemblies; and the troubles of state histories in the next few years helped to convince the men who met at Philadelphia in 1787 that the representative accumulation of legislative power had gone too far for the public good—too far for the safety of the very interests that government had been instituted to protect.

This great store-house of the legislative power was invaded by the makers of the Constitution. The entire building was taken down and laboriously rebuilt. The rich and treasured contents in due course were divided up and parcelled out between separate branches of the new government, each of which was given a separate constitutional base, each of which was equal in its own sphere to the others.

When James Madison, in the brilliant essay forming the fifty-first of *The Federalist Papers,* observed that in a republican government the legislative authority necessarily predominated, he was no longer engaged in affirming the truths of the past; his business now was to explain and justify the elaborate steps that had been taken to keep that power under restraint. A significant section of the whole work was devoted to the task of convincing the earnest but often rather simple adherents of that great prescription for liberty, the separation of powers, that the new Constitution did in fact adequately conform to their demands.

Madison and his generation owed more to Locke, the American, than they could reasonably hope to repay. But two of his principles, which had served so well in the past, were now finally repealed. The grand Whig doctrine of legislative supremacy disappeared from the law of the American Constitution; the written instrument itself acquired the supremacy. As of old in Britain and in the separate states, the law-making power was divided between the two Houses, each planted securely on different foundations. Locke, however, had also claimed that the legislative power must remain "sacred and unalterable in the hands where the community have once placed it," a depository where it would be as safe from the predatory designs of the multitude as it would from the king. The makers of the Constitution rejected that doctrine too, advancing in turn an even higher claim: henceforth the legislative power would cease to be supreme, and the supreme power itself would be alterable.

After 1787 constitutional government in America developed on lines so different from those of Britain as to suggest the working of different principles, even the defence of different values. Yet the contrasts between forms of government were wider and more striking than the different objects those forms were meant to represent. In Britain nothing happened to interfere with the political sovereignty of Parliament. No new crisis, no internal conflict, posed any challenge to the government that could not be dealt with within the framework of the existing system. When the long-delayed movement towards parliamentary reform achieved its limited aims in 1832 the sting could be drawn from the resentment of the more influential sections of the disfranchised and unrepresented by extending the suffrage and redrawing the map of the constituencies—by amending the system of representation; and further reforms would simply carry the same demands further forward. It was perfectly natural that the ministers of the Crown should remain members of Parliament answerable, as they had been since the Glorious Revolution, to a manageable majority in the House of Commons. To have defined them as the "executive" and to have separated them from the Commons, so far from being a safeguard to liberty, would have taken them beyond the control of the representatives of the people. Nothing would have been more dangerous; no one who understood English liberty would have suggested it.

It was not so in America. The engrossment of legislative power by the colonial legislature actually culminated in the Revolution, which in turn meant the final separation between the representative government and the "executive" office of the royal Governor, who had become the symbol of an alien and hostile power.

In the new state constitutions both power and sentiment weighed overwhelmingly in favour of the legislatures, and governors were retained as vestigial emblems of sovereignty, so weakened as to appear in some cases merely as emblems of political impotence. Yet the Governor was still the "executive", charged with certain duties and set aside, in accordance with the dogma of the separation of powers, in his separate compartment. Never could a governor be trusted with power over the Assembly—to do that would be to risk a repetition of all the corruption to which the British Constitution had succumbed in the eighteenth century.

It was the direct result of this situation that when the makers of the Federal Constitution created a national executive, a headship of the Union which was also to be an active department of government, they separated that department from the legislature. Technically speaking it would still have been possible to place the President and the secretaries of departments in the Senate—greater difficulties than that were surmounted in the Convention; a form of government responsible to a congressional majority could have been brought into being as the foundation of the new Constitution. But this was a technical rather than a true historical possibility. It was far from clear at the time that the cabinet system of responsible government was to develop as the leading principle of the British parliamentary system, and much of the contemporary evidence suggested the advisability of avoiding rather than imitating the British method. Beyond this, in any case, the history of representative government in America had already, and very effectively, brought about the separation between representative and executive branches; that state of affairs had not been recently proposed, but had been reached as a result of a long process; and the experience of that process, accentuated by the legislative sovereignty tried out in most of the states, had confirmed in American minds the truth of the doctrine to which in theory they already subscribed. The executive was thus separated from the genuinely legislative functions of government in America as a result of the American engrossment of those functions. Thence the executive was driven upwards into a separate department. This was the final stage in the long cycle, marking the end of the doctrine of legislative supremacy and the beginning of the national phase of American government.

The guardianship of the law of the Constitution fell, eventually and logically, to the Supreme Court. The fact that the Court has interpreted that law in different ways under the influence of differing kinds of pressure or persuasion does nothing to detract from its duty, or its authority, to judge the constitutional issues that involve the meaning of republican government. Republican government, in whatever form, unquestionably involves political representation, and when political representation is impaired or denied then the resulting grievance is by its very nature a constitutional grievance which lies with the Supreme Court. When the suffrage franchise is denied the Constitution is expressly violated; and when a section of the electorate maintains that it is impaired by an unrepresentative apportionment of seats in the legislature, then (whether the plaintiffs are right or wrong in the case) the principle of representation, on which all republican forms of government are founded, is affected. Both kinds of case call equally for the justice that, in the last resort, only the Supreme Court can give: both kinds, to use its own language, are "justiciable." The determination of the Supreme Court in *Baker* v. *Carr,* which arose from the grievance of mal-apportionment in Tennessee in 1962 and in which the Court accepted this responsibility to preside over the representative character of republican government, was fully consistent with its historic guardianship.

The Role of the Lower Houses of Assembly in Eighteenth-Century Politics

——Jack P. Greene

The rise of the representative assemblies was perhaps the most significant political and constitutional development in the history of Britain's overseas empire before the American Revolution. Crown and proprietary authorities had obviously intended the governor to be the focal point of colonial government with the lower houses merely subordinate bodies called together when necessary to levy taxes and ratify local ordinances proposed by the executive. Consequently, except in the New England charter colonies, where the representative bodies early assumed a leading role, they were dominated by the governors and councils for most of the period down to 1689. But beginning with the Restoration and intensifying their efforts during the years following the Glorious Revolution, the lower houses engaged in a successful quest for power as they set about to restrict the authority of the executive, undermine the system of colonial administration laid down by imperial and proprietary authorities, and make themselves paramount in the affairs of their respective colonies.

Historians have been fascinated by this phenomenon. For nearly a century after 1776 they interpreted it as a prelude to the American Revolution. In the 1780's the pro-British historian George Chalmers saw it as the early manifestation of a latent desire for independence, an undutiful reaction to the mild policies of the Mother Country.[1] In the middle of the nineteenth century the American nationalist George Bancroft, although more interested in other aspects of colonial history, looked upon it as the natural expression of American democratic principles, simply another chapter in the progress of mankind.[2] The reaction to these sweeping interpretations set in during the last decades of the nineteenth century, when Charles M. Andrews, Edward Channing, Herbert L. Osgood, and others

From *Journal of Southern History*, XXVII (November 1961), 451–474. Copyright 1961 by the Southern Historical Association. Reprinted by permission of the Managing Editor. This is a slightly revised edition of the article as it appeared in the *Journal of Southern History*.

[1] George Chalmers, *An Introduction to the History of the Revolt of the American Colonies* (2 vols., Boston, 1845), I, 223–26, and II, 226–28, particularly, for statements of Chalmers' position.

[2] George Bancroft, *History of the United States* (14th ed., 10 vols., Boston, 1854–1875), III, 1–108, 383–98, particularly.

began to investigate in detail and to study in context developments from the Restoration to the end of the Seven Years' War. Osgood put a whole squadron of Columbia students to work examining colonial political institutions, and they produced a series of institutional studies in which the evolution of the lower houses was a central feature. These studies clarified the story of legislative development in each colony, but this necessarily piecemeal approach, as well as the excessive fragmentation that characterized the more general narratives of Osgood and Channing, tended to emphasize the differences rather than the similarities in the rise of the lower houses and failed to produce a general analysis of the common features of their quest for power.[3] Among later scholars, Leonard W. Labaree in his excellent monograph *Royal Government in America* presented a comprehensive survey of the institutional development of the lower houses in the royal colonies and of the specific issues involved in their struggles with the royal governors, but he did not offer any systematic interpretation of the general process and pattern of legislative development.[4] Charles Andrews promised to tackle this problem and provide a synthesis in the later volumes of his magnum opus, *The Colonial Period of American History*, but he died before completing that part of the project.[5]

As a result, some fundamental questions have never been fully answered, and no one has produced a comprehensive synthesis. No one has satisfactorily worked out the basic pattern of the quest; analyzed the reasons for and the significance of its development; explored its underlying assumptions and theoretical foundations; or assessed the consequences of the success of the lower houses, particularly the relationship between their rise to power and the coming of the American Revolution. This essay is intended to suggest some tentative conclusions about these problems, not

---

[3] Herbert L. Osgood, *The American Colonies in the Seventeenth Century* (3 vols., New York, 1904–1907) and *The American Colonies in the Eighteenth Century* (4 vols., New York, 1924–1925). For Edward Channing's treatment see *A History of the United States* (6 vols., New York, 1905–1925), II. Representative of the studies of Osgood's students are William R. Shepherd, *History of Proprietary Government in Pennsylvania* (New York, 1896); Newton D. Mereness, *Maryland As a Proprietary Province* (New York, 1901); W. Roy Smith, *South Carolina as a Royal Province, 1719–1776* (New York, 1903); Charles L. Raper, *North Carolina: A Study in English Colonial Government* (New York, 1904); William H. Fry, *New Hampshire As a Royal Province* (New York, 1908); Edwin P. Tanner, *The Province of New Jersey, 1664–1738* (New York, 1908); Edgar J. Fisher, *New Jersey As a Royal Province, 1738–1776* (New York, 1911); and Percy S. Flippin, *The Royal Government in Virginia, 1624–1775* (New York, 1919).

[4] Leonard W. Labaree, *Royal Government in America* (New Haven, 1930), 172–311, particularly. Two other illuminating studies by Labaree's contemporaries are A. B. Keith, *Constitutional History of the First British Empire* (Oxford, 1930), which is legalistic in emphasis, and John F. Burns, *Controversies Between Royal Governors and Their Assemblies in the Northern American Colonies* (Boston, 1923), which fails to tie together in any satisfactory way developments in the four colonies it treats.

[5] Charles M. Andrews, "On the Writing of Colonial History," *William and Mary Quarterly*, 3rd ser., I (January, 1944), 29–42. The line of interpretation that Andrews would probably have followed is briefly developed in his brilliant *The Colonial Background of the American Revolution* (New Haven, 1924), 3–65.

to present ultimate solutions. My basic research on the lower houses has been in the Southern royal colonies and in Nova Scotia. One of the present purposes is to test the generalizations I have arrived at about the Southern colonies by applying them to what scholars have learned of the legislatures in the other colonies. This procedure has the advantage of providing perspective on the story of Southern developments. At the same time, it may serve as one guidepost for a general synthesis in the future.

Any student of the eighteenth-century political process will sooner or later be struck by the fact that, although each of the lower houses developed independently and differently, their stories were similar. The elimination of individual variants, which tend to cancel out each other, discloses certain basic regularities, a clearly discernible pattern—or what the late Sir Lewis Namier called a morphology—common to all of them. They all moved along like paths in their drives for increased authority, and although their success on specific issues differed from colony to colony and the rate of their rise varied from time to time, they all ended up at approximately the same destination. They passed successively through certain vaguely defined phases of political development. Through most of the seventeenth century the lower houses were still in a position of subordination, slowly groping for the power to tax and the right to sit separately from the council and to initiate laws. Sometime during the early eighteenth century most of them advanced to a second stage at which they could battle on equal terms with the governors and councils and challenge even the powers in London if necessary. At that point the lower houses began their bid for political supremacy. The violent eruptions that followed usually ended in an accommodation with the governors and councils which paved the way for the ascendancy of the lower houses and saw the virtual eclipse of the colonial executive. By the end of the Seven Years' War, and in some instances considerably earlier, the lower houses had reached the third and final phase of political dominance and were in a position to speak for the colonies in the conflict with the imperial government which ensued after 1763.

By 1763, with the exception of the lower houses in the corporate colonies of Rhode Island and Connecticut, which had virtually complete authority, the Pennsylvania and Massachusetts houses of representatives were probably most powerful. Having succeeded in placing its election on a statutory basis and depriving the Council of direct legislative authority in the Charter of Privileges in 1701, the Pennsylvania House under the astute guidance of David Lloyd secured broad financial and appointive powers during the administrations of Daniel Gookin and Sir William Keith. Building on these foundations, it gained almost complete dominance in the 1730's and 1740's despite the opposition of the governors, whose power and prestige along with that of the Council declined rapidly.[6] The Massachusetts House, having been accorded the unique privilege of sharing in the selection of the Council by the royal charter in 1691, already had a strong tradition of legislative supremacy inherited from a half century of corporate experience. During the first thirty years under the new charter first the benevolent policies of Sir William Phips and William Stoughton and then wartime conditions during the tenures of Joseph Dudley and Samuel Shute enabled the House, led by Elisha Cooke, Jr., to extend its authority greatly. It emerged from the conflicts over the salary question during the 1720's with firm control over finance, and the Crown's abandonment of its demand for a permanent revenue in the early 1730's paved the way for an accommodation with subsequent governors and the eventual dominance of the House under Governor William Shirley after 1740.[7]

The South Carolina Commons and New York House of Assembly were only slightly less powerful. Beginning in the first decade of the eighteenth century, the South Carolina lower house gradually assumed an ironclad control over all aspects of South Carolina government, extending its supervision to the minutest details of local administration after 1730 as a succession of governors, including Francis Nicholson, Robert Johnson, Thomas Broughton, the elder William Bull, and James Glen offered little determined opposition. The Commons continued to grow in stature after 1750 while the Council's standing declined because of the Crown policy of filling it with placemen from England and the Commons' successful attacks upon its authority.[8] The New York House of Assembly began to demand greater authority in reaction to the mismanagement of Edward Hyde, Viscount Cornbury, during the first decade of the eighteenth century. Governor Robert Hunter met the challenge squarely during his ten-

---

[6] Developments in Pennsylvania may be traced in Shepherd, *Proprietary Government*, *op. cit.*; Benjamin Franklin, *An Historical Review of Pennsylvania* (London, 1759); Roy N. Lokken, *David Lloyd: Colonial Lawmaker* (Seattle, 1959); Sister Joan de Lourdes Leonard, *The Organization and Procedure of the Pennsylvania Assembly, 1682–1772* (Philadelphia, 1949); Winifred T. Root, *The Relation of Pennsylvania with the British Government, 1696–1765* (Philadelphia, 1912); and Theodore Thayer, *Pennsylvania Politics and the Growth of Democracy, 1740–1776* (Harrisburg, Pa., 1953). On Rhode Island and Connecticut see David S. Lovejoy, *Rhode Island Politics and the American Revolution, 1760–1776* (Providence, 1958), and Oscar Zeichner, *Connecticut's Years of Controversy, 1754–1775* (Chapel Hill, N.C., 1949).

[7] Useful studies on Massachusetts are Robert E. Brown, *Middle-Class Democracy and the Revolution in Massachusetts, 1691–1780* (Ithaca, N.Y., 1955); Martin L. Cole, The Rise of the Legislative Assembly in Provincial Massachusetts (unpublished Ph.D. thesis, State University of Iowa, 1939); Thomas Hutchinson, *The History of the Colony and Province of Massachusetts-Bay*, Lawrence S. Mayo, ed. (3 vols., Cambridge, Mass., 1936); and Henry R. Spencer, *Constitutional Conflict in Provincial Massachusetts* (Columbus, O., 1905).

[8] The best published study on South Carolina is Smith, *South Carolina As a Royal Province*. Also useful are David D. Wallace, *The Life of Henry Laurens* (New York, 1915); Jack P. Greene, The Quest for Power of the Lower Houses of Assembly in the Southern Royal Colonies, 1730–1763 (unpublished Ph.D. thesis, Duke University, 1956); and M. Eugene Sirmans, "The South Carolina Royal Council, 1720–1763," *William and Mary Quarterly*, 3rd ser., XVIII (July, 1961), 373–92.

year administration beginning in 1710, but he and his successors could not check the rising power of the House. During the seven-year tenure of George Clarke beginning in 1736, the House advanced into the final stage of development. Following Clarke, George Clinton made a vigorous effort to reassert the authority of the executive, but neither he nor any of his successors was able to challenge the power of the House.[9]

The lower houses of North Carolina, New Jersey, and Virginia developed more slowly. The North Carolina lower house was fully capable of protecting its powers and privileges and competing on equal terms with the executive during the last years of proprietary rule and under the early royal governors, George Burrington and Gabriel Johnston. But it was not until Arthur Dobbs' tenure in the 1750's and 1760's that, meeting more regularly, it assumed the upper hand in North Carolina politics under the astute guidance of Speaker Samuel Swann and Treasurers John Starkey and Thomas Barker.[10] In New Jersey the lower house was partially thwarted in its spirited bid for power during the 1740's under the leadership of John Kinsey and Samuel Nevill by the determined opposition of Governor Lewis Morris, and it did not gain superiority until the administrations of Jonathan Belcher, Thomas Pownall, Francis Bernard, and Thomas Boone during the Seven Years' War.[11] Similarly, the Virginia Burgesses vigorously sought to establish its control in the second decade of the century under Alexander Spotswood, but not until the administrations of Sir William Gooch and Robert Dinwiddie, when first the expansion of the colony and then the Seven Years' War required more regular sessions, did the Burgesses finally gain the upper hand under the effective leadership of Speaker John Robinson.[12]

---

[9] Developments in New York can be followed in Carl L. Becker, *The History of Political Parties in the Province of New York, 1760–1776* (Madison, 1909); Milton M. Klein, "Democracy and Politics in Colonial New York," *New York History*, XL (July 1959), 221–46; Lawrence H. Leder, *Robert Livingston, 1654–1728, and the Politics of Colonial New York* (Chapel Hill, N.C., 1961); Beverly McAnear, Politics in Provincial New York, 1689–1761 (unpublished Ph.D. thesis, Stanford University, 1935); Irving Mark, *Agrarian Conflicts in Colonial New York, 1711–1775* (New York, 1940); William Smith, *The History of the Late Province of New York* (2 vols., New York, 1829); and Charles W. Spencer, *Phases of Royal Government in New York, 1691–1719* (Columbus, O., 1905).

[10] Useful analyses of North Carolina are Raper, *North Carolina, op. cit.*, and Desmond Clarke, *Arthur Dobbs Esquire, 1689–1765* (Chapel Hill, N.C., 1957).

[11] New Jersey developments can be traced in Donald L. Kemmerer's excellent study, *Path to Freedom: The Struggle for Self-Government in Colonial New Jersey, 1703–1776* (Princeton, 1940).

[12] Among the more useful secondary works on Virginia are Flippin, *Royal Government, op. cit.*; Bernard Bailyn, "Politics and Social Structure in Virginia," in James M. Smith, ed., *Seventeenth-Century America: Essays on Colonial History* (Chapel Hill, N.C., 1959), 90–115; Lucille Blanche Griffith, The Virginia House of Burgesses, 1750–1774 (unpublished Ph.D. thesis, Brown University, 1957); Ray Orvin Hummel, Jr., The Virginia House of Burgesses, 1689–1750 (unpublished Ph.D. thesis, University of Nebraska, 1934); David J. Mays, *Edmund Pendleton, 1721–1803* (2 vols., Cambridge, Mass., 1952); Charles S. Sydnor, *Gentlemen Freeholders: Political Practices in Washington's Virginia* (Chapel Hill, N.C., 1952); Thomas J. Wertenbaker, *Give Me Liberty: The Struggle for Self-Government in Virginia* (Philadelphia, 1958); and David Alan Williams, Political Alignments in Colonial Virginia, 1698–1750 (unpublished Ph.D. thesis, Northwestern University, 1959).

Among the lower houses in the older colonies, only the Maryland House of Delegates and the New Hampshire House of Assembly failed to reach the final level of development in the period before 1763. The Maryland body made important advances early in the eighteenth century while under the control of the Crown and aggressively sought to extend its authority in the 1720's under the leadership of the older Daniel Dulany and again in the late 1730's and early 1740's under Dr. Charles Carroll. But the proprietors were usually able to thwart these attempts, and the Delegates failed to pull ahead of the executive despite a concerted effort during the last intercolonial war under the administration of Horatio Sharpe.[13] In New Hampshire, the House had exercised considerable power through the early decades of the eighteenth century, but Governor Benning Wentworth effectively challenged its authority after 1740 and prevented it from attaining the extensive power exercised by its counterparts in other colonies.[14] It should be emphasized, however, that neither the Maryland nor the New Hampshire lower house was in any sense impotent and along with their more youthful equivalent in Georgia gained dominance during the decade of debate with Britain after 1763. Of the lower houses in the continental colonies with pre-1763 political experience, only the Nova Scotia Assembly had not reached the final phase of political dominance by 1776.[15]

The similarities in the process and pattern of legislative development from colony to colony were not entirely accidental. The lower houses faced like problems and drew upon common traditions and imperial precedents for solutions. They all operated in the same broad imperial context and were affected by common historical forces. Moreover, family, cultural, and commercial ties often extended across colony lines, and newspapers and other printed materials, as well as individuals, often found their way from one colony to another. The result was at least a general awareness of issues and practices in neighboring colonies, and occasionally there was even a conscious borrowing of precedents and traditions. Younger bodies such as the Georgia Commons and Nova Scotia Assembly were particularly indebted to their more mature counterparts in South Carolina and Massachusetts Bay.[16] On the executive side, the similarity in attitudes, assumptions, and policies among the governors can be traced to large measure to the fact that they were all subordinate to the same central

---

[13] On Maryland see two excellent studies, Charles A. Barker, *The Background of the Revolution in Maryland* (New Haven, 1940), and Aubrey Land, *The Dulanys of Maryland* (Baltimore, 1955).

[14] New Hampshire developments can be followed in Fry, *New Hampshire*, op. cit., and Jeremy Belknap, *History of New Hampshire* (3 vols., Boston, 1791–1792).

[15] On Georgia see W. W. Abbot, *The Royal Governors of Georgia, 1754–1775* (Chapel Hill, N.C., 1959), and Albert B. Saye, *New Viewpoints in Georgia History* (Atlanta, 1943). John Bartlett Brebner, *The Neutral Yankees of Nova Scotia* (New York, 1937), is the best study of developments in that colony.

[16] On this point see Abbot, *ibid.*, and Brebner, *ibid.*

authority in London, which pursued a common policy in all the colonies.

Before the Seven Years' War the quest was characterized by a considerable degree of spontaneity, by a lack of awareness that activities of the moment were part of any broad struggle for power. Rather than consciously working out the details of some master plan designed to bring them liberty or self-government, the lower houses moved along from issue to issue and from situation to situation, primarily concerning themselves with the problems at hand and displaying a remarkable capacity for spontaneous action, for seizing any and every opportunity to enlarge their own influence at the executive's expense and for holding tenaciously to powers they had already secured. Conscious of the issues involved in each specific conflict, they were for the most part unaware of and uninterested in the long-range implications of their actions. Virginia Governor Francis Fauquier correctly judged the matter in 1760. "Whoever charges them with acting upon a premeditated concerted plan, don't know them," he wrote of the Virginia burgesses, "for they mean honestly, but are Expedient Mongers in the highest Degree." [17] Still, in retrospect it is obvious that throughout the eighteenth century the lower houses were engaged in a continuous movement to enlarge their sphere of influence. To ignore that continuity would be to miss the meaning of eighteenth-century colonial political development.

One is impressed with the rather prosaic manner in which the lower houses went about the task of extending their authority, with the infrequency of dramatic conflict. They gained much of their power in the course of routine business, quietly and simply extending and consolidating their authority of passing laws and establishing practices, the implications of which escaped both colonial executives and imperial authorities and were not always fully recognized even by the lower houses themselves. In this way they gradually extended their financial authority to include the power to audit accounts of all public officers, to share in disbursing public funds, and eventually even to appoint officials concerned in collecting and handling local revenues. Precedents thus established soon hardened into fixed principles, "undoubted rights" or "inherent powers," changing the very fabric of their respective constitutions. The notable absence of conflict is perhaps best illustrated by the none too surprising fact that the lower houses made some of their greatest gains under those governors with whom they enjoyed the most harmony, in particular Keith in Pennsylvania, Shirley in Massachusetts, Hunter in New York, and the elder and younger Bull in South Carolina. In Virginia the House of Burgesses made rapid strides during the 1730's and 1740's under the benevolent government of Gooch, who discovered early in his admin-

---

[17] "Fauquier to Board of Trade," June 2, 1760, in Colonial Office Papers (London, Public Record Office), Series 5/1330, folios 37–39.

istration that the secret of political success for a Virginia governor was to reach an accord with the plantation gentry.

One should not conclude that the colonies had no exciting legislative-executive conflicts, however. Attempts through the middle decades of the eighteenth century by Clinton to weaken the financial powers of the New York House, Massachusetts Governors Samuel Shute and William Burnet to gain a permanent civil list, Benning Wentworth to extend unilaterally the privilege of representation to new districts in New Hampshire, Johnston to break the extensive power of the Albemarle Counties in the North Carolina lower house, Dinwiddie to establish a fee for issuing land patents without the consent of the Virginia Burgesses, and Boone to reform South Carolina's election laws each provided a storm of controversy that brought local politics to a fever pitch.[18] But such conflicts were the exception and usually arose not out of the lower houses' seeking more authority but from the executives' attempts to restrict powers already won. Impatient of restraint and jealous of their rights and privileges, the lower houses responded forcefully and sometimes violently when executive action threatened to deprive them of those rights. Only a few governors, men of the caliber of Henry Ellis in Georgia and to a lesser extent William Henry Lyttelton in South Carolina and Bernard in New Jersey, had the skill to challenge established rights successfully without raising the wrath of the lower houses. Clumsier tacticians—Pennsylvania's William Denny, New York's Clinton, Virginia's Dinwiddie, North Carolina's Dobbs, South Carolina's Boone, Georgia's John Reynolds—failed when pursuing similar goals.

Fundamentally, the quest for power in both the royal and the proprietary colonies was a struggle for political identity, the manifestation of the political ambitions of the leaders of emerging societies within each colony. There is a marked correlation between the appearance of economic and social elites produced by the growth in colonial wealth and population on the one hand and the lower houses' demand for increased authority, dignity, and prestige on the other. In the eighteenth century a group of planters, merchants, and professional men had attained or were rapidly acquiring within the colonies wealth and social position. The lower houses' aggressive drive for power reflects the determination of this new elite to attain through the representative assemblies political influence as well. In another but related sense, the lower houses' efforts represented a movement for autonomy in local affairs, although it is doubtful that many of the members recognized them as such. The lower houses wished to

---

[18] The details of these disputes can be traced in Smith, *History of New York, op. cit.,* II, 68–151; Hutchinson, *History of Massachusetts Bay, op. cit.,* 163–280; Labaree, *Royal Government,* 180–185; Lawrence F. London, "The Representation Controversy in Colonial North Carolina," *North Carolina Historical Review,* XI (October, 1934), 255–270; Jack P. Greene, ed., "The Case of the Pistole Fee," *Virginia Magazine of History and Biography,* LXVI (October, 1958), 399–422, and "The Gadsden Election Controversy and the Revolutionary Movement in South Carolina," *Mississippi Valley Historical Review,* XLVI (December, 1959), 469–492.

strengthen their authority within the colonies and to reduce to a minimum the amount of supervision, with the uncertainties it involved, that royal or proprietary authorities could exercise. Continuously nourished by the growing desire of American legislators to be masters of their own political fortunes and by the development of a vigorous tradition of legislative superiority in imitation of the imperial House of Commons, this basic principle of local control over local affairs in some cases got part of its impetus from an unsatisfactory experience early in the lower houses' development with a despotic, inefficient, or corrupt governor such as Thomas, Lord Culpeper, or Francis, Lord Howard or Effingham, in Virginia, Lionel Copley in Maryland, Sir Edmund Andros in Massachusetts, Seth Sothell in North Carolina, or the infamous Cornbury in New York and New Jersey.

With most of their contemporaries in Great Britain, colonial Americans were convinced that men were imperfect creatures, perpetually self-deluded, enslaved by their passions, vanities, and interests, confined in their vision and understanding, and incapable of exercising power over each other without abusing it. This cluster of assumptions with the associated ideals of a government of laws rather than of men and of a political structure that restrained the vicious tendencies of man by checking them against each other was at the heart of English constitutionalism. In Britain and in the colonies, wherever Englishmen encountered a seeming abuse of power, they could be expected to insist that it be placed under legal and constitutional restraints. Because the monarchy had been the chief offender in seventeenth-century England, it became conventional for the representative branch to keep an especially wary eye on the executive, and the Glorious Revolution tended to institutionalize this pattern of behavior. The necessity to justify the Revolution ensured both that the specter of Stuart despotism would continue to haunt English political arenas throughout the eighteenth century and that representative bodies and representatives would be expected—indeed obliged—to be constantly on the lookout for any signs of that excess of gubernatorial power that would perforce result in executive tyranny. When colonial lower houses demanded checks on the prerogative and sought to undermine executive authority, they were, then, to some extent, playing out roles created for them by their predecessors in the seventeenth-century English House of Commons and using a rhetoric and a set of ground rules that grew out of the revolutionary conditions of Stuart England. In every debate, and in every political contest, each American legislator was a potential Coke, Pym, or Hampden and each governor, at least in legislators' minds, a potential Charles I or James II.

But the lower houses' quest for power involved more than the extension of legislative authority within the colonies at the expense of the colonial executives. After their initial stage of evolution, the lower houses learned that their real antagonists were not the governors but the proprietors or Crown officials in London. Few governors proved to be a match for the representatives. A governor was almost helpless to prevent a lower house from exercising powers secured under his predecessors, and even the most discerning governor could fall into the trap of assenting to an apparently innocent law that would later prove damaging to the royal or proprietary prerogative. Some governors, for the sake of preserving amicable relations with the representatives or because they thought certain legislation to be in the best interest of a colony, actually conspired with legislative leaders to present the actions of the lower houses in a favorable light in London. Thus, Jonathan Belcher worked with Massachusetts leaders to parry the Crown's demand for a permanent revenue in the 1730's, and Fauquier joined with Speaker John Robinson in Virginia to prevent the separation of the offices of speaker and treasurer during the closing years of the Seven Years' War.

Nor could imperial authorities depend upon the colonial councils to furnish an effective check upon the representatives' advancing influence. Most councilors were drawn from the rising social and economic elites in the colonies. The duality of their role is obvious. Bound by oath to uphold the interests of the Crown or the proprietors, they were also driven by ambition and a variety of local pressures to maintain the status and power of the councils as well as to protect and advance their own individual interests and those of their group within the colonies. These two objectives were not always in harmony, and the councils frequently sided with the lower houses rather than with the governors. With a weakened governor and an unreliable council, the task of restraining the representative assemblies ultimately devolved upon the home government. Probably as much of the struggle for power was played out in Whitehall as in Williamsburg, Charleston, New York, Boston, or Philadelphia.

Behind the struggle between colonial lower houses and the imperial authorities were two divergent, though on the colonial side not wholly articulated, concepts of the constitutions of the colonies and in particular of the status of the lower houses. To the very end of the colonial period, imperial authorities persisted in the views that colonial constitutions were static and that the lower houses were subordinate governmental agencies with only temporary and limited lawmaking powers—in the words of one imperial official, merely "so many Corporations at a distance, invested with an Ability to make Temporary By Laws for themselves, agreeable to their respective Situations and Climates." [19] In working out a political system for the colonies in the later seventeenth century, imperial officials had institutionalized these views in the royal commissions and instructions.

---

[19] Sir William Keith, "A Short Discourse on the Present State of the Colonies in America with Respect to the Interest of Great Britain," 1729, in Colonial Office Papers (London, Public Record Office), Series 5/4, folios 170–171.

Despite the fact that the lower houses were yearly making important changes in their respective constitutions, the Crown never altered either the commissions or instructions to conform with realities of the colonial political situation and continued to maintain throughout the eighteenth century that they were the most vital part of the constitutional structure of the royal colonies. The Pennsylvania and to a lesser extent the Maryland proprietors were less rigid, although they also insisted upon their theoretical constitutional and political supremacy over the lower houses.

Colonial lower houses had little respect for and even less patience with such a doctrinaire position, and whether or not royal and proprietary instructions were absolutely binding upon the colonies was the leading constitutional issue in the period before 1763. As the political instruments of what was probably the most pragmatic society in the eighteenth-century Western World, colonial legislators would not likely be restrained by dogma divorced from reality. They had no fear of innovations and welcomed the chance to experiment with new forms and ideas. All they asked was that a thing work. When the lower houses found that instructions from imperial authorities did not work in the best interests of the colonies, that they were, in fact, antithetic to the very measures they as legislatures were trying to effect, they openly refused to submit to them. Instructions, they argued, applied only to officials appointed by the Crown.

> Instructions from his majesty, to his governor, or the council, are binding to them, and esteemed as laws or rules; because if either should disregard them, they might immediately be displaced,

declared a South Carolina writer in 1756 while denying the validity of an instruction that stipulated colonial councils should have equal rights with the lower houses in framing money bills. "But, if instructions should be laws and rules to the people of this province, then there would be no need of assemblies, and all our laws and taxes might be made and levied by an instruction." [20] Clearly, then, instructions might bind governors, but never the elected branch of the legislature.

Even though the lower houses, filled with intensely practical politicians, were concerned largely with practical political considerations, they found it necessary to develop a body of theory with which to oppose unpopular instructions from Britain and to support their claims to greater political power. In those few colonies that had charters, the lower houses relied upon the guarantees in them as their first line of defense, taking the position that the stipulations of the charters were inviolate, despite the fact that some had been invalidated by English courts, and could not be altered by executive order. A more basic premise which was equally applicable to all colonies was that the constituents of the lower houses, as

---

[20] *South Carolina Gazette,* May 13, 1756.

inhabitants of British colonies, were entitled to all the traditional rights of Englishmen. On this foundation the colonial legislatures built their ideological structure. In the early charters the Crown had guaranteed the colonists "all privileges, franchises and liberties of this our kingdom of England . . . any Statute, act, ordinance, or provision to the contrary thereof, notwithstanding." [21] Such guarantees, colonials assumed, merely constituted recognition that their privileges as Englishmen were inherent and unalterable and that it mattered not whether they stayed on the home islands or migrated to the colonies. "His Majesty's Subjects coming over to America," the South Carolina Commons argued in 1739 while asserting its exclusive right to formulate tax laws, "have no more forfeited this their most valuable Inheritance than they have withdrawn their Allegiance." No "Royal Order," the Commons declared, could "qualify or any wise alter a fundamental Right from the shape in which it was handed down to us from our Ancestors." [22]

One of the most important of these rights was the privilege of representation, on which, of course, depended the very existence of the lower houses. Imperial authorities always maintained that the lower houses existed only through the consent of the Crown,[23] but the houses insisted that an elected assembly was a fundamental right of a colony arising out of an Englishman's privilege to be represented and that they did not owe their existence merely to the King's pleasure.

> Our representatives, agreeably to the general sense of their constituents [wrote New York lawyer William Smith in the 1750's] are tenacious in their opinion, that the inhabitants of this colony are entitled to all the privileges of Englishmen; that they have a right to participate in the legislative power, and that the session of assemblies here, is wisely substituted instead of a representation in parliament, which, all things considered, would, at this remote distance, be extremely inconvenient and dangerous.[24]

The logical corollary to this argument was that the lower houses were

---

[21] For instance, see the provision in the Maryland charter conveniently published in Merrill Jensen, ed., *English Historical Documents: American Colonial Documents to 1776* (New York, 1955), 88.

[22] James H. Easterby and Ruth S. Green, eds., *The Colonial Records of South Carolina: The Journals of the Commons House of Assembly* (8 vols., Columbia, 1951–1961), *1736–1739* (June 5, 1739), 720.

[23] This view was implicit in most thinking and writing about the colonies by imperial authorities. For the attitude of John Carteret, Lord Granville, an important figure in colonial affairs through the middle decades of the eighteenth century, see Benjamin Franklin to Isaac Norris, March 19, 1759, as quoted by William S. Mason, "Franklin and Galloway: Some Unpublished Letters," American Antiquarian Society, *Proceedings*, n. s., XXXIV (1925), 245–46. Other examples are Jack P. Greene, ed., "Martin Bladen's Blueprint for a Colonial Union," *William and Mary Quarterly*, 3rd ser., XVII (October, 1960), 516–530, by a prominent member of the Board of Trade, and Archibald Kennedy, *An Essay on the Government of the Colonies* (New York, 1752), 17–18, by an official in the colonies.

[24] Smith, *op. cit.*, I, 307.

equivalents of the House of Commons and must perforce in their limited
spheres be entitled to all the privileges possessed by that body in Great
Britain. Hence, in cases where an invocation of fundamental rights was
not appropriate, the lower houses frequently defended their actions on the
grounds that they were agreeable to the practice of the House of Commons. Thus in 1755 the North Carolina Lower House denied the right of
the Council to amend tax bills on the grounds that it was "contrary to
Custom and Usage of Parliament." [25] Unintentionally, Crown officials encouraged the lower houses to make this analogy by forbidding them in
the instructions to exercise "any power or privilege whatsoever which is
not allowed by us to the House of Commons . . . in Great Britain." [26]

Because neither fundamental rights nor imperial precedents could be
used to defend practices that were contrary to customs of the mother
country or to the British constitution, the lower houses found it necessary
to develop still another argument: that local precedents, habits, traditions,
and statutes were important parts of their particular constitutions and
could not be abridged by a royal or proprietary order. The assumptions
were that the legislatures could alter colonial constitutions by their own
actions without the active consent of imperial officials and that once the
alterations were confirmed by usage they could not be countermanded by
the British government. They did not deny the power of the governor to
veto or of the Privy Council to disallow their laws but argued that imperial
acquiescence over a long period of time was tantamount to consent and
that precedents thus established could not be undone without their approval. The implication was that the American colonists saw their constitutions as living, growing, and constantly changing organisms, a theory
which was directly opposite to the imperial view. To be sure, precedent
had always been an important element in shaping the British constitution,
but Crown officials were unwilling to concede that it was equally so in
determining the fundamental law of the colonies. They willingly granted
that colonial statutes, once formally approved by the Privy Council, automatically became part of the constitutions of the colonies, but they officially took the position that both royal instructions and commissions, as
well as constitutional traditions of the mother country, took precedence
over local practice or unconfirmed statutes.[27] This conflict of views persisted throughout the period after 1689, becoming more and more of
an issue in the decades immediately preceding the American Revolution.

---

[25] Journals of the Lower House, January 4–6, 1755, William L. Saunders, ed., The Colonial Records of North Carolina (10 vols., Raleigh, 1886–1890), V, 287.
[26] Leonard W. Labaree, ed., Royal Instructions to British Colonial Governors, 1670–1776 (2 vols., New York, 1935), I, 112–113.
[27] For a classic statement of the imperial argument by a modern scholar see Lawrence H. Gipson, The British Empire Before the American Revolution (10 vols., Caldwell, Idaho, and New York, 1936–1961), III (rev.), 275–281.

In the last analysis it was the imperial denial of the validity of the constitutional defenses of the lower houses that drove colonial lawmakers to seek to extend the power of the lower houses at the very time they were insisting—and, in fact, deeply believed—that no one individual or institution should have a superiority of power in any government. No matter what kind of workable balance of power might be attained within the colonies, there was always the possibility that the home government might unleash the unlimited might of the parent state against the colonies. The chief fear of colonial legislators, then, was not the power of the governors, which they could control, but that of the imperial government, which in the circumstances they could never hope to control, and the whole movement for legislative authority in the colonies can be interpreted as a search for a viable constitutional arrangement in which the rights of the colonists would be secured against the preponderant power of the mother country. The failure of imperial authorities to provide such an arrangement or even to formalize what small concessions they did make, meant, of course, that the search could never be fulfilled, and the resulting anxiety, only partly conscious and finding expression through the classic arguments and ringing phrases of English political struggles of the seventeenth century, impelled the lower houses and the men who composed them relentlessly through the colonial period and was perhaps the most important single factor in the demand of patriot leaders for explicit, written constitutions after the Declaration of Independence.

It is nonetheless true that, if imperial authorities did not grant the validity of the theoretical arguments of the lower houses, neither did they make any systematic or concerted effort to force a rigid compliance with official policies for most of the period after 1689. Repressive measures, at least before 1763, rarely went beyond the occasional disallowance of an offending statute or the official reprimand of a rambunctious lower house. General lack of interest in the routine business of colonial affairs and failure to recognize the potential seriousness of the situation may in part account for this leniency, but it is also true that official policy under both Walpole and the Pelhams called for a light rein on the colonies on the assumption that contented colonies created fewer problems for the administration. "One would not Strain any point," Charles Delafaye, secretary to the lords justices, cautioned South Carolina's Governor Francis Nicholson in 1722, "where it can be of no Service to our King or Country." "In the Plantations," he added, "the Government should be as Easy and Mild as possible to invite people to Settle under it." [28] Three times between 1734 and 1749 the ministry failed to give enthusiastic support to measures introduced into Parliament to insure the supremacy of instructions over

---

[28] Delafaye to Nicholson, January 22, 1722, in Papers Concerning the Governorship of South Carolina (Houghton Library, Harvard University, Cambridge, Mass.), bMs Am 1455, Item 9.

colonial laws.[29] Though the Calverts were somewhat more insistent upon preserving their proprietary prerogatives, in general the proprietors were equally lax as long as there was no encroachment upon their land rights or proprietary dues.

Imperial organs of administration were in fact inadequate to deal effectively with all the problems of the empire. Since no special governmental bodies were created in England to deal exclusively with colonial affairs, they were handled through the regular machinery of government—a maze of boards and officials whose main interests and responsibilities were not the supervision of overseas colonies. The only body sufficiently informed and interested to deal competently with colonial matters was the Board of Trade, and it had little authority, except for the brief period from 1748 to 1761 under the presidency of George Dunk, Earl of Halifax. The most useful device for restraining the lower houses was the Privy Council's right to review colonial laws, but even that was only partly effective, because the mass of colonial statutes annually coming before the Board of Trade made a thorough scrutiny impossible. Under such arrangements no vigorous colonial policy was likely. The combination of imperial lethargy and colonial aggression virtually guaranteed the success of the lower houses' quest for power. An indication of a growing awareness in imperial circles of the seriousness of the situation was Halifax's spirited, if piecemeal, effort to restrain the growth of the lower houses in the early 1750's. Symptomatic of these efforts was the attempt to make Georgia and Nova Scotia model royal colonies at the institution of royal government by writing into the instructions to their governors provisions designed to insure the continued supremacy of the executive and to prevent the lower houses from going the way of their counterparts in the older colonies. However, the outbreak of the Seven Years' War forced Halifax to suspend his activities and prevented any further reformation until the cessation of hostilities.

Indeed, the war saw a drastic acceleration in the lower houses' bid for authority, and its conclusion found them in possession of many of the powers held less than a century before by the executive. In the realm of finance they had imposed their authority over every phase of raising and distributing public revenue. They had acquired a large measure of independence by winning control over their compositions and proceedings and obtaining guarantees of basic English Parliamentary privileges. Finally, they had pushed their power even beyond that of the English House of Commons by gaining extensive authority in handling executive affairs, including the right to appoint executive officers and to share in formulating executive policy. These specific gains were symptoms of developments of much greater significance. To begin with, they were symbolic

---

[29] For a discussion of these measures see Bernard Knollenberg, *Origin of the American Revolution, 1759–1766* (New York, 1960), 49.

of a fundamental shift of the constitutional center of power in the colonies from the executive to the elected branch of the legislature. With the exception of the Georgia and Nova Scotia bodies, both of which had less than a decade of political experience behind them, the houses had by 1763 succeeded in attaining a new status, raising themselves from dependent lawmaking bodies to the center of political authority in their respective colonies.

But the lower houses had done more than simply acquire a new status in colonial politics. They had in a sense altered the structure of the constitution of the British Empire itself by asserting colonial authority against imperial authority and extending the constitutions of the colonies far beyond the limitations of the charters, instructions, or fixed notions of imperial authorities. The time was ripe for a re-examination and redefinition of the constitutional position of the lower houses. With the rapid economic and territorial expansion of the colonies in the years before 1763 had come a corresponding rise in the responsibilities and prestige of the lower houses and a growing awareness among colonial representatives of their own importance, which had served to strengthen their long-standing, if still imperfectly defined, impression that colonial lower houses were the American counterparts of the British House of Commons. Under the proper stimuli, they would carry this impression to its logical conclusion: that the lower houses enjoyed an equal status under the Crown with Parliament. Here, then, well beyond the embryonic stage, was the theory of colonial equality with the mother country, one of the basic constitutional principles of the American Revolution, waiting to be nourished by the series of crises that beset imperial-colonial relations between 1763 and 1776.

The psychological implications of this new political order were profound. By the 1750's the phenomenal success of the lower houses had generated a soaring self-confidence, a willingness to take on all comers. Called upon to operate on a larger stage during the Seven Years' War, they emerged from that conflict with an increased awareness of their own importance and a growing consciousness of the implications of their activities. Symptomatic of these developments was the spate of bitter controversies that characterized colonial politics during and immediately after the war. The Gadsden election controversy in South Carolina, the dispute over judicial tenure in New York, and the contests over the pistole fee and the two-penny act in Virginia gave abundant evidence of both the lower houses' stubborn determination to preserve their authority and the failure of Crown officials in London and the colonies to gauge accurately their temper or to accept the fact that they had made important changes in the constitutions of the colonies.

With the shift of power to the lower houses also came the development in each colony of an extraordinarily able group of politicians. The lower houses provided excellent training for the leaders of the rapidly maturing colonial societies, and the recurring controversies prepared them for the problems they would be called upon to meet in the dramatic conflicts after 1763. In the decades before Independence there appeared in the colonial statehouses John and Samuel Adams and James Otis in Massachusetts Bay; William Livingston in New York; Benjamin Franklin and John Dickinson in Pennsylvania; Daniel Dulany the younger in Maryland; Richard Bland, Richard Henry Lee, Thomas Jefferson, and Patrick Henry in Virginia; and Christopher Gadsden and John Rutledge in South Carolina. Along with dozens of others, these men guided their colonies through the debate with Britain, assumed direction of the new state governments after 1776, and played conspicuous roles on the national stage as members of the Continental Congress, the Confederation, and, after 1787, the new federal government. By the 1760's, then, almost every colony had an imposing group of native politicians thoroughly schooled in the political arts and primed to meet any challenge to the power and prestige of the lower houses.

Britain's "new colonial policy" after 1763 provided just such a challenge. It precipitated a constitutional crisis in the empire, creating new tensions and setting in motion forces different from those that had shaped earlier developments. The new policy was based upon concepts both unfamiliar and unwelcome to the colonists such as centralization, uniformity, and orderly development. Yet it was a logical culmination of earlier trends and, for the most part, an effort to realize old aspirations. From Edward Randolph in the last decades of the seventeenth century to the Earl of Halifax in the 1750's colonial officials had envisioned a highly centralized empire with a uniform political system in each of the colonies and with the imperial government closely supervising the subordinate governments.[30] But, because they had never made any sustained or systematic attempt to achieve these goals, there had developed during the first half of the eighteenth century a working arrangement permitting the lower houses considerable latitude in shaping colonial constitutions without requiring crown and proprietary officials to give up any of their ideals. That there had been a growing divergence between imperial theory and colonial practice mattered little so long as each refrained from challenging the other. But the new policy threatened to upset this arrangement by implementing the old ideals long after the conditions that produced them had ceased to exist. Aimed at bringing the colonies more closely under imperial control, this policy inevitably sought to curtail the influ-

---

[30] On this point see Charles M. Andrews, *The Colonial Period of American History* (4 vols., New Haven, 1934–1938), IV, 368–425; Michael Garibaldi Hall, *Edward Randolph and the American Colonies, 1676–1703* (Chapel Hill, N.C., 1960); Arthur H. Basye, *Lords Commissioners of Trade and Plantations, 1748–1782* (New Haven, 1925); and Dora Mae Clark, *The Rise of the British Treasury: Colonial Administration in the Eighteenth Century* (New Haven, 1960).

ence of the lower houses, directly challenging many of the powers they had acquired over the previous century. To American legislators accustomed to the lenient policies of Walpole and the Pelhams and impressed with the rising power of their own lower houses, the new program seemed a radical departure from precedent, a frontal assault upon the several constitutions they had been forging over the previous century. To protect gains they had already made and to make good their pretensions to greater political significance, the lower houses thereafter no longer had merely to deal with weak governors or casual imperial administrators; they now faced an aggressive group of officials bent upon using every means at their disposal, including the legislative authority of Parliament, to gain their ends.

Beginning in 1763 one imperial action after another seemed to threaten the position of the lower houses. Between 1764 and 1766 Parliament's attempt to tax the colonists for revenue directly challenged the colonial legislatures' exclusive power to tax, the cornerstone of their authority in America. A variety of other measures, some aimed at particular colonial legislatures and others at general legislative powers and practices, posed serious threats to powers that the lower houses had either long enjoyed or were trying to attain. To meet these challenges, the lower houses had to spell out the implications of the changes they had been making, consciously or not, in the structures of their respective governments. That is, for the first time they had to make clear in their own minds and then to verbalize what they conceived their respective constitutions in fact were or should be. In the process, the spokesmen of the lower houses laid bare the wide gulf between imperial theory and colonial practice. During the Stamp Act crisis in 1764–1766 the lower houses claimed the same authority over taxation in the colonies as Parliament had over that matter in England, and a few of them even asserted an equal right in matters of internal policy.[31] Although justified by the realities of the colonial situation, such a definition of the lower houses' constitutional position within the empire was at marked variance with imperial ideals and only served to increase the determination of the home government to take a stricter tone. This determination was manifested after the repeal of the Stamp Act by Parliament's claim in the Declaratory Act of 1766 to "full power and authority" over the colonies "in all cases whatsoever."[32]

---

[31] See the sweeping claim of the Virginia House of Burgesses to the "Inestimable Right of being governed by such Laws respecting their-internal Polity and Taxation as are devised from their own Consent" in objecting to Grenville's proposed stamp duties. Henry R. McIlwaine and John P. Kennedy (eds.), *Journals of the House of Burgesses in Virginia* (13 vols., Richmond, 1905–1913), *1761–1765*, 302–304 (December 18, 1764). The protests of all the lower houses against the Stamp Act are conveniently collected in Edmund S. Morgan, ed., *Prologue to Revolution: Sources and Documents on the Stamp Act Crisis, 1764–1766* (Chapel Hill, N.C., 1959), 8–17, 46–69.

[32] Danby Pickering, ed., *The Statutes at Large from Magna Carta to the End of the Eleventh Parliament of Great Britain, Anno 1761, Continued to 1806* (46 vols., Cambridge, Eng., 1762–1807), XXVII, 19–20.

The pattern over the next decade was on the part of the home government one of increasing resolution to deal firmly with the colonies and on the part of American lawmakers a heightened consciousness of the implications of the constitutional issue and a continuously rising level of expectation. In addition to their insistence upon the right of Parliament to raise revenue in the colonies, imperial officials also applied, in a way that was increasingly irksome to American legislators, traditional instruments of royal control like restrictive instructions, legislative review, the governors' power to dissolve the lower houses and the suspending clause requiring prior approval of the Crown before laws of an "extraordinary nature" could go into effect. Finally Parliament threatened the very existence of the lower houses by a measure suspending the New York Assembly for refusing to comply with the Quartering Act in 1767 and by another altering the substance of the Massachusetts constitution in the Massachusetts Government Act in 1774. In the process of articulating and defending their constitutional position, the lower houses acquired aspirations well beyond any they had had in the years before 1763. American representatives became convinced in the decade after 1766 not only that they knew best what to do for their constituents and the colonies and that anything interfering with their freedom to adopt whatever course seemed necessary was an intolerable and unconstitutional restraint but also that the only security for their political fortunes was in the abandonment of their attempts to restrict and define Parliamentary authority in America and instead to deny Parliament's jurisdiction over them entirely by asserting their equality with Parliament under the Crown. Suggested by Richard Bland as early as 1766, such a position was openly advocated by James Wilson and Thomas Jefferson in 1774 and was officially adopted by the First Continental Congress when it claimed for Americans in its declarations and resolves "a free and exclusive power of legislation in their several provincial legislatures, where their right of representation can alone be preserved, in all cases of taxation and internal polity." [33]

Parliament could not accept this claim without giving up the principles it had asserted in the Declaratory Act and, in effect, abandoning the traditional British theory of empire and accepting the colonial constitutional position instead. The First Continental Congress professed that a return to the *status quo* of 1763 would satisfy the colonies, but Parliament in 1774–1776 was unwilling even to go that far, much less to promise them exemption from Parliamentary taxation. Besides, American legislators now aspired to much more. James Chalmers, Maryland planter and later loyalist who was out of sympathy with the proceedings of American patriots between 1774 and 1776, correctly charged that American leaders had "been constantly enlarging their views, and stretching them beyond

---

[33] Worthington C. Ford and others, eds., *Journals of the Continental Congress* (34 vols., Washington, 1904–1937), I, 68–69 (October 14, 1774).

their first bounds, till at length they have wholly changed their ground." [34] Edward Rutledge, young delegate from South Carolina to the First Continental Congress, was one who recognized that the colonies would not "be satisfied with a restoration of such rights only, as have been violated since the year '63, when we have as many others, as clear and indisputable, that will even then be infringed." [35] The simple fact was that American political leaders, no matter what their professions, would not have been content to return to the old inarticulate and ambiguous pattern of accommodation between imperial theory and colonial practice that had existed through most of the period between 1689 and 1763. They now sought to become masters of their own political fortunes. Rigid guarantees of colonial rights and precise definitions of the constitutional relationship between the mother country and the colonies and between Parliament and the lower houses on American terms—that is, imperial recognition of the autonomy of the lower houses in local affairs and of the equality of the colonies with the mother country—would have been required to satisfy them.

No analysis of the charges in the Declaration of Independence can fail to suggest that the preservation and consolidation of the rights and powers of the lower houses were central in the struggle with Britain from 1763 to 1776, just as they had been the most important issue in the political relationship between Britain and the colonies over the previous century and a half. Between 1689 and 1763 the lower houses' contests with royal governors and imperial officials had brought them political maturity, a considerable measure of control over local affairs, capable leaders, and a rationale to support their pretensions to political power within the colonies and in the Empire. The British challenge after 1763 threatened to render their accomplishments meaningless and drove them to demand equal rights with Parliament and autonomy in local affairs and eventually to declare their independence. At issue was the whole political structure forged by the lower houses over the previous century. In this context the American Revolution becomes in form, if not in essence, a war for political survival, a conflict involving not only individual rights as traditionally emphasized by historians of the event but assembly rights as well.

---

[34] Candidus [James Chalmers], *Plain Truth: Addressed to the Inhabitants of America* (London, 1776), 46.
[35] Rutledge to Ralph Izard, Jr., October 29, 1774, in A. I. Deas, ed., *Correspondence of Mr. Ralph Izard of South Carolina* (New York, 1844), 22–23.

IV The Relevance of Mr. Jefferson: To the Kennedy-Johnson Era; To the Nixon Era

Introduction Since his death, which occurred with strikingly dramatic symbolism on July 4, 1826, Thomas Jefferson, has held a peculiar fascination as a person, philosopher, and statesman for each succeeding generation of Americans. John Adams, who, almost unbelievably, also died on July 4, 1826, declared at the very end, "Thomas Jefferson still survives." And Jefferson has survived as an image for Americans. Merrill Peterson, in *The Jefferson Image in the American Mind* (1960), has set forth for us what Jefferson has meant to the generations of Americans since his time: whether as a symbol and image to follow or to turn away from, to inspire or to corrupt.

In the two essays reprinted here emphasis is on the relevance of the past to the present, to the discovery of a usable past in its best sense, but not in the sense so often used today. The first essay appeared in the summer of 1961 and must have been written a few months after the inauguration of John F. Kennedy as President of the United States; [1] the second essay is a reprint of a presidential address before the Southern Historical Association two days after the election of Richard M. Nixon as President of the United States.[2]

Both essays are by Dumas Malone, author of a multivolumed life of Thomas Jefferson and Thomas Jefferson Foundation Biographer in Residence at the University of Virginia. The first essay seeks relevance for the 1960's and the second relevance for the 1970's.

Perhaps characteristically the first essay deals primarily with the ideals of Jefferson, his timeliness, though recognizing throughout that much in Jefferson is irrelevant because of the passage of almost a century and three quarters from the day of his inauguration on March 4, 1801. When, late in life, Jefferson made known those achievements by which he wished to be remembered and judged, he listed no public office though he had been a burgess in the Virginia assembly, governor of Virginia, ambassador to France, Secretary of State, Vice President, and President of the United States for two terms. Rather he asked to be remembered and judged as author of the Declaration of Independence, achiever of the Virginia Statute on Religious Freedom, and founder of the University of Virginia. The first enshrines in classic language the idea of the equality of all men as human beings; the second, some of the language of which is inscribed on the Jefferson Memorial in Washington, declares hostility against every sort of tyranny over the minds of men; and the third embodies an undying faith in intelligence and knowledge as the guardians of men's destinies. As Dumas Malone phrases it, "He left us no road map, but more than

---

1 "The Relevance of Mr. Jefferson," *Virginia Quarterly Review,* XXXVII (Summer, 1961), 332–349.
2 "Presidential Leadership and National Unity. The Jefferson Example," *Journal of Southern History,* XXXV (February–November, 1969), 3–17.

any public man in our history he pointed to the star by which our course should be guided."

The second essay deals with Jefferson as a functioning president, at a time when many of the customs and precedents growing out of the Constitution and the growth of political parties had scarcely taken any form at all. It was in the infancy of the nation, and Jefferson had few guidelines to follow in the critical areas of relations with Congress and with foreign governments, the directions in which he would reach out to his constituents to gain their approval and public support—his constituents being the people of the United States—and how to maintain national security and establish a united nation after the bitter and vituperative politics of the late 1790's. These are the problems that have faced every subsequent president. Jefferson, in 1801, stood as a new president and head of a party that had never formed an administration; Nixon, in 1968, was a new president and the head of a party that had not formed an administration for almost a decade, and Jefferson like Nixon had served as Vice President. Yet in those very areas where Jefferson toiled and triumphed, Nixon very largely failed. Jefferson retired with honor to Monticello; Nixon, a resigned president, retired to San Clemente. Professor Malone and the American people in 1969 could hardly have foreseen or imagined these massive and tragic dissimilarities.

The Relevance of Mr. Jefferson
—*Dumas Malone*

I

In almost the last year of his long life, replying to a query about the Declaration of Independence, Thomas Jefferson wrote a letter which is worth recalling. Certain people, especially people who did not care for his politics, had suggested that in fact that famous document was not original. When he was eighty-two years old he made a statement about its objects—that is, his own objects in writing it—which I quote in part:

> Not to find out new principles, or new arguments, never before thought of, not merely to say things which had never been said before; but to place before mankind the common sense of the subject. . . .

The present utterance can hardly be compared to the immortal Declaration, and I do not presume to address it to all mankind, but, without pretense of originality, I hope to set forth the common sense of the matter in dealing with Mr. Jefferson himself. While many true and wonderful things have been said about this inexhaustible man since his death, a considerable number of things have been said that should really be described as nonsense. Perhaps it would be fairer to say of many of these that they are partial truths which have been paraded as whole truths, deriving from the law and gospel. At all events, confusion is confounded when an historic personage is quoted on opposite sides in a contemporary controversy, as Mr. Jefferson repeatedly has been. Instances will quickly come to mind in connection with the presidential campaign of 1960, when it was solemnly announced that he would have voted for both candidates; or in connection with the New Deal, which he is said both to have opposed and favored.

It is not my purpose to declare which side he was on, since I really have no way of knowing. Also, I recognize the likelihood that I should arrive at the pleasant conclusion that he always agreed with me. The proneness of the human mind to rationalize can hardly be exaggerated. In view, however, of the well-authenticated fact that contradictory statements have been made about him ever since his death I am disposed to ask certain questions. What meaning does he really have for *us* in our present situation? Are his words and actions relevant to *our* circumstances, or irrelevant? If he is relevant in certain respects and irrelevant in

From *Virginia Quarterly Review*, XXXVII (Summer 1961), 332–349. Reprinted by permission.

others, what is the ground of distinction? How is anyone to know? On this confused situation I should like to turn what the late William S. Gilbert called "the hose of common sense." Surely the common sense of the matter is to try to distinguish between these words and actions which related solely or primarily to his own time, and those which have the quality of timelessness. That is, we need to separate what is or may be properly regarded as dateless from what is necessarily dated.

In this connection, I do not need to focus attention on him as a human being. Human nature seems to have changed little in the course of re-corded history, and human personality defies barriers of space and time. In spirit we can live intimately with persons from the past whenever their words and deeds are sufficiently recorded for us to know them. We soon forget that their clothes were unlike ours and that they wore their hair quite differently. We have to allow for changes in manners and morals, and even when they employ our own language we may detect a certain quaintness in their speech. But the common denominator of human nature and individual experience is so large that great personalities can speak to us across the generations, even across the centuries, in language that is understandable since it is the language of life itself.

By precept and example the father of the University of Virginia can still teach anyone who will take the trouble to listen to him and observe him. Many things can we learn from him about the fine art of living. Not the least of these is that once an apostle of equality lived a notably elevated life, an extraordinarily rich, perennially interesting, endlessly generous, and ceaselessly useful life, in a society which he himself had made more democratic. He exemplified excellence, not the dull level of mediocrity; individuality, not unthinking conformity. He dared to build his house upon a mountain and to be himself, surveying the universe in personal inde-pendence. As a human being he has real meaning for our time: in his own person he reminds us what man can do with freedom.

Though human nature and human personality seem to be the most constant factors in history except the earth and the waters round it, along with the seasons and the tides, they manifest themselves in widely varying circumstances, of course, and no human being of either the past or the present can be fully understood apart from his particular environment. We should be foolish to assume that Mr. Jefferson would make precisely the same domestic arrangements at Monticello if he were living there now as he made a hundred and fifty years ago; or that, if one of his grandchildren became ill today, he would be as dubious as he was then about the value of medical services; presumably he would not now suggest that doctors may do more harm than good. We can appreciate the realism which enabled him to appraise them so well in his day, but we should be unwise to seek his *specific* advice in the conduct of our personal affairs, medical or otherwise.

Anything that may be said about considering a human being, in his personal life, on the background of his own environment has to be heavily underlined when we speak of him as a public man. We *have* to view statesmen, past and present, in their own settings of time, place, and circumstance. To do otherwise would be to render them a grave injustice. For forty years, with only a few interruptions, Mr. Jefferson was a public official—burgess, delegate, governor, minister to a foreign country, secretary of state, vice president, and president. During all these years he was dealing with current public affairs and day-to-day problems. More than most statesmen, he tried to take the long view and to guide his steps by enduring principles, and if he had not done so better than most men his fame would have been less enduring. Nonetheless, he could not escape the necessity, and no statesman ever can, of adjusting policies to the existing situation. Public affairs are not conducted in a vacuum. It is of the utmost importance, therefore, to seek a fair understanding of the public situation he had to face.

Since he devoted a very large part of his time and labors to foreign relations, and world affairs are of such vital concern to us today, we can profitably take a quick look at the general world situation in his era. Even in his slow-moving age that situation changed, to be sure, but certain of its features were relatively constant during most of his public life. Some of these features were so similar to what we ourselves have faced that his age seems positively familiar. Most of his career was set on a background of general war. The conflict which broke out in Europe when he was secretary of state and lasted, with only slight interruption, considerably beyond his presidency, if not world war in our sense, came nearer being that than any that our planet was to know until the twentieth century. In his day this planet was a less dangerous place than it has been in our era of world war, total war, cold war, and threat of nuclear destruction. Furthermore, because of the slowness of movement and communication, peril was less imminent. There was not the same sense of desperate urgency, and statesmen could be less hurried. That is one thing the statesmen of this day can deeply envy them. Nonetheless, the dangers faced in the two eras were strikingly similar, even if in our time they have been greatly intensified.

His age was one of revolution which touched virtually all parts of the globe that our country was concerned with. Indeed, it was commonly regarded as *the* age of revolution until our generation pre-empted the title. In our day the revolutionary spirit has spread to continents which were still slumbering in his time. It has taken on social and economic forms which were little dreamed of by our forefathers when they proclaimed revolution in the name of political independence, and which were not approached even in revolutionary France. But his time was also one of great political and considerable social convulsion. Thus one can say that, in its international aspects, no other period in American history can so fitly be compared to ours as the age of Washington and Jefferson. I have been particularly struck with what may be called the psychological parallels. Human nature being much the same, personal and social reactions to war and revolution show a great deal of similarity. This is frequently reflected in language: many of the things that were said in manifestos and resolutions, in newspapers and in private letters, sound like utterances of our time if you change the names and places.

There were numerous differences, however, and we can readily recognize the paramount importance of one of them. The position from which Mr. Jefferson and others charged with the national interest and security viewed a warring and revolutionary world was virtually the reverse of the one our leaders now occupy. The potential giant of the West was then only a stripling, a weakling among the Powers, while today our Republic is in all respects gigantic. They had to lead from weakness, where we can lead from strength. The policy which will always be associated with the names of Washington and Jefferson was to keep out of the raging power struggle in so far as possible, regardless of personal predilections one way or the other, regardless of ideology. Thus was born the classic American doctrine of neutrality or non-involvement, which, despite occasional aberrations, endured for generations. It arose from the necessities of national security, and its wisdom at that time cannot be doubted. Everybody knows that the policy has been completely reversed in our century, also because of the necessities of national security.

What does this signify about the bearing of the acts, the policies, the words of Mr. Jefferson on the world problems of our day? Can we really learn anything from him? In my opinion, we can learn much. As an example I will cite the year 1793, when the European war broadened so as to threaten us, when the French Revolution passed into its greatest excesses, when this young Republic entered upon its historic policy of neutrality. To consider the activities of Mr. Jefferson, the Secretary of State, in one of the most momentous years in modern history, observing his incessant labors, his extraordinary patience amid frustrations, his unflagging patriotism, and his basic wisdom, is to share a tremendous experience. Regarding the controversy into which he, a friend of France, was drawn in 1793 with the insolent envoy of the French revolutionary government, one of the greatest of his successors in the office of Secretary of State, John Quincy Adams, said that his papers on that controversy "present the most perfect model of diplomatic discussion and expostulation of modern times." This was American diplomacy at one of its highest points, revealing rare skill and a realistic appraisal of the existing situation which should command the admiration of anyone dealing with international problems in any age.

Yet the policy at which President Washington and Secretary Jefferson arrived has had to be repudiated in our century, when at length we reluctantly assumed the rôle of world leadership which destiny imposed upon us. Conceivably it might have been reversed sooner, to the advantage of mankind, but for the sad human proclivity to learn the wrong lessons from history and miss the right ones. As an exemplar of the skillful and realistic conduct of foreign affairs, which he generally was, Mr. Jefferson is very relevant. So far as specific policies go, however, time has rendered him quite irrelevant. To be sure, some people in our century have sought specific answers to the problems of contemporary foreign policy in the Neutrality Proclamation of 1793, Washington's Farewell Address of 1796, and Jefferson's First Inaugural of 1801. In a world that has been turned upside down, that sort of reliance on sharply dated pronouncements, wonderful as they were when written, hardly seems the common sense of the matter. Indeed, one is inclined to ask, as Elmer Davis used to: "How silly can you be?"

II

Now let us turn from the world situation to the home scene. When we fly on the wings of the spirit back into Mr. Jefferson's America, of course we can recognize many landmarks—the configuration of the coasts, the rivers flowing to the sea, the mountains on the western horizon. We can quickly perceive that he and his contemporaries were persons of like passions and vanities with ourselves. In his day political organization— party organization, for example—was rudimentary from our point of view, but the minds of politicians worked very much as they do right now and they used the same sort of wiles—slogans, name-calling, and various devices designed to show that they were more honest and more patriotic than their rivals. All of this is very familiar and should make us feel at home. But it is difficult for us to realize how few people there were or how scattered, and how slowly they got around. When Jefferson became President the population of New York did not greatly exceed that of present-day Charlottesville. If he could see the national metropolis today he would no doubt regard it as an incredible monstrosity. It took him ten days to come home to Albemarle from Philadelphia; and the post rider from Richmond was so erratic that he sometimes didn't get to Charlottesville with the mail for three weeks, although Mr. Jefferson insisted that the roads were generally passable to a carriage and always, he believed, to a man on horseback. Getting out of one's locality and keeping in touch with the outside world was an exceedingly difficult thing, and it is no wonder that so much government devolved upon the county court in Virginia, or that the town meeting was so important in New England. To a degree which is hard for us to conceive, emphasis *had* to be laid on the locality and the self-reliance of individuals. By our standards that society was amazingly simple, delightfully simple, though by the same standards life was extraordinarily inconvenient and must often have been extremely dull.

The fact is that the series of non-political revolutions which have so profoundly affected the physical conditions of existence and have transformed our economy and society occurred *after* Mr. Jefferson's public career was over. The industrial revolution had begun in Europe by his time, but it did not really get started in this country until the very end of his presidency, and even then our industries were only infants. The successive revolutions in transportation and communication all came later. Fulton's steamboat, the *Clermont*, plied the Hudson in his second term, but it has been aptly said that Jefferson, like Nebuchadnezzar, never saw anything faster than a horse.

It would be rather absurd for me to attempt to describe the various revolutions in science and technology which have followed one upon another with ever-increasing speed. I have had difficulty in adjusting my mind to the ones that have occurred in my own lifetime, finding some of them utterly bewildering. Indeed, I escape from them nearly every day into the age of Mr. Jefferson. The air seems clearer there, and the unhurried pace leaves more time for thought. In the uncrowded country there were no huge factories—scarcely any at all, in fact; there were no immense aggregations of capital and formidable organizations of labor. There were sailing vessels in the harbors and merchants in the ports and inland centers, but nearly all the workers in this farflung country were tillers of the soil. This was no Golden Age of health, comfort, and convenience, but perhaps it may be regarded as a sort of heyday of individualism. Human beings may have been dwarfed by the vastness of the land, though relatively few had traveled over much of it; they were *not* dwarfed by any of the works of man.

Almost exactly one hundred and sixty years ago the raw-boned country gentleman who had been chosen head of this predominantly agricultural republic delivered his first inaugural address in the Senate chamber, the only part of the capitol that was yet finished in the straggling wilderness village that went by the name of Washington. It is said that few in the audience could hear him, he spoke so low; but his speech could be read afterwards in the newspapers, and it proved to be one of the few to which historians recur. Does it have any present bearing on *our* problems?

It was admirably suited to its particular circumstances. One of the important conflicts in the previous campaign had been over the right to oppose, to criticize the existing government—a thing the group in power had sought to prevent by means of the notorious Sedition Act. Historians often say that, whatever else Jefferson's election signified, it vindicated the legitimacy of political opposition. But terrible things had been predicted if this man should be elected; Bibles might be confiscated. Accordingly, he felt impelled to speak words of reassurance, and some of these are still fresh after more than a century and a half. He announced one principle which he called sacred and which may be regarded as timeless, I think, in any self-governing society: "that though the will of the majority is in all cases to prevail, that will, to be rightful, must be reasonable; that the minority possess their equal rights, which equal laws must protect, and to violate which would be oppression." It is a great pity that Abraham Lincoln did not quote those words in *his* first inaugural. They would have been eminently appropriate then, as they would have been on January 20, 1961.

There are other nuggets of abiding wisdom in Mr. Jefferson's address, and there is some deeply moving language. I am most concerned here, however, with what he said in the year 1801 about the way he meant to conduct the government. Since he never wrote anything like a systematic treatise on government but scattered his ideas throughout his profuse writings, the things he said here have been regarded by many as a handy summary of his working political philosophy. Judging from this address, he believed that the federal government should devote itself largely to the conduct of foreign affairs, which were always important in his era. With special reference to domestic matters he summed up federal functions in a passage which has been quoted for more than a century and a half:

> Still one thing more, fellow citizens—a wise and frugal government, which shall restrain men from injuring one another, which shall leave them otherwise free to regulate their own pursuits of industry and improvement, and shall not take from the mouth of labor the bread it has earned. This is the sum of good government. . . .

That is, the federal government, outside the conduct of foreign relations, was to be little more than a policeman and an umpire. It was to grant special privileges to none and secure equal and exact justice for all—an obligation requiring diligence as well as forbearance—but if we take these words at their face value its functions were to be essentially negative. From the vantage point of today, the "sum of good government" as thus described is very small.

Even at that time some intelligent people thought it dangerously small. Midway in his first term his ancient antagonist, Alexander Hamilton, lamented that the Constitution was a "frail and worthless fabric," despite all his own efforts to prop it up. He believed that under Jefferson's interpretation the government could withstand no serious strain; and he had little hope that it would further the economic development of the country in the directions he himself had pointed. Hamilton wanted to stimulate that part of the economic society now described as "business," which by modern standards was then little more than rudimentary. He was particularly interested in banks, the facilitation of trade, the creation of fluid capital; and if anyone deserves to be described as the father of American capitalism surely it is Hamilton. He wanted to use the government, and when in office he did use it, for the development of business. He thought Jefferson uninformed in these matters—indifferent, even hostile to this development. In my opinion, he did not fully understand his great rival; it seems to me that the bitter feeling of the Eastern merchants and emerging financiers of that time toward Jefferson went beyond the point of reason. He certainly knew little about banks and deplored speculation in securities; to him property pre-eminently was real property, that is, land; but he unquestionably knew a great deal about foreign commerce, and he was an economic nationalist in his own way. Nonetheless, I think I can understand why to the Hamiltonians he often seemed an old-fashioned farmer who was blind to the wave of the future. It can be argued that John Marshall did not sufficiently recognize the flexibility of his distant kinsman in the face of actual circumstances. Yet it is not hard to see why the Chief Justice sought to counter the centrifugal tendencies he perceived in the Jeffersonian philosophy by asserting through a long generation the scope of national authority.

How well adjusted the policies of President Jefferson really were to the conditions of his own time is a matter of historical judgment. In his own person he was certainly not negative or lethargic; this incessantly active and extraordinarily dynamic man cannot be rightly regarded as the historical prototype of Calvin Coolidge. Actually, his administration was more economical than Coolidge's, but if anybody should be disposed to think that his main service was that of counting pennies in the Executive Mansion, or that his rôle was primarily that of a caretaker, that person should take a look at the map. There was a large element of luck in the Louisiana Purchase, as well as some theoretical inconsistency on Jefferson's part—or at least this has been alleged; but no one can properly deny to him the credit for doubling the area of his country. The domestic consequences of his actions were to prove momentous. He left to his successor a different country from the one he had begun to govern at the age of fifty-eight; and just as soon as new states began to emerge from this huge domain the Union began to be a different sort of Union. The balance of power within it was bound to shift, and in the long run it shifted decisively against his own Virginia. There was no little irony in the course of later events, but this majestic achievement, this creation of what he happily termed an "empire for liberty," makes it impossible to think of him as the caretaker of an old order, or as one whose main function was to put brakes to the wheels of progress.

One of his undoubted purposes, as expressed in his own words, was to "lead things into the channel of harmony between the governors and governed," and in this he was conspicuously successful. He gave his countrymen what most of them wanted, and I think he gave his country what it then needed most—which was mainly a chance to grow without either aid or interference. The immediate task and the dominant desire was to possess the land. He handed out no subsidies to farmers or anybody else, but to his land-hungry generation he pointed the door of unparalled opportunity, seeking to maintain approximate equality of opportunity but otherwise largely leaving human nature to take its course. He hoped that the vast preponderance of his countrymen would be self-supporting farmers, whom he regarded as the best citizens and the freest and happiest men on earth. His countrymen liked the idea; indeed, they embroidered it into a legend which long survived the circumstances which gave it birth. It became a myth which invested agricultural problems of later generations with nostalgia.

What present reality is there in his pronouncement of one hundred and sixty years ago about limiting the functions of government? Does this mean today that the federal government ought to be small even though everything else has become gigantic—that the best way to solve our national political and economic problems is to set down a pigmy among the giants? And all this in a time of world crisis to which we can see no end? It would hardly be fair to Mr. Jefferson to claim that he would favor that degree of impotence. This is not to say that he would like all of our huge organizations, or any of them. The processes of consolidation in all departments of life have been greatly accelerated in our time by the series of wars and crises we have gone through. Mr. Jefferson would certainly not rejoice that we have had to adjust all our institutions to the needs of these, and he might not like the way we have done it. Very likely he would approve of Lord Acton's well-known dictum: "Power tends to corrupt; absolute power corrupts absolutely." His entire career reflects his distrust of power as well as his undying concern for freedom, and it is just as true now as it ever was that the price of liberty is eternal vigilance. But when speaking of the threat of tyranny, he kept on talking about kings, who are not much of a menace now. Tyranny changes its face from age to age, and every era has to decide for itself where the greatest and most imminent danger to the freedom of the individual really lies. The contradiction which we face arises from the dreadful circumstance that the very survival of liberty at home and abroad depends on the employment of power such as Mr. Jefferson never dreamed of and which inevitably carries within itself a threat to personal freedom. We can't expect him to resolve this contradiction. He would be bewildered by this strange new world, this wonderful and terrible new world. In his day he was an alert sentinel and generally, though not always, a sagacious guide. But he is well beyond the age of retirement and we can't expect him to chart our course for us.

He himself summed things up sufficiently in one of the most important of his sayings: "The earth belongs always to the living generation." Whatever opinions he may have held at one time or another about specific problems, he held tenaciously to the conviction that the present need not and should not be guided by the dead hand of the past. We can learn greatly from past experience, but we must not ask too much of history. It often provides suggestive analogies, but rarely if ever can we find in it an answer to a specific question, a precise solution for a contemporary problem. It offers us no detailed road map to guide the traffic of today. The common sense of the matter is that the particular policies or methods Mr. Jefferson announced one hundred and sixty years ago are now essentially irrelevant, if not wholly so. The same can be said, of course, of the historic policies of George Washington and Abraham Lincoln. And the saying goes for Queen Elizabeth I, Julius Caesar, Alexander the Great, and Pericles, though the careers of all of them are well worth studying.

III

The undiscriminating use of the past has had unfortunate consequences on Mr. Jefferson's reputation. This incessant builder, who was ceaselessly striving to advance knowledge and improve society, has often been cast in the rôle of perpetual obstructionist. One of the signers of the Declaration of Independence was known as "the great objector"; that was not Mr. Jefferson, though no one more than he insisted on the right of any man to object to anything on the merits of the case. There is an even greater danger than that of judging him unfairly: in stressing what is actually irrelevant, people tend to overlook or disregard acts and words of his which do have the ring of timelessness and are applicable to our age or any other. He left us no road map, but, more than any public man in our history, he pointed us to the star by which our course should be guided. It would be a pity if, while following some ancient and long-abandoned trail, we should fail to see what is shining overhead.

He has left us in no doubt whatever about the way to separate the temporary from the enduring elements in his heritage to posterity. He explicitly stated that he wanted no public offices listed on his tombstone—not even the Presidency of the United States. He knew that his official actions were necessarily dated, that policies could not be expected to last forever. He wanted to be remembered for words and deeds which had the quality of timelessness about them, and there can be no possible doubt that he made a wise selection.

The Declaration of Independence, which he listed first, has a date, to be sure—our most famous date since it marks the birthday of our Republic; and this was identified with him all the more irrevocably when he died fifty years later on July 4, as though by Divine Providence. Part of the document itself is unmistakably dated: historians do not accept all those charges against King George III as eternal truth. But the part of the Declaration we know best and prize most was undoubtedly regarded by its author as timeless and universal. How can you date truths which you regard as eternal and self-evident? By virtue of their birth into the world as human beings, all men are equal—not in status certainly, and surely not in ability, but in rights. The implications of the assertion that everybody is a human being and should be treated as one were not fully perceived by all who approved the historic pronouncement of our national faith, but these words have gone ringing down the generations. They were still vibrant words when we answered the mad ravings of Adolf Hitler and countered the arrogant cruelty of the German Nazis. (At the time many historians must have reflected, as I surely did, that history offers no more striking antithesis than that between Adolf Hitler and Thomas Jefferson.) No ways and means are specified in the great Declaration; these must be determined by every living generation for itself in the light of its own circumstances. But those phrases, which we have heard a hundred times, have in them the perennial freshness of the spring; today as in 1776 they breathe undying faith in human beings. Many people, many high-minded people, find it hard to extend that faith to groups they have long regarded as "lesser breeds without the law"; and it is difficult indeed to uphold the freedom and dignity of all men when so many are unworthy and so many abuse their freedom. But we need not look to our historic Declaration for soothing words, for words that condone complacency or excuse any form of arrogance. We can find there no specific solution for any of our immediate problems, but we can find an eternal summons to proceed upon unfinished tasks.

To this timeless document we can also turn for a sense of values—for an everlasting criterion by which to judge all human institutions. So far as my knowledge and judgment go, history provides none better. Man was not made for government, but government was made for man; and the final criterion of its actions or its inaction is the degree to which it supports the freedom, upholds the dignity, and promotes the happiness of individual human beings. This is our answer to Communism and to any form of totalitarianism, whether of the right or left. Man was not made for organization—business, labor, professional, or any other; these were made for man, and the only proper test of them is what they do for him. We should think of this when we consider these giants of government, of business, of labor which our society has nurtured, and which so often seem to dwarf human beings. Surely the purpose of government should never be to augment power for its own sake, of business to produce profits solely for themselves, of labor to increase wages merely for the sake of wages. What is the product worth in terms of human happiness? When change is not productive of human happiness, surely it is not progress. This is no mere matter of material things, though no one can question their importance. "Man shall not live by bread alone," was said by a greater teacher than Mr. Jefferson. The challenge of our times and of all times is to humanize institutions— *all* institutions.

The Virginia act establishing religious freedom was adopted by the General Assembly on a particular date, but the date is unimportant. Actually, Jefferson drew his bill some years before it was passed, and it is just as fresh in the twentieth century as it was on the day he drew it. Here, even more clearly than in the Declaration, perhaps, can one perceive the essence of his philosophy. Above all things, he was a champion of the freedom of the human spirit, and by this he meant even more than the right to worship God in any way one likes—supremely important as that is. He meant the entire freedom of the mind, the sacred right of any man to his own opinions, whether these be popular or not, whether they be moderate or radical or conservative. There was no mistake in choosing the key quotation for the Jefferson Memorial and in putting it as a motto on a postage stamp. He was eternally hostile to all tyrannies but most of all to tyranny over the human mind. I sometimes wonder if some of the people who take his name on their lips really like this, the most typical of all Jefferson quotations. I doubt if the Communists even begin to comprehend it, but surely it is in his insistence on the freedom of men to think that he becomes most dangerous to the monolithic state and the philosophy of complete conformity.

The University of Virginia, with which he ended his select list of memorable achievements, was chartered on a particular date, and we are not yet warranted in describing it as immortal. But in the Western world universities have been exceedingly long-lived; they flow on like so many streams, and this one may be expected to flow as long as our civilization shall endure. Besides being virtually timeless, any university, to be worthy of its name, must in spirit be universal. In his own lovely county, amid its eternal hills, this lifelong student institutionalized his undying faith in intelligence and knowledge. Nothing that he ever did was more characteristic of this inveterate builder—of this ardent farmer who prized the harvest of the mind beyond all others. If I understand him aright, he would not expect his academic heirs to pay much heed to specific things he once said about courses and regulations, but he would want them to apply to their life and learning the final tests of value. Not only does learning languish in the air of conformity and complacency; not only does it fail if it does not liberate the spirit; learning becomes a sterile thing when it loses its humanity.

Nothing is immutable but "the inherent and inalienable rights of man," he said. "The earth belongs always to the living generation." Times change, needs change, policies and methods change with them. But human beings remain, always. And the star of liberty still shines over Monticello. That star and the people it shines on are what he would most want us to see.

Presidential Leadership and National Unity: The Jeffersonian Example

—*Dumas Malone*

It is my purpose to consider here the exercise of the presidential office by Thomas Jefferson with special reference to certain aspects of this which seem to have relevance today. To be sure, the similarity between his situation and that of a President in our time may appear less noteworthy than the contrast. At his first inauguration he walked from his lodgings to the one section of the Capitol that was completed. At his second he rode down Pennsylvania Avenue, accompanied only by his secretary and a groom. He spoke of the "splendid misery" of the presidential office, but it was not marked by much splendor in his day. As the country is more powerful now, so is the President; and his problems have become so enormous and so complex as to beggar description. No early President assumed such an awesome task. But Jefferson had important functions and problems in common with all his successors. He had to deal with Congress and with foreign governments; while retaining the support of his own partisans he had to establish rapport with his constituents, the people of the United States; and at all times he had to maintain the security and essential unity of the country. I think it worth inquiring how this particular President did, or tried to do, some of these things.[1]

From the *Journal of Southern History,* XXXV (1969), 3–17. Copyright 1969 by the Southern Historical Association. Reprinted by permission of the Managing Editor.

[1] I do not refer to relations between the executive and the judiciary because of lack of time and also because the struggle in our own day has not been between the President and the Supreme Court but between Congress and that body.

In his day and for a century thereafter the President was inaugurated on March 4. Unless he should call Congress in special session it would not meet until fall. Jefferson had nine months before first encountering that loquacious body. He designated the period between congressional sessions as a "blessed interim" and spoke with dread of his annual "winter campaign." Whenever the Great Council of the Nation, as he often called Congress, was in town it presented a problem—generally his major problem. So it was at the beginning of our government, so it is now, and so in all probability it will ever be.

Any and every President in dealing with the legislative branch is faced with difficulties imposed by the constitutional separation of powers. (As is well known, the basic reason for the adoption of this system was fear of tyranny rather than desire for effectiveness. It was designed to prevent bad things from happening, not to facilitate positive government, the need for which was little anticipated.) Hardly anybody questioned the desirability of the separation of powers at the time of Jefferson's accession. Members of his own party had emphasized it during their years in opposition. That party came into being in reaction against the policies of the leader most conspicuously identified with the consolidation of governmental power, Alexander Hamilton, who was also the only leader of the first rank in this period who clearly favored positive government. Jefferson, whose early public career had centered on resistance to tyranny, could not have been expected to doubt the wisdom of the division of powers; and the circumstances of the delivery of his first presidential message could have been interpreted as a clear sign that he would encroach in no way on the independence of Congress. Indeed, Hamiltonians feared that the era of legislative dominance of the federal structure had returned.

Instead of delivering his message in person, the third President sent it by his secretary, Captain Meriwether Lewis. There were practical reasons for this procedure. He wrote much better than he spoke, and he said he was consulting the convenience of the legislators, as no doubt he was, along with his own. He was well aware, however, that his followers would welcome this abandonment of a ceremony that derived from colonial practices and smacked of royalty. He was making an antimonarchical gesture and disarming potential critics of presidential authority within his own party in advance.

He himself was convinced that concentration of authority was extremely dangerous. He would have thoroughly approved of the dictum of Lord Acton regarding the tendency of power to corrupt. But his experience as war governor of his state, when he had little power, had been traumatic; and he by no means shared the extreme fear of the executive that was written into the early state constitutions. In fact he was as opposed to legislative omnipotence as John Adams and sought to attain balance in government as in personal life. He started with high hopes that relations between the co-ordinate executive and legislative branches would be harmonious, and in his relations with Congress throughout his administration he was characteristically punctilious; but as Chief Executive he bore more responsibility than anybody else for making this experiment in self-government succeed, for enabling this new nation to endure. And, like all other Presidents, he was faced with the insistent practical problem of performing his own functions effectively.

One of his major functions was in fact legislative. The President has the power to veto acts of Congress, thus exercising a negative influence on legislation. But, while President Washington disapproved two bills, Jefferson, like John Adams, vetoed none. (Franklin D. Roosevelt vetoed 631).[2] On the positive side, the President was enjoined not only to inform Congress of the state of the Union but also to recommend legislation. The practical question was whether or not he should content himself with doing so in a formal message, and Jefferson concluded that he could not. Summing things up after five years of experience, he said that if he thus limited himself the result would be "a government of chance & not of design." This he said in a letter in which, perhaps more than anywhere else, he stressed the importance of having in the House of Representatives a man "in the confidence & views of the administration" who would see that measures recommended by the President should get a hearing.[3] That such a person should have been at the same time the recognized leader of a legislative body jealous of its prerogatives was certainly not inevitable; it might even have been regarded by constitutional purists as contradictory. After he had ceased to play this dual role John Randolph referred indignantly to "backstairs counsellors," and the President had to be constantly on guard lest he be charged with encroachment on the prerogatives of Congress. Actually, the majority in the House and Senate did not formally elect a floor leader as yet, and Jefferson did not limit his representations to a single person in either case; as a rule he and his cabinet members explained things to the chairmen of the committees to which particular recommendations would be referred. This was ad hoc procedure, and, although precedents were established, relations between the executive and the legislature were not really institutionalized.

The business of the House was controlled by the chairmen of committees, who were appointed at this time by the Speaker, Nathaniel Macon.[4] He had named his intimate friend John Randolph chairman of

---

[2] These figures are from Carlton Jackson, *Presidential Vetoes 1792–1945* (Athens, Ga., 1967), viii–ix.
[3] Jefferson to Barnabas Bidwell, July 28, 1806, in Thomas Jefferson Papers (Library of Congress, Washington, D.C.).
[4] Good discussion in Barnabas Bidwell to Jefferson, July 28, 1806, *ibid.*

the Ways and Means Committee and thus opened the door of influence to that brilliant and erratic congressman. And, as a result of maneuvering into which we need not enter here, Randolph remained as chairman of this key committee after he had ceased to enjoy the confidence and share the views of the administration. Jefferson was confronted with a congressional Establishment that he had no recognized power to control, just as any President is today. (We might observe in passing that if the constitutional separation of powers has reduced the danger of centralized tyranny throughout our history, it certainly has not removed the danger of lesser tyrannies.) Operating in this constitutional framework and doctrinal atmosphere, he conveyed information to Congress by informal as well as formal means but sought to avoid the impression of bringing pressure to bear on that self-conscious body. Under these circumstances this unusually tactful man could hardly have escaped the charge of being devious.

Despite the difficulties which are inherent in our divided government and which were accentuated by continuing fears of executive power, he was one of the most successful of Presidents in his relations with Congress. Except for James K. Polk, who had a more positive program and was not subjected to the ordeal of a second term, perhaps no other President prior to Woodrow Wilson was equally successful in getting through Congress the measures he favored. His grip weakened toward the end of his administration, and his relations with the legislators were never as harmonious as he would have liked, but he gained from them a remarkable degree of co-operation.

That is, he gained it from the congressional majority. The hardcore Federalists were not merely unco-operative; they were irreconcilable. His success was inseparable from his leadership of his own party. Neither of his predecessors in the first office was the recognized head of a party, and few of his successors were to be. He had no rival within his party after his election. Aaron Burr may have been a potential rival, but he eliminated himself by consorting with and relying on the Federalists. Jefferson was notably successful in retaining the loyalty of factions which warred against each other. The defection of John Randolph in the first congressional session of his second term was sensational, but that vitriolic orator carried only a handful of followers with him. The spirit of brotherly love certainly did not pervade the party; there were fierce factional struggles, especially in Pennsylvania and New York. But, except for John Randolph's tiny band and occasional dissenters, all hailed Jefferson as chief. Without attempting to explain this situation adequately, I must content myself with saying here that his partisans recognized that he was their most valuable political asset and saw in loyalty to him their surest bond.

Apparently he did not need to engage in arm-twisting—an operation at which, in fact, he was not adept. As a rule, a clear understanding of his wishes was enough for his supporters. On some highly controversial questions he appears to have deliberately refrained from putting his prestige on the line. The question of the Yazoo claims, on which his own mind may have been divided as the minds of his followers undoubtedly were, is a case in point. On certain other matters he was noncommittal, and he may be criticized for not risking enough. But, as he said privately before his first Congress met, there was wisdom in Solon's remark that "no more good must be attempted than the nation can bear . . ."; and his highly sensitized political antennae warned him against asking too much of a legislative majority which was even more economy-minded than he was.[5] This was not a time when many people expected the federal government to do much. With respect to unmistakable measures of the administration, his legislative record was exceedingly high.

He was no party boss, even on the national level. His political enemies saw his hand in everything, to be sure; but, while he made a special point of keeping himself informed and was always available as a confidant and encourager, he was chiefly concerned to maintain party unity and, besides trying to keep out of party squabbles, he left management to others. On several occasions he suggested to particular men that they run for Congress, but, by and large, he followed a policy of laissez faire. His trust of his followers was too uncritical at times, but it was rewarded by their extraordinary loyalty.

Disunity within his party did not become a serious problem until after it had become preponderant. At the outset, and again toward the end of his administration, a more pressing problem was that of maintaining essential national unity. His concern over this is abundantly reflected in his first inaugural, in which he said: "We are all republicans: we are all federalists." He had good reason to be troubled by the intransigence of his foes, especially the politicos of New England who had refused to concede his election. He had long been aware of separatist tendencies in the West, and throughout his administration he sought to remove the causes of discontent in that region. This problem did not arise from political differences, for the trans-Appalachian region was predominantly Jeffersonian, and in attempting to solve it he was at no disadvantage because he was the chieftain of a part that had consistently identified itself with Western interests.

The situation with respect to New England was very different. There at the beginning of his administration his followers constituted a weak minority, despised and bitterly resented by the Establishment. He himself cherished no illusion that he could come to terms with the Establishment,

---

[5] Jefferson to Dr. Walter Jones, March 31, 1801, in Andrew A. Lipscomb and Albert E. Bergh (eds.), *The Writings of Thomas Jefferson* (20 vols., Washington, 1903, 1904), X, 256.

which to his mind represented the union of church and state, but he would unquestionably have denied that he was indifferent to the interests of the region and its people as a whole. From the beginning of his Presidency he sought to gain support for his government in New England; and, stimulated and encouraged by him, his party grew greatly in that previously disaffected region until, at the time of the Embargo, it appeared that his policies were injurious to it. He had never been able to crack the Connecticut nutmeg, however, and the bitterness of the Federalist irreconcilables had shown little sign of diminution.

I am not convinced that the dilemma which this situation presented was clearly perceived by Jefferson. The recalcitrance of the hard-line Federalists was a real danger to the Union, but to have destroyed the opposition altogether would have been to create a one-party system. His implacable foes in the land of steady habits and elsewhere among "the wise, the rich, and the good" (as the New England Federalists regarded themselves) viewed him as the head of a party to which they were bitterly opposed rather than as the President of a united country who deserved a degree of loyalty by virtue of his official position. In our own century there were people in New England and elsewhere who had the same feeling about Franklin D. Roosevelt. There is a certain incompatibility between the roles of chief of state and party chieftain; and under our system this basic contradiction can never be fully resolved. George Washington, as he began to be identified with a party toward the end of his administration, became the object of partisan attack instead of the universal praise to which he was accustomed. But, while Washington detested parties and remained above the conflict between them as long as he could, Jefferson was unquestionably a party man and a rarity among Presidents in the degree of his party leadership. I do not believe that he ever lost sight of the national interest, and I am sure that he exercised a moderating influence on his own partisans; but some of the extremists among them pressed him from the left while Federalist die-hards belabored him from the right, and he did not always succeed in maintaining his equilibrium. Opinions may be expected to differ respecting his presidential performance, but in my judgment he was notably successful during at least three-fourths of it in attaining and maintaining the balance he sought. (If this interpretation is correct, no doubt both our New Left and our New Right will disapprove of him.)

Throughout Jefferson's Presidency foreign policy was a sharply divisive issue. In looking back on this period one is impressed with the absence of bipartisanship. It is true that Federalist Senator John Quincy Adams, who had favored the Louisiana Purchase, even supported the Embargo, but he was disowned by his own party as a consequence. The opposition of Federalist senators to the foreign policy of "that man" in the President's

House was virtually automatic, and foreign diplomats did not hesitate to exploit this division to the advantage of their own countries.

Also, there was some conflict regarding the respective functions and responsibilities of the executive and legislative branches in foreign affairs. Jefferson never doubted that, under the Constitution, the conduct of external affairs was an executive function; and he had had too much experience in the Continental Congress to believe they could be effectively directed by a legislative body or even by one of its committees. As an experienced diplomat he recognized that premature publicity could easily wreck crucial negotiations. He expected to be granted wide discretion, believing that in no other way could the diplomacy of the country be conducted. When negotiations had been completed, however, or had reached a stage when it seemed safe to report them, he promptly communicated full information to the legislators. One is impressed by the quickness with which important diplomatic documents were revealed. Even when they were communicated in confidence, their tenor soon became widely known. The secrets of the government were often shared with the British minister by Federalist senators, and legislators have never been noted for their silence. It would seem that effective diplomacy and participatory democracy are incompatible.

While it appears that the *conduct* of foreign affairs cannot be safely democratized and that delicate diplomatic negotiations cannot be successfully carried on in the white light of publicity, there can be no possible doubt that in a self-governing society foreign *policy* has to be generally acceptable to the sovereign people. It does not have to be acceptable day by day, and one wonders if the samplings of immediate reactions to particular events as reported on television screens and elsewhere in our publicity-ridden society have any real significance or value. In the long run, however, foreign policy has to be approved. No President ever realized this more fully than Jefferson, to whom popular sovereignty was the distinctive principle of our government.

On the pages of history he appears in this period as a man of peace, not war. The author of the Declaration of Independence can hardly be designated a pacifist, and numerous utterances and actions of his show that he was not for peace at any price during his Presidency. (I am not referring to the Tripolitan War, which he regarded as an action against piracy.) In the most crucial situations, however, when confronted with a choice between war and a peaceful alternative, he chose the latter. His foreign policy was brilliantly successful in his first term, when, because of good luck as well as wise foresight, he acquired the province of Louisiana. But his effort to cause the boundaries of this imperial domain to be defined by peaceful negotiation and to acquire West Florida in the process were dismally unsuccessful. And his recourse to economic reprisals in defense of American maritime rights led many of his countrymen to conclude that the cure was worse than the disease. It may be that his inveterate optimism and patriotic zeal caused him in both instances to seek more than he should have expected to gain by formal agreement, and he undoubtedly made tactical mistakes in both cases, but the fact remains that in each of them the course he pursued was an alternative to war. In neither case was his policy thoroughly satisfactory to his constituents; nor has it been generally applauded by scholars who have examined it since his time. I am afraid we all tend to judge foreign policy in terms of its immediate success or failure, though this may have been chiefly owing to forces wholly beyond presidential control. And rarely do we allow sufficiently for alternatives which were rejected, partly because the rejects are often out of sight, partly because human beings are not invariably fair-minded. But at least we should recognize that at times a President must choose between alternatives no one of which is intrinsically desirable. The only choice may be between a greater and a lesser evil.

Jefferson faced such a situation more than once on the southern border, but the presidential dilemma can be more clearly seen in the better-known circumstances that occasioned the ill-fated Embargo. The grave infringements on American rights in the course of the titanic duel between Great Britain and France would have warranted war against either power, but the Mistress of the Seas was inevitably the greater offender. Perhaps our government asked too much of a country involved in what it regarded as a death struggle, but we may doubt if the American public would have been content with lesser demands. At any rate, diplomacy failed and Jefferson then faced a dilemma. He himself was not entirely averse to war, and at times he seems to have expected it. But there was some question about which country we ought to fight; and, while it would have been logical to fight the British, a war against them would have been bitterly opposed in New England—except possibly in the days immediately following the outrage committed on the *Chesapeake* by the *Leopard*. All the rest of the time war might have been expected to divide the country. We may well doubt if any policy could have met the demands of this situation. A neutral country caught in the cross fire of contending major powers is in a most unenviable situation. Some historians have regarded the Embargo as a noble experiment that failed. As an economic substitute for war it may be described as forward-looking, but it also looked backward to the nonimportation and non-exportation agreements of the American Revolution. It can best be regarded as a choice between alternatives, all of which were unpalatable; and its fate leads one to wonder if human beings are really willing to pay the high price of peace.

An American President today can lead from strength which was only potential in those days, but, like Jefferson, he may be forced to choose between alternatives no one of which is desirable in itself. Accordingly he may expect to be damned if he does and damned if he doesn't. In an age when wars are waged without being declared and speed is often of the essence, he may have to act without waiting to feel the pulse of public opinion. By so doing he may stay the march of totalitarianism or even save mankind from nuclear destruction; but, on the other hand, he may dangerously commit us. Thus he and our self-governing society with him face a continuing dilemma. He bears a burden of responsibility far greater than that of Jefferson, but his power to control the actions of other countries is sharply limited. We have to view his actions with a keenly critical eye, but in fairness we should be aware of his difficulties. As the architect of foreign policy in a revolutionary age his lot is not a happy one.

It is now obvious that no President can do much in either the foreign or the domestic field without popular support. Jefferson perceived this more clearly than either of his predecessors had done. He may have been unjust in his judgment that Hamilton relied on force and corruption as European governments did, but he perceived that popular support was the only alternative. During at least three-fourths of his Presidency he had this to a notable degree. The voices of his political enemies were strident and their tones bitter, but the preponderant majority of his countrymen stood behind him. No doubt this was chiefly because of their approval of policies which were designed to lighten the burdens of ordinary mortals and widen their opportunities, though they did not offer positive benefits of the modern sort. But there can be no question of his enormous personal popularity; and one cannot help wondering how this could have been attained by this intellectual who loathed crowds, cherished privacy, and built his house upon a mountain. There are numerous references to his amiability, and throughout life he made a fine art of friendship. With rare exception those who knew him well liked him, but few people actually knew him. Besides his two inaugurals and his addresses to Indian delegations, he made virtually no speeches while President; he made no good-will tours, as Washington and Monroe did; and very few of his countrymen, relatively, ever saw him. In our day a President is subjected to indecent exposure, but this one was almost invisible. Employing the language of our own generation we may ask: What was his image, and how was it projected?

In the first place it should be noted that, while no military hero, he was recognized as a distinguished patriot of the American Revolution. He was very fond of referring to the "spirit of 1776," and the jealousy with which he and his friends guarded his patriotic image is shown by the pains they took to meet the charges arising from his conduct and misfortunes as war governor of his commonwealth. (The worst of these were without foundation, and most of them were unjust.)

By the "spirit of 1776," however, he meant more than national patriotism, just as he regarded the Declaration of Independence as more than a national manifesto. His contemporaries probably did not identify that document with him personally to the same degree that we do; but I think it safe to say that he was regarded by his followers and many others as the foremost champion of the principles and ideals that are set forth in it. There has been some scholarly effort in our own day to demonstrate that his record as a libertarian was not unsullied. This may be conceded in his case as in that of others charged with the responsibility of governing the country. In fairness, however, his alleged aberrations should be examined in their own setting of time and circumstance and viewed in perspective. Although political enemies, whose records as friends of individual freedom could not suffer comparison with his, sought to make political capital of inconsistencies on his part, actual or alleged, they did not succeed in erasing the general impression that he laid major emphasis on the well-being of individual citizens. He had to guard their security as well as their freedom, and in organized society hardly any freedom can be safely regarded as absolute. But, through a long life and highly controversial career, he recognized and emphasized, as few public men have done, the dignity and sanctity of human personality. At times his enemies tried to cast him in the role of autocrat; but only during the Embargo, when the curtailment of economic freedom by govern-mental action was indisputable, do they appear to have had much success. The role of autocrat did not fit him, and he had none of the manner of a tyrant.

It should not be supposed that his past services to human liberty were forgotten during his Presidency, but the designation that suggests the prevailing view of him was that of "The Man of the People." Actually, the term "democrat" was rarely on his own lips at this time or any other; he called himself a republican—that is, an antimonarchist and a believer in self-government. He called his party "Republican," not Democratic Republican, as historians have so generally come to do in order to dis-tinguish it from the Republican party of our day. He unquestionably belonged to the intellectual elite of his time, and his manner of life accorded with the practices and traditions of the landed gentry of Virginia to which he belonged by birth and education. The revolt against gentility had not gone as far as it went later, but the fact that a person of his tastes and status should have been hailed as the man of the people does seem surprising.

His enemies had an explanation. They claimed that, besides ignobly catering to the multitude in his policies and public procedure, he affected for political purposes a plainness, even a boorishness, which was unnatural to him personally and unbecoming in a President. These critics had little ground for complaint about the dinners in the President's House. At his generous table senators and congressmen consumed food prepared by a French chef and served by liveried retainers and drank in vast quantity wines that their host had imported. At one dinner, however, he wounded the sensibilities of a freshly arrived British minister by ignoring protocol, and a *cause célèbre* ensued. The episode of Anthony Merry was probably the most comical of Jefferson's Presidency, and I regret that I can make only passing reference to that tempest in his teapot. Unlike his predecessors, he was accessible to visitors at any time —that is, until he set out on his daily horseback ride, unattended by a groom; this was just before his three-o'clock dinner. What was most remarked upon was that he received his visitors, including foreign ministers, in any sort of dress. Why should a cultivated gentleman, occupying the highest post in the country, do such things?

Henry Adams, who relished paradox, played up this apparent contradiction for considerably more than it was worth. Jefferson's contemporary critics saw demagoguery in it. But these seeming vagaries can be largely explained in more human terms. Elderly widowers, deprived of feminine supervision, often become indifferent to dress; and, except on formal occasions, members of the Virginia gentry showed little concern about their external appearance. (The same has often been said of the Proper Bostonians.) This particular widower, who hated the cold and lived in a big barn of a house, dressed for warmth and comfort during his working hours, and his visitors, including occasional diplomats, had to take him as they found him. He seems to have been well dressed for dinner unless this was merely a family affair. As President Jefferson was disposed to conduct himself just as he would have at Monticello. Since he was following his own custom, he was not assuming a false front. His dislike of ceremonies of all sorts and of the artificial distinctions that he had observed in royal courts was genuine, but he was well aware of the past objections of his own followers to presidential formality, and in dispensing with it to the extent he did he may have been putting on something of an act.

No doubt it was fortunate for him that his physical image could not be projected on the television screen. The modern microphone could have made his voice more audible than it was at his two inaugurals, but his gift was not for speaking. It was for writing, and he projected his personality to his countrymen effectively in his huge personal correspondence. People constantly wrote to him—all sorts and conditions of men —and to an amazing number of them he responded with his own pen. He wrote any number of off-the-record letters to political supporters in all parts of the country who voluntarily sent him information and shared their problems with him. He also discussed vaccination with Dr. Benjamin Waterhouse and gardening with nurserymen and horticulturists, exchanging plants as well as ideas. He was constantly consulted by men of learning and frequently by students, and it would also seem that anybody who had observed something of interest in the natural world or the realm of knowledge or who had invented something he hoped might be useful felt free to communicate with the President of the United States. As one person said, they believed that "the mild and philanthropic *Jefferson*" might be addressed "with the freedom and familiarity of a *fellow citizen & friend.*" [6] He did not really have time for what Charles Willson Peale called "the minutiae of the public good," and he received fantastic and ludicrous suggestions, but his countrymen had sensed that he was interested in anything and everything that bore on human happiness and well-being. Certain clerical foes of his in New England called him the "man of sin," but he received many letters and resolutions of thanks from those who had benefited from the religious freedom he had done so much to further. The hundreds of recipients of private letters from his hand had good reason to regard him as not merely a friend to mankind in general but to individual human beings. This was not mass appeal, and communication was painfully slow in those days, but reports of his invariable friendliness got around.

A major reason for his personal appeal in my opinion, was his genuine respect for human personality. He treated his major associates, especially Madison and Gallatin, not as subordinates but as his peers, rightly believing that they would never take advantage of him. The same cannot be said of the attitude and conduct of General James Wilkinson, and Jefferson was never at his best in dealing with aggressive self-seekers. He could be tough when he thought it necessary, but he may not have thought that often enough. Very many of his correspondents were far from being his peers, except in their human rights, but it would be difficult to find anything condescending or patronizing in his letters to the humblest of them. Though certainly not unaware of the dark side of human nature, he never lost faith in human beings. That faith endeared him to his fellow citizens and constitutes one of the most precious parts of his rich legacy to posterity. Judging from what the newspapers have told us in recent months and years, human nature has shown no marked improvement since his time; but if he were here now I have no doubt that he would continue to steer his bark with hope in the head, leaving fear astern.

His persistent faith in human beings seems all the more notable in view of the fact that he was subjected to personal attacks which have

6 Samuel Elliott to Jefferson, November 1802, in Jefferson Papers. This particular correspondent was asking for a favor.

rarely been matched in presidential history. Since I cannot enter into these here, I will merely observe that the charges of immorality that were raised against him during his Presidency were manifestly political in origin and motivation and will express my own judgment that, except for one episode of his young manhood which he himself admitted to his friends, they were quite unwarranted. I have no doubt whatever that he was an unusually clean and genuinely good man. He himself followed a policy of ignoring personal attacks, and I will do that here. However, I want to commend to our generation the distinction he drew between private and public conduct. This was that a man's private life is his own affair and of no proper concern to the public except as it bears on his public acts. That such a distinction will commend itself to the American people in an age when the President lives in a goldfish bowl seems most unlikely; and the chances are that personal abuse will continue to be a perquisite of the presidential office—a sort of "fringe benefit" in reverse.

Obviously, the problems of our next President will be magnified many times because of the enormous increase in the size and complexity of everything in the last century and a half. Jefferson lived in what we used to call *the* age of revolution, but our age is far more revolutionary. To study his conduct of the Presidency is to enjoy a richly rewarding and highly educational experience, but no one can rightly expect to find in his record detailed guidance for a President today. Far more memorable than his specific acts, policies, and methods is the spirit in which he conducted his high office. Recognizing the danger of power, he exercised it with notable restraint and was not corrupted by it; and he strove to be to all men, and in the fullest sense, humane. He deserves emulation on other grounds, but in these respects, above all, he offers a shining example to his successors in our generation or any other.

V 1776 and 1976: New Directions or Conservative Continuations?

Introduction July 4, 1976, will be the bicentenary of the Declaration of Independence. Scholars, politicians, journalists, opinion makers in general, and the man-in-the street have already begun, rhetorically and seriously to gauge the progress of the Spirit of '76 during the past two centuries. Many thoughtful men and women have tended to see the American Revolution as essentially conservative—as no great break with the past, but rather, instead of pointing the American people toward new directions, legitimizing conservative continuations. This school of thought has contended that the American Revolution does not dwell at all in the world of the French Revolution, the Russian Revolution, the Chinese Revolution, or the Cuban Revolution.

Other thoughtful men and women, while recognizing significant differences between revolutions at different times and in different places, have been more sanguine about the thrust of this American "empire for liberty"—to use Jefferson's felicitous phrase. They have seen its consequences not in the context of conservative continuations, but rather as impelling the nation over all the long years since 1776 in new and hopeful directions, despite occasional setbacks and aberrations.

Among the latter, Cecelia Kenyon unabashedly subtitles her essay presented here "An Old Fashioned Interpretation." This is most refreshing. Her tone is strong. For her the Revolution ". . . precipitated the one great creative period in the political and constitutional history of the United States, and its ramifications were not limited to the single theme of more or less democratization of political structure. . . . For all its pluralistic diversity the American Revolution was still a revolution, and it was radical." Its radicalism can be seen in its consequences: a new nation was founded; republican government was launched; republican government was fused with a new and exciting federalism; and the philosophies of individualism and equality—so modern, so dynamic, so disruptive—were exhibited in working form to a world that was perhaps not so candid. She does not deny but fully acknowledges that the past had contributed much, but not all that much. The founders ". . . had some fine old bricks to start with, and they knew it. Nevertheless, what they designed and partly built from these bricks was not Georgian. It was American, and they knew that too."

Gordon S. Wood, author of the much acclaimed *The Creation of the American Republic* (1969), gave an address entitled ("The American Revolution: Political Integration of the Enslaved and the Disenfranchised,") on January 9, 1974 before a joint session of the Kentucky state legislature at Frankfort, Kentucky. He, like Cecelia Kenyon, sees the American Revolution as radical, particularly in the democratic context, and he details the significance of this legacy for nineteenth- and twentieth-century America. Its legacy goes beyond America: "The profoundest revolution of the past 200 years has been this introduction of

138

ordinary people into the political process. For America and the rest of the Western world, this Revolution was most dramatically expressed at the end of the eighteenth century—"the age of the democratic revolution," as it has been called. "The democratization of American politics, save for the black and the slave, was accomplished in the half century following the Revolution. In Western Europe it was not accomplished until near the end of the nineteenth century, and since 1945 we have observed the Third World ". . . in a hurried even desperate effort . . . to catch up with modern democratic States." The Revolution meant that the United States was the first modern nation ". . . to have a democratic revolution and to establish a republic, in which citizenship and political participation belonged to the whole community." The effect of this was to legitimate the participation of the people in the political process and to make the people sovereign, and henceforward ". . . it was not enough for elected officials to be simply *for* the people; they had to be *of* the people as well."

But this political integration of the disenfranchised had one sad exception: it did not include the black, whether free or slaves. Wood remarks "this greatest anomaly" and justly comments: "There is perhaps no greater irony in the democratization of American politics in the first half of the 19th century than the fact that as the white man gained the vote the black man lost it." This enormous contradiction of revolutionary ideals put such a strain upon the national fabric that ". . . sooner or later those contradictions had to tear the country apart." The result of this has been that in the last generation ". . . largely under the impetus of the Civil Rights movement but going beyond that, we have witnessed a heightened interest in political and voting rights and have drawn out the logic of the principles concerning the suffrage and representation first articulated in the Revolution 200 years ago."

Republicanism and Radicalism
in the American Revolution:
An Old-Fashioned Interpretation
—*Cecelia M. Kenyon** *

I

Although the American Revolution was a central and decisive phenomenon in the national life of the American people, taken comfortably for
granted by its heirs and nominally commemorated by a convenient summer holiday, its nature and significance continue to puzzle historians who
seek to know it well. From the very beginning, it was believed by those
who participated in it—on the western side of the Atlantic—to be a quite
remarkable event, not merely because it was their revolution, but because
it seemed to them to introduce a new phase in the political evolution of
mankind, and therefore to be touched with universal significance. This
native estimate was not entirely parochial. There was considerable interest
in the American experiment among contemporary Europeans, and the
volumes of commentary written by visitors in the nineteenth century indicate that this interest was not merely ephemeral. In more recent times,
Americans have been reminded of their Revolutionary heritage by later
rebels against colonial rule, who have sometimes seemed to find the
America of 1776 more inspiring than the America of 1962. Thus the Revolution was, and continues to be, an event of enduring importance. And
yet, in spite of generations of study, its essential nature remains obscure.
In fact, as its two-hundredth anniversary approaches, there seems to be
more uncertainty about its meaning, more diversity in interpretation, than
ever before. For the last two generations, scholars have debated such
questions as the relationship between the Declaration of Independence
and the Constitution, what the real causes of the Revolution were, whether
it was essentially a colonial revolt or an internal struggle for power,
whether it was radical or conservative—indeed, whether, in fact, it was
actually a revolution. Among these and other issues, a crucial one over
which there has been much confusion is whether the Revolution was

From Cecelia Kenyon, "Republicanism and Radicalism in the American Revolution,"
William and Mary Quarterly, Third Series, XIX (April 1962), 153–182. Reprinted by permission of the author.

* Miss Kenyon is a member of the Department of Government, Smith College. An earlier
version of this article was presented at the Seminar on the American Revolution, sponsored
by Colonial Williamsburg, Inc., Williamsburg, Virginia, Sept. 9, 1960.

radical or conservative. The purpose of this article is to consider some of the intellectual forces which have contributed to this confusion, to suggest a way by which some of this confusion may be resolved, and to analyze the Revolution with respect to its radical and conservative immediate aspects and long-range implications.

II

Among the factors responsible for this confusion, one of the most important is sheer lack of accurate and precise knowledge. Not until very recently, for example, have we really known much about the suffrage or about actual participation in politics.[1] It has taken nearly two centuries for historians to learn the historiographical lessons implicit in Madison's Tenth *Federalist* and to begin to dig out the extraordinarily complex interest groups involved in the ratification of the Constitution.[2] As more knowledge accumulates, so should our understanding of the total Revolutionary situation increase in both depth and breadth.

Yet the facts do not reveal themselves spontaneously, nor do they always speak for themselves. A second factor which has contributed to confusion has been the attempt to impose upon the Revolution too simple a pattern of interpretation. It is natural and inevitable for historians and political scientists to fit the ideas, the institutions, the political, social, and economic developments of the period into a unified and coherent whole. No mere listing of these elements, without classification and an effort to see their various interrelationships, would be intelligible. The hazard of this process of intellectual construction is as natural and familiar as the process itself. It is that the pattern may distort reality even as it illuminates it. Such has been the result of the inclination to view the conflicts and debates of the Revolution as if the parties to them were divided naturally into pairs of opposites. We speak of the American and British position, of Loyalists and Patriots, of radicals and conservatives, of democrats and aristocrats, of Federalists and Anti-Federalists. There is much validity in this categorization, because there were times during the period between 1765 and 1789 when the alternative choices of action were reduced to two: one did or did not sign the Declaration of Independence; one voted for or against the Constitution of 1787. Furthermore, there was some degree of consistency and continuity in the positions taken by various men over an ex-

---

[1] See, for example, Robert E. Brown, *Middle-Class Democracy and the Revolution in Massachusetts, 1691–1780* (Ithaca, 1955); Richard P. McCormick, *Experiment in Independence: New Jersey in the Critical Period, 1781–1789* (New Brunswick, N. J., 1950), and *The History of Voting in New Jersey . . .* (New Brunswick, N. J., 1953); J. R. Pole, "Suffrage Reform and the American Revolution in New Jersey," New Jersey Historical Society, *Proceedings,* LXXIV (Newark, 1956), 173–194; "Suffrage and Representation in Massachusetts: A Statistical Note," *William and Mary Quarterly,* 3d Ser., XIV (1957), 560–592.

[2] See Forrest McDonald, *We the People: The Economic Origins of the Constitution* (Chicago, 1958), esp. iv.

tended period of time. Yet I believe that it is a mistake to see the Revolution from its early stages to its later ones as a movement involving issues over which men divided naturally into two clearly defined groups, radical and conservative, more or less constant in composition.

Among the intellectual forces which have operated to incline American historians toward this dichotomous analysis of the Revolutionary period are two, one conscious, one perhaps unconscious. The first is that inspired by the Populist critique of the Constitution during the 1890's, and later elaborated into a full-blown interpretation according to which the Declaration of Independence represented and embodied the spirit of democracy which characterized the early stages of the Revolution, while the Constitution was the product of a successful conservative and antidemocratic reaction.[3] Charles A. Beard's *Economic Interpretation of the Constitution*[4] was not identical with this interpretation, but it tended to absorb and reinforce it by seeming to present impressive evidence for its validity. An economic interpretation does not necessarily have to be dichotomous, but Beard's was, and it was Beard who exercised a dominant influence over more than a generation of American historians. Why Beard and his followers should have accepted a Hamiltonian rather than a Madisonian view of politics is not easy to explain, but the results of this acceptance do seem reasonably clear. It has exercised an enormous influence both in the selection and interpretation of facts, and has tended to create a simplified pattern to describe and explain what was in reality a very complex set of political phenomena.

This historiographical factor has probably been reinforced by a second one, much less visible, and probably impossible to document. It is the unconscious conditioning effect on Americans of a two-party political system. Only twice within a century has a third party threatened the dominance of the two major parties, and each was strictly a one-shot flash never repeated. To be sure, each of the major parties has its internal cleavages, of which informed students of politics as well as politicians are well aware. Still, Americans do think of politics in terms of two parties, and this conception, I suspect, has had its influence on the way in which we visualize our past. A dualistic party system seems to us so normal that we tend to think of it as part of a natural political order.

It was not so for the men of the Revolution. We do not yet have sufficient evidence to know to what extent their aversion to parties was negated by their tendency to form and use them. The attitude of the most articulate spokesmen is unequivocal and unmistakable, and it appears to have been rather pervasive. As such, it was itself a factor in Revolutionary

---

.[3] See C. Edward Merriam, *A History of American Political Theories* (New York and London, 1903), and J. Allen Smith, *The Spirit of American Government* . . . (New York, 1907).

[4] Charles A. Beard, *An Economic Interpretation of the Constitution of the United States* (New York, 1913).

politics and must be taken into consideration. What I am proposing is that in analyzing the Revolution, we adopt something of the intellectual habit of its makers and consider the implications of their dislike and distrust of parties. One such implication is obvious; they thought of parties as reflecting or magnifying selfish interests. Another is equally obvious and for our purposes perhaps more significant. Their ideal of politics appears to have involved not the division of the body of citizens into more or less permanent groupings held together by similar views on a composite cluster of principles and/or interests, but rather *ex tempore* majorities and minorities formed by the issue of the moment and undistorted by pre-existing organization not related to the instant issue. This ideal was matched and perhaps countered by a recognition of economic and other factors which tended to divide society into relatively stable, though not necessarily politically organized or active, groups, whose influence might, nonetheless, be felt in politics. Some of the new constitutions adopted during the period specifically recognized an economic class division in their property qualifications for officeholding. Similarly, in several of the states, and certainly in the national debate of 1787–88, there was present an awareness of two major classes, and it was assumed by both sides that these classes would sometimes have different economic and political interests. At the same time, the pre-Revolutionary arguments against the British theory of virtual representation, and the later debates over the ratification of the Constitution, expressed the necessity of making the representative assembly reflect a multiplicity of interests and opinions among the voters rather than a dualistic division along party or factional lines. Thus it seems quite clear that the Americans of the Revolutionary period did not have a consistent, systematic theory of the political process, and especially not of political parties. It seems a safe hypothesis to suggest that in this respect there would very likely be a reciprocal relationship between political thought and political behavior. We should not read the pattern of later political divisions back into the eighteenth century, any more than we should read their substance.

It would be remarkable indeed if a simple dichotomous pattern could really fit so complex a phenomenon as the Revolution. It was, as revolutions go, a rather peculiar one. In the first place, no revolution was intended; the colonists wanted merely a redress of grievances as British subjects and had no plans either for independence or for the formation of republican government. In the second place, there were thirteen separate colonies or states involved, and, though they may not have been as different from one another as their members believed them to be, the differences were sufficient to make the impact and the aftermath of the Revolution far from identical in each of them. In the third place, the Revolution was both the creator of and the fruit of the emergence of first a growing consciousness that the British continental colonies constituted a separate community with interests different from those of the mother country and later a spirit of nationalism and eventually of national unity. In the fourth place, the Revolution was accomplished with remarkably little internal coercion and remarkably great decentralization of leadership. No central committee, party, government, or army ever possessed or exercised a preponderance either of power or authority at any time during the period from 1765 to 1789. In short, Americans found themselves in 1776 in a position for which they were not prepared and for which they had no plans. When the decision for independence was taken, they had been in armed revolt for over a year and, during this period, had been living either without formal, recognized governments or with governments of dubious legitimacy and authority. It is necessary to understand this combination of a complex situation and complex political attitudes before proceeding to an analysis of republicanism and radicalism during the American Revolution.

A third factor contributing to the confusion over the nature of the Revolution has been our inability to achieve a precise and meaningful terminology with which to analyze and categorize the phenomena we have sought to describe. There has been no general agreement among scholars about the meaning of words such as radical, conservative, liberal, or democratic, and there has been a notable lack of rigor in the way we have applied them to the Revolutionary era. In particular, I would object that the common use of the terms *radical* and *conservative* to denote respectively populist and anti-populist divisions within the Revolutionary party has tended to obscure the nature of the changes which took place in America during the last quarter of the eighteenth century.

There are several major difficulties involved in an identification of *democratic* and *radical*. In the first place, the word *democratic* is too loose. It is not easy to get a precise yardstick for democracy in the Revolutionary period, or to find among the articulate men of the age one whose views were purely and consistently democratic by any standard. Benjamin Franklin, for example, is usually associated with the radical democrats of Pennsylvania because he was a believer in unicameralism. In the Philadelphia Convention, Franklin was opposed to a salary in excess of expenses for the President, and this arrangement in effect would have restricted that office to the relatively wealthy. James Wilson and Gouverneur Morris both advocated the direct, popular election of the President—on its face a radically democratic proposal—but neither was identified with the populist party in his state, and Morris was very closely associated with Alexander Hamilton. Thomas Jefferson devised a comprehensive plan of reform for the state of Virginia, aimed, as he said, at uprooting the last remnants of aristocracy there. But Jefferson was a staunch believer in separation of powers and therefore can scarcely qualify as a democrat for those who tend to identify democracy with the absence of separation of powers or the concentration of power in the legislative branch of the government.

Similarly, Jefferson's objections to the Constitution of 1787 did not touch the distribution of powers between the central government and the states, and he cannot therefore fit into the association of democracy with localism. In short, the identification of radicalism with democracy or localism fails to provide a clear and precise definition as a tool for analyzing the Revolution.

In the second place, such an identification involves a chain of assumptions of dubious validity. The definition of radical in terms of democracy assumes that the latter was the central issue of the period, that it operated as a primary determinative force in lining up men on other issues which were derivative from it and which were therefore of secondary importance, that its effect, in short, was to produce a polarization of opinion. Was democracy an ideological and dynamic force which operated in this manner? I think not, or at least not consistently. For example, the separation of church and state was a fundamental change. If democracy and radicalism were identical, then the more democratic party should have been in favor of this separation. The opposition to the clause in the Constitution which prohibited religious tests for officeholding suggests that such was not the case. The legal effect of this clause was to establish equality of eligibility for all men, regardless of their religious or nonreligious beliefs or associations. It also, by implication, broadened the potential choice of the electorate, in comparison with the situation in a number of the state governments. In other words, it prohibited a religious monopoly of officeholding, and it prohibited restraints on the free choice of the electorate. These factors are frequently associated with democratic government, yet they were not desired by some of the opponents of the Constitution who criticized that document, on other grounds, as having an aristocratic bias. I submit that these opponents were not democratic on this issue and that the association of radicalism with Revolutionary democracy assumes a unity, consistency, and rationality in political thought which is rarely found even in the most sophisticated and systematic of theorists.

This is not to deny that the association of *radical* with *democratic* has considerable historical justification. In America, as elsewhere, one element of political evolution in the eighteenth and nineteenth centuries was the extension of power and privilege to the majority of the population. With respect to this element, the populist parties of the Revolution may be called radical, though the recent studies of the suffrage requirements indicate that reformist would be more accurate. There were other movements, however, in the direction of nationalism, of individualism, of industrialization that were certainly in the literal sense radical, though none of them was by necessary and exclusive logic connected with democracy. In fact, the advocates of nationalism and industrialism during the last quarter of the eighteenth century in America were frequently in opposition to the advocates of populism and/or democracy. If one accepts the identification

146 – Cecelia M. Kenyon

of radicalism with the latter, then it would seem to follow that nationalism and industrialism were conservative movements. Put in these general terms, this sounds like a ridiculous conclusion, for both were to become major movements of the nineteenth and twentieth centuries, both produced radical changes, and both have been called "revolutions." Similarly, we are accustomed to having the Constitution described as the product of a conservative reaction, although it was unquestionably a great step in the direction of nationalism. Hamilton's financial program had industrialization as one of its purposes, and, though there are probably few historians who would call him a conservative on this particular matter, there is still considerable reluctance to associate him with Revolutionary radicalism. It is men like Thomas Paine and the authors of the Pennsylvania constitution whom that term is more likely to bring to mind. The tendency to define *radical* purely in terms of populist groups makes it difficult to classify changes which were fundamental but not overtly or immediately democratic. If we are to continue to accept this kind of terminology, then we must recognize that it is a very parochial kind of history we write, one which foreign students of America must find difficult to translate into terms which are meaningful to them. And we must recognize that such terminology does not lend itself to precise comparative and analytical studies.

A third major difficulty stemming from the identification of radicalism and democracy is that it inhibits a precise analysis of the issues which arose during the period and of the groups who divided over them. Once a group is labeled democratic or radical on one issue, there is a tendency to assume that whatever stand it took on others was also democratic or radical. Conversely, once a particular policy is associated with a democratic or radical group, it may take on the coloring of that group. Both tendencies may result in distortion, confusion, or a limited presentation of reality. Consider the latter, with respect to the issue of paper money. There must be thousands of graduates of American history courses who associate paper money during the Revolution with radicalism, and radicalism with the *demos*. Yet it is perfectly clear that paper money was supported in some states by the upper classes also. Were the South Carolina planters who supported paper money radicals and democrats? Or was paper money radical only when supported by some groups and opposed by others? Radical in Rhode Island but not in South Carolina? The former tendency, the labeling of ideas and institutions in terms of the assumed character of their advocates or opponents, makes objective analysis and comparison awkward if not impossible.

Two examples may serve to make this difficulty clear. It has been a common interpretation of the Revolutionary period to associate democracy with opposition to separation of powers and checks and balances, partly because the Pennsylvania insurgents of 1776 were a populist group who seized power from a former privileged group and who then established a constitution which did not follow the principle of separation of powers. If this and other similar groups opposed this principle and favored instead a concentration of authority in the legislature, then the latter form must be democratic and the former not. But if this categorization is accepted, then how are we to describe the changes which took place in state constitutions in the period from about 1820 to 1860? An almost universal trend was the creation of an independent executive, popularly elected; the election of other administrative officers was also common and, to a lesser extent, so was the election of judges. These changes were made partly in the name of democracy, and we are familiar with them under the label of the "long ballot." It is perfectly obvious, though not so frequently noted, that they meant a relative decrease in the authority of the legislature and—especially the independent executive—an increase in separation of powers. Were these later constitutions, then, antidemocratic, or at least less democratic than those of the Revolutionary period which did not have an executive independent of the legislature, elected directly by the people? Such a conclusion is certainly possible, but it does involve difficulties. One of them is that not only have our state and federal contitutions continued to be undemocratic, but that there has been no substantial popular demand to have them otherwise. The fundamental methodological point is that a definition of radical in terms of Revolutionary democracy does not provide an adequate tool for comparative analysis of ideas and institutions during different periods in our own political evolution, or of similar ones in different countries. For that, we need a more objective and less relativistic concept.

My second example illustrates another facet of the same need. The Constitution of 1787 was opposesd by groups who have been commonly regarded as more democratic than its advocates, and this interpretation has been partly responsible for the opinion that the Constitution itself was undemocratic. One specific argument against ratification was that the proposed system of representation would prejudice the election of men of "the people" and that the lower house of the national legislature would not truly represent the people. In short, the Constitution, even in its then most democratic feature, would not really be democratic at all. Are we to accept this contemporary opinion and conclude that the Constitution was undemocratic in this most fundamental and simple respect? The reasoning back of this opinion was the belief that large constituencies would necessitate pre-election organization and that the organized electoral majority would not return a legislative majority which faithfully reflected the real, unorganized constituent majority. If we accept the reasoning and the conclusions of the Anti-Federalists on this point, then we must conclude that the House of Representatives is not and has never been democratic; that the Senate, since the Seventeenth Amendment, has been even less democratic (since the constituencies of Senators are entire states); and that the Presidency (with the entire nation as its constituency) is and has been least democratic of all. If the two-thirds of our government which is constituted by popular election is not democratic, then it must of course follow that the United States is not a democracy, has never been one since 1789, and can never be one. Again, this is a perfectly possible and reasonable conclusion. But I do not think that it is a very useful one. We ought not to accept as historiographical tools the opinions of Revolutionary polemicists. The prediction of the Anti-Federalists on this particular point, even in terms of their own conception of democracy, may have been wrong; the election of 1800 suggests the distinct possibility that it was. More importantly, their conception of democracy may be one which cannot be appropriately applied to the study of the whole range of American history. If Revolutionary democracy has these limitations as a definitional tool, then surely it is folly to define *radical* by associating it with this *democracy*.

It is for this reason that I have chosen to use the term *radical* in its strict and formal sense, unassociated with any substantive concept such as democracy, majoritarianism, unicameralism, or localism. Similarly, I would use the term *conservative* in a comparable sense, to refer to an attitude, position, tendency, or policy involving or favoring preservation or continuation of some element or elements in the existing situation, but not identifying it exclusively with any of those elements. The Revolution was not a monolithic or even a dualistic affair. It precipitated the one great creative period in the political and constitutional history of the United States, and its ramifications were not limited to the single theme of more or less democratization of political structure. It was a pluralistic phenomenon involving different sectors of change. Men and groups might be opposed to some changes and in favor of others. Men who were in favor of democracy in the sense of majority rule were not always in favor of such liberal and individualistic measures as complete freedom of religion. Men who sided with what appeared to be the populist party on some issues did not do so on others. Men who joined together on some particular issue, such as adoption or rejection of the Constitution, did so for different reasons and with different motives. In order to analyze all of these issues and their interrelationships, we need a terminology which is capable of expressing subtle as well as gross distinctions, nonsubstantive as well as substantive concepts. Thus I would use *radical* to indicate a fundamental change; *democratic* to denote a political system in which authority is derived from the majority of adult inhabitants, all of whom enjoy the suffrage and may use it at regular and reasonably frequent intervals and all of whom are legally eligible for office; *populist* to indicate a more or less self-conscious group, movement, attitude, or achievement on behalf of the majority conceived of in terms of the mass of the people; and *liberal* to indicate the values of individual rights, freedom, or happiness.[5] Accordingly, there could be radical democrats, radical populists, radical liberals, or any combination of these three substantive positions or their opposites. Similarly, a man or group can be radical on one issue, conservative on another. Or a particular policy or set of institutions can be partly radical, partly conservative. Such a terminology, like many definitions, reflects the outlook of the user. In this case, it reflects a conception of the Revolution as composed of pluralistic factors which do not fall together in a dichotomous pattern. Its parts were diverse, and its major ideological and institutional results were eclectic composites. Very few of the ingredients were totally new, and none of the finished products had that rational symmetry characteristic of systematic political philosophy. They were the products of compromise, of adaptation, sometimes of improvisation. Nevertheless, the Revolution did shape the future development of American politics and government. It selected and accentuated certain ingredients in the British and colonial heritage, rejected others, and made of the whole something that was fundamentally new and different. For all its pluralistic diversity, the American Revolution was still a *revolution,* and it was radical.

III

In the later years of their lives, John Adams and Thomas Jefferson both had occasion to comment on the nature of the Revolution, in which each had played a major role. Both left no doubt that after nearly fifty years they still regarded it, as they had in the beginning, as the fundamental change in the history of the American people. Adams emphasized the death of loyalty, affection, and allegiance toward the King of England and toward England itself. *"This radical change in the principles, opinions, sentiments, and affections of the people was the real American Revolution."* [6] Jefferson expressed a hope for the universal realization of the principles of the Declaration of Independence: "May it be to the world, what I believe it will be, (to some parts sooner, to others later, but finally to all,) the signal of arousing men to burst the chains under which monkish ignorance and superstition had persuaded them to bind themselves, and to assume the blessings and security of self-government." [7] Both men were

---

[5] It may be objected that these definitions, especially that of *democratic* or *democracy,* do not correspond to the meanings the words conveyed in America at the time of Revolution. I would agree that one should be aware of contemporary usage. Otherwise the ideas expressed in a given age will be misunderstood. However, if the historian himself uses words only and always in their historical sense, he will find it difficult to analyze, compare, and evaluate different but similar ideas and institutions in different countries and in different periods. I do not offer the above definitions as absolutes, but as functional tools for the purposes of analysis and comparison.

[6] Letter to Hezekiah Niles, Feb. 13, 1818, in Adrienne Koch and William Peden, eds., *The Selected Writings of John and John Quincy Adams* (New York, 1946), 204.

[7] Letter to Roger C. Weightman, June 24, 1826, in Paul Leicester Ford, ed., *The Works of Thomas Jefferson* (New York and London, 1904–5), XII, 477.

in their eighties at the time of these remarks, and one may be tempted to make some allowance for the inclination of old men to exaggerate the importance of an event which they had helped to bring about. I am prepared to accept their opinion, and have accordingly described this article as an old-fashioned interpretation. The Revolution was radical in its four principal achievements: independence; the establishment of republican government and the identification of republicanism with political right; the crystallization of the individualism and equalitarianism of the Declaration of Independence into an operative as well as a formal political philosophy; the extension of the principle and practice of republicanism to a large and heterogeneous population by combination with a new form of federalism.

Of these four results, the first was prior to all the rest and the one most consciously and immediately felt to be radical. The decision to declare formal separation from Great Britain was a difficult one, taken only after a long period of deliberation and after the colonies had been in armed revolt against the mother country for more than a year. Nearly three-quarters of the colonists were of British descent, and the vast majority of these were accustomed to thinking of themselves as Englishmen. Their resistance to the Stamp Act and subsequent colonial regulations had not been motivated by a desire for independence, but by a desire to maintain their rights as Englishmen. Independence was a last resort, a means to secure these rights as men, and as Americans. Once accepted as the only means to get what they wanted, the decision for independence inexorably produced consequences other than the achievement of their original goal. The United States developed as an independent nation, not as British colonies nor as a constituent member of the British Commonwealth. We take this fact so much for granted today that it is difficult to conceive of what our political, economic, social, and even geographical development might have been had the colonists achieved their goals within the Empire, or had the Revolution been unsuccessful. It is tempting to speculate about the possible "might-have-beens" had the long years of protest resulted in either of these eventualities. But the facts are that we did win our independence, and that we did so with revolutionary violence. Colonial political ideas and practice had already deviated to some extent from British patterns; the institution of independent governments widened the gap and produced a markedly different political tradition.

IV

The most important, as well as the most immediate, change was the formal establishment of republican governments. Throughout most of the period of colonial protest, there had been little criticism of the British constitution or of its aristocratic and monarchical elements as such. The main thrust of American argument had been directed toward Parliament rather than the King, and primarily toward the House of Commons rather than the House of Lords. It was almost inevitable that Americans would not carry their arguments further, given the fact that the issue of taxation was at the heart of colonial opposition. The habitual professions of allegiance, devotion, and loyalty to their gracious Sovereign which accompanied colonial petitions, resolutions, and acts of defiance were both formal and traditional, but they were not completely insincere. As long as Americans believed that the crux of their problem was legislative and not administrative, they could not but consider Parliament as the central opponent; as long as they believed that their aims could be achieved within the Empire, there was no reason for hostility to the institution of the Crown. The Americans were not republicans in either a formal or an ideological sense before 1776. Within a few months, they were, and have remained so ever since. Once the decision for independence was made, there seems to have been no serious question that any other form of government was either possible or desirable. Certainly it would have been difficult for all thirteen states to agree on a single monarch for them all, and the spectacle of thirteen separate embassies touring Europe and interviewing prospective candidates suggests that common sense as well as *Common Sense* had something to do with the American choice of republicanism.

This quick transition from monarchy to republic in form and belief was accomplished with relative ease. The question whether it was a radical change is difficult to answer. In its actual and immediate effect on the general population, it was not. Almost from the very beginning, with some exceptions of time and place, monarchy had rested lightly upon the colonists. George III and his predecessors were weeks away by sea, and in most of the colonies most of the time, the royal governors were effectively limited in the exercise of their authority by the power of the purse and the difficulty of enforcing unpopular measures in the face of concerted opposition without adequate and reliable military forces. Above all, there had been the long years of salutary neglect. It would be too much to say that the American colonies were autonomous republics before 1776, but their governments had been far more republican than that of the home country, and they had long been accustomed to governing themselves with relatively little interference or assistance from the other side of the Atlantic. The transition from monarchy to republic did not therefore bring with it pervasive and fundamental changes, either in private or public life. In this sense, the establishment of republican governments was not a radical change, and it is not remarkable that it took place so quickly and easily.

What is more remarkable is the rapid shift in attitude and belief. Within a very short period of time, Americans developed an ideological attachment to republicanism, and this change was a radical one, with radical and far-reaching consequences. Before 1776, the prevailing opinion in America had been that the ends of government—liberty, justice, happiness, and the public good—could be secured within the framework of monarchy. To be sure, they meant a limited or mixed monarchy, and they emphasized the central importance of constitutionalism. Still, they assumed the compatibility of monarchy with good government. After 1776, they tended to associate all the characteristics of good government with republicanism, and with republicanism only. To be sure, there were dissenters, of whom Alexander Hamilton was the most illustrious. But the preponderant opinion, the genius, to use Madison's word,[8] was clear and unambiguous: good government meant republican government. Thus there emerged an element of rigidity in American political thinking which has never disappeared and scarcely, if ever, been relaxed. The idea was so central and so fixed in the public mind, and the fear and distrust of other forms of government so great (perhaps inconsistently), that a guarantee of republican government to each state was written into the Constitution of 1787. More important, the idea has continued to dominate the American attitude toward politics and has been an important element in the formation of foreign policy. This identification of republican or democratic government with political right was a change both in substance and in intellectual outlook from pre-Revolutionary thought, and its consequences have been radical and far-reaching. Americans have regarded themselves, and have been regarded, as an essentially pragmatic people, but the preference for republicanism which crystallized at the time of the Revolution has constituted an ideological, doctrinaire element in their political outlook which has rarely been questioned. It may also be suggested that the ideological habit thus acquired has been extended to other areas and has become a major factor in American political thinking. Like republicanism, socialism, imperialism, and colonialism are all terms which have become stereotypes for Americans, frequently exercising a powerful ideological force at odds with our alleged pragmatism.

Thus I would suggest that the actual establishment of republican governments in 1776–80 was not a radical change, but that its intellectual consequences were. What is puzzling is the reason for the sudden and virtually complete revolution in attitude. There was, of course, the influence of Paine's critique of monarchy in *Common Sense*. There was the fact that the potential counterinfluence of the losing Loyalists was virtually eliminated by their exodus during and after the war. There was the psy-

---

[8] Alexander Hamilton, James Madison, and John Jay, *The Federalist*, ed. Benjamin Fletcher Wright (Cambridge, Mass., 1961): "The first question that offers itself is, whether the general form and aspect of the government be strictly republican? It is evident that no other form would be reconcilable with the genius of the people of America; with the fundamental principles of the Revolution; or with that honorable determination which animates every votary of freedom, to rest all our political experiments on the capacity of mankind for self-government." The Thirty-ninth Essay, p. 280.

chological necessity in the midst of war for an ideal that would inspire, sustain, and justify the participants and their actions. None of these reasons seems quite adequate, but the last was probably the most important. For the concept of republicanism, linked with the modified Lockeian ideals of the Declaration of Independence, provided a truly revolutionary doctrine with universal significance. Had the Revolution been merely a fight for independence, it would have remained a parochial affair of interest only to Great Britain and possibly to her continental rivals as convenient material for troublemaking. It was the genius of the Americans to see this, and once committed, to transform what might have remained a petty rebellion within the Empire into a symbol for the liberation of all mankind. Republicanism was an integral part of the symbol, and both contributed to and drew strength from it. The Revolution in its origins was a conservative movement to resist what were believed to be the pernicious innovations of George III and his Parliament. After 1776 it was, and was believed to be by its makers, truly radical.

V

The philosophy associated with republicanism and with the Revolution was also radical. It was the philosophy drawn from Locke's *Second Treatise,* but it was Lockeianism with an American gloss. A survey of Revolutionary literature both before and after 1776 reveals a number of modifications in and deviations from the original treatise which the Americans made as they used the great philosopher for their polemical purposes. The most familiar was the substitution in the Declaration of Independence of the *pursuit of happiness* for *property.* Another somewhat less familiar and certainly less clearly defined change was the American refusal to make a sharp distinction between the state of nature and civil society. These and other differences were apparent before the final break with England. The establishment of republican governments induced still other differences, of which the most important were an emphasis on equality, an intensification of individualism, and the identification of Locke with republicanism. The result was a subtle but substantial simplification and radicalization of the doctrine of the *Second Treatise.*

None of the separate changes was radical in the sense of being completely new or unrooted in the original *Treatise* or in the seventeenth-century body of thought upon which Locke drew. Nor was their sum more radical than the ideas set forth by the Levellers of the Civil War or their English heirs. Furthermore, the ideas were rooted in the colonial past and were therefore not unfamiliar. Yet the total complex was radical in implication and operation, especially when linked with the belief in, as well as the practice of, republicanism.

The most important of the changes was the American tendency to blur the differences which Locke had either stated or implied between the state of nature and the state of civil society. The concept of a state of nature was familiar to American thinkers before Locke wrote the *Second Treatise*, and, in American Puritan thought, it more closely resembled the Hobbesian version than the Lockeian. Americans emphasized the innate selfishness of man and the consequently hostile competition of a society in which men lived without the external restraints of law and government. Like Hobbes and Locke, they used the concept as a justification of government. What they did not do was to accept the idea that government could or would provide a completely impartial judge.[9] Their long experience in colonial self-government had taught them the inevitability of factious disputes and the difficulty if not the impossibility of securing impartial legislators and governors. Furthermore, the basis of their case against Parliamentary taxation and against the British theory of virtual representation had been the assumption that men in politics pursue their selfish interests and, in doing so, influence governmental policy. Accordingly, long before Madison's famous Tenth *Federalist*, Americans had questioned the likelihood, though not the ideal, of government as an impartial judge. Perhaps because their governments were already more republican than anything Locke knew, they were more acutely aware of "the people" as a collectivity of different and sometimes competitive groups and individuals than he was.

Similarly, because they expected men to behave selfishly in civil society, whether in or out of the government, they were also more rigorous than Locke was in attempting to insure that the rights men were entitled to in the state of nature were actually enjoyed in civil society. Locke had left the rights of the individual in an ambiguous if not precarious position. He stated that the consent of the majority could be taken for the consent of the individual and that, for generations other than the original contracting one, consent might be no more than tacit acceptance of the status quo. Locke also said that the original contractors might select hereditary monarchy or aristocracy as the form of government. Furthermore, the only kind of revolution Locke defined as a legitimate one was a revolution by the majority of the people. Thus, although he provided for protection of majority rights against monarchical or aristocratic infringement, he did not provide, either in the ordinary operation of government or through revolutionary means, for the protection of individual or minority rights against a majority or against a government supported by a majority. These rights would be secure only if the majority acted in accordance with the dictates of natural law. Locke seems to have assumed that it would so act, though

---

[9] James Otis, "The Rights of the British Colonies Asserted and Proved" (1764), in Charles F. Mullett, ed., *Some Political Writings of James Otis* (Columbia, Mo., 1929), I, 54: "The necessity of a common, indifferent and impartial judge, makes all men seek one; though few find him in the *sovereign power*, of their respective states or any where else in *subordination* to it."

he did not assume that individuals would always do so. The Americans were more consistent and more pessimistic. They did not assume that the behavior of groups of men, whether minorities or majorities, would be more virtuous than that of individuals. In the decade of constitutional protest before Lexington and Concord, the Americans found Locke very congenial and useful, for in the *Second Treatise* the problem of securing liberty is treated almost entirely in terms of the people against the government. Since the colonists were not represented in Parliament, their position was more or less that of Locke's "people," while Parliament's was that of Locke's "government." But the Americans did not ignore the fact that Parliament also represented the people of England and thus was, in another sense, a Lockeian "majority." James Wilson's case against Parliamentary authority over the colonies rested not only on the argument that the members of Parliament were not bound to Americans by mutual or identical interests, but on the assumption that members of Parliament *were* bound in this way to their English constituents and could therefore be held accountable by the latter.[10] It followed that the interests of Americans and of Englishmen were different. By implication, therefore, the people of England were responsible for Parliamentary oppression, not just Parliament itself. Americans constituted a minority in the Empire of which they regarded themselves members, and their demand for legislative autonomy under the Crown was, in one sense, a means to protect their minority rights and interests.

Thus, in their collective relationship to Parliament, the colonists had had some experience with governmental policies which represented, from their point of view, a self-interested and dominant faction of the Empire. Far more important in determining their political attitudes, however, was their long experience in internal colonial politics. Long before the natural rights doctrine of the *Second Treatise* was generally accepted, the existence of factions had been recognized and deplored, and eventually accepted.[11]

---

[10] See the emphatic statement to this effect in Wilson's "On the Legislative Authority of the British Parliament" (1774), in Bird Wilson, ed., *The Works of the Honorable James Wilson, L.L.D. . . .* (Philadelphia, 1804), III, 211: "The interest of the representatives is the same with that of their constituents. Every measure, that is prejudicial to the nation, must be prejudicial to them and their posterity. They cannot betray their electors, without, at the same time, injuring themselves. They must join in bearing the burthen of every oppressive act; and participate in the happy effects of every wise and good law. Influenced by these considerations, they will seriously and with attention examine every measure proposed to them; they will behold it in every light, and extend their views to its most distant consequences."

[11] The development of American colonial thought on this subject is reflected in various of the Election Sermons given in New England in the latter part of the 17th century and the first two-thirds of the 18th. Note the variety as well as the similarity of views expressed in these three sermons: "Take heed of any Sinister Aims in whatsoever Laws do pass: Laws made to strengthen a particular separate interest, never did Good, but Hurt to a Body-Politick: that which may serve the present turn, may in a little time prove more Mischievous, than ever it was Advantageous." (Samuel Willard, *The Character of a Good Ruler . . .* [Boston, 1694], 27.) "*Where there are Envyings and Strifes,* Animosities and Divisions, *there is Confusion and every Evil Work.* Where these Govern, if men can but Obtain their particular Ends and Desires, Advance their Party, Confound their Op-

The Americans had advanced far beyond the point where they could view the problems of liberty and its opposite *simply* in terms of the people against the government. Their political ideas reflected not only the influence of Locke, but also the lessons of their greater experience in self-government. Accordingly, while Locke himself was ambiguous as to how and to what extent the rights of the individual or of minorities would be protected in civil society, his avowed disciples were not. They emphasized the necessity of securing the rights derived from the state of nature against both a monarch and a legislative majority in a civil society. The fear of majority oppression, which has been so persistent and pervasive a factor in American politics, was thus firmly rooted in colonial experience and in the movement of protest which resulted in revolution and independence. When combined with another major modification in the original Locke, this position led the Revolutionists to a radical individualism.

This modification was the substitution of the *pursuit of happiness* for *property* in the Lockeian trilogy of rights. The substitution was not a mere linguistic one made in the Declaration of Independence for rhetorical effect. The colonists had included happiness as one of the natural and fundamental rights in polemical literature of the preceding decade. John Dickinson, for example, had gone so far as to suggest that the constitutionality of Parliamentary statutes be measured by their tendency to make the people of America happy.[12] So indefinite a concept was obviously impossible as a legal test, but the idea of happiness as an end of government was firmly rooted in colonial attitudes before 1776. It was, furthermore, a far more individualistic end than the protection of property.[13]

---

posers they are Content, what Prejudices soever the Publick Suffers: Than all the good Offices that make Society Valuable are Intercepted, and Fierceness, and Provocations, and Injuries Succeed." (Timothy Cutler, *The Firm Union of a People Represented* . . . [New-London, 1717], 33.) "Every large community is constituted of a number of little societies, in which there will be different branches of business. These, whatever pains are taken to prevent it, will have their different connections, and form separate interests; it is vastly difficult for those who govern, to keep the balance so exactly poized that neither part may be injured; but much more, to prevent jealousies and suspicions that things are carried by favor and affection." (Andrew Eliot, *A Sermon Preached before His Excellency Francis Bernard* . . . [Boston, 1765], 14.)

[12] See John Dickinson, *The Political Writings of John Dickinson* . . . (Wilmington, Del., 1801), I, 332, 395.

[13] I do not mean to imply that the exclusion of *property* from the Declaration of Independence meant that Americans had ceased to regard it as a natural right to be secured by government. They had not; many of them probably continued to regard it as superior or prior to that of the pursuit of happiness, while the majority saw no conflict between the two. The line of reasoning to which I would call attention is exemplified in John Dickinson's *An Address to the Committee of Correspondence in Barbados* (Philadelphia, 1766), and in his *Letters from a Farmer in Pennsylvania to the Inhabitants of the British Colonies* (Boston, 1768). From the former: "KINGS or parliaments could not give the rights essential to happiness, as you can confess those invaded by the Stamp Act to be. We claim them from a higher source—from the King of kings, and Lord of all the earth. . . . It would be an insult on the divine Majesty to say, that he has given or allowed any man or body of men a right to make me miserable. If no man or body of men has such a right, I have a right to be happy. If there can be no happiness without freedom, I have a right to be free. If I cannot enjoy freedom without security of property, I have a right to be thus secured." pp. 4–5. From the *Letters from a Farmer*: "Let these truths be indelibly impressed

Property was a tangible, objective element, while happiness was a subjective goal dependent on individual interpretation. Also, the assertion of a right to happiness had strong equalitarian implications. The concept of property as a right to be protected and fostered by government may be and has been interpreted to mean the protection of property already vested in individuals. It may therefore mean the preservation of the *status quo,* and the *status quo* may be an aristocratic one. This seems to have been Locke's intention, for there is nothing in the *Second Treatise* to suggest that he had an economic or social revolution in mind. The idea of the pursuit of happiness necessarily had both dynamic and equalitarian implications, and these have played a substantial role in American politics. The situation at the time of the Revolution was not such as to lead to an explosive implementation of these implications, but the implications were there, and to some extent recognized and acted upon. Since happiness is a subjective state, no individual can decide for another what will promote his happiness. If happiness is really an end of government, and if all men have by nature an equal right to the pursuit of it, then it follows logically that every man should have a voice in the determination of public policy. Thus the two American modifications—the emphasis on happiness rather than property, and the greater concern for the actual implementation of rights in civil society—led to a democratization of Locke as well as to an unequivocal individualism.

The relationship between the ideal of individual happiness and the recognition of factions in society was an important one. As I have indicated before, the Americans had become thoroughly familiar with the existence and operation of factious divisions in society, and they had come to accept with considerable equanimity the fact that self-interest was a primary political motive. They therefore could not, as Locke for the most part did, think and write of "the people" as a corporate whole more or less distinct from the government. Such a dichotomy was not absent from their thought, but because they had already had experience with a relatively high degree of representative government, they were aware of government

---

on our minds—that we cannot be happy without being free—that we cannot be free, without being secure in our property—that we cannot be secure in our property, if, without our consent, others may, as by right, take it away—that taxes imposed on us by Parliament, do thus take it away. . . ." p. 137. Dickinson is here clearly placing happiness as a right logically prior to property and even to liberty, which stand in relation to it as means to end. James Wilson also emphasized happiness rather than property, stating that, "the happiness of the society is the *first* law of every government." Wilson, *Works,* III, 206.

By placing the *pursuit of happiness* in the Declaration, and omitting *property,* Jefferson gave official sanction to these views. If the Declaration had lapsed into obscurity, this departure from Locke's trilogy might not have· been particularly important, except for the historical record. But the Declaration did not become an historian's document merely. It became an ideological force, and this helped to make Jefferson's substitution operative in actual political life. Of course one may also raise the question whether the Declaration would have had the influence that it has had, if the substitution had not been made. Needless to say, the omission of *property* from the Declaration did not keep it from becoming a dominant, if not the dominant, right during certain periods of United States history.

as a tool of the stronger faction among the people. This realistic or pessimistic attitude toward human nature has come to be associated with conservatism, but it had a logical connection with the radical implications of
the Declaration of Independence. It embodied the American view that the
same defects of human nature which Locke and Hobbes had used to
explain the transition from the state of nature to civil society would still
be present in the latter condition and would still jeopardize the ends for
which government was instituted. The connection was succinctly stated
in Jefferson's First Inaugural Address: "Some times it is said that Man
cannot be trusted with the government of himself. Can he then be trusted
with the government of others? Or have we found angels in the form of
kings to govern him?" [14] In other words, the imperfection of man was
itself an argument for republican government. By logical extension, it
was also an argument for a democratic republic. For if all men were
equally entitled to the rights of life, liberty, and the pursuit of happiness,
and if self-interest was a universal characteristic of human nature, then
all men must be given the opportunity of defending their rights against
encroachment by others. Thus, although the colonists had not set out with
the intention of establishing republicanism, once they had done so, as a
corollary of independence, the pessimistic strain in their thought provided
ideological reinforcement for practical accomplishment. Similarly, the
establishment of republican governments served to accentuate the equalitarian and individualistic content of their official philosophy.

This philosophy was one of radical individualism, and it was accepted,
I think, by the majority of Americans at the time, including many of those
who are frequently regarded as conservatives. Without abandoning completely the concept of a common good or public interest or justice, they
tended to regard the pursuit of self-interest as legitimate and sought primarily to avoid an overwhelming concentration of power behind a single
interest, whether it be upper or lower class, urban, rural, northern, southern, or other. It was the refusal of Thomas Paine and Alexander Hamilton
to accept this individualism which made both of them alien to the prevailing political attitude. Paine was a radical democrat, but he could not
stomach the rough and tumble politics of his colleagues in Pennsylvania,
who pursued what he regarded as selfish interests with little restraint.
Similarly, Hamilton could not recognize opposition to his policies as
legitimate because he interpreted the national interest in terms of corporate greatness, while his opponents interpreted it in terms of individual
satisfaction. Paine and Hamilton, therefore, were both conservative in
their attitude toward the proper ends of government and the proper
political behavior of individual citizens. The individualism which they
rejected was not new in theory. It was clearly explicit in *The Leviathan*,
present though somewhat obscured in the *Second Treatise*, and had been

---

[14] Ford, ed., *Works of Jefferson*, IX, 196.

an increasing element in both colonial thought and practice. With the coming of the Revolution it became manifestly operative, and has continued to exert a decisive influence in American politics.

This individualism, rooted in colonial experience but transformed by the break with Britain and the establishment of republican governments, had ramifications which influenced the nature of our political tradition and served further to set it apart from that of the mother country. These ramifications, though some of them did not become apparent until much later, help to illuminate the radical effects of the Revolution.

As I have suggested in the preceding pages, the individualism of the early republic was associated with equalitarianism in civil society as well as in the state of nature. Of this, the Revolutionists were themselves aware. They were less aware of the relativistic implications of the theory summarized in the Declaration, and of the extent to which that theory gave philosophical justification to the egoism which they so frequently and habitually deplored, but which they accepted as an ordinary ingredient of politics. The relativism of the Declaration can be summarized briefly. Two of the central rights, to which all men are entitled, are not amenable to objective definition or delimitation. The *liberty* of the trilogy was to some extent defined in the specific terms of traditional procedural liberties associated with the British constitution or common law, and in the newer substantive terms of freedom of speech, press, and religion. There were also attempts, by Jefferson and Paine, for example, to classify rights into primary and secondary categories, the latter being subject to social or political regulation. Except for the allegedly absolute rights of the first order, a man's liberty was commonly said to extend so far as it did not interfere with or jeopardize the similar liberties of other men. This sounds like a good enough common-sense definition. However, the Revolutionary American conception of society as composed of selfish individuals and groups whose interests would frequently be in conflict, suggests the impossibility of using that common-sense definition in practice with any degree of precision. If, that is to say, men's interests habitually and *normally* come into conflict, then this formula is not altogether relevant or applicable. Somewhat the same thing is true of the third right in the triology, the pursuit of happiness. It is an even more subjective right than liberty. And unless one assumes a very harmonious society, the happiness of different individuals are likely to come in conflict with each other. If all individuals possess these rights equally, and if they are an integral end of government, then there is no logical criterion by which such conflicts can be adjudicated. There is no way to define justice objectively, and there is great difficulty in defining the substantive common good objectively, except perhaps in some obvious crisis of national preservation. What is left is political relativism, combined with a philosophy of natural rights which tended to provide a justification of political and ethical egoism.

I do not think the men of the Revolution were fully aware of the trend of their thought. They continued to think in terms of justice and the general welfare and to deplore man's tendency toward self-interest and bias. Their hostility to parties is in itself an indication of their belief in a common good to which all men owed their allegiance. Nevertheless, the relativism implicit in natural rights doctrine had undermined the operative force of the common good by making it difficult if not impossible to define. This difficulty of defining justice or the common interest would, paradoxically and ironically, encourage the propensity to use ideological stereotypes in political debate.

Had the Americans been imbued with a strong sense of nationalism, or had their security not been so easily achieved by the happy windfall of Louisiana and the physical barrier of the Atlantic Ocean, this relativism might have been balanced by a concern for national defense or perhaps national glory. As it was, the same individualism which produced the relativism contributed to the really profound inclination toward isolation and withdrawal from international affairs. It is perhaps ironical that the Declaration of Independence, written partly for the purpose of securing foreign aid, should have had so strong an influence in the direction of concentration on domestic affairs. Yet I think it did. If the primary function of government is believed to be the protection of individual rights, and if by the grace of history and geography this can be done in the absence of serious and continuous threats from abroad, then it is natural that the people involved should be primarily occupied with immediate and domestic concerns. If, furthermore, they have another ocean to aim at, with nothing much in between but a few savages, and if they regard themselves as the world's torchbearers for a great ideal, whatever ambitions they may have for national and imperial greatness may be satisfied with a minimum awareness of or involvement in the affairs of other nations. There was very little to keep Americans constantly aware of one of the traditional functions of statehood—defense against external danger. This fact, plus the nature of our federal system, inhibited the emergence of a sense of national interest transcendent of individual, group, and sectional interests which would supply content for the concept of the common good. There was thus no strong compensatory factor, such as the mystique of the British Empire, to offset the relativism and individualism implicit in Revolutionary doctrine.

These factors, combined with the Revolutionary acceptance of egoism, gradually brought about a major divergence in the American attitude toward politics from the heritage which the colonists had shared with the home country. At the time of the Revolution, in America as in Britain, politics was an occupation regarded with respect and engaged in by men of distinguished qualities. It was, to use modern sociological terminology, a prestige occupation. To be sure, this condition was due in part to the property qualifications for officeholding. in some colonies and states considerably stiffer than those for voting. But far more important, both ambition and a sense of responsibility drew men of wealth and learning into colonial, state, and federal office. It was Jefferson's intention and hope that his scheme of education would, among other things, provide a reservoir of political leaders—a kind of aristocracy of talent. This concept of aristocratic leadership was undermined in a number of ways. Historically as well as philosophically, it had been linked with belief in an objective good, and it was this link which the idea of happiness as an end of government tended to negate. For if individual happiness—or self-interest— is an end of government, then one man's opinion is as good as another. Thus, though the concept of the public good as a composite of individual and group interests does not require the rejection of wisdom and virtue as a qualification for the exercise of political authority, it does promote a powerful alternative—identity of opinion and interest, or the willingness to give the voter what he wants. To be sure, this was not a peculiarly American phenomenon, as Burke's experience with the electors of Bristol indicates. Furthermore, there was a touch of the Burkeian theory of representation in that of the authors of the Constitution, especially in their attitude toward the Senate. Nevertheless, the realism concerning political motivation and behavior which characterized the American attitude, as it was summarized in the Tenth *Federalist,* expressed something very close to a theory of pressure group politics. And it is this kind of politics which, by and large, has dominated the American tradition. However, Americans have never been completely comfortable with it, and their uneasiness has produced a reliable scapegoat. At the time of the Revolution, dissatisfaction found expression and release in the almost universal dislike and distrust of parties, a tribute to the lost ideal of a transcendent public good. Gradually, this antipathy was extended to the men who manned and ran the parties, the politicians. There has thus been a peculiar schizophrenia in the American political mind. On the one hand, we have engaged in pressure and partisan politics continuously and with vigor; on the other, we despise the men who act as brokers to carry out our demands, whether honestly or corruptly. Even now, a sure way of winning popular approval is to create the image that one is not a politician. Something of the same attitude is involved in the American reaction to the word and the fact of bipartisanship; it gives a comfortable sense of satisfied virtue. This distrust and contempt for politicians is no doubt partially attributable to the personal corruption of individuals, but it has more profound causes, and one of these is the somewhat obscurely felt dissatisfaction with the relativism and its consequent pressure group politics which have as their basis the radical individualism of the Declaration of Independence.

VI

Equally radical was the Revolution's culmination, the creation and adoption of the Constitution of 1787. There had been federations of states before, both in ancient and modern times, and the idea of a central government had become familiar in America with the Albany Plan, the first two Continental Congresses, and the Articles of Confederation. What was new was the direct control over the central government exercised by the electorate, the relative independence of that government with respect to the governments of the constituent states, and its direct authority over the individual citizens of those states. This was a government so new that, as its critics gibed, it lacked a name. It was, in the strict meaning of the word, radical.

Its opponents perceived this fact from the very beginning, and both the spirit and substance of their polemics provide evidence of a typically conservative stance. They argued that the Philadelphia Convention had gone too far, that they had exceeded their instructions, that there was no necessity for an entirely new frame of government, and that a little patching up of the Articles of Confederation would have been sufficient. They pointed out that what was proposed had never been done before and bewailed the loss of resistance to innovation which the Revolution itself had induced in the people. They paraded a succession of imaginary horribles, and they said that the authors of the Constitution had based their scheme of government on too optimistic a vew of human nature. Furthermore, they saw quite clearly that the Constitution, if adopted, would bring about a new kind of politics in which large-scale organization would be a major factor, and they identified the old, familiar, personal politics with liberty and responsible government. Most important and most significant, they denied that the principle and practice of republicanism could be made operative over the area and population then embraced by the thirteen separate states. Their position, both with respect to the *status quo* of 1776–87 and with that of the pre-Revolutionary experience of self-government, was the conservative one in the great debate over ratification.[15]

It was the Founding Fathers who were the true radicals. In the very first number of *The Federalist,* Hamilton struck a radical stance when he stated that the question for decision was whether mankind could deter-

---

[15] This interpretation is presented at some length in my article, "Men of Little Faith: The Anti-Federalists on the Nature of Representative Government," *Wm. and Mary Qtly.,* 3d Ser., XII (1955), 3–43.

mine its government by deliberate choice or must continue to be subject to the forces of accident and chance.[16] Indeed, the whole idea of drafting a constitution for an entire nation and then submitting it to conventions chosen by the people for ratification or rejection was radical in the extreme, though the example of Massachusetts had provided a precedent for a similar procedure on a much smaller scale. Scholars may argue until doomsday as to whether the Constitution was democratic or not, but they are less likely to argue as to whether it was a new departure in political institutions. It must rank with the establishment of republican government and the philosophy of the Declaration of Independence as one of the great and radical achievements of the Revolution.

VII

The establishment of a new nation, the initiation of the first great modern experiment in republican government, the combination of this experiment with an entirely new kind of federalism, the crystallization in operative form of a political philosophy of individualism and equality —these were the results of the American Revolution. Together with the Revolutionary experience itself, they gave decisive shape to the American political tradition and, in particular, operated to differentiate it from that of the mother country and from those of the older British Commonwealths which won their independence in a later period and without revolution. The relatively short period of intensive opposition and resistance to imperial impositions, the realistic recognition of egoism as a general cause of these, the emphasis in the Declaration on the rights of the individual combined to fix in the American mind an ineradicable fear and distrust of government and government officials, even when popularly elected. This general fear was more profound and more enduring than the specific fear of the executive which stemmed from colonial experience with nonelective governors, and helped to sustain the system of separation of powers, which was also rooted in colonial institutions. Later, the individualist relativism implicit in the Declaration, added to this recognition of egoism, accentuated the distrust of politicians, and reduced the prestige of government as a career. To fear and distrust of government, there was thus added contempt. The American attitude toward government as a necessary evil (and probably more evil than necessary) goes back to the Revolution. It has, perhaps paradoxically, continued to find expression in the strong localist conservatism which helped precipitate the Revolution and later provided much of the opposition to the Constitution. Our Revolutionary experience also both embodied and encouraged that peculiar combination of pragmatism and appeal to ideological principles which has character-

[16] Hamilton, Madison, and Jay, *The Federalist*, ed., Wright, 89.

ized American political thinking. The men of 1776 did not set out to establish republicanism, but once they had done so as a means of securing the rights of life, liberty, and the pursuit of happiness, republicanism itself became a principle of political right. So it has been with later concepts. We have not asked only whether policies would or would not contribute to the realization of these rights; we have asked whether the policies were democratic or antidemocratic, socialist or laissez-faire. Our political tradition has involved the interaction of pragmatic and ideological attitudes and thus has reflected the spirit of 1776.

That spirit was not a particularly radical one, certainly not when compared with that of the French Revolution, the Soviet Revolution of 1917, or the nationalist revolutions of the present time. It had a profoundly conservative aspect, and the radicalism it involved was of a very sober variety. Apart from the recent revival of conservatism and the consequent desire to establish its roots in the political foundation of the nation, there are excellent reasons for regarding the American Revolution as conservative—at least in some respects.

It was a limited revolution, and it was primarily a political movement. There were some social and economic repercussions, but there was no concerted, deliberate attempt at wholesale reconstruction of society or of the habits and everyday lives of the people. There was no American Robespierre or Lenin; Thomas Paine, who looked like a radical in the American context, was imprisoned in France because of the moderate position he took there. The American leaders, even while initiating radical changes, acted with sobriety and, with some exceptions, exhibited a political sophistication based on experience in politics other than as revolutionists.

Most important of all, the Revolution began as a movement of conservative protest, and none of its results represented a total break with the colonial past. Independence had been preceded by a long enjoyment of considerable autonomy; long before Paul Revere ordered lanterns hung in the Old North Church, John Winthrop had mounted a cannon on Beacon Hill to repel any British attempt to seize the Charter of the Colony. Before Thomas Paine ridiculed the British Monarchy in *Common Sense*, the colonists had put a bridle on their governors. The ideas expressed in the second paragraph of the Declaration of Independence were not quite so firmly rooted in colonial experience, and the fact of their formal acceptance gave them an operative force they had previously lacked. But if we are to believe Thomas Jefferson, even they had become embedded in the American mind. The one thing which was most truly radical was the new federalism of the Constitution of 1787. Even it had been preceded by the lesser authority of the Empire and the experience of intercolonial cooperation preceding the war and under the Articles of Confederation. And it was combined with a structure of government, many of whose elements were familiar, because they, too, were rooted in colonial institutions.

So it seems to me that we must conclude that the American Revolution was partly radical and partly conservative. If I may borrow a figure from the great Greek so despised by the author of the Declaration of Independence, the character of the Revolution was the character of the men who made it writ large.[17] Their attitude toward the past was selective. Part of it they wished to preserve, part of it they wished to abandon. They were quite self-conscious about the newness of their enterprise and referred to it frequently as an experiment, but they never had the slightest inclination to repudiate the whole of their British heritage or of their colonial past. They had some fine old bricks to start with, and they knew it. Nevertheless, what they designed and partly built from these bricks was not Georgian. It was American, and they knew that too.

Revolution and the Political Integration of the Enslaved and Disenfranchised
—*Gordon S. Wood*

The radical character of the American Revolution is a subject of some historical controversy. Yet in one important respect there can be no denying its radicalism. The Revolution transformed the American colonies into republics, which meant that ordinary people were no longer to be considered "subjects" to be ruled as they were under a monarchy. They were thereafter to be citizens—participants themselves in the ruling process. This is what democracy has come to mean for us.

The profoundest revolution of the past 200 years has been this introduction of ordinary people into the political process. For America and the rest of the Western world, this Revolution was most dramatically expressed at the end of the eighteenth century—"the age of the democratic

From Gordon S. Wood, *Revolution and the Political Integration of the Enslaved and Disenfranchised*. Copyright 1974 by the American Enterprise Institute as part of the American Enterprise Institute's Lecture Series on American Bicentennial.

[17] In a letter to John Adams in 1814, Jefferson criticized *The Republic* severely and speculated as to the reasons for Plato's reputation. His general estimate of the great philosopher is suggested by these references scattered throughout a lengthy passage: "the whimsies, the puerilities, and unintelligible jargon of this work," "nonsense," "foggy mind;" he also concluded that Plato's dialogues "are libels on Socrates." Jefferson to John Adams, July 5, 1814, in Ford, ed., *Works of Jefferson*, XI, 396–398.

revolution," as it has been called.[1] This bringing of the people into politics extended through the next fifty years in the United States, while in Western Europe it took much longer, requiring at least the greater part of the nineteenth century. And of course for the rest of the world the process is still going on. In fact since 1945 with the emergence of new nations and the Third World, we have been witnessing what has been called a "participation explosion,"[2] the rapid incorporation into the political process of peoples who had hitherto been outside of politics, in a hurried, even a desperate, effort by underdeveloped nations to catch up with the modern democratic states.

More than anything else this incorporation of common ordinary people into politics is what sets the modern world apart from what went on before. Americans were in the vanguard of this development. Our assumption of the leadership of the democratic nations is not simply based on our preponderance of power since 1945. Ever since the American Revolution we have claimed the leadership of the Free World, even when we were an underdeveloped nation ourselves and our claims were treated with bemused contempt by Europe. Our assertions of leadership were based on our priority in time: we were the first modern nation to have a democratic revolution and to establish a republic in which citizenship and political participation belong to the whole community. The French Revolution and all the other European revolutions of the nineteenth century were in our eyes merely examples or species of the revolutionary genus that we had created. Part of the explanation for the intensity of the ideological confrontation between the United States and the Soviet Union since the Communist Revolution of 1917 comes from the Soviet Union's claim that it has created a new revolutionary tradition, a new revolutionary genus, one which threatens to usurp our position in the vanguard of history.

We Americans have never been able to figure out why the rest of the world has had such a hard time catching up with us. Because the process of creating a republican citizenry seemed so simple for us, we have believed it ought to be simple for others. It seems to us to be merely a matter of allowing the people to vote. Because voting is the most obvious means by which the people participate in politics, we have tended to emphasize the right to vote as the necessary and sufficient criterion of democratic politics. But this is a mistake. The suffrage is clearly a prerequisite for democratic politics, but it is hardly all there is to it. It is important for us in our bicentennial celebrations to examine our Revolution and its heritage and to seek to understand the sources of our political practice and values. Only with knowledge of the conditions

[1] R. R. Palmer, *The Age of the Democratic Revolution: A Political History of Europe and America, 1760–1800*, 2 vols. (Princeton: Princeton University Press, 1959, 1964).
[2] Gabriel A. Almond and Sidney Verba, *The Civic Culture: Political Attitudes and Democracy in Five Nations* (Boston: Little, Brown & Co., Inc., 1965), p. 2.

that underlie the principle of consent in our polity can we confront the world and the future. Voting is in fact only the exposed tip of an incredibly complicated political and social process. How this process came about and how the people became involved in politics are questions that lie at the heart of the American Revolution.

I

The American Revolution was both a consequence and a cause of democracy. It came to mark a decisive change in the way political activity was carried on in America. It gave new legitimacy to the involvement of common people in politics. It was not, however, simply a matter of enfranchising new voters. Although the franchise in colonial America was confined by property qualifications as it was in eighteenth century England, property owning was so widespread that the colonists enjoyed the broadest suffrage of any people in the world: perhaps 80 percent of white adult males could vote. Yet the fact remains that most of those enfranchised did not exercise the right. The social structure and social values were such that colonial politics, at least when compared to politics in post-revolutionary America, were remarkably stable, and the percentage of the people actually voting and participating in politics remained small—much smaller even than today. In the eighteenth century the legal exclusion of the propertyless from the franchise was based not on the fear that the poor might confiscate the wealth of the aristocratic few, but on the opposite fear: that the aristocratic few might manipulate and corrupt the poor for their own ends. Established social leaders expected deference from those below them, and generally got it and were habitually reelected to political office. There were no organized political parties and no professional politicians in today's sense of those words. Established merchants, wealthy lawyers, and large planters held the major offices and ran political affairs as part of the responsibility of their elevated social positions. It was rare for a tavern keeper or small farmer to gain a political office of any consequence. Men were granted political authority in accord not with their seniority or experience in politics but with their established economic and social superiority. Thus Thomas Hutchinson, son of a distinguished Boston mercantile family, was elected to the Massachusetts House of Representatives at the age of twenty-six and almost immediately became its speaker. Social and political authority was indivisible and men moved horizontally into politics from the society, rather than (as is common today) moving up vertically through an exclusively political hierarchy.

Yet politics in eighteenth-century colonial America was unstable enough in many areas that members of the elite struggled for political power and precedence among themselves. The social hierarchy was sufficiently confused at the top that it was never entirely clear who was destined to hold political office and govern. It was obvious that well-to-do lawyers or merchants were superior to, say, blacksmiths, but among several well-to-do lawyers or merchants superiority was not so visible and incontestable. These were the conditions that led to the formation of political factions —the shifting conglomerations of competing elites that characterized much of eighteenth-century colonial politics. While some members of the elite sought the leverage of the Crown in gaining and wielding political power, others turned to the only alternative source of political authority recognized in eighteenth century Anglo-American political theory—the people.

In the half century before the Revolution these competing elites found themselves, as a tactical device, invoking "the people" to offset the power of the Crown and to gain political office. In the process they steadily mobilized elements of the population that had not been involved in politics earlier. This popularization of politics during the decades before the Revolution can be traced in various ways—in the rise in voter participation, the increase in contested elections, the resort to caucuses, tickets and other forms of political organization, and the growth of campaign propaganda and professional pamphleteering. This is how democracy began to develop. It was not the result of the people arousing themselves spontaneously and clamoring from below for a share in political authority. Rather democracy was created from above: the people were cajoled, persuaded, even frightened into getting involved. Each competing faction tried to outdo its opponents in posing as a friend of the people, defending popular rights and advancing popular interests. Yet over time what began as a pose eventually assumed a reality that had not been anticipated. The people having been invoked could not easily be laid to rest. By the middle decades of the eighteenth century, American politics was on the verge of a radical transformation—a radical transformation that was both expressed and amplified by the Revolution.

The Revolution made the people sovereign. The practices of mobilizing the people into politics that had begun before the Revolution now increased dramatically, as political leaders competed with each other for the power and endorsement that being a friend of the people brought. First the authority of the English government was challenged for its inability to represent not only the American people but its own people as well. Then in America all authority was challenged by what eventually seemed to be ceaseless appeals to the people. For no institution seemed capable of embodying their will. The Revolution so intensified the people's dominance in politics that there could never thereafter be any escaping from them. In America's new republican consciousness there could be nothing else in politics—no orders, no estates, no lords, no court, no monarch, not even rulers in the traditional sense—only the people. How they expressed themselves, how they participated in government, how they gave their consent, how they were represented were questions that preoccupied Americans in the Revolution and ever after.

During the Revolution Americans put together an idea of popular representation in government that we have never lost. The controversy and debate with England in the 1760s exposed a basic Anglo-American difference of experience and viewpoint concerning representation—a difference that only widened with the Revolution. For their part the English clung to what they called "virtual representation." England's eighteenth-century electorate comprised only a small proportion of its population and bore little relation to shifts in that population. The electoral districts were a hodgepodge left over from centuries of history. Thus ancient rotten boroughs like Old Sarum, completely depopulated by the eighteenth century, continued to send members to the House of Commons while newer large cities like Manchester and Birmingham sent none. Such apparent anomalies were justified on the not unreasonable grounds that each member of Parliament should represent not any particular locality but the whole community. Parliament, as Edmund Burke said, was not "a *congress* of ambassadors from different and hostile interests . . . but . . . a *deliberative* assembly of *one* nation, with *one* interest, that of the whole."[3] To the English what made a member of Parliament representative was not voting or the electoral process, which were considered incidental, but the mutuality of interests that presumably existed between the representative and the people. This mutuality of interests tied the people to the representative even without the exercise of the franchise. Hence the English thought of the members of Parliament as virtually representing all those who did not vote for them —including the colonists.

To the Americans, however, whose experience in politics had developed differently from that of the mother country, representation possessed an actual and local character. Their electoral districts were not the consequence of history going back to time immemorial but were recent and regular creations that bore a distinct relation to changes in their population. When a new county or a town was created by the colonists, it was usually granted immediate representation in the legislature. Thus Americans came to think of their legislatures as precisely what Burke denied they should be—as congresses of ambassadors from different and contending localities and interests, of all whose consent had to be real and explicit. Hence they could not accept the British contention that they were virtually represented, like the people of Manchester, in the English Parliament and therefore capable of being taxed by it. In the course of a century and a half the American colonists had developed such a keen awareness of the individuality of their interests that they could not understand how anyone could speak for them in whose election they had no voice. Such a sense of particularity put a premium on voting as

---

[3] Edmund Burke, "Speech to the Electors of Bristol" (1774), *The Works of the Right Honorable Edmund Burke,* rev. ed. (Boston: Little, Brown & Co., Inc., 1865–66), vol 2, p. 96.

the sole measure of representation and on ensuring that all participated equally in the process of consent.

The ramifications of these ideas about representation were immense and we are still feeling their effects today. During the Revolution and in the years following, they led, first, to heightened demands for an expansion of the suffrage and, second, to the growing notion of "one man, one vote," a notion which has resulted in continual attempts to relate representation to demographic changes. Finally the belief that voting itself was the sole criterion of representation has in time transformed all elected officials, including governors and members of upper houses, into other kinds of representatives of the people, standing in a sometimes awkward relationship to the original houses of representatives.

This extreme localism and the demand for actuality of representation had more than constitutional importance. It had social implications of even greater significance for the character of our politics. Even before the revolutionary turmoil had settled, some Americans were arguing that mere voting by ordinary men was not a sufficient protection of ordinary men's interests, if only members of the elite were being elected. It was coming to be thought that in a society of diverse and particular interests men from one class or group, however educated and respectable, could not be acquainted with the needs of another class or group. Wealthy college-educated lawyers or merchants could not know the concerns of poor farmers or small tradesmen. The logic of the actuality of representation expressed in the Revolution required that ordinary men be represented by ordinary men. It was not enough for elected officials to be simply *for* the people; they now had to be *of* the people as well.

Such an idea constituted an extraordinary transformation in the way people looked at the relation between government and society; it lay at the heart of the radicalism of the American Revolution. It was strengthened by a powerful ideological force—equality—the most important and corrosive doctrine in American culture. At the outset of the Revolution, equality to most American leaders had meant an equality of legal rights and the opportunity to rise by merit through clearly discernible ranks. But in the hands of competing politicians seeking to diminish the stature of their opponents and win votes, the idea of equality was expanded in ways that few of its supporters had originally anticipated to mean in time that one man was as good as another. This meaning of equality soon dissolved the traditional identity between social and political leadership and helped to give political power to the kinds of men who had hitherto never held it. Politics became egalitarian after the Revolution in ways it never had been before, and the political upstarts—obscure men with obscure backgrounds—launched vigorous attacks on the former attributes of social superiority—names, titles, social origins, family connections— and bragged that their own positions were based not on relatives or friends but only on what their money had made for them.

We have a particularly illuminating example of the new attitudes in the case of a William Thompson, an unknown tavern keeper of Charleston, South Carolina, of the early 1780s. John Rutledge, a distinguished social and political leader in South Carolina, had sent a female servant to Thompson's tavern to watch a fireworks display from the roof. Thompson denied the servant admittance and sent her back to Rutledge, who was furious and requested that Thompson come to his house and apologize. Thompson refused and, believing his honor affronted by Rutledge's arrogant request, challenged Rutledge to a duel. Now the social likes of Rutledge did not accept challenges from tavern keepers, so Rutledge went to the South Carolina House of Representatives, of which he was a member, and demanded that it pass a bill banishing Thompson from the state for insulting a member of its government. Thompson took to the press for his defense and in 1784 made what can only be described as a classic expression of American egalitarian resentment against social superiority—a resentment voiced, as Thompson said, not on behalf of himself but on behalf of the people, or "those more especially, who go at this day, under the opprobrious appellation of, the *Lower Orders of Men.*"

Thompson was not merely attacking the few aristocratic "Nabobs" who had humiliated him; he was actually assaulting the entire idea of a social hierarchy ruled by a gentlemanly elite. In fact he turned prevailing eighteenth century opinion upside down and argued that the social aristocracy was peculiarly *unqualified* to rule politically. Rather than preparing men for political leadership in a free government, said Thompson, "signal opulence and influence," especially when united "by intermarriage or otherwise," were really "calculated to subvert *Republicanism.*" The "persons and conduct" of the South Carolina "Nabobs" like Rutledge "in *private* life, may be unexceptionable, and even amiable, but their pride, influence, ambition, connections, wealth, and political principles," Thompson argued, "ought in *public* life, ever to exclude them from *public confidence.*" All that was needed in republican leadership, said Thompson, was "being *good, able, useful, and friends to social equality,*" for in a republican government "consequence is from the *public opinion,* and not from *private fancy.*" In the press Thompson sardonically recounted how he, a tavern keeper, "a *wretch* of no higher rank in the Commonwealth than that of Common-Citizen," had been debased by what he called "those *self-exalted* characters, who affect to compose the *grand hierarchy* of the State, . . . for having dared to dispute with a John Rutledge, or any of the NABOB *tribe.*" The experience had been degrading enough to Thompson as a man but as a former militia officer it had been, he said, "insupportable"—indicating how revolutionary military service affected social mobility and social expectations. Undoubtedly, said Thompson, Rutledge had "conceived me his inferior." But like many others in these years—tavern keepers, farmers, petty merchants, small-time lawyers, former militia officers—Thompson could no longer "comprehend the *inferiority*." [4]

Many new politicians in the decades following, likewise not being able to comprehend their inferiority, used the popular and egalitarian ideals of the Revolution to upset the older social hierarchy and bring ordinary people like themselves into politics. This was not always easy, for, as some politicians complained, "the poorer commonality," even when they possessed the legal right to vote, seemed apathetic to appeals and too accepting of traditional authority. Their ideas of government had too long been "rather aristocratical than popular." "The rich," said one polemicist, "having been used to govern, seem to think it is their right," while the common people, "having hitherto had little or no hand in government, seem to think it does not belong to them to have any." [5] To convince the people that they rightfully had a share in government became the task of egalitarian politicians in the decades after the Revolution, giving birth in the process to modern democratic politics. This democratization of politics involved not only the legal widening of the electorate, but also the extension of practices begun before the Revolution in activating those who legally could but often did not vote.

More and more offices, including judgeships, were made directly elective and everyone, it seemed, was now "running"—not, as earlier, simply "standing"—for election. New acts of persuasion using cheap newspapers and mass meetings were developed, and politics assumed carnival-like characteristics that led during the nineteenth century to participation by higher percentages of the electorate than ever again was achieved in American politics. In such an atmosphere of stump-speaking and "running" for office the members of the older gentry were frequently at a considerable disadvantage. In fact by the early nineteenth century being a gentleman or professing the characteristics of a gentleman became a liability in elections in some parts of the country, and a member of the gentry campaigning for votes was forced to take off his white gloves if he wanted to beat the tavern keeper who was calling him an aristocratic dandy.

One of the most graphic examples of this kind of change in American politics occurred in the 1868 election campaign for the fifth congressional district of Massachusetts—Essex County, the former center of Massachusetts Brahminism but by the mid-nineteenth century increasingly filled by Irish immigrants. The campaign was essentially between Richard Henry Dana, Jr., a well-to-do and Harvard-educated descendant of a distinguished Massachusetts family and author of *Two Years Before the Mast*, and Benjamin Butler, son of a boardinghouse keeper who had

---

[4] Gordon S. Wood, *The Creation of the American Republic, 1776–1787* (Chapel Hill: University of North Carolina Press, 1969), pp. 482–483.
[5] Philadelphia, *Pennsylvania Evening Post*, July 30, 1776, quoted in David Hawke, *In the Midst of a Revolution* (Philadelphia: University of Pennsylvania Press, 1961), p. 187.

never been to college and one of the most flamboyant demagogues American politics has ever produced. (One gets some idea of Butler's standing with the Massachusetts elite by realizing that he was the first governor of Massachusetts in over two centuries not invited to a Harvard College commencement.) In the congressional campaign Butler showed Dana what nineteenth century electoral politics was all about. While Dana was talking to tea groups about bond payments, Butler was haranguing the Irish shoe workers of Lynn, organizing parades, turning out the fire and police departments, hiring brass bands, distributing hundreds of pamphlets and torches, and charging his opponent with being a Beau Brummel in white gloves. Dana was simply no match for him. When Dana was finally forced to confront audiences of workingmen, he gave up talking about bonds and even doffed his white gloves, trying desperately to assure his audiences that he too worked hard. All the while Butler was making fun of his efforts to make common cause with the people. During one speech Dana told the Irish shoe workers that when he spent two years before the mast as a young sailor he too was a laborer who didn't wear any white gloves: "I was as dirty as any of you," he exclaimed. With such statements it is not surprising that Dana ended up with less than 10 percent of the vote in a humiliating loss to Butler.[6]

The rise of egalitarian politics, evident in Butler's campaigning, was the result not only of an expanded electorate but also of the final collapse of the older social hierarchy and the traditional belief in elite rule. It was this kind of change in the first half of the nineteenth century that made the rise of political parties both necessary and possible. Indeed, the United States was the first nation to develop modern political parties. The broadened electorate and the end of any sort of automatic assumption of political leadership by the social elite required new instruments for the mobilization of voters and the recruitment of leaders. Individuals, cut loose from traditional ties to the social hierarchy, were now forced to combine in new groups for political ends. Political office no longer was set by social ascription but rather was won by political achievement within the organization of a party and through the winning of votes. By vying for political leadership and competing for votes, new men—not necessarily as flamboyant as Butler but having the same social obscurity and doomed in any other kind of society to remain in obscurity —were fed into the political process and rose not because they became gentry but because they knew how to appeal to the people.

It was the American Revolution that helped to make possible and to accelerate these changes in our politics. As a result of this republican Revolution, Americans could not easily legitimize any status other than that of citizen. The people were all there was in politics and all of the people were equal. Any sort of unequal restrictions on the rights of

---

[6] Samuel Shapiro, " 'Aristocracy, Mud, and Vituperation': The Butler–Dana Campaign," *New England Quarterly*, vol. 31 (1958), pp. 340–360.

citizenship—on the right to run for office or to vote, for example—were anomalies, relics of an older society, that now had to be done away with. In the early decades of the nineteenth century the permissive ideas of representation, citizenship, and equality encouraged competing political parties to search out groups of people hitherto uninvolved in the political process and bring them in—renters denied the suffrage because they were not freeholders, poor men who lacked the necessary property qualifi- cations, or newly arrived immigrants, anyone who might become a voter and supporter of the party, or even one of its leaders. If they could not yet legally vote, the vote could be given them. If they could legally vote but did not, then they could be convinced they ought to. In these ways American politicians in the decades following the Revolution worked to establish universal manhood suffrage and democratic politics.

We take these developments for granted and easily forget how far ahead of the rest of the world the United States was in the early nineteenth century. Tavern keepers and weavers were sitting in our legislatures while Europeans were still trying to disentangle voting and representa- tion from an incredible variety of estate and corporate statuses. In 1792 Kentucky entered the union with a constitution allowing universal manhood suffrage. A generation later the English were still debating whether voting was a privilege confined to a few; in fact England had to wait until 1867 before workingmen got the vote and became, in Glad- stone's words, "our fellow subjects." Indeed, in many parts of the world today the people are still waiting to become citizens, full participants in the political process.

II

Yet, as we all too well know, America's record in integrating the people into politics has not been entirely a success story. The great anomaly amidst all the revolutionary talk of equality, voting, and representation was slavery. Indeed, it was the Revolution itself, not only with its appeal to liberty but with its idea of citizenship of equal individuals, that made slavery in 1776 suddenly seem anomalous to large numbers of Americans. What had often been taken for granted earlier in the eighteenth century as part of the brutality of life—regarded as merely the most base and degraded status in a society of infinite degrees and multiple ranks of freedom and unfreedom—now seemed conspicuous and peculiar. In a republic, as was not the case in a monarchy, there could be no place for degrees of freedom or dependency. In the North, where slavery was considerable but not deeply rooted, the exposure of the anomaly worked to abolish it: by 1830 in the northern states there were less than 3,000 black slaves out of a northern black population of over 125,000.[7] In the South the suddenly exposed anomaly of slavery threw

[7] Arthur Zilversmit, The First Emancipation: The Abolition of Slavery in the North (Chicago: University of Chicago Press, 1967), p. 222.

southern whites, who had been in the vanguard of the revolutionary movement and among the most fervent spokesmen for its libertarianism, onto the defensive and gradually separated them from the mainstream of America's egalitarian developments.

Yet the very egalitarianism of America's republican ideology—the egalitarianism that undercut the rationale of slavery—worked at the same time to inhibit integrating the free black man into the political nation. Since republican citizenship implied equality for all citizens, a person once admitted as a citizen into the political process was put on a level with all other citizens and regarded as being as good as the next man. With the spread of these republican assumptions northern whites began to view black voters with increasing apprehension, unwilling to accept the equality that suffrage and citizenship dictated. In 1800 in many states of the North free Negroes possessed the right to vote (often as a result of the general extension of the franchise that took place during the Revolution), and they exercised it in some areas with particular effectiveness. But in subsequent years, as the electorate continued to expand through changes in the law and the mobilization of new voters, the blacks found themselves being squeezed out. There is perhaps no greater irony in the democratization of American politics in the first half of the nineteenth century than the fact that as the white man gained the vote the black man lost it. During the heyday of Jacksonian democracy white populist majorities in state after state in the North moved to eliminate the remaining property restrictions on white voters while at the same time concocting new restrictions to take away the franchise from Negro voters who had in some cases exercised it for decades. No state admitted to the union after 1819 allowed blacks to vote. By 1840, 93 per cent of northern free Negroes lived in states which completely or practically excluded them from the suffrage and hence from participation in politics.[8]

This exclusion of blacks from politics was largely a consequence of white fears of the equality that republican citizenship demanded. But it was also a product of competitive democratic politics. In some states, like Pennsylvania, Negro exclusion was the price paid for lower-class whites' gaining the right to vote—universal manhood suffrage having been opposed on the grounds it would add too many blacks to the electorate. In other states, like New York, exclusion of the Negro from the franchise was an effective way for Democratic party majorities to eliminate once and for all blocs of Negro voters who had tended to vote first for Federalist and then for Whig candidates. Since the Democratic party, as the spokesman for the popular cause against elitism, was in the forefront of the move to expand the suffrage, it seemed to be good politics for the party not only to attract new voters to its ranks but

---

[8] Leon F. Litwack, *North of Slavery: The Negro in the Free States, 1790–1860* (Chicago: University of Chicago Press, 1961), p. 75.

to take away voters who supported its opponents. It was this kind of political pressure that led to the peculiar situation in some states where immigrant aliens were granted the right to vote before they became citizens whereas Negroes born and bred in the United States had theirs abolished—a development often based on a shrewd assessment by politicians of what particular parties the new immigrants and the blacks would support.

For a republican society it was an impossible situation and Americans wrestled with it for over a half century. Federal officials in the first half of the nineteenth century could never decide the precise status of free Negroes, sometimes arguing that blacks were not citizens in having the right to vote but were citizens in having the right to secure passports. Others tried to discover some sort of intermediate legal position for free blacks as denizens standing between aliens and citizens. But the logic of republican equality would not allow these distinctions, and sooner or later many sought escape from the dilemma posed by Negro disfranchisement by denying citizenship outright to all blacks, whether slave or free, the position Chief Justice Taney tried to establish in the Dred Scott decision of 1857. The suffrage had become sufficiently equated with representation in America so that if a person was not granted the right to vote then he was not represented in the community; and not being represented in a republican community was equivalent to not being a citizen. In the end enslaved blacks without liberty and free blacks without citizenship were such contradictions of the revolutionary ideals that sooner or later those contradictions had to tear the country apart.

When northerners came to debate methods of southern reconstruction at the end of the Civil War, they moved reluctantly but steadily toward Negro enfranchisement, impelled both by the logic of the persisting ideals of the Revolution and by the circumstances of politics. Although some historians have believed that the Republican party's espousal of Negro suffrage in the late 1860s was based on a cynical desire to recruit new voters to the party, it was obviously based on much more than that. In terms of political expediency alone the Republicans' sponsorship of Negro suffrage ran the risk even in the North of what we have come to call "white backlash." Many advocates of Negro suffrage sincerely believed, as Wendell Philips put it, that America could never be truly a united nation "until every class God has made, from the lakes to the Gulf, has its ballot to protect itself." [9]

Yet there can be no doubt that black enfranchisement after the Civil War was fed, like all reforms, by political exigencies, and that many northerners and Republicans favored it grudgingly and only as a means of preventing the resurgence of an unreconstructed Democratic South

---

[9] James M. McPherson, "The Ballot and Land for the Freedmen, 1861–1865," in Kenneth M. Stampp and Leon F. Litwack, eds., *Reconstruction: An Anthology of Revisionist Writings* (Baton Rouge: Louisiana State University Press, 1969), p. 138.

that would threaten the dominance of the Republican party. Hence there resulted an awkward gap between the Fourteenth Amendment, which defined citizenship for the first time and gave it a national emphasis which it had hitherto lacked, and the Fifteenth Amendment, which enfranchised the Negro but unfortunately linked his enfranchisement not to his citizenship but to his race. This linkage allowed a state to impose any voting qualifications it chose so long as they were not based on race, creating a tangled situation that twentieth-century Americans are still trying to unravel.

III

Although Americans have hesitated to make the connection between citizenship and the right to vote explicit and unequivocal, everything in American history has pointed toward that connection. During the past decade or so, largely under the impetus of the civil rights movement but going beyond that, there has been heightened interest in political and voting rights, and the logic of principles concerning suffrage and representation first articulated in the Revolution 200 years ago has been drawn out. Voting rights acts and the anti-poll tax amendment of the mid-1960s were based on a deeply rooted belief that no nation like ours could in conscience exclude any of its citizens from the political process. It was the same legacy from the Revolution that led the Supreme Court in a series of reapportionment decisions to apply the idea of "one man, one vote" to congressional and state legislative electoral districting. Large and unequal campaign contributions are of such concern precisely because they seem to negate the effects of an equal suffrage and to do violence to equality of participation in the political process. Despite an electorate that at times seems apathetic, interest in the suffrage and in the actuality and equality of consent has never been greater than it is today. Such a concern naturally puts a terrific burden on our political system, but it is a burden we should gladly bear (and many other nations would love to have it), for it bespeaks an underlying popular confidence in the processes of politics that surface events and news headlines make us too easily ignore.

In fact, concern with the suffrage and with the formal rights of consent has assumed such a transcendent significance that it has sometimes obscured the substance of democratic politics and has led to an exaggeration of the real power of the legal right to vote. The suffrage has become such a symbol of citizenship that its possession seems necessarily to involve all kinds of rights. Thus acquiring the vote has often seemed an instrument of reform, a means of solving complicated social problems. The women's rights movement of the nineteenth century—premised on the belief, as one woman put it in 1848, that "there is no reality in any power that cannot be coined into votes"—came to focus almost exclusively on the gaining of the suffrage.[10] And when the Nineteenth Amendment giving women the franchise was finally ratified in 1920 and did not lead to the promised revolution, the sense of failure set the feminist movement back at least a half century—a setback from which it has only recently been recovering. Even today this formal integration into the political process through the suffrage continues to be regarded as a panacea for social ills. Certainly this assumption lay behind the response to the youth rebellions of the late 1960s and the eventual adoption of the Twenty-sixth Amendment granting eighteen-year-olds the vote.

This special fascination with politics and this reliance on political integration through voting as a means of solving social problems are legacies of our Revolution, and they are as alive now as they were 200 years ago. The Revolution not only brought ordinary people into politics. It also created such a confidence in the suffrage as the sole criterion of representation that we have too often forgotten just what makes the right to vote workable in America. In our dealings with newly developing nations we are too apt to believe that the mere institution of the ballot in a new state will automatically create a viable democratic society, and we are confused and disillusioned when this rarely happens.

The point is that we have the relationship backwards. It is not the suffrage that gives life to our democracy; it is our democratic society that gives life to the suffrage. American society is permeated by the belief in (and to an extraordinary extent by the reality of) equality that makes our reliance on the ballot operable. As historians in the past two decades have only begun to discover, it was not the breadth of the franchise in the nineteenth century that created democratic politics. The franchise was broad even in colonial times. Rather it was the egalitarian process of politics that led to the mobilization of voters and the political integration of the nation. It was the work of countless politicians recruited from all levels of society and representing many diverse elements, attempting to win elections by exhorting and pleasing their electors, that in the final analysis shaped our democratic system. Any state can grant the suffrage to its people overnight, but it cannot thereby guarantee to itself a democratic polity. As American history shows, such a democracy requires generations of experience with electoral politics. More important, it requires the emergence of political parties and egalitarian politicians—none of whom have too much power and most of whom run scared—politicians whose maneuverings for electoral advantage, whose courting of the electorate, and whose passion for victory result in the end in grander and more significant developments than they themselves can foresee or even imagine. Politicians are at the heart of our political system, and insofar as it is democratic they have made it so.

10 Chilton Williamson, *American Suffrage from Property to Democracy, 1760–1860* (Princeton: Princeton University Press, 1960), p. 279.

VI The Confederation Period: Federalist (Radical) Versus Nationalist (Conservative)

Introduction There are two conflicting interpretations of the historical meaning of the Confederation Period (1781–1789). One view emerges from a particular approach to the revolutionary background. This approach to the problem sees the basic issues of the 1760's as a struggle between radicals and conservatives for the control of the colonial governments, though the two united, somewhat uneasily, in the struggle for American liberty against British oppression. According to this view the Declaration of Independence was a radical victory, with the conservatives either opposed or reluctant. The struggle over the Articles of Confederation was a struggle between federalist (states rights advocates) and nationalists, and the adoption of the Articles, with their emphasis upon states rights, was a victory for the federalists. The whole of the history of the United States under the Articles was a further conflict between federalists, most of whom "believed, as a result of their experience with Great Britain before 1776 and of their reading of history, that the states could be best governed without the intervention of a powerful central government," and the nationalists, who "declared that national honor and prestige could be maintained only by a powerful central government." Further, these two groupings differed from each other in that the federalists emphasized the beneficent operation of government by legislative authority, and the nationalists emphasized government by the executive and judicial branches. The adoption of the federal Constitution (1787–1788), according to this interpretation, is the culminating victory for the nationalist cause. Professor Merrill Jensen is the outstanding advocate of this interpretation; his views are represented below in two selections from his book *The New Nation* (1950).

The Jensen interpretation has been challenged in recent years, largely upon the basis that it is too simplistic, that it sets up fixed categories and imposes these categories upon the historical reality. The new view contends that the historical reality of the Confederation Period was much more complex and diffuse, that individuals in the main did not remain fixed in their categories of federalist (radical) or nationalist (conservative). They crossed these lines on different issues, and this makes a uniform interpretation unreal and unhistorical, because it forces rigidity upon a differentiated historical development. An example of this type of critique of Jensen is supplied below in the article by Professor Richard Morris, "The Confederation and the American Historian." A problem in semantics arises in using Jensen and Morris as conflicting interpretations. For Jensen, federalist (radical) and nationalist (conservative) are the opposites; for Morris, antifederalist (radical) and federalist (conservative) are the opposites, though Morris does not accept these strict categories.

The Confederation Period: Perspectives and Significance[*]
—*Merrill Jensen*

The Confederation Period in American History

This book is an account of the first years of the new nation that was born of the American Revolution. Like every other segment of time, the history of the United States from 1781 to 1789 was an integral part of the past in which it was rooted and of the future into which it was growing. It was a time when men believed they could shape the future of the new nation, and since it was also a time in which they disagreed as to what that future should be, they discussed great issues with a forthrightness and realism seldom equalled in political debates. The history of the Confederation is therefore one of great inherent importance for the study of human society if for no other reason than that during it men debated publicly and even violently the question of whether or not people could govern themselves.

Aside from its inherent importance, the history of the Confederaton has been of enormous significance to one generation of Americans after another in the years since then. Repeatedly Americans have turned to that history in the course of innumerable social and political struggles. They have done so because it was during those years that the Articles of Confederation were replaced by the Constitution of 1787. In order to explain their Constitution, Americans have appealed to the history of the period out of which it came. In the course of such appeals, sometimes honestly for light and guidance and sometimes only for support of partisan arguments, Americans have usually found what they sought. As a result the "history" has been obscured in a haze of ideas, quotations, and assumptions torn bodily from the context of fact that alone gives them meaning. Again and again political opponents have asserted that the founding fathers stood for this or that, while their writings have stood idly and helplessly in volumes on shelves or have lain buried in yellowed manuscripts and newspapers.

Since the founding fathers themselves disagreed as to the nature of the history of the period and as to the best kind of government for the new nation, it is possible to find arguments to support almost any interpretation

Composite of excerpts reprinted by permission of the publisher from *The New Nation* by Merrill Jensen. Copyright, 1950 by Alfred A. Knopf, Inc.

[*] The over-all title for the selections from this work was supplied by the editor.

one chooses. It is not surprising therefore that conflicting interpretations have filled thousands of pages and that all this effort has never produced any final answers and probably never will, for men have ever interpreted the two constitutions of the United States in terms of their hopes, interests, and beliefs rather than in terms of knowable facts.

The conflict of interpretation has been continuous ever since the first debates over the Articles of Confederation in the summer of 1776. Men then differed as to the kind of government which should be created for the new nation. They continued to debate the issue during the 1780's. The members of the Convention of 1787 differed as to the need for and the amount of constitutional change. When the Constitution was submitted to the public in October 1787 the controversy rose to new heights. Men talked in public meetings and wrote private letters and public essays in an effort to explain, justify, or denounce what the Convention had done. They disagreed as to what had happened since the war. Some said there had been chaos; others said there had been peace and prosperity. Some said there would be chaos without the new Constitution; others that there would be chaos if it were adopted.

Once it was adopted Thomas Jefferson and Alexander Hamilton, with two opposed ideals of what the United States should be, laid down two classic and contradictory opinions of the nature of the Constitution. These two basic interpretations may be simply stated. Jefferson held that the central government was sharply limited by the letter of the Constitution; that in effect the states retained their sovereign powers except where they were specifically delegated. Hamilton argued in effect that the central government was a national government which could not be restrained by a strict interpretation of the Constitution or by ideas of state sovereignty. These rival interpretations did not originate with Hamilton and Jefferson, for they had been the very core of constitutional debate ever since the Declaration of Independence, and even before it, for that matter.

Jefferson and his followers used the states rights idea to oppose the plans of the Federalists when they passed the Alien and Sedition Acts in 1798. But when Jefferson became president and purchased Louisiana, he justified his actions by constitutional theories that even Hamilton hardly dared use. Meanwhile Jefferson's opponents seized upon his earlier theories in a vain attempt to block the expansion of the United States. They did so again during the War of 1812 when the Federalists of New England became out-and-out exponents of "states rights" and threatened secession because they were opposed to the war.

In the decades before the Civil War, Daniel Webster and John C. Calhoun carried on the dispute, each having changed sides since his youthful years in politics. Webster, who had been a states rights spokesman during the War of 1812, became the high priest of nationalism, while Calhoun, a leading nationalist in 1812, became the high priest of the states rights idea which he elaborated to defend the slave-owning aristocracy of the South.

The Civil War itself was the bloody climax of a social conflict in which the ultimate nature of the Constitution was argued again and again in seeking support for and arguments against antagonistic programs. But even the Civil War did not finally settle the constitutional issue. The stresses and strains that came with the rise of industrial and finance capitalism produced demands for social and regulatory legislation. The passage of such legislation by the states involved the interpretation of the nature of the Constitution, for business interests regulated by state governments denied their authority and appealed to the national courts. Those courts soon denied the power of regulation to state legislatures. Then, when regulatory laws were passed by the national government, the regulated interests evolved a "states rights" theory that limited the power of the central government, and the national courts once more agreed.

Throughout American history the courts have drawn boundary lines between state and national authority. The pose of judicial impartiality and finality assumed by the courts cannot hide the fact that they have shifted those boundary lines with the shifting winds of politics, and always with sufficient precedents, if not with adequate grace. As a result they had created by 1900 a legal and constitutional no man's land in which all sorts of activity could be carried on without effective regulation by either state or national governments.

The crash of American economy in 1929 once more posed in imperative terms the problem of the nature of the Constitution. How should it, how could it deal with the potentiality of chaos inherent in unemployment, starvation, and bankruptcy, and ultimately, the loss of faith in the utility of the economic and political foundation of the society itself.

As the national government began to act where, plainly, state and local governments had failed to or were unable to act, the question of constitutionality was raised. For a time the courts once more listened to and heeded states rights constitutional theories which were expounded by opponents of the New Deal. New Deal lawyers, in turn, adopted as weapons John Marshall's nationalistic interpretations of the Constitution for ends which Marshall himself would have fought to the death. President Roosevelt, in his fight on the Supreme Court, declared that the Constitution was not a lawyer's document; yet some of the ablest lawyers who ever lived in America wrote it. New Deal publicists wrote tracts in the guise of history to prove that there had been a "national sovereignty" in the United States from the beginning of the Revolution. Therefore, they argued, the courts could not stop the New Deal from doing what needed doing by following a strict interpretation of the Constitution. Both the New Dealers and the

Republicans insisted that they were the sole heirs of the legacy of Thomas Jefferson, while Alexander Hamilton went into an eclipse from which he has not yet emerged.

The most recent appeal to the history of the Confederation Period has come from those who support some form of world government. Adequate arguments for such a government can be found in twentieth-century experience, but, like most men, its backers turn to history for analogies and lessons.

When the League of Nations was set up at the end of the First World War men turned to American history after the American Revolution as a parallel experience. At that time books were written to show the "chaos" of the Confederation Period and the happy solution that came with the Constitution of 1787. Among them was a book by a great authority on international law with the title *James Madison's Notes of Debates in the Federal Convention of 1787 and their Relation to a More Perfect Society of Nations*. The book was widely distributed by the Carnegie Endowment for International Peace. This and other books like it had little relation to the realities of world politics in the 1920's and 1930's, but despite this supporters of the United Nations and of various plans of world government have again turned to the history of the American states after the American Revolution.

The most notable appeal has been that of Clarence Streit. In his book *Union Now* he analyzes the history of our past as he sees it. He calls the Articles of Confederation a "league of friendship." He says, paraphrasing John Fiske, that by 1786 there was universal depression, trade had well-nigh stopped, and political quackery with cheap and dirty remedies had full control of the field. Trade disputes promised to end in war between states. Territorial disputes led to bloodshed. War with Spain threatened. The "league" could not coerce its members. Secession was threatened by some states. Congress had no money and could borrow none. Courts were broken up by armed mobs. When Shay's Rebellion came, state sovereignty was so strong that Massachusetts would not allow "league" troops to enter the state, even to guard the "league's" own arsenal. Streit goes on to say that the idea of turning a league into a union was not even seriously proposed until the Convention opened in May 1787. And then, he says, within two years the freedom-loving American democracies decided to try out this invention for themselves. Streit goes on to argue that it would be just as easy to secure union of the democracies now as it was for the American democracies to achieve a union then. Some things made it difficult then; some make it so now. Some made it easy then; some make it easy now.

Many men have followed in Streit's footsteps. His book was first published in 1939. In 1940 Federal Union Incorporated published a pamphlet called *It Must be done Again; the Case for World Federal Union . . . illustrated by excerpts from John Fiske's Critical Period, etc.*

In the February issue of 1945, the *Reader's Digest* published an article called "Our Post War Problems of 1787" which was still another summary of John Fiske's *The Critical Period of American History.* In May 1945, the *Saturday Review of Literature* had an editorial called "Where do we go From Here?" They urged John Fiske's *Critical Period* as timely reading for the constitutional convention of the United Nations then meeting in San Francisco. The *Review* argued that American experience in the eighteenth century was analogous, despite those who pointed to the disparities. It declared that the crucial lesson offered by American experience was that unified government is not created by similarities, but by differences. But the *Review* was willing, for the sake of argument, to agree that even if the American colonies (it called them that instead of states) offer no valid parallel, even then the basic question is how to control differences. The answer, said the *Review,* is that the historical fact remains that "only government has been able to control war."

One more example will suffice, not only to show how the proponents of world government continue to use what they call "history," but to show how they too swing with the tide. On 12 March 1948 Federal Union took a full page in the *New York Times* to advertise this proposition in a headline: "By Hamilton's 'Stroke of Genius' Plan . . . we can stop Stalin Now . . . and avert Freedom's suicide." Hamilton's plan was "boiled down" to the following statement: "Unite democracies by federal union and have the Union not only replace their currencies with its currency but assume each democracy's public debt." The advertisement goes on to give the traditional story of how Hamilton saved public credit, saved money, cut government expenses, and so on. Thus a litter of ideas, fathered by hope and ignorance, are set before the public as historical fact.

Even if it can be granted that most appeals to the history of the Confederation have been sincere, let it also be said that they have seldom been infused with any knowledge of the period or its problems. The result has been the drawing of lessons the past does not have to teach. This is a luxury too expensive in an age when men have discovered how to unhinge the very force that holds matter itself together but have advanced very little beyond cave men in their notions of how to live peacefully with one another.

Yet it is little wonder that such false lessons have been drawn in the twentieth century because most of them have come from John Fiske's *The Critical Period of American History,* a book of vast influence but of no value as either history or example. Fiske, a philosopher and popular lecturer, wrote the book "without fear and without research," to use the words of Charles A. Beard. As long ago as 1905, Andrew C. McLaughlin, an impeccably conservative historian of the Constitution who wrote a far better book on the same period, said that Fiske's book was "altogether without scientific standing, because it is little more than a remarkably skilful adaptation of a very few secondary authorities showing almost no evidence of first hand acquaintance with the sources."

The story told by Fiske and repeated by publicists and scholars who have not worked in the field—and some who have, for that matter—is based on the assumption that this was *the* "critical period" of American history during which unselfish patriots rescued the new nation from impending anarchy, if not from chaos itself. The picture is one of stagnation, ineptitude, bankruptcy, corruption, and disintegration. Such a picture is at worst false and at best grossly distorted. It is therefore important to attempt a history which makes an effort to examine the sources, which is concerned with the nature of political and economic problems rather than with proving that one side or another in the innumerable political battles of the period was "right" or "wrong." Nothing is to be gained by following a "chaos and patriots to the rescue" interpretation. We have too long ignored the fact that thoroughly patriotic Americans during the 1780's did not believe there was chaos and emphatically denied that their supposed rescuers were patriotic. The point is that there were patriots on both sides of the issue, but that they differed as to desirable goals for the new nation. At the same time, of course, there were men as narrow and selfish on both sides as their political enemies said they were.

If one approaches the history of the Confederation in this way, if one tries to see it as men who lived in it saw it and to write of it in their terms, one may achieve some semblance of reality. It is not the task of the historian to defend or attack the various groups of men whose conflicts were the essence of the period, but to set forth what they believed and what they tried to achieve. This can be illustrated no better than in the definition of terms. Throughout this book the words "federalist" and "nationalist" are used to describe two opposed bodies of opinion as to the best kind of central government for the United States. In so doing I have followed the members of the Convention of 1787. Those men believed that the Articles of Confederation provided for a "federal" government and the majority of them wanted to replace it with a "national" government. The fact that the men who wanted a national government called themselves Federalists after their work was submitted to the public is relevant to the history of politics after 1787, not to the discussion of the nature of the central government prior to and during the Convention of 1787.

Whatever the confusion since then, there was none at the time. Gouverneur Morris stated the issue concisely in the Convention when he "explained the distinction between a federal and a national, supreme government; the former being a mere compact resting on the good faith of the parties; the latter having a complete and compulsive operation." This explanation was in answer to those members of the Convention who wanted to know what Edmund Randolph meant in his opening speech when he spoke of the "defects of the federal system, the necessity of transforming it into a national efficient government. . . ."

The issue was not, as has been argued from time to time, whether there was a "nation" before the adoption of the Constitution of 1787. That was not the question at all during the 1780's. There was a new nation, as the men of the time agreed: they disagreed as to whether the new nation should have a federal or a national government. They did so from the outset of the Revolution and men have continued to do so ever since. The Constitution of 1787 was, as Madison said, both national and federal. And while this fact has led to innumerable conflicts of interpretation, it has also been a source of strength; for as one political group after another has gotten control of the central government it has been able to shape the Constitution to its needs and desires. Thus with the single exception of the Civil War, peaceful change has always been possible, and as long as Americans are willing to accept the decisions of ballot boxes, legislatures, and courts, the Constitution will continue to change with changing needs and pressures. . . .

The Significance of the Confederation Period

The foregoing pages indicate that the Confederation Period was one of great significance, but not of the kind that tradition has led us to believe. The "critical period" idea was the result of an uncritical acceptance of the arguments of the victorious party in a long political battle, of a failure to face the fact that partisan propaganda is not history but only historical evidence. What emerges instead is a much more complex and important story in which several themes are interwoven. It was a period of what we would call post-war demobilization, of sudden economic change, dislocation, and expansion, and fundamental conflict over the nature of the Constitution of the United States. Each of these themes is so interwoven with the others that any separation is arbitrary but, taken separately or together, they are better keys to an understanding of the period than the traditional one.

At the end of the war Americans faced innumerable problems arising from it. What should be done with war veterans? Should the Loyalists return to their homes? What should be our relations with foreign friends and foes? Should commerce be free or should there be discrimination, and if so, against whom and for whose benefit? How would peace affect the economy? How should the war debt be paid? What kind of taxes should be levied to pay it, and who should pay them? When the war-boom collapsed, why did it? What should the state or central governments, or both, do about it? Should government encourage one form of economic enterprise over another or should it keep hands off? What about discontented groups: should government ignore them, cater to them, or forcibly suppress those who might revolt?

Such questions or others like them have probably been asked after every great war in history. They were asked, debated, and given various solutions during the 1780's. The significance of those debates and solutions has often been misunderstood. This is no better illustrated than in the case of the national debt during the 1780's which is usually discussed only in terms of depreciation and nonpayment of interest. Actually much more was involved than this. The debt was fantastically low compared with the national debt of today—about twelve dollars per capita as compared with seventeen hundred—and the nation had vast untouched natural resources with which to pay it. Multitudes of accounts had to be reduced to simple forms so that they could be paid, and this the Confederation government managed to do. But even more important than the economics of the national debt was its politics: should it be paid by the states or the central government? A fundamental assumption of every political leader was that the political agency which paid the debt would hold the balance of power in the new nation. Hence, the supporters of a strong central government insisted that the national debt must be paid by Congress while their opponents insisted that it should be divided among the states and paid by them. The latter group was on the way to victory by the end of the 1780's, for they were supported by clamoring creditors. The result was that one state after another assumed portions of the national debt owing to its citizens. Thus the traditional story is so out of context as to be virtually meaningless. This is true of other traditions as well. Most of the ports of the world were open, not closed, to American citizens. Reciprocity and equal treatment of all United States citizens was the rule in the tonnage and tariff acts of the states, not trade barriers.

To say that many of the pessimistic traditions are false is not to say that all Americans were peaceful and satisfied. The holders of national and state debts wanted bigger payments than they got. The merchants wanted more government aid than was given them. The farmers, hit by high taxes and rigid collection of both taxes and private debts, demanded relief in the form of lower taxes and government loans from state legislatures. Such demands kept state politics in an uproar during the 1780's. However, the often violent expression of such discontents in politics should not blind us to the fact that the period was one of extraordinary economic growth. Merchants owned more ships at the end of the 1780's than they had at the beginning of the Revolution, and they carried a greater share of American produce. By 1790 the export of agricultural produce was double what it had been before the war. American cities grew rapidly, with the result that housing was scarce and building booms produced a labor shortage. Tens of thousands of farmers spread outwards to the frontiers. There can be no question but that freedom from the British Empire resulted in a surge of activity in all phases of American life. Of course not all the problems of the new nation were solved by 1789—all have not yet been solved—but there is no evidence of stagnation and decay in the 1780's. Instead the story is one of a newly free people who seized upon every means to improve and enrich themselves in a nation which they believed had a golden destiny.

Politically the dominating fact of the Confederation Period was the struggle between two groups of leaders to shape the character of the state and central governments. The revolutionary constitutions of the states placed final power in the legislatures and made the executive and judicial branches subservient to them. The members of the colonial aristocracy who became Patriots, and new men who gained economic power during the Revolution deplored this fact, but they were unable to alter the state constitutions during the 1780's. Meanwhile they tried persistently to strengthen the central government. These men were the nationalists of the 1780's.

On the other hand the men who were the true federalists believed that the greatest gain of the Revolution was the independence of the several states and the creation of a central government subservient to them. The leaders of this group from the Declaration of Independence to the Convention of 1787 were Samuel Adams, Patrick Henry, Richard Henry Lee, George Clinton, James Warren, Samuel Bryan, George Bryan, Elbridge Gerry, George Mason and a host of less well known but no less important men in each of the states. Most of these men believed, as a result of their experience with Great Britain before 1776 and of their reading of history, that the states could be best governed without the intervention of a powerful central government. Some of them had programs of political and social reform; others had none at all. Some had a vision of democracy; others had no desire except to control their states for whatever satisfactions such control might offer. Some were in fact as narrow and provincial as their opponents said they were. However, the best of them agreed that the central government needed more power, but they wanted that power given so as not to alter the basic character of the Articles of Confederation. Here is where they were in fundamental disagreement with the nationalists who wanted to remove the central government from the control of the state legislatures.

The nationalist leaders from the Declaration of Independence to the Philadelphia convention were men like Robert Morris, John Jay, Gouverneur Morris, James Wilson, Alexander Hamilton, Henry Knox, James Duane, George Washington, James Madison, and many lesser men. Most of these men were by temperament or economic interest believers in executive and judicial rather than legislative control of state and central governments, in the rigorous collection of taxes, and, as creditors, in strict payment of public and private debts. They declared that national honor and prestige could be maintained only by a powerful central government. Naturally, not all men who used such language used it sincerely, for some were as selfish and greedy as their opponents said they were. The nationalists frankly disliked the political heritage of the Revolution. They deplored the fact there was no check upon the actions of majorities in state legislatures; that there was no central government to which minorities could appeal from the decisions of such majorities, as they had done before the Revolution.

There were men who veered from side to side, but their number is relatively small and their veering is of little significance as compared with the fact that from the outset of the Revolution there were two consistently opposed bodies of opinion as to the nature of the central government. There was, of course, a wide variation of belief among adherents of both points of view. There were extremists who wanted no central government at all and others who wanted to wipe out the states entirely. There were some who wanted a monarchy and others who would have welcomed dictatorship. But such extremists are not representative of the two great bodies of men whose conflict was the essence of the years both before and after 1789.

While the federalist leaders gradually moved to a position where they were willing to add specific powers to the Articles of Confederation, the nationalist leaders campaigned steadily for the kind of government they wanted. During the war they argued that it could not be won without creating a powerful central government. After the war they insisted that such a government was necessary to do justice to public creditors, solve the problems of post-war trade, bring about recovery from depression and win the respect of the world for the new nation. Meanwhile their experience with majorities in state legislatures merely intensified their desire. They became desperate as state after state in 1785 and 1786 adopted some form of paper money that could be loaned on farm mortgages and be used to pay taxes, and in some cases private debts as well. When they were able to hold off such demands and farmers revolted, as in Massachusetts, they were thoroughly frightened.

They looked upon such events as evidence of the horrors of unchecked democracy and they said so in poetry, private letters, newspaper essays, and public speeches. The problem, they said, was to find some refuge from democracy. They worked hard to control state legislatures and they were often successful, but such control was uncertain at best, for annual elections meant a constant threat of overturn and the threat was realized repeatedly.

We may not call it democracy, but they did. Edmund Randolph put their case bluntly in his opening speech in the Convention of 1787. He

said, "our chief danger arises from the democratic parts of our constitutions
. . . None of the [state] constitutions have provided a sufficient check
against the democracy. The feeble senate of Virginia is a phantom. Maryland has a more powerful senate, but the late distractions in that state,
have discovered that it is not powerful enough. The check established in
the constitutions of New York and Massachusetts is yet a stronger barrier
against democracy, but they all seem insufficient." Outside the Convention
General Knox was saying that a "mad democracy sweeps away every
moral trait from the human character" and that the Convention would
"clip the wings of a mad democracy." James Madison in the *Federalist
Papers* argued that the new Constitution should be adopted because a "republican" form of Government was better than a "democracy."

The debate was white-hot and was carried on with utter frankness. It
was white-hot because for a moment in history self-government by
majorities within particular political boundaries was possible. Those
majorities could do what they wanted, and some of them knew what they
wanted. Democracy was no vague ideal, but a concrete program: it meant
definite things in politics, economics, and religion. Whatever side of the
controversy we take, whether we think the majorities in state legislatures
governed badly or well—the fact to face is that men of the 1780's believed
that the issue was democracy as a way of government for the United
States of those days.

They faced the issue squarely. They thought hard and realistically about
the problems of government. They understood that society is complex and
that the truth about it is multifold rather than simple. James Madison
summed it up as well as it has ever been done. There are, he said, many
passions and interests in society and these will ever clash for control of
government and will ever interpret their own desires as the good of the
whole. Men like Madison and John Adams believed, as Madison said, that
the "great desideratum which has not yet been found for Republican governments seems to be some disinterested and dispassionate umpire in disputes between different passions and interests in the state." In the tenth
number of *The Federalist,* after citing various origins of political parties,
Madison said that "the most durable source of factions [parties] has been
the various and unequal distribution of property. Those who hold and
those who are without property have ever formed distinct interests in
society. Those who are creditors and those who are debtors, fall under a
like discrimination. A landed interest, a manufacturing interest, a mercantile interest, a monied interest, with many lesser interests, grow up of
necessity in civilized nations, and divide them into different classes, actuated by different sentiments and views. The regulation of these various
and interfering interests forms the principal task of modern legislation,
and involves the spirit of party and faction in the necessary and ordinary
operations of the government."

The constitutional debate of the 1780's was thus carried on by men with a realistic appreciation of the social forces lying behind constitutional forms and theories, by men who were aware of the relationship between economic and political power. This realistic approach was lost sight of in the nineteenth century by romantic democrats who believed that once every man had the right to vote the problems of society could be solved. It was lost sight of too by those who came to believe in an oversimplified economic interpretation of history. In a sense they were as romantic as the democrats, for they assumed a rationality in the historic process that is not always supported by the evidence.

If the history of the Confederation has anything to offer us it is the realistic approach to politics so widely held by the political leaders of the time, however much they might differ as to forms of government and desirable goals for the new nation. Throughout the Confederation men with rival goals pushed two programs simultaneously. The federalists tried to strengthen the Articles of Confederation; the nationalists tried to create a new constitution by means of a convention, and thus avoid the method of change prescribed by the Articles of Confederation. The movement to strengthen the Articles failed on the verge of success; the movement to call a convention suceeded on the verge of failure. The failure of one movement and the success of the other, however, we may interpret them, is one of the dramatic stories in the history of politics.

The Confederation Period and the American Historian
—*Richard B. Morris*

Plautus tells us that "one eyewitness is worth ten hearsays," but I am not sure that he would have left us this counsel if he had lived during the Confederation period of American history. In this era the eyewitnesses themselves failed to see eye to eye. In fact, the two opposing views of the post-Revolutionary years which are held by historians of the twentieth century can be traced directly to the Founding Fathers. The first we might call the Washington-Madison-Hamilton approach, accepted by most historians of the post-Revolutionary generation, and developed by George Bancroft, John Fiske, John B. McMaster, and with some reservations by Andrew C. McLaughin. The other is the approach of certain Antifederalist

From *William and Mary Quarterly*, XIII (April 1956), 139–156. Reprinted by permission.

leaders, an approach adopted by Henry B. Dawson, by J. Allen Smith, by the early Charles A. Beard, and by the more recent Merrill Jensen.

If one could read the minds of the majority of the Founding Fathers in 1787—and an abundant and ever-increasing quantity of first-hand documentation makes this a less formidable effort than it seems on its face—he might be very much surprised indeed that any issue should have arisen in historiography about the years of the Confederation. The majority of the Founders saw a clear drift toward anarchy culminating in a crisis. Constantly needled by such correspondents as Henry Knox and David Humphreys, Washington's alarm at the weaknesses of the Confederacy was deepened as the disorders in Massachusetts in the fall of 1786 seemed to portend a crisis for the nation. "I predict the worst consequences from a half-starved, limping government, always moving upon crutches and tottering at every step," he wrote. On August 1, 1786, he asserted: "I do not conceive we can long exist as a nation without having lodged somewhere a power which will pervade the whole Union in as energetic a manner as the authority of the State governments extends over the several states." On October 22 he wrote David Humphreys: "But for God's sake tell me what is the cause of all these commotions? . . . I am mortified beyond expression that in the moment of our acknowledged independence we should by our conduct verify the predictions of our transatlantic foe, and render ourselves ridiculous and contemptible in the eyes of all Europe." Nine days later he wrote Henry Lee, "To be more exposed in the eyes of the world, and more contemptible than we already are, is hardly possible." [1] On November 5 he told James Madison, "We are fast verging to anarchy and confusion!" [2]

Others than the New England Federalists, who were closest to Shays' Rebellion and understandably perturbed, shared Washington's views about the state of the nation. Henry Lee declared: "We are all in dire apprehension that a beginning of anarchy with all its calamitys has approached, and have no means to stop the dreadful work." [3] In December of 1786 Madison wrote Jefferson of "dangerous defects" in the Confederation. [4] During the fall of 1786 John Jay kept writing Jefferson that "the inefficacy of our Government becomes daily more and more apparent," and intimated that the Shaysites had more "extensive" objectives than the immediate redress of grievances. [5] Edmund Randolph, who oscillated between Federalism and Antifederalism, wrote Washington in March of 1787, "Every day brings forth some new crisis"; and he expressed doubt whether Con-

---

[1] *The Writings of George Washington from the Original Manuscript Sources, 1745–1799,* ed. J. C. Fitzpatrick (Washington, 1931–44), XXVIII, 502; XXIX, 27, 34.

[2] *Ibid.,* XXIX, 51.

[3] Henry Lee to George Washington, Oct. 17, 1786, *Letters of Members of the Continental Congress,* ed. E. C. Burnett (Washington, 1921–33), VIII, 486.

[4] *The Papers of Thomas Jefferson,* ed. Julian P. Boyd (Princeton, 1950–   ), X, 574.

[5] *Ibid.,* p. 489.

gress could survive beyond the current year.[6] No one at the Constitutional Convention was more explicit than Randolph in spelling out the defects of the government, which he considered "totally inadequate to the peace, safety, and security of the Confederation" and which he repeatedly denounced for its "imbecility." [7]

For the classic contemporary view of the alarming weaknesses of the Confederation we must turn to *The Federalist.* Therein Hamilton, a consistent viewer-with-alarm during this period, attacks the Confederation government as inefficient, asserts that the country had "reached almost the last stage of national humiliation," speaks disparagingly of "the present shadow of a federal government," views the Confederacy as dying, and urges ratification of the Constitution to prevent anarchy, civil war, and "perhaps the military despotism of a victorious demagogue." [8] It would be easy to pile up assertions in similar vein from the pens of Knox and the two Morrises.

These Federalist worthies were in general agreement that the weaknesses of the Confederation could be attributed to financial muddling by the states; to English dumping; to the loss of the British West Indian market; to paper money; to stay laws; to state tariffs; but, above all, to a lack of coercive power by a central authority. Observers in charge of foreign affairs, notably Jay and John Adams, felt that this was the most critical spot in the American system of government. "I may reason till I die to no purpose," declared Adams in June 1785. "It is unanimity in America which will produce a fair treaty of commerce." [9]

In eloquence, prestige, and even in numbers among the leadership the Federalist view of conditions had impressive support, but it was far from universally held. George Clinton, the bête noire of the nationalist leaders, was quoted as intimating that the calling of a Constitutional Convention was "calculated to impress the people with an idea of evils which do not exist." [10] At the Convention, Gunning Bedford of Delaware expressed a complacent view of the government of the Confederacy, and at the Pennsylvania ratifying convention Antifederalists under the leadership of William Findley, Robert Whitehill, and John Smilie asserted that the people along with the legislature had been frightened into consenting to a state convention by unfounded talk of impending anarchy.

Thus there was a division of opinion in 1787 about conditions in the Confederation, and there never has ceased to be down to the present day. More recent writers who look at the Confederation through Antifederalist

---

[6] *The Writings of George Washington* . . . , ed. Jared Sparks (Boston, 1834–37), IX, 243 n.
[7] *Records of the Federal Convention of 1787,* ed. Max Farrand (New Haven, 1911–37), I, 19, 24, 25.
[8] See especially *Federalist* 1, 15, 16, and 85.
[9] Adams to Jay, June 26, 1785, *Works of John Adams,* ed. C. F. Adams (Boston, 1850–56), VIII, 276.
[10] *Advertiser,* New York, July 21, 1787.

spectacles are buoyed up by the fact that Franklin and Jefferson were not as disturbed about conditions as other contemporaries. Yet Jefferson, as he was passing through Boston on his way to France, found "the conviction growing strongly that nothing could preserve the confederacy unless the bond of union, their common council, should be strengthened." [11] It is perhaps especially significant that when Franklin, Jefferson, and Robert R. Livingston expressed in writing a more roseate view of conditions than other Founding Fathers, they were making these observations to foreigners —to Frenchmen or to Englishmen. They were seeking to reassure friends and well-wishers of America abroad that this country was not headed for a collapse. Such assertions must be discounted as skillful propaganda. In France, for example, Jefferson reassured Démeunier that the United States was in no danger of bankruptcy and that, with certain minor exceptions, "the Confederation is a wonderfully perfect instrument." [12] Similarly, when Franklin wrote to M. Le Veillard on March 6, 1786, that "America never was in higher prosperity," [13] commodity prices had steadily dropped— they were to decline thirty per cent between 1785 and 1789; farm wages were shrinking and were to fall to a low of forty cents a day by 1787; mortgage foreclosures and judgments for debts in central and western Massachusetts had reached an all-time high; and in the Valley of Virginia, as Freeman Hart has pointed out, executions more than doubled between 1784 and 1788.[14] In fact, the only economic index that showed an upturn was that for foreign trade, for in commerce the worst of the depression set in a bit earlier than in other lines and showed a more complete recovery by 1788. Again, when Livingston wrote Lafayette in April 1787 that commodity prices and wages were higher than before the war, he was evading the real issue of how far they had dropped since the coming of the peace.[15]

This double standard of correspondence—one line for Americans, the other for foreign well-wishers—is revealed in the writing of that arch-pessimist, George Washington. It is true that he was somewhat more candid with his old friend Lafayette, whom he wrote on August 15, 1786, that he chose to remain silent on domestic affairs "since I could not disguise or palliate, where I might think them erroneous." [16] Yet two weeks earlier he had written two letters which are very nearly contradictory to each other.

---

[11] Jefferson to Madison, July 1, 1784, *Jefferson Papers,* VII, 356.

[12] *Jefferson Papers,* X, 14 ff.

[13] *Complete Works of Benjamin Franklin,* ed. John Bigelow (New York, 1887–88), IX, 300–301.

[14] Freeman H. Hart, *The Valley of Virginia in the American Revolution* (Chapel Hill, 1942), pp. 123–125. For evidence from the court records of sharply mounting indebtedness in central and western Massachusetts, see R. B. Morris, "Insurrection in Massachusetts," in *America in Crisis,* ed. Daniel Aaron (New York, 1952), p. 24. On the steady upsurge of insolvency in Connecticut during the entire Confederation period, see *Public Records of the State of Connecticut (1776–1796),* eds. C. J. Hoadly and L. W. Labaree (Hartford, 1894–1951), VII, xv, xvi.

[15] R. R. Livingston Papers, Bancroft Transcripts, New York Public Library.

[16] Washington, *Writings,* ed. Fitzpatrick, XXVIII, 521.

On August 1 he wrote the Chevalier de la Luzerne a reassuring letter to counteract reports of the American situation circulating in Europe. "In short," he concluded his picture of domestic America, "the foundation of a great empire is laid, and I please myself with a persuasion, that Providence will not leave its work imperfect." On the same day, however, he wrote John Jay, then Secretary for Foreign Affairs, expressing the doubt that the nation could exist much longer unless stronger powers were lodged with the central government.[17]

Even the younger generation, men who could scarcely be accused of strong Federalist attachments, accepted the Federalist view of the glaring weaknesses of the Confederation. Consider, for example, Andrew Jackson, who was admitted to practice law the year the Constitutional Convention met in Philadelphia. In his Proclamation against Nullification Jackson declared in 1832: "But the defects of the Confederation need not be detailed. Under its operation we could scarcely be called a nation. We had neither prosperity at home nor consideration abroad. This state of things could not be endured, and our present happy Constitution was formed, but formed in vain if this fatal doctrine prevails." [18]

Jackson's view of the Confederation period was the view of the nationalist commentators on the Constitution and of the nationalist historians. It was expounded by James Wilson and Nathaniel Chipman, by Nathan Dane, and most notably by Joseph Story and George Ticknor Curtis, who gave formal expression to the views of Daniel Webster. In his *History of the Origin, Formation, and Adoption of the Constitution,* first published in 1854, Curtis begins by declaring: "The Constitution of the United States was the means by which republican liberty was saved from the consequences of impending anarchy. . . ." Paraphrasing the Founding Fathers, Curtis saw the Confederation as "a great shadow without the substance of a government. . . ." He saw the whole period as replete with "dangers and difficulties," full of "suffering and peril." [19]

Curtis' view of the Confederation interlude was fully shared by the nationalist historians writing in the generation or two following the adoption of the Constitution. Most distinguished of this group, George Bancroft—whose literary career spans the period from the Age of Jackson to the Age of Chester A. Arthur—put off writing about the post-Revolutionary era until the closing years of his life. His *History of the Formation of the Constitution of the United States of America* was not published until 1882. As might be expected, Bancroft viewed the period from a nationalist or continental point of view. He stressed the "helplessness" of Congress, whose "perpetual failures" he considered "inherent and incurable." To Ban-

---

[17] *Ibid.,* pp. 501, 502.

[18] *Compilation of the Messages and Papers of the Presidents, 1789–1902,* ed. J. D. Richardson (Washington, 1903), II, 643.

[19] George Ticknor Curtis, *History of thhe Origin, Formation, and Adoption of the Constitution of the United States* . . . (New York, 1854), I, xi, 233, 234, 330.

croft "no ray of hope remained" but from the convention summoned at Annapolis.[20] Nevertheless, he treats the Massachusetts debtors with sympathy and understanding, approves of Bowdoin's lenity toward the Shaysites, and reviews the economic decline which set in at the start of the period in sober language, in sharp contrast with the more intemperate treatment of the insurrection by his contemporary Richard Hildreth, who had surveyed the period many years earlier.[21]

Perhaps the historian who coined the term "critical period" to describe the Confederation interlude was William Henry Trescot. In his rather temperate and fair-minded *Diplomatic History of the Administrations of Washington and Adams,* published in 1857, he asserted: "Indeed, it would be more correct to say, that the most critical period of the country's history embraced the time between the peace of 1783 and the adoption of the constitution in 1788." [22] This point of view was adopted by Frothingham, by Schouler, and by von Holst. The last-named spoke of "the contemptible impotence of congress. . . ." This was strong language, but Washington had used it before him.[23]

The classic exposition of the Federalist approach is found in John Fiske's *The Critical Period of American History, 1783–1789.* His title has fastened upon an epoch in American history a popular nomenclature that dies hard. The first edition appeared in 1888, not too long after the appearance of Bancroft's *Last Revision.* The title and theme of the book were suggested by the fact of Tom Paine's stopping the publication of the "Crisis," on hearing the news of the treaty of peace in 1783. Now, Paine said, "the times that tried men's souls are over." Fiske does not agree with Paine. The next five years, he contends, were to be the most critical time of all. Fiske used the term "critical" first to settle the question whether there was to be a national government or a group of small city-states. Secondly, he used the term to describe what he regarded to be the utter incompetence of the states and the federal government to deal with the problem of postwar reconstruction. To Fiske the drift "toward anarchy" was only checked by the eleventh-hour ratification of the federal Constitution.[24]

---

[20] George Bancroft, *History of the Formation of the Constitution of the United States of America* (New York, 1885), I, 262–266.

[21] *Ibid.,* pp. 274–275; Richard Hildreth, *The History of the United States of America* (New York, 1848–51), III, 472–477.

[22] William Henry Trescot, *The Diplomatic History of the Administrations of Washington and Adams: 1789–1801* (Boston, 1857), p. 9. Long before Trescot, however, Richard Henry Lee, a leading Antifederalist, wrote, Oct. 8, 1787: "I know our situation is critical, and it behoves us to make the best of it." "Letters of the Federal Farmer," Letter I, in *Pamphlets on the Constitution of the United States,* ed. P. L. Ford (Brooklyn, 1888), p. 280.

[23] Richard Frothingham, *The Rise of the Republic of the United States* (Boston, 1910. First published in 1872), pp. 583ff.; James Schouler, *History of the United States of America under the Constitution* (revised ed., New York, 1894), I, 13ff.; H. von Holst, *The Constitutional and Political History of the United States,* trans. John J. Lalor and Alfred B. Mason (Chicago, 1889–92), I, 37.

[24] John Fiske, *The Critical Period of American History, 1783–1789* (Boston and New York, 1888), pp. 55–57, and Chap. IV, *passim.*

It has become the fashion of latter-day historians to criticize Fiske's scholarship. McLaughin concedes that "there are not many errors in fact in the book," but insists that "as an authority the work is altogether without scientific standing, because it is little more than a remarkably skilful adaptation of a very few secondary authorities, showing almost no evidence of first-hand acquaintance with the sources." [25] Yet McLaughlin himself shows surprisingly little acquaintance with the sources when he describes economic conditions in the Confederation and gives the reader a string of generalizations entirely unsupported by statistical evidence or other business documentation. But the issue is not whether Fiske used first-hand sources, but whether he produced a valid synthesis. As one who has conducted graduate seminars for some time, I am not unaware of the fact that a good many people saturate themselves in the primary sources but are utterly unable to interpret them intelligently. Whether or not William Macdonald's appraisal of Fiske's book as "the best comprehensive account of the period" [26] still stands today, John Fiske's approach to the era had an enormous impact both upon the public and upon fellow historians. John Bach McMaster adopts it without reservations. In his *History of the People of the United States* he refers to the "disaffected," meaning the Shaysites, "associating for evil purposes," as opposed to "the better-minded," equally active in forming societies "for good purposes." [27] His treatment might well have been written by George R. Minot, clerk of the Massachusetts lower house, whose contemporary account of Shays' Rebellion betrays the fears of the conservative element as to the broader implications of the insurrection.[28] McMaster excoriates Clinton and New York for particularist tendencies. Save for Rhode Island, no state behaved worse than New York, McMaster contends.[29]

Other writers, while generally accepting the nationalist synthesis of the period, have approached the Confederation years in a somewhat more objective spirit than did Fiske and most of his predecessors. In the editor's introduction to Andrew C. McLaughlin's volume in the old *American Nation* series, Albert Bushnell Hart expresses doubt whether Fiske's "critical period" was "really a time of such danger of national dissolution as people then and since have supposed." He views the McLaughlin volume as showing "a more orderly, logical, and inevitable march of events than has commonly been described." [30] McLaughlin sees little or no justification for the constant lament about poverty in this period. "Some tribulation there

---

[25] Andrew C. McLaughlin, *The Confederation and the Constitution, 1783–1789,* in *The American Nation: A History,* ed. Albert Bushnell Hart, X (New York and London, 1905), 319–320.
[26] William Macdonald, in *The Literature of American History: A Bibliographical Guide* . . . , ed. J. N. Larned (Boston, 1902), p. 156.
[27] John Bach McMaster, *A History of the People of the United States, From the Revolution to the Civil War* (New York, 1883–1913), I, 313.
[28] *History of the Insurrection in Massachusetts in 1786* . . . (Worcester, 1788).
[29] *History,* I, 369–370.   [30] McLaughlin, *The Confederation and the Constitution,* p. xv.

was," he concedes, "but that the country was forlorn, destitute, and poverty-stricken is far from the truth." He sees indications of an upturn in trade by 1786. However, on the constitutional and diplomatic aspects of the period there is little difference between McLaughlin and Fiske. Referring to the humiliating relations with the Barbary states, McLaughlin asserts: "All this, like everything else one touches during the dismal period, discloses the helplessness of the confederacy." Toward the Shaysites he is far less sympathetic than Bancroft. "The vicious, the restless, the ignorant, the foolish—and there were plenty of each class—were coming together to test the strength of the newly established government of Massachusetts." The result, as he sees it, was "nothing short of civil war," but its virtue was that it disclosed the dangers, helped to bring about a reaction, discredited extreme democratic tendencies, and thereby aided the men who sought to inject vigor into the union.[31] Thus, those who were led by the editor of the series to believe that they were going to read a revisionist book were to find that it was essentially conventional in interpretation. Similarly, Edward Channing, in his *History of the United States*, published some years after McLaughlin, stresses the "helplessness" of the existing government and its failure to win respect either at home or abroad, but finds evidence of a business upthrust before the new Constitution went into operation.[32]

The Antifederalist or pro-democratic interpretation (and I need hardly say that the two terms are not necessarily equated) was perhaps first, among nineteenth-century historians, expounded by Henry B. Dawson, a learned military historian of the American Revolution, who also devoted himself to studying the role of the masses in that war, and had a penchant for picking controversial issues which he fought with relish and passion. In an article in the *Historical Magazine* in 1871, Dawson attempted to refute John Lothrop Motley, who, in a celebrated letter to the London *Times* written during the Civil War, had asserted that the Confederation was a period of "chaos," in which the absence of law, order, and security for life and property was "as absolute as could be well conceived in a civilized land." These were reckless and false accusations, Dawson charged. He traced their origin to distinguished men of the Confederation period who had spread them "for selfish or partisan motives." He accused these leaders of having "nullified the established law of the Confederacy and violently and corruptly substituted for it what they styled the Constitution of the United States." Dawson had made extreme and curiously unbalanced charges but failed to substantiate them. The significance of the attack, however, lies far less in the kind of evidence adduced than in its formulation of the notion that the Federalists conspired to falsify the true conditions of the period in a deliberate effort to create panic and under-

---

[31] *Ibid.*, pp. 71, 107, 156, 161.
[32] Edward Channing, *A History of the United States* (New York, 1916–26), III, 491, 414–415, 426–427.

mine the government of the Confederation. Oddly enough, the criminal statistics Dawson cites for New York State not only are inconclusive regarding lawlessness, but point directly opposite to what Dawson believed. They indicate that in New York City and County there were almost twice as many indictments between 1784 and 1789 as there were for the first five years under the new federal government.[33] Concerning law and order, Dawson may very well have been on the right track, but somewhere along the path he lost the scent.

Despite the intemperate character of his attack, Dawson had touched off certain doubts as to the reportorial objectivity both of the Founding Fathers and of later historians. These were again raised in 1907, when J. Allen Smith, in his *The Spirit of American Government*, attacked on a second front, contending that the Constitution was the result of a counter-revolution. To him the Declaration of Independence spelled sweeping changes in the American form of government, changes manifest in an omnipotent legislature and the overthrow of the system of checks and balances which had been derived from the English constitution, with its characteristic blending of monarchical, aristocratic, and democratic elements. To Smith the chief feature of the Articles of Confederation was the entire absence of checks and balances, the vesting of all power in a single legislative body, unchecked by a distinct executive or judiciary. The fact that the power which was vested in the continental legislature was ineffectual did not disturb him. His main point, though, was that such democratic changes had been wrought by radical forces and that the conservatives, once they had a chance to assess the situation, set about, in more or less conspiratorial fashion, to redress the balance. The Constitutional Convention was called, according to Smith, not only to impart vigor to the government but to institute an elaborate system of constitutional checks. The adoption of this system he calls a "triumph of a skillfully directed reactionary movement."[34] The idea that the adoption of the Constitution was the result of a struggle among interest groups was pressed by Arthur F. Bentley in *The Process of Government* (1908), in language which stemmed from Madison's *Federalist* 10, and in a more naked form by A. M. Simons' *Social Forces in American History* (1911).

The most significant amplification of the Smith-Bentley-Simons approach came in 1913 from the pen of Charles A. Beard. In his *An Economic Interpretation of the Constitution of the United States* Beard concedes that "interpretative schools seem always to originate in social antagonism," but he prefers the road which explains proximate or remote causes and relations to the so-called "impartial" history which surveys outward

---

[33] Henry B. Dawson, "The Motley Letter," *Historical Magazine*, 2nd Ser., IX (Mar., 1871), 157ff.

[34] J. Allen Smith, *The Spirit of American Government: A Study of the Constitution, Its Origin, Influence, and Relation to Democracy* (Chautauqua, 1911), p. 37.

events and classifies and orders phenomena.[35] Beard was profoundly influenced by the Turnerian school, which substituted for the states'-rights interpretation of our history a recognition of social and economic areas, independent of state lines, which acted as units in political history. For the period of the Confederation the most important Turnerian contribution was Orin C. Libby's *Geographical Distribution of the Vote of the Thirteen States on the Federal Constitution,* an original and searching study published as far back as 1894. Beard found that nationalism cut across state lines, that it was created by a welding of economic interests of creditors holders of personalty—especially public securities—, manufacturers, shippers, commercial groups, and speculators in western lands. While this majestic formula helped explain why people were Federalists, it has failed dismally in explaining differences between Federalists and Antifederalists. Recent studies by Robert Thomas of the property interests of members of the ratifying convention in Virginia have failed to turn up any significant differences between the two parties either in the kind and quantity of their property-holdings or in their relative status as creditors or debtors. On the other hand, Jackson T. Main asserts that the Virginians who favored greater centralization were found in pro-creditor areas, the Northern Neck and much of the Tidewater, while the opposition came from the debtor Piedmont. After 1785, Main contends, the Shenandoah Valley counties, which had previously voted with the Piedmont on most issues, now supported a grant to Congress of power over commerce. But the picture is at best hardly clean-cut or conclusive.[36]

Beard suggested that general social conditions were prosperous and that the defects of the Articles did not justify the "loud complaints" of the advocates of change. In short, Beard found that the "critical period" was really not so critical after all, but, drawing upon Dawson's article, "a phantom of the imagination produced by some undoubted evils which could have been remedied without a political revolution." [37] Save for a quotation from Franklin, Beard fails to document this crucial generalization.

Lest anyone should carry away with him the view that Beard opposed the Constitution, as did J. Allen Smith, it might be well to point out that in his *Supreme Court and the Constitution,* published the previous year, he praised the Constitution and furnished historical precedents for judicial review. In later years he drew further and further away from any monolithic economic interpretation of the period. Although his *Rise of American Civilization* adhered to the approach of his *Economic Interpretation,*

---

[35] Charles A. Beard, *An Economic Interpretation of the Constitution of the United States* (New York, 1949), pp. 3–4.
[36] Robert E. Thomas, "The Virgnia Convention of 1788: A Criticism of Beard's *An Economic Interpretation of the Constitution*," *Journal of Southern History,* XIX (1953), 63–72. Jackson T. Main, "Sections and Politics in Virginia, 1781–1787," *William and Mary Quarterly,* 3rd Ser., XII (1955), 96–112.
[37] Beard, *An Economic Interpretation of the Constitution,* pp. 47–48.

as did Parrington's treatment in *Main Currents in American Thought*, Beard by 1935 completely repudiated economic determinism. In *The Republic* (1943) he considered the adoption of the Constitution as the alternative to military dictatorship. In his *Basic History of the United States* (1944) he defended checks and balances as curbs on despotic powers, whereas in his earlier *Rise of American Civilization* he insists that checks and balances dissolved "the energy of the democratic majority." [38] In *The Enduring Federalist*, published in 1948, he refers to the Congress of the Confederation as "a kind of debating society," and describes conditions in the Confederation period in language which would have gratified Fiske and perhaps shocked Bancroft.[39] In short, by the end of his career, Beard, the confirmed nationalist and isolationist, had moved a long way from the Beard of pre-World War I days.

But it is the unreconstructed Beard who still captures the imagination of our younger scholars. Today the chief disciple of J. Allen Smith and the early Beard is Merrill Jensen. In two significant books, *The Articles of Confederation*, published in 1940, and a more amplified treatment of the same problem, *The New Nation*, which appeared in 1950, Professor Jensen expounds learnedly and at length the argument that the Federalist party was organized to destroy the kind of democratic government and economic practice made possible by the Articles of Confederation.[40] Jensen sees the Articles as a constitutional expression of the philosophy of the Declaration of Independence, the Constitution as a betrayal of those principles. To Jensen the Articles were designed to prevent the central government from infringing upon the rights of the states, whereas the Constitution was designed to check both the states and the democracy that found expression within state bounds. As Jensen sees it, the Confederation government failed, not because it was inadequate, but because the radicals failed to maintain the organization they had created to bring about the American Revolution. He speaks of the radicals as having won "*their* war," but the fact remains that it was as much the war of the conservatives; probably a good deal more so.

Mr. Jensen finds conspiracy and betrayal at various levels. He suggests that the conservatives might well have betrayed the diplomatic objectives of the Revolution were it not for the integrity of Jay and Adams. He deplores the fact that radical leaders of the Thomas Burke-Richard Henry Lee-Sam Adams vintage quit the field and left it to what General Horatio

---

[38] Charles A. Beard and Mary R. Beard, *The Rise of American Civilization* (New York, 1930. First published in 1927), I, 326.

[39] Beard, *The Enduring Federalist* (New York, 1948), pp. 27–30.

[40] *The Articles of Confederation: An Interpretation of The Social-Constitutional History of the American Revolution, 1774–1781* (University of Wisconsin, 1940. Second printing with additional foreword, 1948). *The New Nation: A History of the United States During the Confederation, 1781–1789* (New York, 1950).

Gates, scarcely an objective or disinterested patriot, called "the rapacious graspers of power and profit." Gates was one grasper of power who just missed the brass ring. Mr. Jensen sees this revolutionary group outnumbered by 1781, and worn down by defeat. Then from 1781 to 1783 the government revolved around Robert Morris and his satellites, for all practical purposes a dictatorship in Mr. Jensen's eyes. But when we look more closely at these counterrevolutionaries, the sharp line between radicals and conservatives seems to fade away. Who was more radical than Alexander McDougall in Sons-of-Liberty days? Yet it was he who headed a delegation of officers to Congress in the winter of 1783. Perhaps Hamilton was not far wrong when he defended the Morris faction as not only "the most liberal," but as "the men who think continentally." The issue does not seem to have been one between radicals and conservatives, but between extreme particularists of the Clinton stripe and continental nationalists of varying shades and degrees.

Mr. Jensen is most effective in recounting the constructive steps taken in the Confederation period to repair federal and state finances. He points out that the Confederation actually managed to reduce the principal of its debt, and praises the states for their role in paying the national debt. Mr. Jensen points to the rapid amortization of state debts as evidence of the ability of the states to put their financial houses in order without much help from a central government. There is no doubt whatsoever that the states had now largely assumed the debt-funding function that the federal government had proven incapable of shouldering. Dr. E. J. Ferguson's studies of the assumption of the federal debts by the states reveal the considerable progress that was made in that direction in the Confederation period.[41] But, in terms of more recent ideas of economic planning, it would now seem that states like Massachusetts made the mistake of a too rapid amortization of the state debt, thereby initiating a sharp deflationary thrust. Even a conservative like Governor Bowdoin urged in 1786 a more gradual plan of amortization than that which the property-conscious legislature had enacted.

In short, the Beard-Jensen approach has served to present the Confederation period in a more constructive light, to give greater recognition to signs of economic expansion in the period and to the stabilizing role of the states, particularly in financial matters. As Allan Nevins has pointed out, when the new federal government went into effect, in no state was the debt appallingly high, and in some it was already low.[42] Mr. Jensen is doubtless correct in arguing that in most states the forces of law and

---

[41] E. J. Ferguson, "State Assumption of Federal Debt During the Confederation," *Mississippi Valley Historical Review,* XXXVIII (1951), 403.
[42] Allan Nevins, *The American States During and After the American Revolution* (New York, 1927), p. 541.

order never lost the upper hand. In New York that arch-Antifederalist George Clinton personally led the troops of the state against the insurrectionary Shays. In most cases—and Maryland is an excellent example—the disgruntled elements confined their efforts to obtaining relief in a legal manner through legislative action.

In truth, the real difference between the nationalist and Antifederalist schools of historiography turns neither on the extent of the depression nor on the amount of anarchy in the "critical period," but springs from a deep divergence in interpreting the American Revolution and the issues for which it was fought. Mr. Jensen sees the radical party in the Revolution as comprising the town masses and the frontier groups. As he views it, the radicals fought for an internal revolution; those conservatives who reluctantly supported the war merely wanted independence from England. In fact, this school of historiography depicts the American Revolution as essentially a civil war among the Whigs. In this version there seems to be little or no room for Tories, for redcoats, or for Hessians. This formula fails to explain why New York City and Philadelphia were hotbeds of Loyalism, why the regulators of Carolina and the levelers of upstate New York were Tories, or why debtors and creditors, hard-money men and paper-money men, suffrage expansionists and suffrage restrictionists were arrayed on the same side. It fails to explain the prominent role of the Whig conservative elite in bringing about the Revolution or to lay the foundation for understanding why in so many areas the radicalism of the leadership was that of the Gironde, not the Mountain.[43]

In the last analysis the view that the course of the Confederation period was determined by a counterrevolutionary movement, which, through the instrumentality of the Constitutional Convention, nipped democracy in the bud, hinges upon one's ideas about the American Revolution. Unless one is ready to accept the thesis that the group that started the war were libertarians and democrats and were supplanted by a conservative authoritarian party, one cannot give uncritical adherence to the Smith-Beard-Jensen approach to the Confederation period. The facts simply will not support the argument that the democratic forces originally seized control of the movement in the states. Even in the short run, these forces were unsuccessful in every state save Pennsylvania and Georgia. In New Jersey, then as now hospitable to democracy, the Constitution, as Mr. McCormick

[43] For examples from New England, see Lee N. Newcomer, *The Embattled Farmers: A Massachusetts Countryside in the American Revolution* (New York, 1953); Oscar Zeichner, *Connecticut's Years of Controversy, 1750–1776* (Chapel Hill, 1949). Robert E. Brown, *Middle-Class Democracy and the Revolution in Massachusetts, 1691–1780* (Ithaca, N. Y., 1955), demonstrates that in Massachusetts the property qualification for voting did not bar the majority of adult males from taking part in elections. He opposes the view of an "internal revolution" on the ground that democracy was already established. It is unlikely, however, that a re-examination of the nature and extent of the franchise and other so-called democratic indices in most of the remaining twelve states will support his concluding speculation that the "common man . . . had come into his own long before the era of Jacksonian Democracy."

has demonstrated,[44] was welcomed by all classes because it promised needed financial relief. In that state a western conservative coalition brought about deflationary policies, but not until the very end of the period under review. But the counterrevolution, if the halting of the left-ward swing of the pendulum deserves that appellation, was gradual and mild. States like Delaware and Maryland, as John A. Munroe [45] and Philip Crowl [46] have shown us, did not have a counterrevolution, because there never was the kind of democratic upthrust that characterized the early Revolutionary years in Pennsylvania.

The failure of the so-called democratic forces, as Elisha P. Douglass has recently restated for us,[47] is a tribute to the vigorous Revolutionary leadership of the Whig conservative forces and their awareness of the fundamental issues at stake. It was the Whig conservatives, not the regulators in North Carolina or the back-country insurgents in Massachusetts, who took the lead in the movement toward independence. Only where the Whig elite seemed timorous and unwilling to move from protest to revolution did the democratic and back-country forces have any chance of seizing power. That was the case in Pennsylvania, where the conservatives had abdicated their political leadership, and to a lesser degree in Georgia, where the story still remains to be spelled out and where the democratic victory was by no means as clear-cut as in Pennsylvania.

The Burke-Bryan-Lee-Clinton forces that comprised the so-called "democratic" party in the Revolutionary years—just what did they stand for? What kind of democracy did they want? The touchstone of their democracy seems to have been an advocacy of a unicameral legislature, a popularly elected judiciary, and a weak executive—and very little else. In some respects the Whigh conservatives held more advanced views than did the radicals. Judged by present-day standards the majoritarians were not always liberal. Back-country enthusiasts of the Great Awakening, they were by no means as ready to tolerate non-Protestant religious beliefs as were the deistically-minded Whig leaders. In fact, some of the most revealing evidence presented by Mr. Douglass is that which indicates that left-wing Protestants of Pietist or evangelical inclinations were fundamentalists in outlook and often basically conservative on political issues. It was they who tried to curb the political rights of non-Protestants, and in Pennsylvania it was the so-called radicals who enacted a law restricting freedom of expression. No, the majoritarians did not always act in democratic ways, nor did they seem always willing to abide by the will of the majority. Witness the shocking abuse of power by the radicals in Pennsylvania who established the state constitution by fiat and did not dare submit it to the

[44] Richard P. McCormick, *Experiment in Independence: New Jersey in the Critical Period, 1781–1789* (New Brunswick, 1950).
[45] *Federalist Delaware, 1775–1815* (New Brunswick, 1954).
[46] *Maryland During and After the Revolution* (Baltimore, 1942).
[47] *Rebels and Democrats* (Chapel Hill, 1955)

people. In fact, they went so far as to require the people to take an oath to support the constitution as a prerequisite to exercising the franchise.

Much has been made of the distrust of the masses held by the Whig conservatives, of the views of men like Jay that "the mass of men are neither wise nor good." But many of the Antifederalists shared similar views. Take Samuel Chase, who, as Philip Crowl has shown us, was instrumental in framing Maryland's ultraconservative constitution, and is alleged to have been unstinting in his praise of the aristocratic features of that document, particularly of the electoral college for choosing senators. His desertion to the Antifederalist camp is perhaps best explained by his financial reverses, but he did not linger in it too long. In the federal Convention the Antifederalist John F. Mercer had opposed allowing the people to participate, declaring, "The people cannot know and judge of the characters of Candidates. The worst possible choice will be made." [48] Elbridge Gerry, who refused to sign the Constitution, asserted that "the evils we experience flow from the excess of democracy" and expressed concern at "the danger of the levilling [sic] spirit." [49] In New York the bulwark of Antifederalism was the landowner, with his rural isolation, his dread of the federal impost, and his jealousy of sharing political power. True, he was supported in his opposition to the Constitution by tenants and small farmers, but the Antifederalist leaders of that state had little faith in the people. At the New York Convention George Clinton criticized the people for their fickleness, their tendency "to vibrate from one extreme to another." It was this very disposition, Clinton confessed, against which he wished to guard. [50]

The Antifederalists were not poured out of one democratic mold,[51] any more than the Federalists represented a unitary point of view about how to strengthen the central government. As Robert East has demonstrated,[52] there was a wide breach between the Bowdoin-Adams kind of federalism in Massachusetts and the Cabot-Pickering stripe of particularism, with its strong sectional and anti-Southern overtones. There was an even wider gulf between the democratic nationalism of Franklin and the authoritarian nationalism of Hamilton.

On the pro-democratic side of the Federalist ledger must be credited the position of the Whig conservatives in support of certain basic human rights which they conceived as fundamental and not subject to change at

---

[48] *Records of the Federal Convention of 1787*, ed. Max Farrand (New Haven, 1911–37) II, 205.

[49] *Ibid.*, I, 48.

[50] *Debates in the Several State Conventions on the Adoption of the Federal Constitution, . . . Together with the Journal of the Federal Convention . . .* , ed. Jonathan Elliot (Philadelphia, 1881), II, 359.

[51] The reader is referred to the provocative article by Cecelia M. Kenyon, "Men of Little Faith: The Anti-Federalists on the Nature of Representative Government," *William and Mary Quarterly*, 3rd Ser., XII (1955), 3–43.

[52] "The Massachusetts Conservatives in the Critical Period," in *The Era of the American Revolution*, ed. R. B. Morris (New York, 1939), pp. 349–391.

the caprice of majority rule. Fortunately for the evolution of American democracy, the principles of the conservative revolutionaries and their so-called democratic opponents were largely complementary to each other. Although almost everywhere the radicals were defeated in their efforts to seize the machinery of Revolution, the liberative effects of the war proved a deterrent to the kind of social revolution which would have enshrined class hatreds and ensured violent reaction.[53]

Yes, the American Whigs were divided in the years of the Revolution on almost all issues except that of political independence from Great Britain. Since diverse and even divergent interests forged the Whig alliance, it was only to be expected that the victory of the patriots would settle no single social or economic issue except freedom from British mercantilist controls, hardly an unmixed blessing in the years of the Confederation. Despite the efforts of J. Franklin Jameson to consider the American Revolution as a social movement, the fact is that the great internal social reforms lay ahead. As Harrison Gray Otis once wrote to a friend of Revolutionary days: "You and I did not imagine when the first war with Britain was over that the revolution was just begun."[54] Similar sentiments were expressed by Dr. Benjamin Rush on an earlier occasion. In his "Address to the People of the United States on the Defects of the Confederation" Rush declared: "The American war is over; but this is far from being the case with the American Revolution."[55]

Indeed, the imposition of a vitalized federalism and the tightening of the bonds of union precipitated a greater revolution in American life than did separation from England. To those who view the adoption of a system of republican federalism as constituting a more thoroughgoing break with the political system of the past than did that earlier severing of the tenuous bonds of empire—and there is impressive evidence in the Confederation interlude of our history to substantiate this interpretation—the Federalists, not the Antifederalists, were the real radicals of their day.

---

[53] "Was there ever a revolution brought about, especially so important as this, without great internal tumults and violent convulsions!" Sam Adams asked rhetorically. *The Writings of Samuel Adams*, ed. H. A. Cushing (New York, 1904–08), III, 304.

[54] Samuel Eliot Morison, *The Life and Letters of Harrison Gray Otis* (Boston and New York, 1913), I, 49.

[55] Reprinted in H. Niles, *Principles and Acts of the Revolution in America* (Baltimore, 1822), p. 402.

VII *The Constitution: Economic Determinism or Eighteenth-Century Political Theory?*

Introduction Each generation of Americans interprets the Constitution in the light of its own problems in an effort to bring the force of the Constitution to bear upon the "felt needs of mankind." Both majorities and minorities have sought protection within the Constitution's hospitable bounds. In the years before the Civil War the great constitutional issues related to the nature of the federal union, the relations of the states to the federal government, the powers and relative positions of the three branches of the government, and the protection of sectional minorities under the federal form of government. The emphasis was upon a legalistic, political science, and political theory point of view.

In the years following the Civil War, with the emergence of a new industrial order, with the businessman, the banker, and the railroad magnate emerging to an ever more dominant place and the corporate form of business enterprise everywhere gaining ground, the old traditional interpretations were no longer relevant. To the new ruling groups associated with the new industrial order, as Douglass Adair has pointed out, "the greatest glory of the American system established by the Constitution was its political and economic conservatism." It was Hamilton with his supposed businessman's philosophy of government and respect for property who was the hero among the founding fathers, and not the agrarian James Madison. Emerging out of the hard times of the 1890's and growing in strength down to the First World War, the Progressive Movement came to develop an interpretative faculty respecting American life and American institutions that sought to use the new tools of the social sciences. The Supreme Court in Muller vs. Oregon (1908) began to accept the findings of social workers and social scientists as relevant material to consider in the decisions of the Court.

This was the characteristic intellectual climate in which Charles A. Beard came to maturity, and this "younger Beard" published in the year 1913 his epoch-making *An Economic Interpretation of the Constitution*, from which two excerpts setting forth the fundamentals of interpretation follow. Beard's main thesis, that economic motives and interests dominated "the founding fathers" in drawing up the new federal Constitution in 1787, led scholars, in the main, during the twenties and thirties to subscribe to an economic interpretation of history. Beard declared in the most forthright manner that his inquiry "is based upon the political science of James Madison, the father of the Constitution and later President of the Union he had done so much to create." He then went on to quote from Madison's *Federalist No. 10* and concluded: "Here we have a masterly statement of the theory of economic determinism in politics."

Since the end of the Second World War, Beard's thesis has been subjected to sweeping criticism by R. E. Brown, Forrest McDonald,

Cecelia Kenyon, Douglass Adair, and others. Adair in particular is highly critical of Beard's use of Madison's *Tenth Federalist* as the major documentary source for his theory that economic determinism, primarily, motivated the founding fathers. Adair declares: "In the process of studying the evolution of Madison's ideas it will become apparent that it is highly anachronistic to tag his theory 'anti-democratic' in the nineteenth- or twentieth-century meaning of the term. Madison's *Tenth Federalist* is eighteenth-century political theory directed to an eighteenth-century problem; and it is one of the great creative achievements of that intellectual movement that later ages have christened 'Jefferson democracy.' "[1] The second piece below is a most persuasive exposition of Madison's political theory and its relation to the formation of our federal constitution.

---

[1] "The Tenth Federalist Revisited," *William and Mary Quarterly,* VIII (January 1951), 67.

An Economic Interpretation of the Constitution of the United States

—*Charles A. Beard*

This volume was first issued in 1913 during the tumult of discussion that accompanied the advent of the Progressive party, the split in Republican ranks, and the conflict over the popular election of United States Senators, workmen's compensation, and other social legislation. At that time Theodore Roosevelt had raised fundamental questions under the head of "the New Nationalism" and proposed to make the Federal Government adequate to the exigencies created by railways, the consolidation of industries, the closure of free land on the frontier, and the new position of labor in American economy. In the course of developing his conceptions, Mr. Roosevelt drew into consideration the place of the judiciary in the American system. While expressing high regard for that branch of government, he proposed to place limitations on its authority. He contended that "by the abuse of the power to declare laws unconstitutional the courts have become a law-making instead of a law-enforcing agency." As a check upon judicial proclivities, he proposed a scheme for "the recall of judicial decisions." This project he justified by the assertion that "when a court decides a constitutional question, when it decides what the people as a whole can or cannot do, the people should have the right to recall that decision when they think it wrong." Owing to such declarations, and to the counter-declarations, the "climate of opinion" was profoundly disturbed when *An Economic Interpretation of the Constitution* originally appeared.

Yet in no sense was the volume a work of the occasion, written with reference to immediate controversies. Doubtless I was, in common with all other students, influenced more or less by "the spirit of the times," but I had in mind no thought of forwarding the interests of the Progressive party or of its conservative critics and opponents. I had taken up the study of the Constitution many years before the publication of my work, while a profound calm rested on the sea of constitutional opinion. In that study I had occasion to read voluminous writings by the Fathers, and I was struck by the emphasis which so many of them placed upon economic interests as forces in politics and in the formulation of laws and constitutions. In particular I was impressed by the philosophy of politics set forth by James Madison in Number X of the *Federalist* . . . which seemed to furnish a clue to practical operations connected with the formation of the Constitution—operations in which Madison himself took a leading part.

Madison's view of the Constitution seemed in flat contradiction to most of the theorizing about the Constitution to which I had been accustomed in colleges, universities, and legal circles. It is true, older historians, such as Hildreth, had pointed out that there had been a sharp struggle over the formation and adoption of the Constitution, and that in the struggle an alignment of economic interests had taken place. It is true that Chief Justice Marshall, in his life of George Washington, had sketched the economic conflict out of which the Constitution sprang. But during the closing years of the nineteenth century this realistic view of the Constitution had been largely submerged in abstract discussions of states' rights and national sovereignty and in formal, logical, and discriminative analyses of judicial opinions. It was admitted, of course, that there had been a bitter conflict over the formation and adoption of the Constitution; but the struggle was usually explained, if explained at all, by reference to the fact that some men cherished states' rights and others favored a strong central government. At the time I began my inquiries the generally prevailing view was that expressed recently by Professor Theodore Clarke Smith: "Former historians had described the struggle over the formation and adoption of the document as a contest between sections ending in a victory of straight-thinking national-minded men over narrower and more local opponents." How some men got to be "national-minded" and "straight-thinking", and others became narrow and local in their ideas did not disturb the thought of scholars who presided over historical writing at the turn of the nineteenth century. Nor were those scholars at much pains to explain whether the term "section," which they freely used, meant a segment of physical geography or a set of social and economic arrangements within a geographic area, conditioned by physical circumstances.

One thing, however, my masters taught me, and that was to go behind the pages of history written by my contemporaries and read "the sources." In applying this method, I read the letters, papers, and documents pertaining to the Constitution written by the men who took part in framing and adopting it. And to my surprise I found that many Fathers of the Republic regarded the conflict over the Constitution as springing essentially out of conflicts of economic interests, which had a certain geographical or sectional distribution. This discovery, coming at a time when such conceptions of history were neglected by writers on history, gave me "the shock of my life." And since this aspect of the Constitution had been so long disregarded, I sought to redress the balance by emphasis, "naturally" perhaps. At all events I called my volume "an economic interpretation of the Constitution." I did not call it "the" economic interpretation, or "the only" interpretation possible to thought. Nor did I pretend that it was "the history" of the formation and adoption of the Constitution. The reader was warned in advance of the theory and the emphasis. No attempt was made to take him off his guard by some plausible formula of completeness and comprehensiveness. I simply sought to bring back into the mental picture of the Constitution those realistic features of economic conflict, stress, and strain, which my masters had, for some reason, left out of it, or thrust far into the background as incidental rather than fundamental.

When my book appeared, it was roundly condemned by conservative Republicans, including ex-President Taft, and praised, with about the same amount of discrimination, by Progressives and others on the left wing. Perhaps no other book on the Constitution has been more severely criticized, and so little read. Perhaps no other book on the subject has been used to justify opinions and projects so utterly beyond its necessary implications. It was employed by a socialist writer to support a plea for an entirely new constitution and by a conservative judge of the United States Supreme Court to justify an attack on a new piece of "social legislation." Some members of the New York Bar Association became so alarmed by the book that they formed a committee and summoned me to appear before it; and, when I declined on the ground that I was not engaged in legal politics or political politics, they treated my reply as a kind of contempt of court. Few took the position occupied by Justice Oliver Wendell Holmes, who once remarked to me that he had not got excited about the book, like some of his colleagues, but had supposed that it was intended to throw light on the nature of the Constitution, and, in his opinion, did so in fact.

Among my historical colleagues the reception accorded the volume varied. Professor William A. Dunning wrote me that he regarded it as "the pure milk of the word," although it would "make the heathen rage." Professor Albert Bushnell Hart declared that it was little short of indecent. Others sought to classify it by calling it "Marxian." Even as late as the year 1934, Professor Theodore Clarke Smith, in an address before the American Historical Association, expressed this view of the volume, in making it illustrative of a type of historical writing, which is "doctrinaire" and "excludes anything like impartiality." He said: "This is the view that American history, like all history, can and must be explained in economic terms. . . . This idea has its origin, of course, in the Marxian theories." [1] Having made this assertion, Professor Smith turned his scholarly battery upon An Economic Interpretation of the Constitution.

Now as a matter of fact there is no reason why an economic interpretation of the Constitution should be more partisan than any other interpre-

---

[1] American Historical Review, April, 1935, p. 447.

tation. It may be employed, to be sure, to condemn one interest in the conflict or another interest, but no such use of it is imposed upon an author by the nature of the interpretation. Indeed an economic analysis may be coldly neutral, and in the pages of this volume no words of condemnation are pronounced upon the men enlisted upon either side of the great controversy which accompanied the formation and adoption of the Constitution. Are the security holders who sought to collect principal and interest through the formation of a stronger government to be treated as guilty of impropriety or praised? That is a question to which the following inquiry is not addressed. An answer to that question belongs to moralists and philosophers, not to students of history as such. If partiality is taken in the customary and accepted sense, it means "leaning to one party or another." Impartiality means the opposite. Then this volume is, strictly speaking, impartial. It supports the conclusion that in the main the men who favored the Constitution were affiliated with certain types of property and economic interest, and that the men who opposed it were affiliated with other types. It does not say that the former were "straight-thinking" and that the latter were "narrow." It applies no moralistic epithets to either party.

On the other hand Professor Smith's statement about the conflict over the Constitution is his *interpretation* of the nature of things, in that it makes the conflict over the Constitution purely psychological in character, unless some economic content is to be given to the term "section." In any event it assumes that straight-thinking and national-mindedness are entities, particularities, or forces, apparently independent of all earthly considerations coming under the head of "economic." It does not say how these entities, particularities, or forces got into American heads. It does not show whether they were imported into the colonies from Europe or sprang up after the colonial epoch closed. It arbitrarily excludes the possibilities that their existence may have been conditioned if not determined by economic interests and activities. It is firm in its exclusion of other interpretations and conceptions. Whoever does not believe that the struggle over the Constitution was a simple contest between the straight-thinking men and narrower and local men of the respective sections is to be cast into outer darkness as "Marxian" or lacking in "impartiality." Is that not a doctrinaire position?

Not only is Professor Smith's position exclusive. It is highly partial. The men who favored the Constitution were "straight-thinking" men. Those who opposed it were "narrower" men. These words certainly may be taken to mean that advocates of the Constitution were wiser men, men of a higher type of mind, than the "narrower" men who opposed it. In a strict sense, of course, straight-thinking may be interpreted as thinking logically. In that case no praise or partiality is necessarily involved. A trained burglar who applies his science to cracking a safe may be more logical than an impulsive night watchman who sacrifices his life in the performance of duty. But in common academic acceptance a logical man is supposed to be superior to the intuitional and emotional man.

Nor is there exactness in such an antithesis as "straight-thinking" and narrowness. Narrowness does not, of necessity, mean lack of straight-thinking. Straight-thinking may be done in a narrow field of thought as well as in a large domain. But there is a true opposition in national-mindedness and local-mindedness, and the student of economic history merely inquires whether the antithesis does not correspond in the main to an economic antagonism. He may accept Professor Smith's psychological antithesis and go beyond it to inquire into its origins. But in so doing he need not ascribe any superior quality of intellect to the one party or the other. To ascribe qualities of mind—high or low—to either party is partiality, dogmatic and doctinaire partiality. It arbitrarily introduces virtues of intellectual superiority and inferiority into an examination of matters of fact.

In the minds of some, the term "Marxian," imported into the discussion by Professor Smith, means an epithet; and in the minds of others, praise. With neither of these views have I the least concern. For myself I can say that I have never believed that "all history" can or must be "explained" in economic terms, or any other terms. He who really "explains" history must have the attributes ascribed by the theologians to God. It can be "explained," no doubt, to the satisfaction of certain mentalities at certain times, but such explanations are not universally accepted and approved. I confess to have hoped in my youth to find "the causes of things," but I never thought that I had found them. Yet it has seemed to me, and does now, that in the great transformations in society, such as was brought about by the formation and adoption of the Constitution, economic "forces" are primordial or fundamental, and come nearer "explaining" events than any other "forces." Where the configurations and pressures of economic interests are brought into an immediate relation to the event or series of events under consideration, an economic interpretation is effected. Yet, as I said in 1913, on page 195, "It may be that some larger world process is working through each series of historical events; but ultimate causes lie beyond our horizon." If anywhere I have said or written that "all history" can be "explained" in economic terms, I was then suffering from an aberration of the mind.

Nor can I accept as a historical fact Professor Smith's assertion that the economic interpretation of history or my volume on the Constitution had its origin in "Marxian theories." As I point out in Chapter 1 of my *Economic Basis of Politics,* the germinal idea of class and group conflicts in history appeared in the writings of Aristotle, long before the Christian era, and was known to great writers on politics during the middle ages and modern times. It was expounded by James Madison, in Number X of the *Federalist*, written in defense of the Constitution of the United States, long before Karl Marx was born. Marx seized upon the idea, applied it with rigor, and based predictions upon it, but he did not originate it. Fathers of the American Constitution were well aware of the idea, operated on the hypothesis that it had at least a considerable validity, and expressed it in numerous writings. Whether conflicting economic interests bulk large in contemporary debates over protective tariffs, foreign trade, transportation, industry, commerce, labor, agriculture, and the nature of the Constitution itself, each of our contemporaries may decide on the basis of his experience and knowledge.

Yet at the time this volume was written, I was, in common with all students who professed even a modest competence in modern history, conversant with the theories and writings of Marx. Having read extensively among the writings of the Fathers of the Constitution of the United States and studied Aristotle, Machiavelli, Locke, ond other political philosophers, I became all the more interested in Marx when I discovered in his works the ideas which had been cogently expressed by outstanding thinkers and statesmen in the preceding centuries. That interest was deepened when I learned from an inquiry into his student life that he himself had been acquainted with the works of Aristotle, Montesquieu, and other writers of the positive bent before he began to work out his own historical hypothesis. By those who use his name to rally political parties or to frighten Daughters of the American Revolution, students of history concerned with the origins of theories need not be disturbed.

For the reason that this volume was not written for any particular political occasion but designed to illuminate all occasions in which discussion of the Constitution appears, I venture to re-issue it in its original form. It does not "explain" the Constitution. It does not exclude other explanations deemed more satisfactory to the explainers. Whatever its short-comings, the volume does, however, present some indubitable facts pertaining to that great document which will be useful to students of the Constitution and to practitioners engaged in interpreting it. The Constitution was of human origin, immediately at least, and it is now discussed and applied by human beings who find themselves engaged in certain callings, occupations, professions, and interests. . . .

Historical Interpretation in the United States

Broadly speaking, three schools of interpretation have dominated American historical research and generalization. The first of these, which may be justly associated with the name of Bancroft, explains the larger achievements in our national life by reference to the peculiar moral endowments of a people acting under divine guidance; or perhaps it would be more correct to say, it sees in the course of our development the working out of a higher will than that of man. There is to be observed in the history of the struggle for the Constitution, to use Bancroft's words, "the movement of the divine power which gives unity to the universe, and order and connection to events." [2]

Notwithstanding such statements, scattered through Bancroft's pages, it is impossible to describe in a single phrase the ideal that controlled his principles of historical construction, because he was so often swayed by his deference to the susceptibilities of the social class from which he sprang and by the exigencies of the public life in which he played a by no means inconspicuous part. Even telling the whole truth did not lie upon his conscience, for, speaking on the question of the number of Americans who were descendants from transported felons and indented servants, he said that "Having a hand full, he opened his little finger." [3]

Nevertheless, Bancroft constantly recurs in his writings to that "higher power" which is operating in human affairs, although he avoids citing specific events which may be attributed to it. It appears to him to be the whole course of history, rather than any event or set of events, which justifies his theory. "However great," he says, "may be the number of those who persuade themselves that there is in man nothing superior to himself, history interposes with evidence that tyranny and wrong lead inevitably to decay; that freedom and right, however hard may be the struggle, always prove resistless. Through this assurance ancient nations learn to renew their youth; the rising generation is incited to take a generous part in the grand drama of time; and old age, staying itself upon sweet Hope as its companion and cherisher, not bating a jot of courage, nor seeing cause to argue against the hand or the will of a higher power, stands waiting in the tranquil conviction that the path of humanity is still fresh with the dews of morning, that the Redeemer of the nations liveth." [4]

The second school of historical interpretation, which in the order of time followed that of Bancroft, may be called the Teutonic, because it ascribes the wonderful achievements of the English-speaking peoples to the peculiar political genius of the Germanic race. Without distinctly repudiating the doctrine of the "higher power" in history, it finds the secret to the "free" institutional development of the Anglo-Saxon world in innate racial qualities.

The thesis of this school is, in brief, as follows. The Teutonic peoples were oginally endowed with singular political talents and aptitudes; Teutonic tribes invaded England and destroyed the last vestiges of the

---

[2] The History of the Constitution of the United States (1882 ed.), Vol. II, p. 284.
[3] American Historical Review, Vol. II, p. 13.　　[4] Bancroft, op. cit., Vol. I, p. 6.

older Roman and British culture; they then set an example to the world in the development of "free" government. Descendants of this specially gifted race settled America and fashioned their institutions after old English models. The full fruition of their political genius was reached in the creation of the Federal Constitution.

For more than a generation the Teutonic theory of our institutions deeply influenced historical research in the United States; but it was exhausted in the study of local government rather than of great epochs; and it produced no monument of erudition comparable to Stubbs' *Constitutional History of England*. Whatever may be said of this school, which has its historical explanation and justification,[5] it served one exceedingly useful purpose: it was scrupulously careful in the documentation of its preconceptions and thus cultivated a more critical spirit than that which characterized the older historians.[6]

The third school of historical research is not to be characterized by any phrase. It is marked rather by an absence of hypotheses. Its representatives, seeing the many pitfalls which beset the way of earlier writers, have resolutely turned aside from "interpretation" in the larger sense, and concerned themselves with critical editions of the documents and with the "impartial" presentation of related facts. This tendency in American scholarship has been fruitful in its results, for it has produced more care in the use of historical sources and has given us many excellent and accurate surveys of outward events which are indispensable to the student who would inquire more deeply into underlying causes.[7]

Such historical writing, however, bears somewhat the same relation to scientific history which systematic botany bears to ecology; that is, it classifies and orders phenomena, but does not explain their proximate or remote causes and relations. The predominance of such a historical ideal in the United States and elsewhere is not altogether inexplicable; for interpretative schools seem always to originate in social antagonisms.[8]

---

[5] It has been left to a Russian to explain to Englishmen the origin of Teutonism in historical writing. See the introduction to Vinogradoff, *Villainage in England*. W. J. Ashley, in his preface to the translation of Fustel de Coulanges, *Origin of Property in Land*, throws some light on the problem, but does not attempt a systematic study.

[6] Note the painstaking documentation for the first chapters in Stubbs' great work.

[7] What Morley has said of Macaulay is true of many eminent American historical writers: "A popular author must, in a thoroughgoing way, take the accepted maxims for granted. He must suppress any whimsical fancy for applying the Socratic elenchus; or any other engine of criticism, scepticism, or verification to those sentiments or current precepts or morals which may in truth be very equivocal and may be much neglected in practice, but which the public opinion of his time requires to be treated in theory and in literature as if they had been cherished and held *semper, ubique, et ab omnibus*." *Miscellanies*, Vol. I, p. 272.

[8] For instance, intimate connections can be shown between the vogue of Darwinism and the competitive ideals of the mid-Victorian middle-class in England. Darwin got one of his leading ideas, the struggle for existence, from Malthus, who originated it as a club to destroy the social reformers, Godwin, Condorcet, and others, and then gave it a serious scientific guise as an afterthought.

The monarchy, in its rise and development, was never correctly understood as long as it was regarded by all as a mystery which must not be waded into, as James I put it, by ordinary mortals. Without the old régime there would have been no Turgot and Voltaire; Metternich and Joseph de Maistre came after the Revolution.

But the origin of different schools of interpretation in controversies and the prevalence of many mere preconceptions bolstered with a show of learning should not lead us to reject without examination any new hypothesis, such as the theory of economic determinism, on the general assumption of Pascal "that the will, the imagination, the disorders of the body, the thousand concealed infirmities of the intelligence conspire to reduce our discovery of justice and truth to a process of haphazard, in which we more often miss than hit the mark." Such a doctrine of pessimism would make of equal value for the student who would understand, for instance, such an important matter as the origin of the state, Mr. Edward Jenk's severely scientific *History of Politics* and Dr. Nathaniel Johnston's *The Excellency of Monarchical Government, especially the English Monarchy, wherein is largely treated of the Several Benefits of Kingly Government and the Inconvenience of Commonwealths. . . . Likewise the Duty of Subjects and the Mischief of Faction, Sedition, and Rebellion*, published in 1686.

It is not without significance, however, that almost the only work in economic interpretation which has been done in the United States seems to have been inspired at the University of Wisconsin by Professor Turner, now of Harvard. Under the direction of this original scholar and thinker, the influence of the material circumstances of the frontier on American politics was first clearly pointed out. Under his direction also the most important single contribution to the interpretation of the movement for the federal Constitution was made: O. G. Libby's *Geographical Distribution of the Vote of the Thirteen States on the Federal Constitution.*

In a preface to this work, Professor Turner remarks that the study was designed to contribute "to an understanding of the relations between the political history of the United States, and the physiographic, social, and economic conditions underlying this history. . . . It is believed that many phases of our political history have been obscured by the attention paid to state boundaries and to the sectional lines of North and South. At the same time the economic interpretation of our history has been neglected. In the study of the persistence of the struggle for state particularism in American constitutional history, it was inevitable that writers should make prominent the state as a political factor. But, from the point of view of the rise and growth of sectionalism and nationalism, It is much more important to note the existence of great social and economic areas, independent of state lines, which have acted as units in political history, and which have changed their political attitude as they changed their economic organization and divided into new groups." [9]

Although the hypothesis that economic elements are the chief factors in the development of political institutions has thus been used in one or two serious works, and has been more or less discussed as a philosophic theory,[10] it has not been applied to the study of American history at large —certainly not with that infinite detailed analysis which it requires. Nor has it received at the hands of professed historians that attention which its significance warrants. On the contrary, there has been a tendency to treat it with scant courtesy and to dismiss it with a sharpness bordering on contempt.[11] Such summary judgment is, of course, wholly unwarranted and premature; for as Dr. William Cunningham remarks, the validity of no hypothesis can be determined until it has been worked to its utmost limits. It is easier to write a bulky volume from statutes, congressional debates,[12] memoirs, and diplomatic notes than it is to ascertain the geographical distribution and political significance of any important group of economic factors. The theory of economic determinism has not been tried out in American history, and until it is tried out, it cannot be found wanting.

Sadly as the economic factors have been ignored in historical studies, the neglect has been all the more pronounced in the field of private and public law. The reason for this is apparent. The aim of instruction in these subjects is intensely practical; there are few research professorships in law; and the "case" system of teaching discourages attempts at generalization and surveys.[13] Not even the elementary work has been done. There has been no generous effort to describe the merely superficial aspects of the development of private law in the United States. There has been no concerted attempt to bring together and make available to students the raw materials of such a history. Most of the current views on the history of our law are derived from occasional disquisitions of judges which are

---

[9] See also the valuable and suggestive writings on American history by Professor W. E. Dodd, of Chicago University; W. A. Schaper, "Sectionalism in South Carolina," *American Historical Association Report* (1900), Vol. I; A. Bentley, *The Process of Government*; C. H. Ambler, *Sectionalism in Virginia*. There are three works by socialist writers that deserve study: Simons, *Social Forces in American History*; Gustavus Myers, *History of Great American Fortunes* and *History of the Supreme Court*.

[10] See Seligman, *The Economic Interpretation of History*.

[11] Vincent, in his treatise on *Historical Research* (1911), dismisses the economic theory without critical examination.

[12] The *Congressional Record* requires more care in use than any other great source of information on American politics.

[13] Attention should be drawn, however, to the good work which is being done in the translation of several European legal studies, the "Modern Legal Philosophy Series," under the editorial direction of the Association of American Law Schools. Perhaps the most hopeful sign of the times is the growth of interest in comparative jurisprudence. See Borchard, "Jurisprudence in Germany," Columbia Law Review, April, 1912.

all too frequently shot through with curious errors of fact and conception.

Nor has England advanced far beyond us in the critical interpretation of legal evolution—its explanation in terms of, or in relation to, the shifting economic processes and methods in which the law is tangled. It is true that English scholars have produced admirable histories of the law in its outward aspects, such as the monumental work of Pollock and Maitland; and they have made marvellous collections of raw materials, like the publications of the Selden Society. But apart from scattered and brilliant suggestions thrown off occasionally by Maitland [14] in passing, no interpretation has been ventured, and no effort has been made to connect legal phases with economic changes.

In the absence of a critical analysis of legal evolution, all sorts of vague abstractions dominate most of the thinking that is done in the field of law. The characteristic view of the subject taken by American commentators and lawyers immersed in practical affairs is perhaps summed up as finely by Carter as by any writer. "In free, popular states," he says, "the law springs from and is made by the people; and as the process of building it up consists in applying, from time to time, to human actions the popular ideal or standard of justice, justice is only interest consulted in the work. . . . The law of England and America has been a pure development proceeding from a constant endeavor to apply to the civil conduct of men the ever advancing standard of justice." [15] In other words, law is made out of some abstract stuff known as "justice." What set the standard in the beginning and why does it advance?

The devotion to deductions from "principles" exemplified in particular cases, which is such a distinguishing sign of American legal thinking, has the same effect upon correct analysis which the adherence to abstract terms had upon the advancement of learning—as pointed out by Bacon. The absence of any consideration of the social and economic elements determining the thought of the thinkers themselves is all the more marked when contrasted with the penetration shown by European savants like Jhering, Menger, and Stammler. Indeed, almost the only indication of a possible economic interpretation to be found in current American jurisprudence is implicit in the writings of a few scholars, like Professor Roscoe

---

[14] For examples of Maitland's suggestiveness, see the English Historical Review, Vol. IX, p. 439, for a side light on the effect of money economy on the manor and consequently on feudal law. See also the closing pages of his *Constitutional History of England*, where he makes constitutional law in large part the history of the law of real property. "If we are to learn anything about the constitution, it is necessary first and foremost that we should learn a good deal about the land law. We can make no progress whatever in the history of parliament without speaking of tenure; indeed our whole constitutional law seems at times to be but an appendix to the law of real property" (p. 538). Maitland's entire marvellous chapter on "The Definition of Constitutional Law" deserves the most carfeul study and reflection. He was entirely emancipated from bondage to systematists (p. 539).

[15] J. G. Carter, *The Proposed Codification of Our Common Law* (1884), pp. 6–8.

Pound and Professor Goodnow,[16] and in occasional opinions rendered by Mr. Justice Holmes of the Supreme Court of the United States.[17]

What has here been said about our private law may be more than repeated about our constitutional history and law. This subject, though it has long held an honorable position in the American scheme of learning, has not yet received the analytical study which its intrinsic importance merits. In the past, it has often been taught in the law schools by retired judges who treated it as a branch of natural and moral philosophy or by practical lawyers who took care for the instant need of things. Our great commentaries, Kent, Story, Miller, are never penetrating; they are generally confined to statements of fact; and designed to inculcate the spirit of reverence rather than of understanding. And of constitutional histories, strictly speaking, we have none, except the surveys of superficial aspects by Curtis and Bancroft.

In fact, the juristic theory of the origin and nature of the Constitution is marked by the same lack of analysis of determining forces which characterized older historical writing in general. It may be stated in the following manner: The Constitution proceeds from the whole people; the people are the original source of all political authority exercised under it; it is founded on broad general principles of liberty and government entertained, for some reason, by the whole people and having no reference to the interest or advantage of any particular group or class. "By calm meditation and friendly councils," says Bancroft, "they [the people] had prepared a Constitution which, in the union of freedom with strength and order, excelled every one known before. . . . In the happy morning of their existence as one of the powers of the world, they had chosen justice for their guide; and while they proceeded on their way with a well-founded confidence and joy, all the friends of mankind invoked success on their endeavor as the only hope for renovating the life of the civilized world." [18]

With less exaltation, Chief Justice Marshall states the theory, in his opinion in the case of McCulloch v. Maryland: "The government proceeds directly from the people; is 'ordained and established' in the name of the people; and is declared to be ordained 'in order to form a more perfect union, to establish justice, insure domestic tranquillity, and secure the

---

[16] Of the newer literature on law, see the following articles by Professor Roscoe Pound: "Do we need a Philosophy of Law?" Columbia Law Review, Vol. V, p. 339; "Need of a Sociological Jurisprudence," Green Bag, Vol. XIX, p. 607; "Mechanical Jurisprudence," Columbia Law Review, Vol. VIII, p. 605; "Law in Books and Law in Action," American Law Review, Vol. XLIV, p. 12; Professor Munroe Smith, "Jurisprudence" (in the Columbia University Lectures in Arts and Sciences); Goodnow, Social Reform and the Constitution.
[17] Consider, for example, the following remarks by this eminent Justice in his dissenting opinion in the New York Bakery case: "This case is decided upon an economic theory which a large part of the country does not entertain. . . . The Fourteenth Amendment does not enact Mr. Herbert Spencer's Social Statics. . . . General propositions do not decide concrete cases. The decision will depend on a judgment or intuition more subtle than any articulate major premise." 198 U. S. 75.
[18] Op. cit., Vol. II, p. 367.

blessings of liberty' to themselves and to their posterity. The assent of the states, in their sovereign capacity, is implied in calling a convention, and thus submitting that instrument to the people. But the people were at perfect liberty to accept or reject it; and their act was final. . . . The government of the Union, then (whatever may be the influence of this fact on the case) is emphatically and truly a government of the people. In form and in substance it emanates from them. Its powers are granted by them, and are to be exercised directly on them, and for their benefit. . . . It is the government of all; its powers are delegated by all; it represents all, and acts for all." [19]

In the juristic view, the Constitution is not only the work of the whole people, but it also bears in it no traces of the party conflict from which it emerged. Take, for example, any of the traditional legal definitions of the Constitution; Miller's will suffice: "A constitution, in the American sense of the word, is any instrument by which the fundamental powers of the government are established, limited, and defined, and by which these powers are distributed among the several departments for their more safe and useful exercise, for the benefit of the body politic. . . . It is not, however, the origin of private rights, nor the foundation of laws. It is not the cause, but the consequence of personal and political freedom. It declares those natural and fundamental rights of individuals, for the security and common enjoyment of which governments are established." [20]

Nowhere in the commentaries is there any evidence of the fact that the rules of our fundamental law are designed to protect any class in its rights, or secure the property of one group against the assaults of another. "The Constitution," declares Bancroft, "establishes nothing that interferes with equality and individuality. It knows nothing of differences by descent, or opinions, of favored classes, or legalized religion, or the political power of property. It leaves the individual along-side of the individual. . . . As the sea is made up of drops, American society is composed of separate, free, and constantly moving atoms, ever in reciprocal action . . . so that the institutions and laws of the country rise out of the masses of individual thought, which, like the waters of the ocean, are rolling evermore." [21]

In turning from the vague phraseology of Bancroft to an economic interpretation of constitutional history, it is necessary to realize at the outset that law is not an abstract thing, a printed page, a volume of statutes, a statement by a judge. So far as it becomes of any consequence to the observer it must take on a real form; it must govern actions; it must determine positive relations between men; it must prescribe processes and juxtapositions.[22] A statute may be on the books for an age, but unless,

[19] 4 Wheaton, p. 316. No doubt the learned Justice was here more concerned with discrediting the doctrine of state's rights than with establishing the popular basis of our government.
[20] S. F. Miller, *Lectures on the Constitution* (1891), p. 71.
[21] *Op. cit.*, Vol. II, p. 324. [22] See A. Bentley, *The Process of Government.*

under its provisions, a determinate arrangement of human relations is brought about or maintained, it exists only in the imagination. Separated from the social and economic fabric by which it is, in part, conditioned and which, in turn, it helps to condition, it has no reality.

Now, most of the law (except the elemental law of community defence) is concerned with the property relations of men, which reduced to their simple terms mean the processes by which the ownership of concrete forms of property is determined or passes from one person to another. As society becomes more settled and industrial in character, mere defence against violence (a very considerable portion of which originates in forcible attempts to change the ownership of property) becomes of relatively less importance; and property relations increase in complexity and subtlety.

But it may be said that constitutional law is a peculiar branch of the law; that it is not concerned primarily with property or with property relations, but with organs of government, the suffrage, administration. The superficiality of this view becomes apparent at a second glance. Inasmuch as the primary object of a government, beyond the mere repression of physical violence, is the making of the rules which determine the property relations of members of society, the dominant classes whose rights are thus to be determined must perforce obtain from the government such rules as are consonant with the larger interests necesary to the continuance of their economic processes, or they must themselves control the organs of government. In a stable despotism the former takes place; under any other system of government, where political power is shared by any portion of the population, the methods and nature of this control become the problem of prime importance—in fact, the fundamental problem in constitutional law. The social structure by which one type of legislation is secured and another prevented—that is, the constitution—is a secondary or derivative feature arising from the nature of the economic groups seeking positive action and negative restraint.

In what has just been said there is nothing new to scholars who have given any attention to European writings on jurisprudence. It is based in the first instance on the doctine advanced by Jhering that law does not "grow," but is, in fact, "made"—adapted to precise interests which may be objectively determined. It was not original with Jhering. Long before he worked out the concept in his epoch-making book, *Der Zweck im Recht*, Lassalle had set it forth in his elaborate *Das System der erworbenen Rechte*, and long before Lassalle had thought it through, our own Madison had formulated it, after the most wide-reaching researches in history and politics.[23]

In fact, the inquiry which follows is based upon the political science of James Madison, the father of the Constitution and later President of the

---

[23] And before Madison's century, Harrington had perceived its significance. H. A. L Fisher, *Republican Tradition in Europe*, p. 51.

Union he had done so much to create. This political science runs through all of his really serious writings and is formulated in its most precise fashion in *The Federalist* [24] as follows: "The diversity in the faculties of men, from which the rights of property originate, is not less an insuperable obstacle to a uniformity of interests. The protection of these faculties is the first object of government. From the protection of different and unequal faculties of acquiring property, the possession of different degrees and kinds of property immediately results; and from the influence of these on the sentiments and views of the respective proprietors, ensues a division of society into different interests and parties. . . . The most common and durable source of factions has been the various and unequal distribution of property. Those who hold and those who are without property have ever formed distinct interests in society. Those who are creditors, and those who are debtors, fall under a like discrimination. A landed interest, a manufacturing interest, a mercantile interest, a moneyed interest, with many lesser interests, grow up of necessity in civilized nations and divide them into different classes, actuated by different sentiments and views. The regulation of these various and interfering interests forms the principal task of modern legislation, and involves the spirit of party and faction in the necessary and ordinary operations of the government."

Here we have a masterly statement of the theory of economic determinism in politics.[25] Different degrees and kinds of property inevitably exist in modern society; party doctrines and "principles" originate in the sentiments and views which the possession of various kinds of property creates in the minds of the possessors; class and group divisions based on property lie at the basis of modern government; and politics and constitutional law are inevitably a reflex of these contending interests. Those who are inclined to repudiate the hypothesis of economic determinism as a European importation must, therefore, revise their views, on learning that one of the earliest, and certainly one of the clearest, statements of it came from a profound student of politics who sat in the Convention that framed our fundamental law.

The requirements for an economic interpretation of the formation and adoption of the Constitution may be stated in a hypothetical proposition which, although it cannot be verified absolutely from ascertainable data,

---

[24] Number 10.

[25] The theory of the economic interpretation of history as stated by Professor Seligman seems as nearly axiomatic as any proposition in social science can be: "The existence of man depends upon his ability to sustain himself; the economic life is therefore the fundamental condition of all life. Since human life, however, is the life of man in society, individual existence moves within the framework of the social structure and is modified by it. What the conditions of maintenance are to the individual, the similar relations of production and consumption are to the community. To economic causes, therefore, must be traced in the last instance those transformations in the structure of society which themselves condition the relations of social classes and the various manifestations of social life." *The Economic Interpretation of History*, p. 3.

will at once illustrate the problem and furnish a guide to research and generalization.

It will be admitted without controversy that the Constitution was the creation of a certain number of men, and it was opposed by a certain number of men. Now, if it were possible to have an economic biography of all those connected with its framing and adoption,—perhaps about 160,000 men altogether,—the materials for scientific analysis and classification would be available. Such an economic biography would include a list of the real and personal property owned by all of these men and their families: lands and houses, with incumbrances, money at interest, slaves, capital invested in shipping and manufacturing, and in state and continental securities.

Suppose it could be shown from the classification of the men who supported and opposed the Constitution that there was no line of property division at all; that is, that men owning substantially the same amounts of the same kinds of property were equally divided on the matter of adoption or rejection—it would then become apparent that the Constitution had no ascertainable relation to economic groups or classes, but was the product of some abstract causes remote from the chief business of life—gaining a livelihood.

Suppose, on the other hand, that substantially all of the merchants, money lenders, security holders, manufacturers, shippers, capitalists, and financiers and their professional associates are to be found on one side in support of the Constitution and that substantially all or the major portion of the opposition came from the non-slaveholding farmers and the debtors —would it not be pretty conclusively demonstrated that our fundamental law was not the product of an abstraction known as "the whole people," but of a group of economic interests which must have expected beneficial results from its adoption? Obviously all the facts here desired cannot be discovered, but the data presented in the following chapters bear out the latter hypothesis, and thus a reasonable presumption in favor of the theory is created.

Of course, it may be shown (and perhaps can be shown) that the farmers and debtors who opposed the Constitution were, in fact, benefited by the general improvement which resulted from its adoption. It may likewise be shown, to take an extreme case, that the English nation derived immense advantages from the Norman Conquest and the orderly administrative processes which were introduced, as it undoubtedly did; nevertheless, it does not follow that the vague thing known as "the advancement of general welfare" or some abstraction known as "justice" was the immediate, guiding purpose of the leaders in either of these great historic changes. The point is, that the direct, impelling motive in both cases was the economic advantages which the beneficiaries expected would accrue to themselves first, from their action. Further than this, economic interpretation cannot go. It may be that some larger world-process is working through each series of historical events; but ultimate causes lie beyond our horizon.

"That Politics May Be Reduced to a Science": David Hume, James Madison, and the Tenth "Federalist"

—*Douglass Adair*

In June 1783, the war for American independence being ended, General Washington addressed his once-famous circular letter to the state governors with the hopeful prophecy that if the Union of the States could be preserved, the future of the Republic would be both glorious and happy. "The foundation of our Empire was not laid in the gloomy age of Ignorance and Superstition," Washington pointed out, "but at an Epocha when the rights of mankind were better understood and more clearly defined, than at any former period; the researches of the human mind after social happiness, have been carried to a great extent, the treasures of knowledge, acquired by the labours of Philosophers, Sages, and Legislators, through a long succession of years, are laid open for our use, and their collected wisdom may be happily applied in the Establishment of our forms of Government . . . At this auspicious period, the United States came into existence as a Nation, and if their Citizens should not be completely free and happy, the fault will be intirely their own."

The optimism of General Washington's statement is manifest; the reasons he advances for this optimism, however, seem to modern Americans a century and a half later both odd and naive, if not slightly un-American. For Washington here argues in favor of "the Progress of the Human Mind." Knowledge gradually acquired through "researches of the human mind" about the nature of man and government—knowledge which "the gloomy age of Ignorance and Superstition" did not have— gives Americans in 1783 the power to new-model their forms of government according to the precepts of wisdom and reason. The "Philosopher"

From *Huntington Library Quarterly*, XX (August 1957), 343–360. Reprinted by permission. Delivered at the Conference of Early American History at the Henry E. Huntington Library, February 9, 1957.

as Sage and Legislator, General Washington hopes, will preside over the creation and reform of American political institutions.

"Philosopher" as written here by Washington was a word with hopeful and good connotations. But this was 1783. In 1789 the French Revolution began; by 1792 "philosophy" was being equated with the guillotine, atheism, the reign of terror. Thereafter "philosopher" would be a smear-word, connoting a fuzzy-minded and dangerous social theorist—one of those impractical Utopians whose foolish attempts to reform society according to a rational plan created the anarchy and social disaster of the Terror. Before his death in 1799 Washington himself came to distrust and fear the political activities of philosophers. And in time it would become fashionable among both French conservatives and among all patriotic Americans to stress the sinister new implications of the word "philosophy" added after 1789 and to credit the French philosophers with transforming the French Revolution into a "bad" revolution in contrast to the "good" non-philosophical American Revolution. But this ethical transformation of the word still lay in the future in 1783. Then "philosophy" and "philosopher" were still terms evoking optimism and hopes of the high tide of Enlightenment on both sides of the Atlantic.

Dr. Johnson in his *Dictionary* helps us understand why Washington had such high regard for philosophy as our war for independence ended. "Philosophy," according to the lexicographer, was "knowledge natural or moral"; it was "hypothesis or system upon which natural effects are ex--plained." "To philosophize," or "play the philosopher," was "to search into nature; to enquire into the causes of effects." The synonym of "Philosophy" in 1783 then was "Science"; the synonym of "Philosopher" would be our modern word (not coined until 1840) "Scientist," "a man deep in knowledge, either moral or natural."

Bacon, Newton, and Locke were the famed trinity of representative great philosophers for Americans and all educated inhabitants of Western Europe in 1783. Francis Bacon, the earliest prophet of philosophy as a program for the advancement of learning, had preached that "Knowledge is Power" and that Truth discovered by Reason through observation and free inquiry is as certain and as readily adapted to promote the happiness of human life, as Truth communicated to mankind through God's direct revelation. Isaac Newton, "the first luminary in this bright constellation," had demonstrated that Reason indeed could discover the laws of physical Nature and of Nature's God, while John Locke's researches into psychology and human understanding had definitely channeled inquiry toward the discovery of the immutable and universal laws of Human Nature. By the middle of the eighteenth century a multitude of researchers in all the countries of Europe were seeking, in Newtonian style, to advance the bounds of knowledge in politics, economics, law, and sociology. By the middle of the century the French judge and *philosophe* Montesquieu had produced a compendium of the behavioral sciences, cutting across all these fields in his famous study of *The Spirit of the Laws.*

However, Washington's assurance that already scientific knowledge about government had accumulated to such an extent that it could be immediately applied to the uses of "Legislators," pointed less toward France than toward Scotland. There, especially in the Scottish universities, had been developed the chief centers of eighteenth-century social science research and publication in all the world. The names of Francis Hutcheson, David Hume, Adam Smith, Thomas Reid, Lord Kames, Adam Ferguson, the most prominent of the Scottish philosophers, were internationally famous. In America the treatises of these Scots, dealing with history, ethics, politics, economics, psychology, and jurisprudence in terms of "system upon which natural effects are explained," had become the standard textbooks of the colleges of the late colonial period. At Princeton, at William and Mary, at Pennsylvania, at Yale, at King's, and at Harvard, the young men who rode off to war in 1776 had been trained in the texts of Scottish social science.

The Scottish system, as it had been gradually elaborated in the works of a whole generation of researchers, rested on one basic assumption, had developed its own special method, and kept to a consistent aim. The assumption was "that there is a great uniformity among the actions of men, in all nations and ages, and that human nature remains still the same, in its principles and operations. The same motives always produce the same actions; the same events follow from the same causes. . . . Would you know the sentiments, inclinations, and course of life of the Greeks and Romans? Study well the temper and actions of the French and English . . ."—thus David Hume, presenting the basis of a science of human behavior. The method of eighteenth-century social science followed from this primary assumption—it was historical-comparative synthesis. Again Hume: "Mankind are so much the same, in all times and places, that history informs us of nothing new or strange in this particular. Its chief use is only to discover the constant and universal principles of human nature, by showing men in all varieties and situations, and furnishing us with materials from which we may form our observations and become acquainted with the regular springs of human action and behavior." [1]

---

[1] David Hume, "Of Liberty and Necessity," in *An Enquiry Concerning Human Understanding* (London, 1748). An examination of the social theory of the Scottish school is to be found in Gladys Bryson, *Man and Society: The Scottish Inquiry of the Eighteenth Century* (Princeton, 1945). Miss Bryson seems unaware both of the position held by Scottish social science in the curriculum of the American colleges after 1750—Princeton, for example, where nine members of the Constitutional Convention of 1787 graduated, was a provincial carbon-copy, under President Witherspoon, of Edinburgh—and of its influence on the revolutionary generation. For a brilliant analysis of Francis Hutcheson's ideas and his part in setting the tone and direction of Scottish research, as well as the trans-Atlantic flow of ideas between Scotland and the American colonies in the eighteenth century, with a presuasive explanation of why the Scots specialized in social science formulations that were peculiarly congenial to the American revolutionary elite, see Caroline Robbins, "When It Is That Colonies May Turn Independent," *William and Mary Quarterly*, 3d ser., Vol. XI (April, 1954), pp. 214–251.

Finally, the aim of studying man's behavior in its comparative-historical manifestations was for the purpose of prediction—philosophy would aid the legislator in making correct policy decisions. Comparative-historical studies of man in society would allow the discovery of the constant and universal principle of human nature, which, in turn, would allow at least some safe predictions about the effects of legislation "almost as general and certain . . . as any which the mathematical sciences will afford us." "Politics" (and again the words are Hume's) to some degree "may be reduced to a science."

By thus translating the abstract generalizations about "philosophy" in Washington's letter of 1783 into the concrete and particular type of philosophy to which he referred, the issue is brought into new focus more congenial to our modern understanding. On reviewing the specific body of philosophical theory and writing with which Washington and his American contemporaries were familiar, we immediately remember that "the collected wisdom" of at least some of the Scottish academic philosophers was applied to American legislation during the nineteenth century. It is obvious, for example, that the "scientific predictions," based on historical analysis, contained in Professor Adam Smith's *An Inquiry into the Nature and Causes of the Wealth of Nations* (London, 1776), concerning the role of free enterprise and economic productivity, was of prime significance in shaping the relations of the state with the American business community, especially after 1828. Washington's expectations of 1783 were thus accurate in the long-run view.[2]

It is the purpose of this paper, however, to show that Washington's immediate expectations of the creative role of "philosophy" in American politics were also accurate in the period in which he wrote. It is thus the larger inference of the following essay that "philosophy," or "the science of politics" (as defined above), was integral to the whole discussion of the necessity for a *more* perfect Union that resulted in the creation of the American Constitution of 1787.

It can be shown, though not in this short paper, that the use of history in the debates both in the Philadelphia Convention and in the state ratifying conventions is not mere rhetorical-historical window-dressing, concealing substantially greedy motives of class and property. The speakers were making a genuinely "scientific" attempt to discover the "constant and universal principles" of any republican government in regard to liberty, justice, and stability.

In this perspective the three hundred pages of comparative-historical research in John Adams's *Defence of the Constitutions of the United States*

---

[2] The theoretical and prophetic nature of Adam Smith's classic when it was published in 1776 is today largely ignored by both scholars and spokesmen for the modern American business community. In 1776, however, Smith could only theorize from scattered historical precedents as to how a projective free enterprise system might work, because nowhere in his mercantilist world was a free enterprise system of the sort he described on paper actually operating.

(1787), and the five-hour closely argued historical analysis in Alexander Hamilton's Convention Speech of June 18, 1787, were both "scientific" efforts to relate the current difficulties of the thirteen American republics to the universal tendencies of republicanism in all nations and in all ages. History, scientifically considered, thus helped *define* both the nature of the crisis of 1787 for these leaders and their audience, and also determined in large part the "reforms" that, it could be predicted, would end the crisis. To both Adams and Hamilton history proved (so they believed) that sooner or later the American people would have to return to a system of mixed or limited monarchy—so great was the size of the country, so diverse were the interests to be reconciled that no other system could be adequate in securing both liberty and justice. In like manner Patrick Henry's prediction, June 9, 1788, in the Virginia Ratifying Convention, "that one government [i.e., the proposed constitution] cannot reign over so extensive a country as this is, without absolute despotism" was grounded upon a "political axiom" scientifically confirmed, so he believed, by history.

The most creative and philosophical disciple of the Scotitsh school of science and politics in the Philadelphia Convention was James Madison. His effectiveness as an advocate of a new constitution, and of the particular constitution that was drawn up in Philadelphia in 1787, was certainly based in large part on his personal experience in public life and his personal knowledge of the conditions of America in 1787. But Madison's greatness as a statesman rests in part on his ability quite deliberately to set his limited personal experience in the context of the experience of men in other ages and times, thus giving extra reaches of insight to his political formulations.

His most amazing political prophecy, formally published in the tenth *Federalist,* was that the size of the United States and its variety of interests could be made a guarantee of stability and justice under the new constitution. When Madison made this prophecy the accepted opinion among all sophisticated politicians was exactly the opposite. It is the purpose of the following detailed analysis to show Madison, the scholar-statesman, evolving his novel theory, and not only using the behavioral science techniques of the eighteenth century, but turning to the writings of David Hume himself for some of the suggestions concerning an extended republic.

It was David Hume's speculations on the "Idea of a Perfect Commonwealth," first published in 1752, that most stimulated James Madison's thought on factions.[3] In this essay Hume disclaimed any attempt to substitute a political Utopia for "the common botched and inaccurate govern-

---

[3] David Hume, *Essays, Moral, Political, and Literary* (London, 1875). Madison apparently used the 1758 edition, which was the most complete printed during the Scot's lifetime, and which gathered up into two volumes what he conceived of as the final revised version of his thoughts on the topics treated. Earlier versions of certain of the essays had been printed in 1742, 1748, 1752; there are numerous modern editions of the 1758 printing. All page references to Hume in this article are to the 1875 edition.

ments" which seemed to serve imperfect men so well. Nevertheless, he argued, the idea of a perfect commonwealth "is surely the most worthy curiosity of any the wit of man can possibly devise. And who knows, if this controversy were fixed by the universal consent of the wise and learned, but, in some future age, an opportunity might be afforded of reducing the theory to practice, either by a dissolution of some old government, or by the combination of men to form a new one, in some distant part of the world." At the very end of Hume's essay was a discussion that could not help being of interest to Madison. For here the Scot casually demolished the Montesquieu small-republic theory; and it was this part of his essay, contained in a single page, that was to serve Madison in new-modeling a "botched" Confederation "in a distant part of the world." (I, 480–481, 492.)

Hume concluded his "Idea of a Perfect Commonwealth" with some observations on "the falsehood of the common opinion, that no large state, such as France or Great Britain, could ever be modelled into a commonwealth, but that such a form of government can only take place in a city or small territory." The opposite seemed to be true, decided Hume. "Though it is more difficult to form a republican government in an extensive country than in a city; there is more facility, when once it is formed, of preserving it steady and uniform, without tumult and faction."

The formidable problem of first unifying the outlying and various segments of a big area had thrown Montesquieu and like-minded theorists off the track, Hume believed. "It is not easy, for the distant parts of a large state to combine in any plan of free government; but they easily conspire in the esteem and reverence for a single person, who, by means of this popular favour, may seize the power, and forcing the more obstinate to submit, may establish a monarchical government." (I, 492.) Historically, therefore, it is the great leader who has been the symbol and engine of unity in empire building. His characteristic ability to evoke loyalty has made him in the past a mechanism both of solidarity and of exploitation. His leadership enables diverse peoples to work for a common end, but because of the power temptations inherent in his strategic position he usually ends as an absolute monarch.

And yet, Hume argued, this last step is not a rigid social law as Montesquieu would have it. There was always the possibility that some modern leader with the wisdom and ancient virtue of a Solon or of a Lycurgus would suppress his personal ambition and found a free state in a large territory "to secure the peace, happiness, and liberty of future generations." ("Of Parties in General," I, 127.) In 1776—the year Hume died—a provincial notable named George Washington was starting on the career that was to justify Hume's penetrating analysis of the unifying role of the great man in a large and variegated empire. Hume would have exulted at the discovery that his deductive leap into the future with a scientific prediction was correct: all great men who consolidated empires did not necessarily desire crowns.

Having disposed of the reason why monarchies had usually been set up in big empires and why it still was a matter of free will rather than necessity, Hume then turned to the problem of the easily founded, and unstable, small republic. In contrast to the large state, "a city readily concurs in the same notions of government, the natural equality of property favours liberty,[4] and the nearness of habitation enables the citizens mutually to assist each other. Even under absolute princes, the subordinate government of cities is commonly republican. . . . But these same circumstances, which facilitate the erection of commonwealths in cities, render their constitution more frail and uncertain. Democracies are turbulent. For however the people may be separated or divided into small parties, either in their votes or elections; their near habitation in a city will always make the force of popuplar tides and currents very sensible. Aristocracies are better adapted for peace and order, and accordingly were most admired by ancient writers; but they are jealous and oppressive." (I, 492) Here, of course, was the ancient dilemma that Madison knew so well, re-stated by Hume. In the city where wealth and poverty existed in close proximity, the poor, if given the vote, might very well try to use the power of the government to expropriate the opulent. While the rich, ever a self-conscious minority in a republican state, were constantly driven by fear of danger, even when no danger existed in fact, to take aggressive and oppressive measures to head off the slightest threat to their power, position, and property.

It was Hume's next two sentences that must have electrified Madison as he read them: "In a large government, which is modelled with masterly skill, there is compass and room enough to refine the democracy, from the lower people, who may be admitted into the first elections or first concoction of the commonwealth, to the higher magistrates, who direct all the movements. At the same time, the parts are so distant and remote, that it is very difficult, either by intrigue, prejudice, or passion, to hurry them into any measures against the public interest." (I, 492.) Hume's analysis here had turned the small-territory republic theory upside down: *if* a free state could once be established in a large area, it would be stable and safe from the effects of faction. Madison had found the answer to Montesquieu. He had also found in embryonic form his own theory of the extended federal republic.

Madison could not but feel that the "political aphorisms" which David

---

[4] Hume seems to be referring to the development in cities of a specialized product, trade, or industrial skill, that gives the small area an equal interest in a specific type of economic activity. All the inhabitants of Sheffield from the lowly artisan to the wealthiest manufacturer had an interest in the iron industry; every dweller in Liverpool had a stake in the prosperity of the slave trade. It was this regional unity of occupation that Hume was speaking of, not equality of income from the occupation, as is shown by the latter part of his analysis.

Hume scattered so lavishly in his essays were worthy of his careful study. He re-examined the sketch of Hume's perfect commonwealth: "a form of government, to which," Hume claimed, "I cannot in theory discover any considerable objection." Hume suggested that Great Britain and Ireland—"or any territory of equal extent"—be divided into a hundred counties, and that each county in turn be divided into one hundred parishes, making in all ten thousand minor districts in the state. The twenty-pound freeholders and five-hundred-pound householders in each parish were to elect annually a representative for the parish. The hundred parish representatives in each county would then elect out of themselves one "senator" and ten county "magistrates." There would thus be in "the whole commonwealth, 100 senators, 1100 [*sic*] county magistrates, and 10,000 . . . representatives." Hume would then have vested in the senators the executive power: "the power of peace and war, of giving orders to generals, admirals, and ambassadors, and, in short all the prerogatives of a British King, except his negative." (I, 482–483.) The county magistrates were to have the legislative power; but they were never to assemble as a single legislative body. They were to convene in their own counties, and each county was to have one vote; and although they could initiate legislation, Hume expected the senators normally to make policy. The ten thousand parish representatives were to have the right to a referendum when the other two orders in the state disagreed.

It was all very complicated and cumbersome, but Hume thought that it would allow a government to be based on the consent of the "people" and at the same time obviate the danger of factions. He stated the "political aphorism" which explained his complex system.

The lower sort of people and small proprietors are good judges enough of one not very distant from them in rank or habitation; and therefore, in their parochial meetings, will probably chuse the best, or nearly the the best representative: But they are wholly unfit for county-meetings, and for electing into the higher offices of the republic. Their ignorance gives the grandees an opportunity of deceiving them.[5]

This carefully graded hierarchy of officials therefore carried the system of indirect elections to a logical conclusion.

Madison quite easily traced out the origin of Hume's scheme. He found it in the essay entitled "Of the First Principles of Government." Hume had been led to his idea of fragmentizing election districts by his reading of

---

[5] *Essays*, I, 487. Hume elaborated his system in great detail, working out a judiciary system, the methods of organizing and controlling the militia, etc. The Scot incidentally acknowledged that his thought and theories on the subject owed much to James Harrington's *Oceana* (London, 1656), "the only valuable model of a [perfect] commonwealth that has yet been offered to the public." For Hume thought that Sir Thomas More's *Utopia* and Plato's *Republic* with all other utopian blueprints were worthless. "All plans of government, which suppose great reformation in the manners of mankind," he noted, "are plainly imaginary." *Ibid.*, 481.

Roman history and his contemplation of the historically verified evils incident to the direct participation of every citizen in democratical governments. The Scotsman had little use for "a pure republic," that is to say, a direct democracy. "For though the people, collected in a body like the Roman tribes, be quite unfit for government, yet when dispersed in small bodies, they are more susceptible both of reason and order; the force of popular currents and tides is, in a great measure, broken; and the public interest may be pursued with some method and constancy." (I, 113.) Hence, Hume's careful attempts to keep the citizens with the suffrage operating in thousands of artificially created electoral districts. And as Madison thought over Hume's theoretic system, he must suddenly have seen that in this instance the troublesome corporate aggressiveness of the thirteen American states could be used to good purpose. There already existed in the United States local governing units to break the force of popular currents. There was no need to invent an artificial system of counties in America. The states themselves could serve as the chief pillars and supports of a new constitution in a large-area commonwealth.

Here in Hume's *Essays* lay the germ for Madison's theory of the extended republic. It is interesting to see how he took these scattered and incomplete fragments and built them into an intellectual and theoretical structure of his own. Madison's first full statement of this hypothesis appeared in his "Notes on the Confederacy" written in April 1787, eight months before the final version of it was published as the tenth *Federalist*.[6] Starting with the proposition that "in republican Government, the majority, however composed, ultimately give the law," Madison then asks what is to restrain an interested majority from unjust violations of the minority's rights? Three motives might be claimed to meliorate the selfishness of the majority: first, "prudent regard for their own good, as involved in the general . . . good"; second, "respect for character"; and finally, religious scruples.[7] After examining each in its turn Madison concludes that they are but a frail bulwark against a ruthless party.

In his discussion of the insufficiency of "respect for character" as a curb on faction, Madison again leans heavily upon Hume. The Scot had stated paradoxically that it is "a just *political* maxim *that every man must be supposed a knave:* Though at the same time, it appears somewhat strange, that a maxim should be true in *politics,* which is false in *fact* . . . men are generally more honest in their private than in their public capacity, and will go greater lengths to serve a party, than when their own private interest is alone concerned. Honour is a great check upon mankind: But

---

[6] *Federalist*, X, appeared in *The New York Packet*, Friday, Nov. 23, 1787. There are thus three versions of Madison's theoretic formulation of how a properly organized republic in a large area, incorporating within its jurisdiction a multiplicity of interests, will sterilize the class conflict of the rich versus the poor: (1) the "Notes" of Apr. 1787; (2) speeches in the convention during June 1787; and (3) the final polished and elaborated form, in the *Federalist*, Nov. 1787.

[7] James Madison, *Letters and Other Writings*, 4 vols. (Philadelphia, 1867), I, 325–326.

where a considerable body of men act together, this check is, in a great measure, removed; since a man is sure to be approved of by his own party . . . and he soon learns to despise the clamours of adversaries." [8] This argument, confirmed by his own experience, seemed to Madison too just and pointed not to use, so under "Respect for character" he set down: "However strong this motive may be in individuals, it is considered as very insufficient to restrain them from injustice. In a multitude its efficacy is diminished in proportion to the number which is to share the praise or the blame. Besides, as it has reference to public opinion, which, within a particular society, is the opinion of the majority, the standard is fixed by those whose conduct is to be measured by it." [9] The young Virginian readily found a concrete example in Rhode Island, where honor had proved to be no check on factious behavior. In a letter to Jefferson explaining the theory of the new constitution, Madison was to repeat his category of inefficacious motives,[10] but in formally presenting his theory to the world in the letters of Publius he deliberately excluded it.[11] There was a certain disadvantage in making derogatory remarks to a majority that must be persuaded to adopt your arguments.

In April 1787, however, when Madison was writing down his first thoughts on the advantage of an extended government, he had still not completely thought through and integrated Hume's system of indirect elections with his own ideas. The Virginian, nevertheless, had not dismissed the subject from his thoughts. He had taken a subsidiary element of Hume's "Perfect Commonwealth" argument and developed it as the primary factor in his own theorem; but he was also to include Hume's major technique of indirect election as a minor device in the constitution he proposed for the new American state. As the last paragraph of "Notes on the Confederacy" there appears a long sentence that on its surface has little organic relation to Madison's preceding two-page discussion of how "an extensive Republic meliorates the administration of a small Republic."

An auxiliary desideratum for the melioration of the Republican form is such a process of elections as will most certainly extract from the mass of the society the purest and noblest characters which it contains; such as will at once feel most strongly the proper motives to pursue the end of their appointment, and be most capable to devise the proper means of attaining it.[12]

---

[8] "Of the Independency of Parliament," *Essays*, I, 118–119.   [9] *Letters*, I, 326.
[10] *Ibid.*, p. 352. To Thomas Jefferson, Oct. 24, 1787.
[11] In Madison's earliest presentation of his thesis certain other elements indicating his debt to Hume appear that have vanished in the *Federalist*. In the "Notes on the Confederacy" the phrase "notorious factions and oppressions which take place in corporate towns" (*Letters*, I, 327) recalls the original starting point of Hume's analysis in the "Perfect Commonwealth." Also the phraseology of the sentence: "The society becomes broken into a greater variety of interests . . . which check each other . . ." (*ibid.*), varied in the letter to Jefferson to: "In a large society, the people are broken into so many interests" (*ibid.*, 352), is probably a parallel of Hume's "The force of popular currents and tides is, in a great measure, broken." ("First Principles of Governments," *Essays*, I, 113.)
[12] *Letters*, I, 328.

This final sentence, with its abrupt departure in thought, would be hard to explain were it not for the juxtaposition in Hume of the material on large area and indirect election.

When Madison presented his thesis to the electorate in the tenth *Federalist* as justification for a more perfect union, Hume's *Essays* were to offer one final service. Hume had written a scientific analysis on "Parties in General" as well as on the "Parties of Great Britain." In the first of these essays he took the position independently arrived at by Madison concerning the great variety of factions likely to agitate a republican state. The Virginian, with his characteristic scholarly thoroughness, therefore turned to Hume again when it came time to parade his arguments in full dress. Hume had made his major contribution to Madison's political philosophy before the Philadelphia Convention. Now he was to help in the final polishing and elaboration of the theory for purposes of public persuasion in print.

Madison had no capacity for slavish imitation; but a borrowed word, a sentence lifted almost in its entirety from the other's essay, and above all, the exactly parallel march of ideas in Hume's "Parties" and Madison's *Federalist, X*, show how congenial he found the Scot's way of thinking, and how invaluable Hume was in the final crystallizing of Madison's own convictions. "Men have such a propensity to divide into personal factions," wrote Hume, "that the smallest appearance of real difference will produce them." (I, 128.) And the Virginian takes up the thread to spin his more elaborate web: "So strong is this propensity of mankind to fall into mutual animosities, that where no substantial occasion presents itself, the most frivolous and fanciful distinctions have been sufficient to kindle their unfriendly passions and excite their most violent conflicts." [13] Hume, in his parallel passage, presents copious examples. He cites the rivalry of the blues and the greens at Constantinople, and recalls the feud between two tribes in Rome, the Pollia and the Papiria, that lasted three hundred years after everyone had forgotten the original cause of the quarrel. "If mankind had not a strong propensity to such divisions, the indifference of the rest of the community must have suppressed this foolish animosity [of the two tribes], that had not any aliment of new, benefits and injuries. . . ." (I, 128–129.) The fine Latinity of the word "aliment" [14] apparently caught in some crevice of Madison's mind, soon to reappear in his statement, "Liberty is to faction what air is to fire, an aliment, without which it in-

---

[13] *The Federalist*, ed. Max Beloff (Oxford and New York, 1948), No. X, p. 43. Hereafter page references to the *Federalist* will be to this edition.

[14] L. *alimentum*, fr. *alere* to nourish. Food; nutriment; hence, sustenance, means of support.—SYN. see PABULUM. This word is not a common one in 18th century political literature. Outside of *The Federalist* and Hume's essay I have run across it only in Bacon's works. To the man of the 18th century even the cognate forms "alimentary" (canal), and "alimony," so familiar to us in common speech, were still highly technical terms of medicine and law.

stantly expires." [15] So far as his writings show, he never used the word again; but in this year of 1787 his head was full of such words and ideas culled from David Hume.

When one examines these two pages in which Hume and Madison summed up the eighteenth century's most profound thought on party, it becomes increasingly clear that the young American used the earlier work in preparing a survey on faction through the ages to introduce his own discussion of faction in America. Hume's work was admirably adapted to this purpose. It was philosophical and scientific in the best tradition of the Enlightenment. The facile damnation of faction had been a commonplace in English politics for a hundred years, as Whig and Tory vociferously sought to fasten the label on each other. But the Scot, very little interested as a partisan and very much so as a social scientist, treated the subject therefore in psychological, intellectual, and socio-economic terms. Throughout all history, he discovered, mankind has been divided into factions based either on personal loyalty to some leader or upon some "sentiment or interest" common to the group as a unit. This latter type he called a "Real" as distinguished from the "Personal" faction. Finally he subdivided the "real factions" into parties based on "interest," upon "principle," or upon "affection." Hume spent well over five pages dissecting these three types; but Madison, while determined to be inclusive, had not the space to go into such minute analysis. Besides, he was more intent now on developing the cure than on describing the malady. He therefore consolidated Hume's two-page treatment of "personal" factions, and his long discussion of parties based on "principle and affection" into a single sentence. The tenth *Federalist* reads: "A zeal for different opinions concerning religion, concerning government, and many other points, as well of speculation as of practice; [16] an attachment to different leaders ambitiously contending

---

[15] *Federalist,* p. 42. Compare Hume's remarks: "In despotic governments, indeed, factions often do not appear; but they are not the less real; or rather, they are more real and more pernicious, upon that very account. The distinct orders of men, nobles and people, soldiers and merchants, have all a distinct interest; but the more powerful oppresses the weaker with impunity and without resistance; which begets a seeming tranquility in such governments." (I, 130.) Also see Hume's comparison of faction to "weeds . . . which grow most plentifully in the richest soil; and though absolute governments be not wholly free from them, it must be confessed, that they rise more easily, and propagate themselves faster in free governments, where they always infect the legislature itself, which alone could be able, by the steady application of rewards and punishments, to eradicate them" (I, 127–128); and notice Madison's "The regulation of these various and interfering interests forms the principal task of modern legislation, and involves the spirit of party and faction in the necessary and ordinary operations of the government." (*Federalist,* p. 43.)

[16] This clause of Madison's refers to Hume's "parties from *principle,* especially abstract speculative principle," in the discussion of which he includes "different political principles" and "principles of priestly government . . . which has . . . been the poison of human society, and the source of the most inveterate factions." Hume, in keeping with his reputation as the great sceptic, feels that while the congregations of persecuting sects must be called "factions of principle," the priests, who are "the prime movers" in religious parties, are factions out of "interest." The word "speculation" that appears in Madison is rendered twice as "speculative" in Hume. (I, 130–132.)

for pre-eminence and power; [17] or to persons of other descriptions whose fortunes have been interesting to the human passions,[18] have, in turn, divided mankind into parties, inflamed them with mutual animosity, and rendered them much more disposed to vex and oppress each other than to cooperate for their common good." [19] It is hard to conceive of a more perfect example of the concentration of idea and meaning than Madison achieved in this famous sentence.

It is noteworthy that while James Madison compressed the greater part of Hume's essay on factions into a single sentence, he greatly expanded the quick sketch of the faction from "interest" buried in the middle of the philosopher's analysis. This reference, in Madison's hands, became the climax of his treatment and is the basis of his reputation in some circles as the progenitor of the theory of economic determinism. Hume had written that factions from interest "are the most reasonable, and the most excusable. When two orders of men, such as the nobles and people, have a distinct authority in a government, not very accurately balanced and modelled, they naturally follow a distinct interest; nor can we reasonably expect a different conduct, considering that degree of selfishness implanted in human nature. It requires great skill in a legislator to prevent such parties; and many philosophers are of opinion, that this secret, like the *grand elixir*, or *perpetual motion*, may amuse men in theory, but can never possibly be reduced to practice." (I, 130.) With this uncomfortable thought Hume dismissed the subject of economic factions as he fell into the congenial task of sticking sharp intellectual pins into priestly parties and bigots who fought over abstract political principles.

---

[17] Here is Hume's "Personal" faction, "founded on personal friendship or animosity among such as compose the contending parties." Hume instances the Colonesi and Orsini of modern Rome, the Neri and Bianchi of Florence, the rivalry between the Pollia and Papiria of ancient Rome, and the confused mass of shifting alliances that marked the struggle between Guelfs and Ghibellines. (I, 128–129.)

[18] This phrase, which is quite obscure in the context, making a separate category of a type of party apparently just covered under "contending leaders," refers to the loyal bitter-end Jacobites of 18th-century England. These sentimental irreconcilables of the Squire Western ilk made up Hume's "party from *affection*." Hume explains: "By parties from affection, I understand those which are founded on the different attachments of men towards particularly families and persons, whom they desire to rule over them. These factions are often very violent [Hume was writing only three years before Bonnie Prince Charlie and the clans had frightened all England in '45]; though, I must own, it may seem unaccountable, that men should attach themselves so strongly to persons, with whom they are no wise acquainted, whom perhaps they never saw, and from whom they never received, nor can ever hope for any favour." (I, 133.)

The fact that Madison includes this category in his paper satisfies me that, when he came to write the tenth *Federalist* for publication, he referred directly to Hume's volume as he reworked his introduction into its final polished form. One can account for the other similarities in the discussion of faction as a result of Madison's careful reading of Hume's works and his retentive memory. But the inclusion of this "party from affection" in the Virginian's final scheme where its ambiguity indeed detracts from the force of the argument, puts a strain on the belief that it resulted from memory alone. This odd fourth classification, which on its face is redundant, probably was included because Hume's book was open on the table beside him, and because James Madison would leave no historical stone unturned in his effort to make a definitive scientific summary.

[19] *Federalist*, X, pp. 42–43.

Madison, on the contrary, was not satisfied with this cursory treatment. He had his own ideas about the importance of economic forces. All that Hume had to say of personal parties, of parties of principle, and of parties of attachment, was but a prologue to the Virginian's discussion of "the various and unequal distribution of property," throughout recorded history. "Those who hold, and those who are without property, have ever formed distinct interests in society. Those who are creditors, and those who are debtors, fall under a like discrimination. A landed interest, a manufacturing interest, a mercantile interest, a moneyed interest, with many lesser interests, grow up of necessity in civilized nations, and divide them into different classes actuated by different sentiments and views." [20] Here was the pivot of Madison's analysis. Here in this multiplicity of economic factions was "the grand elixir" that transformed the ancient doctrine of the rich against the poor into a situation that a skillful American legislator might model into equilibrium. Compound various economic interests of a large territory with a federal system of thirteen semi-sovereign political units, establish a scheme of indirect elections which will functionally bind the extensive area into a unit while "refining" the voice of the people, and you will have a stable republican state.

This was the glad news that James Madison carried to Philadelphia. This was the theory which he claimed had made obsolete the necessity for the "mixed government" advocated by Hamilton and Adams. This was the message he gave to the world in the first *Federalist* paper he composed. His own scientific reading of history, ancient and modern, his experience with religious factions in Virginia, and above all his knowledge of the scientific axiom regarding man and society in the works of David Hume, ablest British philosopher of his age, had served him and his country well. "Of all men, that distinguished themselves by memorable achievements, the first place of honour seems due to Legislators and founders of states, who transmit a system of laws and institutions to secure the peace, happiness, and liberty of future generations." (I, 127.)

---

[20] *Federalist*, X, p. 43.

VIII *Alexander Hamilton: Realist or Idealist?*

Introduction

"Every day proves to me more and more, that this American world was not made for me." So Hamilton wrote to Gouverneur Morris in February 1802. Two and one half years later he was dead by the pistol of Aaron Burr.

In the century and a half since Hamilton's death, his reputation in "this American world" has gone through a cyclical rise and fall. To the men of his own generation, whether political friend or foe, his name and reputation were formidable and imposing; as Jefferson said, he was "a host unto himself." In the age of Jackson, with the emergence of populistic democracy, Hamilton and the ideas he stood for fell into eclipse. In the period from the end of the Civil War to the turn of the century, characterized by the triumph of industrial America and the protective tariff, the Hamiltonian tradition supplied a congenial rhetoric, though applied to an industrial order whose leaders Hamilton would have found quite of his taste. "I hate money-making men," he once cryptically observed.

The whole climate of opinion of the early twentieth century, marked by the rise of the Progressive Movement, was antipathetic to the legacy of Hamilton's ideas. "A very great man, but not a great American," was the verdict of Woodrow Wilson. In the years between the great wars of this century, Hamilton was variously estimated by Hoover Republicans and Roosevelt New Dealers, the former approving Hamilton and the latter disapproving him. In our own day, with the triumph of a big superintending national government and the effort to implement a "realistic foreign policy," the tradition he stood for has come to seem a reinvigorated orthodoxy. His bicentenary, celebrated in 1957 —two years too late—gave stimulus to a substantial addition to Hamiltonian scholarship in the works of Broadus Mitchell, Louis Hacker, Leonard White, and Hans Morgenthau, to mention a few. A great project to edit and publish his writings has been started under the general editorship of Harold C. Syrett.

The new scholarship has been generally favorable to Hamilton, but there are dissentient voices, and his place has not been fixed even for our generation. He is an enigmatic political and social philosopher despite the apparent clarity of his clean, strong prose style.

The selections presented here are illustrative, though certainly not exhaustive, of the diversity of contemporary interpretation. Saul K. Padover's representation and estimation of Hamilton may be characterized as traditional and eclectic; Cecelia M. Kenyon's interpretation of Hamilton as "the Rousseau of the Right," as an idealist rather than a realist in his views of politics and society, is brilliantly novel and conflicts in a most marked degree with the Padover interpretation.

244

The Controversial Mr. Hamilton
—*Saul K. Padover*

I

Of all the outstanding Founding Fathers, Alexander Hamilton is the one who has never been fully enshrined as a hero acceptable to all his countrymen. There are few if any divisions of opinion in regard to Washington or Franklin or Jefferson; these are widely accepted, although with varying degrees of admiration. But not so Hamilton. Admired for generations by conservatives (who perhaps did not always understand him), he has been consistently assaulted by liberals.

As late as 1948, nearly a century and a half after Hamilton's death, a distinguished historian found it necessary to complain that the name of Hamilton "still arouses choking emotions in the bosoms of all 'right thinkers' who confine their knowledge and thinking to the Anti-Federalist tradition." [1] In brief, as he was during his short and stormy life, so Hamilton has remained after a tragic death—a figure of paradox and controversy.

Much of the difficulty lies in Hamilton's character. There was something turbulent and explosive about him. Contemporaries were struck by his restlessness and lack of personal serenity. He gave the impression of a man who could not curb his feelings—or his tongue. "My heart," he once said to General Henry Knox, "has always been the master of my judgment." He could be sweet-tempered to some people and unbearably arrogant to others. On occasion he could be gentle and diplomatic, but more often he was ruthless and aggressive. The consistent pattern of Hamilton's character was one of outer unquietness and inner disharmony.

His life, although not, as we shall see, his basic ideas, reflected this internal imbalance. Deeply attached to his wife and family, he was, nevertheless, capable of an unsavory amorous adventure (which he admitted publicly). Scrupulously honest himself, he winked at the peculations of friends. Under lasting obligation to Washington, he made insulting and slighting remarks about the General. A bitter enemy of the "visionary" and "chimerical" Jefferson, he nevertheless helped him decisively in the election to the Presidency in 1801. A humble-born British colonial, he openly sang the praises of Britain's aristocracy. A lifelong believer in monarchy as the best form of government, he fought magnificently for the

From pp. 1–23 *The Mind of Alexander Hamilton*, arranged by Saul K. Padover. Copyright 1958 by Saul K. Padover. Harper & Row, Publishers, Incorporated. Reprinted by permission.

[1] Charles A. Beard, *The Enduring Federalist*, 1948, p. 10.

adoption of the Federal Constitution. Filled with contempt for democracy, he gave the American Republic loyal and invaluable support. Rejecting dueling as unchristian, he permitted himself to be drawn into a duel that killed him. This by no means exhausts the list of paradoxes.

The judgment of contemporaries—especially political opponents—reflects awareness of Hamilton's inconsistencies, as well as, of course, his great gifts. Jefferson's final evaluation of his enemy, written fourteen years after Hamilton's death, has the merit of fairness. "Hamilton," he wrote (in 1818), "was, indeed, a singular character. Of acute understanding, disinterested, honest, and honorable in all private transactions, amiable in society, and duly valuing virtue in private life, yet so bewitched and perverted by the British example, as to be under thorough conviction that corruption was essential to the government of a nation."

James Madison, a milder critic, after paying tribute to Hamilton's "intellectual powers of the first order," made a similar point. "If," Madison said of his collaborator on *The Federalist*, "his theory of government deviated from the republican standard he had the candor to avow it, and the greater merit of cooperating faithfully in maturing and supporting a system which was not his choice." And John Quincy Adams, whose father was one of Hamilton's pet aversions (and vice versa), summarized the paradoxical character of John Adams' enemy in the following terms:

> [Hamilton's] talents were of the highest order, his ambition transcendent, and his disposition to intrigue irrepressible. His consciousness of talent was greater than its reality. . . . His valor was deliberate and undaunted; his experience in war not inconsiderable; the powers and resources of his mind extraordinary; his eloquence, both of speaking and writing, in the very first style of excellence; he had within him to a great degree that which subdues the minds of other men, perhaps the first of all qualities for the commander of an army. But he was of that class of characters which cannot bear a rival—haughty, overbearing, jealous, bitter and violent in his personal enmities, and little scrupulous of the means which he used against those who stood in the way of his ambition.

II

Hamilton's background helps to an understanding of his character. Psychologically, his birth and parentage must have left an ineradicable scar on his life. For, like William the Conqueror, Leonardo da Vinci, Erasmus, and many another famous man, Alexander Hamilton was born illegitimate.

There has been much confusion about Hamilton's early dates and parentage. Recent researchers, however, especially in the Danish State Archives at Copenhagen, have helped to clear up some obscure points. We now know, for example, that Hamilton was two years older than he claimed or perhaps knew. His mother died on February 19, 1768, and in that year the court, when it settled her small estate, noted that she had a son, Alexander, who was "thirteen years of age." If he was thirteen in 1768, then the year of his birth was 1755 instead of 1757, which is usually given in the history books. This year's celebration of Hamilton's 200th anniversary is thus two years late.

There is some obscurity about the early period of his life. What is indisputable is that he was born in Nevis, the smallest (sixty square miles) of the Leeward Islands in the British West Indies. Beyond that, the record is not full. His mother was Rachel Faucette, variously spelled as Faucitt, Fawcette, Fawcet, Fotzet; she was the daughter of an impecunious island family. Sometime about 1745, when Rachel was around sixteen, she married an older man named John Michael Levine—or Lawein or Leweine or Lavine or Lavien—said to be a Danish Jew. The marriage to Levine, who had a small plantation in nearby St. Croix, lasted about five years; after giving birth to a son, Peter, Mrs. Levine, at the age of around twenty-one, left her husband.

Sometime after abandoning her husband, Rachel Levine set up household with an itinerant Scotsman named James Hamilton, about whom not much is known, except that he was a drifter and a failure. Although without benefit of clergy, the ménage seemed to have been respectable and continued for a few years. Then James Hamilton, after having sired Alexander and one older boy, somehow drifted away, out of the family's life. On February 25, 1759, about four years after Alexander's birth, John Michael Levine sued his wife Rachel for divorce in the court of St. Croix. Levine charged that she had "absented herself from him for nine years and gone elsewhere, where she has begotten several illegitimate children." Rachel Levine—legally she was never Mrs. Hamilton—thus accused of desertion and adultery, did not contest the suit and, on June 25, 1759, the court granted the divorce but, under Danish law, denied Rachel the right to remarry. Alexander, therefore, could not be made legitimate.

After the death of his mother, the thirteen-year-old Alexander was for a while supported by relatives. Then he entered the counting house of a local businessman named Nicholas Cruger, and by the time he was fifteen was in charge of the establishment. But Alexander was too proud and ambitious to be satisfied with a clerkship in a colonial shop. At the age of fourteen he wrote to his intimate young friend, Edward Stevens:

> To confess my weakness, Ned, my ambition is prevalent, so that I contemn the grovelling condition of a clerk or the like, to which my fortune, etc., condemns me, and would willingly risk my life, though not my character, to exalt my station. I am confident, Ned, that my youth excludes me from any hopes of immediate preferment; nor do I desire it; but I mean to prepare the way for futurity.

In this youthful letter we see the germs of the later Hamilton—pride, ambition, desire for place and prestige, iron determination to achieve his goals. While clerking, he read incessantly, taught himself the indispensable art of disciplined writing, and learned to speak French fluently. "*Il parle et écrit parfaitement bien la langue*," a French traveler, the Marquis de Chastellux, said of him after he met him in the United States. This knowledge of French not only marked him as an educated gentleman, but was to be useful to Hamilton when he had to deal with Lafayette and other French officers when he was aide to General Washington, whose knowledge of that tongue was close to zero.

Soon young Hamilton was ready to break out of the narrow confines of his insular world. Sometime in September or October, 1772, he sailed from St. Croix to Boston, whence he went to New York. Apart from a little money given to him by his aunts on the island, his most precious material possessions were letters of introduction to influential Americans. Among the most important of them was one from his teacher Hugh Knox, a Presbyterian clergyman who had studied at Princeton, to William Livingston, member of a prominent New Jersey family, later governor of his state and a delegate, as was Hamilton, to the Constitutional Convention in 1787.

Hamilton was seventeen when he came to America, a frail boy of small stature, reddish-haired and blue-eyed. He was full of fire, precocious, energetic, and burning with desire to make his name and place in this new world. After a year at boarding school in New Jersey, he entered King's College (now Columbia University) in New York. King's was not much of a college in those days. It had a total faculty of three, one of whom, Myles Cooper, was the president; another, Samuel Clossy, taught in the medical school; and the third, John Vardill, taught nearly everything, including rhetoric, philosophy, theology, disputation, and what is today known as economics and sociology or their equivalents. The underlying ideas of the curriculum at King's College, as was also the case in the rest of America, were natural law and Old Testament ethics. These were given as "self-evident truths." Central to this universe was the enshrinement of property and its institutions as virtually sacred to man in civilized society. There is no reason to assume that Hamilton, then or later, questioned for a moment the immutability of those principles.

Hamilton did not require much intellectual guidance or help at King's College. He was, to say the least, as quick, as perceptive, as articulate as any of his elders at the college. A mind of immense discipline and retentive power, he read voraciously and with a concentration that was oblivious to everything except the world of hard facts and logical construction. His brain stored everything away in an orderly fashion, ready for use when the time came; thus in later years the busy Hamilton's utterances and writings impressed people by their scholarship. He sharpened his mind to become an instrument of marvelous precision. He learned to express his thoughts in a lean and muscular style, without subtlety or adornment. In his type of mental structure there was no room for originality or the exploration of new avenues of thought or for questioning of major premises. Hamilton acquired his basic ideas early in life and he never changed them. Blunt, tough, and practical, he had no understanding for dreamers, visionaries, or imprecise idealists.

At nineteen, after a year at King's College, Hamilton was ready for a life of action. This was the year 1774, when the colonies were on the threshold of the great crisis that was to lead to war and, ultimately, independence. Young Hamilton entered upon the historic scene in an America that was in a state of agitation and uncertainty. Although antagonized by British imperial policy, the leading men in the colonies did not yet quite know what course to pursue. Few as yet thought of complete independence from Great Britain; but at bottom they no longer felt themselves to be Englishmen. They were something new, something they did not yet altogether understand. There was no American nation—only undercurrents of nationalism. But the crisis was rapidly evolving and, as Hamilton soon found out, men had to take sides. The young man from the island of Nevis promptly joined what is known as the "popular cause," that is, the side that challenged the absolute authority of the British crown over the colonies and that was ready, if necessary, to cut the umbilical cord with the mother country.

Hamilton began to contribute political articles to Holt's *New York Journal, or General Advertiser* in 1774. At the end of the year, when he was not yet twenty, he published his first important work, a major contribution to the literature of the American Revolution. This consisted of two pamphlets, *A Full Vindication of the Measures of the Congress from the Calumnies of their Enemies* (14,000 words) and *The Farmer Refuted* (35,000 words). Following the fashion of the times, they were written anonymously as answers to widely read articles by Samuel Seabury, who, under the pen name of "A Westchester Farmer," eloquently defended the British colonial system. Hamilton's polemics against Seabury were so brilliantly conceived and maturely reasoned that contemporaries, when they learned the name of the author, could not believe that they had before them the work of a stripling just out of college.

III

When hostilities broke out between the colonies and Great Britain, Hamilton enlisted and became a captain of artillery. He attracted the attention of Nathanael Greene, one of the ablest generals of the Revolutionary War, who in turn introduced him to George Washington, who was having trouble with incompetent adjutants. As usual, Hamilton made a great impression and in March, 1777, the commander in chief of the American Revolutionary forces appointed him aide-de-camp with the rank of lieutenant colonel. Of General Washington's seven aides-de-camp, Hamilton was by far the best equipped—he wrote many of the General's important military papers and letters—and certainly the one most appreciated by the commander. Despite his icy reserve and aloofness, General Washington referred affectionately to the youthful Colonel Hamilton as "my boy."

It is a commentary on Hamilton's personality that he did not, then or ever, reciprocate Washington's affection and admiration. Indeed, Hamilton was one of the few contemporaries and collaborators of the General who was unimpressed by his true greatness. Hamilton never showed any understanding of the paramount quality that made Washington so impressive a figure, namely, the General's towering character, a mixture of unshakable strength, balance, dignity, and fairness. Hamilton, the insecurely born, seems to have had an instinctive dislike of Washington, the big man who so easily loomed as a father image to so many people. "Our dispositions," Hamilton frankly admitted, "are the opposites of each other." The two were in sharp contrast. The tall General was slow-minded, deliberate, shy, inarticulate in speech, modest, and without any sparkle; the little colonel was quick-witted, intellectually arrogant, self-assured, and brilliant. Washington was apparently unaware that his young aide-de-camp harbored anything but friendly feelings toward him; he continued to respect and admire the younger man throughout his life.

After about four years as aide-de-camp, Colonel Hamilton broke with Washington. The decision to do so was not sudden; it had been in his mind for some time. Hamilton had long been fretting at what he considered his position as an underling. In view of his insatiable ambition, it is also possible that he was jealous and resentful of Washington's high military position and reputation. As a matter of fact, Hamilton, who fancied himself fit to command armies, secretly disparaged Washington's military abilities and his knowledge of the art of war. The twenty-six-year-old colonel, thirsting for martial glory which he could not attain so long as he was chained to a desk at headquarters, soon found an opportunity abruptly to leave "the General's family," as he put it. The story, as related by Hamilton to his father-in-law, General Philip Schuyler (whose daughter Elizabeth he married on December 14, 1780), is self-revealing.

One day in February, 1781, at headquarters in New Windsor, as Washington passed Hamilton on the stairs, the General said that he wanted to see him. Hamilton replied he would do so immediately, as soon as he had delivered something to his fellow adjutant, Colonel Tench Tilghman. On his way to Washington's room, Hamilton was stopped by General Lafayette and the two young officer friends had a brief conversation. Suddenly General Washington appeared at the head of the stairs and spoke up angrily: "Colonel Hamilton, you have kept me waiting at the head of the stairs these ten minutes. I must tell you, sir, you treat me with disrespect."

Hamilton, sure that his conversation with Lafayette had lasted only about two minutes, snapped back: "I am not conscious of it, sir; but since you have thought it necessary to tell me so, we part."

"Very well, Sir," said Washington, "if it be your choice."

An hour later, Colonel Tilghman came with a conciliatory message from General Washington, assuring Hamilton of his "great confidence" in him and explaining that the regrettable incident "could not have happened but in a moment of passion." Would Colonel Hamilton forget the whole thing and return to his duties? Hamilton adamantly refused. He would not only not resume his post but also would not see the General. He was through, he said.

"Perhaps," he explained to his father-in-law, "you may think I was precipitate in rejecting the overture made by the General. . . . I assure you, my dear Sir, it was not the effect of resentment; it was the deliberate result of maxims I had long formed for the government of my own conduct." He went on to say that he disliked the General and that for the last three years he neither felt nor professed any friendship for him. He considered Washington merely a connection that might be useful. "He was an Egis," Hamilton was to say cold-bloodedly after Washington's death in 1799, "very essential to me."

> I always disliked the office of aide-de-camp [Hamilton continued his explanation] as having in it a kind of personal dependence. I refused to serve in this capacity with two major-generals at an early period of the war. Infected, however, with the enthusiasm of the time, an idea of the General's character, *which experience taught me to be unfounded*, overcame my scruples, and induced me to accept his invitation to enter into his family. It was not long before I discovered he was neither remarkable for delicacy nor good temper. . . . I was always determined, if there should ever happen a breach between us, never to consent to an accommodation.

Hamilton's petulance and antipathy found no responsive echo in George Washington. Although the younger man never showed the General any warmth or affection, Washington continued to be unfailingly generous toward Hamilton. Three-quarters of a year after the breach between them, in the autumn of 1781, Hamilton, yearning for a chance to distinguish himself on the field of battle before the war was over, asked General Washington to permit him to lead a small storming party during the siege of Yorktown. The General gave him his chance—and Hamilton had his brief moment of military glory, which he felt he needed for the record. After the Revolutionary War, when Hamilton was rising rapidly as a prominent lawyer and politician in New York, he asked Washington in Mount Vernon to scotch a rumor spread by his enemies that he, Hamilton, had "palmed" himself off on Washington as aide-de-camp and had been dismissed from his service. Washington promptly gave him his clearance, saying, "I do . . . explicitly declare that both charges are entirely unfounded" and that "quitting was altogether . . . your own choice."

As President, he appointed the youthful Hamilton to the second highest position in his Cabinet and gave him staunch support throughout a stormy administration. When the time came for Washington to retire from public life, it was to Hamilton that he turned, in 1796, for help in the drafting of the Farewell Address. And in 1798, when war with France seemed imminent and the country was mobilizing for it, George Washington used his immense influence to have President John Adams appoint Hamilton major general and second in command, a post the latter hungrily coveted and clamored for, thereby by-passing and antagonizing older and more experienced officers. Yes, as Hamilton wrote to the widowed Martha Washington early in 1800, her husband had always been useful to him.

IV

But the usefulness worked both ways. Just as Washington had been essential to Hamilton's career, so Hamilton was to the early history of the United States. What greatness there was in Hamilton came out in the years of the formation of the Constitution and the first Washington administration. It was the period when the American national structure was built, and Hamilton was beyond doubt one of its indispensable architects. Here, paradoxically enough, his foreign birth played a not inconsiderable role, for it gave him the kind of perspective most native Americans still lacked. For the leading men of the day did not yet think of themselves as citizens of America. They were, rather, Virginians, Pennsylvanians, New Yorkers, Carolinians, and so forth; their loyalties and roots were in their native states. It was therefore with some difficulty that they could identify with a political unit larger than the state; when they finally moved from the native state to the union of states, they did so slowly, reluctantly, and with many grave reservations.

Not so Hamilton. He had no native roots in America. He was not emotionally attached to any single state. He could not, indeed, understand how anybody could have strong attachments to a comparatively small political entity such as Rhode Island or Delaware or New Jersey or, for that matter, New York. To his logical mind, it made no sense to continue the existence of separate and independent states when, instead, they could combine and transform themselves into a powerful "American empire," as he liked to call it. He saw the vision of such a union from the beginning. As a young staff officer during the Revolution, he had firsthand experience with the shocking incompetence that prevailed under the loose government of the Congress. His sense of order was outraged by the political weakness, the local intrigues, the disunity, the parochial patriotism of the Confederation. Referring to the self-oriented states, he wrote early in the Revolutionary War: "This pernicious mistake must be corrected."

And so he became one of the prime agents in the movement for an effective federal union. He had two main objectives. The first was the creation of a united nation, which, he frankly hoped, would eliminate the individual states. The second was the establishment of a centralized government with power to defend property and to maintain order in the face of potentially turbulent radical forces. Both of these goals were more difficult of achievement than would appear to a twentieth-century observer. For Hamilton was aware, and painfully aware, that public opinion in general was against a strong national union and that the Revolutionary War had unleashed popular forces that were outspokenly hostile to any rule by the rich and the aristocratic.

The delegates to the Constitutional Convention, which sat in Philadelphia from May to September, 1787, consisted mostly of the well-to-do; they shared Hamilton's awareness of the prevailing anti-authoritarian temper of the American people, which they all dreaded. Like Hamilton, the majority of them—only thirty-nine of the fifty-five chosen delegates attended the sessions more or less regularly—were conservative in their economics and politics. With exceptions, they distrusted the people, as did Hamilton, who was more blunt and candid than most.

A fellow delegate, William Pierce of Georgia, has left the following sketch of Hamilton at the Convention:

> Colo. Hamilton is deservedly celebrated for his talents. He is . . . a finished Scholar. To a clear and strong judgment he unites the ornaments of fancy. . . . He is rather a convincing Speaker, than a blazing Orator. Colo. Hamilton requires time to think—he enquires into every part of his subject with the searchings of phylosophy, and when he comes forward he comes highly charged with interesting matter, there is no skimming over the surface of a subject with him, he must sink to the bottom to see what foundation it rests on. . . . His eloquence is not so diffusive as to trifle with the senses, but he rambles just enough to strike and keep up the attention. He is . . . of small stature, and lean. His manners are tinctured with stiffness, and sometimes with a degree of vanity that is highly disagreeable.

During the first weeks of the convention, Hamilton was mostly a silent member. He listened to various proposals, including those that provided for a mere patching up of the Articles of Confederation, instead of a new Constitution. He was increasingly depressed as the delegates, still state-oriented, at first refused to face boldly the central problem that confronted them, namely, the creation of a strong national union with a totally new Constitution.

Hamilton finally lost patience with what he thought was mere shilly-shallying and one day he rose and delivered a major speech in which he cut across all those currents of doubt and bluntly focused attention on the political realities as he saw them. James Madison, in his journal of the Convention, thus briefly summarized Hamilton's long and brilliant speech:

> This view of the subject almost led him [Hamilton] to despair that a republican government could be established over so great an extent [of American territory]. He was sensible, at the same time, that it would be unwise to propose one of any other form. In his private opinion, he had no scruple in declaring . . . that the British Government was the best in the world; and that he doubted much whether any thing short of it would do in America. He hoped gentlemen of different opinions would bear with him in this, and begged them to recollect the change of opinion on this subject which had taken place, and was still going on. It was once thought that the power of Congress was amply sufficient to secure the ends of their institution. The error was now seen by everyone. The members most tenacious of republicanism . . . were as loud as any in declaiming against the vices of democracy. This progress of the public mind led him to anticipate the time when others . . . would join in the praise bestowed by Mr. Necker on the British Constitution, namely, that it is the only government in the world, "which unites public strength with individual security."

Much of Hamilton's reputation as a "reactionary" derives from this particular speech at the Convention. In the course of it, and secure in the feeling that he was protected by the secrecy that covered the proceedings and debates, he uttered many sentiments which, while familiar doctrine to his upper-class contemporaries, are shocking to democratic American ears today. It was in the Constitutional Convention that Hamilton used the expression: "Take mankind in general, they are vicious." He also remarked: "The voice of the people has been said to be the voice of God; and, however generally this maxim has been quoted and believed, it is not true to fact. The people are turbulent and changing; they seldom judge or determine right."

These are, indeed, extreme statements, uttered in the heat of oratory. As Martin Van Buren comments in his *Autobiography*, Hamilton, "absorbed in the egotism and . . . vanity which have been the lot of great orators in all ages," blindly threw himself "headlong upon the Convention and recklessly proclaimed sentiments at variance with . . . what experience has since shown to be the riveted feeling of the American people." Standing by themselves, Hamilton's utterances in the Convention would condemn him as a hopelessly narrow politician, unworthy of consideration as a leader of men in a republic. But in proper context they merely underline a well-reasoned and consistently held political philosophy, although one that was voiced without tact and without regard for general public opinion.

One may reject Hamilton's view of mankind and his theory of political society as too Hobbesian and needlessly myopic; but one must grant him that he did have a clearly defined philosophy which had the merit of candor and which he had the courage to proclaim and defend. In a negative way, Hamilton may perhaps be given some credit for the fact that his outspoken antidemocratic views, by irritating contemporaries who believed in democracy, provoked them to a truly vigorous and searching defense of their democratic faith. This can certainly be said of Jefferson, who was not infrequently angered by Hamilton's candidly and repeatedly uttered contempt for democracy, which he labeled a "poison." Jefferson could barely control his aversion when he heard Hamilton, at his own dinner table (as he relates in his diary, April, 1791), proclaim that the British monarchical-aristocratic system, precisely *because it was corrupt,* was the "most perfect government which ever existed."

How did so superlatively intelligent a man as Hamilton justify such a view? He did so on the basis of what he conceived to be psychology. His political philosophy, which also shaped his economic principles and policies, was based on a firmly held view of human nature. Indeed, it is not possible to understand his political beliefs without a knowledge of his psychological assumptions. For central to Hamilton's thought was the conception of man as a corrupt and selfish animal, motivated by the worst passions, such as greed and selfishness. "The passions . . . of avarice, ambition, interest," he told his fellow delegates at the Constitutional Convention, ". . . govern most individuals, and all public bodies." Not a tactful observation under the circumstances, but a truly Hamiltonian one!

Here, of course, is the crucial idea on which Hamilton parted company with democrats, then and forever. For underlying the democratic belief is confidence in the virtue and potentialities of the average human being, as well as, according to the Jeffersonians, in his perfectibility, through education and other means. Without such an assumption about human nature, democracy, or any other polity that calls for even a limited amount of self-government, becomes impossible and, in fact, a contradiction in terms. For how can the corrupt and the selfish be expected to rule, with any prospect of success or stability, over others who are no less corrupt and selfish? For that matter, how can *any* government endure if *all* people are morally rotten? Did not an assumption of total human depravity lead to the pigsty type of government?

As Jefferson, probably thinking of Hamilton and his followers, put it in his First Inaugural Address: "Sometimes it is said that man cannot be trusted with the government of himself. Can he, then, be trusted with the government of others? Or have we found angels in the forms of kings to govern him? Let history answer this question."

Hamilton, it must be said, was consistent and logical in his views on government. Since human passions were a fact of nature and could not be altered, he proposed that they be recognized as such and harnessed for useful political ends. It was, he said, "a principle of human nature" that political institutions must be founded on "men's interests." He could, therefore, see no other way to build a successful government except through an appeal to what he called "avarice and ambition."

> Political writers [he argued] . . . have established it as a maxim, that, in contriving any system of government, and fixing the several checks and controls of the constitution, *every man ought to be supposed a knave;* and to have no other end, in all his actions, but private interest. By this *interest we must govern him;* and, by means of it, make him co-operate to public good, notwithstanding his insatiable avarice and ambition. Without this, we shall in vain boast of the advantages of any constitution.

Although his generalizations about human nature and behavior applied to all men, Hamilton, nevertheless, made a distinction between the few and the many, between the "rich and well born" and the mass of the people. The many, he said, were "turbulent and uncontrollable," driven by nothing but blind passion, and hence too imprudent to be entrusted with governmental power. The few, on the other hand, while also motivated by greed and selfishness, had enough sense and education to judge matters and, in consequence, could be depended upon to realize that their own best interests lay in using political power responsibly. It was not that he had any special affection for or illusion about the wealthy—"I hate money making men," he once blurted out in a letter to an intimate friend—but that he thought they were a safer depository of power than the equally base and selfish common people. Having no illusions about what motivated the greedy upper classes, Hamilton suggested that their loyalty to the new government be won through special privileges and economic advantages—through what he called "a dispensation of . . . regular honors and emoluments."

More than that. He proposed that the rich be given "a distinct, permanent share in the government," to serve as an unalterable check on whatever democratic institutions might develop in the future. To keep the "imprudence of democracy" in leash, he advocated the establishment of a permanent Senate and an Executive for life. Both were to be chosen indirectly, through electors or governors in the states (if there must be individual states), from the ranks of the economically superior individuals in the community.

Would not such a lifelong Executive be a monarch to all intents and purposes? That, countered Hamilton, was a matter of definition; if, he argued, you choose an Executive for, say, seven years, what have you? You have a seven-year monarch, but still a monarch, or whatever you care to call him. So what difference did it make, particularly if he be an excellent man and on his good behavior?

Again, was not a Senate chosen for life too dangerous? If human nature was as depraved and avaricious as Hamilton said it was, how could a handful of senators be safely entrusted with unrestrained power? Not so, said Hamilton. Precisely because they were assured of lifelong positions, special privileges, and conspicuous honors, the senators would have no motive for corruption or temptation for radical changes. In other words, give this elite everything and it would have no reason to ask for anything more. This was likewise true of the lifelong Executive. Assure his position for ever and remunerate him richly, and he will give you loyal service. Such, Hamilton pointed out, had been the experience of Great Britain, with its marvelous system of Lords and hereditary crown. As he told his fellow delegates at the Convention (June 18, 1787):

> The British . . . House of Lords is a most noble institution. Having nothing to hope for by a change, and a sufficient interest by means of their property, in being faithful to the national interest, they form a permanent barrier against every pernicious innovation, whether . . . on the part of the crown or Commons. No temporary Senate will have firmness enough to answer the purpose. . . .
>
> As to the Executive . . . no good one could be established on republican principles. . . . The English model was the only good one on this subject. The hereditary interest of the King was so interwoven with that of the nation, and his personal emoluments so great, that he was placed above the danger of being corrupted.

But would the American people tolerate a class government? Public opinion, Hamilton admitted, was hostile to anything resembling hereditary rule or domination by the wealthy. He felt, however, that once the people realized that it was to their advantage to have an elite in office, their hostility would melt away. Furthermore, he said, the mass of the people would not be completely powerless or totally disfranchised, since there was a general feeling—which he shared, although with reluctance—that, as a sop to the people, at least the lower legislative chamber should be popularly elected. The House of Representatives, with its periodic and frequent elections, would thus give the common people a certain amount of control over their rulers. So what reason would the masses have to complain?

A popularly chosen lower chamber, Hamilton knew, raised two important questions. One was that the congressmen elected by the people might be dangerous and irresponsible democrats. The other was that the

House of Representatives might not truly represent the various classes in the country and hence would lead to discontent. Hamilton argued that the chances were that, even in the democratic lower chamber, the representatives would come from the ranks of the well-to-do and the educated. Would such upper-class individuals truly be able to represent, and hence satisfy, the less privileged people? Yes, said Hamilton. Only the rich and the educated, he was convinced, could know what was good for the others and, therefore, could best represent them for their common interest. This is the way he stated his argument in *The Federalist* (No. 35):

> The representative body . . . will be composed of landholders, merchants, and men of the learned professions. But where is the danger that the interests and feelings of the different classes of citizens will not be understood or attended to by these three descriptions of men? Will not the landholder know and feel whatever will promote or insure the interest of landed property? And will he not, from his own interest in that species of property, be sufficiently prone to resist every attempt to prejudice or encumber it? Will not the merchant understand and be disposed to cultivate, as far as may be proper, the interests of the mechanic and manufacturing arts, to which his commerce is so nearly allied? Will not the man of the learned profession, who will feel a neutrality to rivalships between the different branches of industry, be likely to prove an impartial arbiter between them, ready to promote either, so far as it shall appear to him conducive to the general interests of the society?

Who, Hamilton asked, was in a better position to understand the problems and feelings of the people as a whole than the individual who has had a chance to travel and to study? The impecunious and the uneducated did not, of necessity, possess an enlarged view and hence could not be expected to be as good a representative as the one who had opportunities to widen his intellectual and political horizon.

> Is the man [Hamilton asked rhetorically] whose situation leads to extensive inquiry and information less likely to be a competent judge of their [national problems] nature, extent, and foundation than one whose observation does not travel beyond the circle of his neighbors and acquaintances? Is it not natural that a man who is a candidate for the favor of the people, and who is dependent on the suffrages of his fellow-citizens for the continuance of his public honors, should take care to inform himself of their dispositions and inclinations, and should be willing to allow them their proper degree of influence upon his conduct? This dependence, and the necessity of being bound . . . by the laws to which he gives his assent, are the true, and they are the strong chords of sympathy between the representative and the constituent.

These Hamiltonian ideas, forming in their sum a kind of aristocratic republicanism, were not, in the last analysis, acceptable to the Constitutional Convention. While the majority of the delegates agreed with much of what Hamilton said and believed, virtually all of them being members of the well-to-do and professional classes, they yet sensed that public opinion would reject a government from which the common people would be, as Hamilton desired, to a large extent excluded. And, as Hamilton's Federalists were to discover to their sorrow a decade later, the "rich and well born" were too few in numbers to impose their will permanently on the sprawling, restless, energetic, independent, rapidly growing population of farmers, frontiersmen, and workers.

Unlike Hamilton, the delegates to the Constitutional Convention were mostly native-born, with roots and relations in their home communities; hence they were able almost instinctively to understand, without necessarily sharing, the outlooks and feelings of their neighbors. The delegates knew that there were limits to American tolerance and patience, and that the Hamiltonian proposals for the creation of what in effect would have amounted to a permanent ruling class went beyond anything that a fiercely individualistic people would tolerate. The Convention, moreover, contained a small group of what today would be called liberals—among them such personalities as Benjamin Franklin, James Wilson, and, to a lesser degree, James Madison—who warned their colleagues not to push things to an extreme. As Franklin once dryly reminded the delegates, it was the common people who had fought and died in the Revolutionary War. If they were good enough to fight for independence, were they not also good enough to have a voice in their own government?

Fortunately for all concerned, Hamilton was not present during some of the most crucial debates at the Convention. For about two months, during July and August, he was absent from Philadelphia. Sensing that he could not sway the delegates, he had left the Convention in a mood of near despair. "I own to you, Sir," he wrote to the Convention's presiding officer, General Washington, on his way back to New York, "that I am seriously and deeply distressed at the aspect of counsels which prevailed when I left Philadelphia. I fear that we shall let slip the golden opportunity of rescuing the American empire from disunion, anarchy, and misery."

In his absence, however, the delegates abated their antidemocratic position and, despite serious doubts, agreed to a number of compromises which, in their total, added up to the granting of a considerable share of potential power to the people. This was not to Hamilton's liking; in his eyes, the Constitution's democratic features—the periodic election of the President and the senators, for example—made it fundamentally defective. He found it so when he returned to Philadelphia, as the Constitution was ready for signing in September. But, as a practical man, the delegate from New York signed it.

General Hamilton [his friend Gouverneur Morris recalled years after Hamilton signed the Constitution] hated republican government, because he confounded it with democratical government, and he detested the latter, because he believed it must end in despotism, and be, in the meantime, destructive to public morality. . . . His study of ancient history impressed on his mind a conviction that democracy ending in tyranny is, while it lasts, a cruel and oppressive domination.

Why, then, did Hamilton sign a Constitution that called for the creation of a republican government for which he had the deepest distrust? He did so because, first, it was better than nothing, and, second, because the upper classes might yet be able to shape it to their own ends. He hoped that in some future crisis, war, for example, this "frail and worthless fabric," as he later called the Constitution, might be transformed into a powerful instrument that would help the ruling elements of the country curb the centrifugal and democratic forces then at large in America.

V

At this point, in September, 1787, when the Constitution was made public and was submitted to the states for ratification, began Hamilton's great services to the United States. In a short span of some eight years, from 1787 to 1795, his contributions to America were to be of paramount importance. In that period of time, he was pre-eminent in the fight for the adoption of the Constitution, wrote the majority of the *Federalist* papers in its defense, and, finally, as the first Secretary of the Treasury, laid the durable foundations of the fiscal and economic policies of the United States. Although he lived for nearly another decade after his resignation from President Washington's Cabinet in January, 1795, his great work was over by the time he was forty.

The Constitution, so patiently and painfully hammered out in Philadelphia during a period of sixteen weeks, met with a storm of opposition throughout the country as soon as it was made public. Just as Hamilton did not like it because it was too democratic, so the American people in general objected to it because it was not democratic enough. It was this widespread popular hostility to the Constitution that contributed to the nerving and steeling of Hamilton's will in its defense; for clearly an instrument so detested by the masses must after all have something good in it.

Hamilton threw himself into the championship of the Constitution with characteristic energy and unmatched brilliance. A proper appreciation of his achievements in that crucial struggle, however, calls for an understanding of the main currents of opinion that swirled and eddied around the controverted document.

Three major streams of opinion can be discerned. They may be described, for the sake of simplicity, as conservative, popular, and liberal. The first gave the Constitution wholehearted support. The second was hostile. The third had reservations.

The conservative viewpoint, the position taken by Hamilton's rich and well-born, ranged from total approval because it was a perfect instrument to endorsement because it was the best under the circumstances. The whole position was perhaps best summarized by George Washington, when he said: "The Constitution . . . is not free from imperfections, but there are as few radical defects in it as could well be expected."

Popular opinion showed opposition to the Constitution on two main grounds. First, by providing for a central government, it threatened the independence of the individual states, which were regarded as bulwarks of personal liberty; second, the proposed new federal system appeared to be an instrument of the rich for the oppression of the poor, particularly since the latter were not represented at the Convention. Patrick Henry was the most eloquent exponent of this viewpoint. In his violent, and nearly successful, attack on the Constitution in the Virginia Ratification Convention, Henry described it as "extremely pernicious, impolitic and dangerous." Others argued that the Constitution would "take away all we have—all our property"; that it contained "no proper restriction of power"; that it was "founded on the principles of monarchy"; and that it was "like a mad horse" that would run away with its rider. As one opponent said in the New York State Constitutional Convention, anybody who trusted this new-fangled Constitution was like a man getting on a horse without a bridle; he would "justly be deemed a mad man, and deserve to have his neck broken."

Finally, there was the liberal opposition. This group, while granting that the Constitution contained a number of good features, objected to the absence of a Bill of Rights. The Constitution, the liberals said, provided safeguards for the protection of property but not for liberty—an oversight which, by the way, aroused the most hostility and which in the end forced its defenders to promise a Bill of Rights at the first opportunity. The liberal viewpoint was most articulately voiced by Jefferson, who, in a famous letter to his friend James Madison (December 20, 1787), wrote:

> I like much the general idea of framing a government, which should go on of itself. . . . I like the organization of the government into legislative, judiciary and executive. I like the power given the legislature to levy taxes. . . . I approve the greater House being chosen by the people directly. . . . I am captivated by the compromise of the opposite claims of the great and little States. . . . There are other good things. . . .
>
> I will now tell you what I do not like. First, the omission of a Bill of Rights, providing clearly, and without the aid of sophism, for free-

262 – Saul K. Padover

dom of religion, freedom of the press, protection against standing armies, restriction of monopolies, the eternal and unremitting force of the habeas corpus laws, and trials by jury. . . . To say . . . that a Bill of Rights was not necessary, because all is reserved in the case of the general government which is not given . . . is surely a *gratis dictum*. . . . It would have been much more just and wise to have concluded the other way . . . and to have established general right instead of general wrong. Let me add that a Bill of Rights is what the people are entitled to against every government on earth . . . and what no just government should refuse, or rest on inferences.

Hamilton was acutely aware of all these voices of approval, hostility, and criticism; and in one of the great tours de force in the history of political thought, he faced them head on. He lost no time in plunging into the national debate on the subject. About two weeks after the Constitution was signed in Philadelphia, he published, in the New York *Independent Journal* of October 2, 1787, the first of the famous articles in its defense. The series continued, in the *Journal* and in other New York publications, until April, 1788, in which year all the articles, including those written by Hamilton's callaborators, John Jay and James Madison, were published in book form under the title of *The Federalist*.

Of the eighty-five *Federalist* papers, Hamilton wrote fifty-one by himself and three in collaboration with Madison. The authorship of twelve is uncertain; they were written either by Hamilton or by Madison. In any case, the bulk of the contributions were Hamilton's.[2]

This is not the place to laud the virtues of *The Federalist*. The work has been sufficiently and rightly praised by many others in the past. Written in the heat of the campaign for the ratification of the Constitution, and designed as a polemic against its critics, *The Federalist* has, nevertheless, become not only an American classic but also a major contribution to the world's literature of political science. In its searching and far-ranging analysis of the principles of free government, as well as of the mechanics of republicanism in general, *The Federalist* has probably no equal in any language. "It is," Chancellor James Kent said of it in his *Commentaries on American Law* (Vol. I, 1826), "equally admirable in the depth of its wisdom, the comprehensiveness of its views, the sagacity of its reflections, and the fearlessness, patriotism, candor, simplicity, and elegance, with which its truths are uttered and recommended."

Considering Hamilton's deep-rooted prejudices against democracy and republicanism, it is ironic to reflect that in *The Federalist* he wrote what

[2] *By Hamilton:* Nos. 1, 6–9, 11–13, 15–17, 21–36, 59–61, 65–85; *by Hamilton and Madison:* Nos. 18–20; *by Hamilton or Madison:* Nos. 49–58, 62–63.
Of the rest of the nineteen papers, Madison wrote fourteen (Nos. 10, 14, 37–48), and Jay five (Nos. 2–5, 64).

is probably still the best and most powerfully reasoned defense of the institution of free government. His *Federalist* essays show unusual moderation and a profound grasp of republicanism, if not democracy, the latter of which, he argued, was embodied in the Constitution since, in the last analysis, it derived its power from the people. In pleading that the Constitution be given a chance, Hamilton showed that he was capable of rising above personal bias to statesmanlike heights.

Hamilton threw himself into the battle for the Constitution not because he loved republicanism but because he hated anarchy. He was revolted by the prevailing disunity and by the, to him, senseless pretensions to independence on the part of the thirteen individual states. Rejection of the Constitution, he was convinced, would not lead to a better one at some future date, but to chaos and possibly military dictatorship. Thus the great opportunity to create a free and powerful nation, which was, he said, America's destiny, would be forever lost. In his final plea for the adoption of the Constitution, Hamilton, citing David Hume on the desirability of moderation in political affairs, wrote in the concluding paragraph of the last (No. 85) *Federalist* paper:

> These judicious reflections contain a lesson of moderation to all the sincere lovers of the Union, and ought to put them upon their guard against hazarding anarchy, civil war, a perpetual alienation of the States from each other, and perhaps the military despotism of a victorious demagogue. . . . It may be in me a defect of political fortitude, but I acknowledge that I cannot entertain an equal tranquility with those who affect to treat the dangers of a longer continuance in our present situation as imaginary. A nation without a national government, is, in my view, an awful spectacle. The establishment of a Constitution, in time of profound peace, by the voluntary consent of a whole people, is a prodigy, to the completion of which I look forward with trembling anxiety. . . . I dread the more the consequences of new attempts, because I know that powerful individuals, in this and in other States, are enemies to a general national government in every possible shape.

While the *Federalist* papers were coming out, friends of the Constitution, perhaps strengthened and inspired by Hamilton's writings, won ratification victories in seven states. Delaware, Pennsylvania, and New Jersey ratified in December, 1787; Georgia and Connecticut, in January, 1788; Massachusetts and Maryland, in February and April. Two more states were needed to make up the nine required to put the Constitution into effect. Of the remaining six states, some, like the Carolinas, had too small a population to be politically potent, and others, like Rhode Island, were hostile to the Constitution; the latter, indeed, did not ratify until long after the Federal Government was established. Everything, therefore, now depended upon the two most populous and influential States, Virginia and New York. Rejection of the Constitution there would have been a disaster.

For a while it did look as if both pivotal states, where the Ratification Conventions met in June, 1788, would turn down the Constitution; and Hamilton, who kept in contact with Madison in Virginia, was filled with anxiety at the outcome of the contest. After a sharp struggle, on June 25, thanks largely to the eloquence of Madison and the prestige of Washington, the Constitution squeezed through the Virginia Convention by the narrow vote of 89 to 79. Now it was up to New York—and to Alexander Hamilton.

The situation in New York State was bad, and Hamilton girded himself for what was, beyond a doubt, the most important battle of his political career. For New York opinion was inimical to the Constitution, and the state's Ratification Convention, which met at Poughkeepsie, reflected this hostility. "The anti-Federal party," Hamilton informed Madison in a mood of unhappiness and pessimism, "have a majority of two thirds in the Convention, and . . . about four sevenths in the community." Of the sixty-five delegates, only nineteen were known to be willing to vote for the Constitution; forty-six were opposed to it. Dreading that nonadoption would lead to "disunion and chaos," Hamilton took on the seemingly hopeless task of winning over the hostile delegates. For seven days, between June 20 and June 28, he poured himself out in a torrent of oratory, logic, and political analysis so formidable that his audience was dazzled and overcome. It was not a vain effort. In the end, nearly a dozen reluctant delegates were won over by Hamilton's forensic performance—just enough to give victory to the Constitution. The final vote—by far the slimmest of all the states—stood 30 for and 27 against. It was mainly the triumph of one lone individual, a young man of only thirty-three, who was truly, in Jefferson's words, "a host unto himself."

Thus the Constitution went into effect, and on April 30 in the following year George Washington was inaugurated first President of the new union. For the post of Secretary of the Treasury, which turned out to be the most crucial position in the Cabinet, the President selected his former aide-de-camp, the brilliant Alexander Hamilton. It was in some ways a strange appointment, for Hamilton, whose reputation was primarily that of a lawyer-politician and orator, had no special experience in finance or economics. As it turned out, he needed no previous experience. A careful student of Adam Smith, he grasped the whole economic picture with his usual acuteness, and by applying his disciplined mind and energies to unaccustomed problems, he arrived at clearly defined conclusions and decisive recommendations.

For more than five years, from September, 1789, to January, 1795, Hamilton served as Secretary of the Treasury, and in that critical period he laid the foundations of fiscal and economic policies that have remained substantially the same ever since. Only George Washington himself excelled him in the durability of his achievements as the early builder of the Republic.

Alexander Hamilton:
Rousseau of the Right
—Cecelia M. Kenyon

The thesis of this paper is suggested in the title. It is that Hamilton's political thought was characterized by a heavy emphasis on a concept central to Rousseau's theory, the general will or the public good; that for Hamilton, as for Rousseau, this public good was morally and politically prior to private, individual ends, with which it was occasionally if not frequently in conflict; that the content of this public good as Hamilton visualized it was alien to the prevailing will of the majority of Americans in the early years of the Republic; that Hamilton was never able to reconcile his political ideal with his announced view of political reality; and that, as a result, his political theory is confused, contradictory, and basically unrealistic.

It is no light matter to charge Alexander Hamilton with a lack of realism. His writings are filled with references to what has been called the "dark side of humanity"; none of his contemporaries excelled him in constant emphasis on self-interest as man's dominant political motive, or in warnings against the evil passions of man's nature. Every undergraduate knows that Hamilton had a "pessimistic" conception of human nature. Every undergraduate knows, too, that the new government established under the Constitution desperately needed its finances put in order, and that Hamilton accomplished this. How, then, can such a man be called unrealistic? My argument is that Hamilton was not able to accept with equanimity the political facts of life as he saw them, or to relate them successfully to the political ideals he pursued. There remained within his thought an unresolved tension between what he believed man was, and what he believed man ought to be. Such a tension is not of course unusual, but the distance between the *is* and the *ought* in Hamilton's ideas was extreme.

This tension can best be examined by comparing the Hamilton of the

Reprinted with permission from the *Political Science Quarterly*, June 1958, Vol. LXXIII, No. 2, 161–178.

Federal Convention with the Hamilton of the Federalist party. They are the same man, but not quite the same thinker.

In his speech of June 18, 1787, Hamilton presented his plan of a political system proper for America. He wanted to do two things: to transfer the attachment of the people from the governments of their separate states to that of the Union; and to construct that government in such a way that it would not be wrecked by the turbulence of democracy and the imprudence of the people.

In the first part of the speech Hamilton analyzed those "great and essential principles necessary for the support of government," [1] and found that all of them then operated in favor of the states rather than of the Union. These principles of political obedience were several—interest, love of power, habit, force, influence. In order to make them support the nation rather than the separate states, Hamilton advocated an almost complete transfer of sovereignty from the latter governments to the former. This proposal is significant because of its apparent assumption that those very passions by which the people were so strongly attached to their state governments might remain sufficiently quiescent to permit the reduction of the states to the position of administrative provinces. It was the most drastic proposal of Hamilton's career and suggests his affinity with the classical tradition of the Legislator as well as his propensity—usually restrained—for Draconian measures.

In the second part of the speech Hamilton defended that part of his plan which provided for a senate and an executive elected for life. These were to serve as checks on the people's will, which would be represented in a popularly elected lower house with limited tenure. The reports of Madison and Yates differ somewhat, and for that reason I shall quote both versions of the crucial passage, beginning with that of Madison.

> In every community where industry is encouraged, there will be a division of it into the few and the many. Hence, separate interests will arise. There will be debtors and creditors, etc. Give all power to the many, they will oppress the few. Give all power to the few, they will oppress the many. Both, therefore, ought to have the power, that each may defend itself against the other. To the want of this check we owe our paper-money instalment laws, etc. To the proper adjustment of it the British owe the excellence of their constitution. Their House of Lords is a most noble institution. Having nothing to hope for by a change, and a sufficient interest, by means of their property, in being faithful to the national interest, they form a permanent barrier against every pernicious innovation whether attempted on the part of the Crown or of the Commons. No temporary Senate will have firmness enough to answer the purpose.[2]

---

[1] Max Farrand, *Records of the Federal Convention* (New Haven, 1911), vol. I, p. 365.
[2] Farrand, *Records*, vol. I, p. 371.

All communities divide themselves into the few and the many. The first are the rich and well-born, the other the mass of the people. The voice of the people has been said to be the voice of God; and however generally this maxim has been quoted and believed, it is not true in fact. The people are turbulent and changing; they seldom judge or determine right. Give, therefore, to the first class a distinct, permanent share in the government. They will check the unsteadiness of the second, and, as they cannot receive any advantage by a change, they therefore will ever maintain good government. Can a democratic Assembly, who annually revolve in the mass of the people, be supposed steadily to pursue the public good? Nothing but a permanent body can check the imprudence of democracy. Their turbulence and uncontrolling disposition requires checks.[3]

I believe these statements constitute the cornerstone of Hamilton's theory. They were made in the course of debates not intended for publication, and in defense of a system which Hamilton should have known had little chance of being adopted. Here Hamilton was his own advocate, not as in *The Federalist*, advocate of a system which he believed to be less than second best. These statements, therefore, require careful explication.

There is, to begin with, the familiar division of men into the few and the many, or the rich and the well-born, and the mass of the people. There is the further assumption that the interests of these two classes will be different, that they will be in conflict with each other at least part of the time, that the the political behavior of each class will be motivated by its interests, and that each class will oppress the other if it gets the chance and has the power to do so. Hamilton does not want this last to happen: "Both, therefore, ought to have the power, that each may defend itself against the other." It was not, then, a class government that Hamilton sought, at least not in the sense of one that had as its end the direct and deliberate promotion of class interests.

Thus far, there is no real difficulty in interpreting Hamilton. But the remainder of the passage, whether as reported by Madison or Yates, is less clear because it is, or appears to be, elliptical. In the second part of the passage, Hamilton suggests that the few will be more reliable in the cause of good government than the many. They, then, should have a share in the governing process, not only to protect their class interests, but in order to secure the national interest. Why will the few be the better guardians of this interest than the many? There seem to be two reasons, though neither is fully expounded.

In both the Madison and Yates versions, Hamilton expresses hostility to change and implies, if he does not explicitly state, that change is inimical to the "national interest" (Madison) or "good government" (Yates). This attitude is accompanied by the assertion that the upper class will be

---

[3] *Ibid.*, p. 382. Cf. Hamilton's notes prepared for the speech, pp. 387–388.

opposed to change. Therefore, the upper class will be the safer guardian of the public interest, not because its members are fundamentally more virtuous than "the people," but because on this particular issue—of change —their separate, class interest coincides with the public interest. It is also suggested (in the Madison but not in the Yates version) that the property of the Lords keeps that body faithful to the national interest in Britain.

This is a curious and revealing passage. Consider first the attitude toward change. It seems inconsistent with most of Hamilton's own career, for who among his contemporaries was more constantly in the vanguard of reform than he? He was an ardent Revolutionist; he was wholeheartedly in support of the movement for a new Constitution; his proposals as Secretary of the Treasury envisioned a deliberate effort to effect profound changes in the nature of American society; and the very speech in which he expressed this hostility to change was the speech in which he was recommending changes in the existing system far too drastic for his colleagues to accept. In comparison, the fluctuating policies followed by some of the States between 1776 and 1787, and which were so deplored by Hamilton and the other delegates, were the merest piddling. Hamilton was not alone in his quest for stability, but the attitude expressed in this speech, coupled with his own ardent support of sweeping changes, does call for a bit of explaining.

Again, I think, it reveals Hamilton as the modern prototype of the Legislator: take whatever measures are necessary to establish good Laws, and then guard against the undermining forces of future change. It is an attitude which cannot be reconciled with the theory of conservatism expounded by Burke three years later, for not only does it call for radical reconstruction, but it is hostile to the gradual, piecemeal process of adaptation which Burke accepted as characteristic of the natural life of society.

Consider next the assumption implicit in the relationship Hamilton posited between the national interest, the interest of the upper classes, good government, and an inclination or disinclination toward change. He assumes, first, that change is not compatible with good government. He assumes, second, that the upper classes will not be inclined toward change. These two assumptions are explicit. There is a third assumption which is implicit: good government is that which favors or protects the interests of these classes, but not the interests of the many—for it is they who are most likely to advocate change. It is therefore difficult to escape the conclusion that no matter how pure and patriotic Hamilton was in intent, he nevertheless tended to associate good government and the national interest with the interest of the rich, the well-born, and the few.

The exact nature of this relationship is difficult to pin down. The national interest is apparently regarded as both different from and separate from that of the many, and different from though not always separate from that of the few. It is, in short, distinct. It is the Hamiltonian counterpart of the Rousseauan general will, that will of the community toward its corporate good, something quite distinct from the will of all, which is the sum of individual and group private, self-interested wills. For Hamilton, this national interest was the primary end of government.

What we are concerned with here, then, is the fundamental question in any political theory: the end of government. It is a question which was not much discussed during the debate over ratification, and its answer was assumed and accepted rather than reached by any genuinely search-ing analysis even during the Revolutionary debate. This answer was more or less ready-made, and packaged in the doctrine of natural law and natural rights. Now this doctrine is ambivalent in its implications with respect to individuals and social unity. If the emphasis is on natural *law*, as it was during the medieval period, the doctrine tends in the direc-tion of harmony and consensus. But if the emphasis is on *rights*, and especially if happiness is included among the rights, then the doctrine tends toward individualism. It cannot do otherwise, and it was no mere whim which led Rousseau to reject natural rights doctrine as the basis for his state.

Some political thinkers in America in the eighteenth century realized the ethical implications of their accepted doctrine quite fully, and others did not. Jefferson was among those who did. His poetic passages on the virtues of agrarianism really boil down to a belief that this way of life was the one in which men could most easily fulfill their self-interest with-out being driven to do so by means which corrupted their integrity or injured their fellows. If Jefferson had an "optimistic" view of human nature, it was because his expectations and hopes were limited not only by a recognition of egoism but by an acceptance of it as ethically legiti-mate.

Tom Paine, though fully committed to the doctrine of natural rights as a justification for freedom, was not aware of and was not committed to its egoistic ethical implications. Thus his apologia for unicameralism:

> My idea of a single legislature was always founded on a hope, that whatever personal parties might be in the state, they would all unite and agree in the general principles of good government—that these party differences would be dropped at the threshold of the state house, and that the public good, or the good of the whole, would be the governing principle of the legislature within it.
>
> Party dispute, taken on this ground, would only be, who should have the honor of making the laws; not what the laws should be.[4]

---

[4] Philip S. Foner (ed.), *The Complete Writings of Thomas Paine* (New York, 1945), from *Dissertations on Government*, vol. 2, p. 409.

Implicit in this lost hope is the Rousseauan concept of the ideal citizen, he who distinguishes between his private interest and the public good, suppresses the former, and votes wholeheartedly for the latter.

It is my belief that this was also Hamilton's ideal, that he never abandoned it as the standard for judging political behavior, even though he fully realized that it was not in accord with the facts of human nature. This standard, essentially a non-liberal standard, was the springboard of his bitter attacks on the reason and virtue of the people. Thus I would argue that the real difference between Hamilton's and Jefferson's conceptions of human nature and their respective estimates of the people's capacity for self-government lay not in what either believed man actually to be, but in what each thought man ought to be and do. As far as politics was concerned, Jefferson thought man should pursue his happiness; Hamilton thought he should seek the national interest. One called for egoistic behavior, the other for altruistic. It was Hamilton who was the greater idealist, Jefferson the greater realist.

Yet Hamilton strove mightily for realism. His method was ambitious, arrogant, and in the great tradition of Plato, Machiavelli and Rousseau. It was the method of the Legislator. The following passages indicate the spirit of Hamilton's belief that man's nature could and should be molded for his own good as well as for that of the state.

> Take mankind in general, they are vicious, their passions may be operated upon. . . . Take mankind as they are, and what are they governed by? Their passions. There may be in every government a few choice spirits, who may act from more worthy motives. One great error is that we suppose mankind more honest than they are. Our prevailing passions are ambition and interest; and *it will ever be the duty of a wise government to avail itself of the passions, in order to make them subservient to the public good; for these ever induce us to action.*[5]
>
> The true politician . . . takes human nature (and human society its aggregate) as he finds it, a compound of good and ill qualities, of good and ill tendencies. . . .
>
> With this view of human nature he will not attempt to warp or disturb from its natural direction, he will not attempt to promote its happiness by means to which it is not suited . . . but he will seek to promote his action according to the bias of his nature, to lead him to the development of his energies according to the scope of his passions, and erecting the social organization on this basis he will favor all those institutions and plans which tend to make men happy according to their natural bent, which multiply the sources of individual enjoyment and increase of national resources and strength.[6]

---

[5] Farrand, *Records,* vol. I, pp. 388–389 (as reported by Yates). Emphasis added.

[6] Richard B. Morris (ed.), *Alexander Hamilton and the Founding of the Nation* (New York, 1957). Quotation from "Defence of the Funding System," dated 1795–1799 in a hand other than Hamilton's, pp. 313–314.

This is the spirit of the Legislator, though, to be sure, infinitely less ruthless than that of Plato or Rousseau. It implies wisdom on the one hand, malleability on the other, and an essentially manipulative relationship between the two. In modern times this sort of thing goes by the name of social engineering. Before and during the eighteenth century, it was usually associated with some form of benevolent despotism. Hamilton's problem, like Rousseau's, was to adapt it to republican government. The difficulty for each was the same: the people had the power but not the wisdom, while the leaders had the wisdom but not the power. How, then, could the people be made to follow wisdom? Rousseau's answer was simple: let the Legislator claim for his plans the authority of the gods.

Hamilton's answer was not so simple. *The Federalist Papers* were an appeal to reason, to self-interest, and to patriotism. Most of his other publicist ventures were similar. In spite of all his diatribes about the weakness of man's reason and the dominance of man's passions, Hamilton never abandoned hope that the better side of man's nature might be reached and might respond. Even the misguided *Caesar Letters*,* if indeed they were his, represented an appeal to the people's reason. This was the idealist in Hamilton, relatively pure and certainly indestructible.

His financial program both reveals and represents the other major facet in his answer to the problem of the Legislator. It reflects Hamilton the blundering realist. It is sometimes said that, having failed to secure a permanent share in the structure of government for the upper classes, Hamilton sought to secure their attachment to the new government through his financial program. I believe this is correct. It was a long-term policy and it is succinctly stated in a sentence chosen by Professor Morris to head one of the selections in his excellent anthology. "The only plan that can preserve the currency is one that will make it the *immediate* interest of the moneyed men to cooperate with government in its support." [7] The emphasis on the word *immediate* was Hamilton's. Nearly a decade passed after this was written before he became Secretary of the Treasury, and during that period his fiscal theories were elaborated and matured. But the basic principle remained the same: the private interest of the moneyed class must be made the ally of the national interest. Selfish interest must be made to support the public good. And how? By having the moneyed class's bread buttered by the government. There

---

* Two letters appearing in the New York *Daily Advertiser* on October 1 and 15, 1787 over the signature of Caesar constitute the Caesar Letters. They were attributed by Paul Leicester Ford to Hamilton and have often been used to show that Hamilton distrusted the people and that his most desired form of government was a dictatorship or a monarchy. Recent scholarship throws strong doubt on Hamilton's authorship of the Caesar Letters. See J. E. Cooke, "Alexander Hamilton's Authorship of the 'Caesar' Letters." *William and Mary Quarterly*, XVII (January 1960), 78–85. *Editor's note.*

[7] *Op. cit.*, pp. 335 and 339. From a letter "To a Member of Congress." See Morris' notes for date (probably 1779 or 1780) and addressee.

would, then, be no conflict between its interest and the general welfare. So far, so good. By catering to its self-interest, one class is led to do what is right. This is a fine exercise in political realism.

But what of the other class, the "many" of the June 18th speech in the Convention? In that speech Hamilton implied, though he did not explicitly state, that the interests of the two classes, the few and the many, would be in conflict with each other. Logically, then, any policy which served the interests of the few would injure or at least jeopardize the interests of the many. It is true that Hamilton believed that his fiscal policies would serve the national interest, and it is also true that he believed they would ultimately serve the self-interest of the many. But he *did* emphasize the necessity of attaching the *immediate* interest of the moneyed class to the government, and he had stated, in *The Federalist*, that men in general were much more likely to act in accordance with what they believed to be their immediate interests than their long-run interests.[8] Logically, therefore, he ought to have expected widespread opposition to the policies he advocated as Secretary of the Treasury, and equally logically he ought to have accepted such opposition with equanimity.

That he did not is well known. His letters and papers of the 1790's are filled with blasts against Jefferson, blasts against the people, blasts against factionalism, and laments about the lack of patriotism in everyone except himself and a few kindred Federalists. Hamilton was genuinely shocked, and he should really not have been. For consider what he had done. In his Convention speech he had posited the existence of two classes, with probably conflicting interests. In the Convention and elsewhere—innumerable times—he had argued that men are dominated by self-interest. He had occasionally, though not consistently, suggested that the upper classes were more likely to be patriotic than the mass of the people.[9] Nevertheless, he had sought the support of this group, not by appealing to their patriotism, altruism, or even long-run interest, but by appealing deliberately to their *immediate* self-interest. It was to them that he held out the carrot. And it was the other class, the many, the mass of the people, upon whom he now called for patriotism, and/or appreciation of long-run self-interest. It was from this class that he now expected and demanded the greater exercise of both reason and virtue. In so doing, he was not logical, he was not realistic, and he led his party straight down the road to extinction.

There were times during the late 1790's and early 1800's when he half-

---

[8] Number 6. In the Modern Library edition at p. 30.

[9] H. C. Lodge (ed.), *The Works of Alexander Hamilton* (New York, 1885), vol. VII, p. 241. In the eighth number of his "Examination of Jefferson's Message to Congress of December 7, 1801," Hamilton wrote that the safety of the Republic depended, among other things, "on that love of country which will almost invariably be found to be closely connected with birth, education, and family."

realized what he had done and cast about for practical solutions. In 1799 he advocated road-building as a method of courting the people's good will. It was a measure "universally popular." He also advocated the institution of a society with funds for the encouragement of agriculture and the arts. Such a program, he wrote, would "speak powerfully to the feelings and interests of those classes of men to whom the benefits derived from the government have been heretofore the least manifest." [10]

Before commenting on this proposal, I should like to place beside it a passage from another attempt by Hamilton to explain his party's failure to win popular support.

Nothing is more fallacious than to expect to produce any valuable or permanent result in political projects by relying merely on the reason of men. Men are rather reasoning than reasonable animals, for the most part governed by the impulse of passion. This is a truth well understood by our adversaries, who have practised upon it with no small benefit to their cause; for at the very moment they are eulogizing the reason of men, and professing to appeal only to that faculty, they are courting the strongest and most active passion of the human heart, vanity! It is no less true, that the Federalists seem not to have attended to the fact sufficiently; and that they erred in relying so much on the rectitude and utility of their measures as to have neglected the cultivation of popular favor, by fair and justifiable expedients. [11]

These comments reveal the very deep conflict in Hamilton's thought. In the later one (1802), Hamilton saw his party's error in having relied "so much on the rectitude and utility of their measures, as to have neglected the cultivation of popular favor, by fair and justifiable expedients." In the earlier letter, Hamilton admitted that the benefits of the new government had thus far not been "manifest" to certain classes—in the context, the many. In both letters, the two Hamiltons show through: the idealist, sure of the rightness of his policies and regretful that the people were neither rational nor virtuous enough to accept them on their merits; the realist, ever ready to seek support by the enlistment of man's worse (but never worst) nature. He had deliberately done the latter to win the moneyed class over to his side in the early 1790's. Now, at the end of the decade, he proposed to do the same thing for the majority. But it was a classic case of too little, too late. He had, in effect, made a partnership between the national interest and a special class interest. I am not sure whether he intended this partnership to be permanent and exclusive. He did intend it to be universally benevolent; its fruits were meant to trickle down and

---

[10] Lodge, *Works*, vol. VIII, pp. 518–519. From a letter to Jonathan Dayton, 1799.
[11] *Ibid.*, p. 597. From a letter to James A. Bayard, April 1802.

be enjoyed by everyone. Yet there remains that implicit assumption of the June 18th speech: a desire for change is more likely to exist among the many than the few, because good government will leave the interests of the many unsatisfied. There is an ambivalence in Hamilton's theory which I find it impossible to resolve.

My primary interest is not to decide whether he was or was not a class theorist, however. His political ideas are significant and rewarding because they reflect and illumine a difficult stage in the evolution of liberal democratic thought.

As I have suggested earlier, Hamilton's basic difference from Jefferson, and I think from most Americans of the era, was his rejection of the ethical egoism implicit in natural rights doctrine. This difference ought not to be exaggerated. No American of the age was an advocate of unrestrained self-interest, and the concept of a general interest which may be separate from and in conflict with private interests was generally present. It was at the root of the Revolutionary generation's distrust of faction. Nor, on the other hand, did Hamilton advocate or desire an absolute subjection of the individual to the state. It was rather that Hamilton, like Paine, was more extreme in his condemnation of egoism and in fact represented an older view of the proper end of government.

This older view was pre-individualistic, pre-modern. It was the medieval view that government existed for the good of society, and its end therefore was the common good. One of the things that distinguishes modern theory from medieval is the greater difficulty modern theorists face in defining this concept, the common good. There are a number of reasons for this; among them are the greater unity of medieval society by virtue of Christianity, and the relative rôles of legislative and customary law in the governing process. The point is that the existence of a common good was assumed in the earlier period, and its content was easier to define. But introduce into the political system the concept of ethical individualism combined with the practice of legislative determination of policy, and the difficulty of defining the common good is obvious—by hindsight. It was not obvious in the sixteenth century, or the seventeenth. It became increasingly obvious to Americans in the first three quarters of the eighteenth century because they were virtually self-governing communities and met the problem in the everyday conduct of their affairs. Madison's Tenth *Federalist* was the culmination of a long and painful process of thought on this subject. Madison, and I think he was here accurately reflecting the dominant opinion of his contemporaries, seems to hover ambivalently between two conceptions: (1) that of an ever elusive public good somehow distinct from the clashing of selfish and private interests; (2) that of the public good as a reconciliation or compromise of these same interests.

Hamilton clung more closely to the former view. One of the reasons may have been his late arrival as a practitioner of republicanism. In this respect he was very like Tom Paine, and I think a comparison of their lives from the time of their arrival in this country will show their fundamental kinship, though one was politically of the Right, the other of the Left. Each devoted himself without reserve to the service of his country. For each of them this entailed a sacrifice of the private interests common to most men —property, or at least greater property for both, and for Hamilton, the welfare of his family. For him, the sacrifice in the end was extreme. Among the documents he wrote before the duel there is one which concludes with a sentence profoundly symbolic of his entire life. After recounting his abhorrence of the practice on religious and ethical grounds, his unwillingness to give grief to his wife and children, his feeling of responsibility to his creditors, his intention of reserving fire on the first and perhaps even the second shot, Hamilton concluded: "The ability to be in future useful, whether in resisting mischief or in effecting good, in those crises of our public affairs which seem likely to happen, would probably be inseparable from a conformity with public prejudice in this particular." [12] He was indeed a patriot.

At every step of his career (except possibly the row with Washington), Hamilton—and Paine—put country first, self second. In a sense this was not sacrifice but fulfillment of their deepest desires. But in so far as it was fulfillment, it marked them off from other men. Each was in essence a political being, intensely so; each realized his nature, his self-interest, in devoting himself to the public good. The personality of each reinforced his conception of this public good as something better than and different from a mere reconciliation of individual and group interests. Neither ever ceased to regard his standard of political behavior as the standard proper for every man. For Paine, this meant an ever recurring optimism punctuated with bitter disillusion. For Hamilton, it meant a steady and self-nourishing pessimism. Both were idealists, and both shared the same ideal: a Rousseauistic community in which men were citizens first and individuals second. Hamilton knew his ideal was incapable of realization, and he sought a substitute which might still achieve the same goal—a government that governed in the national interest. The substitute was an alliance of upper-class interests with the national interests.

Jefferson and Madison opposed him partly because of the nature of the alliance, partly because the content of his conception of the public good was too nationalistic for their tastes. I do not think either he or they ever fully realized the more theoretical, and I think more fundamental, difference between them. The difference was subtle but profound. Jefferson and

---

[12] Morris, *op. cit.,* p. 608.

Madison were committed to the ethical individualism implicit, in natural rights theory: the end of the government as the protection of life, liberty, and the pursuit of happiness. This doctrine recognizes the political legitimacy of egoism. Hamilton was only partly committed to the doctrine. The basic difference between him and most of his contemporaries was that his conception of the public good was the older, corporate one, and theirs was the newer one in which the corporate element, though still present, had given ground to individualism.

The tension between these two concepts, a corporate and an individualistic public good, can be observed throughout the Revolutionary period. It underlay the colonial opposition to the British theory of virtual representation; it was central to the debates in the Federal Convention, and it was a major element in the ratification controversy. During the latter, James Winthrop seemed to be speaking directly to Hamilton when he wrote, "It is vain to tell us that we ought to overlook local interests. It is only by protecting local concerns that the interest of the whole is preserved." [13] This was the spirit of the future of American politics: local interests, sectional interests, class interests, group interests, individual interests. The conflict, compromise, or sometimes reconciliation of these interests was to be the main determinant of public policy, not the Hamiltonian ideal of a transcendent national interest, not the Rousseauan ideal of an overriding general will.

Here lay the heart of Hamilton's dilemma. As a genuine patriot of his adopted country, he was loyally committed to the practice of republican government. His grave doubts about the success of the experiment stemmed from his rejection of ethical individualism coupled with his acceptance of egoism as a fact of political life. The real trouble was that his end was incompatible with the means which, as a patriot, he had to accept. Logically, he should have ended up with some sort of philosopher-king theory, and he did have leanings in that direction. Since he was not a closet-philosopher, this way out of the dilemma was closed. There was really no way out. The way he chose, an alliance of one special interest group with what he conceived to be the national interest, simply stimulated opposition to the latter because he *had* linked it to the former. So he intensified in both groups the selfishness which was his enemy, and encouraged the growth of factions which he so deplored. That he was regarded by his contemporary opponents as a representative of class interests is perhaps regrettable, but their misunderstanding of him and his motives was no greater than his misunderstanding of them and theirs. They were wrong in believing him to be an oligarch, but they were right in believing that his political ideals were opposed to theirs. His were

---

[13] From the *Agrippa Letters*, in P. L. Ford (ed.), *Essays on the Constitution of the United States* (Brooklyn, 1892), p. 17.

corporate, theirs individualistic. His end was not logically anti-republican, but, in the context of public opinion at the time, it was bound to make him doubtful that it could be achieved under republicanism. It was unlikely that the people, left to themselves, would faithfully pursue the national interest. They needed a Legislator. Hamilton volunteered for the job.

In this aspect of his thought—means rather than ends—I would again argue that Hamilton's ideas were subtly but profoundly different from those of most of his contemporaries. They all talked a lot about man's passions and emphasized the necessity of taking these into account when constructing a constitution. I think Hamilton had a much more ambitious opinion concerning the extent to which these passions could be actively used—manipulated—by politicians. Consider the benevolent passage quoted above in which he outlined the principles a wise politician must follow if he would lead the people toward the achievement of their happiness and the national interest. Consider his injunction that "it will ever be the duty of a wise government to avail itself of the passions, in order to make them subservient to the public good. . . ." Consider his proposal in the Convention to transfer sovereignty from the state governments to the national government in order to transfer the people's passions from the former to the latter. And consider his tendency during the 1790's to regard the people as dupes who had been led astray by designing politicians. All this adds up to a fairly consistent picture. The people are clay in the hands of the potter, but the potter may be either wise and virtuous, or shrewd and vicious. The former will give them what they ought to have, the latter will pretend to give them what they think they want.

As a Legislator, Hamilton was initially successful. The conditions which existed during and shortly after the inauguration of the new government were congenial for the exercise of his special talents. Afterwards, his effectiveness as politician and statesman declined with remarkable rapidity. Both his ends and his means were alien to the ideals and the experience of the people he sought to lead. Their ideals were liberal and individualistic, and their practice of self-government had rendered them impervious to the benevolent molding Hamilton had in mind to impose upon them. They would govern themselves. It was inevitable that he should be rejected.

Though his corporate idealism and manipulative methods be rejected, the central problem for which he offered them as solutions cannot be ignored. That problem is basic: how, in a nation governed by the people, is agreement on the public good to be obtained and put into effect? In this process, what is and should be the relationship between wisdom and public opinion, between private interest and national interest? These were fundamental questions when Hamilton grappled with them, and they still are.

We have not yet worked out a satisfactory theory that will tell us precisely when the individual is ethically obligated to sacrifice his interests or when he may legitimately refuse to do so. Hamilton's plea for altruism in politics is relevant and salutary. The pursuit of selfish individual or group interests unrestrained by any sense of the general welfare may produce such bitter and divisive competition as to destroy the unity and consensus which sustain individual freedom as well as national strength.

Yet the Hamiltonian ideal, of each citizen placing the national interest before his own, is not without its dangers. It places an indefinite limitation on the exercise of individual freedom. There must be limits, of course, but this limit is an abstraction, and abstractions, when reified, are powerful forces to set against the solitary right and will of the individual. The national interest, with some exceptions such as sheer survival, will always be an elusive concept, its substance difficult to determine. Therefore there are practical reasons for refusing to concede it a permanently and categorically preferred position in all contests with individual, separate interests.

These practical reasons are merely corollaries of the main one. The main one is the ethical priority of the individual and his welfare as the proper and ultimate end of government. To this end, the national interest is logically and ethically secondary; to this end, the national interest must stand in the relationship of means. At least it must if one still accepts the Declaration of Independence as a statement of the purposes of American government. Hamilton mistook the means for the end, and tipped the scale too far in the direction of the national interest. In so doing he gave it ethical priority over the demands of the individual.

Such a priority seems to necessitate resort to manipulative techniques in order to induce the individual to forego what he conceives to be his own interest. Thus Plato resorted to the persuasion of the myth of the metals, Rousseau to the authority of the gods. In his idealistic moods, Hamilton appealed to reason; in his self-consciously realistic moods, he attempted a calculated alliance between the national interest and selfish class interests. This was bound not only to accentuate conflict between factions, but to obscure the national interest itself. Hamilton's idealism was thus vitiated by a would-be realistic policy which was both shrewd and obtuse at the same time.

The fault lay in the man himself. Hamilton's idealism was genuine and profound. It was also touched with arrogance. His penchant for what he regarded as realism was a fundamental trait of his character; he liked to think of himself as a skillful maneuverer of men's emotions. Thus his realism was likewise touched with arrogance. It may be that this dual arrogance was subjectively justified—Hamilton *was* a superior individual. But in the politics of republican government, such arrogance may operate to blind its possessor to that which he must see and understand if he is to achieve a successful blend of idealism and realism. That is the nature of man, or, more specifically, the motivation and behavior of the voter. It was Hamilton's fortune to serve his country well for a brief and crucial period in its history; it was his fate to be rejected by the countrymen whose ideals he did not share, and whose politics he did not understand.

IX *The War of 1812: The Issues Versus the Consequences*

Introduction   The two pieces of historical writing on the War of 1812 offered here do not contradict, but rather supplement each other. We see, in the first selection, the issues in international relations that brought Great Britain and the United States into war in June, 1812. In the second selection, we see the consequences in America of the divisiveness of public opinion and the resulting factionalism ". . . that made it (the war) an almost fatal test of the sturdiness of the nation. . . ."

Bradford Perkins, in a chapter entitled "This Unnatural War" taken from the second of four volumes he has devoted to Anglo-American relations, presents to us, with luminous detail and just criticism, the issues involved in the Anglo-American embroglio in the final months before the outbreak of the war, with appropriate retrospective comment.[1] This account gives us a sense of immediacy, motion, and specifics. The scene is not viewed from afar but is incontinentally thrust into the living room, and the men, events, and policies become alive. Perkins writes in his preface: "I believe scholars have over-emphasized the tangible, rational reasons for actions and, while not ignoring, have given too little heed to such things as national pride, sensitivity, and frustration, although the evidence of this sort of thing leaps to the eye. Emotion, chance, and half choices often mold the relations between states as much or more than cool reason. Such clearly was true in the years between 1805 and 1812."

Samuel Eliot Morison, in the second selection, focuses on domestic dissent within the United States during the war years 1812–1814.[2] He states: "Plenty of books there have been on the causes of the war, and a few good articles on its military, naval, and diplomatic history, but nothing of consequence on political, economic, or other internal matters during the war. It has generally been assumed that Henry Adams had said the last word on these aspects." Yet he believes that the war so divided public opinion in the United States and led to such bitter utterances against the administration of President Madison and to the formation of policies which, if successful, would have led to secession, that had the war continued well into 1815 it might have precipitated a civil war within the United States. So grave was the internal crisis that Morison believes that the War of 1812 was ". . . the most unpopular war that this country has ever waged, not even excepting the Vietnam conflict." He cites a press conference of President Lyndon Johnson of November 17, 1967, in which our late besieged president compared his dilemma to that of his predecessor Madison, although the context in which President Johnson made the comparison was historically inaccurate as Professor Morison pointed out in a letter

---

[1] *Prologue to War* (1961).   [2] *Dissent in Three American Wars* (1970), pp. 3–31.

to the Boston *Globe* of January 27, 1967. This essay was originally presented before the Massachusetts Historical Society as part of a series on Dissent in Three American Wars in 1968–1969. The other wars considered were the Mexican War by Frederick Merk, and the Spanish-American War with the Philippine Insurrection by Frank Freidel.

"This Unnatural War"
—Bradford Perkins

Although America's declaration of war came only after seven years of controversy and as many months of noisy congressional action, it surprised Great Britain and the United States. The English, who did not want war, were serenely confident of the result. "We cannot fear a war with any power in the world," the *Times* commented, ". . . but it is not unmanly to say, that we regret the sad necessity . . . of carrying the flame and devastation of war to a part of the world which has not seen a hostile foot for thirty years." [1] After repeal of the Orders in Council, Britain discounted all bad news from the United States, sure that America would abandon notions of a quixotic struggle when she learned of her great victory over the chief symbol of discord.

Even news of the declaration of war caused only muted debate in Britain. Henry Brougham expected a speedy armistice, and Alexander Baring advised him to support the government on existing issues, confident that Madison could not continue the war for two weeks after news of repeal arrived. The *Sun* unreasonably complained that, in his war message, "Mr. MADDISON recapitulates all the subjects of complaint against this country, . . . but he cautiously avoids answering any of the charges that have been preferred against the American Government." In an editorial lacking its usual splenetic fire, the *Courier* answered Madison point by point and warned that war might continue despite England's surrender of the orders. The *Morning Chronicle*, while complaining that the Americans had acted precipitately and objecting that "there is, in Mr. MADISON's paper, a querulous spirit, which betrays more of the littleness of the lawyer than the enlarged and national indignation of a Statesman," let its chief criticism fall upon the ministry. The *Chronicle* asserted "that our mode of proceeding towards America has been most irritating to her, as well as most injurious to ourselves—that the charge against us, of obstinate perseverance in error, from pride rather than conviction, is just . . . —and that we have, in truth, more reason to impute to our own imbecile Councils, all the calamities that may spring from this unnatural war, than to the influence of the French on the councils of America." The *Caledonian*

Originally published by the University of California Press, reprinted by permission of the Regents of the University of California.

1 *Times* (London), June 5, 1812.

Mercury and the *Times* agreed that, with the orders repealed, impressment was too "paltry an affair for two great nations to go to war about." Madison's message, the *Times* stated, "sums up all her grievances against us; and to speak candidly, she makes a fair shew." [2] Only later did humiliating naval defeats, the threat to Canada, and America's refusal to make peace after learning of the revocation of the orders ignite British anger against President Madison.

No such mildness characterized the American reaction to the declaration of war. Many moderates, whatever their desires prior to June 18, quietly supported the war once it had come. The joyful celebration of war men and the strident complaint of Federalists made up for their silence. A drunken celebrant, driving Winfield Scott's gig, twice tipped the young officer into the ditch. Republican centers like Richmond congratulated themselves on the impending "new harvest of political advantage and national glory." A Virginian, assigning too much personal credit to the President, wrote him: "You have politically regenerated the nation, and washed out the stain in their national character, inflicted on it by England." A mass meeting at Germantown resolved to support the war, since "it hath pleased the Almighty Ruler of the universe to suffer the perfidious outrages of the British government to render it necessary, once more, for the American people to struggle for their 'sovereignty and independence.' " In many New England seaports church bells tolled a dirge, shops closed, and ships' flags flew at half-mast. Bostonians hissed two prowar congressmen, and another was mobbed at Plymouth. The *Connecticut Courant* summed up the Federalist reaction, saying the war "was commenced in folly, it is proposed to be carried on with madness, and (unless speedily terminated) will end in ruin." [3] Many found consolation only in the conviction that it made Republican defeat certain.

The mixed reaction in New York perhaps best characterized the national mood. The *Evening Post* bitterly criticized the administration, and Moses Austin's wife wrote him that war "has come like an Electrick shock upon the great part of the people who have been two sanguine, in regard to peace Measures." Mrs. Austin added that most people were prepared to unite behind the government, and another observer, after noting that the city overwhelmingly opposed war, added, "but there are not wanting those who rejoice." "Pepal here are more reasonable about the war measure than what I esspected," John Jacob Astor wrote to his friend Gallatin, "& alltho many disapprove of the manner and time it was declared all agree

[2] Brougham to Grey, Aug. 2, 1812, Henry Brougham, *The Life and Times of Henry Lord Brougham* (2 vols.; Edinburgh, 1871), II, 27–28; Baring to Brougham, Aug. 1, 1812; *ibid.*, II, 36–39; *Sun* (Londdon), July 31, 1812; *Courier* (London), July 31, 1812; *Morning Chronicle* (London), July 31, 1812; *Caledonian Mercury* (Edinburgh), Aug. 3, 1812; *Times*, July 31, 1812.
[3] Wirt to Monroe, June 21, 1812, James Monroe MSS, Library of Congress; William Pope to Madison, July 10, 1812, James Madison MSS, Library of Congress; *Aurora* (Philadelphia), Aug. 12, 1812; *Connecticut Courant* (Hartford), June 30, 1812.

that we have plenty cause." [4] The silent, negative support extended to the government spoke volumes for the ineptitude of Congress and the President during the winter.

Five weeks after the declaration of war America learned that the Orders in Council had been repealed. Noting particularly that Castlereagh had reserved the right to restore the system in May, 1813, if French or American conduct so required, Madison interpreted the development as a trick to turn America from war. War Hawk journals quickly shifted to impressment and indemnities for past seizures. Attacking Alexander Baring, one of America's best English friends, for saying the orders were America's only major complaint, the Lexington *Reporter* wrote that "we will take the liberty to inform him that whenever peace is made, he will find that the SCALPS and lives of the FARME[R]S in the western world will not again be abandoned to British savages, and that the liberty of our seamen will have some weight in the scale." The *National Intelligencer* soon quieted the *Reporter*'s fears that the administration would be "deceived by this trap of our eternal enemies." On August 25 it contrasted conditional British repeal with the absolute revocation of the French edicts and added, "A public act of one belligerent, *so deliberately framed, so worded,* is in derogation from and *violation* of our standing neutral rights. A war against such inadmissible pretensions . . . is a war for the freedom, sovereignty and independence of . . . the American Union." "It should take more to make peace than to prevent war," Jefferson declared. "The sword once drawn, full justice must be done." [5] A concession which, if known in time, would have prevented war, utterly failed to move the two nations toward peace. The Americans raised their terms, and England angrily rejected what seemed an attempt at extortion.

The war continued for two and a half years, and for nearly 150 years it has challenged those who seek to explain its coming. Contemporary Federalists found a simple explanation in alleged Republican subserviency to France. A New York dominie declared God had brought on war so that the young republic might chastise the British government, "a *despotic usurpation—A superstitious combination of civil and ecclesiastic power— A branch of the grand antichristian apostacy—Erastian in its constitution and administration*—and *Cruel in its policy.*" [6] Actually, neither

---

[4] *New-York Evening Post,* June 20, 1812; Maria A. Austin to Moses Austin, June 23, 1812, Eugene C. Barker, ed., *The Austin Papers,* I, American Historical Association, *Annual Report, 1919,* Vol. II (Washington, 1924), p. 214; Arthur E. Roorbach to Livingston, June 24, 1812, Robert R. Livingston MSS, New-York Historical Society; Astor to Gallatin, June 27, 1812, Albert Gallatin MSS, New-York Historical Society.

[5] Madison to Gallatin, Aug. 8, 1812, Henry Adams, ed., *The Writings of Albert Gallatin* (3 vols.; Philadelphia, 1879), I, 523; *Reporter* (Lexington, Ky.), Aug. 23, 1812; *National Intelligencer* (Washington), Aug. 25, 1812; Jefferson to Robert Wright, Aug. 8, 1812, Andrew A. Lipscomb and Albert E. Bergh, eds., *The Writings of Thomas Jefferson* (Memorial ed.; 20 vols.; Washington, 1903–1904), XIII, 184.

[6] Alexander McLeod, *A Scriptural View of the Character, Causes and Ends of the Present War* (New York, 1815), p. 97.

God nor Napoleon seems an adequate explanation for the war, and historians have sought to establish the importance of more mundane influences.

Most nineteenth-century historians emphasized British outrages against American commerce. Admiral Mahan said that the orders "by their enormity dwarfed all previous causes of complaint, and with the question of impressment constituted a vital and irreconcilable body of dissent which dragged the two states into armed collision." Henry Adams apparently considered this maritime emphasis inadequate, but, as Warren Goodman suggests in an able historiographical article, he modified rather than abandoned the traditional view, although he did hint that Canadian-directed imperialism played a part.[7] Despite a dislike of Jefferson and Madison so bitter that he sometimes doctored the evidence, Adams' volumes remain the most complete, often the best written, and, when used with proper caution, the most useful survey of the entire period. After a lapse of some years, A. L. Burt reëmphasized maritime causes in a graceful summary of the era.

For two decades before the appearance of Burt's work in 1940, scholars sought to explain the motives of the West, the section that most unanimously supported war. Louis M. Hacker, then in a Marxist phase, suggested that a greedy desire for fertile Canadian farm land lay behind the façade of arguments for national honor. Julius W. Pratt contradicted Hacker's position, largely by disproving the central hypothesis, that there was no longer good agricultural land on the American side of the frontier.[8] Then, following a line already sketched by Dice R. Anderson, Pratt in his turn suggested a bargain between frontiersmen and Republicans of the North, who desired Canada, and Southerners, who wanted to absorb Florida. Sectional jealousies, Pratt concluded, broke down this alliance only after it had brought on war. Pratt found it difficult to demonstrate a real bargain, and there is reason to believe that the South did not almost universally desire the acquisition of Florida, as he maintained. But not without merit is Pratt's thesis that Western Anglophobia was stirred by the menace of Indian warfare believed to be inspired by Canadian authorities.[9] Finally, George R. Taylor put forward the argument that the West, economically overextended and suffering from depression from 1808 onward, blamed its troubles on the restrictive edicts of Europe and advo-

---

[7] Alfred T. Mahan, *Sea Power in Its Relation to the War of 1812* (2 vols.; Boston, 1905), I, 2; Warren H. Goodman, "The Origins of the War of 1812: a Survey of Changing Interpretations," *Mississippi Valley Historical Review*, XXVIII (1941–1942), 173. Including texts and general histories, Goodman examined forty-three treatments of the subject.

[8] Louis M. Hacker, "Western Land Hunger and the War of 1812: a Conjecture," *Mississippi Valley Historical Review*, X (1923–1924), 365–395 *passim*; Julius W. Pratt, "Western Aims in the War of 1812," *ibid.*, XII (1925–1926), 45–50 and *passim*.

[9] Dice R. Anderson, "The Insurgents of 1811," American Historical Association, *Annual Report, 1911*, I (Washington, 1913), 167–176; Julius W. Pratt, *Expansionists of 1812* (New York, 1925), pp. 12–14 and *passim*.

cated war to break down this barrier to prosperity. In April, 1812, Augustus J. Foster anticipated this interpretation: "The Western States having nothing to lose by war, . . . [are] clamorous for it, . . . being likely even to gain in the Exports of their produce while the exportation of that of the Atlantic shall be impeded." [10] Moreover, there was always the chance that war, or even the threat of war, would drive England to surrender the orders.

Hacker billed his suggestion "a conjecture," and Pratt and Taylor specifically noted that they were dealing, in the former's words, "with one set of causes only." Still, despite Pratt's coördinate interest in Southern ambitions for Florida, the researches of these scholars concentrated attention upon the West. The war came to bear the mark of the West, although only nine congressmen—a mere one of each nine voting for war—came from Western states. Taylor's suggestion that the West sought war to regain an export market might just as legitimately have been applied to other agricultural areas of the country, particularly the South, as Goodman, Burt, and Margaret K. Latimer have recently noted.[11] Studies of Western motivation, despite the caveats of their authors, have distorted the image of events leading to the War of 1812.

In his biography of the President, Irving Brant attempts to refurbish Madison's reputation. Attention is so narrowly concentrated on the President and on events with which he dealt that many important developments in Europe and America are slighted. Brant clearly shows the President's technical diplomatic ability. He does not equally clearly disprove Henry Adams' contention that, by emphasizing America's right to demand repeal of the orders as a consequence of alleged French repeal,

Madison had been so unfortunate in making the issue that on his own showing no sufficient cause of war seemed to exist. . . . Great Britain was able to pose before the world in the attitude of victim to a conspiracy between Napoleon and the United States to destroy the liberties of Europe. Such inversion of the truth passed ordinary bounds, and so real was Madison's diplomatic mismanagement that it paralyzed one-half the energies of the American people.[12]

As Brant claims, Madison recognized that peace might become impossibly costly, but in 1812 he abandoned with great reluctance what Samuel

---

[10] George R. Taylor, "Agrarian Discontent in the Mississippi Valley Preceding the War of 1812," *Journal of Political Economy*, XXXIX (1931), 471–505 passim; Foster #28 to Castlereagh, April 23, 1812, Foreign Office Archives, Public Record Office, FO 5/85.

[11] Goodman, *op. cit.*, p. 184; Alfred L. Burt, *The United States, Great Britain, and British North America from the Revolution to the Establishment of Peace after the War of 1812* (New Haven, 1940), pp. 306–307; Margaret K. Latimer, "South Carolina—a Protagonist of the War of 1812," *American Historical Review*, LXI (1955–1956), 914–929 passim.

[12] Henry Adams, *History of the United States during the Administrations of Jefferson and Madison* (9 vols.; New York, 1889–1891), VI, 398–399.

Flagg Bemis has perceptively called his "strategy of auctioning the great belligerents out of their respective systems of retaliation."[13] Perhaps Napoleon and Perceval acted foolishly in rejecting the bids Madison put forward during the auction; perhaps the President calculated more accurately the mutual benefits of accommodation. Still, it is one of the supreme functions of the statesman to weigh the intangibles as well as the tangibles, to expect illogical and prejudiced reactions along with coolly calculated ones. When Irving Brant declares that "President Madison to be successful . . . needed to deal with men whose understanding matched his own,"[14] he really confesses the political failure of his hero.

Madison never firmly controlled the Congress; he often lost command of his own Cabinet; frequently he seemed to drift rather than to direct policy. John Adams, fiercely challenged during the disintegration of Federalism, at least remained firm. In the spring of 1812 the congressional delegate from Mississippi Territory wrote that "the Executive is much censured by all parties for the tardiness of its advances to meet the *tug of war,* and the tenure of Mr. Madison's continuance in the presidential chair, in my opinion, depends upon the success of our hostile preparations." Yet the President did not forcefully support the cause of those whose loyalty had to be preserved for the impending election, nor did he speak out in favor of a course that might have maintained the peace he cherished. He reigned but he did not rule. After the declaration of war Jonathan Roberts wrote: "The world are pleased to suppose I am on good terms at the White House which by the way is no advantage for the cry of mad dog is not more fatal to its victim than the cry of executive connexion here."[15] Madison won reëlection, but he was the least respected victor the country had yet known.

The war came, not because of the President, but despite him. The war came, not for any single reason, but from the interplay of many. The nation did not want war, and surely it did not embark gleefully on a great crusade. Tired of the self-flagellation and the disgrace that had marked the years since 1805, propelled by the fear of ridicule for inconsistency and by an honest interest in the nation's honor, a sufficient number of congressmen allowed themselves to support war. Justification for a declaration of war was not wanting, and the long-term results were probably beneficial. Still, the war came just when the United States might have enjoyed without a struggle the immense benefits of the neutrality in which so much Christian forbearance (or cowardice) had been invested. Neither

---

[13] Samuel F. Bemis, *John Quincy Adams and the Foundations of American Foreign Policy* (New York, 1949), p. 181.
[14] Irving Brant, *James Madison:.the President* (Indianapolis, 1956), p. 483.
[15] George Poindexter to William C. Mead, April 10, 1812, Bernard Mayo, ed., *Henry Clay, Spokesman of the New West* (Boston, 1937), p. 512; Roberts to Matthew Roberts, July 1, 1812, Jonathan Roberts MSS, Historical Society of Pennsylvania.

side sought the War of 1812, and in the short run it was tragically unnecessary.

The United States did not go to war to add new states to the Union. A very few ebullient men from the North may have desired this. For sectional reasons the South and the West opposed it. A few advance agents of manifest destiny believed, as the Reverend McLeod put it in 1815, that the war was "a contest, not only to prevent the recolonization of these states, but also in the Providence of God for extending the principles of *representative democracy*—the blessings of liberty, and the rights of self-government, among the colonies of Europe." Even McLeod counted more on the imperialism of ideas than on military conquest. For most Americans Canada was but a means to an end, "a blow that might have given a speedier termination to the controversy," as Niles put it. At most, the occupation of the British provinces seemed the best means to reduce the enemy's power. A loyal Republican paper in Virginia commented:

> The great advantages to be derived from the acquisition of those possessions will not accrue so much from the tenure of them as a conquest, . . . but from the very important consequences which their loss will occasion to Britain; and among these consequences we may reckon the suppression of a great deal of smuggling, the curtailment . . . of the British fur trade and the disseverance of the West India Islands from Great Britain.[16]

So feeble was the desire for permanent incorporation of Canada within the Union that within six weeks after the destruction of British power in Upper Canada at the battle of the Thames in 1813, the Western militia had returned to their homes.

From the opening of the war session, both supporters and enemies of war proclaimed that an attack upon Canada would be the principal American offensive. Congress ostensibly tailored the new army to the requirements of this campaign. All the Republicans, at least, believed that even the slightest effort would result in victory. "In four weeks from the time that a declaration of war is heard on our frontier," John C. Calhoun declared, "the whole of Upper and a part of Lower Canada will be in our possession." When Federalists complained that their opponents sought to establish a standing army that might menace American liberties, Trenton's *True American* replied, "It will be a *moving, fighting, conquering,* army—and as soon as its duty is done, it will be disbanded."[17] Had Bermuda or Jamaica been vulnerable to attack by a flotilla of Jefferson's

---

[16] McLeod, *op. cit.*, p. 220; *Niles' Weekly Register* (Baltimore), March 28, 1812; *Virginia Argus* (Richmond), Nov. 11, 1811.

[17] *Annals*, 12th Cong., 1st sess., p. 1397; *True American* (Trenton), May 18, 1812. Later in the war, however, many Americans, including Madison and Monroe, were tempted by the dream of incorporating Canada into the United States.

gunboats, the War Hawks would have been equally satisfied to invade them.

Even Indian warfare did not inspire important demands for Canadian conquest in the winter of 1811–12. "Much of that resentment against the British, which prevailed so strongly in the western states," a Kentucky historian of the war stated, ". . . may fairly be attributed to this source." Even this Western chronicler, however, declared that the Orders in Council became more intolerable than any other source of complaint against England.[18] After Tippecanoe desultory warfare took place along the frontier, but most Indian tribes remained at peace until General Hull surrendered his army to Isaac Brock in the summer of 1812. Although Grundy and the Lexington *Reporter* remained irate, the Indian menace played a comparatively minor part in congressional debates until the very end of the session, when all complaints against Britain were being brought together to support a declaration of war. At that time congressmen emphasized Britain's interference in American affairs rather than the material consequences to one section.

The most important, most justified American complaints against England sprang from Britain's exercise of her maritime power. Substantively, through the loss of seamen, ships, and cargoes, America suffered greatly from impressment, blockades, and the Orders in Council. The sovereign spirit and the self-respect of the American nation suffered perhaps even more every time a seaman was removed from beneath the Stars and Stripes or a merchant vessel was haled to trial before an admiralty court that paid scant heed to international law. The penalties of neutrality are often dear, and perhaps only the weak, the phlegmatic, or the noble are capable of enduring them. Jefferson and Madison might fit into one or the other of these categories. Ultimately the nation felt taxed beyond endurance. However necessary to British prosecution of the contest with Napoleon impressment and attacks upon neutral commerce might be, they finally brought war with America. Fortune rather than justice postponed the outbreak of war beyond the gloomiest days of Britain's struggle, when American entry might well have played an important part.

Impressment, Frank A. Updyke has observed, was "the most aggravating and the most persistent" American grievance. By 1812 the press gangs had been at work for twenty years. In many instances—probably even the majority—the British forcibly recalled a king's subject to his allegiance rather than kidnapped an American. More often than was generally admitted, the Admiralty released mariners mistakenly seized. Still, impressment formed an ultimately intolerable insult to national sovereignty. When, during the war, the Federalist legislature of Massachusetts undertook an

---

[18] Robert McAfee, *History of the Late War in the Western Country* (Lexington, Ky., 1816), pp. 2, 7.

investigation to show that very few seamen had been impressed, John Quincy Adams angrily and accurately declared the question irrelevant:

> No Nation can be Independent which suffers her Citizens to be stolen from her at the discretion of the Naval or military Officers of another. . . . The State, by the social compact is bound to *protect* every one of its Citizens, and the enquiry how many of them a foreign Nation may be allowed to rob with impunity is itself a humiliation to which I blush to see that the Legislature of my native state could defend. . . . The principle for which we are now struggling is of a higher and more sacred nature than any question about taxation can involve. It is the principle of personal liberty, and of every social right.[19]

Failures of American arms and a European peace that halted impressment caused Adams, along with Madison and Monroe, to accept a peace silent on impressment. In principle, however, he was correct. America might well have gone to war on this issue, perhaps at the time of the *Chesapeake* affair.

Although officially the American government made very little of impressment from 1808 onward, the people could not forget it. During the war session, and particularly in the spring, impressment aroused more and more heat. *Niles' Register*, which began publication in 1811, rallied opinion on this issue. "Accursed be the American government, and every individual in it," an imprecation ran, "who . . . shall agree to make peace with Great Britain, until ample provision shall be made for our impressed seamen, and security shall be given for the prevention of such abominable outrages in the future." A Quid and a Republican who hoped to avoid war told Foster this was the most ticklish problem to explain to their constituents, and even the stanchly antiwar senator, Thomas Worthington, found impressment almost impossible to tolerate. "He says," Foster wrote in his diary, "he would rather live on a Crust in the Interior than live degraded." Foster, who repeatedly suggested that modification of the orders would prevent a declaration of war, nevertheless recognized the renewed importance accorded to impressment. On April 23 he wrote, "Very inflammatory paragraphs and letters on the subject . . . have lately been circulated in the American papers, and as the causes of war become more closely canvassed, that arising out of the practice of impressment seems to be dwelt upon with considerable vehemence." [20] When war approached, the War Hawks had a singularly effective propaganda point

---

[19] Frank A. Updyke, *The Diplomacy of the War of 1812* (Baltimore, 1915), p. 3; Adams to Plumer, Aug. 13, 1813, Adams Family MSS (microfilm), Massachusetts Historical Society, Vol. CXXXIX.

[20] *Niles' Register*, April 18, 1812 (italics omitted); journal entries, April 19, 22, May 24, 1812, Foster journal, Augustus J. Foster MSS, Library of Congress; Foster #28 to Castlereagh, April 23, 1812, FO 5/86.

in this violation of the rights of individual Americans who deserved better of their country.

Both the British government and the Federalists later complained that the President only resuscitated the impressment issue after the Orders in Council had disappeared. They pointed out that, particularly in the Erskine negotiations, the administration had allowed impressment to pass in silence. In 1813 Lord Castlereagh described it as "a cause of war, now brought forward as such for the first time." [21] These criticisms showed only that the administration had been backward in defending the rights of citizens, or that the President and Congress had been willing for a time to exchange the kidnaping of Americans for the benefits of neutrality. Neither Lord Castlereagh nor Timothy Pickering, who as secretary of state had himself vehemently protested the practice, should have been surprised that the American people considered impressment an insult.

Even more than impressment, with which congressmen and newspaper editors often coupled them, the Orders in Council showed Britain's contemptuous disdain for American protests against her use of sea power. The forcible enlistment of seamen could be expressed in dramatic human terms. The Orders in Council more massively and more selfishly assaulted the United States. Their material cost was impressive. Although the number of seizures actually fell after 1808, the year beginning in October, 1811, saw an increase of nearly 50 per cent. The orders and the *Essex* case had long since reduced the reëxport trade to a shadow of its former size. After a spurt stimulated by Macon's Bill #2 and the Cadore letter, the export of native American produce fell drastically after the spring of 1811. By far the greatest proportion of this decline came in exports to Britain, particularly because return cargoes were forbidden and the United Kingdom suffered from glut. [22] Agriculturists and plantation owners, some shipowners, and the average congressman ascribed the decline to Britain's Orders in Council, which prevented Americans from developing the presumably lucrative Continental market. At the same time, particularly because the British permitted their own subjects to trade with Europe under license, the Orders in Council seemed humiliating. Since at least November, 1807, the English had presumed to legislate not only for their own people but also for the commercial world. Economic necessity and national right alike cried out against the Orders in Council.

Everyone in Washington during the months from November to June placed the Orders in Council at the head of the list of American grievances. Louis Sérurier and Augustus Foster, Federalists and Republicans were in agreement. When the British minister asked Chauncey Goodrich, a Federalist senator, "what was required of us by Men of fair Views, he replied,

---

[21] *Hansard*, XXIV, 371.
[22] Adam Seybert, *Statistical Annals . . of the United States of America* (Philadelphia, 1818), pp. 79–80, 93, 112–113.

take off the Orders in Council and come to some Arrangement about Impressment." In November President Madison considered British maritime policy the transcendent issue between the two countries. Porter's report declared that the orders "went to the subversion of our national independence" and were "sapping the foundation of our prosperity." [23] Throughout the winter congressmen assailed the orders, drowning out the "whip-poor-will cry" for Canada of which John Randolph spoke. Repeal, Madison noted years later, would have postponed war and led to renewed negotiations on impressment "with fresh vigor & hopes, under the auspices of success in the case of the orders in council." The orders, he told Jared Sparks in 1830, were the only issue sturdy enough to bear a declaration of war.[24]

The strength of this issue depended in part upon the reinforcement provided by impressment and other grievances, the flying buttresses of the central structure. Had the orders stood alone as a British challenge, war would probably not have come in 1812. But they became the key to the drive for war. No other factor, not even impressment, which most directly affected Northeasterners, struck all sections so impartially. Not even impressment exceeded the orders as a threat to America's position as a sovereign power. The Orders in Council were four years old when the Twelfth Congress met, going on five when America declared war. Why this delay? A natural desire to escape war partly explains it. Unreal faith in the power of trade boycotts, more justified expectations from the Erskine agreement, optimism engendered by the Cadore letter, hope that the Prince of Wales would replace his insane father's ministers with more friendly men, the anticipated impact of American measures of preparedness in Great Britain—all these counseled delay. When war ultimately came in June, 1812, the Orders in Council were the central issue. The requirements of consistency and a growing realization that American honor had been nearly exhausted were the immediate precipitants.

Since at least 1806 the United States government, and more particularly Republican congressmen, had proclaimed that America would not settle for whatever neutral trade the belligerents chose to let her enjoy. Profitable as such trade might be (and it often was extremely rewarding), the United States would demand its rights. Of course Jefferson, and especially Madison, did not demand utter surrender from their opponents, and they did not press certain claims they considered comparatively insignificant. In principle, however, they insisted that Britain and France recognize American rights and tailor their policies to them. Commercial pressure

---

[23] Journal entry, May 18, 1812, Foster MSS; Madison to Adams, private, Nov. 15, 1811, Gaillard Hunt, ed., *The Writings of James Madison* (9 vols.; New York, 1900–1910), VIII, 166–167.

[24] Madison to Wheaton, Feb. 26–27, 1827, Hunt, *op. cit.*, IX, 273; journal entry, April 18[–23], 1830, Jared Sparks MSS, Houghton Library, Harvard University.

failed, political bargaining did not succeed, pleas for justice rebounded hollowly across the Atlantic. Still America maintained her claims, and the only remaining weapon to secure them was military power. The War Hawk Congress initiated preparedness, and the administration discreetly encouraged it, in the hope that England would surrender to this weapon what she had denied to boycotts, bargaining, and complaint.

Once embarked upon this course it became almost impossible to turn back. Many who voted for military measures without wanting war found it difficult to recede from the ground they had taken. The 10,000–man army proposed by the House of Representatives had an ostensible military purpose, but its supporters valued it chiefly as a demonstration of American determination. "We are not at war yet tho' David R. Williams hopes in god we soon shall be. Till we are at war I shall not go above 10,000 additional troops," Jonathan Roberts wrote in December. As time passed, Roberts became more and more bellicose. In February he wrote, "There seems to be no disposition to relax our war measures but I believe every body would be exceeding glad to remain at peace." A month later he stated, "I am well convinced we have no hope of peace but by vigorous preparations for War," but he added that he was ready to vote for war.[25] As the spring passed, Roberts found his Quaker principles weakening, and he attended meetings very infrequently. In May and June this man, who had come to Washington determined that affairs should be forced to a solution and yet still hopeful war could be avoided, found himself more and more firmly committed to the cause of the War Hawks. The logic of the situation carried the Pennsylvanian and many of his colleagues forward.

In May John Randolph declared that, although many members of the majority would not follow the same course if they had it to do over again, "they have advanced to the brink of a precipice, and not left themselves room to turn." John Smilie admitted as much, arguing that while he would have preferred a further attempt at commercial coercion he now felt it necessary to go on toward war, since "if we now recede we shall be a reproach among nations." Willis Alston of North Carolina told Foster in March that Congress "should have originally taken another Course, now too late. it would have been better to protest against the belligerents & let Commerce thrive, this should have been done from the Beginning." Alston voted with the War Hawks on every important roll call. Speaker Clay and his supporters counted on and made frequent, effective reference to consistency in the closing months of the session. "After the pledges we have made, and the stand we have taken," Clay asked his colleagues, "are we now to cover ourselves with shame and indelible disgrace by retreating from the measures and ground we have taken?" Remembering the reputation of the Tenth Congress, many representatives felt that the

---

[25] Roberts to Matthew Roberts, Dec. 20, 1811, Feb. 3, March 2, 1812, Roberts MSS.

296 - Bradford Perkins

answer was as obvious as Clay pictured it. Thus legislators who were really
"scarecrow men" came to support a declaration of war. James A. Bayard,
one Federalist who had foreseen this danger from the beginning, chided a
friend for his shortsightedness, saying, "You have thought the thing all
along a jest & I have no doubt in the commencement it was so, but jests
sometimes become serious & end in earnest." [26] So it was in 1812.

Consistency in congressmen, in a party, or in an administration became
national honor when applied to the country as a whole. Since the acquisition of Louisiana in 1803, America had endured a steady diet of diplomatic humiliation. Jefferson, Madison, and the Congresses of their time
attempted to reverse European policy by applying economic pressure.
This tactic failed because Congress lacked staying power and Republican
leaders underestimated the strength of emotions abroad. Defeats continued. Napoleon's announcement of repeal merely worsened the situation,
for his cynical contempt and the gullibility of the American administration
soon became apparent. Republicans had jeopardized the nation character and the reputation of the United States; they had created a situation
from which war was almost the only honorable escape; they had encouraged England, where unfortunately such encouragement was too little
needed, to act almost as though Lord Cornwallis had won the battle of
Yorktown. "We have suffered and suffered until our forbearance has been
pronounced cowardice and want of energy," a friend wrote Jonathan
Roberts. Although talk of honor perhaps came too easily to the lips of
some patriotic orators, the danger was real. When John C. Calhoun asserted that "if we submit to the prentensions of England, now openly
avowed, the independence of this nation is lost. . . . This is the second
struggle for our liberty," he scarcely exaggerated. When a Republican
Fourth of July meeting at Boston toasted "The War—The second and last
struggle for national freedom—A final effort to rescue from the deep the
drowning honor of our country," the sentiment was apt.[27]

In his first annual message after the outbreak of war, President Madison
declared:

> To have shrunk under such circumstances from manly resistance would
> have been a degradation blasting our best and proudest hopes; it would
> have struck us from the high rank where the virtuous struggle of our
> fathers had placed us, and have betrayed the magnificent legacy which
> we hold in trust for future generations. It would have acknowledged
> that on the element which forms three-fourths of the globe we inhabit,

[26] *Annals,* 12th Cong., 1st sess., pp. 1403, 1592; journal entry, March 18, 1812, Foster MSS;
Calhoun to Virgil Maxcy, May 2, 1812, Robert L. Meriwether, ed., *The Papers of John C.
Calhoun,* I (Columbia, S.C., 1959), 101; *Annals,* 12th Cong., 1st sess., p. 1588; Bayard to
Rodney, June 11, 1812, James A. Bayard Letterbook of Letters to Caesar A. Rodney, New
York Public Library.
[27] Thomas J. Rogers to Roberts, March 22, 1812, Roberts MSS; *Annals,* 12th Cong., 1st
sess., p. 1399; *Independent Chronicle* (Boston), July 6, 1812.

and where all independent nations have equal and common rights, the Americans were not an independent people, but colonists and vassals.

A year after the war ended, Henry Clay similarly stressed the theme of national honor and self-respect. "We had become the scorn of foreign Powers, and the contempt of our own citizens," he said. ". . . Let any man look at the degraded condition of this country before the war; the scorn of the universe, the contempt of ourselves. . . . What is our present situation? Respectability and character abroad—security and confidence at home. . . . our character and Constitutions are placed on a solid basis, never to be shaken." Years later, Augustus J. Foster philosophically wrote: "This war was certainly productive of much ill-blood between England and America, but in the opinion of the Speaker, Mr. Clay, and his friends it was as necessary to America as a duel is to a young naval officer to prevent his being bullied and elbowed in society. . . . Baleful as the war has been, I must confess that I think in this respect something has been gained by it." [28] The President, the Speaker, and the envoy, who stood at the center of affairs during the war session, effectively summarized the one unanswerable argument for war. All the insults suffered by the United States, even the most important of them all, the Orders in Council, posed a greater threat in the realm of the spirit than in the world of the accountant and the merchant, the seaman and the frontiersman.

That war became imperative in June, 1812, does not mean that the American people desired it or that it could not have been avoided by greater wisdom in earlier years. Castlereagh's statement, in 1813, that "Great Britain has throughout acted towards the United States of America, with a spirit of amity, forbearance, and conciliation," [29] was simply preposterous. While the policy of England was far less rigid than Americans often suggested, the self-righteous spirit of messianism engendered by the Napoleonic wars and a woeful underestimation of the price of American good will combined to prevent a reconciliation Jefferson and Madison eagerly desired. In America, most of the Federalists served their country ill, for, blinded by their own hatred of Napoleon and their inveterate contempt for the politicians who had displaced them, they sabotaged peaceful American resistance to British outrages and repeatedly declared that the Republicans lacked the fortitude to go to war. Roberts wrote in his memoirs, "There had all along been an idea cherish'd by the opposition, that the majority would not have nerve enough to meet war. This I believe, mainly induc'd Britain to persist in her aggressions. If she could have been made to believe . . . that we were a united people, & would act as such,

---

[28] James D. Richardson, ed., *A Compilation of the Messages and Papers of the Presidents* (Washington, 1897), I, 520; *Annals*, 14th Cong., 1st sess., pp. 777, 783; Richard B. Davis, ed., *Jeffersonian America: Notes on the United States of America . . by Sir Augustus John Foster, Bart.* (San Marino, 1954), pp. 4–5.
[29] *Hansard*, XXIV, 364.

war might have been avoided." The *Independent Chronicle* complained with a good deal of justice, "In every measure of government, the federal faction have rallied in opposition, and urged the Ministry to persist in their Orders. They forced the United States to the alternative, either to *surrender their independence,* or *maintain it by War.*"[30] American disunion was clear enough, the desire to avoid war quite obvious. Despite the temporary and transparent policy advocated by Quincy, the Federalists contributed to that disunion and to British stubbornness.

Still, the Republican chieftains must bear primary responsibility for the war and the factionalism that made it an almost fatal test of the sturdiness of the nation they themselves had done so much to build. Whereas Washington and Adams kept objectives and means in harmony with one another, their successors often committed the United States to seek absolute right with inadequate weapons. Compromise, when sought, was usually offered at an impossible time. The justice of American demands is nearly undeniable, but the two Virginians, who prided themselves on the coolness of their logic, failed to perceive that justice was not a weapon in itself. They provided it with insufficient support, and they expected warring powers to view collateral problems with the same coolness that America exhibited. Economic warfare rested upon a rigid, mechanical conception of international trade. Although it was, of course, felt by the belligerents, it proved far more harmful to America, economically and morally, and served chiefly to convince Europe of the cowardice of the United States.

The two presidents secured not one important diplomatic objective after 1803. They scarcely challenged the development of factionalism within the Republican party, factionalism that deprived Congress of any real sense of direction. They provided public opinion with far too little leadership. They and their followers often spoke loudly and carried no stick at all. When at last a small group of congressmen declared that the time for half measures had ended and carried a majority with them down the road toward war, neither Great Britain nor the American people believed the destination would be reached. Thus British concession was discouraged and national union made impossible. In a state of military and psychological unpreparedness, the United States of America embarked upon a war to recover the self-respect destroyed by Republican leaders. Old John Taylor of Caroline wrote to the Secretary of State on the day of the declaration of war, "May God send you a safe deliverance."[31]

[30] Memoirs (photostat), II, 14, Roberts MSS; *Independent Chronicle,* July 16, 1812.
[31] Taylor to Monroe, June 18, 1812, William E. Dodd, ed., "Letters of John Taylor, of Caroline County, Virginia," *John P. Branch Papers,* II (Richmond, 1908), 342.

Dissent in the War of 1812

——*Samuel Eliot Morison*

In working over sources for my *Harrison Gray Otis, Urbane Federalist* (1969) I was astonished to find how little work had been done on the internal history of the War of 1812 since my *Harrison Gray Otis, Federalist* came out in 1913. Plenty of books there have been on the causes of the war, and a few good articles on its military, naval, and diplomatic history, but nothing of any consequence on political, economic, or other internal matters during the war. It has generally been assumed that Henry Adams had said the last word on those aspects. My second biography of Otis includes an attempt to set forth some of the anti-war trends in Massachusetts, especially the potentially dangerous "Reunion of the Original Thirteen States" movement promoted by John Lowell.

In my opinion the most unpopular war that this country has ever waged, not even excepting the Vietnam conflict, was our second war with Great Britain. The declaration on June 18, 1812, passed by only 79 to 49 in the House, and 19 to 13 in the Senate. Eight out of ten New England senators, eleven out of fourteen New York representatives, voted against it. Although the South and West in general were keen for the war, their enthusiasm did not last. The War Department could never build up the regular army to half its authorized strength and obtained only 10,000 one-year volunteers out of 50,000 authorized. Henry Clay boasted that he could conquer Canada with Kentucky militia alone, but Kentucky furnished only 400 recruits in 1812. Thomas Jefferson said that the conquest of Canada would be only a matter of marching—but it turned out to be a matter of fighting as well, since the Canadians, French as well as British, instead of "rising as one man" to "throw off the British yoke" (as the Secretary of War, William Eustis of Roxbury, Massachusetts, predicted), showed a perverse disposition to fight for King and Country. Interestingly enough, the loyal minority in New England more than made up for the discouraging stand of the Federalist state governments; those five states provided the regular army with nineteen regiments as against fifteen from the middle states and ten from the southern states.

Reprinted by permission of the publishers from Samuel Eliot Morison, Frederick Merk, and Frank Friedel, *Dissent in Three American Wars*, Cambridge, Mass.: Harvard University Press, copyright, 1970, by the Massachusetts Historical Society.

After Hull's surrender of Detroit in 1812 had shown that the war would be no walkover, it became heartily disliked throughout the country. You might say that it was our most popular war when it was over and our most unpopular while it lasted.

The notion that only Yankee Federalists opposed the war is pure myth. Robert Smith, a Maryland merchant-shipowner who served in Jefferson's and Madison's cabinets, issued a public address against the war and sent a copy to Chief Justice Marshall, who replied in part: "All minor considerations should be waived . . . and the great division between the friends of peace & the advocates of war ought alone to remain. . . . All who wish peace ought to unite in the means which may facilitate its attainment." Senator Beveridge, Marshall's biographer, admits that the chief justice opposed the war as bitterly as did Harrison Gray Otis or Timothy Pickering and that most of the southern Federalists were of the same mind. But the Yankee Federalists called down most of the postwar odium on themselves because they alone controlled state governments and were able to turn state rights against the nation.

After Congress declared war, the lower house of the Massachusetts General Court issued an address to the people, saying, "Organize a *peace party* throughout your Country, and let all other party distinctions vanish." Governor Caleb Strong followed this up by proclaiming a public fast to atone for a declaration of war "against the nation from which we are descended, and which for many generations has been the bulwark of the religion we profess."

The war slogan of the administration, "Free Trade and Sailors' Rights," seemed mere hokum to Federalists and to the shipowning community generally; they were making big money in neutral trade, and the number of impressments of native-born American seamen was small. Fundamentally, it seemed wicked and unchristian to Federalists to attack England when she was "the world's last hope" against the tyrant Napoleon. As Harrison Gray Otis wrote, "The most intelligent and respectable men in the country . . . tremble for the prosperity and fate of Britain, and consider her . . . as the Bulwark of the liberties of this country and mankind." That belief happened to be correct in 1812. Napoleon had suppressed every vestige of liberty in Western Europe save in England, Portugal, and recalcitrant Spain. Within a week after America declared war on Great Britain, his grand army entered Russia. England's cause in 1812, as in 1914 and 1939, was that of the free world.

Certain old and important Republican families of Massachusetts, such as Adams, Gerry, Austin, and Crowninshield, supported the war; but most of the old families were anti-war Federalists. The Harvard Corporation—President Kirkland, Treasurer Davis, Fellows Lathrop, Lowell, Phillips, Gore, and Chauncey—was 100 percent anti-war. This they publicly proclaimed at Commencement in 1814 by conferring honorary degrees on John Lowell, the secessionist; H. G. Otis, leader of the New England Convention movement; Judge Isaac Parker, who advised Governor Strong to withhold militia; and Chief Justice Tilghman of Pennsylvania, who had defied the federal government in the Olmstead case.[1]

The Massachusetts Federalists maintained a policy of giving the war minimum support consistent with obedience to the laws (as interpreted by themselves) in the hope of promoting a speedy peace. Governor Strong decided whether to honor presidential requisitions for militia, and refused most of them. So did every other New England governor except Gilman of New Hampshire. There was a certain justification for this localism.[2] In July 1812, almost every regular unit garrisoning coastal forts marched off to invade Canada, leaving the New England coast defenseless except for militia. Distrustful as the state administrations were of the Washington government, they refused requisitions not merely to spite the "little man in the Palace," as they called President Madison,[3] but because the militia, who elected their own officers, balked at being placed under officers of the regular army. General Winfield Scott of Virginia wrote in his *Memoirs* what nobody dared to say during the war, that Madison refused commissions to Federalist gentlemen who wanted to serve, and in New England "there were but very few educated Republicans." Hence the Yankees selected for commissions "consisted mostly of coarse and ignorant men. In the other States . . . the appointments consisted, generally, of swaggerers, dependants, decayed gentlemen and others fit for nothing else, which always turned out *utterly unfit for any military purpose whatsoever.*"

Boston Federalists condescended to celebrate American naval victories, since they regarded the United States Navy as a Federalist creation which the Jeffersonians had starved and neglected. A naval ball at the Exchange Coffee House on State Street in March 1813 was the only public function during the war when both parties got together. There was dancing from 8:00 to 11:00, and "a sumptuous supper," at which seven hundred were able to sit down at once. As the Boston *New England Palladium* reported: "The splendor of the ball was never equalled in this town, and we believe never was surpassed in the United States. Commodores Rodgers and Bainbridge and Capt. Hull, with their respective ladies . . . and most of the other naval officers in town, augmented the brilliancy, as much as they increased the enjoyments of the evening."

---

1 For the Olmstead case, see a valuable and much neglected work, Herman V. Ames, *State Documents on Federal Relations* (Philadelphia, 1906), 45–52.

2 See Ames, 54–64, for the constitutional side of this contest between the New England states and the federal government.

3 It is a curious human trait to avoid mentioning by name someone you bitterly hate. Most of us remember Franklin D. Roosevelt's being called "That man [or: That ————] in the White House"; and, a generation earlier, the editor of a New York newspaper gave orders to his staff never to mention the name of Theodore Roosevelt.

A service of plate was presented by Boston to Commodore Oliver H. Perry after his victory on Lake Erie, but, according to the diary of the Rev. William Bentley, "Commodore Perry passed through Salem this day towards Portsmouth. No notice was given of his visit and no ceremonies passed." Salem, Newburyport, and Essex County generally (always excepting Marblehead!) were solidly anti-war. The Republican press reported that a five-star, five-stripe flag was displayed by the Sea Fencibles of Newburyport and that a mob there tried to liberate British prisoners brought in by the privateer *Grand Turk*.

In celebrating American naval victories, the Boston Federalists spent far less energy and enthusiasm than over two European events, the retreat of Napoleon from Moscow, and the entrance of the Allies into Paris. The festivities to celebrate the Russian victory opened on March 25, 1813 in King's Chapel. A choir sang Handel's *Hallelujah Chorus*, the Rev. William Ellery Channing offered a prayer which "united the elegance, and what the French call the *onction* of Fénelon, with the simplicity of the Apostolick Age," and the Rev. James Freeman delivered an extraordinary discourse composed of passages from the Old Testament so cunningly woven together as to appear a prophecy of recent events. Harrison Gray Otis presided at a public dinner in the Exchange Coffee House, where President Kirkland of Harvard invoked the Lord's blessing. At the first toast, to "Alexander the Great," a transparency representing the Emperor as "The Deliverer of Europe" was unveiled, an orchestra played the imperial Russian anthem, and everyone rose and cheered.

Similarly, in 1814, Boston sang no hallelujahs for Macdonough's naval victory on Lake Champlain but held a "Splendid and Solemn Festival" on June 15 to commemorate the "downfall of the Tyrant" Napoleon. In the evening the State House was illuminated, a band played in the colonnade, red-hot shot and "carbonic comets" were fired from Boston Neck, and the John Hancock mansion was adorned with transparencies showing fleurs-de-lys and "Honor to the Allies." We were then supposed to be fighting the principal ally, England.

Celebrations of this sort were not confined to Boston, or even to New England. The New York Federalists had them too, and John Randolph of Roanoke wrote to Josiah Quincy declaring that Boston had done herself proud.

Whatever Boston Federalists were able to effect by resolutions and celebrations paled in comparison with the results of their financial policy. Various factors resulting from the war gave New England a monopoly of manufactured and imported goods, and a large part of the specie in the country migrated to Boston banks. These institutions, with one exception, were controlled by Federalists, and Philadelphia financial circles were similarly constituted. A good understanding existed between the financial powers of Philadelphia and Boston (New York, apparently, did not count) to withhold subscriptions to government loans until assured of peace, hoping thus to force President Madison to abandon his strategy of conquering Canada. And they nearly succeeded in bankrupting their government at a very critical period.

On April 4, 1814 Congress authorized a new loan of $25 million. Otis and the Philadelphia bankers David Parish and Charles Willing Hare were eager to subscribe. Money had become plentiful in both cities and hard to place; Washington would get the money somehow; they hated to miss an opportunity for safe and lucrative investment. The Philadelphians argued that subscribing to loans was no greater encouragement of the war than paying customs duties on imports and pointed out that Federalists would not be exempt from the baleful consequences of a collapse of the government and a total prostration of public credit. The leading merchant-financiers of Boston, including George Cabot, John Phillips, Samuel Eliot, Theodore Lyman, and Thomas Handasyd Perkins, thrashed the matter out at a private meeting. Otis argued the Philadelphia case but Cabot countered (so he wrote to Otis five years later) "on the ground that the war was *absolutely unjust*"; hence "we ought never to *volunteer* our services in a cause which we believe to be morally wrong." The meeting then voted to help the government financially only upon receiving definite assurances from Washington that satisfactory instructions had been given to the peace commissioners. Like any self-respecting government, it refused to give this information, and the loan proved a failure without Federalist support. Boston took up only $1 million of the loan; but Virginia, a state which shouted most loudly for the war, subscribed only $200,000.

By the close of 1813, another act of government enhanced the woes of maritime New England. Contraband trade, especially in Maine and Georgia, had assumed such proportions that Congress passed a general embargo act even more severe than Jefferson's, prohibiting all coasting trade and fishing outside harbors. "Madison's Embargo" aroused the most indignant protests in eastern Maine, where the only way to get about was by water. The voters of Deer Isle passed resolutions denouncing Madison's embargo as "the utmost stench of despotism"; Belfast declared that the sufferings, injuries, and oppressions "under the present Dynasty are tenfold greater" than those of 1775–76; Ellsworth compared Madison to Bonaparte; the voters of Gouldsborough complained that even sleighs carrying food for their families were stopped and searched for contraband by Madison's minions; Castine asked, "Shall Massachusetts be . . . obliged to carry on this war forever to gratify the malignity of a few individuals directed by 'an unseen hand'?"—Napoleon, of course. Maine was the hottest part of the anti-war bloc in 1813–14.[4] Cyrus King, brother

---

4 These two resolutions are in the Massachusetts Archives (State House, Boston).

to Rufus King, ran for Congress from a Maine district and won, on an extremist platform. In a widely quoted speech he said, "If a simple king of England, by his corrupt servants, chastised New England with whips, the administration here chastised her with scorpions. . . . The states of New England can never be satellites."

Only because moderate Federalist leaders such as Otis, Josiah Quincy, and James Lloyd acted as brakes did the Massachusetts General Court avoid confrontation with the Union during the winter session of 1813–14. Senator Timothy Pickering, stung by the sneers of his Washington colleagues that Massachusetts might bluster but dared not act, spurred on his followers. Francis Blake, state senator from Worcester, delivered a glowing eulogy of Great Britain, declaring that if our Constitution permitted embargoes, he preferred the British, "monarchy and all." Samuel Fessenden of New Gloucester, Maine, announced that "it was time to take our rights into our own hands. . . . We ought to establish a custom house by law, and the sooner we come at issue with the general government the better." One who heard this speech wrote that "these ravings of a political maniac were received with manifest applause." But, he adds, Harrison Gray Otis threw cold water upon them.

By the spring of 1814, so violent had become the feeling against war and embargo that Massachusetts Republicans dared not go before the people on a platform of unqualified support of the war and the administration. They nominated for governor Samuel Dexter, who in an open letter proclaimed himself still a Federalist, announced that on the policy of commercial restriction he "differs radically from the party called Republican, and *he desires that they should know it*," and that his only quarrel with the Federalists arose from their aggressive pacifism. Caleb Strong won his tenth election easily; and, more significant, 360 Federalists and only 156 Republicans were elected to the lower house of the General Court.

Presently there developed a situation even more critical and alarming to New England than before. The British government, relieved in Europe by the collapse of Napoleon's empire, prepared to overwhelm its only remaining enemy by invasions and raids at every vulnerable point of the American coast and frontier. Hitherto New England had not been invested by sea, but in June 1814 British men-of-war blockaded her ports and began minor raiding attacks on several points along our coast. On July 7, armed barges from a warship off Boston Light raided the harbor and carried off five small sloops. Moose Island and Eastport, Maine, were captured on July 11, and the inhabitants were required to take an oath of allegiance to King George. On August 30–31 Boston learned details of the Battle of Bladensburg, the capture of Washington, and the burning of the Capitol. On September 4 Sir George Prevost invaded New York at Lake Champlain with the finest British army ever sent to America. On the same day it became known in Boston that a formidable naval expedition (three ships of the line, two frigates, three more warships, and ten transports lifting 3,500 soldiers) under Lieutenant General Sherbrook had occupied Castine, raided Bangor, and taken possession of eastern Maine. Almost everyone assumed that Sherbrook would next attack Boston.

With the federal government a fugitive from Washington, national integrity threatened at every point, the regular army undermined by desertion, and several states forced to provide for their own defense, the Union has never been so weak, or national prestige so low, as in that first week of September 1814.

The war department did indeed offer to undertake the recovery of Castine and eastern Maine, if Massachusetts would undertake to furnish troop-lift for 5,000 men, raise them, feed and pay them, to be reimbursed after the war. Governor Strong refused, as no such expedition was militarily feasible. With the entire New England coast blockaded by the enemy, no armed ship could even get at the British in Castine, where no fewer than fourteen ships of the Royal Navy were constantly maintained, and where several thousand redcoats garrisoned Fort George and nearby redoubts. Strong well remembered the futile, disastrous attempt to recapture Castine during the War of Independence; and he pointed out that without a superior naval force—and most of the ships of the United States were then blockaded in harbor—any such attempt in 1814 would be doomed to certain defeat and merely expose the inhabitants to violent reprisals.[5]

As a result of this startling series of events in the summer of 1814, Governor Strong summoned the already elected General Court for a special session on October 5. In his opening speech the governor described the state's situation in the most gloomy terms. His speech was referred to a joint committee of which H. G. Otis was chairman. "Otis's Report," submitted in three days' time, exhorted all citizens to unite "in repelling our invading foe," but deplored "the destructive policy by which a state of unparalleled national felicity has been converted into one of humiliation, of danger, and distress." He recommended that a convention of the New England states be summoned immediately, to deal with the grievances of that section and to do something about local defense.

Otis's Report became the subject of a long-winded, acrimonious debate

---

[5] George A. Wheeler, *Castine Past and Present* (Boston, 1896) blames Strong; anyone who reads Mahan's account of naval events in 1814 will endorse the Governor's wisdom. Cf. Richard Hildreth, *The History of the United States of America*, 6 vols. (New York, 1876), VI, 538, who adds that the selection of General Henry Dearborn to head this dubious enterprise was considered "a deliberate insult." Nobody has yet written a candid history of eastern Maine under this British occupation. From what I can gather, the people at large welcomed it as an alternative to the embargoes, etc., of the Madison administration and made good money trading with Nova Scotia.

in the General Court. "Monarchy and all" Blake proposed to prohibit the federal government from collecting duties, excises, or other taxes in Massachusetts. Otis declared he was "extremely sorry for this," believed it to be "very injurious to our national government," and persuaded the Worcester senator, much against his will, to withdraw his motion. Leverett Saltonstall, the young member from Salem, made an able speech defending Governor Strong's stand on the militia problem. He attempted to answer the charge of poor timing at a period of national peril by quoting 2 Corinthians 6:2: "Now is the accepted time; behold, now is the day of salvation." Saltonstall admitted the Union to be in danger, but that was not New England's fault. Unless we make an effort, the Union "will soon as naturally fall asunder, as ripe fruit falling from our trees." [6] John Holmes of Maine, ablest orator on the Republican side, answered Saltonstall in a speech that took two and a half hours to deliver and in which he called Otis "the flippant orator, the pretty man." Nevertheless, Otis's Report passed the state senate on October 12 by a vote of 22 to 12 and passed the house four days later by 260 to 20. A letter of invitation was sent to the other New England state governors to be represented at Hartford, and those of Rhode Island and Connecticut promptly accepted.

Exactly what was the Hartford Convention expected to accomplish? The official objectives were to draft constitutional amendments to protect New England interests and to agree with the federal government to let the states conduct their own defense. But was that really all? John Quincy Adams and the Republicans charged that the whole thing was a secession plot, to be initiated by concluding a separate peace with Great Britain. We may confidently deny that charge, since all evidence points to the fact that Otis, George Cabot, and their colleagues wished to avoid secession at any cost; but anti-war sentiment had gone very, very far indeed.

That fall, Congressmen who had voted for the war were bawled at as "war hawks" and hustled on the streets of Boston and Plymouth. And at the congressional elections in early November every district in Massachusetts proper, and six out of seven in Maine, elected an anti-war Federalist candidate. Even Joseph Varnum's safe Middlesex district, despite a ringing appeal by Samuel Hoar and John Keyes to show its "indignation" over the Hartford Convention, went Federalist. Even John Holmes of Maine, the Republican leader in the General Court, went down to defeat. Never had the Federalists enjoyed so nearly a clean sweep. A writer in the Republican Boston *Patriot* of December 7 admitted that at least half the people of Massachusetts were for disunion and warned that if it came to that the Bay State, ruled by "Blakes, Quincys,

[6] Boston *Weekly Messenger*, Nov. 18, 1814. I consulted this and other newspapers of 1814 at the Boston Athenaeum and the Massachusetts Historical Society.

Pickerings and Saltonstalls," would have to live off the export of "potash, mules, grindstones and pine boards." And an earthquake shock on November 30, first to be felt in Boston since 1783, convinced many of the godly that the Almighty intended to give the "Headquarters of Good Principles" a good shaking-up.

Most of the proposals which Otis and Cabot regarded as dangerous, and which they hoped would whistle out to sea when the Convention met, were for seizing customs houses, impounding federal revenues, declaring neutrality, nullifying conscription,[7] and the like. Such action would certainly have brought a direct confrontation between state and federal governments, which Otis and other moderate Federalists wished above all to avoid.

One threat which they knew nothing about was Governor Strong's secret mission to lay the grounds for an armistice, or separate peace, with Great Britain. This intrigue seems to have been the personal diplomacy of the supposedly simple, straightforward sage of Northampton, whose speeches had been published under the title *Piety and Patriotism.* Canny Caleb was too cagey to put anything down in writing, but he sent Thomas Adams, Federalist member of the General Court from occupied Castine, to General Sir John Sherbrooke at Halifax in mid-November 1814 with oral instructions to ascertain the "views" of the British government in the event of a direct clash between himself and Madison. Sir John wrote to Lord Bathurst, the Colonial Secretary, on November 20 that he hoped His Majesty's government would profit from any such opportunity to break up the American Union. Bathurst replied from London on December 13, 1814, that if Madison did not ratify the peace treaty, which he expected would shortly be signed (and was signed on Christmas Eve), and the war went on, Sir John had authority to sign an armistice with the New England states and to furnish them with logistic support to help defend themselves from the expected "resentment of the American Executive." But he must not promise troops.[8]

Politically, the most dangerous element in the situation was the movement for a new union of the original thirteen states only, initiated by John Lowell.

"Jack" Lowell was one of the most able, attractive, and imprudent of

---

[7] There was a tremendous uproar in New England over the conscription bill of Senator Giles of Virginia, which failed to pass, and over his bill to allow the enlistment of boys under eighteen without their parent's consent, which did pass. The Connecticut legislature threatened to nullify it if the administration attempted to enforce it. Ames, *State Documents,* 76.

[8] The British documents on Caleb Strong's mission are in the *American Historical Review,* 43 (1938), 553–566; see also Massachusetts Historical Society, *Proceedings,* LXIX (1947–1950), 218, note 25. No name is mentioned, and the governor gave the man no credentials; but as Sir John Sherbrooke describes him as a well-known citizen of eastern Maine and a member of the General Court, I infer that Thomas Adams, representative of Castine, was the man. One of the Republican newspapers of Boston in late 1814 has a squib about Adams crossing the British lines concealed in a double-bottomed wagon.

the Federalist leaders. Son of Judge John Lowell, first of that distinguished family to move to Boston from Newburyport, and of Sarah Higginson, he married Rebecca Amory; his half-brother Francis C. Lowell, whose mother was a Cabot, married a Jackson; there you have the nucleus of the famous Essex Junto. As John T. Morse, Jr., wrote, Cabots, Lowells, Lees, Jacksons, and Higginsons "knew each other well in Essex County and had a satisfying belief that New England morality and intellectuality had produced nothing better than they were; so they . . . intermarried very much, with a sure and cheerful faith that in such alliances there could be no blunders." [9] There certainly was no blunder in this case. Jack's only son John Amory Lowell married (1) his cousin Susanna Jackson and (2) his cousin Elizabeth Cabot Putnam; from them A. Lawrence Lowell, Percival Lowell, Amy Lowell, Ralph Lowell, and McGeorge Bundy are descended.

Jack Lowell was a man of wealth and of public spirit, a founder of the Massachusetts General Hospital, the Athenaeum, and other old Boston institutions; and his son John Amory Lowell became the No. 1 trustee of the famous Lowell Institute. In the pretty, rural scenery of Roxbury, John Lowell had a country estate famous for horticulture and hospitality. In every aspect of life except the political, Lowell was altogether admirable; but in politics he justified nicknames applied by the local Jeffersonians: "Crazy Jack" or "The Boston Rebel."

After writing two of the most powerful anti-administration pamphlets —Mr. Madison's War and Perpetual War, the Policy of Mr. Madison— accusing the President of refusing any reasonable peace settlement, Jack Lowell furthered a proposal so idiotic that it would hardly be worth serious consideration had it not been seriously promoted in the Federalist press. It amounted to a pistol-point reorganization of the Union. He announced it in a now very rare pamphlet of 1813, Thoughts in a Series of Letters, in Answer to a Question respecting the Division of the States, by a Massachusetts Farmer.[10]

Lowell's plan was this: the New England Convention should draft a new federal constitution so drawn as to safeguard maritime, commercial, and New England interests. This new constitution should be presented as an ultimatum to the original thirteen states only. In other words, kick the West out of the Union!

Lowell argued that the Louisiana Purchase violated "the great original

---

9 Memoir of Colonel Henry Lee (Boston, 1905), 9.

10 Copy in the Massachusetts Historical Society. No place or date on the pamphlet, the substance of which probably first appeared in a Federalist newspaper, but I have not found it. The only reference I have seen to it in any secondary work is in John S. Barry, The History of Massachusetts, 3 vols. (Boston, 1857), III, 419, note 3. It is attributed to Lowell in Ralph R. Shaw and Richard H. Shoemaker, American Bibliography, Preliminary Checklist for 1813 (New York, 1962), 262 (which locates copies in seven other institutions), and there are so many phrases identical with those of Lowell's earlier pamphlets that there can be no doubt of his authorship.

compact," [11] bringing in a horde of ignorant congressmen determined "to prostrate our commerce." He compared the old thirteen states to a benevolent merchant with a large family who took into his house a needy stranger. This man "began to usurp authority . . . and succeeded so well (his host being a peaceable man)" as to persuade him to take in three or four more comrades, farmers, and moonshiners, who insisted on their host's giving up his proper business and joining them in growing corn and distilling whiskey! Whilst a separation of the West "*must* take place, and the sooner the better*," Lowell hoped we might "soon again embrace our elder sister Virginia." The Westerners hate Great Britain, hate commerce, hate New England, and the Navy is an "object of their implacable hatred." We can never recover our ancient prosperity while they wield the lash. And he concludes that to unite "the original thirteen states . . . appears to be the last hope of our country."

Lowell predicted in a letter to Pickering that the eight eastern states outside New England would dare not interfere. As for pro-war Yankee Republicans, Lowell fatuously assumed that they would go along in order to be relieved from paying Madison's war taxes!

Senator Timothy Pickering in Congress took up the idea with enthusiasm, as did Gouverneur Morris of New York and Charles Carroll of Maryland. Assuming that General Pakenham's expeditionary force would defeat Andrew Jackson's army, Pickering wrote, "From the moment that the British possess New Orleans, the Union is severed." The West would embrace British sovereignty—or at least protection—to secure a Mississippi outlet, as it had often threatened to do in the past, and the rest of the original thirteen would be forced to join New England on New England's terms.

This wild scheme cannot be dismissed as a personal aberration of "Crazy Jack." Every Federalist newspaper of Boston but one promoted it as a platform for the Hartford Convention.[12] The Boston *Gazette* predicted in its number of November 17 that by July 4, 1815, "If James Madison is not out of office, a new form of government will be in operation in the eastern section of the Union." The *Columbian Centinel*, oldest and most respectable of the Boston Federalist press, promoted Lowell's scheme in a series of violent articles called "The Crisis"; and, before they were finished, started another series by a writer who chose the pseudonym "Epaminondas"—the Theban general who had detached several states from the Athenian Confederacy. "Epaminondas" urged the Hartford Convention "not to be entangled by the cobwebs of a compact

---

[11] The compact theory of the Federal Constitution, even the very words of the Virginia and Kentucky Resolves of 1798, were continually being thrown in the teeth of the Republicans by the Federalist newspapers; and Frank Maloy Anderson argued in his "Forgotten Phase" article (Mississippi Valley Historical Association, *Proceedings*, VI [1912–13], 176–188) that this was a deliberate attempt to ripen secessionist sentiment.

[12] I have not, however, examined the *Repertory*.

which has long since ceased to exist." He declared that the Union, once a blessing, had under Madison become a curse; that New England was not afraid of secession—look at how a little country, Holland, "threw off the yoke of Spain (our Virginia)." [13]

Already on November 9 the *Centinel* had announced Connecticut's and Rhode Island's acceptance of the invitation to Hartford as "Second" and "Third Pillar of a New Federal Edifice Raised," accompanying the text by a cut showing three columns, with room for a couple more. Thus in 1788 the *Centinel* had announced successive state ratifications of the federal Constitution. A witty writer in the Republican *Yankee* for December 9 said that the *Centinel's* three pillars looked like snuff bottles in an apothecary's window; so for good Republicans the Hartford conclave became the "Snuff Bottle Convention."

On November 26 the *Centinel* sketched out a whole scheme of action for the Hartford Convention "to do to save the country." "The bond of union is already broken by you, Mr. Madison." No more federal taxes should be paid until our just claims are heard. Conclude a separate peace with Great Britain to which the other states will be invited to adhere. Call a new federal convention of Northern States *only* to form a new federal constitution, which the South Atlantic States *alone* will be invited to join.[14]

And this scheme had some support outside New England, even from the press. The *Federal Republican* of Georgetown, D.C., printed an open letter to President Madison in early November: "Do immediate justice to all the reasonable claims of New England," it said. "Withdraw . . . your disgraced and incompetent generals." New England "has been driven off by every species of oppression. . . . Do you imagine that a people thus injured, insulted, abused and libelled, can possibly feel toward you any sentiment but that of deep and fixed detestation?" [15]

In the midst of all this excitement, life went on much as usual in Boston. There is a notice in the *Centinel* of December 12, 1814: "The Cotillion Party will meet at Concert-Hall on the evening of Tuesday the 15th at 6.30. H. Codman, Secretary."

Why, then, after all this fulminating, did nothing happen? Because the state legislatures had taken care to appoint to the Hartford Convention only moderate men, like George Cabot, Joseph Lyman, H. G. Otis, and Benjamin Hazard. John Lowell, in a letter to Pickering, denounced these members as timid and time-serving; not one really strong character, he said, had been sent to Hartford. And, as he feared, the Convention issued a moderate, statesmanlike Report condemning violent action.

---

[13] *Columbian Centinel*, Dec. 21–28, 1814.
[14] Quoted from "Refederator" articles in the Boston *Daily Advertiser*. "Refederator" I believe to have been John Lowell.
[15] Quoted in the Boston *Gazette*, Nov. 10, 1814.

"To attempt upon every abuse of power to change the Constitution would be to perpetuate the evils of revolution," said the Report. The main cause of New England's woes has been the "fierce passions which have convulsed the nations of Europe," entering "the bosoms of our citizens"; with Napoleon's fall these should subside. And the war has proved to the interior states the value of maritime power.

But the war was still going on when the Convention adjourned on January 5, 1815 (news of the Peace of Ghent, signed on Christmas Eve, did not reach the United States until February 13). So Governor Strong appointed a committee consisting of H. G. Otis, William Sullivan, and Thomas Handasyd Perkins to go to Washington and persuade the Madison administration to hand over federal funds for the defense of Massachusetts against the enemy. That, too, had been recommended by the Hartford Convention. Nowadays, nobody thinks twice of efforts to obtain federal funds for local use; but this unprecedented effort was denounced as treasonable. The loyal Republicans got out an amusing cartoon of the three respectable gentlemen sailing to Washington in a vessel built on the lines of a chamber pot, flying a five-striped ensign with the cross of St. George in the canton. Otis is saying, "Damn me, Tom, she's sprung a leak!" To which Perkins replies, "Who's afraid? Did you ever know a ship like ours fill from her *own* bottom?"

News of the Peace of Ghent and the Battle of New Orleans, arriving in Washington exactly when the "three ambassadors" did, rendered their mission futile and ridiculous.

A curious view of this mission, to the effect that its object was to promote the secession of New England, was given by President Lyndon B. Johnson in his press conference of November 17, 1967. The President is reported [16] to have said:

"There has always been confusion, frustration, and differences of opinion when there is a war going on. . . . That was true when all of New England came down to secede in Madison's administration in the War of 1812, and stopped in Baltimore. They didn't quite make it because Andrew Jackson's results in New Orleans came in.

"They were having a party there that night. The next morning they came and told the President they wanted to congratulate him—that they thought he was right all along, although they had come from Boston to Baltimore in a secessionist mood."

Pathetic indeed. President Johnson, comparing himself wistfully with President Madison at lowest ebb, hoped that a spectacular victory like General Jackson's would shortly bring peace, so that by Christmas the

---

16 Boston *Globe*, Nov. 18, 1967; and, on the 27th, letter by me deferentially correcting this extraordinary theory of events—Otis, under whose leadership the Hartford Convention had rejected secession before it adjourned on January 5, arriving in Washington to demand secession on February 14!

"hawks" could triumph over the "doves." Alas, there was to be no Peace of Christmas Eve 1967, or 1968 or 1969.

A myth of a New England secession plot's having been thwarted by the Treaty of Ghent and General Jackson's victory was started by administration organs almost immediately, as a smoke screen to cover Madison's mismanagement of the war. This myth, although shown to be false by every serious historian of the United States for the last 150 years, is so pleasing to people who dislike New England that many to this day continue to believe it. Presumably, President Johnson imbibed it from his school history in Texas.

We may amuse ourselves, at this safe distance, by discussing what might have happened if the war had continued well into 1815. It does not unduly strain the imagination to predict that if Madison's administration had been stubborn about ratifying the Treaty of Ghent, a very serious situation would have arisen. As a result of Governor Strong's secret diplomacy, the British authorities at Halifax had the green light from London to intervene if Madison refused to ratify the treaty, and if the New England states asked for help. Halifax was given permission to conclude an armistice with New England; and, in the event that those states were invaded by federal forces, to provide them with logistic support. There would have been a civil war, with Yankee militia supported by the Royal Navy, Canadian militia, and perhaps a fresh British expeditionary force.

Of course this is pure fantasy. Remembering the haste with which both governments ratified the Treaty of Ghent, and the fact that the British recalled General Pakenham's expeditionary force from Louisiana without even knowing whether it had won or lost, it is clear that the Peace of Christmas Eve 1814 was inevitable. And peace caused the entire sectional movement in New England, based as it was on false premises, to collapse. Everyone of both parties rejoiced over the end of this unpopular war, and New England "rebels" turned their minds to other topics.

Jack Lowell now employed his polemical pen to attack the conservatives in religion. His pamphlet *Are You a Christian or a Calvinist?* started a controversy that convulsed the Congregational churches of New England and led to the secession of orthodox churches from those that had gone liberal.

So ended the most unpopular war in our history. But because of Jackson's victory at New Orleans, the American people came to believe that they had won it, and that whatever setbacks had occurred were the fault of those nasty New England Federalists.

X The American West as Symbol and Myth: Poetic Inspiration or Pragmatic Perspective?

Introduction In 1950 Henry Nash Smith published his seminal study *Virgin Land: The American West as Symbol and Myth.* Smith brought to his study of the American West the conceptual tools of symbol and myth that had never, heretofore, been employed as a methodology in the manner in which Smith employed them. Not only was the methodology new and exciting, but its realization in Smith's writing, eloquent and imaginative, marked the publication of his book as an event in American historiography.

Smith defined his terms: "The terms 'myth' and 'symbol' occur so often in the following pages that the reader deserves some warning about them. I use the words to designate larger or smaller units of the same kind of thing, normally an intellectual construction that fuses concept and emotion into an image. The myths and symbols with which I deal have the further characteristic of being collective representations rather than the work of a single mind. I do not mean to raise the question whether such products of the imagination accurately reflect empirical fact. [See Barry Marks, "The Concept of Myth in Virgin Land," *American Quarterly,* V (Spring 1955), 71–76.] They exist on a different plane. But as I have tried to show, they sometimes exert a decided influence on practical affairs."[1] The materials upon which Smith based his study were primarily literary materials. This thematic treatment of myth and symbol from a chapter of his book, "The Agricultural West in Literature," is the first essay below.

Rush Welter, though he acknowledges his debt to Smith's insights and judges *Virgin Land* to be the main work in the field, is yet critical of the realities of the myths and symbols that Smith evokes as giving any whole image of the West as Americans conceived it. He states that "the predominantly literary antithesis that Henry Nash Smith has traced in *Virgin Land* may not have influenced the American people as much as their novels and some of their congressional rhetoric may suggest."[2]

In the second piece of writing below, Welter develops his criticism still further: "The themes that Smith and others trace are too nearly poetic in their inspiration, too nearly conventional in their application, to be trustworthy guides to the pragmatic perspective with which most Americans contemplated their lives. Above all, they are too restricted to account for various images of the West as a country that real people might inhabit; and they do not always differentiate the West that was to be occupied and farmed and ultimately to be industrialized from the majestic natural phenomenon that still surrounds

---

[1] *Virgin Land,* Preface, p. v.

[2] Rush Welter, "The Frontier West as Image of American Society: Conservative Attitudes Before the Civil War," *Mississippi Valley Historical Review,* XLVI (1960), 594.

Westerns on television and in movies." Welter concludes that between 1776 and 1860 Americans came to view the West as "an almost limitless extension of the social and economic and political values they associated with their country at large."

The Agricultural West in Literature

—*Henry Nash Smith*

I. Cooper and the Stages of Society

The Wild West beyond the frontier lent itself readily to interpretation in a literature developing the themes of natural nobility and physical adventure, but the agricultural West, as we have already remarked, proved quite intractable as literary material. The myth of the garden and the ideal figure of the Western yeoman were poetic ideas, as Tocqueville rightly called them, but they could not be brought to fictional expression. The difficulty lay in the class status of the Western farmer. The Declaration of Independence had proclaimed that all men were created equal, and American political institutions had reflected a general acceptance of the proposition in the widespread removal of property qualifications for the franchise as early as the 1820's and 1830's. But there was a lag of half a century between the triumph of the idea of equality in politics and its embodiment in imaginative literature.

The early literary characters in the pattern of Leatherstocking did not really bear upon the problem because they were outside society. In his capacity as Indian fighter and hunter the Western hero could be celebrated without regard to class lines. But we have noted how slowly the Western hunter gained sufficient social standing to be allowed to marry the heroine. This fictional emancipation of the Wild Westerner was not clearly worked out before the late 1870's.

The yeoman had an even harder struggle to achieve full status in literature. Cooper, for all his delight in Leatherstocking and his theoretical approval of political equality, stoutly resisted the tendency to break down distinctions between social classes. Indeed, as he became aroused over the "Anti-Rent War" in upstate New York he concluded that even in the political sphere the cult of the yeoman had been carried too far. He declared in 1848 that politicians eager for votes had made the small farmer into an idol before which they fell down in worship. "We can see citizens in these yeomen," continued the crusty novelist, "but not princes, who are to be especially favored by laws made to take from others to bestow on them." [1] The cult seemed to him a phase of the "bastard democracy" that was coming into favor, a movement to seek for the sovereign people in the

---

[1] *The Oak Openings; or, The Bee-Hunter*, 2 vols. (New York, 1848), I, 154.

gutters, "forgetting that the landlord has just as much right to protection as the tenant, the master as the servant, the rich as the poor, the gentleman as the blackguard." [2] In his Littlepage trilogy, Cooper had roundly denounced the tenants in the Hudson Valley who had resorted to violence in protest against a system of tenures that made it difficult for small farmers to acquire title to land. The ideal of the yeoman society was obviously incompatible with Cooper's aristocratic ideal of a society dominated by great landed proprietors.

Few writers of Cooper's generation were as frank as he in stating their conservative social bias. Perhaps they were not even conscious of it. But it was evidently at work as a force inhibiting the use of the small farmer as a character in fiction. James K. Paulding is a case in point. More than a decade after he had celebrated the career of Basil in *The Backwoodsman* he turned again to the agricultural West in his novel *Westward Ho!* published in 1832. Although the novelist acknowledges Flint's *Recollections of the Last Ten Years* as his source of information about the Mississippi Valley, [3] he builds his plot around a group of plantation gentry who migrate from Virginia to Kentucky; the only character really belonging to the West is the old hunter Ambrose Bushfield, a composite of Leatherstocking and Daniel Boone. [4] The story contains no characters representing the yeoman class.

The expatriate sculptor Thomas Buchanan Read's determined effort to depict an Arcadian West in his long blank verse narrative *The New Pastoral* (1855) shows even more clearly how difficult it was to devise a literary interpretation of the movement of the agricultural frontier into the Mississippi Valley. Read has an ample store of the clichés of agrarian theory. With his oaten pipe, he announces, he plans to celebrate the sweetly contended middle state between the hut and the palace, "The simple life of nature, fresh from God!" He will write of the great mass of Western farmers who labor that the structure of society may be sustained, for these folk are morally superior to the idle rich in their purple and fine linen. [5] But how can this claim be made good? Read follows a group of emigrants from rural Pennsylvania overland to Pittsburgh, down the Ohio to Cincinnati, and on into the Indiana forest. As they carve their homes from the wilderness civilization sweeps onward, and soon a golden harvest waves where once dark forests stood. But the poet is hard pressed for incident. He turns in desperation to a wilder West by describing a buffalo hunt and the lassoing of wild horses, and presents an elaborate metrical version of the standard vision of the Mississippi Valley in the future with

---

[2] *Ibid.*, I, 113.   [3] *Westward Ho! A Tale*, 2 vols. (New York, 1832), I, 4.
[4] Bushfield had been a companion of Boone (*ibid.*, I, 70); he was a loyal retainer of Colonel Dangerfield (I, 71); he felt crowded by the advance of settlement (I, 179–181); he wished to be able to fell a tree near his house for fuel (I, 184); and finally he fled to a remote military post on the Missouri River (II, 193).
[5] *The New Pastoral* (Philadelphia, 1855), p. vi.

its cheerful farms, quiet herds, cities, steamboats, a Pacific railway, and a great metropolis on the Lakes.

> *Onward still*
> *The giant movement goes with rapid pace,*
> *And civilization spreads its arms abroad;*
> *While the cleared forest-lands look gladly up,*
> *And nod their harvest plumes.*[6]

Of the actual process of agricultural settlement we have little except an account of the malaria among the farmers. Two of the patriarchs of the colony at last give up and make their way back to Pennsylvania—"Too stern the battle for such souls as theirs."[7] The whole performance is remarkably tame, despite Read's ingratiating fluency. As in the case of Paulding's *The Backwoodsman,* the trouble lies not in the poet so much as in an unfortunate lack of congruence between the materials and the literary mode he has chosen. His conventionally bland manner can not convey the coarse and salty reality of his subject, and he is evidently convinced only in theory of the dignity of his characters.

Mrs. Caroline A. Soule's *Little Alice,* to mention only one further effort at a mild and cheerful interpretation of agricultural settlement in the West, is likewise a failure. The author states in her preface that the novel is the fruit of "four years of actual pioneer life in the valley of the Upper Des Moines, of emigrant life in a cabin on the prairie."[8] She is perfectly convinced that frontier farmers are noble and that the process of advancing the agricultural frontier yields vast consequences for the good of mankind. The guests at a wedding, for example, are bathed in an aura of primitive sentiment:

> Fifty sturdy pioneers, clad in clean homespun, stood about in various attitudes, their frank open faces radiant with light from their honest hearts. Upon the mossy logs, sat as many noble women, their coarse garments betokening thrift and neatness, while their pleasant faces told of their sympathy with the fair girl whose bridal they had come to witness.[9]

Mrs. Soule asserts that in the earliest period of settlement, hardship and danger promote the spirit of mutual aid to such an extent that "the brotherhood of men is recognized as an actual as well as an ideal thing."[10] Fifteen years later the community shows many evidences of change,

> but thank heaven, only a bright, beautiful change, which has brought hundreds of struggling, debt-ridden, homeless and hungry men and women from the crowded cities of older States, and given them peace

---

[6] *Ibid.,* p. 208.   [7] *Ibid.,* pp. 215–217, 225, 233–234, 237.
[8] *Little Alice; or, The Pet of the Settlement. A Story of Prairie Land* (Boston, 1863), p. iii
[9] *Ibid.,* p. 143.   [10] *Ibid.,* p. 56.

and plenty, houses and lands, while they in grateful return have "made the wilderness and the solitary place glad for them; and the desert to rejoice, and blossom as the rose."[11]

Yet the story that is intended to exhibit the process is as unconvincing as Read's poem. The hero and heroine are recent arrivals from New England, formerly wealthy and very genteel. Uncle Billy, an "old and experienced hunter" speaking a strong dialect, is a benign Leatherstocking whose frontier skills are employed in the fashion prescribed by Wild Western convention.[12] Mrs. Soule also provides a female counterpart of Uncle Billy in the charitable but uneducated Grandma Symmes.[13] These characters represent the Western flavor of the book; but they are distinctly subordinate, just as Leatherstocking was subordinate to Cooper's gentry. The scheme of values in the novel is organized about the superiority of the hero and heroine, whose merits have nothing to do with the West or with agriculture. For all her four years on the prairie, Mrs. Soule can not find the literary means to embody the affirmation of the agrarian ideal that her theory calls for.

These early efforts to deal with the agricultural West in literature prove that the frontier farmer could not be made into an acceptable hero. His sedentary and laborious calling stripped him of the exotic glamor that could be exploited in hunters and scouts of the Wild West. At the same time his low social status made it impossible to elaborate his gentility. Whatever the orators might say in glittering abstractions about the virtues of the yeoman, the novelists found themselves unable to control the emotions aroused by the Western farmer's degraded rank in the class system. Since class feeling about the yeoman is the crux of the literary problem presented by the agricultural West, we are obliged to look as closely as possible into prevalent notions concerning the place of the West and its people in American society.

Such an inquiry leads back once again to the contrast between civilization and savagery that lay at the root of the distinction between the Wild West and the domesticated or agricultural West. The frontier of agricultural settlement was universally recognized as the line separating civilization from savagery; but the structure of civilized society within the frontier was conceived according to two contrasting schools of thought. The agrarian tradition that stemmed from Jefferson held up as its ideal simple agricultural communities in which an approximate equality of wealth prevailed, and in which social stratification was accordingly kept to a minimum. But the equalitarian overtones of this ideal were by no means acceptable to the country as a whole. The concept of a classless society appealed only to a radical minority, and was constantly in danger of being obliterated by the much older and deeper belief in social stratifi-

---

[11] *Ibid.*, p. 236.   [12] *Ibid.*, pp. 18, 67, 28.   [13] *Ibid.*, p. 45.

cation. The situation could hardly have been otherwise. Equalitarianism, especially social and economic equalitarianism, was a recent and perhaps transient notion deriving in large part from French radical thought of the eighteenth century. The ideal of social subordination, of a hierarchy of classes, of a status system, had the weight of centuries behind it. Still more important for the imaginative interpretation of American life was the fact that the assumptions underlying the class structure of English society permeated the genre of the sentimental novel, which was built about the genteel hero and heroine. There was no coherent literary tradition embodying equalitarian assumptions.

The belief in the Western farmer's social inferiority was further strengthened by certain ideas derived from the New England theocratic tradition. From this standpoint, all emigrants were actually or potentially criminal because of their flight from an orderly municipal life into frontier areas that were remote from centers of control. The attitude had developed naturally out of the Puritan devotion to social order maintained by church and state as coöperating agencies. A sermon preached before a Boston congregation by the Reverend Thomas Barnard in 1758 states the theocratic case against the backwoodsman quite clearly. Religion, he said, will flourish most where the arts of peace are cultivated, "especially Industry, among those born for Labour." For a quiet steady life in an orderly community keeps alive a regard for whatever is virtuous and pious, facilitates attendance upon public worship, tends to implant clear notions of justice and a regard for property, and leads men toward a proper submission to their civil rulers. On the other hand, when people wander into the wilderness and settle far apart from one another, the result is "Savageness of Temper, Ignorance, Want of the Means of Religion; (which will attend a solitary State and distant Neighborhood)." Worse still, when a plenty of free land allows men to support themselves "by the spontaneous Products of Nature with Little Labour; Experience has shewn, that Habits of Idleness and Intemperance have been contracted, much to the public Damage." [14]

This general view is so familiar it hardly needs elaborate illustration, but a few later comments may be mentioned to indicate the persistence of the Eastern belief in frontier depravity. The most famous among such statements is that of the Reverend Timothy Dwight, President of Yale, who wrote a characterization of the *"foresters, or Pioneers"* of Vermont on the basis of his travels in the state in 1798 and 1806. Such men, in the opinion of the noted divine, had proved too idle, talkative, passionate, and shiftless to acquire either property or reputation in stable communities, and therefore wished to escape the restraints of law, religion, morality, and government. Unable to adjust themselves to the social state, "they become at

---

[14] *A Sermon Preached in Boston, New-England, before the Society for Encouraging Industry, and Employing the Poor, September 20, 1758* (Boston, 1758), pp. 10–11, 13.

length discouraged: and under the pressure of poverty, the fear of a gaol, and the consciousness of public contempt, leave their native places, and betake themselves to the wilderness." [15] Dwight distinguishes between such dissolute foresters and the virtuous farmers who establish orderly communities after the first pioneers have moved on, but he implies that most settlers in the farther West are of the depraved class which he has described in Vermont.

> The class of men, who have been the principal subject of these remarks [he asserts], have already straggled onward from New-England, as well as from other parts of the Union, to Louisiana. In a political view, their emigration is of very serious utility to the ancient inhabitants. . . . The institutions, and habits, of New-England, more I suspect than those of any other country, have prevented, or kept down, this noxious disposition; but they cannot entirely prevent either its existence, or its effects. In mercy, therefore, to the sober, industrious, and well-disposed, inhabitants, Providence has opened in the vast Western wilderness a retreat, sufficiently alluring to draw them away from the land of their nativity. We have many troubles even now: but we should have many more, if this body of foresters had remained at home.[16]

These characteristics of life in new settlements continued to be especially clear to New Englanders who had enjoyed the advantages of theological training. The tradition was so explicit that even the young and relatively radical Unitarian minister James Freeman Clarke, who had been exposed to Transcendentalism and had gone out to Louisville with vaguely evangelistic aims, struggled in vain against it. In a review of Mann Butler's *History of the Commonwealth of Kentucky* and James Hall's *Sketches of History, Life, and Manners, in the West*, Clarke allowed the West a "genius deep, rich, strong, various, and full of promise," but he was alarmed at the fact that this genius was unbridled, undirected, and ungoverned. Western mothers encouraged their children to fight, women favored duelling, grave judges gambled, and vice ate into the heart of social virtue. The West needed religious restraint, it needed moral principle, it needed greater respect for law and a disposition to follow duty as pointed out to it by wise guidance—presumably from New England.[17]

The covert class bias characteristic of this attitude appears even more clearly in a review of Caroline M. Kirkland's *Forest Life* by Cornelius C. Felton, of Harvard, in 1842. A population was growing up in the West, according to the reviewer, "with none of the restraints which fetter the characters of the working classes in other countries." No feudal feeling of loyalty tempered the natural overflow of passion or restrained the full growth of individual humors. Each man in the West considered himself a

[15] *Travels; in New-England and New-York,* 4 vols. (New Haven, 1821–1822), II, 459.
[16] *Ibid.,* II, 461–462.   [17] *North American Review,* XLIII, 27–28 (July, 1836).

sovereign by indefeasible right, and had no idea anyone else was his better in any respect.[18]

To the theocratic suspicion of the Western farmer as a rebellious fugitive from society must be added the unfavorable view of him derived from the idea of civilization and progress. The conception of civilization, like the word itself, had first gained currency in the middle decades of the eighteenth century in the writings of Turgot and Rousseau.[19] Its most persuasive formulation came in the 1790's with Condorcet's *Esquisse d'un tableau historique des progrès de l'esprit humain*, which was immediately translated into English and had two editions in the United States before 1825.[20] The most influential aspect of Condorcet's theory of civilization was the notion that all human societies pass through the same series of social stages in the course of their evolution upward from barbarism toward the goal of universal enlightenment. He divided the history of the human race into ten epochs, the first nine stretching from the dawn of existence to the foundation of the French Republic, the tenth embracing the glorious future opened up for mankind by the triumph of Reason. The most important of these epochs for social theory were the earliest, which comprised the union of autonomous families who subsisted mainly by hunting, into "hordes"; the domestication of animals, inaugurating the pastoral stage of society; and the transition from a pastoral to an agricultural stage. Other writers developed the idea that civilization actually began when a given society adopted an agricultural way of life.[21]

Although in Europe the successive stages of society were naturally thought of as succeeding one another in time, so that primitive conditions could be studied only through historical and archeological research, the situation in America was quite different. When the theory of civilization became current in this country many observers were struck by its applicability to the actual state of affairs in the West. The comment was frequently made that in America one could examine side by side the social stages that were believed to have followed one another in time in the long history of the Old World. William Darby, for example, wrote in his *Emigrant's Guide* in 1818 that a journey from New Orleans westward to the Sabine showed man in every stage of his progress, from the most

---

[18] *Ibid.*, LV, 511 (October, 1842).

[19] The origins of the conception and its currency in the United States are traced in Charles A. and Mary Beard, *The Rise of American Civilization*, Volume IV: *The American Spirit: A Study of the Idea of Civilization in the United States* (New York, 1942).

[20] Philadelphia, 1796, and Baltimore, 1802.

[21] This point, for example, was frequently made by missionaries working with Western Indians (*Twenty-Sixth Annual Report of the American Board of Commissioners for Foreign Missions*, Boston, 1835, p. 99; *Twenty-Seventh Annual Report*, Boston, 1836, pp. 95–96). William Tooke, an English traveler in Asia cited by William Darby (*View of the United States*, Philadelphia, 1828, p. 321), had asserted that the transition from a migratory pastoral life to agriculture "determines the boundary between civilized and barbarous nations" (*View of the Russian Empire during the Reign of Catherine the Second*, 3 vols., London, 1799, III, 230). Volney made the same point with regard to the Bedouins of Arabia (*Travels through Egypt and Syria*, Eng. trans., 2 vols., New York, 1798, I, 231).

civilized to the most savage. New Orleans represented the summit of cultivation, refinement, and luxury. The plantations of the lower Mississippi likewise offered "all that art, aided by wealth, can produce." In Attacapas and Opelousas parishes the glare of luxury vanished, and in its stead the traveler encountered substantial, independent farmers living in rough though comfortable houses. In the western parts of Opelousas parish could be found pastoral hunters who recalled to the imagination the primitive ages of history. Still farther west, along the Sabine, the way of life of the scattered inhabitants suggested "the utmost verge of inhabited earth, and the earliest dawn of human improvement." [22]

In 1824 the *Port Folio* of Philadelphia quoted a remark to this same effect made by the British traveler Adam Hodgson after a journey from west to east across the United States. "I have seen the roving hunter acquiring the habit of the herdsman," said Hodgson; "the pastoral state merging into the agricultural, and the agricultural into the manufacturing and commercial." [23] Jefferson himself, whom Hodgson had visited at Monticello,[24] a short time later expounded the theory at length.

> Let a philosophic observer [he wrote] commence a journey from the savages of the Rocky Mountains, eastwardly towards our sea-coast. These he would observe in the earliest stage of association living under no law but that of nature, [subsisting] and covering themselves with the flesh and skins of wild beasts. He would next find those on our frontiers in the pastoral state, raising domestic animals, to supply the defects of hunting. Then succeed our own semi-barbarous citizens, the pioneers of the advance of civilization, and so in his progress he would meet the gradual shades of improving man until he would reach his, as yet, most improved state in our seaport towns. This, in fact, is equivalent to a survey, in time, of the progress of man from the infancy of creation to the present day.[25]

One or two examples from imaginative literature will be enough to indicate how widespread the theory was. In his *Francis Berrian*, published serially in 1825–1826, Timothy Flint causes the hero to remark that when he traveled westward from Natchitoches into Texas he "had occasion to experiment the truth of the remark, that in traveling towards the frontier, the decreasing scale of civilization and improvement exhibits an accurate illustration of inverted history." Berrian felt that he had traveled down six centuries in as many days. The half-savage settlers on the remote frontier, who lived as much by hunting as by agriculture, were "the inter-

---

[22] *The Emigrant's Guide to the Western and Southwestern States and Territories* (New York, 1818), pp. 61–62.

[23] *Port Folio*, Fourth [Fifth] Series, XVII, 214 (March, 1824).

[24] Adam Hodgson, *Letters from North America*, 2 vols. (London, 1824), I, 318–319.

[25] *Writings*, ed. H. A. Washington, VII, 377–378 (Monticello, September 6, 1824).

mediate race between savage and civilized man." [26] A final illustration
may be taken from Cooper's *The Prairie* (1827):

> The gradations of society, from that state which is called refined to that
> which approaches as near barbarity as connexion with an intelligent
> people will readily allow, are to be traced from the bosom of the states,
> where wealth, luxury and the arts are beginning to seat themselves, to
> those distant and ever-receding borders which mark the skirts and an-
> nounce the approach of the nation, as moving mists precede the signs
> of the day.[27]

This theoretical statement introduces the character of Ishmael Bush, a
Kentucky backwoodsman who represents Cooper's deepest penetration
into the problem of the agricultural frontier, and well deserves to stand as
the counterpart of Leatherstocking, the Child of the Forest. Whereas
Leatherstocking has a natural virtue and an exotic splendor derived from
his communion with untouched nature, Bush and his sons are at war with
nature. They are the very axemen from whom Leatherstocking has fled
halfway across the continent. Cooper is so eager to make this symbolic
point that he has Bush's sons chop down a grove of trees conjured up for
the purpose in the midst of the treeless great plains.[28] Although Leatherstocking and Bush figure in the same novel, they belong to entirely distinct
conceptual systems. The line that divides them is the agricultural frontier.
Leatherstocking, living beyond the frontier and following the vocation of
a hunter and trapper, is not a member of society at all. Bush, the husbandman, belongs to society; his "connexion with an intelligent people" is his
participation in the Social Compact to which Leatherstocking is not a
party.

But if Bush has a place in the scheme of civilization that flowers at the
top into Cooper's gentry, he represents the lowest of its stages, at a great
remove from the level of refinement.[29] He is a wanderer—Cooper's readers
would not have missed the biblical allusion in his name; and he also
arouses suspicion as a propertyless member of the lowest social class. He is
just such a backwoodsman as Barnard and Dwight had described. He is
clad in "the coarsest vestments of a husbandman," but wears "a singular
and wild display of prodigal and ill-judged ornaments" that bespeak a
half-barbaric taste. The lower part of his face is "coarse, extended, and
vacant," while the upper part is "low, receding, and mean." His manner
is characterized by apathy and indolence, although it is evident that he
has great muscular strength. He is, in short, half animal, as Cooper insists

[26] *Francis Berrian; or, The Mexican Patriot*, 2 vols. (Boston, 1826), I, 39.
[27] *The Prairie* (Philadelphia, 1827), I, 88. [28] *Ibid.*, I, 26, 103.
[29] Cooper calls the Bush group "semi-barbarous" (*ibid.*, I, 165), which was Jefferson's
word for American settlers just within the frontier, immediately above the pastoral Indians
in the scale of social stages.

in a simile: "... he suffered his huge frame, to descend the gentle declivity, in the same sluggish manner that an over fatted beast would have yielded to the downward pressure."[30] The novelist makes Bush the accomplice of his brother-in-law Abiram White, slave-stealer by trade, who has abducted the heroine Inez de Certavallos and is keeping her prisoner in one of the wagons of Bush's train. And we learn that Bush has shot a deputy sheriff who tried to evict him and fifty other squatters from a tract of land back in Kentucky.[31] This act of rebellion seems somehow vastly more sinister than Leatherstocking's defiance of the law in *The Pioneers*, which was motivated by feudal loyalty to his patron Major Effingham.

All these traits of Bush are in perfect accord with conservative theory. Yet the character has an interest for Cooper that defies theory. The idea of Bush's barbarism, along with its connotations of mere criminality, carries a suggestion of moral sublimity. It is related to the moral beauty of Leatherstocking as the somber and tormented landscapes of Salvator Rosa seemed to Cooper and his contemporaries to be related to the mild and smiling landscapes of their other favorite Claude Lorrain. In exploring this esthetic aspect of Bush, Cooper was able to view him for the moment, so to speak, purely, without judging him by the criterion of refinement or the theory of social stages, and in consequence was led to write one of the best sequences in all the Leatherstocking series. Near the end of the story, Ishmael as patriarch of his tribe sets about administering justice for the murder of his son Asa. A dim acquaintance with the Scriptures has left in his mind the barbaric notion that an eye for an eye is the law of God. When the murderer is revealed to be his wife's brother Abiram, the law of God comes into conflict with primitive clan loyalty, but Ishmael and his wife consult the Scriptures and come to the conclusion that Abiram must die. If Leatherstocking is notable for his intuitive ability to distinguish right from wrong, Ishmael too has his terrifying sense of justice. Abiram's craven pleas for one more hour of life suggest the grim expedient of binding his arms, tying a noose about his neck, and leaving him upon a narrow ledge from which as his strength fails he must in the end cast himself. That night, in a setting of wind and drifting clouds intended to suggest Salvator's style, Ishmael and his wife return to the place of execution, cut down the swinging body, and bury it.[32] The same sense of justice had earlier led Bush, after ponderous meditation, to release Inez of his own volition.[33]

Cooper's perception of values in Ishmael Bush's character that sprang from the conditions of life in a primitively agricultural West, yet could

---

[30] *Ibid.*, I, 16–17, 20. At I, 166 Ishmael is again compared to "a well-fed and fattened ox," and is said to be a member of "a race who lived chiefly for the indulgence of the natural wants. . . ."
[31] *Ibid.*, I, 78.   [32] *Ibid.*, II, 237–248.   [33] *Ibid.*, I, 222.

not be accounted for by reference to the ideas of civilization and refinement, pointed the way toward a more adequate literary treatment of the
agricultural frontier. But the idea of civilization was so deeply rooted in
American thought that it could not be cast aside overnight. Writers who
sought to deal with the agricultural West therefore continued for decades
to waver between a direct response to their materials and the attitude of
reserve or disapproval of Western coarseness dictated by the prevalent
social theory. Cooper himself found the problem persistently challenging,
although he did not advance very far toward solving it. In *Home as Found*,
published in 1838, he returned to the Cooperstown whose early history he
had chronicled in *The Pioneers* fifteen years before. He did not try again
to draw a Western character on the scale of Ishmael Bush, but he did
undertake an elaborate theoretical analysis of what happens in the wake
of agricultural settlement in the wilderness.

The goal toward which all such communities evolve is in his opinion
clear enough: it is the establishment of a secure class of gentry whose
ownership of land confers on them the wealth and the leisure that are
indispensable to the flowering of the higher graces of human nature. This
social ideal obviously depends upon what Cooper calls a "division into
castes," and can not be realized under the conditions of rough equality
that prevail in the earliest stages of settlement. It is true that he has a
rather unexpected Arcadian dream of the adventurous first years, when
for a time "life has much of the reckless gaiety, careless association, and
buoyant merriment of childhood." But this is a transient phase. Only
when gradations of social station, based on differences in inherited wealth,
have become clearly marked, does the society reach its final and ordered
stability.[34]

Cooper, a consistent and explicit conservative in social theory despite
his carefully limited endorsement of political democracy, was quite willing
to acknowledge that refinement and gentility were conceivable only in
members of an upper class with enough wealth to guarantee its leisure,
and a sufficiently secure social status to give it poise and assurance. The
form of the sentimental novel suggested exactly these assumptions. But
other novelists who tried to deal with the agricultural West felt themselves
under some compulsion to extend the application of the sounding platitudes of democracy and equality from politics to social and economic life.
They therefore faced a continual struggle to reconcile their almost instinctive regard for refinement with their democratic theories and their desire
to find some values in the unrefined West.

The conflict would not be resolved so long as they clung to the theory
of civilization with its fixed series of social stages. For the West could have
only one place in such a scheme: it was primitive and therefore unrefined.
This was indeed its defining characteristic. In proportion as the West lost

---

[34] *Home as Found*, 2 vols. (Philadelphia, 1838), I, 180–183

its primitive character it became indistinguishable from the East and there was no basis for a characteristic Western literature. Writers who were attracted by Western materials had an obscure awareness that the unprecedented adventure of agricultural settlement in the Mississippi Valley was somehow worthy of imaginative interpretation. The theory of progress and civilization, on the other hand, could take no account of novelty except as an increase of enlightenment in the most advanced societies. Abstract and rationalistic as it was, it implied that only the most advanced stage of social development produced characters worthy of admiration. The theory offered little ground for finding a value in America as contrasted with Europe, or in the American West as contrasted with the American East. From Cooper's day to that of Hamlin Garland, writers about the West had to struggle against the notion that their characters had no claim upon the attention of sophisticated readers, except through their alarming or at best their picturesque lack of refinement.

II. From Caroline Kirkland to Hamlin Garland

Literary historians have long been accustomed to find Joseph Kirkland and Hamlin Garland important because they contributed "the bitterness of the frontier" to the development of realism in fiction.[35] It is more relevant here to ask a different question about these men. What were their origins? From what literary background did they proceed? Since there are no absolute beginnings or endings in the history of literature, Kirkland and Garland can be considered the culmination of one development just as profitably as they can be considered the pioneers of another. To see in them nothing except a prophetic mood of disillusionment is to oversimplify a rich and suggestive chapter in the history of American thought. Whatever their shortcomings as artists, they signalize a slow but far-reaching change in literary attitudes toward the Western farmer. In the early nineteenth century, as we have seen, the farmer could be depicted in fiction only as a member of a low social class. By 1890 he could be presented as a human being, unfortunate perhaps, but possessed of dignity even in his tribulations. The purpose of the present chapter is to trace this process through the work of representative writers who dealt with the agricultural West during the half century between the last of the Leatherstocking novels and *Main Travelled Roads*.[36]

---

[35] Vernon L. Parrington, *The Beginnings of Critical Realism in America* (*Main Currents in American Thought*, Volume III, 1930), reprint ed. (New York, n. d.), p. 288.

[36] Ludwig Lewisohn's comment greatly overstates the case, but suggests the importance of this development for American literature: "It took genuine courage, genuine independence of mind to give literary treatment to the rude peasantry that peopled the Mississippi Valley. And it is from the treatment of this peasantry that our modern literature takes its rise. . . . The germs of our period of national expression are to be found in those few writers like Edward Eggleston and E. W. Howe who, whether consenting to it or resisting it, made the collective life of the American people the substance of serious literature" (*The Story of American Literature*, New York, 1932, p. 276).

The earliest of these was Mrs. Caroline M. Kirkland. A native of New York, she spent five years in southern Michigan during the late 1830's and early 1840's while her husband took a fling at land speculation and town building. On the basis of this exposure to the West Mrs. Kirkland wrote three books: *A New Home–Who'll Follow?* (1839), *Forest Life* (1842), and *Western Clearings* (1845), besides minor sketches and stories dealing with the same materials. Her books were widely read, and deserved to be, for they have the merits of clear observation and lively reporting. They are also a valuable repository of upper-class Eastern attitudes toward the raw West.

As a grand-daughter of Samuel Stansbury, the Loyalist poet of the Revolutionary period, Mrs. Kirkland had an assured social standing that made it impossible for her to identify herself with the free-and-easy outlook and customs of the Michigan frontier.[37] Instead, she conceived of herself as a traveler who happened to have made an unusually long sojourn in the wilderness "beyond the confines of civilization."[38] Her first book is cast in the form of letters to cultivated friends back home. She realizes these sophisticated readers will hardly be able to believe that Western backwoodsmen "are partakers with themselves of a common nature."[39] The Western indifference to class lines arouses in her by turns a lively amusement and something not far from indignation. She is greatly annoyed with people who pretend to believe in the principle of social equality. To carry out such doctrines in practice would, she assures us, "imply nothing short of a lingering mental martyrdom to the cultivated and the refined."[40]

Yet she responds almost in spite of herself to the generosity and kindness of the pioneer farmers. She says she always returns from her little excursions about the countryside with an increased liking for the people.

> There is after all [she explains] so much kindness, simplicity and trustfulness—one catches so many glimpses of the lovelier aspect of our common nature—that much that is uncouth is forgotten, and much that is offensive is pardoned. One sees the rougher sort of people in their best light, and learns to own the "tie of brotherhood."[41]

To her second volume of sketches she prefixed six Spenserian stanzas in praise of Sympathy, "Nature's blest decree," which she had learned from the Wizard of the North. The master had taught her that the backwoodsman was human after all:

---

[37] The fullest account of Mrs. Kirkland's life and work is Langley Carleton Keyes, "Caroline M. Kirkland. A Pioneer in American Realism," Unpublishedd Doctor's Dissertation, Harvard University, 1935. The social position of the Stansburys is discussed on p. 96.
[38] *A New Home—Who'll Follow? or Glimpses of Western Life,* by Mrs. Mary Clavers (pseud.) (first published 1839; 4th ed., New York, 1850), p. 3.
[39] *Ibid.,* pp. 7, 8.   [40] *Forest Life,* 2 vols. (New York, 1842), I, 122.   [41] *Ibid.,* I, 209.

The power that stirred the universal heart
Dwells in the forest, in the common air—
In cottage lone, as in th' o'er burdened mart—
For Nature's painter learned from Nature all his art.[42]

If the reader will compare this sentimental theory of the nobility of humble Western farmers—reminiscent of Timothy Flint's preface to *George Mason*—with the kittenish remark which opens Mrs. Kirkland's first volume ("I intend to be 'decidedly low'")[43] he will recognize how instructive a confusion of attitudes her writing exhibits.

The contradictions between her high-flown theory and her instinctive revulsion from the crudities of backwards Michigan are reflected in her vain struggle to find a satisfactory literary form. The structure of her books is extremely simple. She writes as if she were keeping a travel diary in which, as a cultivated outsider, she makes notes concerning the natives of a strange land. The form is that which comes naturally to the first explorers of a new area. Hundreds of such narratives had been written about the West by travelers with no literary pretensions. But Mrs. Kirkland uses the strategy of writing in the first person to keep her sensibility constantly before the reader and to emphasize her detachment from her surroundings. She takes it for granted that her readers share with her a higher social status than that of the natives and underlines the assumption by plentiful literary allusions and quotations, plus a sprinkling of French and Italian phrases that authenticate her implied claim to rank as a bluestocking cast among unlettered country folk.

But she can not be permanently content with so simple a literary form and tries valiantly to devise something more complicated. In her three volumes are interpolated perhaps a dozen pieces of fiction that she tries to endow with a plot. The experiments range from the brief autobiography put into the mouth of the admirable Mrs. Danforth in *A New Home*[44] to the more ambitious efforts which Mrs. Kirkland was encouraged to make by the success of her first book. *Forest Life* contains, for example, the tale of how the worthy young backwoodsman Seymour won the hand of Caroline Hay, daughter of the greatest landowner in the country,[45] and an account of an English couple named Sibthorpe which ends up in the epistolary mode of the previous century.[46] Several of the sketches in *Western Clearings* threaten to become plotted narratives, such as the story of the shiftless Silas Ashburn who is still not base enough to resort to illegal violence against a man he considers an enemy,[47] or "Ambuscades," which relates how the enthusiastic huntsman Tom Oliver forgot to hunt and became a hard-working farmer through love of Emma Levering.[48]

---

[42] *Ibid.*, I, 7.   [43] *A New Home*, p. 9.   [44] *Ibid.*, pp. 29–31.
[45] *Forest Life*, I, 237–250, II, [3]–45.   [46] *Ibid.*, II, 46–146.
[47] *Western Clearings* (New York, 1845), pp. 66–86.   [48] *Ibid.*, pp. 118–143.

Despite the variety of these experiments in fiction, it cannot be said that Mrs. Kirkland succeeded in finding an adequate form for her Western materials. She could not discover any dependable plot structure except a love story, and her lovers develop toward the stereotypes of the sentimental tradition. In proportion as they are worked into a plot they lose any Western characteristics they may have had at the outset. There is no progress toward overcoming the lack of coherence between materials and form that constituted her literary problem. She demonstrated that the agricultural West offered interesting and even challenging themes for fiction but she could not find a satisfactory method for dealing with them.

During the next two decades the obvious strategy of writing a conventional love story against a Western background was adopted by a number of women novelists, including Mrs. Metta V. Victor, her sister Mrs. Frances Fuller Barritt, and Mrs. Caroline A. Soule, who has been mentioned before. Mrs. Victor's *Alice Wilde, the Raftsman's Daughter. A Forest Romance,* issued in 1860 as Number 4 of Beadle's Dime Novels, conducts the elegant and cultivated Philip More of New York to a remote region of the West. Although the sophisticated Virginia, likewise of New York, cannot understand why he wishes to throw himself away upon "a rude and uncultivated community," [49] Philip falls in love with Alice, daughter of the raftsman David Wilde. The father speaks a strong dialect but the daughter's speech is correct; her rusticity is indicated mainly by the fact that she dresses in the style of twenty years before.[50] After the hero has declared his love, Alice is sent to a seminary at Centre City for a little polishing. Mrs. Victor's conception of the problem she is dealing with is indicated in Alice's exclamation to her fiancé: ". . . you had pride, prejudice, rank, fashion, every thing to struggle against in choosing me." [51] That the triumph of love over these obstacles was widely approved is indicated by the enormous sale of the novel—250,000 copies in the United States, besides an immense run in England.[52]

In *The Backwoods Bride. A Romance of Squatter Life* [53] Mrs. Victor seized upon a conflict growing more directly out of agricultural settlement on the frontier. The elegant and cultivated Harry Gardiner has bought a large tract of government land in Michigan in the 1840's. When he comes out to take possession he finds that numerous squatters have settled on it, including Enos Carter, father of the beautiful seventeen-year-old Susan.[54] Although Mr. Gardiner has bought the land as a speculaton, his noble nature leads him to offer to sell to the squatters at the price he gave for it. But the squatters, perhaps under the influence of George Henry Evans,

---

[49] *Alice Wilde*, p. 72.   [50] *Ibid.*, p. 20.   [51] *Ibid.*, pp. 77, 81.
[52] Advertisement on p. [30] of Edward S. Ellis, *The Frontier Angel,* New and Old Friends, No. 7 (New York, 1873).
[53] Beadle's Dime Novels, No. 10 (1860)   [54] *Ibid.*, pp. [9] ,11, 14.

are convinced that "in the new country men are entitled to all they could cultivate. . . ." [55] Enos Carter states their position eloquently:

God made this earth to be free to all; and whoever takes wild land, and clears it, and cultivates it, makes it his own—he's a right to it. What right have these men that never did a day's work in their lives, coming along and takin' the bread out of our mouths? [56]

Mrs. Victor allows this very real conflict to develop to the point where a mob, including Enos, tries to break into Gardiner's hotel room to lynch him, whereupon the young hero kills one of the mob with a pistol.[57] But the author is not willing to follow through the issue she has stated, and takes refuge in a reconciliation which leaves Gardiner the squatters' candidate for Congress.[58] He can marry Susan without too great violation of the proprieties because her father was once better off and she retains some gentility from her childhood in rural New York.

Mrs. Victor returns to the problem of the social status of Western farmers in *Uncle Ezekiel and his Exploits on Two Continents*, but this time the roles of hero and heroine are reversed. Edith Lancaster, daughter of an upper-class Englishman, is brought through great exertions of the author to an Illinois prairie. Amos Potter, son of a squatter, does not have his father's backwoods dialect but is still too humble in status to satisfy Edith's father, who takes her to his London mansion.[59] There she pines for her Western lover until the eccentric Uncle Ezekiel, a character in the humorous Down East tradition, manages to reunite the young people and reconcile the father to the match.[60]

Mrs. Barritt, in her *East and West; or, the Beauty of Willard's Mill*, simplifies the problem at the expense of probability by creating an Iowa heroine of impeccable gentility. Although Minnie Willard, the miller's daughter, is unsophisticated in comparison with the urbane Constance, her highbred visiting cousin from New York, the country girl has the elegant accomplishments of writing verses and sketching in charcoal.[61] Fletcher Harris, an artist sent on tour by an Eastern magazine, falls in love with Minnie and draws a picture entitled "The Fawn of the Prairie" that celebrates a lyric moment described in one of Minnie's poems.[62] Yet before this marriage can take place Minnie must be sent to New York to become cultivated by looking at pictures and hearing music.[63] The heroine of Mrs. Barritt's *The Land Claim. A Tale of the Upper Missouri* is established as genteel by being made the daughter of an Englishwoman of noble family who eloped with the gardener and came to America; in the end the heroine is restored to her grandfather, Sir Deming.[64] It will be recalled that

---

[55] *Ibid.*, p. 17.   [56] *Ibid.*, p. 19.   [57] *Ibid.*, p. 23.   [58] *Ibid.*, p. 98.
[59] Beadle's Dime Novels, No. 16 (1861), p. 103.   [60] *Ibid.*, pp. 103, 119–120.
[61] Beadle's Dime Novels, No. 35 (1862), pp. 9, 41.   [62] *Ibid.*, pp. 58–59.
[63] *Ibid.*, pp. 84–85.
[64] Beadle's Dime Novels, No. 39 (1862), pp. 9, 95.

Margaret Belden, heroine of Mrs. Soule's *Little Alice,* could be presented as refined despite her backwoods setting because she had been reared in an affluent New England home.

Each of these authors cleaves to the theory of social stages which places the West below the East in a sequence to which both belong. The West has no meaning in itself because the only value recognized by the theory of civilization is the refinement which is believed to increase steadily as one moves from primitive simplicity and coarseness toward the complexity and polish of urban life. The values that are occasionally found in the West are anomalous instances of conformity to a standard that is actually foreign to the region. This principle is exemplified in the Western heroines, who seem to be worthy of admiration only in proportion as they have escaped from the crudity and vulgarity of their surroundings, either by virtue of birth elsewhere, or through the possession of an implausble innate refinement. The occasional half-hearted tendency to contrast Western freshness with Eastern oversophistication will be recognized as a remnant of the dying theory of cultural primitivism. It is quite inconsistent with the cult of refinement that furnished the intellectual framework for sentimental fiction.

The first step toward solving the literary problem of the agricultural West was to find some means of escape from the assumption that the East was the standard of value and that Westerners were of inferior social status. If novelists were to deal with the West on its own terms, they would have to adopt some criterion besides that of refinement and would have to rid themselves of their unconscious devotion to class distinctions. In practice this meant getting rid of the theory of social stages.

The stories and sketches of Alice Cary of Ohio, published during the 1850's, are the earliest body of writing in which the relation of the West to the East has ceased to be the major problem. It is significant that Miss Cary was the first native of the Ohio Valley who attempted to interpret the region in fiction. With all its shortcomings, her work supports Edward Eggleston's statement that she was the founder of the tradition of honest interpretation of the West.[65] Transmitted through Eggleston to Hamlin Garland, her repudiation of the conventional way of looking at sectional relationships was destined to have important literary consequences. Her indifference toward the East appears to have sharpened her eye for detail and to have helped her achieve moments of direct reporting that still seem sharp and fresh. But her writing suffers from defects that fully account for the neglect into which it has fallen. She is seldom free of conventional sentiment and often verges toward a familiar kind of religiosity. The schoolmaster in the sketch "Two Visits," [66] whose hands evince his gentle

---

[65] *The Hoosier School-Master. A Novel* (New York, 1871), p. [5].

[66] *Clovernook or Recollections of Our Neighborhood in the West. Second Series* (first published 1853; New York, 1884), pp. 109–145.

origin if indeed his glossy black curls, pale complexion, great melancholy eyes, and fondness for Coleridge were not more than sufficient indications, is pure claptrap. Like Emmeline Grangerford in *Huckleberry Finn*, he shows his gentility by sketching; and like her, he prefers funerary subjects. His masterpiece is a drawing of the grave of his first love, with himself kneeling by it.[67]

Furthermore, Miss Cary's literary method impedes the full development of her characters. She takes over Mrs. Kirkland's habit of writing in the first person and is seldom able to get herself out of the picture. She cannot refrain from occasional reminders that she too is a lady who knows her Spenser and Milton, and is qualified to make judgments concerning refinement or the lack of it in people and houses. In abandoning the intellectual framework offered by the theory of social stages, she was not able to construct any coherent theory to take its place. She asserts that "the independent yeoman, with his simple rusticity and healthful habits, is the happiest man in the world," but this judgment is supported by the condescending line from Gray which she quotes immediately afterward: "When ignorance is bliss, 'tis folly to be wise." [68] She believes that her Western farm and village characters are the "humbler classes" and that she is writing the simple annals of the poor, in contrast with other lady authors who "have apparently been familiar only with wealth and splendor, and such joys or sorrows as come gracefully to mingle with the refinements of luxury and art . . ."

> In our country [she continues], though all men are not "created equal," such is the influence of the sentiment of liberty and political equality, that
>
> *All thoughts, all passions, all delights,*
> *Whatever stirs this mortal frame,*
>
> may with as much probability be supposed to affect conduct and expectation in the log cabin as in the marble mansion; and to illustrate this truth, to dispel that erroneous belief of the necessary baseness of the "common people" which the great masters in literature have in all ages labored to create, is a purpose and an object in our nationality to which the finest and highest genius may wisely be devoted; but which may be effected in a degree by writings as unpretending as these reminiscences of what occurred in and about the little village where I from childhood watched the pulsations of the surrounding hearts.[69]

---

[67] *Ibid.*, p. 143.   [68] *Ibid.*, p. 25.

[69] *Ibid.*, pp. 363–364. The Preface to the First Series of Clovernook sketches (New York, 1851, reprint, 1852), pp. v–vi, makes the same point about the failure of city dwellers to sympathize with poor and humble farm people. Although Miss Cary does not consider all Westerners socially inferior (Cincinnati, for example, has an upper class), she is vividly conscious of class differences between urban and rural populations.

This is perhaps a little more explicit than Flint's and Mrs. Kirkland's statements of similar ideas, and Miss Cary came nearer than they did to realizing her program in fiction. But her sketches are still not consistently organized about her thesis. They reveal an interesting but in the end annoying instability of attitude in the author.

The sketch which contains the touching portrait of the schoolmaster, for example, begins as a contrast between the overaustere household of the prosperous Knights and the charming household of the poorer Lytles. But before she is done, Miss Cary manages to insert the death and funeral of little Henry Hathaway, the courtship and marriage of Hetty Knight, and the death of Kitty Lytle, presumably from heartbreak. The author is not sure where her interest lies or what she is trying to do. To mention only one other example, the sketch "Charlotte Ryan" deals with the daughter of the "last" family in the neighborhood who, brought up in poverty, goes for a visit with relatives near Cincinnati, encounters true elegance for the first time, suffers for her rusticity in the presence of the splendid Mr. Sully Dinsmore, is taken to some vague but glittering greater city by other friends, becomes herself the cynosure of all eyes at the ball, and snubs Mr. Dinsmore in return for his cruelty to her back in Ohio. But Charlotte is no happier in her silks than she had been in her homespun.[70]

Miss Cary's most ambitious effort to deal with the countryside about Cincinnati in fiction is *Married, Not Mated,* published in 1856. This confused work seems to have grown out of an autobiographical reminiscence; one of the young ladies introduced in Part II carries the remainder of the narrative in the first person. The nearest approach to a thread of plot is the story of how the headstrong Annette Furniss of Cincinnati determines to escape from domestic monotony by marrying Henry Graham, a young farmer who supplies the family with butter. Annette is a selfish creature and is really in love with Henry's unpleasant brother Stafford. The marriage therefore fails and Henry dies. By calling her hero a farmer Miss Cary seems to promise a study of rural Western character. There is a faint suggestion that Henry Graham's language and dress need to be refined by the power of love, but he is never made to speak dialect and his character is so profoundly genteel that one cannot take him seriously as a Westerner. He reads poetry, for example, in a secluded grove, and leaves a strip of willows standing along a brook because they improve the landscape. The actual work of the farm is carried on offstage by hired hands. The only labor Henry performs is the sentimental task of tending the grave of Annette's sister Nellie.[71]

The latter half of the novel wanders off into a tedious character sketch of the pompous Mr. Peter Throckmorton and a desperately comic study

70 *Clovernook* (Second Series), pp. 245–280.
71 *Married, Not Mated; or, How They Lived at Woodside and Throckmorton Hall* (New York, 1856), pp. 67, 97, 266, 270.

of the cures undertaken in his behalf by a series of amateur and professional physicians. And there are other grotesque things in the book. It is nevertheless oddly interesting, in part because Miss Cary stumbles almost accidentally into a remarkable technical experiment by telling the story of Henry and Annette from several points of view, in part because she manages to render directly observed depths of squalor and neurosis, but most of all because of the character of Raphe Muggins. Raphe appears first as an adolescent backwoods waif serving the Graham household as maid of all work; later she is married and rearing a vigorous family. She and her husband are of the folk and there is no doubt in the author's mind that they belong to a social class distinct from that of the Grahams. Yet Raphe is made much more real than any other character in the story. Miss Cary not only reproduces her robust speech at length, but admires her shrewd and healthy insight into the tortured lives of the Grahams, and uses Raphe's successful marriage as a foil for the introspective complications of the principal characters. The author's unpatronizing affection for this very ungenteel Western woman all but breaks down the literary convention that consigns the character to an inferior status.[72]

Despite Miss Cary's occasional triumphs, Edward Eggleston's work marks a distinct advance toward the discovery of literary values in the agricultural West. It is true that he was no more able than Miss Cary to get beyond the accepted dogma that a novel is a love story; all his heroes and heroines exhibit a stereotyped variety of sentimental virtue. It is also true that his novels contain traces of the old *a priori* doctrine of Western inferiority. One of the principal themes of *The Hoosier School-Master*, for example, is the desire of Bud Means to "get out of this low-lived Flat Crick way of livin'" by putting in "his best licks for Jesus Christ."[73] Eggleston remarks with approval that Patty Lumsden, heroine of *The Circuit-Rider*, was saved by her pride "from possible assimilation with the vulgarity about her."[74] The character Nancy Kirtley in *Roxy*, studied in considerable detail, is intended as a representation of "that curious poor-whitey race which is called 'tarheel' in the northern Carolina, 'sand-hiller' in the southern, 'corn-cracker' in Kentucky, 'yahoo' in Mississippi and in California 'pike.'" These backwoodsmen, like most of the Means family in *The Hoosier School-Master*, resemble Ishmael Bush in *The Prairie*. They are coarse, illiterate, lawless—in a word, "half-barbarous." Eggleston, like Cooper, is interested in the type, and his conclusions deserve quotation:

They never continue in one stay, but are the half gypsies of America, seeking by shiftless removals from one region to another to better their

[72] Miss Cary's other fictional efforts (*Hager. A Story of To-Day*, [New York, 1852; "second edition," 1852]; *The Bishop's Son. A Novel* [New York, 1867]) show no change in the rather confused pattern of her attitudes toward Western farmers.
[73] *Hoosier School-Master*, pp. 122, 125.
[74] *The Circuit-Rider: A Tale of the Heroic Age* (New York, 1874), p. [173].

wretched fortunes, or, more likely to gratify a restless love of change and adventure. They are the Hoosiers of the dark regions of Indiana and the Egyptians of southern Illinois. Always in a half-barbarous state, it is among them that lynchings most prevail. Their love of excitement drives them into a daring life and often into crime. From them came the Kentucky frontiersmen, the Texan rangers, the Murrell highwaymen, the Arkansas regulators and anti-regulators, the ancient keelboatmen, the more modern flat-boatmen and raftsmen and roustabouts, and this race furnishes, perhaps, more than its share of the "road agents" that infest the territories. Brave men and generous men are often found among them; but they are never able to rise above Daniel Boones and Simon Kentons.[75]

After Mark Bonamy has been led into sin by Nancy, he has a momentary impulse to give up all his past life and go with her to Texas, where he may live out his degradation with no reproach from any moral censor. Among the fugitive criminals and bankrupts there he may hope to become a leader and thus make some sort of a life for himself.

This Nance was a lawless creature—a splendid savage, full of ferocity. Something of the sentiment of Tennyson's "Locksley Hall" was in him. He would commit moral suicide instead of physical,—release the animal part of his nature from allegiance to what was better; and, since he had failed in civilized life, he might try his desperate luck as a savage. It was easier to sink the present Bonamy in the wild elements of the South-western frontier, than to blow out his brains or drown himself.[76]

Evidently, Eggleston is willing to go as far as any New England clergyman in painting the lawless savagery of the remote frontier. And though he considers Indiana more civilized than Texas, vestiges of a dark earlier barbarism linger even there. After all, Nancy belongs to Indiana as much as Mark does. In the West of his fiction Eggleston finds petty political corruption, dishonest manipulation of the preëmption law, and a sordid devotion to profit at any cost.[77] He notes that the greatest wealth of postfrontier communities has come not from hard work but from land speculation.[78] Whiskey Jim, the sympathetic Minnesota stage driver in The Mystery of Metropolisville, remarks that the West isn't the country of ideas, but of corner lots. "I tell you," he exclaims, "here it's nothin' but per-cent."[79]

It is rather odd that, holding such conventional views of Western depravity and "materialism," Eggleston should nevertheless have been so thoroughly convinced that the region deserved literary treatment. In the preface to The Hoosier School-Master he remarks:

[75] Roxy (New York, 1878), p. 183.   [76] Ibid., p. 343.
[77] Hoosier School-Master, p. 163; The Mystery of Metropolisville (New York, 1873), p. 93.
[78] Hoosier School-Master, p. 29.   [79] Mystery of Metropolisville, p. 21.

It used to be a matter of no little jealousy with us, I remember, that the manners, customs, thoughts, and feelings of New England country people filled so large a place in books, while our life, not less interesting, not less romantic, and certainly not less filled with humorous and grotesque material, had no place in literature. It was as though we were shut out of good society. And, with the single exception of Alice Cary, perhaps, our Western writers did not dare speak of the West otherwise than as the unreal world to which Cooper's lively imagination had given birth.[80]

But this does not take us very far, and it is certainly not an adequate analysis of Eggleston's attitude toward his Hoosiers. A year later he prefaced *The End of the World* with a quotation from Principal John C. Shairp's lecture on Wordsworth that relates how the poet found "pith of sense and solidity of judgment," as well as the essential feelings and passions of mankind, in greater simplicity and strength among humble country folk.[81] But this too fails to get at Eggleston's own attitude. For one thing, Wordsworth's theory would imply that the Kirtleys (and with them, Wesern poor whites as a class), as primitive children of nature, are even more admirable than the Mark Bonamys and the Ralph Hartsooks who have acquired a certain degree of literacy and cultivation. Eggleston's acceptance of the theory of progressive refinement through successively higher social stages prevented him from accepting the implications of Wordsworth's attitude. The conception of nature as a source of spiritual value could have little meaning for him. If his intense although undogmatic piety had allowed him to entertain the idea, he would still have found it in conflict with the deterministic notions he had taken over from Taine and Darwin.[82]

Since Eggleston's statement of his intentions is so meager we must make our own inferences from his work. It has been often remarked that before he began *The Hoosier School-Master* he had written a brief notice of a translation of Taine's *Philosophy of Art in the Netherlands* for *The Independent*.[83] The debt cannot have been great, but there are a few indications in the novels that Taine had given him at least an inkling of a pure pictorial feeling for common and familiar scenes, without overtones of moral or social evaluation. Chapter VI of *Roxy* is entitled "A Genre Piece." It relates how the young minister Whittaker spent an evening with Roxy

---

[80] *Hoosier School-Master*, p. [5].
[81] *The End of the World. A Love Story* (New York, 1872), p. 8.
[82] Eggleston remarks of Nancy Kirtley that she had only "something which a sanguine evolutionist might hope would develop into a conscience, by some chance, in many generations" (*Roxy*, p. [346]). His interest in and eventual acceptance of Darwin's position is discussed by his biographer William P. Randel (*Edward Eggleston, Author of The Hoosier School-Master* [New York, 1946], pp. 11, 218). In *The Faith Doctor* Eggleston referred to Darwin as "the intellect that has dominated our age" (Randel, *Eggleston*, p. 196). He publicly accepted Darwin in 1887 (*ibid.*, p. 218).
[83] Randel, *Eggleston*, p. 123.

and her father the shoemaker, and began to fall in love with her. Eggleston apparently wishes to call attention to the visual image of these figures grouped in a kitchen. A clearer example of the novelist's exploitation of pure visual interest is a passage in *The Circuit Rider* which describes Patty Lumsden spinning. Our sculptors, Eggleston remarks, ought to realize that in "mythology and heroics" Americans can never be anything but copyists. If they would turn to our own primitive life they would find admirable subjects like the girl spinning—an activity that reveals as no other can the grace of the female figure. Eggleston adds that the kitchen of the Lumsden home would make a genre subject good enough for the old Dutch masters.[84]

It is refreshing to find even so slight a hint that crude Western materials could be viewed disinterestedly, without the apparatus of theory that had so often beclouded the vision of observers like Mrs. Kirkland. But so long as the achievement was limited to the plane of visual perception, it could not have very far-reaching consequences for literary attitude and method. The borrowing of effects from painting had long been an established convention in writing about the West. Many authors, for example, had invoked the paintings of wild Salvator Rosa to convey their response to Western landscapes felt to be picturesque and sublime.[85] Merely to turn from Salvator to Dutch masters of "realism" was not a startling advance in literary practice. What was requisite was an extension of the technique of disinterested observation to the sphere of ethics, to the psychological interior of the characters as contrasted with their outer appearance or the houses they lived in.[86]

Taine did not help Eggleston very far along this road. The novelist's religiosity and recurrent retreats into sentimentalism lend a strongly archaic air to his work. Yet he did make a beginning. The aspect of his fiction that proved most valuable to the writers who came after him and is most interesting nowadays is his sincere feeling for the "folk"—for the characteristic traits of human beings in a specific geographical and social setting. This is the germ at once of what has been called his "realism" and of the interest in social history that eventually led him to abandon fiction altogether.

The notion that the lore and the mores of the backwoodsman might be interesting without reference to his functions as a standard-bearer of prog-

---

[84] *The Circuit Rider*, pp. 55–56.
[85] Some instances: George W. Kendall, *Narrative of the Texan Santa Fe Expedition*, 2 vols. (New York, 1844), I, 216–217; Francis Parkman, *The California and Oregon Trail: Being Sketches of Prairie and Rocky Mountain Life* (New York, 1849), p. 187; Thomas B. Thorpe, *Spirit of the Times*, X, [361] (1840).
[86] If the term "realism" has any use in the vocabulary of literary criticism—and until a Professor Lovejoy discriminates the half-dozen or more current senses of the word it will probably continue to confuse more things than it clarifies—it might well be made to designate precisely these aspects of Dutch pictorial method transferred to the sphere of psychological analysis.

ress and civilization, or his alarming and exciting barbarism, or his embodiment of a natural goodness, was quite late in appearing. Although travelers had reported a few snatches of the songs of French Canadian *voyageurs* and an occasional tall tale from the Far West, especially from the 1830's onward, apparently the first indications of an interest in the folklore of the agricultural West are contained in Alice Cary's work. Since her attitude toward these materials is at once complicated and highly suggestive for the future, it deserves more than a passing glance.

In describing her visit to the household of the grim Mrs. Knight, Miss Cary tells how Sally and Jane Ann, left alone for a few moments with their guest, entertain her by reciting riddles: "Four stiff-standers, four down-hangers, two crook-abouts, two look-abouts, and a whisk-about"; "Through a riddle and through a reel, Through an ancient spinning wheel . . ."; "Long legs, short thighs, Little head, and no eyes"; and "Round as an apple, deep as a cup, And all the king's oxen can't draw it up." They have begun a counting-out rime ("Oneary, oreary, kittery Kay . . .") when their mother comes in and angrily sends them away as if they had been misbehaving. The problem here is of course to define Miss Cary's own attitude toward the charming bits of folklore she has recorded. "Mrs. Knight," she remarks, "had been mortified when she found her daughters indulging in the jargon I have reported, and so imprisoned them, as I have described; but if she had accustomed herself to spend some portion of the day devoted to scolding the children, in their cultivation, few punishments of any kind would have been required. If they had known anything sensible, they would probably not have been repeating the nonsense which seemed to please them so." Miss Cary offered to bring over "some prettily illustrated stories . . . which might please her little girls. . . ." [87]

The riddles and counting-out rime are, then, jargon and nonsense, which should be replaced in the children's minds by systematic cultivation through proper children's books—perhaps the Peter Parley series. Yet Miss Cary is interested enough in the rimes to set them down, as apparently no one before her had done. Furthermore, she considers it deplorable that Mrs. Knight refuses to allow her older girls to attend play-parties where the games depend on folk songs:

Many a time [she writes] had the young women gone to bed with aching hearts to hear in dreams the music of—

> *We are marching forward to Quebec*
> *And the drums are loudly beating,*
> *America has gained the day*
> *And the British are retreating.*

---

[87] *Clovernook* (Second Series), pp. 116–117, 121–122.

> *The wars are o'er and we'll turn back*
> *And never more be parted;*
> *So open the ring and chose another in*
> *That you think will prove true-hearted.*[88]

Despite her lapse into a conventionally obtuse attitude concerning the children's rimes, Miss Cary was at least vaguely aware that the nonliterary culture of the Western folk embodied some value.[89]

Eggleston likewise describes a game involving choice of a true-love to the accompaniment of chanted verses ("Oats, peas, beans, and barley grow . . .") of which he reports three stanzas.[90] He perceives that this material raises a literary issue of some consequence, although he does not succeed very well in stating the case for the use of it. People who enjoy society novels, he declares, will consider "these boisterous, unrefined sports" a far from promising beginning for a story. Readers find it easy to imagine heroism, generosity, and courage in people who dance on velvet carpets, but difficult to ascribe similar merits to crude backwoodsmen. This hardly seems a satisfactory statement of the issue. What he is feeling for is a value in the mores of the folk comparable to the pictorial values he could perceive in his backwoods interiors. But he argues instead somewhat irrelevantly that people crude enough to play rowdy kissing games may nevertheless be quite heroic: "the great heroes, the world's demigods, grew in just such rough social states as that of Ohio in the early part of this century." And this leads to a little homily for the benefit of sophisticated readers:

> There is nothing more important for an over-refined generation than to understand that it has not a monopoly of the great qualities of humanity, and that it must not only tolerate rude folk, but sometimes admire in them traits that have grown scarce as refinement has increased. So that I may not shrink from telling that one kissing-play took the place of another until the excitement and merriment reached a pitch which would be thought not consonant with propriety by the society that loves round-dances with *roués*, and "the German" untranslated—though, for that matter, there are people old-fashioned enough to think that refined deviltry is not much better than rude freedom, after all.[91]

---

[88] *Ibid.*, pp. 119–120.

[89] In "Mrs. Wetherbe's Quilting Party" the play-party is a functional part of the plot. The "plays" include the nonmusical "Hunting the Key" as well as "rude rhymes, sung as accompaniments to the playing." Three specimens of the rimes are quoted: "O Sister Phoebe," "Uncle Johnny's sick-a-bed," and a four-line stanza announcing, "My love and I will go, / And my love and I will go, / And we'll settle on the banks / Of the pleasant O-h-i-ó (*Ibid.*, pp. 50–51).

[90] *The Circuit Rider*, p. 22.

[91] *Ibid.*, p. 21. Volney, among others, had long before compared American Indians to "the nation so much extolled of ancient Greece and Italy"—intending of course to belittle the Greeks and Romans (*A View of the Soil and Climate of the United States of America*, [1803], trans. Charles Brockden Brown [Philadelphia, 1804], p. 410). The theory that the American West exhibited all the stages of social development lent itself easily to the discovery of a "heroic" age at some point in the Mississippi Valley.

While it is far from clear that the same New Yorkers enjoyed reading German with Margaret Fuller and dancing round-dances, the mere fact that Eggleston can conceive of overrefinement liberates him partially from the inadequate literary theories of the 1870's. At least he has realized that folk rimes and games are more than jargon and nonsense, since they represent a tradition "that has existed in England from immemorial time." [92] If the culture of the folk attested a continuity of social evolution reaching far back into the past, it acquired a new dignity. It had a historical dimension that could never be accounted for by the abstract and schematic and even antihistorical theory of uniform progress through fixed social stages. This way of looking at illiteracy and barbarism offered a valid means of escape from the theory of civilization and refinement, and suggested how Western farmers could be rescued from their degraded social status.

The gradual emergence of a new conception of the Western folk in Eggleston and his successors can be traced clearly in the changing attitudes toward language, which after all was the most intimate, the most flexible, the most characteristic and suggestive of all the aspects of folk culture. What were literary interpreters of the agricultural West to do with vernacular speech?

We are familiar with the role of dialect in the tradition of Cooper, and indeed in sentimental fiction generally, as a simple and unambiguous badge of status. No "straight" character could be allowed to speak dialect, and every character who used dialect was instantly recognizable as having a low social rank. In books of more or less direct reporting, like Mrs. Kirkland's, the upper-class observer regales his presumably upper-class readers by rendering the outlandish speech of the natives as a foil for his own elegant rhetoric. Similarly, the heroes and heroines of fiction who come into the West from outside are distinguished from the natives by their correct and elevated diction. If a Westerner is to be made into a hero, like Cooper's Ben Boden the bee hunter in *The Oak Openings*, the author must take pains to tidy up the character's speech. The first notable departure from this simple set of literary conventions is in the work of Miss Cary, where indifference to the contrast between East and West lessens her interest in speech as a badge of social and sectional status. Although she makes a few experiments in transcribing the Western vernacular, she is capable of reporting the speech of characters living in abject poverty, in a remote rural area, without self-conscious attention to dialect at all, using an easy, colloquial style for people of quite various classes.[93]

But if it was a necessary first step to cease exploiting dialect as a badge

---

[92] *The Circuit Rider*, p. 22.

[93] Mrs. Wetherbe, in "Mrs. Wetherbe's Quilting Party," whom Miss Cary admires, is given a marked dialect (*Clovernook*, Second Series, pp. 18–19, etc.), but the poverty-stricken family in "Ward Henderson" do not speak in dialect (*ibid.*, pp. 346–360). The strongly sentimental atmosphere of this story has perhaps exerted a refining influence on the language of the characters.

of status, the achievement was merely negative. The effort to discover positive values in the culture of the folk would obviously suggest some affirmative use of the vernacular. The analogy of Dutch genre painting would imply a pure esthetic concern with dialect, a delight in the object for its own sake without insisting on its meaning as a badge of status or (what amounted to the same thing) as an index of refinement or the lack of it. There is evidence that the germ of Eggleston's first novel, *The Hoosier School-Master*, was precisely such an interest in the folk speech of southern Indiana. The novelist's biographer has found a list of "Hoosierisms" jotted down by Eggleston in February, 1863, eight years before the novel was published.[94] Eggleston was corresponding with James Russell Lowell about this list of dialect terms in January, 1870, and the Harvard professor's enthusiasm doubtless did much to convince him that his linguistic interest was reputable from a scholarly and literary standpoint.[95] Years later, in an issue of *The Critic* honoring Lowell's seventieth birthday, Eggleston wrote that Lowell had been his master more than anyone else. "His magnanimous appreciation of the first lines I ever printed on the subject of American dialect and his cordial encouragement and wise advice gave me heart to go on. . . ." [96] The indebtedness had been acknowledged long before in the preface to *The Hoosier School-Master* by a reference to the "admirable and erudite preface to the Biglow Papers."

> To Mr. Lowell [Eggleston asserted] belongs the distinction of being the only one of our most eminent authors and the only one of our most eminent scholars who has given careful attention to American dialects. But while I have not ventured to discuss the provincialisms of the Indiana backwoods, I have been careful to preserve the true *usus loquendi* of each locution, and I trust my little story may afford material for some one better qualified than I to criticize the dialect.[97]

The attitude of a linguist cannot be compared with that of a genre painter, but they have in common the fact that neither is primarily concerned with ethical judgments of his materials.

If *The Hoosier School-Master* was indeed the leader of the procession of American dialect novels, as Eggleston later asserted,[98] the fact may arouse mixed emotions in modern readers. For much of the dialect writing produced by the local color school in the two decades following the appearance of Eggleston's novel is both unskilful and patronizing. "In all use of dialect," remarked George Philip Krapp, "there is probably present some sense of amused superiority on the part of the conventional speaker as he views the forms of the dialect speech. . . ." [99] The generalization

---

[94] Randel, *Eggleston*, p. 79.   [95] *Ibid.*, p. 105.
[96] *Ibid.*, p. 187. It is not clear what publication Eggleston had in mind.
[97] *Hoosier School-Master*, p. 6.   [98] Randel, *Eggleston*, p. 126.
[99] *The English Language in America*, 2 vols. (New York, 1925), I, 229.

certainly applies to run-of-the-mill local color writing, which depends for too many of its effects upon the supposed quaintness of the illiterate natives of various American regions. But despite this danger in the literary use of dialect, it opened up pathways of advance in two directions. On the one hand, the perception that the speech of Western backwoodsmen exemplified the historian's principle that "all which is partakes of that which was" [100] saved it from being considered merely crude, coarse, and unrefined. The discovery added a dignity to the uneducated folk which they could never have acquired within the framework of the theory of progress and civilization. In *Roxy* Eggleston causes the Swiss-American girl Twonnet (Antoinette) to defend the use of "right" for "very" by pointing out to the young minister Whittaker, a gradute of Yale, that "right" occurs in this sense in the Bible; indeed, she even goes on to make the revolutionary suggestion that Yale itself, students and faculty, has it own local dialect.[101] This was a novel way of conceiving the differences between Eastern and Western speech.

The other line of literary development opened up by the growing respect for Western dialect is merely hinted at in Eggleston's work. This is the creation of an American literary prose formed on the vernacular. Whitman had been a pioneer in this respect, but Eggleston found Whitman merely "coarse." [102] And he had little more respect for Mark Twain, whose *Huckleberry Finn* was the first masterpiece of vernacular prose.[103] Yet Eggleston was moving with the current. His style has far fewer literary flourishes than that of Mrs. Kirkland, and on at least one occasion, when his own use of a provincialism (the word "hover" as a transitive verb to describe the action of a hen brooding her chicks) was pointed out to him by a proofreader, he let it stand, merely adding a note to the effect that the word was so used "at least in half the country." [104] Later in his career he became even more fully aware of the potential richness of folk speech as a literary medium. In 1888, commenting on James Whitcomb Riley's language, he wrote very shrewdly: "As dialect it is perfectly sound Hoosier but a little thin. He has known it more among villagers than among rustics. He has known it at a later period than I did, and the tremendous—almost unequalled vigor of the public school system in Indiana must have washed the color out of the dialect a good deal." [105]

Eggleston's scientific interest in the speech of Western farmers was carried even farther by Joseph Kirkland in *Zury, the Meanest Man in Spring*

---

[100] Edward Eggleston, "Folk-Speech in America," *Century Magazine*, XLVIII, 870 (October, 1894).

[101] *Roxy*, pp. 426–427.

[102] Eggleston remarks that if the Backwoods Philosopher in *The End of the World* had known Whitman's work, he would have assigned the poet to the "Inferno" section of his library along with Swinburne, *Don Juan*, and "some French novels" (p. 44).

[103] Eggleston wrote to his wife in 1888, after meeting Mark Twain, that he was "only a good clown after all" (Randel, *Eggleston*, p. 184).

[104] *The End of the World*, p. 37 and note.   [105] Randel, *Eggleston*, p. 184.

County (1887) and *The McVeys* (1888).[106] The plots of these novels are
dominated by Anne Sparrow, a New England school teacher who brings
an unexampled cultivation and refinement to rural Illinois, but the character of the avaricious Zury Prouder is well observed in the period before he
is regenerated by Anne's virtue, and the speech of the countryside is reported with care and skill. Kirkland's ear for what people actually said was
keener than that of any other writer who has dealt with the agricultural
West, except Sinclair Lewis. In addition to accurate phonetic notations, he
made the discovery that in conversation people often use an elliptical syn-
tax and altogether omit various kinds of unemphatic words.

But Zury is more than a dialect. He gives the impression of having been
created through the accumulation of tall tales about stinginess just as the
legendary Davy Crockett was created through accumulation of tales about
coon-hunting, fighting, and drinking whiskey. Kirkland says he is repeating stories told by a man who once worked for Zury and later delighted
his comrades in the Union army with them; some of the yarns, he adds,
have already found their way into print.[107] The political speech which
Zury makes with the assistance of Anne is a masterpiece of vernacular
prose filled with shrewd anecdotes, like those of Lincoln, which Kirkland
greatly admired.[108] If the novelist's simultaneous devotion to folklore and
to female gentility led him to consummate one of the strangest matings in
all literature by marrying Zury to Anne Sparrow—a transaction as odd as
would have been the marriage of Davy Crockett to Miss Alcott's Jo March
—he was nevertheless aware that the folk elements in Zury held a new and
vital kind of literary interest. Kirkland makes the point explicitly. Anne's
daughter Margaret edits the "Third Page" of the *Springville Bugle,* a
section given over to book reviews, anecdotes, pointed paragraphs, and
editorials. She and her cultivated friend Dr. Strafford notice that whenever Zury has spent an evening with them her writing is much improved.
"How is it, Margaret?" asks Strafford. "How does he help us so much?"

> "Well [she replies, evidently speaking for the author], as nearly as I
> can make out, it is the *tone* he gives our thoughts. If I read too much,
> the T. P. grows eastern and literary. If I leave it to you, it is scientific
> and political; but when Mr. Prouder is the inspiration, it is frontierish,
> quaint, common-sensical, shrewd, strong, gay, and—I don't know what
> all." [109]

---

[106] Kirkland told Hamlin Garland he was trying to improve on Eggleston, although he
did not specify in what respect (*Roadside Meetings* [New York, 1930], p. 111).

[107] *Zury: The Meanest Man in Spring County. A Novel of Western Life* (Boston, 1887),
pp. 80–81. I have not been able to trace this allusion.

[108] *Ibid.*, pp. 348–356. Kirkland explains in a note that one of the illustrations in the
speech—based on feeding a calf—is derived from a stump speech of "Representative
Horr, of Michigan" (p. 352 n.).

[109] *The McVeys: An Episode* (Boston, 1888), p. 339.

Despite the soft spot in the vicinity of the word "quaint," this is not a bad statement of the qualities that Eggleston and Kirkland were beginning to discover in their Western folk.

But neither the rendering of dialect nor the use of folklore proved after all to be the decisive factor in the complex literary evolution preceding the appearance of Hamlin Garland's *Main Travelled Roads* in 1891. It is true that when Garland was writing his memoirs toward the end of his long life he began his account of this movement by discussing the earliest uses of the "New World's vernacular"—in a few of Leatherstocking's speeches, in the *Biglow Papers,* and in Whittier, Bret Harte, and John Hay.[110] But he passes at once to a discussion of E. W. Howe. This transition is remarkable because Howe was not interested in reporting dialect The Western farm people of his stories have a colorless diction that tends toward conventional rhetoric, rather than the carefully constructed dialect of Eggleston's or Kirkland's characters. Garland refers to Howe's "strong, idiomatic Western prose," [111] but this is not the same thing as dialect and Garland does not probe further into the interesting problem of an American vernacular literary prose as contrasted with the reported speech of characters held distinct from the narrator.

The letter to Howe which Garland wrote in July, 1886, congratulating him on his novel *Moonlight Boy,* is a valuable document for the study of the various trends and currents that were at work in this important decade. It touches upon a number of attitudes and literary procedures that Garland endorsed, and develops a literary credo of some dimensions. Howe is for Garland one of the representative names standing for "local scene and character painting," the only one who represents the prairie West. He has depicted "homely, prosaic people in their restricted lives," not viewing them from a distance as picturesque, but writing "as from among them." [112] The pattern of the travel narrative, as in Mrs. Kirkland's sketches, has disappeared along with the status system that elevated Easterners above Westerners. In Howe's first and best book, *The Story of a Country Town* (1883), the narrator who speaks in the first person is a young man looking back upon his own bleak childhood in the prairie West.

But the most important trait of Howe's work is the constant note of sadness and disillusionment that bespeaks the fading of the dream of an agrarian utopia. *The Story of a Country Town* is a sardonic commentary on the theme of going West to grow up with the country. Through an eccentric character named Lytle Biggs, who sometimes speaks for the author, Howe attacks the cult of the yeoman as explicitly as Cooper had attacked it, although from a somewhat different standpoint. The notions

---

[110] *Roadside Meetings,* pp. 90–94.   [111] *Ibid.,* p. 95.   [112] *Ibid.,* pp. 94–95.

that there is a peculiar merit in agricultural labor and that farmers are more virtuous than other men, Biggs declares to be falsehoods circulated by politicians for their own advantage.[113] Howe's West offers neither color to the observer from without nor consolations to the people themselves. It is a world of grim, savage religion, of silent endurance, of families held together by no tenderness, of communities whose only amusement is malicious gossip. Howe's farmers seem on the whole to be prosperous enough, but some not easily analyzed bitterness has poisoned the springs of human feeling. The Reverend John Westlock, father of the narrator, a stern minister and successful farmer, runs away with a woman he does not love after years of a strange silent battle with himself. Jo Erring, the narrator's closest friend, is destroyed by insane jealousy. The symbol that dominates the opening and the close of the novel is a great bell in the steeple of Fairview church which is used to announce deaths in the community, and is also tolled by the winds "as if the ghosts from the grave lot had crawled up there, and were counting the number to be buried the coming year. . . ." [114]

Garland described this book as "a singularly gloomy, real yet unreal, narrative written in the tone of weary and hopeless age." [115] It is at this point that Howe differs most clearly from Joseph Kirkland, who considered the novel too melodramatic and told Garland that Howe's country town "never had any existence outside of his tired brain." [116] Yet the description of Zury's childhood in Kirkland's own novel is dark and bitter, as is the characterization of the half-insane Hobbs in *The McVeys*, with its end in the ghastly lynching scene; and both Mrs. Kirkland (in her shocked description of the death of a girl from an attempted abortion) [117] and Miss Cary (in her sketch of the newsboy Ward Henderson) [118] had included ominous shadows in their pictures of the West. These shadows had no doubt been somewhat blurred, but in devoting himself to a prolonged exploration of the dark recesses of his own childhood, Howe was merely developing hints in the works of his predecessors. The self-castigating Westlock is only a degree more neurotic than Mrs. Knight in Miss Cary's sketch, and both characters are thwarted by a grim and colorless environment.

Although Howe's extreme conservatism made him unsympathetic with the efforts of Western farmers to organize themselves for political action in the Farmers' Alliance,[119] the stories collected in *Main Travelled Roads* owe more to Howe's melancholy than to Kirkland's rather cold fidelity to

---

[113] *The Story of a Country Town* (Boston, 1883), pp. 239–240.   [114] *Ibid.*, p. 3.
[115] *Roadside Meetings*, p. 94.   [116] *Ibid.*, p. 111.   [117] *A New Home*, pp. 173–176.
[118] *Clovernook* (Second Series), pp. 346–360.
[119] Lytle Biggs is an unscrupulous man who organizes chapters of the Alliance to make money for himself. He cynically tells the farmers how industrious, honest, and oppressed they are in order to win their favor (*Story of a Country Town*, p. 240). The character of Biggs is not sympathetic but here he seems to be voicing Howe's own views.

linguistic fact or his use of a tall-tale tradition. Garland did practice faithfully the lesson of exact description, and despite his lack of a good ear for language he worked hard at transcribing the actual speech of his characters. But the method was with him only a means of bringing home to his readers the farmers' sufferings. Many years later he wrote that his point of view when he came back in 1887 to his old homes in Iowa and South Dakota "was plainly that of one who, having escaped from this sad life, was now a pitying onlooker." "That my old neighbors were in a mood of depression," he continued, "was evident. Things were going badly with them. Wheat was very low in price and dairying had brought new problems and new drudgery into their lives. Six years had made little improvement in farm conditions." [120] The visit coincided with the collapse of the great Western boom. Garland's success as a portrayer of hardship and suffering on Northwestern farms was due in part to the fact that his personal experience happened to parallel the shock which the entire West received in the later 1880's from the combined effects of low prices in the international wheat market, grasshoppers, drought, the terrible blizzards of the winter of 1886–1887, and the juggling of freight rates that led to the Interstate Commerce Act in 1887.

In Garland, Howe's undefined sadness, which had no acknowledged connection with economic distress, came into focus about the creed of Henry George's Single Taxers. "There was nothing humorous about the lives of these toilers," he wrote of his trip West in 1887. "On the contrary, I regarded them as victims of an unjust land system. An immense pity took possession of me. I perceived their helplessness. They were like flies in a pool of tar." [121] In the Preface to *Jason Edwards,* a novel written for Benjamin Flower's *Arena* in 1891 and dedicated to the Farmers' Alliance, Garland states his interpretation of what had happened in the agricultural West:

For more than a half century the outlet toward the free lands of the West has been the escape-valve of social discontent in the great cities of America. Whenever the conditions of his native place pressed too hard upon him, the artisan or the farmer has turned his face toward the prairies and forests of the West. . . . Thus long before the days of '49, the West had become the Golden West, the land of wealth and freedom and happiness. All of the associations called up by the spoken word, the West, were fabulous, mythic, hopeful.[122]

But the hopeful myth had been destroyed. With an element of exaggeration that can certainly be forgiven a novelist if it appeared also in the historian Frederick Jackson Turner, Garland declared, "Free land is gone. The last acre of available farmland has now passed into private or cor-

---

[120] *Roadside Meetings,* p. 113.   [121] *Idem.*
[122] *Jason Edwards, An Average Man* (Boston, 1892), p. [v].

porate hands." [123] His story is an apologue on the closing of the safety valve. Jason Edwards, a Boston mechanic, takes his family to the Western prairies in search of the free land promised by advertising circulars, only to find that all land within thirty miles of a railroad has been taken up by speculators. After five years of desperate struggle to pay interest and get title to his farm, Edwards is prostrated by a hailstorm that destroys his wheat just before harvest. The family return to Massachusetts in defeat under the protection of Alice Edward's fiancé, a Boston newspaperman. The evil forces oppressing the farmer are represented by Judge S. H. Balser, land agent, who falsifies the evidences of a boom in order to market his lands, and sits back collecting his interest while Edwards and other farmers grind themselves to illness and despair in their fields.[124] Reeves, the fiancé, points the moral of the tale: "So this is the reality of the dream! This is the 'homestead in the Golden West, embowered in trees, beside the purling brook!' A shanty on a barren plain, hot and lone as a desert. My God!" [125]

In view of actual conditions in the West, the ideal of the yeoman society could be considered nothing but a device of propaganda manipulated by cynical speculators. Yet Garland continued to hope that the ideal might be realized. He endorsed the single-tax program because he saw in it a means to this end. Ida Wilbur, the radical lecturer who voices many of Garland's ideas in *A Spoil of Office,* announces to the hero Bradley Talcott:

I believe in thickly settled farming communities, communities where every man has a small, highly cultivated farm. That's what I've been advocating and prophesying, but I now begin to see that our system of ownership in land is directly against this security, and directly against thickly-settled farming communities. The big land owners are swallowing up the small farmers, and turning them into renters or laborers.[126]

The social theories which shaped Garland's early stories are evident enough. Land monopolists had blighted the promise of the West; the single tax would eliminate the speculator and allow the yeoman ideal to be realized. But Garland was seldom able to integrate his theories with the materials he had gathered by personal experience and observation. The radical ideas occur as concepts. They are seldom realized imaginatively— perhaps never fully except in "Under the Lion's Paw," which exhibits a shrewd landowner exploiting a tenant.[127] Garland's strength lay rather in a simple humanitarian sympathy that was entirely congruous with the sentimental tradition. His description of an imaginary painting on the wall of Howard McLane's apartment in "Up the Coulé" expresses an emotion deeper than his conscious doctrines. The picture is "a sombre landscape

[123] *Ibid.,* p. [vi].   [124] *Ibid.,* pp. 103, 111.   [125] *Ibid.,* p. 142.
[126] *A Spoil of Office. A Story of the Modern West* (Boston, 1892), p. 152.
[127] *Main-Travelled Roads. Six Mississippi Valley Stories* (Boston, 1891), pp. 217–240.

by a master greater than Millet, a melancholy subject, treated with pitiless fidelity." It evidently has a portentous meaning for him:

A farm in the valley! Over the mountain swept jagged, gray, angry, sprawling clouds, sending a freezing, thin drizzle of rain, as they passed, upon a man following a plough. The horses had a sullen and weary look, and their manes and tails streamed sidewise in the blast. The plough-man clad in a ragged gray coat, with uncouth, muddy boots upon his feet, walked with his head inclined toward the sleet, to shield his face from the cold and sting of it. The soil rolled away black and sticky and with a dull sheen upon it. Near by, a boy with tears on his cheeks was watching cattle, a dog seated near, his back to the gale.[128]

This plowman is neither the yeoman of agrarian tradition, nor a picturesque rural swain, nor a half-barbarian like Ishmael Bush, nor an amusingly unrefined backwoodsman, nor even a victim of a perverted land system. His most direct relation is to nature, and even though this relation is one of conflict, it confers on him a certain dignity and tends to enlarge his stature by making him a representative of suffering humanity, of man in general. Garland's early stories are not a literary achievement of the first or even of the second rank, but they mark the end of a long evolution in attitudes. It had at last become possible to deal with the Western farmer in literature as a human being instead of seeing him through a veil of literary convention, class prejudice, or social theory.

The Frontier West as Image of American Society, 1776-1860
——*Rush Welter*

After three decades of controversy, American historians find themselves still embroiled in a bitter and often fruitless quarrel over the significance of the frontier in American history. Presumably, the critics of Turner's frontier hypothesis will ultimately win their campaigns to discredit his interpretation, for it is vulnerable both as an intellectual system and as a doctrine appropriate to an earlier and simpler world than the chaos in

---

[128] *Ibid.,* pp. 96–97.

From *Pacific Northwest Quarterly,* LII (January 1961), 1–6. Reprinted by permission. This paper is a slightly revised version of one read at the Mississippi Valley Historical Association meeting in Louisville in April 1960.

which we now live. Yet the very tenacity of Turner's hold on his defenders, together with the narrowness with which some of his critics have attacked his doctrines, suggests that a complete victory for Turner's opponents would deprive us of a valuable perspective on our past. Under the circumstances it seems appropriate to attempt a somewhat different evaluation of the Americans' frontier experience, to seek to remove it equally from the realm of too-generous sentiment and from that of literal-minded historiography.

The purpose determines the method and scope of this essay. Instead of insisting that the frontier be understood institutionally, as an economic or a political or a social influence on American life, we may choose to evaluate it in terms of its influence on American thought. This paper is a beginning, a preliminary exploration of the possibilities. Its purpose is not to argue the Turner thesis, but to illuminate it. Its data will be, not evidence that Turner was or was not an accurate historian, but attitudes expressed by American writers before he was born.

Other scholars have already explored some of the same ground. Chief among them is Henry Nash Smith, whose *Virgin Land* marked a new departure in frontier scholarship, and whose methods of studying imaginative literature and sub-literature have worked a near-revolution in American cultural history, not to mention other fields of endeavor.[1] Yet it is probably fair to say that in employing the techniques of literary analysis Smith and his followers have sometimes obscured as well as illuminated American thought. That is, they have demonstrated beyond all question that literary stereotypes influenced American writing and hence American thinking about the West; but they have tended to ignore other perspectives in which Americans saw the region.

For example, *Virgin Land* shows us how literary conventions stemming at least from the 18th century helped to shape the West in American eyes, making it seem variously a vast commercial empire, an ambiguous naturalistic refuge, or a perpetual agrarian utopia. Other studies, focused instead on religious imagery, have emphasized the extent to which the same region also appeared to give reality to the Biblical garden or the Biblical wilderness, and so to present Americans with a unique challenge and a unique opportunity to work out their religious destiny on a new stage.[2] But it is at least arguable that Americans saw the West in other terms as well, less arbitrary and less exaggerated.

The themes that Smith and others trace are too nearly poetic in their inspiration, too nearly conventional in their application, to be trustworthy

---

[1] Henry Nash Smith, *Virgin Land: The American West as Symbol and Myth* (Cambridge, Mass., 1950).

[2] See particularly George H. Williams, "The Wilderness and Paradise in the History of the Church," *Church History*, XXVIII (1959), 3–24.

guides to the pragmatic perspectives with which most Americans ordinarily contemplated their lives. Above all, they are too restricted to account for various images of the West as a country that real people might inhabit; and they do not always differentiate the West that was to be occupied and farmed and ultimately to be industrialized from the majestic natural phenomenon that still surrounds the Westerns on television and in the movies.

I suggest, instead, that between 1776 and 1860, far from being bound by literary or religious conventions in their views of the West, Americans came to see in it an almost limitless extension of the social and economic and political values they associated with their country at large. This proposition invites extended empirical inquiry, but there is already evidence enough to suggest that it is worth developing here in outline form. Indeed, the most difficult problem may be to formulate its terms clearly and accurately, for if they are formulated effectively, everyone should be able to test them in his own reading of primary sources.

To begin, we should restrict our inquiry so far as possible to an examination of what eastern writers made of the West. Thanks in large part to eastern condescension, which Smith among others documents, Westerners and western spokesmen often felt the need to describe their section and its prospects in exaggerated and overoptimistic terms. But while their views were undoubtedly significant expressions of American opinion, they also have the defect—for our purposes here—not only of special pleading, but also of irrelevancy. It can hardly be surprising that Westerners should have advocated the claims of their region to recognition and national approbation. It is both significant and surprising, however, that Easterners should so often have agreed with them. If we are to look anywhere for evidence that the West held special meanings for Americans before the Civil War, we can well afford to focus on eastern sources.

Within the range of eastern opinion, in turn, it is most striking that eastern conservatives—men representing unmistakable orthodoxy in religion or politics or social theory—should have seen the West in a favorable light. I have already urged, in a recent issue of the *Mississippi Valley Historical Review*, that after a notorious early reluctance to accept the West on any terms whatsoever, these conservatives came close to adopting it as their own.[3] That essay is concerned, among other things, with why their views shifted; the important point here is that they did.

Meanwhile, of course, more tolerant Easterners had long since identified the western frontier with the persistence and expansion of valued American institutions. This identification was evident in the writings of

[3] Rush Welter, "The Frontier West as Image of American Society: Conservative Attitudes before the Civil War," *Mississippi Valley Historical Review*, XLVI (1960), 593–614.

both Benjamin Franklin and Thomas Jefferson, who believed that a vast reserve of unsettled land would perpetuate our liberal institutions by protecting us against the growth of cities and the effects of poverty; but the image of the West soon transcended their pastoral and republican dream.

On the one hand, it took shape in the doctrines of manifest destiny: as early as 1819 Representative George F. Strother of Virginia protested against potential limitations on western settlement in the name of civilization, progress, religion, and all the social virtues.[4] On the other hand, it also entered profoundly into the doctrines of Jacksonian democracy. Indeed, Albert K. Weinberg's study, *Manifest Destiny*, suggests indirectly that the two phenomena—manifest destiny and Jacksonian democracy—were closely related through their common western orientation; and while other studies show that the relationship was by no means exact, it is hardly possible to ignore the extent to which each drew on western prospects and resources.[5]

Nevertheless, the categories of manifest destiny and Jacksonian democracy do not exhaust the perspectives in which Americans held the frontier West. For one thing, they do not take sufficient account of the distinctly utilitarian values eastern commentators placed upon the region. These were evident in an essay on the public domain that appeared in the *American Quarterly Review* for December, 1829.

> When we consider the unexampled rapidity with which the western states have acquired population and importance, we are surprised, not only at that fact, but at the inadequate ideas which have heretofore prevailed as to the magnitude and resources of that country. We are a travelling and a calculating people, and it seems strange that those who visited the western wilds in early times, should not have foreseen the events which have since transpired. That they did make golden reports we are aware; but contrary to all experience, those reports have fallen short of the truth, and all that has been dreamt and prophesied in relation to this region, by its most sanguine admirers, has been more than realized.[6]

Moreover, it illustrated these remarks, not by reference to a land of milk and honey, nor even to a yeoman's paradise, but by remarking on the growth of Lexington, Kentucky, and on the flourishing state of the West generally.

The same article also serves to point up another significant characteristic of the eastern perspective on the West: any practical estimate of the area focused of necessity on its habitable, usable regions. The proposition

---

[4] As quoted by Albert K. Weinberg, *Manifest Destiny: A Study of Nationalist Expansionism in American History* (Gloucester, Mass., 1958), 80.

[5] *Ibid.*, 116–117.

[6] *American Quarterly Review*, VI (1829), 263.

is self-evident, but perhaps it needs to be stated in order to counterbalance the emphasis that has been placed upon literary valuations of the West. Indeed, if we may trust the impressions of a European observer, Easterners saw in the West nothing but regions that would one day be like their own. According to Alexis de Tocqueville,

> In Europe people talk a great deal of the wilds of America, but the Americans themselves never think about them; they are insensible to the wonders of inanimate nature and they may be said not to perceive the mighty forests that surround them till they fall beneath the hatchet. Their eyes are fixed upon another sight: the American people views its own march across these wilds, draining swamps, turning the course of rivers, peopling solitudes, and subduing nature. This magnificent image of themselves does not meet the gaze of the Americans at intervals only; it may be said to haunt every one of them in his least as well as in his most important actions and to be always flitting before his mind.[7]

Even so, to refer to the eastern perspective on the West as if it were reducible solely to utilitarian terms is to miss important characteristics of the frontier image. We must acknowledge that even the most practical writers often endowed the region with certain imaginary attributes, and that it is impossible to understand the place it occupied in American thought without recognizing this fact. Let us see, then, what relatively prosaic eastern imaginations did with the plastic image of the West.

It is already evident that eastern commentators often looked forward to an uncomplicated horizontal extension of eastern political institutions into the frontier areas. The doughty Jacksonian journalist, Francis Grund, spelled out this concept in 1837:

> Every new colony of settlers contains within itself a nucleus of republican institutions, and revives, in a measure, the history of the first settlers. Its relation to the Atlantic states is similar to the situation of the early colonies with regard to the mother country, and contains the elements of freedom.[8]

Of course, Grund's conservative contemporaries were more apprehensive than he over the actual or the potential consequences of westward migration; but despite differences of emphasis, spokesmen for different points of view generally agreed that the West was a promising arena for most of the advantageous institutions of the East.

---

[7] Alexis de Tocqueville, *Democracy in America*, ed. Phillips Bradley (New York, 1945), II, 74.

[8] Francis J. Grund, *The Americans, in their Moral, Social, and Political Relations* (Boston, 1837), 208.

By the same token, the westward extension of political institutions also connoted, for many eastern spokesmen, a simultaneous reduplication of the economic opportunities that had already opened up in the East. Grund suggested as much; so did the *Democratic Review* when, in October, 1847, it sponsored territorial expansion at the expense of Mexico:

> Occupation of territory by the people is the great movement of the age, and until every acre of the North American continent is occupied by citizens of the United States, the foundation of the future empire will not have been laid. . . . That which constitutes the strength of the Union, the wealth and independence of its people, is the boundless expanse of territory laid open to their possession; and the more rapidly it is overrun by needy settlers, the greater is the security, that it will be equally and extensively distributed, and the more impossible it becomes for any section or clique to exercise "control over them," or to encroach upon the rights they enjoy under our constitution.[9]

As this passage suggests, most of the commentators who invoked the economic possibilities of the West focused their attention on its agricultural opportunities. They did not entirely limit their hopes to agriculture, as the writers I have already cited and the contemporary guidebooks attest.[10] But it is true that the agricultural West achieved special importance in eastern thought because of the safety-valve doctrine. As Carter Goodrich and Sol Davison pointed out twenty-six years ago, both those who feared the effect of free lands and those who saw benefits in them agreed that western lands would maintain high wages for eastern workingmen. (They also suggested that only partisans of other solutions to contemporary social and industrial problems, for example Matthew Carey, were likely to quarrel with the basic premise.) [11] Whether agricultural or not, however, the West seemed to offer apparently unlimited opportunities to Easterners to pursue their own well-being; it seemed made to order for American democrats and American entrepreneurs.

As the safety-valve doctrine particularly implies, moreover, the relatively accurate and relatively neutral appreciation of the West as an underpopulated and underexploited region was easily metamorphosed into a more optimistic and more exaggerated image. Not only did the newness of the region connote opportunities that could not be duplicated in the more settled areas of the country, as eastern writers often suggested, but its vast extent augured an almost endless succession of similar opportuni-

---

[9] "New Territory versus No Territory," *The United States Magazine, and Democratic Review*, XXI (1847), 291–92.

[10] See, for example, Samuel R. Brown, *The Western Gazetteer; or Emigrant's Directory* (Auburn, N. Y., 1817), and [Robert Baird], *View of the Valley of the Mississippi; or the Emigrant's and Traveller's Guide to the West* (Philadelphia, 1832).

[11] Carter Goodrich and Sol Davison, "The Wage-Earner in the Westward Movement, I," *Political Science Quarterly*, L (1935), 169–74.

ties, guaranteeing the distant future as well as supporting present hopes. It also held out much the same kind of promise for our social and political institutions, a promise that is reflected in Francis Grund's remark that

> The western states, from their peculiar position, are supposed to develope all the resources and peculiarities of democratic governments, without being driven to excesses by the opposition of contrary principles. Their number too augments the intensity of republican life by increasing the number of rallying points, without which the principle of liberty would be too much weakened by expansion.[12]

This was the sort of hope that ultimately influenced the passage of the Homestead Act; but the Homestead Act only documents a broader phenomenon, the constant identification of American prosperity and national well-being in the future with the continued existence of a frontier West.

The image of a West that would perpetually sustain and strengthen established social and political institutions also supported an imaginative identification between the West and the whole nation's character and destiny. The doctrines of manifest destiny undoubtedly played a large part in establishing this wider identification, but they do not satisfactorily define it. For the fundamental meaning of manifest destiny lay in the ways in which it committed Americans to further territorial expansion, whereas what we are concerned with here is their perspectives on territory they had already begun to occupy. The view I am pursuing was better represented by de Tocqueville's report on the Americans' self-image, or by the English review of 1821 that Turner quotes in "Middle Western Pioneer Democracy": "Others appeal to history: an American appeals to prophecy; and with Malthus in one hand and a map of the back country in the other, he boldly defies us to a comparison with America as she is to be."[13]

Nor are we compelled to rely upon foreign observers for evidence of this American proclivity. It was implicit, for example, in Representative Orin Fowler's apostrophe to the American character in 1852. During the debate on the Homestead Bill, the Massachusetts Whig exclaimed:

> What indomitable enterprise marks the character of our people! What immense forests have disappeared, and given place to cultivated towns, thriving villages, and wealthy cities! Agriculture, and manufactures, and commerce, and schools, and public buildings, and houses of public worship; all these testify to our matchless enterprise. The rapidity of our progress throws all Eastern countries into the shade. We build steamboats for the Sultan of Turkey, and railroads for the Autocrat of Russia; and our enterprise extends to the icebergs of the poles—to India, China, and Japan.[14]

---

[12] Grund, *The Americans*, 209.
[13] Frederick Jackson Turner, *The Frontier in American History* (New York, 1920), 345.
[14] 32nd Cong., 1st Sess., *Congressional Globe* (March 31, 1852), Appendix, 396.

Even more pointedly, during the 1840's the *Democratic Review* paid tribute to the West because it promised to create a truly American civilization, untrammeled by European influences; while more conservative sources had long since proclaimed, more ambiguously but no less insistently, that its development would decide the fate of the nation.[15]

The corollary of these present satisfactions and future hopes was a belief that in some sense the West had already made unique contributions to American life. Representative Fowler's paean of praise verges on making this assertion; other commentators were more nearly explicit. In particular, they portrayed the West as the breeding ground of a new sort of man, whose qualities would one day influence the whole United States. The tendency was already at work in the *American Quarterly Review* for June, 1829, when, in a review of Timothy Flint's *Condensed Geography and History of the Western States,* it pointed out that "The pioneers are a people peculiar to our country," and went on to describe the backwoodsmen sympathetically yet factually as brave, hardy, indolent, honest, generous, improvident, independent, sagacious, "and capable, when excited, of powerful bodily exertions." [16] The same tendency was even more apparent in the writings of James H. Lanman, the Connecticut businessman who spent several years in Michigan during the late 1830's, and who reported in *Hunt's Merchant's Magazine* in 1840 that

> The people of the west are generous, though crude, unmindful from habit of the luxuries of life, endowed with great boldnes and originality of mind, from the circumstances under which they are placed. They are, from the various elements of which they are composed, in a state of amalgamation, and from this amalgamation a new and valuable form of American character will spring up.[17]

But the most striking statement of this sort came from the prominent Baptist missionary, J. M. Peck, who developed in the columns of the *Christian Review* for January, 1851, what reads like a primitive version of the Turner thesis. The American people, Peck said, made up of "Puritans" and "Cavaliers," and of Germans, French, Irish, Scots-Irish, and Welsh, are mingling in the West and being molded by their experience there into a new civilization. They characteristically display "great energy, and the spirit of enterprise," intense patriotism, "strong social feelings," "high-toned republicanism, or strong democratic tendencies," a zeal for education, a universal spirit of improvement, and (thanks to itinerant evangelists and the impact of religious revivals) an "increasing influence of pure

---

[15] "The Poetry of the West," *Democratic Review,* IX (1841), 24–25; and see Welter, *loc. cit.*

[16] *American Quarterly Review,* V (1829), 356.

[17] James H. Lanman, "The Progress of the Northwest," *The Merchant's Magazine and Commercial Review,* III (1840), 39.

Christianity." "The feelings of honor, the abhorrence of falsehood, and entire frankness of Western Character," Peck concluded, "only need to be animated by deep, ardent, and intelligent piety to make us what we ought to be." [18]

Neither Lanman nor Peck was a wholly reliable spokesman for eastern attitudes, the former because he remained a western booster even after he had returned to the East, the latter because as a western missionary he obviously portrayed the region in heightened terms. But the critical fact here is not the extent to which these men may have been swayed by their western experience; it is, rather, the way in which they chose to communicate that experience to eastern readers. Moved by western prospects, they virtually identified the United States with its frontier heritage. The West was their country because they were Americans.

At the same time, contemporary critics of these western images often lent them unintended force. For example, Orestes Brownson took issue with the safety-valve doctrine; but in doing so—as a radical social commentator dissenting from contemporary opinion—he only confirmed its authority.[19] Similarly, Horace Bushnell bitterly attacked westward emigration from Connecticut, but in such terms as to minimize his most trenchant criticisms. He told the Hartford County Agricultural Society in 1846:

> If you will sacrifice everything here above the range of raw physical necessity, and consent to become a barbarian as regards all the refinements of life, you will see how it is that the emigrant is able to get a start and why he is supposed to do it so much more easily at the West. . . . The first generation can hardly be said to live. They let go life, throw it away, for the benefits of the generation to come after them.[20]

Who in America was likely to see only the hardships and to ignore the promise that even Bushnell's words held out?

Finally, southern spokesmen went out of their way during the 1850's to challenge the images of homestead and democracy that spokesmen for the North had attached to the West; but (as Henry Nash Smith has suggested) their attack on these values only demonstrated the futility of their own imagination, their inability to substitute their own projection of a plantation West for the more characteristic northern image of a fee-simple empire.[21] Before the Civil War, those who challenged the frontier West as an image of American society did battle with most of their countrymen.

---

[18] J. M. Peck, "Elements of Western Character," *Christian Review*, XVI (1851), 89–90, 93–94, 95.

[19] *Boston Quarterly Review*, III (1840), 372.

[20] As quoted by Clarence H. Danhof, "Economic Validity of the Safety Valve Doctrine," *Journal of Economic History*, I, *Supplement* (December, 1941), 101, n. 17.

[21] Smith, *Virgin Land*, Chaps. 13 and 15.

Dissenters and advocates together support the proposition, therefore, that on many levels and in many ways the frontier West both dramatized and lent independent meaning to a wide range of prevalent social attitudes. Before 1860 a good many Americans, eastern as well as western, believed that the West was a unique possession of the American republic and a unique influence on its past, its present, and its future. They saw in it not simply a struggle between nature and civilization, not merely an agrarian haven, but a model and a vision of themselves.

Indeed, with someone like the Reverend J. M. Peck in mind, it is not too much to suggest that these ante-bellum commentators on the West adumbrated most of the elements of Turner's frontier hypothesis well before its author was born. For that matter, some of Turner's critics have argued that various elements of the frontier thesis were not completely novel, but they have not pursued their discovery far enough to make it fruitful. I suggest that, far from undermining Turner's place in our historiography, these elements point the way toward a fuller appreciation of his work. If Turner somehow gathered together in his writings many of the perspectives in which Americans of fifty or seventy-five years before him had seen the West, the fact may be a tribute as well as a criticism. For Turner was—as he set out to be—an American poet as well as a historian: what he wrote captured historic images that others lost sight of.

Furthermore, placing Turner's work in this broader perspective also has the effect of diminishing some of the criticisms that have been leveled against his intelligence. It is true, for instance, that Turner did not successfully distinguish between the frontier as a line, the frontier as a section, and the frontier as a process; but the confusion was part of our tradition, and he did not create it. It is also true that he was vague and hortatory, rather than precise and empirical, in his descriptions of the relationship the West bore to the rest of the United States; but again the attitude and the confusion it encouraged did not originate with him. Finally, it is true that Turner was guilty of thinking in terms of closed space and that in various ways the categories of his frontier theory have limited public debate on crucial political issues. But here, too, it is neither accurate nor relevant to charge him with the whole responsibility for the defects of American social thought. Indeed, if we acknowledge that his thinking embodied traditional valuations of the frontier, we should not find it surprising that he portrayed the crisis of the 1890's in terms of the frontier's disappearance. The frontier was what Americans imagined as well as what they experienced.

I do not mean to argue that Turner was always an adequate historian of the United States, nor to excuse his shortcomings by labeling him a poet wherever it is inconvenient to defend him as a scholar. But I do suggest that those who have criticized Turner for being derivative and confused have often missed the logical implication of their arguments: his images of the frontier West embodied a wide range of historic American attitudes. If we were to concentrate on sorting out these attitudes, to use Turner's work as a kind of retrospective guidebook to ideas as well as events, we might make great strides in understanding the way Americans thought well before his time.

XI Slavery: The Tannenbaum-Elkins Interpretation Versus More Recent Research

Introduction Frank Tannenbaum in a modestly sized but most important book, *Slave and Citizen: The Negro in the Americas* (1974), and Stanley Elkins in a somewhat larger and certainly more controversial book, *Slavery: A Problem in American Institutional and Intellectual Life*—first edition 1959, second edition 1968, though the latter is identical with the former save for an appendix—created a new canon of historical interpretation. The chief thrust of both books was a comparison of slavery as it existed in the ante-bellum United States and as it existed in Latin America. Elkins, in very large measure, took over Tannenbaum's seminal idea (i.e., that, because of institutional protections, slavery in Latin America, was much less harsh than in the ante-bellum South), but he developed the new canon of historical interpretation in stronger, more awesome tones, which have something of an absolutist quality, and which have tended to overshadow Tannenbaum's less doctrinaire book.

Elkins begins his study with a consideration of what he regards as the largely deinstitutionalized character of American life in the Age of Jackson. He asks: "Why should the American of, say, 1830 have been so insensitive to institutions and their function?" He then shows us a church that was fragmented while religion remained vital, a bar that was democratized and lacked institutional restraints, a politics of deference and tradition succeeded by a politics of diffusion and mass movement, and a Hamiltonian capitalism succeeded by a brash, speculative, and individualist Jacksonian capitalism. "Thus for the American of that day it was the very success of his society—of capitalism, of religious liberalism and political democracy—that made it unnecessary for him to be concerned with institutions." He quotes with approval Henry James' apostrophe to America, "no church."

The absence of the restraining influence of ancient and honored institutions embodying the wisdom and agony of the centuries, in Elkins' view, brought unmitigated capitalism, centering around the production of staples in the American South, into a brutal confrontation with unmitigated slavery. He studies the "four major legal categories" of American slavery: "term of servitude," "marriage and the family," "police and disciplinary powers over the slave," and "property and other civil rights." He concludes that because of the lack of interposing institutions in American life that might have mitigated and muted the master's arbitrary power over the slave, there emerged a slave system with few, if any, restraints upon the master and with fewer, if any, protections for the slave. Because of this almost unbridled and uncushioned master-slave relationship, "American slavery was unique in the sense that, for symmetry and precision of outline, nothing like it had ever previously been seen." It was a "closed" system with no effective scrutiny and inquiry from without,

362

and with the abrasive, direct confrontation of master and slave, with full and arbitrary power for the one and only abject subordination for the other, that led to the destruction of the slave personality and its infantilization.

In order to show the uniqueness of American Negro slavery, Elkins examines slavery in Latin America. Here he finds the safeguards of ancient institutions, primarily the Crown and the Church, interposing themselves between master and slave and, to a degree, humanizing that relationship. "For all the cruelty and bigotry of this quasi-medieval society (in Latin America), the balance between property rights and human rights stand in a vastly different ratio—much to the advantage of human rights—from that seen in the American South." Elkins then examines the same "four legal categories" of slavery previously studied in the American context in the Latin American context. He finds that the restraining hand of a more institutionalized form of life in Latin America made slavery a more tolerable institution, though one still cruel and degrading. Human personality might survive better in a "contract in which the master owned a man's labor but not the man."

Elsewhere in his book, Elkins confronts us with another dimension of comparative history. He adduces the concentration camp in Nazi Germany as a model for the examination of another brutal confrontation. While declaring that the American plantation "was not even in a metaphysical sense a 'concentration camp'; nor was it even 'like' a concentration camp," Elkins seeks to throw light upon the breakdown of human personality and its infantilization in the concentration camp as, in some ways, analogous to what occurred on the American plantation in the ante-bellum South. This gives us a sense of the brooding extrapolation of his study.

The Tannenbaum–Elkins thesis has been the subject of much praise and much criticism. As examples of this revisionist literature—so quickly does revisionism begin—two pieces of historical writing are presented here.

The first is an article by Arnold A. Sio,[1] who also uses the comparative dimension, though in this case it is a comparison of slavery in the United States with Roman slavery. The essayist sets himself three tasks ". . . to distinguish between the property and racial components in the status of the ante-bellum slave through a comparison with Roman slavery where the status involved a property but not a racial component. This is followed by a consideration of the evidence for a personal component in the definition of the slave status in the United States. The essay concludes with some re-examination of the status of the slave in Latin America in terms of the three components." (Sio earlier identifies the three components as the legal status of the slave, the relations of masters and slaves, and the relationship between these two facets of the institution.) The general effect of the

---

[1] "Interpretations of Slavery: The Slave Status in the Americas," *Comparative Studies in Society and History*, VII (April, 1965), 289–308.

study is to raise some very large doubts about the validity of the Tannenbaum–Elkins thesis. In his last paragraph Sio looks forward to further comparative studies of the institution of slavery in the United States and Latin America.

That need is met by a most penetrating and scholarly study by Carl N. Degler,[2] who, in order to focus the issues sharply, limits his study to the institution of slavery as it existed in Brazil only and then compares Brazilian slavery with American slavery. He states: "If the evidence and argument of this essay are sound, then the explanations of the differences [in North and South America] offered by Tannenbaum and Elkins, at least as far as Brazil is concerned, are not supported by the evidence. But if Tannenbaum's explanation has to be abandoned, his belief that there was a strikingly different attitude toward blacks in Brazil from that in the United States has not been challenged at all. Rather it has been reinforced."

---

[2] "Slavery in Brazil and the United States: An Essay in Comparative History," *American Historical Review*, LXXV (April, 1970), 1004–1028. Somewhat rewritten this article became Chapter II in *Neither Black Nor White: Slavery and Race Relations in Brazil and the United States* (1971). This book goes on past slavery to the examination of the similarities and differences in contemporary race relations in Brazil and the United States.

Interpretations of Slavery:
The Slave Status in the Americas
—*Arnold A. Sio*

Recent interpretations of slavery in the United States suggest that we may be entering a new phase of scholarship on slavery as new approaches and categories are introduced by historians, and as anthropologists and sociologists again take up the study of an institution that was of such concern to their nineteenth century predecessors.

As an assessment of these interpretations, the concern of this essay is with those aspects of the legal status of the slave which appear as problematic or neglected. The purpose is to reformulate, refocus, and clarify rather than to introduce an alternative interpretation or to present new materials.[1]

Although the scholarship on slavery has tended to shift away from the strong moral bias as well as the categories of analysis carried over for so long from the pro-slavery and anti-slavery debates, those aspects of the slavery system traditionally at issue also constitute the problematic aspects in the more recent interpretations. These are the legal status of the slave, the relations of masters and slaves, and the relationship between these two facets of the institution.[2]

I

The concept of slavery covers a considerable variety of social phenomena, but it is generally thought of as the practice of bringing strangers into a society for use in economic production and legally defining them in terms of the category of property. The complete subordination of the slave to

From Arnold A. Sio, "Interpretations of Slavery: The Slave Status in the Americas" from *Comparative Studies in Society and History*, VII (1965), 289–308.
© Copyright by the Society for Comparative Study of Society and History, by permission of Cambridge University Press.

[1] The author wishes to acknowledge his obligations to M. I. Finley, John Hope Franklin, Robert Freedman, and Richard Robbins, among others, who have read and criticized this paper, and to the Research Council of Colgate University for a generous research grant.
[2] See Stanley Elkins, *Slavery* (Chicago, 1959), Chap. I: Kenneth Stampp, "The Historian and Southern Negro Slavery," *American Historical Review*, LVII (April, 1952), pp. 613–24; Richard Hofstadter, "U. B. Phillips and the Plantation Legend," *Journal of Negro History*, XXIX (April, 1944), pp. 109–25.

the will of the master is regarded as a main defining feature of the institution.

> Subordination implies and is an aspect of authority. Authority is the socially recognized right to direct, control or manage some or all of the affairs of a person, or group, or thing. In this sense there is an overlap between property as a bundle of rights over things and the authority which is invested in some person over others as their slaves, with the result that such types of authority are treated as property at law.[3]

Slavery involves the "legal assimilation of interpersonal rights to the norm of property rights over things."[4]

This definition of the legal status of the slave has been taken in many studies as a basis for an interpretation solely in terms of the property component in the status.[5] Thus although the interpretations of slavery in the United States to be discussed in this essay involve both the historical and comparative methods and an emphasis on economic as well as ideological forces, they arrive at a similar conception of the legal status of the slave as property. This conception obscures significant differences between the property and racial components in the status, and circumvents critical evidence pertaining to the personal component in the status.[6]

In this essay an attempt is made to distinguish between the property and racial components in the status of the ante-bellum slave through a comparison with Roman slavery where the status involved a property but not a racial component. This is followed by a consideration of the evidence for a personal component in the definition of the slave status in the United States. The essay concludes with some re-examination of the status of the slave in Latin America in terms of the three components.

The interpretations of Frank Tannenbaum[7] and Stanley Elkins[8] ex-

---

[3] M. G. Smith, "Slavery and Emancipation in Two Societies," *Social and Economic Studies*, III, Nos. 3 and 4 (1954), pp. 245–46.

[4] *Ibid.*, p. 246.

[5] The classic account is H. J. Nieboer, *Slavery as an Industrial System* (Rotterdam, 1910).

[6] Wilbert Moore, "Slave Law and the Social Structure," *Journal of Negro History*, XXVI (April, 1941), pp. 171–202.

[7] *Slave and Citizen* (New York, 1947).

[8] *Slavery.* Chap. 2. This discussion is limited to his treatment of the legal status of the slave. Elkins proposes an alternative to the established approach to slavery in the United States which, taking its stance from the debates over slavery, has been concerned mainly with the rightness or wrongness of the institution considered in terms of categories pertaining to the health and welfare of the slaves. The historical study of slavery has alternated over the years between a pro-slavery and an anti-slavery position, but the purpose and the categories of analysis have remained unchanged. The result has been a continuing confusion of the historical study of slavery with moral judgments about slavery. Elkins proposes discarding this approach and adopting instead the method of comparison as followed by Tannenbaum. Slavery as an evil is taken for granted. Elkins' treatment of slavery as analogous to the concentration camp in its effects on Negro personality is discussed in Earle E. Thorpe, "Chattel Slavery and Concentration Camps," *The Negro History Bulletin*, XXV (May, 1962), pp. 171–76.

emplify the shift away from the moral approach to the institution of slavery and the introduction of new methods and categories. The treatment in both is comparative. Why did slavery in the United States differ in form and consequences from the kind of servitude developed in the Latin American colonies of Spain and Portugal? According to Tannenbaum, there were at least three traditions or historical forces in Latin America which prevented the definition of the slave there solely as property; namely, the continuance of the Roman law of slavery as it came down through the Justinian Code, the influence of the Catholic Church, and the long familiarity of the Iberians with Moors and Negroes.[9] Tannenbaum puts his emphasis on whether, "The law accepted the doctrine of the moral personality of the slave and made possible the gradual achievement of freedom implicit in such a doctrine" and on a universalistic religion, i.e. Catholicism, in preventing the definition of the slave solely as property.[10] In the United States slavery developed in a legal and moral setting in which the doctrine of the moral personality of the slave did not affect the definition of his status in the society. "Legally he was a chattel under the law, and in practice an animal to be bred for market."[11]

In comparing North American and Latin American slavery, Elkins adds to Tannenbaum's earlier treatment. The legal status of the slave in "the liberal, Protestant, secularized, capitalist culture of America" is contrasted with that of the slave in "the conservative, paternalistic, Catholic, quasi-medieval culture of Spain and Portugal and their New World colonies."[12] Elkins concludes that in the absence of such restraining institutions in the United States the search for private gain and profit was unlimited, and the law of slavery developed in such a way as to eliminate the slightest hindrance to the authority of the slaveholder over his slaves. The legal status of the slave developed exclusively in terms of property as the result of the demands of an emerging capitalism. Slavery in the United States was "a system conceived and evolved exclusively on the grounds of property."[13]

For Elkins and Tannenbaum the definitive feature of the legal status of the ante-bellum slave was the centrality of the property component. The rights of personality were suppressed by the law, and the legal subordination of the slave to the authority of the master in the areas of parentage and kinship, property and other private rights, and police and disciplinary power over the slave was developed to such an extent as to make slavery in the United States a unique system.[14] The entire institution became integrated around the definition of the slave as property.

---

[9] Tannenbaum, pp. 43–65.   [10] *Ibid.*, p. 8..   [11] *Ibid.*, p. 82.   [12] *Elkins*, p. 37.
[13] *Ibid.*, p. 55.
[14] *Ibid.*, p. 52. These categories are taken from Elkins, but they are also used by Stampp and Tannenbaum in describing the status of the slave.

368 - Arnold A. Sio

Kenneth Stampp's *The Peculiar Institution* [15] has been viewed as one of the most important and provocative contributions since Ulrich B. Phillips' *American Negro Slavery*.[16] Although it is organized essentially in terms of the categories used by Phillips and other earlier students of slavery, Stampp's study exceeds the earlier work in comprehensiveness, in presenting the response of the slave to the institution, and in its use of the available scientific evidence regarding race. In contrast to Elkins and Tannenbaum, Stampp takes up the social organization of slavery as well as its legal structure. His interpretation of the legal status of the slave is mainly in terms of economic values, and stresses the property component as do Elkins and Tannenbaum.[17] Unlike Elkins and Tannenbaum, however, he finds that the status also contained a personal element, which made for a certain degree of ambiguity in the status.[18]

In these interpretations, the initial status of the Negro is taken as having been neither that of a slave nor that of a member of a racial group against which discrimination was practiced. The status of the Negro as a slave and his status as a member of a racial minority apparently developed concurrently, since there was no tradition of slavery or of racial discrimination in the colonies to inform the initial status of the Negro. The causal connection implied between slavery and racial discrimination is a widely held conception and needs to be reconsidered in the light of recent historical investigation and comparative evidence.

Much more difficult to grasp is the effect of racial discrimination on the definition of the slave status. Elkins refers to "the most implacable race-consciousness yet observed in virtually any society" as affecting the definition of the status, but the stress on economic values in his interpretation obscures any distinction that may have been intended between the property and racial components in the status.[19] Similarly, although Stampp refers to the fact "that chattel slavery, the caste system, and color prejudice" were a part of custom and law by the eighteenth century, no clear distinction is made between those features of the status which are to be attributed to the definition of the slave as property and those which are the consequence of racial discrimination.[20]

Tannenbaum is clearly concerned with the consequences of racial discrimination for the legal status of the Negro as slave and as freedman. He stresses the fact that slavery in the United States meant Negro slavery. In contrast to Latin America, slavery in the ante-bellum South involved "caste," "by law of nature," or "innate inferiority."[21] Slavery systems can be distinguished in terms of the ease and availability of manumission and the status of the freedman, as these indicate whether

---

15 (New York, 1957.)   16 (New York, 1918.)
17 Stampp, Chap. 5.   18 *Ibid.,* pp. 192–93.   19 Elkins, p. 61.
20 Stampp, p. 23.   21 Tannenbaum, pp. 55–56.

or not the law denied the moral personality of the slave.[22] In the United States the conception of the slave as a racial inferior led to severe restrictions on manumission and to a low status for free Negroes. At the same time, however, it is readily apparent from Tannenbaum's comparison with slavery in Latin America that in his view the conception of the antebellum Negro as innately inferior affected all the legal categories defining his status: the extent of the assimilation of his rights to property in law as well as manumission and the status of the freedman.[23] Racial discrimination accentuated the legal definition of the slave as property.

The slave as property is taken as the primary or exclusive component in these interpretations of the legal status of the slave in the United States. For Elkins and Stampp this is the consequence mainly of economic forces, while for Tannenbaum ideological forces are basic. The focus on the definition of the slave as property results in a tendency to fuse the property and racial components, and in a failure to consider the evidence bearing on the personal component in the legal status.

II

While the assimilation to property in law of the rights of slaves was common to slavery in classical antiquity and the United States, slavery in ancient society "was a type unfamiliar to Europeans and Americans of the last two centuries. It had no color line. (Therefore, *pace Aristotles*, it had no single and clearly defined race or slave caste.)" [24] Moreover, the law of slavery in ancient society did not deny the moral personality of the slave as, according to Roman law, the institution of slavery was of the *Ius Gentium* but at the same time contrary to the *Ius Naturale*, for all men were equal under natural law.[25] A comparison with slavery in Rome where slaves were defined as property in law but did not constitute a separate caste in the society, and where the legal suppression of the personality of the slave, as expressed in the attitude toward manumission and the status of the freedman, did not occur, thus provides a method for distinguishing between the property and the racial components in the definition of the legal status. Since the categories of marriage and the family, property and other rights, and police and disciplinary powers over slaves are used by Elkins, Tannenbaum and Stampp in de-

---

[22] *Ibid.*, p. 69. See also William L. Westermann, *The Slave Systems of Greek and Roman Antiquity* (Philadelphia, 1955), p. 154.

[23] Tannenbaum, p. 69.

[24] William L. Westermann, "Slavery and Elements of Freedom in Ancient Greece," *Bulletin of the Polish Institute of Arts and Sciences in America*, I (Jan., 1943), p. 346. See also M. I. Finley, "Between Slavery and Freedom," *Comparative Studies in Society and History*, VI (Apr., 1964), p. 246.

[25] Westermann, *The Slave Systems*, pp. 57, 80; W. W. Buckland, *The Roman Law of Slavery* (Cambridge, 1906), p. 1. The consequent ambiguity in the status of the slave as property and as a person in ancient society is discussed at a later point.

scribing the status of the slave as property in the United States, these will guide the comparison with Rome.[26]

As to marriage and the family in the ante-bellum South, marriages between slaves had no legal standing. "The relation between slaves is essentially different from that of man and wife, joined in lawful wedlock . . . with slaves it may be dissolved at the pleasure of either party, or by the sale of one or both, depending on the caprice or necessity of the owners." [27] The denial of legal marriage meant, in conjunction with the rule that the child follow the condition of the mother, that the off-spring of slaves had no legal father, whether the father was slave or free. The duration of the union between slaves depended on the interests of the master or those of the slaves. The union was subject at any time to being dissolved by the sale of one or both of the slaves. The children of these "contubernial relationships," as they were termed, had no legal protection against separation from their parents. In the law there was no such thing as fornication or adultery among slaves. A slave could not be charged with adultery, and a male slave had no legal recourse against another slave, free Negro, or white person for intercourse with his "wife." Nor could the slave present this abuse as evidence in his defense in a criminal charge of assault and battery, or murder.

Roman slaves were also legally incapable of marriage. Any union between slaves or between slaves and free persons was differentiated as *contubernium* as opposed to *conubium*. A marriage was terminated if either party became enslaved. Infidelity between slaves could not be adultery. Although a slave could be guilty of adultery with a married free woman, it was not possible for an enslaved female to commit the offense, or for it to be committed with her. The inheritance of slavery followed the rule that the child follow the status of the mother, whatever the position of the father. A child born of a free father and a slave mother was a slave and the property of the owner, while the child of a slave father and a free mother inherited the free status of the mother. The children of slaves were the property of the owner of the mother, and, since the economic use of slaves during the Republic was at the discretion of the master, slaves were bought and sold without regard for their families. "There was nothing to prevent the legacy of a single slave away from his connexions." [28]

According to the legal codes of the ante-bellum South, a slave "was unable to acquire title to property by purchase, gift, or devise." [29] A slave

---

[26] Materials for the description of the legal status of the ante-bellum slave are standard and taken from Elkins, Chap. 2; Stampp, Chap. 5; Tannenbaum, p. 69ff; and Helen T. Catterall, *Judicial Cases Concerning Slavery and the Negro* (Washington, 1926). Those for the Roman Republic are taken from the standard work by Buckland; R. H. Barrow, *Historical Introduction to the Study of Roman Law* (Cambridge, 1932); and Rudolph Sohm, *The Institutes* (Oxford, 1907).

[27] *Howard v. Howard*, 6 Jones N.C. 235, December 1858. Catterall, II, p. 221.

[28] Buckland, p. 77.   [29] Stampp, p. 197.

might not make a will, and he could not, by will, inherit anything. Slaves were not to hire themselves out, locate their own employment, establish their own residence, or make contracts for any purpose including, of course, marriage. A slave "can do nothing, possess nothing, nor acquire anything but what must belong to his master." [30] He could engage in financial transactions, but only as his master's agent. A slave could not be a party to a suit, except indirectly, when a free person represented him in a suit for freedom. Slaves might only be witnesses in court in cases involving slaves or free Negroes. When the testimony of a slave was allowed, he was not put under oath as a responsible person. Teaching slaves to read and write was prohibited, and instruction in religion was also subject to legal restrictions.

"Of the slave's civil position," in Rome, "it may be said that he had none." [31] A slave could not make a contract, he could be neither creditor nor debtor, he could not make a will, and if he became free, a will made in slavery was void. Slaves could in no way be concerned in civil proceedings which had to be made in the name of the master. A judgment against a slave was null and void and the pact of a slave was likewise void.

As to his participation in commerce, "his capacity here is almost purely derivative, and the texts speak of him as unqualified in nearly every branch of law". [32] Although the Roman slave could acquire possessions for the master, "the will of the slave and, in fact, his mental faculties in general, operate, in principle, where they operate at all, for the benefit of the master". [33] Legally the slave did not have possessory rights in the property acquired by him or granted to him. The *peculium* assigned to him by the master, to which the slave might add by investment, earnings, gift, interest, produce, or wages existed by the authority of the master and was subject to partial or total recall at the slaveowner's wish. The *peculium* was not alienable by the slave any more than other property. The *peculium* did not change the legal position of the slave. He was still a slave. No legal process which was closed to a slave without *peculium* was available to him if he had one. The *peculium* did not go with the slave upon manumission unless expressly given by the master.

Slaves were legally incapable of prosecution as accusers either on their own behalf or on behalf of others. As a general rule the evidence of slaves was not admissible in court, and when it was taken it was taken by torture, for it could not be received in any other form from slaves. Slaves were excluded from giving testimony on behalf of their masters.

The slave codes of the South supported the "full dominion" of the

---

[30] The Civil Code of Louisiana quoted in John C. Hurd, *The Law of Freedom and Bondage in the United States* (Boston, 1858), II, p. 160.
[31] Buckland, p. 82. [32] *Ibid.*, p. 82. [33] *Ibid*, p. 82.

master in matters of policy and discipline. The slave's relationship with his master was expected to be one of complete subordination. Generally, homicide was the major crime that could be committed against an enslaved individual. The owner of a slave, however, could not be indicted for assault and battery on his own slave. "The power of the master must be absolute to render the submission of the slave perfect." [34] Furthermore, the master was not held responsible for the death of a slave as a consequence of "moderate correction," for "it cannot be presumed that prepensed malice (which alone makes murder felony) should induce any man to destroy his own estate." [35] The master was to recover damages caused by an assault or homicide against his slave.

During the Roman Republic there was no legal limitation on the power of the slaveowner: "his rights were unrestricted." [36] "Except in cases of revolt which endangered the government the Roman state left the problem of the discipline and punishment of slaves to their masters." [37] Sohm writes that as against his master, "a slave had no legal rights whatsoever." [38] In dealing with the offenses of slaves the owner's powers of punishment included corporal punishment, confinement in chains, confinement in the ergasulum, banishment from Rome and Italy, and the death penalty. Slaves, as possessions of value, were protected from mistreatment by persons other than their masters. In case of injury done to a slave "the master had cause of action for damages against the perpetrator." [39] If a slave was enticed into escaping or forcibly removed the owner might resort to both criminal and civil action.

These comparisons suggest that, on the legal evidence which defines the authority of the master in the areas of parentage and kinship, property and other rights, and police and disciplinary power over slaves, there is nothing sufficiently distinctive to distinguish the legal status of the slave as property in the United States from that in Rome.

Arnold Toynbee refers to the "Negro slave immigrant" as having been "subject to the twofold penalization of racial discrimination and legal servitude." [40] A society may extensively assimilate to property in law the rights of slaves, as indeed many have, but yet not restrict the status of slavery to members of a particular group for whom slavery is defined as natural, inevitable, and permanent as occurred in the United States. This was the introduction of caste into the status of the ante-bellum Negro, slave or free.[41] The Negro as slave occupied both a slave status and a

---

[34] State v. Mann, 2 Deveroux 263 (N.C.), December 1829, Catterall, II, p. 57.
[35] Virginia Act of 1669, Hurd, I, p. 232.   [36] Buckland, p. 36.
[37] Westermann, p. 75.   [38] Sohm, p. 166.   [39] Westermann, p. 83.
[40] Arnold J. Toynbee, A Study of History (Oxford, 1934), II, p. 218.
[41] There has been considerable disagreement as to whether the term "caste" is applicable to the American case. It has been insisted that it should be limited to India. The present writer agrees with Everett Hughes who writes: "If we grant this, we will simply have to find some other term for the kind of social category into which one is assigned at birth and from which he cannot escape by action of his own: and to distinguish such

caste status.[42] He was subject to disabilities in addition to those connected with the legal categorization of him as property, and these disabilities continued to define his status as a freedman. Caste law as well as slave law governed the status of the Negro.

The restriction of slavery to the Negro rested on the legal principle that it was a status properly belonging to the Negro as an innately (racially) inferior being. If slavery was a status attaching to a racial inferior, then it was inheritable even where one parent was white. Intermarriage between Negro slaves and whites was prohibited. Racial inferiority, legalized inheritance, and endogamy were related to another principle; namely, that slavery was the presumptive status of every Negro or person of color. The slave status was to follow naturally and inevitably from Negro ancestry.[43]

Although the slave and caste statuses were coextensive for the preponderant majority of ante-bellum Negroes, there were free Negroes in the North and South who, however, continued to be members of the lower caste. Caste was inclusive of the slave and free status. Thus the rule that the child follow the condition of the mother made slaves of the majority of Negroes and members of the lower caste of all Negroes. Negroes, slave or free, were legally prohibited from intermarrying with members of the dominant group. All members of the lower caste were presumed to be slaves unless they could establish that they should be legally free. There was a definite strain in the legal structure to establish slavery and caste as coextensive for all Negroes. The status of the free Negro is evidence of this strain. Although legally no longer an object of property rights, he was legally and socially a member of a lower caste and as such his life chances, whether he lived in the North or South, were held within narrow limits.[44]

Slavery in Republican Rome was not restricted to any particular group who ought properly to occupy the legal status of slaves. The legal restrictions on intermarriage of slave and free, on manumission, and on the

---

social categories from classes or ranked groups, from which it is possible, though sometimes difficult, to rise." Everett C. Hughes and H. MacGill Hughes, *Where Peoples Meet* (Glencoe, 1952), p. 111. Berreman has recently defined the term as to be useful cross-culturally. He defines a caste system "as a *hierarchy of endogamous divisions in which membership is hereditary and permanent.* Here hierarchy includes inequality both in status and in access to goods and services. Interdependence of the subdivisions, restricted contracts among them, occupational specialization, and/or a degree of cultural distinctiveness might be added as criteria, although they appear to be correlates rather than defining characteristics." Gerald D. Berreman, "Caste in India and the United States," *American Journal of Sociology*, LXVI (Sept., 1960), pp. 120–21, cf. Louis Dumont, "Caste, Racism, and 'Stratification,' Reflections of a Social Anthropologist," *Contributions to Indian Sociology*, V (Oct., 1961), pp. 20–43.

[42] Moore, pp. 177–79.

[43] *Ibid.*, 184–88. See also Winthrop D. Jordan, "American Chiaroscuro: The Status and Definition of Mulattoes in the British Colonies," *William and Mary Quarterly*, XIX, No. 2 (April, 1962), pp. 183–200.

[44] John Hope Franklin, *The Free Negro in North Carolina* (Chapel Hill, 1943); Leon F. Litwack, *North of Slavery* (Chicago, 1961).

status of freedmen, though at times severe, were not the consequence of a conception of the slave or former slave as innately inferior. Those who were enslaved in Rome did not constitute a caste in the society for whom the proper and permanent status was conceived to be slavery.[45]

It is not surprising that the highly perceptive Alexis de Tocqueville should have noticed this essential difference between slavery in antiquity and the United States. However, observing that discrimination against the Negro persisted in those parts of the United States where slavery had been abolished, he concluded that slavery must have given "birth" to "prejudice." [46] A causal relationship between slavery and racial discrimination is also implied in the interpretations under discussion.

Setting aside the conventional question as to "why slavery produced discrimination?" Carl Degler has separated the two elements, and, still treating the question historically, asks rather "which appeared first, slavery or discrimination?" His main argument is that from the beginning "the Negro was treated as an inferior to the white man, servant or free." [47] Caste or elements of caste antedated slavery, and as the legal status evolved "it reflected and included as a part of its essence, this same discrimination the white man had practiced against the Negro" from the outset in New England as well as the South.[48]

The colonists of the early seventeenth century not only were well aware of the distinction between indentured servitude and slavery, but they had ample opportunity to acquire the prejudicial attitudes and discriminatory practices against Negroes through the slave trade and from Providence, Bermuda, Barbados, Jamaica, and the Spanish and Portuguese colonies.[49] Moreover, there was the inferior status ascribed to the non-Caucasian Indians and even their enslavement almost from the beginning of English settlement.

The evidence summarized by Degler indicates that Negroes were being set aside as a separate group because of their race before the legal status of slavery became fully crystallized in the late seventeenth century. There was legislation (1) preventing inter-racial marriages and sexual union; (2) declaring that the status of the offspring of a white man and a Negro would follow that of the mother; and (3) establishing civil and legal disabilities applying to Negroes either free or in servitude.[50] As to the

45 Westermann, p. 15, 23.

46 Alexis de Tocqueville, Democracy in America (New York, 1948), I, pp. 358–60.

47 Carl N. Degler, "Slavery and the Genesis of American Race Prejudice," Comparative Studies in Society and History, II (Oct., 1959), p. 52. Cf. Oscar and Mary F. Handlin, "Origins of the Southern Labor System," William and Mary Quarterly, 3rd Ser., VI (April, 1950), pp. 199–222; Winthrop D. Jordan, "Modern Tensions and the Origins of American Slavery," Journal of Southern History, XXVII (Feb., 1962), pp. 18–33.

48 Degler, p. 52.

49 Ibid., pp. 53–56. See also Winthrop D. Jordan, "The Influence of the West Indies on the Origin of New England Slavery," William and Mary Quarterly, XVIII (April, 1961), pp. 243–50.

50 Ibid., pp. 56–62. See also Moore, pp. 177–86.

situation of the Negro in the North, "from the earliest years a lowly differentiated status, if not slavery itself, was reserved and recognized for the Negro—and the Indian, it might be added." [51] Degler concludes that "long before slavery or black labor became an important part of the Southern economy, a special and inferior status had been worked out for the Negro. . . . it was a demand for labor which dragged the Negro to American shores, but the status he acquired cannot be explained by reference to that economic motive." [52]

Turning now to the personal component in the status of the ante-bellum slave, it is apparent that a conception of a legal relationship between persons or groups of persons is implied in the definition of slaves as a caste in the society. As we have seen, the ante-bellum slave was not uniformly regarded in the law as a person. There were certain situations and relationships, however, in which he was not regarded solely as property.

Kingsley Davis has observed that "slavery is extremely interesting precisely because it does attempt to fit human beings into the category of objects of property rights. . . . Always the slave is given some rights, and these rights interfere with the attempt to deal with him solely as property." [53] Westermann found this to be a "constant paradox" in Greek and Roman antiquity, and "inherent in the very nature of the institution." "Theoretically," the slave was a chattel and subject only to the laws pertaining to private property, and in "actuality" he was "also a human being and subject to protective legislation affecting human individuals." [54] Isaac Mendelsohn refers to "the highly contradictory situation" in the slavery systems of the ancient Near East "in which on the one hand, the slave was considered as possessing qualities of a human being, while on the other hand, he was . . . regarded as a thing." [55] Under the law in Greek, Roman, and Near Eastern society the slave had an ambiguous status: he was both an object of property rights and a rudimentary legal person.

As to the personal component in the status of the slave in the United States, Elkins argues that as a consequence of the requirements of capitalistic agriculture "to operate efficiently and profitably," through the rational employment of slaves as economic instruments, any ambiguity in the legal status of the slave as property could not be tolerated.[56] Any rights of personality that remained to the Negro at the end of the seventeenth century had been suppressed by the middle of the eighteenth.[57] However they may differ as to causation, Elkins and Tannenbaum are in agreement that the status of the slave was determinate as property.

[51] Degler, p. 62.
[52] *Ibid.*, p. 62. Jordan, *The Influence of the West Indies*, pp. 243–44, 250.
[53] *Human Society* (New York, 1949), p. 456.   [54] Westermann, p. 1.
[55] *Slavery in the Near East* (New York, 1949), p. 64.   [56] Elkins, p. 49, 53.
[57] *Ibid.*, p. 42.

For Tannenbaum the "element of human personality" had been lost in the definition of the slave in the United States.[58] Stampp, on the other hand, found a "dual character" in the legal codes. The legal authorities "were caught in a dilemma whenever they found that the slave's status as property was incompatible with this status as a person." [59] In a much earlier and very careful treatment of the personal component, Moore found that initially the question as to whether a slave was a person or a piece of property was involved in the difficult issue as to the status of the slave after conversion and baptism. Allowing the slave the privilege of salvation implied a recognition of him as a Christian person, and, by implication, as a legal personality. The idea that conversion and baptism altered the status of the slave as property was not easily changed, and the settling of the difficulty in favor of continued enslavement does not appear to have finally disposed of the matter.[60] "The persistence of this indeterminacy arising out of religious status," concludes Moore, "must be regarded as at least one source of the continued legislative and judicial declarations of the personality of the slave, despite other definitions and implications to the contrary." [61]

There are three aspects to be considered in taking up the matter of the doubtful status of the slave before the law. The most obvious, of course, is that the dual quality is inherent in the status itself. Slaves are conscious beings defined as economic property. On the one hand, the definition of the legal status conceives of them as objects of economic value. On the other hand, the slave as an item of economic value also remains a social object. The values he possesses as a conscious being can be utilized by the master, namely, his body, his skill, and his knowledge. The definition of the slave as a physical object overlaps that of the slave as a social object, since only social objects can perform and have intentions. The value of a slave as property resides in his being a person, but his value as a person rests in his status being defined as property.[62]

The second aspect involves the recognition in the law not only of the humanity of the slave, but also that he may be the subject of rights of his own. In this connection, Stampp has noted a significant juxtaposition of two clauses in the legal code of Alabama in 1853. The first defines the status of the slave as property and establishes the owner's rights to the slave's "time, labor, and services," as well as the slave's obligation to comply with the lawful demands of the master. The second contains the personal element and states the master's obligation to be humane to his slaves and to provide them with adequate food, clothing, and with care

---

[58] Tannenbaum, p. 97.   [59] Stampp, pp. 192–93.   [60] Moore, pp. 195–96.
[61] Ibid., p. 196. See also Charles Sellers, "The Travail of Slavery," in Charles Sellers, ed., The Southerner as American (Chapel Hill, 1960), pp. 40–71.
[62] Talcott Parsons and Neil J. Smelser, Economy and Society (Glencoe, 1956), p. 12.

during illness and old age.[63] Similarly a Kentucky court ruled in one case that "a slave by our code, is not a person, but (negotium) a thing," while in another case in the same state the court considered "slaves as property, yet recognizes their personal existence, and to a qualified extent, their natural rights." [64]

Cases clearly affirming that the slave was a person were also numerous during the ante-bellum period. One judgment in Tennessee held:

A slave is not in the condition of a horse . . . he is made after the image of the Creator. He has mental capacities, and an immortal principle in his nature . . . the laws . . . cannot extenguish his high born nature, nor deprive him of many rights which are inherent in man.[65]

That the slave as an object of property rights was protected by law and by remedies the law provided whereby an owner could recover damages done to his property has already been discussed. A slave was also entitled in his own right to protection from malicious injury to his life and limb. The courts ruled that manslaughter against a slave "exists by common law: because it is the unlawful killing of a human being"; [66] that a slave is "a reasonable creature in being, in whose homicide either a white person or a slave may commit the crime of murder or manslaughter"; [67] and that "Negroes are under the protection of the laws, and have personal rights, and cannot be considered on a footing only with domestic animals." [68] The justification of the legal principle that a crime could be committed against an enslaved individual tended to shift, and in many cases revealed the ambivalence between the conception of the slave as property, and as a person. In a judgment acknowledging that an indictment for an assault upon a slave could be made, a Louisiana court ruled that "Slaves are treated in our law as property, and, also, as persons. . . ." [69] As stated earlier, however, generally homicide was the major crime that could be committed against a slave, and the owner of a slave could not be indicted for assault and battery on his slaves.

Many of the laws also implied that a slave was a legal person in that he was capable of committing crimes and could be held to trial. Cases involving slave crimes were very numerous and frequently they turned on the conception of the slave as a person. In the judgment of a Georgia court in 1854:

[63] Stampp, pp. 192–93. The following discussion is not intended to be comprehensive. For a detailed treatment of the definition of the slave as a person see Moore, pp. 191–202.
[64] *Jarman v. Patterson*, 7 T.B. Mon. 644, December 1828 (Ky.), Catterall, I, p. 311. See also *Catherine Bodine's Will*, 4 Dana 476, Oct. 1836 (Ky.), *Ibid.*, I, pp. 334–35.
[65] *Kennedy v. Williams*, 7 Humphreys, Sept., 1846 (Tenn.), *Ibid.*, II, p. 530.
[66] *Fields v. State*, I Yerger 156, Jan., 1829 (Tenn.), *Ibid.*, II, p. 494.
[67] *Hudson v. State*, 34 Ala. 253, June 1859, *Ibid.*, III, p. 233.
[68] *State v. Cynthia Simmons and Laurence Kitchen*, I Brevard 6, Fall 1794 (So. Car.), *Ibid.*, II, p. 277.
[69] *State v. Davis*, 14 La. An. 678, July 1859, *Ibid.*, III, p. 674.

> . . . it is not true that slaves are only chattels, . . . and therefore, it is not true that it is not possible for them to be prisoners . . . the Penal Code . . . has them in contemplation . . . in the first division . . . as persons capable of committing crimes; and as a . . . consequence . . . as capable of becoming prisoners.[70]

Another court held that a white man could be indicted and convicted as an accessory to a murder committed by a slave. The judgment stated that "Negroes are under the protection of the laws, and have personal rights. . . . They have wills of their own—capacities to commit crimes; and are responsible for offences against society." [71]

Again, however, there were limits on the extent to which the personality of the slave was recognized, and in defining these limits the courts frequently expressed the indeterminate character of the status:

> Because they are rational *human beings,* they are capable of committing crimes; and, in reference to acts which are crimes, are regarded as *persons.* Because they are *slaves,* they are . . . incapable of performing civil acts; and in reference to all such, they are *things;* not persons.[72]

That slaves were held to some of the responsibilities usually expected of persons in society and few of the privileges is further illustrated by the fact that slaves were persons who could abscond and commit capital crimes, but if killed or maimed in capture or put to death by law, the slaveowner was reimbursed for the loss of his property.

The third aspect pertains to the cases of manumission by will, deed, and legislative action; the instances of successful suits for freedom; and the cases of self-purchase—all of which implied evaluation of the slave as a person with some legal capacity:

> They may be emancipated by their owners; and must, of course, have a right to seek and enjoy the protection of the law in the establishment of all deeds, or wills, or other legal documents of emancipation; and so far, they must be considered as natural persons, entitled to some legal rights, whenever their owners shall have declared . . . they . . . be free; and to this extent the general reason of policy which disables slaves as persons, and subjects them to the general reason of mere brute property, does not apply.[73]

Moreover, the presence of free Negroes in the population from the beginning; manumission; suits for freedom; and self-purchase indicated that

---

[70] *Baker v. State,* 15 Ga. 498, July 1854, *Ibid.,* III, p. 35.
[71] *State v. Cynthia Simmons and Laurence Kitchen,* I Brevard 6, fall 1794 (So. Car.), *Ibid.,* II, p. 277.
[72] *Creswell's Executor v. Walker,* 37 Ala. 229, January 1861, *Ibid.,* III, p. 247.
[73] *Catherine Bodine's Will,* 4 Dana 476, October 1836 (Ken.), *Ibid.,* I, pp. 334–35.

slavery did not follow naturally and inevitably from Negro ancestry. The intrusion of the values of liberty and individual achievement into the legal structure meant that race and slavery were not coextensive for all Negroes. The law sanctioned the possibility of slaves legitimately aspiring to and attaining in attenuated form the culture goals of the enslaving group having to do with freedom and individual achievement. The status of the free Negro was real and symbolic evidence of the indeterminacy resulting from the attainment of goals that were presumably denied to Negroes and applicable only to whites.[74]

III

In the interpretations of Elkins, Tannenbaum, and Stampp much has been made of the legal status of the slave as property and the extent to which the rights of slaves were assimilated to property in law. As the preceding discussion has indicated, in the United States where slaves were conceived of as innately inferior they constituted a caste in the society and their rights were extensively assimilated to property in law. In Republican Rome where slaves were not conceived of as innately inferior to the enslaving group and did not form a separate caste an equally extensive assimilation of their rights to property occurred. In contrast to the United States, manumission was easily available to the Roman slave, and the freedman could look forward to assimilation into Roman society.

Although the slave status in Rome was not justified in terms of the innate inferiority of the slave, the assimilation of ownership in slaves to property was comparable to that in the United States. Roman law respected the moral personality of the slave, as reflected in the rules governing manumission and the status of the freed slave, but this did not prevent the assimilation of his rights to property in law.

In so far as the legal categorization of the slave as property is concerned we are dealing with a common social form in Rome and the United States. Caste produced the contrast between the legal structures of the two systems of slavery. The consequence of racial discrimination for the legal structure of ante-bellum slavery was the creation of a hereditary, endogamous and permanent group of individuals in the status of slaves who, moreover, continued as members of a lower caste in the society after freedom. Although the conception of the slave as innately (racially) inferior to the enslaving group had important consequences for manumission and for the status of freedmen, as Tannenbaum has indicated, the comparison with Rome suggests that it did not accentuate the assimilation

---

[74] Wilbert Moore and Robin Williams, "Stratification in the Ante-bellum South," *American Sociological Review*, VII (June, 1942), pp. 343–51. Cf. Douglas Hall, "Slaves and Slavery in the British West Indies," *Social and Economic Studies*, II, No. 4 (December, 1962), pp. 305–18.

of ownership in slaves to property. Racial discrimination does not appear to have affected the legal status of the slave as property.

Now slavery in Rome was not a single social phenomenon historically. Not until the first two centuries of the Empire did significant changes occur in the authority of the master over the rights of slaves. "In their ultimate legal formulation the changes found expression in the Codes of Theodosius and Justinian." [75] Up to that time, although Roman law respected the moral integrity of the slave, the subordination of the slave to the authority of the master was comparable to that in the United States. The slave law that came down through the Justinian Code to influence the Iberian law of slavery, later to be transferred to Latin America, contained not only the doctrine of the moral personality of the slave, but also embodied those changes in later Roman law which had "loosened the strict controls by which the slave element had formerly been bound to the will of the master group." [76]

According to the interpretations of slavery in Latin America by Tannenbaum and Elkins, it was this body of law in conjunction with certain traditions and institutional arrangements that functioned to protect the slaves both from an extensive assimilation to property in law and from a caste status. Some reference will be made in the concluding portion of this essay to the need for a revision of this interpretation on the basis of more recent research.

Considerable variation occurs among slavery systems in the extent to which the slave is assimilated to property in law. Variations in this component are generally taken to be related to "the level of technical development and the accompanying institutional apparatus, including the economic system." [77] Where slavery was a domestic system, as in China and the Near East, the assimilation of the slave to property in law was less extensive than in Rome and the United States where slavery was an industrial system.[78]

The property component in the status of the ante-bellum slave was undoubtedly related to economic values and the labor needs of an emerging capitalism, as Elkins and Stampp have emphasized, but the entire status cannot be derived from the operation of economic values. On the one hand, the extensive assimilation to property in law of the Roman slave did not generate a conception of him as innately inferior and create a caste of slaves and freedmen. On the other hand, the absence of certain institutions and traditions embodying values respecting the moral personality of the slave does not account for the conception of the Negro as inherently inferior and for caste. If these were absent, then the as-

[75] Westermann, p. 140. [76] Ibid., p. 140.

[77] Sidney W. Mintz, Review of Slavery by Stanley Elkins, American Anthropologist, 63 (June, 1961), p. 580.

[78] G. Martin Wilbur, Slavery in China During the Former Han Dynasty (Chicago, 1943), p. 243; Mendelsohn, pp. 121–22.

similation of ownership in slaves to property in law must have caused
racial discrimination and caste. The historical evidence indicates rather
that discrimination against the Negro occurred before the slave status
was fully defined and before Negro labor became pivotal to the economic
system.[79]

In the conception of the legal status of the slave as determinate in
terms of property the slave has neither a juridical nor a moral personality.
The values of the dominant group in the United States that had a bearing
on the law of slavery were, on the one hand, those which legitimatized
slavery and the rigid system of stratification, and on the other hand, those
values pertaining to freedom and individual dignity and worth. Although
there was no complex of laws, traditions, and institutions pertaining to
the institution of slavery as such that embodied these latter values, a
significant element in the general value system of the South was an
ethical valuation of the individual. The legal evidence indicates that
these extra-legal values of the society were expressed in the legal definition
and conception of slavery. The law of slavery shows the existence of an
ethical norm, however vague and rudimentary, attaching value to the
individual.[80]

The interpretation of the legal status of the slave primarily or wholly in
terms of property has implications as well for the conception of the pattern of relations between masters and slaves. In discussing the connection
between the legal structure and the master-slave relationship, David
Potter has observed that "the human relationship within this legal context was complex and multiple." The relation between masters and slaves
had "two faces—a paternalistic manorial one and an exploitative commercial one." [81]

---

[79] That the essential features of a caste status for the Negro may have preceded the
full development of the slave status does not alter the widely accepted proposition that
the initial status of the Negro was not that of a slave but rather that of an indentured
servant or free man. Some aspects of caste appear to have developed later than others,
but the main defining features were fixed early and before the complete development of
the status of slavery. Racial segregation, although obviously foreshadowed in the status of
the free Negro, did not appear as a part of the caste system until the late nineteenth and
early twentieth centuries. The system of restricted contacts between Negroes and whites,
clearly based on the long-standing assumption of the innate inferiority of the Negro, was
simply the latest feature of caste to develop. See C. Vann Woodward, *The Strange Career
of Jim Crow* (New York, 1957).

[80] Moore, pp. 201–02. For another discussion of the alternative value systems and the
resulting conflicts within Southern society and within individuals see Sellers, pp. 51–67.
A similar ambiguity existed in connection with slavery in ancient society. In Roman law
"slavery is the only case in which, in the extant sources . . ., a conflict is declared to
exist between the *Ius Gentium* and the *Ius Naturale*." Buckland, p. 1. "No society," writes
Finley, "can carry such a conflict within, around so important a set of beliefs and
institutions, without the stresses erupting in some fashion, no matter how remote and
extended the lines and connections may be from the original stimulus." M. I. Finley, "Was
Greek Civilization Based on Slave Labour?" in M. I. Finley, ed. *Slavery in Classical Antiquity*
(Cambridge, 1960), p. 162.

[81] David M. Potter, Review of *The Peculiar Institution* by Kenneth Stampp, *Yale Review*,
46 (Winter, 1957), pp. 260–61.

In the interpretations of Tannenbaum, Elkins, and Stampp there is a close correspondence between the legal structure and the pattern of the master-slave relationship. Since, according to these writers, the slave status was governed by instrumental and economic values and not affected by the religious and ethical convictions of the dominant group attaching value to the individual, there was nothing to impede the rational use of slaves as economic instruments. The exploitative commercial pattern was expected to be followed in organizing the relations of masters and slaves. It was normatively and numerically the predominant pattern in the South.

Given this conception of the connection between the legal structure and the relations of masters and slaves, the paternalistic manorial pattern can only be interpreted as a deviation from the expected and approved pattern of the master-slave relationship. It is not interpreted as an equally recognized and approved mode of organizing and managing the relations of masters and slaves, but rather as the result of fortuitous circumstances. It is attributed to the smallness of the plantation or to the "personal factor." [82] According to this interpretation there was nothing in the law to sanction the paternalistic manorial pattern, while the commercial exploitative pattern was clearly compatible with the instrumental use of slaves as sanctioned in the definition of the slave as an object of property rights. Yet, the paternalistic manorial pattern was widespread in the South as an accepted and approved mode of organizing the master-slave relationship and represented, as did the personal component in the legal status, the intrusion of the valuation of the individual into a categorized relationship. [83]

IV

Since the contrast with slavery in Latin America is central to the interpretations of slavery in the United States by Tannenbaum and Elkins,

---

[82] Elkins, pp. 137–38.

[83] The pattern of the master-slave relationships continues to be one of the most problematic and debated aspects of ante-bellum slavery. The exploitative commercial pattern tends to be taken as the predominant pattern and in accordance with the normative prescriptions of ante-bellum society, while the paternalistic manorial pattern is generally treated as the result of the intrusion of non-normative factors, and usually attributed to smallness of size. However, Franklin has pointed out that the bulk of the slaves were on small plantations. If so, then the paternalistic manorial pattern must have been exceedingly widespread. On the other hand, it has also been suggested that this pattern was to be found on the larger holdings. Phillips had this conception of the master-slave relationship on large plantations. It seems likely that both patterns were normative; that is, accepted and approved ways of organizing the master-slave relationship. If this was the case, then further investigation must be directed at ascertaining the determinants of these patterns on the concrete level. Size would be one among several determinants. See John Hope Franklin, *From Slavery to Freedom* (New York, 1952), pp. 185–86. Needless to say, the pattern of the master-slave relationship is significant for the impact of slavery upon the personality of the Negro. If the paternalistic manorial pattern was widely institutionalized in the ante-bellum South, then a very significant number of Negro slaves were able to escape the tendency for the system to absorb the personality. Cf. Elkins, pp. 137–138.

some reference may be made to the more recent studies of slavery and race relations in Latin America and the implications for a comparison with North America. The results of these studies appear to be consistent with those of this essay.

In connection with the interpretations of slavery in Latin America by Elkins and Tannenbaum, Mintz questions whether slavery in Latin America can be treated as a single phenomenon historically.[83a] He points out that once slavery became a part of the industrial plantation system in Cuba and Puerto Rico, for example, an extensive assimilation to property in law of the rights of slaves occurred in spite of an institutional framework protecting the moral personality of the slave. Slavery in Cuba "dehumanized the slave as viciously as had Jamaican or North America slavery." [84] Much the same thing happened in Puerto Rico. Between 1803 and 1873 repressive laws were passed "more and more limiting the slaves' legal, social, economic status." [85] In connection with slavery on the sugar plantations and in the mines of Portuguese Brazil, E. R. Boxer writes that the widely accepted "belief that the Brazilian was an exceptionally kind master is applicable only to nineteenth-century slavery under the Empire" and not to the colonial period.[86] At the same time, however, "one of the few redeeming features in the life of slaves . . . was the possibility of their buying or being given their freedom at some time, a contingency which was much rarer in the French and English American colonies." [87]

As to the racial component in the slave status, investigations of race relations in Brazil, where most of the work has been done, indicate that during the colonial period slavery also involved a caste system between whites and Negro slaves, "based on white supremacy and the institutionalized inferiority of colored slaves." [88] Concubinage was widely practiced, but inter-marriage was rare, "as the system demanded the separation of the two castes and the clearcut distinction of superiors and inferiors." [89] Colonial legislation discriminated against the free Negroes who "were often coupled with enslaved Negroes in the laws." [90] They were prevented from acquiring possessions or participating in activities in

---

[83a] Useful summaries are to be found in Juan Comas, "Recent Research on Race Relations —Latin America," *International Social Science Journal*, XIII, No. 2 (1961), pp. 271–99; Oracy Nogueira, "Skin Color and Social Class," *Plantation Systems of the New World* (Washington, 1959), pp. 164–83; Roger Bastide, "Race Relations in Brazil," *International Social Science Bulletin*, IX, No. 4 (1957), pp. 495–512.

[84] Mintz, p. 581.

[85] *Ibid.*, p. 583. See also O. A. Sherrard, *Freedom from Fear* (London, 1959), p. 75.

[86] *The Golden Age of Brazil* (Berkeley, 1961), p. 173. Gilberto Freyre's *The Masters and the Slaves* (New York, 1946), on which much of the existing conception of slavery in Brazil is based, wrote mainly about domestic slaves.

[87] Boxer, p. 177.

[88] Harley Ross Hammond, "Race, Social Mobility and Politics in Brazil," *Race*, IV, No. 2 (1962), p. 477. See Charles Wagley, "From Caste to Class in North Brazil," in Charles Wagley (ed.), *Race and Class in Rural Brazil* (New York, 1963), pp. 142–156.

[89] *Ibid.*, p. 4.

[90] Boxer, p. 17.

the society "which might tend to place them on a level with whites." [91]
Mulattoes who attained positions of importance in Brazil "did so in spite
of the official and social prejudices which existed against them throughout
the whole of the colonial period." [92]

It is readily apparent from these studies that a much greater similarity
existed between slavery in the United States and Latin America than here-
to-fore suspected. The status of slaves in Latin America, as well as in
Rome and the United States, indicates that whether or not the law
respected the moral personality of the slave, an extensive assimilation
of his rights to property in law occurred under slavery as an industrial
system. Moreover, contrary to the widely held conception, racial discrimination was present in Latin America and had the consequence of
creating a duality in the status of the slave as property and as a member
of a racial caste.[93] These elements were apparently combined to some
extent with a respect for the moral personality of the slave in the law.

Further comparative study of slavery in the United States and Latin
America will enable us to delineate more precisely the differences and
similarities in the property, racial, and personal components of the slave
status in these societies. We may also expect such study to reveal, as this
essay has attempted to do, that economic and ideological forces were
not mutually exclusive in their consequences for the legal structure of
slavery.

---

[91] *Ibid.*, p. 17.   [92] *Ibid.*, p. 17.
[93] Nogueira, pp. 167–176, has attempted to distinguish race prejudice in Brazil from
that in the United States. With reference to the origin of race prejudice in Brazil, James
G. Leyburn, in his discussion of Nogueira's paper, questions whether it was slavery which
produced prejudice. *Ibid.*, p. 181.

Slavery in Brazil and the United States: An Essay in Comparative History
—*Carl N. Degler*

Over twenty years ago Frank Tannenbaum made a comparison of slavery
in the societies of the New World in which he argued that the differences

---

From Carl N. Degler, "Slavery in Brazil and the United States: An Essay in Comparative
History" from *American Historical Review*, LXXV (1970), 1004–1028. Reprinted by permission
of the author.

in contemporary race relations between the United States and Latin America are to be traced to differences in the character of slavery in the two places. A decade later Stanley Elkins built a provocative book upon Tannenbaum's conclusions. More recently, Arnold Sio and David Brion Davis entered strong demurrers to the Tannenbaum–Elkins conclusions by arguing that slavery as an institution was more similar than different throughout the societies of the New World.[1]

These and a number of other writings on the comparative history of slavery in the Western Hemisphere attest to a burgeoning scholarly interest. But throughout the debate one of the prominent difficulties has been the great breadth and diversity of the areas being compared. To make convincing comparisons among some two dozen societies presents obvious problems and is open to the dangers of superficiality. It is the intention here, therefore, to draw a much more restricted comparison, not because the large problem that Tannenbaum raised will finally be resolved by such a limited approach, but simply because two countries are more manageable as variables than two continents. It is also worth noting that Brazil and the United States have the advantage of being the two most important slave societies in the New World. Both had a long history of slavery—only Cuba and Brazil retained slavery longer than the United States—and in both societies slavery occupied an important, if not actually a central, place in the economy.[2]

Mr. Degler, professor of history at Stanford University and a specialist in the social history of the United States, received his Ph.D. in 1952 from Columbia University, where he worked under John A. Krout and Richard B. Morris. He is the author of *Out of our Past: The Forces that Shaped Modern America,* published first in 1959 and in a revised edition in 1970. The present article is part of a larger study of race relations and slavery in the United States and Brazil. In somewhat different form it was presented as a paper at the meeting of the Organization of American Historians in Philadelphia in April, 1969. Mr. Degler wishes to thank Eugene D. Genovese, Richard M. Morse, and Herbert S. Klein, who were commentators on that occasion, for their criticisms.

[1] The books and articles referred to are: Frank Tannenbaum, *Slave and Citizen: The Negro in the Americas* (New York, 1947); Stanley Elkins, *Slavery: A Problem in American Institutional and Intellectual Life* (2d ed., Chicago, 1969), the text of which is identical with the first edition of 1959 except for an added appendix; Arnold Sio, "Interpretations of Slavery: The Slave States in the Americas," *Comparative Studies in Society and History,* VII (Apr. 1965), 289–308; and David Brion Davis, *The Problem of Slavery in Western Culture* (Ithaca, N.Y., 1966).

[2] It has sometimes been said that the diversity of the crops and topography of Brazil resulted in a diversity of slavery that makes it difficult if not impossible to generalize about the institution in that country. It is true that slavery in the northeastern sugar regions was different in style from that practiced in Maranhão on the cotton and rice plantations. Writers on Brazilian history have noted, furthermore, that slavery was much harsher in a newly opened province like Maranhão than in the old and declining sugar areas in the northeast. (See Gilberto Freyre, *Nordeste* [Rio de Janeiro, 1937], 219; and Henry Koster, *Travels in Brazil* [2 vols., 2d ed., London, 1817], II, 292.) But the diversity of crops and terrain and the differences in "styles" of slavery that resulted are well recognized in the United States; the slavery on tobacco farms in Virginia, for example, is often contrasted with the kind of slavery on sugar or cotton plantations in Louisiana. In the United States, moreover, the threat to sell a slave "down the river" reflected a recognition that planters in the newer areas of the Deep South tended to work slaves harder than in the older regions where slavery was more firmly established. Despite their recognitions of regional diversity, however, historians of slavery in the United States have not been

Essentially this essay seeks to answer two quite limited questions: First, in what respects were the systems of slavery in Brazil and the United State alike during their mature years—that is, during the nineteenth century—and in what ways did they differ? Second, to what extent are these differences related to the laws and practices of the state and the Church in Brazil, as both Tannenbaum and Elkins have contended? Even if these questions can be answered with some degree of certainty, it should be said that the large question that Tannenbaum raised and sought to answer in his book will not be settled. But I hope that the ground will be cleared for a new attack upon the problem.

How were the two systems of slavery alike? Tannenbaum and Elkins stress the different legal conceptions of the slave in the United States and in Latin America. Tannenbaum, for example, contrasts the definition of a slave as a chattel in the United States with the more ambiguous definition in Latin America.

> In fact, *the element of human personality was not lost in the transition to slavery from Africa to the Spanish or Portuguese dominions.* He [the Negro] remained a person even while he was a slave. . . . He was never considered a mere chattel, never defined as unanimated property, and never under the law treated as such. His master never enjoyed the powers of life and death over his body, even though abuses existed and cruelties were performed.[3]

Yet an examination of Brazilian and United States law reveals striking similarities in the definition of a slave.

The law in both the United States and Brazil, for example, recognized that a slave was both a human being and a piece of property. As a Tennessee court in 1846 put it,

> A slave is not in the condition of a horse, he is made after the image of the creator. He has mental capacities and an immortal principle in

---

prevented from generalizing about the institution; hence, it would seem to be equally legitimate to ignore the regional differences in Brazilian slavery so long as an effort is made to draw evidence from most of the principal slave areas of the country. The regional differences are certainly there in both societies, but they are refinements rather than essentials. One further statement on the problems of comparison: although the literature on slavery in the United States is voluminous, there being a monograph for virtually every southern slave state, the literature on Brazilian slavery is uneven. For some important slave regions like Maranhão and Minas Gerais, for example, there are no monographic studies on slavery at all; scattered references in travel accounts and general histories must be relied upon. On the other hand, for other areas, like the coffee country to the south, two excellent, recently written monographs are available: Stanley Stein, *Vassouras: A Brazilian Coffee County, 1850–1900* (Cambridge, Mass., 1957); and Emília Viotti da Costa, *Da Senzala à Colônia* (São Paulo, 1966). Of immense importance for its historiographical impact, if nothing else, is the impressionistic, virtuoso performance of Gilberto Freyre, *The Masters and the Slaves* (New York, 1946), which deals primarily with domestic slavery in northeastern Brazil though it purports to speak of slavery in general.

3 Tannenbaum, *Slave and Citizen*, 97–98, 103.

his nature, that constitute him equal to his owner but for the accidental position in which fortune has placed him . . . the laws . . . cannot extinguish his high born nature, nor deprive him of many rights which are inherent in man. . . .[4]

In 1818 a Mississippi court went so far as to observe that "Slavery is condemned by reason and the laws of nature. It exists and can only exist through municipal regulations, and in matters of doubt" the courts must lean in favor of freedom.[5] As late as 1861 an Alabama court concluded that because slaves "are rational beings, they are capable of committing crimes; and in reference to acts which are crimes, are regarded as persons. Because they are slaves, they are . . . incapable of performing civil acts, and, in reference to all such, they are things, not persons."[6]

That last statement is close, in phraseology as well as meaning, to that set forth in Brazilian slave law by its principal authority, Agostino Marques Perdigão Malheiro. "In regard to the penal code," he wrote, "the slave, as subject of the offense or agent of it, is not a *thing*, he is a *person* . . . he is a human entity." Hence he is held personally responsible for crimes. But when he is an "Object or sufferer of a crime" the matter is different. The slave is not indemnified for such injuries, though the master may be. "In the latter case the question is one of *property*, but in the other it is one of *personality*." Perdigão Malheiro makes clear, moreover, that the position of the slave in court was not much different from that of the slave in the United States. No slave in Brazil could enter a complaint himself; it had to be done by his master or by the public authority. Nor could a slave make an accusation against his master. In fact, a slave could not give sworn testimony, only information. Perdigão Malheiro writes that in only three circumstances did a slave have standing in court: in regard to spiritual matters, such as marriage; in regard to his liberty; and in matters of obvious public concern. Only in regard to the first did the legal position of the slave in the United States differ; slave marriages had no legal basis in the United States.[7]

If there was little difference in the conception of the slave in Brazilian and United States law, there was also little difference in the law's supposed protection of the slave's humanity. Despite the general statements of some scholars,[8] both societies had laws protecting the slave against murder, mistreatment, or overwork by his master.[9] The operative question

[4] *Judicial Cases concerning Slavery and the Negro*, ed. Helen T. Catterall (5 vols., Washington, D.C., 1926), II, 530.
[5] Charles Sackett Sydnor, *Slavery in Mississippi* (New York, 1933), 239.
[6] *Judicial Cases concerning Slavery and the Negro*, ed. Catterall, III, 247.
[7] Agostino Marques Perdigão Malheiro, *A Escravidão no Brasil: Ensaio Historico-Juridico-Social* (reprint of 1867 ed., 2 vols., São Paulo, 1944), I, 39–40, 34–45, 67.
[8] See, e.g., Tannenbaum, *Slave and Citizen*, 93.
[9] Kenneth M. Stampp, *The Peculiar Institution: Slavery in the Ante-bellum South* (New York, 1956), 192, summarizes the situation in the United States as follows: "The law

is whether the law or the church in fact interceded between the master and the slave in behalf of the latter. Certainly for the United States the evidence is not convincing. And in Brazil, too, the power of the state or the church to affect the life of the slave seems to have been limited. As Henry Koster, an English planter in Brazil, pointed out early in the nineteenth century, the Brazilian government was a weak reed on which to lean for anything, much less for control over members of the ruling slaveholding class. He tells, for example, of an instance in which one of his own slaves injured the slave of another man, but says that nothing was done about the matter. The owner of the injured slave might have pressed charges, if he so chose, "but the law of itself seldom does anything. Even in the cases of murder the prosecutor . . . has it at his option to bring the trial forward or not; if he can be bribed or otherwise persuaded to give up the accusation, the matter drops to the ground." It is not likely that the state, which was run by slaveholders, would be more energetic in protecting the slave's humanity. Koster writes that occasionally a cruel master was fined for maltreating his slaves, "but," he adds, "I never heard of punishment having been carried farther than this trifling manner of correction." [10] Later in the century another traveler, the German painter John Rugendas, put the matter even more directly. Although there were laws in Brazil limiting the use of the whip and fixing the number of lashes at one time, he wrote in 1835:

these laws have no force and probably may be unknown to the majority of the slaves and masters; on the other hand, the authorities are so removed that in actuality the punishment of the slave for a true or imaginary infraction or the bad treatment resulting from the caprice and the cruelty of the master, only encounters limits in the fear of losing the slave by death, by flight, or as a consequence of public opinion. But these considerations are never sufficient to impede the evil and it is inescapable that examples of cruelty are not lacking, which result in the mutilation and death of slaves.[11]

It is only toward the end of the era of slavery, when the abolitionists

required that masters be humane to their slaves, furnish them adequate food and clothing, and provide care for them during sickness and old age. In short, the state endowed masters with obligations as well as rights and assumed some responsibility for the welfare of the bondsmen." For elaboration of the obligations laid down by law, see *ibid.*, 218–24.

[10] Koster, *Travels in Brazil,* I, 375–76; II, 237; Da Costa, *Da Senzala,* 295–96. Charles Expilly, a French traveler in Brazil in the 1860's, conceded that in the big cities like Rio a slave might occasionally be able to get to the police to complain of bad treatment, but, away from the cities, it was quite different. There, Expilly wrote, the power of the master was like that of "a feudal baron, who exercises in his dominion the highest and the lowest justice." There were no appeals from his sentences. "No guarantee is conceded to the slave." (Charles Expilly, *Mulheres e costumes do Brasil,* tr. Gastão Penalva [São Paulo, 1935], 361.)

[11] João Mauricio Rugendas, *Viagem pitoresca através do Brasil,* tr. Sergio Milliet (3d ed., São Paulo, 1941), 185.

brought cases of mistreatment to court, that Brazilian laws in behalf of the slaves actually protected them.

Both Elkins and Tannenbaum emphasize the role of the Roman Catholic Church in giving the Negro slave in Latin America a higher "moral" position than in the United States.[12] If that means that the Church accepted Negro slaves as members, the churches of the United States did, too. If it means that the Church actively intervened between master and slave in behalf of the latter, then it must be said that in Brazil the interest of the Church in and its power to protect the slave's humanity were as limited as those of the state. For one thing, few plantations had resident priests; most plantations saw a priest only once a year when he came to legalize unions and to baptize. There were not, in fact, enough priests in the country to affect the daily life of the slave, even if they had the interest to do so. As Emilia Viotti da Costa points out, not until 1885 did the archbishop of Bahia rule that no master could prevent a slave from marrying or sell him away from his spouse. Yet even at that late date, a slave could marry against his master's will only if the slave could demonstrate that he knew Christian doctrine—the Lord's Prayer, the Ave Maria, the Creed, and the commandments—understood the obligations of holy matrimony, and was clear in his intention to remain married for life. Furthermore, as in the United States, religion in Brazil was used by churchmen to buttress slavery. One priest told a group of planters: "Confession is the antidote to insurrections, because the confessor makes the slave see that his master is in the place of his father to whom he owes love, respect, and obedience. . . ."[13]

In 1887, on the eve of abolition in Brazil, the abolitionist Anselmo Fonseca wrote a long book castigating the Brazilian Catholic clergy for its lack of interest in the then highly active abolitionist movement in his country. Caustically he observed that in 1871 when Rio Branco fought for the Law of the Free Womb of slave mothers, the Church was silent, for slavery "still had much vitality. . . . It was dangerous to take it on frontally. Why did not the Bishops then show the solidarity and courage and the energy with which in 1873–74 they combated Masonry and the government?" Fonseca draws the interesting contrast between the massive indifference to the plight of the slave on the part of the Brazilian Catholic Church throughout the history of slavery and the activities of Protestant clergymen like William Ellery Channing in behalf of the slave in the United States.[14]

Slave marriages were valid in the eyes of the Brazilian Church; marriages of slaves in Protestant churches in the United States also qualified

---

[12] Tannenbaum, *Slave and Citizen*, 62–64, 98; Elkins, *Slavery*, 73, 76–77.

[13] Da Costa, *Da Senzala*, 250, 271, 249.

[14] Luis Anselmo Fonseca, *A Escravidão, O clero e O abolicionismo* (Bahia, 1887), 440–41, 1–27. The references to Channing are on pages 12–15.

as sacramental acts, though masters, it was understood, were not bound to honor such unions. Given the weakness of the Church's control over slave masters, it is not likely that marriages of slaves in Brazil were any more enduring or protected from disruption through sale than in the United States. In any event, in Brazil only a small proportion of slaves were married by the Church. Early in the nineteenth century the reformer José Bonifacio asked for laws to compel masters to permit slaves to marry freely and to require that at least two-thirds of a master's slaves be married. Yet, forty years later, travelers still reported that few Negroes were married and that "rarely were [marriages] confirmed by a religious act." A traveler in 1841 found only 10 slaves married out of 2,500 on the Isle of Santa Catherina in southern Brazil. In northeastern Brazil, in Rio Grande do Norte, a local document listed only about 5 per cent of the 13,000 slaves in the province in 1874 as married or widowed, though 30 per cent of free persons were married. Of the 660,000 slaves in all of Brazil in 1875, who were 14 years or older, only about 1 out of 6 was recorded as married or widowed.[15]

In the United States the lack of protection for the informal slave family is acknowledged as a fact of slave life. Tannenbaum has summarized it well: "Under the law of most of the Southern states there was no regard for the Negro family, no question of the right of the owner to sell his slaves separately, and no limitation upon separating husband and wife, or child from its mother." [16]

Yet, for most of the nineteenth century, the same generalization is quite accurate for Brazil. Prior to 1869 there was no legal protection for the slave family, though, as was the case in the United States, a vigorous internal slave trade was a powerful cause for the breaking up of many families, whether their ties had been solemnized by the Church or not. The internal slave trade in Brazil was especially active in the middle years of the nineteenth century when the coffee areas in the South were expanding and thousands of slaves were brought down from the economically declining Northeast. One estimate in 1862 put at five thousand per year the number arriving from the North at Rio de Janeiro by coastal shipping alone. A modern authority has cited thirty thousand a year as the number that went from the North to the state of São Paulo between 1850 and 1870.[17]

---

15 *Ibid.*, 268; Fernando Henrique Cardoso and Octávio Ianni, *Côr e mobilidade social em Florianapolis* (São Paulo, 1960), 128–29; Robert Edgar Conrad, "The Struggle for the Abolition of the Brazilian Slave Trade, 1808–1853," doctoral dissertation, Columbia University, 1967, 55–56.
16 Tannenbaum, *Slave and Citizen*, 77.
17 W. D. Christie, *Notes on Brazilian Questions* (London, 1865), 93; Pedro Calmon, *História social do Brasil* (São Paulo, 1937), 151. Roberto Simonsen, "As Consequências economica da abolição," *Revista do Arquivo Municipal de São Paulo*, XLVII (May, 1938), 261, says that in 1888 over two-thirds of the slaves in the Empire were in the provinces

There is little doubt that the disruption of the slave family was common in Brazil at least prior to 1869. Indeed, to take an extreme example, one of the great Brazilian abolitionists, Luis Gama, was sold into slavery by his own white father. Stanley Stein reports that in the 1870's it was not unknown in Vassouras for a planter to sell his mulatto offspring to a passing slave trader.[18] A law passed in 1875, prohibiting the sale of one's own children, suggests that such a practice was known even at that late date.[19] Another sign that the slave family was disintegrating throughout the nineteenth century, at least, is that antislavery reformers like Bonifacio in the early nineteenth century and others as late as 1862 were demanding that ways be found to protect the slave family.[20] In 1854 Baron Cotegipe, who was later to oppose abolition, argued for limitations on the internal slave trade because it disrupted families. "It is a horror, gentlemen," he told the Senate, "to see children ripped from their mothers, husbands separated from wives, parents from children! Go to Law Street . . . and be outraged and touched by the spectacle of such sufferings. . . ." In 1866 Perdigão Malheiro was still asking that the law prevent the separation of married slave couples and children of less than seven years of age. Without such legal protection, he contended, there was little reason to expect the slave family to exist at all.[21]

The fact is that in Brazil prior to 1869 there was no law preventing the disruption of slave families. And even the law passed in 1869 required some nine years of agitation before it was enacted.[22] Most slave states in the U.S., as Tannenbaum has pointed out, never enacted such laws, but a few did. A law of 1829 in Louisiana prohibited the sale of children under ten; apparently it was adhered to by slave traders. Laws in Alabama and Georgia forbade the dissolution of inherited slave families, but not others. In practice, probably most planters in the United States tried to avoid breaking up slave families, though undoubtedly many were disrupted.[23]

Perhaps the most frequently stressed difference between slavery in Latin America and the United States concerns manumission. Yet, even

---

of Rio, Minas Gerais, São Paulo, and those to the south. I am indebted to Professor Richard Graham of the University of Utah for this reference.

[18] Stein, *Vassouras,* 159.

[19] Richard M. Morse, *From Community to Metropolis: A Biography of São Paulo, Brazil* (Gainesville, Fla., 1958), 146; Magnus Mörner, *Race Mixture in the History of Latin America* (Boston, 1967), 117.

[20] Arthur Ramos, *The Negro in Brazil,* tr. Richard Pattee (Washington, D.C., 1939), 58–59.

[21] Maurilio de Gouveia, *História da escravidão* (Rio de Janeiro, 1955), 134; Perdigão Malheiro, *A Escravidão no Brasil,* II, 223.

[22] Da Costa, *Da Senzala,* 271, 385. The law prohibited selling children under fifteen away from their parents. The so-called Law of the Free Womb of 1871, however, lowered the age to twelve.

[23] Joe Gray Taylor, *Negro Slavery in Louisiana* (Baton Rouge, La., 1963), 40–41; Stampp, *Peculiar Institution,* 252, 239–41; Edward W. Phifer, "Slavery in Microcosm: Burke County, North Carolina," *Journal of Southern History,* XXVIII (May 1962), 48.

here, as Davis has pointed out, manumission in Brazil was not unlimited, and in the U.S. it was not absolutely denied.[24] The purchase of freedom by the slave himself, so much emphasized in discussion on Brazilian slavery, was, moreover, far from rare in the United States. Sumner Matison, for example, found several hundred examples of self-purchase. Luther Jackson, studying self-purchase in three cities of Virginia, found twenty examples even at the height of the sectional conflict of the 1850's and despite a law requiring removal of manumitted slaves out of the state.[25]

On the Brazilian side of the comparison it must be said that prior to 1871, despite tradition and the assertions of Tannenbaum and Elkins,[26] there was no law requiring a master to permit a slave to buy his freedom. One American historian of Brazil made a search for such a law, but found none before 1871, when emancipationists insisted upon it; this suggests that the practice of self-purchase was not as firmly protected as has been alleged.[27] It is true that in Brazilian law there were none of the limitations that became increasingly common in the southern United States after 1830. Under Brazilian law emancipation was legal in almost any form: by letter, by will, or by explicit statement at baptism.[28] In Brazil, moreover, there were no statutes requiring the removal of emancipated slaves to other states, though such laws were characteristic of the southern United States. But Brazilian law contained a curious qualification to its otherwise liberal policy on emancipation: freedom might be revoked by the master for ingratitude on the part of the freedman, even if that ingratitude was expressed only orally and outside of the presence of the former master. Perdigão Malheiro, who reports this provision of the law, doubted that it was still valid in 1866. In 1871 the power to revoke freedom was explicitly withdrawn in an anti-slavery law, suggesting that the old provision was not such a dead letter that opponents of slavery were willing to let it remain on the statute books.[29] The provision also raises a question as to whether the law in Brazil was in fact helping to preserve the Negro's moral personality as some modern historians have

[24] Davis, *Problem of Slavery*, 262–64.

[25] Sumner E. Matison, "Manumission by Purchase," *Journal of Negro History*, XXXIII (Apr. 1948), 165; Luther P. Jackson, "Manumission in Certain Virginia Cities," *ibid.*, XV (July 1930), 306.

[26] Tannenbaum, *Slave and Citizen*, 54; Elkins, *Slavery*, 75.

[27] Mary Wilhelmine Williams, "The Treatment of Negro Slaves in the Brazilian Empire: A Comparison with the United States of America," *Journal of Negro History*, XV (July 1930), 331.

[28] Perdigão Malheiro, *A Escravidão no Brasil*, I, 95.

[29] *Ibid.*, 167–68; Gouveia, *História da escravidão*, 396. The Code Noir of Louisiana, which also had liberal provisions for manumission, contained the following restrictions: "We command all manumitted slaves to show the profoundest respect to their former masters, to their widows and children, and any injury or insult offered by said manumitted slaves to their former master, their widows or children, shall be punished with more severity than if it had been offered by any other person." (Quoted in Taylor, *Negro Slavery in Louisiana*, 16.)

argued. At the very least it encouraged masters to think of their Negroes as minors or wards rather than as persons on an equal footing. At worst, it perpetuated in the Negro that sense of subordination and inferiority derived from the degraded status of slavery, thereby counteracting whatever elevating effects might flow from the relative ease of manumission.

Some modern historians, like Tannenbaum and Elkins,[30] have emphasized the slave's right to hold property in Latin America and therefore to be in a position to buy his freedom, as contrasted with the lack of that right in the U.S. In Brazil, however, the law did not permit slaves to possess property, or a peculium, until near the end of the era of slavery. Perdigão Malheiro writes in his treatise on slave law that, as late as 1866, "Among us, no law guarantees to the slave his peculium; nor the disposition overall by the last will, nor the succession. . . ." However, he goes on, most masters tolerated the slave's holding property, generally permitting the slave to use it as he saw fit.[31] The same situation prevailed, by and large, in the United States, where slave property was neither recognized nor protected by law, but in practice was generally recognized by the master. Occasionally the courts would throw a protective arm around the peculium, as in a South Carolina case in 1792, when a slave was held capable of holding property separate from that of his master. On the basis of that case, a half century later, Judge J. B. O'Neall of South Carolina concluded that "by the law of this state a slave might acquire personal property." [32]

Yet, after all these qualifications have been made in the usually optimistic picture of manumission under Brazilian slavery, Brazil still appears to have been more liberal on manumission than was the U.S. And the principal reason for this conclusion is the higher proportion of free Negroes in Brazil than in the United States. Because of the paucity of adequate figures for both countries, a quantitative comparison can be made only for the nineteenth century. In 1817–1818 the number of slaves in Brazil was about three times that of free Negroes and mulattoes.[33] This ratio may be compared with that in the United States in 1860, when the number of free Negroes reached its maximum under slavery. At that date there were eight times as many slaves as free Negroes in the whole of the United States and sixteen times as many slaves if the comparison is made in the slave states only. As slavery came to an end in Brazil the number of free Negroes grew enormously, so that in 1872 the number of free Negroes and colored was more than double that of the slaves.[34]

[30] Tannenbaum, *Slave and Citizen*, 54; Elkins, *Slavery*, 246.
[31] Perdigão Malheiro, *A Escravidão no Brasil*, I, 60.
[32] *Judicial Cases concerning Slavery and the Negro*, ed. Catterall, II, 267, 275, n.
[33] Agostinho Marques Perdigão Malheiro, *A Escravidão no Brasil: ensaio historico-juridico-social* (Rio de Janeiro, 1866), Pt. 3, 13–14.
[34] Raymond Sayers, *Negro in Brazilian Literature* (New York, 1956), 7.

Although it is not the intention of this essay to explain this difference in attitude toward manumission, if only because of the complexity of the issue, at least two suggestions are worth brief examination. One of these is that Brazilian masters were freeing the sick and the old in order to relieve themselves of responsibility and cost. Denunciations in newspapers and laws prohibiting such practices indicate that masters were indeed freeing their infirm, aged, and incurable slaves.[35] Yet it is difficult to believe that such practices, however widespread they appear to be, could have been the principal source of the relatively large free colored population. Infirm, aged, or sick slaves simply would not have been numerous enough or have been able to produce offspring in sufficient numbers to account for the great number of free colored.

Marvin Harris has advanced a more reasonable explanation, in which he emphasizes the differences in the processes of settlement and economic development in Brazil and the United States.[36] In Brazil a freed Negro or mulatto had a place in a society that was only sparsely populated and in a slave economy that was focused upon staple production. Free blacks and mulattoes were needed in the economy to produce food, to serve as slave catchers, militiamen, shopkeepers, craftsmen, artisans, and so forth. They filled the many petty jobs and performed the "interstitial" work of the economy that slave labor could not easily perform and that white labor was insufficient to man. Octavio Ianni, writing about slavery in southern Brazil, and Nelson de Senna, describing conditions in Minas Gerais, emphasize the great variety of occupations filled by free Negroes and mulattoes.[37]

In the southern United States many plantations also allocated their labor in this fashion, that is, by importing food rather than growing it. But the food was produced by a large number of nonslaveholding whites in the South and the Northwest. Virtually from the beginning of settlement in the South there had been more than enough whites to perform all the tasks of the society except that of compulsory labor. In fact, throughout the ante bellum years, as later, the South exported whites to the rest of the nation. Hence, in the U.S. there was no compelling economic reason for emancipation; nor, more importantly, was there any economic place for those who were manumitted. But this demographic

---

35 Da Costa, Da Senzala, 262–63; Stein, Vassouras, 79, n; see also the report of the British minister, August 1852, quoting the effort by the president of the province of Bahia to have the practice stopped by law. The report is given in Christie, Notes on Brazilian Questions, 218–19.

36 Marvin Harris, Patterns of Race in the Americas (New York, 1964), 84–89.

37 Octávio Ianni, As Metamorfoses do escravo (São Paulo, 1962), 175; Nelson de Senna, Africanos no Brasil (Bello Horizonte, Brazil, 1938), 62. Caio Prado Junior, História economica do Brasil (10th ed., n.p., n.d.), 45, asserts that cattle raising in the sertão of the northeast required free men rather than slaves.

or materialist interpretation is not the complete explanation, suggestive as it is. As we shall see later, the relative ease of manumission in Brazil was part of a larger and deeper difference in attitudes between the two societies.

Comparisons between slavery in Brazil and the United States traditionally emphasize the greater rebelliousness of slaves in Brazil. But here, too, the distinction, when examined closely, is not as sharp as has frequently been alleged. The most often mentioned measure of the greater rebelliousness of Brazilian slaves is the large slave hideaway or *quilombo* of Palmares in northeastern Brazil, which, during the seventeenth century, resisted the attacks of government and other troops for more than fifty years. Examples of other *quilombos*, less spectacular or famous than Palmares, are also well documented.[38] It is questionable, however, whether such groups of runaways, no matter how long lived or large scale, ought to be classed as slave rebellions. Generally the *quilombos* neither attempted to overthrow the slave system nor made war on it, except when whites sought to destroy them. Even Palmares would have been content to remain as an African state separate from white society if the government and the *paulistas* had left it alone.[39] Thus, if one is counting armed uprisings against slaveholders, such as took place under Nat Turner in Virginia in 1831, then the total number in Brazil is considerably smaller if one excludes the *quilombos*. For in Brazil, as in the United States, the most common expression of slave unrest was the runaway, not the insurrectionist.

Rumors of revolts were common in both countries, but, except during the last years of slavery and with the exception of a series of revolts in Bahia in the early nineteenth century, slave revolts in Brazil were scattered, and in some areas almost nonexistent. Koster, the English planter, wrote in the early nineteenth century that "Pernambuco has never experienced any serious revolt among the slaves." Modern historians of the coffee region point out that neither slave revolts nor *quilombos* were on anything but a small scale. Da Costa speaks of revolts as "rare in the coffee regions." F. H. Cardoso also found little opportunity for, or evidence of, slave revolts in Rio Grande do Sul. Girão writes that in Ceará Province in the early nineteenth century "fugitives were not common and rebellions very rare." Octavio Eduardo reports that "no series of revolts

---

[38] The fullest and most recent account of Palmares in English is R. K. Kent, "Palmares: An African State in Brazil," *Journal of African History*, VI (No. 2, 1965), 161–75. As his title suggests, Kent argues (pp. 163–64) against depicting Palmares as merely a *quilombo*, but that issue is not important in this discussion. Clovis Moura, *Rebeliões da senzala* (São Paulo, 1959), contains a number of accounts of *quilombos* aside from Palmares.

[39] See Edison Carneiro, *Ladinos e Crioulos (Estudos sôbre o negro no Brasil)* (Rio de Janeiro, 1964), 30–32, for a statement on this point by an authority on Palmares and *quilombos* in general.

occurred in Maranhão as they did in Bahia, although the revolt of the Balaios from 1838 to 1841" attracted runaway slaves to the cause.[40]

On the other hand, general works on slave rebellions in Brazil as a whole emphasize their importance, and a recent study of the sugar areas in São Paulo Province refers to the large number of slave rebellions there.[41] In short, much work remains to be done on the extent and character of slave unrest in Brazil, and it seems safe to say that most of the writing on slave rebellions has not been careful to distinguish between military outbreaks and runaways or between those uprisings striking at the slave system directly and those simply fleeing from it, as, for example, has been done for American slave revolts by Marion Kilson.[42]

In the broadest sense, of course, both slave rebellions and runaways threatened the slave system, for they constituted avenues by which some slaves could escape from the system and raised the expectations of those who remained behind. In this regard, Brazilian slaves had somewhat greater opportunities for escape than had slaves in the United States. Actual revolts may not have been much more numerous in Brazil, but the numbers of slaves involved in those that did take place were greater, just as the size of the *quilombos* were larger than those in the United States. Stein described a revolt in Vassouras, for example, that mobilized three hundred slaves and required federal troops to suppress it. At least two revolts involving several hundred slaves were reported in 1820 in Minas Gerais. In the first half of the nineteenth century in the province of Espírito Santo, uprisings of two hundred and four hundred slaves occurred, though it is not clear whether these were revolts or collective runaways.[43]

The really striking examples of undoubted slave insurrections are the half dozen that erupted in and around the city of Bahia between 1807 and 1835, several of which involved pitched battles between armed slaves and government troops. It is significant that these rebellions occurred in the city, not in the plantation region. They are, moreover, among the few that can be confidently classified as violent attacks upon whites and the

---

[40] Koster, *Travels in Brazil,* II, 258; *Relações raciais entre negros e brancos em São Paulo,* ed. Roger Bastide (São Paulo, 1955), 199; Da Costa, *Da Senzala,* 300–301, 315; Fernando Henrique Cardoso, *Capitalismo e escravidão no Brasil meridional* (São Paulo, 1962), 159–60; Raimundo Girão, *A Abolição no Ceará* (Fortaleza, Brazil, 1956), 42; Aderbal Jurema, *Insurreições negras no Brasil* (Recife, Brazil, 1935), 53–55; Maura, *Rebelioes da senzala,* 65–66; Octavio da Costa Eduardo, *The Negro in Northern Brazil* (New York, 1948), 18.

[41] See, e.g., Jurema, *Insurreições negras no Brasil;* Maura, *Rebeliões da senzala;* and Maria Thereza Schorer Petrone, *A Lavoura canavieira em* (São Paulo, 1968), 121–25. Professor Graham brought the last reference to my attention.

[42] Marion D. de B. Kilson, "Towards Freedom: An Analysis of Slave Revolts in the United States," *Phylon,* XXV (2d Quar., 1964), 175–87.

[43] Da Costa, *Da Senzala,* 304; Maria Stella de Novaes, *A Escravidão e abolição no Espírito Santo* (Vitória, Brazil, 1963), 77.

slave system rather than as flights to a *quilombo*.[44] But, in the history of Brazilian slavery, the Bahian revolts were unusual and, as we shall see, the consequence of special circumstances.

There were true slave revolts in the U.S., too, though they were fewer and generally much smaller in number of participants than in Brazil. Of the three biggest and best-known uprisings, those at Stono, South Carolina, in 1739, New Orleans in 1811, and Southampton, Virginia, in 1831, only the second involved more than one hundred slaves. The *quilombos* in the United States were considerably fewer and smaller in size than those in Brazil.[45] The climate in the U.S. was largely responsible for the smaller number of maroons, or *quilombos*. In most of the United States the winter is simply too harsh for a *quilombo* to survive for very long, whereas the greater part of Brazil lies in the tropics. The frontier area in the United States was, moreover, too well settled and, accordingly, too well policed, especially after the seventeenth century, to provide many opportunities for colonies of runaways. The only example of a *quilombo* approaching the size and endurance of Palmares was the Second Seminole War, during which Indians and runaway blacks held out against the U.S. Army for seven years.[46] It is significant that the struggle took place in the warmest part of the United States and in an area unsettled by whites.

Another difference between the two slave societies was the dependence of the Brazilians upon the African slave trade. Although the foreign slave trade in Brazil was supposedly ended in 1831 by treaty with Great Britain, all authorities agree that importations of slaves continued at high annual rates for another twenty years. Over 300,000 slaves entered Brazil between 1842 and 1851 alone, bringing the total number of slaves in the country to 2,500,000 in 1850, probably the highest figure ever reached.[47] There is also general agreement that the importation of large numbers of slaves into the United States ceased in 1807, with the federal prohibition of the foreign trade. Actually, every one of the slave states themselves had prohibited importation prior to 1800. Only South Carolina reopened the

---

[44] Ramos, *Negro in Brazil*, 34–37. The basic source for the revolts in Bahia is Raymundo Nina Rodrigues, *Os Africanos no Brasil* (2d ed., São Paulo, 1935), Chap. II, but Raymond Kent will soon publish a thorough examination of the revolt of 1835, a copy of which he has kindly permitted me to read in typescript.

[45] Herbert Aptheker, *American Negro Slave Revolts* (New York, 1943), *passim*, and Herbert Aptheker, "Maroons Within the Present Limits of the United States," *Journal of Negro History*, XXIV (April, 1939), 167–84.

[46] See Kenneth W. Porter, "Negroes and the Seminole War, 1835–1842," *Journal of Southern History*, XXX (Nov., 1964), 427–40.

[47] Mauricio Goulart, *Escravidão africana no Brasil* (2d ed., São Paulo, 1950), 249–63; the total figure for slaves is given in Stein, *Vassouras*, 294. Christie (*Notes on Brazilian Questions*, 69–70) insist that when he was writing, in 1865, slaves numbered three million. The lack of a census makes it impossible to arrive at anything more accurate than estimates.

trade before the federal government finally closed it. Thus even before 1807 the influx of native Africans had decreased considerably.

The larger number of recently imported Africans in Brazil all through the history of slavery probably accounts for the greater number of revolts there.[48] Revolts were hard enough to organize and carry out under any circumstances, but they were especially difficult under a slave system like that in the United States where the slaves were principally native and almost entirely shorn of their African culture or identity. In Brazil the presence of thousands of newly arrived Africans, alienated from their new masters and society while often united by their common African tribal culture, was undoubtedly a source of slave rebellion. Stein calls attention to a rash of attempted uprisings in Vassouras in the 1840's just as the number of imported Africans reached its peak. Particularly in the cities were the slaves able to retain their African languages, dances, religious rites, and other customs, even though the authorities, aware of the nucleus such African traits provided for discontent and revolt, attempted to suppress them.[49] It is certainly not accidental that the greatest revolts in Brazil were in the city of Bahia and that they were generally led by Hausa and Yoruba Negroes, who were Muslims. A common African tribal culture, language, and religion provided the necessary cement of organization and the incentives to resistance, which were almost wholly lacking among the slaves in the United States. It is significant that the documents captured from the Bahian rebels in 1835 were written in Arabic script, and, though there is some doubt as to the extent of the religious basis for the revolt, a number of the leaders were clearly Muslims.[50] In the nineteenth century, coffee planters in the southern part of Brazil were so conscious of the dangers of newly arrived slaves from the same African tribal background that they limited their purchases of such slaves to small numbers in order to minimize revolts. C. R. Boxer writes that the diversity of African nations among the slaves in eighteenth-century Minas Gerais was the chief safeguard against the outbreak of revolts.[51]

The connections between Brazil and Africa were so close in the nineteenth century that some slaves, after they earned their freedom or

---

48 Mörner (Race Mixture in the History of Latin America, 76) suggests that most slave revolts were led by African-born slaves.

49 Stein, Vassouras, 145; Da Costa, Da Senzala, 232; Cardoso and Ianni, Côr e mobilidade, 126–27.

50 Ramos, Negro in Brazil, 30–31, 36–37; Donald Pierson, Negroes in Brazil (Chicago, 1942), 39–40; E. Franklin Frazier, "Some Aspects of Race Relations in Brazil," Phylon, III (Third Quarter, 1942), 290. Kent, in the unpublished article referred to in note 44, above, strongly questions the religious basis for the 1835 revolt in Bahia, which heretofore has been the standard interpretation. (See, e.g., Roger Bastide, Les religions africaines au Brésil [Paris, 1960], 146.)

51 Da Costa, Da Senzala, 235, 252; Charles Ralph Boxer, The Golden Age of Brazil, 1695–1750 (Berkeley, Calif., 1962), 176–77.

otherwise gained manumission, elected to return to Africa. One historian, for example, has reported on a number of leaders of nineteenth-century Nigerian society who had been slaves in Brazil, but who after manumission returned to Africa to make a living in the slave trade. So intimate was the connection between Brazil and Africa that until 1905 at least—almost twenty years after abolition—ships plied between Bahia and Lagos, "repatriating nostalgic, emancipated Negroes and returning with West Coast products much prized by Africans and their descendants in Brazil." [52] In striking contrast is the well-known reluctance of Negroes in the United States during the ante bellum years to have anything to do with removal to Africa. That contrast emphasizes once again the overwhelmingly native character of slavery in the U.S. and the dearth of African survivals.

The persistence, and even expansion, of the slave system of the United States without any substantial additions from importations is unique in history. Neither in antiquity nor in Latin America was a slave system sustained principally by reproduction. Even if one accepts the highest figure for smuggling into the United States—270,000 in the fifty years prior to 1860, or about 5,000 a year—the figure can hardly account for the steady and large increase in the slave population recorded by the decennial censuses. For example, in the 1790's, prior to the federal closing of the slave trade, the increase was 30 per cent; in the 1840's the increase was still 28 per cent, while the absolute average annual figures were 20,000 and 70,000, respectively. In short, it seems clear that reproduction was the principal source of slaves for the United States, at least since the first census.[53] One consequence was that the ratio between the sexes was virtually equal, a fact that was conducive to holding slaves in so-called family units as well as to breeding. (It was also conducive to greater control over the slaves.) Thus the ratio between the sexes in Mississippi counties according to the census of 1860 was about the same as among the whites. In 1860 in all of the southern slave states the numerical difference between the sexes was 3 per cent or less of the total, except in Louisiana where the surplus of males was 3.6 per cent. This ratio among the slaves was closer to an absolute balance between the sexes than obtained among the whites themselves in five southern states, where the surplus of males ran between 4 and 8 per cent of the white population.

---

[52] David A. Ross, "The Career of Domingo Martinez in the Bight of Benin," *Journal of African History*, VI (No. 1, 1965), 83. Freyre (*Nordeste*, 130–31) and Da Costa (*Da Senzala*, 56–57, n.) also report blacks returning to Africa and acting as slave traders. See also Donald Pierson, "The Educational Process and the Brazilian Negro," *American Journal of Sociology*, XLVIII (May 1943), 695, n.; and Gilberto Freyre, *Ordem e Progresso* (2d ed., Rio de Janeiro, 1962), 572, n. 33. The close connection between Africa and Brazil is forcefully demonstrated in José Honório Rodrigues, *Brazil and Africa* (Berkeley, Calif., 1965).
[53] The above was written before the publication of Philip D. Curtin, *The Atlantic Slave Trade. A Census* (Madison, Wis., 1969). Curtin, p. 234, estimates that after 1808 the total number of slaves entering the United States directly from Africa was fewer than 55,000.

Thus in both the so-called breeding and consuming regions of the South the sexes were remarkably well balanced.

Although Gilberto Freyre writes of the Brazilian master's interest in the "generative belly" of the female slave, other writers make clear that slave breeding was not important to Brazilian slaveholders. Stein, for example, found a genuine reluctance among slaveholders to breed and rear slaves; the very hours during which male and female slaves could be together were deliberately limited. Lynn Smith cites a number of sources to show that masters consciously restricted slave reproduction by locking up the sexes separately at night.[54]

Undoubtedly the availability of slaves from Africa accounts for some of the lack of interest in slave breeding in Brazil prior to 1851. For within five years after the closing of the slave trade, books began to appear in Brazil advising planters to follow the example of Virginians, who were alleged to be such efficient breeders of slaves that the infants were bought while still in the mother's womb.[55] These exhortations do not seem to have had much effect, however, for twenty years after the end of the African slave trade the slaveholder's customary rationale for not raising slaves was still being advanced:

"One buys a Negro for 300 milreis, who harvests in the course of the year 100 arrobas of coffee, which produces a net profit at least equal to the cost of the slave; thereafter everything is profit. It is not worth the trouble to raise children, who, only after sixteen years, will give equal service. Furthermore, the pregnant Negroes and those nursing are not available to use the hoe; heavy fatigue prevents the regular development of the fetus in some; in others the diminution of the flow of milk, and in almost all, sloppiness in the treatment of the children occurs, from which sickness and death of the children result. So why raise them?" [56]

And apparently infant mortality among slaves was amazingly high, even after the foreign slave trade had ended. One authority on the coffee region has placed it as high as 88 per cent. The census of 1870 revealed that in the city of Rio de Janeiro the mortality of slave children exceeded births by 1.8 per cent; even this shocking figure must have been a minimum since most slaves in Rio were domestic and presumably better cared for than agricultural slaves. Rio Branco, the Brazilian statesman who gave his name to an important emanicipationist law, calculated that on the basis of the excess of slave deaths over births alone slavery would die out

---

[54] Stein, *Vassouras*, 155; T. Lynn Smith, *Brazil, People and Institutions* (Baton Rouge, La., 1963), 130.

[55] Da Costa, *Da Senzala*, 130.

[56] Quoted in Joaquim Nabuco, *O Abolicionismo*, in *Obras completas* (14 vols., São Paulo, 1944–49), VII, 89–90. The book from which Nabuco quoted was published in 1872.

within seventy-five years. And although the British minister at Rio, W. D. Christie, was highly incensed at Brazilian complacency over the persistence of slavery, he had to admit in 1863 in a report to his home government that

> the slave population is decreasing, though not considerably. . . . The mortality among the children of slaves is very great; and Brazilian proprietors do not appear to have given nearly so much attention as might have been expected, from obvious motives of self-interest, to marriages among slaves, or the care of mothers or children.[57]

One undoubted consequence of the continuance of the foreign slave trade was that Brazilian planters made no effort to balance the sexes among the slaves. Since male slaves were stronger and more serviceable, they apparently constituted the overwhelming majority of the importations throughout the history of Brazilian slavery. According to one authority, on some plantations there were no female slaves. For Brazil as a whole he estimates that one Negro woman was imported for each three or four males. The statistics compiled by Stein for Vassouras support that estimate, for he found that between 1820 and 1880, 70 per cent or more of the African-born slaves were males. Robert Conrad, quoting from the records of captured slave ships in the 1830's and 1840's, found ratios of one to four and one to five in favor of males.[58] The heavy imbalance between the sexes meant that once the slave trade was stopped, Brazilian slavery began to decline, for the paucity of women, not to mention the masters' lack of interest in breeding, ensured that the reduction in the foreign supply of slaves would not be easily or quickly made up.

The imbalance between the sexes in Brazil may help also to explain the somewhat greater number of rebellions and runaways in that country as compared with the United States. In the U.S., with slaves more or less divided into family units, for a male slave to rebel or to run away meant serious personal loss, since he probably would have to leave women and children behind. Such a consequence was much less likely in Brazil. One indication that the pairing of the sexes in the United States reduced rebelliousness is provided by a report from São Paulo toward the last years of slavery when masters were quoted as saying about a restless or rebellious slave: "It is necessary to give that Negro in marriage and give him a piece of land in order to calm him down and cultivate responsibility in him." [59]

---

[57] Da Costa, *Da Senzala*, 256; Gouveia, *História da escravidão*, 208; Christie, *Notes on Brazilian Questions*, 102, n.
[58] Rodrigues, *Brazil and Africa*, 159; Stein, *Vassouras*, 155; Conrad, "Struggle for Abolition of the Brazilian Slave Trade," 55.
[59] *Relações raciais entre negros e brancos em São Paulo*, ed. Bastide, 81.

Although it is often said or implied that slavery in Latin America in general was milder than in the United States,[60] there are several reasons for believing that in a comparison between Brazil and the U.S. the relationship is just the reverse. Admittedly such comparisons are difficult to make since the evidence that might be mustered on either side is open to serious doubts as to its representativeness. But this problem can be circumvented in part, at least, if general classes of evidence are used. There are at least three general reasons, aside from any discrete examples of treatment of slaves, suggesting that slavery was harsher in Brazil than in the United States. First, the very fact that slavery in the U.S. was able to endure and expand on the basis of reproduction alone is itself strong testimony to a better standard of physical care. It is true that the imbalance of the sexes in Brazil played a part in keeping down reproduction, but the high mortality of slave children and the care and expense involved probably account for the reluctance to rear slaves in the first place. Moreover, as we have seen, even after the slave trade was closed, the rearing of slave children was still resisted in Brazil. Masters said that it was easier to raise three or four white children than one black child, the difference being attributed to the "greater fragility of the black race." In 1862 a French visitor reported that "the most simple hygienic measures are almost always neglected by the owners of slaves, and the mortality of 'negrillons' is very considerable, especially on the plantations of the interior." [61] Brazilians, in short, simply did not take sufficient care of their slaves for them to reproduce.

Second, there are kinds of severe and cruel treatment of slaves in Brazil that rarely occurred in the United States. A number of Brazilian sources, both during the colonial period and under the Empire in the nineteenth century, speak of the use of female slaves as prostitutes.[62] So far as I know, this source of income from slaves was unknown or very rare in the United States. Brazilian sources also contain numerous references to the use of iron or tin masks on slaves, usually to prevent them from eating dirt or drinking liquor. Indeed, the practice of using masks was sufficiently common that pictures of slaves wearing them appear in books on slavery. I have yet to see such a picture in the literature of slavery in the U.S., and references to the use of the mask are rare, though not unknown.[63] As already noted, Brazilian sources call attention to

---

60 See, e.g., Elkins, *Slavery*, 77–78.

61 Da Costa, *Da Senzala*, 257–58; Élisée Reclus, "Le Brésil et la Colonisation. II," *Revue des deux mondes*, XL (July–Aug. 1862), 391.

62 Boxer, *Golden Age of Brazil*, 138, 165; Gilberto Freyre, *Masters and the Slaves*, 455.

63 See the picture, e.g., in Da Costa, *Da Senzala*, facing p. 240; Gilberto Freyre, *O Escravo nos anúncios de journais brasilieros do seculo xix* (Recife, Brazil, 1963), 100, discusses the use of the mask; Thomas Ewbank, *Life in Brazil* (New York, 1856), 437–38, describes the masks he saw worn on the street. Stampp (*Peculiar Institutions*, 304) notes that masks were sometimes used in the United States to prevent eating clay. There is at least one reference to masks in that compendium of horrors by Theodore Weld, *American Slavery as It Is* (New York, 1839), 76.

another practice that also suggests severe treatment: the freeing of ill, old, or crippled slaves in order to escape the obligation of caring for them. The several efforts to legislate against this practice, much less to put a stop to it, were fruitless until just before the abolition of slavery.[64] Finally, because of the imbalance of the sexes, most slaves in Brazil had no sexual outlets at all.

Though making comparisons of physical treatment may have pitfalls, the effort has value because such comparisons give some insight into the nature of the slave systems in the two countries. Some authorities, like Elkins, for example,[65] argue that a comparative analysis of treatment is not germane to a comparison of the impact of slavery on the Negro, for "in one case [Latin America] we would be dealing with cruelty of man to men, and in the other [the United States], with the care, maintenance, and indulgence of men toward creatures who were legally and morally *not* men. . . ." But this argument collapses, as Davis has pointed out,[66] when it can be shown that the law in Brazil and the United States defined the slave as both a man and a thing. Under such circumstances, treatment can no longer be confidently separated from attitudes. Instead, the way a master treats a slave, particularly *when the slave is a member of a physically identifiable class,* becomes a part of the historian's evidence for ascertaining the attitude of white men toward black men who are slaves, and of the way in which blacks are conditioned to think of themselves. When a master muzzles a slave, for example, he is literally treating him like a dog. The master's behavior, at the very least, is evidence for concluding that he considered his slave on the level with a dog; at the most, his behavior suggests that its source was the belief that the slave was from the beginning no better than a dog. In either case, the master's treatment of the slave is part of the evidence to be evaluated in ascertaining white men's attitudes toward black slaves. Perhaps even more important is the real possibility that a slave who is muzzled or who sees other black men muzzled may well be led to think of himself as a dog, worthy of being muzzled. In short, the treatment accorded black slaves in both societies is relevant to the question of how white men think about black men.

A second reason for making a comparison of physical treatment is to call attention to the importance of the slave trade in accounting for some of the differences between slavery in Brazil and the United States. Brazilians simply did not have to treat their slaves with care or concern when new slaves were obtainable from outside the system. That the slave trade played this role was recognized by Perdigão Malheiro in

---

[64] References to the practice are common. See, e.g., Gouveia, *História, da escravidão,* 179; Perdigão Malheiro, *A Escravidão no Brasil,* II, 220, 348; Da Costa, *Da Senzala,* 263.
[65] Elkins, *Slavery,* 78, n.
[66] Davis, *Problem of Slavery in Western Culture,* 229, n.

1866, after the trade had been stopped for fifteen years. He asserted that since the closing of the traffic from abroad the treatment of slaves in Brazil had improved. No longer, he wrote, did one "meet in the streets, as in other not remote times, slaves with their faces covered by a wire mask or a great weight on the foot. . . ." Slaves were so well dressed and shod, he continued, "that no one would know who they are," that is, they could not be distinguished from free blacks. Two visiting Americans noticed the same change even earlier:

> Until 1850, when the slave-trade was effectually put down, it was considered cheaper, on the country plantations to use up a slave in five or seven years, and purchase another, than to take care of him. This I had, in the interior, from intelligent native Brazilians, and my own observation has confirmed it. But, since the inhuman traffic has ceased, the price of slaves has been enhanced, and the selfish motives for taking greater care of them have been increased.[67]

But it needs to be added that the closing of the foreign slave trade in Brazil had at least one worsening effect upon the lot of the slave. It undoubtedly increased the internal slave trade, thereby enhancing the likelihood of the dissolution of slave families. Prior to 1850 the foreign slave trade probably kept to a minimum the movement of established slaves from one part of the country to another. In the United States, on the other hand, slaves prior to 1850 probably experienced more disruption of families, simply because the foreign slave trade was closed and the opening of new areas in the Southwest provided a growing market for slaves, who had to be drawn from the older regions, especially the upper South.

One of the earliest signs of discrimination against Negroes in seventeenth-century Virginia, Maryland, and even New England was the legal denial of arms to blacks, free or slave, but not to white indentured servants.[68] This discrimination constitutes perhaps the sharpest difference between the slave systems of the U.S. and Brazil. Almost from the beginning of settlement, the Portuguese and then the Brazilians permitted not only Negroes, but slaves themselves, to be armed. Arthur Ramos has even suggested that whites encouraged the slaves to arm themselves.[69] During the wars against the French and the Dutch invaders in the sixteenth and seventeenth centuries, large numbers of slaves and free

---

[67] Perdigão Malheiro, A Escravidão no Brasil, II, 114–15; D. P. Kidder and J. C. Fletcher, Brazil and the Brazilians (Philadelphia, 1857), 132.

[68] Carl N. Degler, "Slavery and the Genesis of American Race Prejudice," Comparative Studies in Society and History, II (Oct. 1959), 57, 64; see also Winthrop D. Jordan, White Over Black: American Attitudes toward the Negro, 1550–1812 (Chapel Hill, N.C., 1968), 71, 125–26. Jordan notes that free Negroes served in all the wars of colonial New England, but that few slaves served in any colonial militias.

[69] Ramos, Negro in Brazil, 157.

Negroes fought on the side of the Brazilians. The Dutch occupation of northeastern Brazil, which entailed almost continuous warfare, lasted for a quarter of a century. Negroes, slave and free, also fought in the War of the Farrapos in southern Brazil against the Empire in the late 1830's. Indeed, as Roger Bastide has written, "the Negro appears in all the civil revolts, the war of the *paulistas* against the Emboabos, the wars of national independence, and one even sees them in the party struggles under the Empire, between royalists and republicans or in the rivalries of political leaders among themselves." Slaves served in the Paraguayan War of 1865–70, often being sent by masters to fight in their places or to win favor with the Emperor. Fugitive slaves also served in the Brazilian army in the nineteenth century. At the end of the Paraguayan War some twenty thousand slaves who had served in the army were given their freedom.[70]

When comparable occasions arose in the United States the results were quite different. During the American Revolution, for example, Henry and John Laurens, leading figures in South Carolina, proposed in 1779 that slaves be enlisted to help counter the military successes of the British in the southern colonies. It was understood that the survivors would be freed. Although the Laurenses were joined by a few other South Carolinians and the Continental Congress approved of the plan, the South Carolina legislature overwhelmingly rejected it. The Laurenses raised the issue again in 1781, but once more the proposal was rejected by both the South Carolina and Georgia legislatures. When the slave South was faced with a struggle for survival during the Civil War it again steadfastly refused to use slave soldiers until the very last month of the war; indeed, the Confederacy rejected even free Negros when they offered their services at the beginning of the war.[71]

That slaves in Brazil were often armed and that they rarely were in the United States is obviously a significant difference between the practices of slavery in the two places. To arm Negro slaves surely affects how one feels about Negroes, whether slave or free. As Octavio Ianni has observed, concerning the use of Negro slaves in the Paraguayan War, Brazilian whites could not help but obtain a new and larger view of Negro capabilities when blacks served as defenders of the nation.[72] How can this difference in practice be explained?

---

[70] Charles R. Boxer, *The Dutch in Brazil, 1624–1654* (Oxford, Eng., 1957), 166–69; Cardoso, *Capitalismo e escravidão*, 153–54, n; Bastide, *Religions africaines au Brésil*, 109; Da Costa, *Da Senzala*, 401. Ianni (*Metamorfoses*, 175–76) cites an example of a slave being sent by his master to serve in place of a white man; after service, he was freed. Rodrigues (*Brazil and Africa*, 45–52) is one of several sources for the figure of twenty thousand slaves freed after the Paraguayan War.

[71] John Alden, *The First South* (Baton Rouge, La., 1961), 37–40; Benjamin Quarles, *The Negro in the American Revolution* (Chapel Hill, N.C., 1961), 60–67. Some slaves, however, were enlisted by their masters in the northern states, usually as substitutes. On the offer of blacks to support the Confederacy, see D. E. Everett, "Ben Butler and the Louisiana Native Guards, 1861–1862," *Journal of Southern History*, XXIV (May 1958), 202–204.

[72] Ianni, *Metamorfoses*, 217.

A part of the explanation is undoubtedly related to the quite dissimilar colonial histories of the two countries. Sixteenth-century Brazil was a tiny, sparsely settled colony, desperately clinging to the coast, yet attractive to foreign powers because of its wealth, actual and potential. At different times during the sixteenth and seventeenth centuries the French and Dutch attempted to wrest the colony from Portugal by actual invasion. Since the mother country was too weak to offer much help, all the resources of the colony had to be mobilized for defense, which included every scrap of manpower, including slaves. The recourse to armed slaves, it is worth noticing, was undertaken reluctantly. For as Ramos writes, Negroes were first used only as a kind of advanced guard, being denied a place in the regular army during the sixteenth and seventeenth centuries. But as the need for soldiers continued and a new generation of Brazilian-born Negroes entered the scene, the whites came to demand that they serve in the armed forces. That the acceptance of Negro troops was the result of circumstances rather than ideology is shown by the fact that the Negroes were usually segregated until the years of the Empire, and even when they were no longer set apart, "whites tended to occupy the military posts of major responsibility." [73] Use of Negroes in the colonial period was, therefore, not the result of the prior acceptance of the colored man as an equal, but of the need of him as a fighter. Throughout the eighteenth century, as before, the law *denied* Negroes and mulattoes the right to carry arms. [74]

In striking contrast is the history of the Negro in the British colonies of North America, where conditions and circumstances of settlement and development differed. In the first fifty years of settlement, when the necessities of defense might have encouraged the arming of slaves, there were very few blacks available. As is well known, in the South white indentured servants made up the great preponderance of the unfree labor supply until the end of the seventeenth century. Even at that time, in both Maryland and Virginia, Negroes constituted considerably less than one-fifth of the population. Meanwhile, the white population, servant and free, had long been more than adequate for purposes of defense. Unlike the situation in Brazil, moreover, colonial Englishmen experienced no foreign invasions and only an occasional foreign threat. In short, neither at the beginning nor at the close of the formative seventeenth century were English colonists under any pressure to use Negroes or slaves as defensive troops. As a consequence they could indulge their acute awareness of their difference in appearance, religion, and culture from Africans by permitting their social institutions to reflect this awareness. Thus in both the southern and northern colonies Negroes were resolutely kept

---

[73] Ramos, *Negro in Brazil*, 151–54.
[74] Mörner, *Race Mixture in the History of Latin America*, 52.

from bearing arms. At one time, in 1652, Massachusetts had enlisted Indians and Negroes in the militia, but in 1656 this policy was reversed by the statement that "henceforth no negroes or Indians, altho servants of the English, shalbe armed or permitted to trayne." In 1660 Connecticut also excluded Indians and "negar servants" from the militia.[75]

There is one exception to the English colonists' attitudes toward the arming of slaves, but it is an exception that proves the rule. Early in the eighteenth century, when South Carolina was weak and threatened by Spanish invasion, slaves were required to be trained in the use of arms and included in an auxiliary militia.[76] The policy, however, was only temporary, since the colony was soon able to protect itself by dependence upon whites alone and the feared invasions did not materialize.

Further differences in attitudes toward Negroes and slaves in the U.S. and in Brazil are the responses that the two societies made to the threat of slave insurrections. In both societies, it should be said, fear of slave revolts was widespread. One of the several measures that whites in the southern United States took to forestall slave insurrections was to place restrictions upon free Negroes, who were widely believed to be fomenters of slave conspiracies and revolts. Thus the uncovering in 1820 of a plot allegedly organized by the free Negro Denmark Vesey moved South Carolina and other southern states to enact new and stricter limitations on the free movement of Negroes. Fear of the free Negro as a potential instigator of slave revolts was also the principal reason for the many restrictions placed upon manumission in the southern states during the nineteenth century. The most common limitation was the requirement that all newly manumitted Negroes must leave the state. At the end of the ante bellum era several southern states so feared the influence of the free Negro that they enacted laws prohibiting manumission; at least one state passed a law requiring the enslavement of all free Negroes found within the state after a certain date.[77] White society obviously saw a connection between the Negro slave and the free Negro; the important thing was not that one was free and the other a slave, but that both belonged to the same race.

In one sense, of course, Brazilian slavery was also racially based. Only Negroes, and, for a while, Indians, were slaves, though in Brazil, as in the U.S., there was an occasional slave who was fair-skinned and with blue

[75] *Records of the Governor and Company of the Massachusetts Bay in New England,* ed. N. F. Shurteff (5 vols., Boston, 1853–54), III., 268, 397; *Public Records of the Colony of Connecticut* [1636–1776] (15 vols., Hartford, Conn., 1850–1890), I, 349. See Jordan, *White over Black,* 122–28, for a survey of legal discrimination against free blacks in the English colonies of North America.

[76] Ulrich B. Phillips, *American Negro Slavery* (New York, 1928), 87.

[77] Stampp, *Peculiar Institution,* 232–35; John Hope Franklin, *From Slavery to Freedom* (New York, 1947), 218–19.

eyes, so that he was a white in everything but status.[78] But in Brazil the connection between the inferior status of slavery and race did not persist into freedom to the same extent that it did in the United States. If slave-holders in the U.S. viewed the free Negro as a potential threat to the slave system, their counterparts in Brazil saw him as a veritable prop to the system of slavery. Many, if not most of the *capitães de mato* (bush captains or slave catchers), for example, were mulattoes or Negroes. One nineteenth-century Brazilian asserted that two-thirds of the overseers, slave catchers, and slave dealers in Bahia were either mulattoes or blacks. Moreover, many free blacks and mulattoes showed little if any interest in abolition, and some, evidently, actively opposed the end of slavery.[79] In Brazil, in other words, more important than race in differentiating between men was legal status. The mere fact that a man was a Negro or a mulatto offered no presumption that he would identify with slaves.

The refusal of Brazilians to lump together free Negroes and slaves is reflected also in their failure to justify slavery on grounds of race. For, contrary to the prevailing situation in the southern United States, in Brazil there was no important proslavery argument based upon the biological inferiority of the Negro. It is true that a racist conception of the black man existed in nineteenth-century Brazil,[80] but defenders of slavery on clearly racist grounds were rare among public supporters of the institution. A Brazilian historian has written that in the debates in the Brazilian legislature concerning the treaty with Britain in 1827 that closed the international slave trade, only one member of that body clearly asserted the racial inferiority of Negroes, though other kinds of defenses of slavery were made.[81] A French commentator in 1862 noted that in Brazil slaveholders "do not believe themselves obliged, like their American colleagues, to invent for the Negro a new original sin, nor to erect a system of absolute distinction between the races, nor to place an in-

---

[78] Freyre (*O Escravo nos anúncios de jornais brasilieros do seculo xix*, 195) cites examples of light-colored slaves in the advertisements for runaways and refers to a royal order of 1773 in which it was said that, much to the shame of humanity and religion, there were slaves who were lighter than their owners, but who were called "Pretos e . . . negras." Freyre also cites an advertisement in a newspaper in 1865 in which the fugitive was described as having blond hair and blue eyes. Stampp (*Peculiar Institution*, 194) refers to blond, blue-eyed runaways in newspaper advertisements in the U. S.
[79] Williams, "Treatment of Negro Slaves in the Brazilian Empire," 327; Da Costa, *Da Senzala*, 29; Pierson, *Negroes in Brazil*, 47, n.
[80] See Stein, *Vassouras*, 133–34; Da Costa, *Da Senzala*, 354–55. Expilly provides probably the most explicit examples of racial arguments in defense of slavery. He quotes one slaveholder as saying that one could free slaves "today, and tomorrow, instead of using this freedom, they will rob and kill in order to satisfy their needs. Only by terror do they perform services. . . . I believe, gentlemen, Negroes would be baffled by freedom. God created them to be slaves." A little later, Expilly quotes the planter as saying, "The Africans represent an intermediate race between the gorilla and man. They are improved monkeys, not men." A priest is also cited as justifying slavery on the grounds that St. Thomas Aquinas claimed "that nature intended certain creatures for physical and moral reasons to be slaves." (Expilly, *Mulheres e costumes do Brasil*, 381–83.)
[81] Rodrigues, *Brazil and Africa*, 151.

surmountable barrier between the offspring of descendants of slaves and of those of free men." [82] The most common defenses of the system were the argument in behalf of property and the assertion that the prosperity of the country depended on slave labor. Some defenders of the institution, even late in the nineteenth century, spoke of it as a "necessary evil," as North Americans had done in the early years of the century. In 1886, as slavery in Brazil was coming under increasing attack from abolitionists, a member of the Brazilian Congress from the coffee district asserted that the planters in his area would have no objection to emancipation if they could be assured of a new, adequate supply of labor, presumably immigrants.[83] Even more dramatic is the fact that some of the principal leaders of the abolition movement who held elective office came from the slaveholding provinces of Brazil. No such willingness to contemplate the wholesale increase in the number of free blacks was thinkable in the slaveholding regions of the United States. Even defenders of slavery in nineteenth-century Brazil spoke of the absence of color prejudice in their country and noted with apparent approval the high position achieved by some Negroes and mulattoes.[84] Leaving aside the assertion that there was no prejudice in Brazil, one would find it difficult indeed to point to a slaveholder in the U.S. in the middle of the nineteenth century who would utter publicly a similar statement of praise for free Negroes as a class.

What may be concluded from this examination of slavery in Brazil and the United States? That there were in fact differences in the practices of slavery in the two countries there can be no doubt. The explanation for those differences, however, as I have tried to show, is to be sought neither in the laws of the Crown nor in the attitude and practices of the Roman Catholic Church in Brazil. The behavior of neither state nor Church displayed any deep concern about the humanity of the slave, and, in any event, neither used its authority to affect significantly the life of the slave. Certainly demographic, economic, and geographic factors account for some of the differences between the two slave systems that have been explored in this essay. But these materialist explanations do not help us to understand the more interesting and profound difference that emerges from the comparison.

This difference becomes evident only as one contemplates the various specific differences in conjunction with one another. In Brazil the slave was feared, but the black man was not, while in the United States the black man as well as the slave was feared. Once this difference in attitude

---

[82] Reclus, "Brésil et la Colonisation," 386.

[83] Da Costa, Da Senzala, 354–56; Cardoso, Capitalismo e escravidão, 280; Florestan Fernandes, A Integração do negro no Sociedade de classes (2 vols., São Paulo, 1965), I, 200, n.

[84] Da Costa, Da Senzala, 358.

is recognized, certain differences between the two systems are recognized as stemming from a common source. Thus the willingness of Brazilians to manumit slaves much more freely than North Americans is clearly a result of their not fearing free blacks in great numbers. (Indeed, in Brazil today, a common explanation for the obviously greater acceptance of blacks in northeastern Brazil than in the southern part of the country is that in the North there is a greater proportion of Negroes than in the South. Just the opposite explanation, of course, is current in the U.S. where it is said that when Negroes constitute a large proportion of the population they are more likely to be tightly controlled or restricted.) Brazilians, therefore, did not restrict manumission in anything like the degree practiced in the slave states of the United States. This same difference in attitude toward the Negro is also evident in the willingness of Brazilian slaveholders to use blacks as slave catchers and overseers, while in the U.S. slaveholders in particular and white men in general could scarcely entertain the idea. Finally, this difference emerges when one asks why the slave trade remained open in Brazil to 1851, but was closed in most of the United States before the end of the eighteenth century. Even before the Revolution, in fact, Englishmen in North America had been seeking ways to limit the number of blacks in their midst, free or slave. In 1772, for example, the Virginia legislature asked the Crown to permit it to check the slave traffic since "The importation of slaves into the colonies from the coast of Africa hath long been considered as a trade of great inhumanity, and under its *present encouragement,* we have too much reason to fear, *will endanger the very* existence of your Majesty's American dominions. . . ." This fear that an unimpeded slave trade was dangerous ran through the history of all the English colonies, especially that of South Carolina. One of colonial South Carolina's several laws calling for limitation on the slave trade advocated encouragement to white immigration as "the best way to prevent the mischiefs that may be attended by the great importation of negroes into the province. . . ." In 1786 North Carolina placed a tax on slaves on the ground that "the importation of slaves into this state is productive of evil consequences, and highly impolitic." [85] The widespread fear of Negroes also explains why all but one of the states prohibited the importation of slaves years before the federal prohibition in 1808. Certainly there was a humanitarian motive behind the movement to stop the African slave trade, but also of great importance was the fear that if the importations were not limited

---

[85] W. E. Burghardt Du Bois, *The Suppressions of the African Slave-Trade to the United States of America, 1638–1870* (New York, 1896), 221, 215, 229. The appendix to this work contains a number of other excerpts from colonial statutes to the same effect. Don B. Kates, Jr., "Abolition, Deportation, Integration: Attitudes toward Slavery in the Early Republic," *Journal of Negro History,* LIII (Jan. 1968), 33–47, contains a number of expressions by white Americans of their opposition to freed Negroes remaining in the United States.

or stopped white men would be overwhelmed by black. For as the founding and the work of the American Colonization Society in the nineteenth century reveal, even those people in the slave states who conscientiously opposed slavery did not want the Negro as a free man in the United States.

In Brazil, on the other hand, the slave trade came to an end principally because of pressures from *outside* the society. For a quarter of a century before 1851 the British government badgered the Brazilians to put an end to the trade. It is easy to believe that without the pressure from the British and the humiliating infringements of Brazilian sovereignty by ships of the Royal Navy the Brazilians would have kept the slave trade open even longer. Apparently Brazilians rarely worried, as did the North Americans, that they would be overwhelmed by blacks.

This article opened with the observation that Tannenbaum's work began a long and continuing scholarly debate over the role that slavery in North and South America had played in bringing about a different place for the Negro in the societies of the Western Hemisphere. If the evidence and argument of this essay are sound, then the explanations of the differences offered by Tannenbaum and Elkins, at least as far as Brazil is concerned, are not supported by the evidence. But if Tannenbaum's explanation has to be abandoned, his belief that there was a strikingly different attitude toward blacks in Brazil from that in the United States has not been challenged at all. Rather it has been reinforced. For if factors like demography, geography, and the continuance of the international slave trade in Brazil help to account for some of the differences in the practices of slavery in the two societies, those same factors do not really aid us in explaining why Brazilians feared slaves but not blacks, while North Americans feared both. What is now needed is a more searching and fundamental explanation than can be derived from these factors alone or found in the practices or laws of state and church regarding the slave. Clearly that explanation will have to be sought in more subtle and elusive places, such as among the inherited cultural patterns and social structures and values of the two countries. For it is the argument of this article that the differences between Brazilian and United States slavery, rather than being the sources of the different patterns of race relations in the two countries are, in fact, merely the consequence themselves of deeper divergences in the culture and history of the two peoples.

XII *The Middle Period in American History: The Age of Jackson Versus the Age of Egalitarianism*

Introduction It has been customary to conceptualize the Middle Period in American history—from the end of the Virginia Dynasty to the Compromise of 1850—as the Age of Jackson, and its ideology and programs as Jacksonian Democracy. It has also been the common habit to see in the two principal parties of the period, Democrats and Whigs, essential differences in principle and theory rather than seeing them as separate only in "partisan rhetoric." This tendency is observable in our historiography at least since 1900 and was probably initiated by the writings of Frederic Jackson Turner. It has found its kind of classic embodiment, though from different points of view, in Arthur Schlesinger's *The Age of Jackson* (1945) and Bray Hammond's *Banks and Politics in America* (1957). The focus of interest for both Schlesinger and Hammond was the creed of the Jacksonians, and for Hammond particularly the creed as it related to the great struggle to "kill" the Second Bank of the United States, in which struggle are grouped the strongest political, economic, social, and even cultural ideologies and folklore of the day. But implicit in the work of both is a sort of consensus by which, even if the two differ about the true interpretation of Jacksonism, they agree that the Jacksonians were essentially different from Whigs and that the whole battle between the parties was not merely "a tale told by an idiot, full of sound and fury and signifying nothing." Schlesinger contends that it was the "hard money," "loco foco" wing of the party that controlled the policy of the administration from the winter of 1833 onward. "Its aim was to clip the wings of commerce and finance by restricting the credit that paper money enabled them to obtain. There would be no debt, no inflation, no demoralizing price changes, there would be no fluctuant or disappearing values and no grinding poverty. The precious metals would impose an automatic and uncompromising limit on the volatile tendencies of trade."[1] This view of the money question had, according to Schlesinger, its greatest appeal not on the frontier, but among laboring men in the eastern cities, and among farmers in the South. These were what Hammond calls "Democrats in principle."

Hammond himself rejects the idea that this group controlled administration policy. To him the real control was exercised by the "Democrats by trade" whose "strength lay with free enterprise, that is with the new generation of businessmen, promoters, and speculators who found the old Hamiltonian order of the Federalists too stodgy and confining,"[2] and that "though their cause was a sophisticated one of enterprisers against capitalist, of banker against regula-

---

[1] Bray Hammond, "Jackson, Biddle, and the Bank of the United States," *Journal of Economic History,* VII (May, 1947), 6.
[2] *Ibid.,* p. 6.

414

tion, and of Wall Street against Chestnut, the language was the same as if they were all back on the farm." Here are differences in ideology and principle among the Jacksonians exhibited and the clear conception expressed that though the Jacksonians differed among themselves they differed far more with the Whigs. The selection below from Bray Hammond's book is illustrative of this historiography of conflict.

Lee Benson, in his book *The Concept of Jacksonian Democracy: New York as a Test Case* (1961), sweeps away the notion that the Middle Period in American history should be labeled the "Age of Jackson" and contends vigorously that it should now be shown forth as the "Age of Egalitarianism." Benson holds that any caption for a period may distort reality "But when we substitute the Age of Egalitarianism for the Age of Jackson, we substitute a general phenomenon for a particular individual, and can go on to substitute the concept of the egalitarian revolution for that of Jacksonian revolution (or Jacksonian Democracy)." Benson is particularly critical of Hammond's manner of portraying the Jacksonians, but he is always cautious to point out that his generalizations come forward from his researches for one state, albeit an important one, New York. Benson's book has importance beyond questions relating to the period he studies, for he here uses, and advocates that other historians should use, the techniques and methodology of quantification.[3]

---

[3] For a rather stringent criticism of Benson's use of material at one point in his study, see Frank O. Gatell, "Money and Party in Jacksonian America: A Quantitative Look at New York City's Men of Quality," *Political Science Quarterly,* LXXXII (June, 1968), 235–252.

The Jacksonians, 1829-1841
—*Bray Hammond*

I

During the half century that ended with General Jackson's election, America underwent changes perhaps the most radical and sweeping it has ever undergone in so short a time. It passed the climacteric separating a modern industrial economy from an older one of handicraft; it passed from colonial weakness through bare independence to actual power and from an unjostled rural culture to the complexities of populousness, sectionalism, urban slums, mechanized industry, and monetary credit. Men who had spent their childhood in a thin line of sea-board colonies, close even in their little cities to the edge of the westward continental wilderness, spent their late years in a tamed and wealthy land spread already to the Missouri and about to extend beyond it. They lived to ride on railways and steamships, to use the products of steam-driven machinery, to dwell in metropolitan centers, and to feel within their grasp and the grasp of their sons more potential and accessible wealth than had ever before excited the enterprise of man.

An outstanding factor in the changes that came about was the flow of immigration from Europe. Between 1790 and 1840 the population grew from 4,000,000 to 17,000,000. In the latter year an average of 230 immigrants entered the country daily. Ten years later it was over 1,000 daily. The area of settlement and exploitation expanded swiftly under the pressure of this movement. While General Jackson was President the federal union came to include twice as many states as it had begun with and held territory that recently had belonged to Spain and France. It was shortly to add regions in the South and West taken from Mexico and regions in the Northwest that Great Britain claimed. Its expansion seemed irresistible.

The changes in social outlook were profound. Steam was generating conceptions of life, liberty, and the pursuit of happiness that were quite alien to Thomas Jefferson's; and the newcomers pushing into the country from Europe had more impatient economic motives than their 18th century predecessors. People were led as they had not been before by visions of money-making. Liberty became transformed into *laisser faire*. A violent,

Selections from Chapter 12, "The Jacksonians" in Bray Hammond, *Banks and Politics in America from the Revolution to the Civil War* (copyright © 1957 by the Princeton University Press; Princeton Paperback, 1967), pp. 326–340, 345–350, and 358–368. Reprinted by permission of Princeton University Press.

aggressive, economic individualism became established. The democracy became greedy, intolerant, imperialistic, and lawless. It opened economic advantages to those who had not previously had them; yet it allowed wealth to be concentrated in new hands only somewhat more numerous than before, less responsible, and less disciplined. There were unenterprising and unpropertied thousands who missed entirely the economic opportunities with which America was thick. There was poverty in the eastern cities and poverty on the frontier. Those who failed to hold their own in the struggle were set down as unfit.

Wealth was won and lost, lost and won. Patient accumulation was contemned. People believed it was not what they saved but what they made that counted. Jay Cooke, one of America's future millionaires, who was scarcely born poor on a farm but primitively at least, in a frontier settlement, was already on his way to fortune in a private banking firm before the age of twenty and writing home about his work with enthusiasm. This was in the winter of 1839–1840. "My bosses are making money fast," he said. "This business is always good, and those who follow it in time become rich. . . . Among our customers are men of every age and every position in society, from the hoary miser to the dashing buck who lives upon his thousands. Through all grades I see the same all-pervading, all engrossing anxiety to grow rich." Something of the same sort, to be sure, was taking place in western Europe and especially in Great Britain. Half the people and most of the money for America's transformation came from there. But though industrial and technological revolution occurred also in the Old World, in the New, where vast resources awaited exploitation, it produced a dazzling, democratic expansion experienced nowhere else. The situation was such that the rallying cry, *"Laissez nous faire!"* expressed the views of Americans perfectly, when translated.

Socially, the Jacksonian revolution signified that a nation of democrats was tired of being governed, however well, by gentlemen from Virginia and Massachusetts. As Professor Sumner observed, what seems to have enchanted people with General Jackson when he became a candidate for President was not any principles or policies he advocated but his breaches of decorum, real or alleged.[1] Economically, the revolution signified that a nation of potential money-makers could not abide traditionary, conservative limitations on business enterprise, particularly by capitalists in Philadelphia. The Jacksonian revolution was a consequence of the Industrial Revolution and of a farm-born people's realization that now anyone in America could get rich and through his own efforts, if he had a fair chance. A conception of earned wealth arose which rendered the self-made man as superior morally to the hereditary well-to-do as the agrarian had been. It was like the conception which led Theodoric the Great to boast

---

[1] Oberholtzer, I, 57–58; Sumner, *Jackson*, 179.

that he held Italy solely by right of conquest and without the shadow of legal, that is, hereditary right. The humbly born and rugged individualists who were gaining fortunes by their own toil and sweat, or wits, were still simple Americans, Jeffersonian, anti-monopolistic, anti-governmental, but fraught with the spirit of enterprise and fired with a sense of what soon would be called manifest destiny. They envied the social and economic advantages of the established urban capitalists, mercantile and financial; and they fought these aristocrats with far more zeal and ingenuity than the agrarians ever had. They resented the federal Bank's interference with expansion of the monetary supply. They found it bestriding the path of enterprise, and with Apollyon's brag but Christian's better luck they were resolved to spill its soul. They democratized business under a great show of agrarian idealism and made the age of Jackson a festival of *laisser faire* prelusive to the age of Grant and the robber barons.

In their attack on the Bank of the United States, the Jacksonians still employed the vocabulary of their agrarian backgrounds. The phraseology of idealism was adapted to money-making, the creed of an earlier generation becoming the cant of its successor. Their terms of abuse were "oppression," "tyranny," "monied power," "aristocracy," "wealth," "privilege," "monopoly"; their terms of praise were "the humble," "the poor," "the simple," "the honest and industrious." Though their cause was a sophisticated one of enterpriser against capitalist, of banker against regulation, and of Wall Street against Chestnut, the language was the same as if they were all back on the farm. Neither the President, nor his advisers, nor their followers saw any discrepancy between the concept of freedom in an age of agrarianism and the concept of freedom in one of enterprise. Only the poets and philosophers were really aware that a discrepancy existed and though troubled by it their vision was far from clear. Notwithstanding their language, therefore, the Jacksonians' destruction of the Bank of the United States was in no sense a blow at capitalism or property or the "money power." It was a blow at an older set of capitalists by a newer, more numerous set. It was incident to the democratization of business, the diffusion of enterprise among the mass of people, and the transfer of economic primacy from an old and conservative merchant class to a newer, more aggressive, and more numerous body of business men and speculators of all sorts.

The Jacksonians were unconventional and skillful in politics. In their assault on the Bank they united five important elements, which, incongruities notwithstanding, comprised an effective combination. These were Wall Street's jealousy of Chestnut Street, the business man's dislike of the federal Bank's restraint upon bank credit, the politician's resentment at the Bank's interference with states' rights, popular identification of the Bank with the aristocracy of business, and the direction of agrarian antipathy away from banks in general to the federal Bank in particular. Destruction of the Bank ended federal regulation of bank credit and shifted the money center of the country from Chestnut Street to Wall Street. It left the poor agrarian as poor as he had been before and it left the money power possessed of more money and more power than ever.

II

By the term "Jacksonian" I mean not merely the President's Democratic supporters, whom he still called Republican, but in particular his closest advisers and sharers in responsibility. These included most of his "Kitchen Cabinet," some of his official Cabinet, and a number of others. Those most responsible for the destruction of the Bank, without whose urgency and help it might not have been undertaken or achieved, were all either business men or closely concerned with the business world. Named in the approximate order of their appearance, they were Duff Green, Samuel Ingham, Isaac Hill, Martin Van Buren, Amos Kendall, Francis Preston Blair, Churchill C. Cambreleng, Roger B. Taney, and David Henshaw— all but Taney being or becoming men of wealth. They did not include Major William B. Lewis, a Tennessee planter, one of the General's oldest friends and the only one of his intimates not openly hostile to the Bank. Others of importance were Thomas Hart Benton, James K. Polk, Levi Woodbury, Benjamin F. Butler, Jacob Barker, Reuben M. Whitney, William Gouge, and James A. Hamilton.

Duff Green was born in Kentucky but as a young man he went on to Missouri, where he became a land speculator and merchant, with a substantial business centering in St. Louis. By the time he left there a decade later, he says: "I had established the first line of stages west of the Mississippi. I had a profitable contract for carrying the mail. I had placed the line under the charge of trustworthy partners, who paid me a large fixed income. I had a valuable business as an attorney. I was the editor and proprietor of a leading paper, giving me considerable profit, and I was investing my income in and adjoining the city of St. Louis." He moved to Washington in 1825, where he owned the *United States Telegraph* and edited it in support of Andrew Jackson for President and in denunciation of the Bank of the United States. Newspaper publishing was apparently a simpler, less specialized, and perhaps more generally profitable form of business then than it has since become. He at first belonged to the Kitchen Cabinet, but before long he was thrust out because he was a friend of John C. Calhoun. Though Duff Green borrowed from the Bank, he approved its destruction. But his dislike of it was offset by his dislike of Amos Kendall and other Jacksonians and by his ties of family and friendship with Mr. Calhoun. He continued a long, successful career in business enterprise, being banker, railway-builder, manufacturer, and promoter in divers fields.[2]

Andrew Jackson's first Secretary of the Treasury was Samuel Ingham of Pennsylvania, farm-born but apprenticed to a paper-maker. He remained active in farming while engaged mainly in paper-manufacturing, coal-mining, railways, and eventually banking. Though primarily a business man he was always active in politics. As Secretary of the Treasury he opened the official assault on the federal Bank.

An assistant of his in the Treasury who instigated the attack was Isaac Hill of New Hampshire, also an appointee of General Jackson's. He was frail and lame, an abusive editorial-writer, an acrid partisan, a publisher, a bank director, a bank president, and a substantial man of business. He too was a member of the Kitchen Cabinet. He failed to be confirmed in his Treasury appointment by the Senate, but promptly got elected a member thereof. As an editor, in Professor Sumner's words, "His main 'principle' was that things were in the hands of an 'aristocracy' and that he ought to organize the 'honest yeomanry' in order to oust that aristocracy from power. . . . He had the rancorous malignity of those men who have been in a contest with persons who have treated them from above downwards." When a candidate for Governor of New Hampshire in 1835 he had to be defended from the "grave reproach" of being wealthy. But if wealthy, it was urged, he had not always been so; "Isaac Hill was born of poor but respectable parentage." He was a self-made man and not one of "those sons of fortune who have been from their very cradle nursed in the lap of luxury, who have never known what it is to grapple with adversity, who have found every wish anticipated and every want supplied almost before it was experienced." Such "may thank their God that they are not as this mechanic," but they "will generally be found, in their race through life, . . . outstripped by those whose experience and whose training have prepared them by their very severity for a certain victory." [3]

Martin Van Buren, President Jackson's first Secretary of State, later Vice President with him, and his successor in the Presidency, was probably the most influential of the President's advisers and highest in his esteem. His father had been a farmer and tavern-keeper of very modest estate, and he himself was without formal education. He achieved polish, eminence, and wealth. In his early career he was an associate of Jacob Barker, a Wall Street banker of more enterprise than substance. He left the bar at the age of forty-six, when he became Governor of New York, "with a competence fairly earned, which his prudence and skill made grow into an ample fortune." Baring Brothers were informed by a New York correspondent, the banker Jonathan Goodhue, 16 March 1837, respecting the new President, that "Mr. Van Buren is a very rich man," with an under-

---

[2] Green, 27, 80–81; Washington *Telegraph,* 11 July 1832.
[3] Sumner, *Jackson,* 186; Bradley, 1, 141–44.

standing of business "vastly better" than General Jackson's.[4] The Albany Regency, the New York political oligarchy of which he was the creative spirit, maintained banks and politics in the most intimate union. Mr. Van Buren sponsored, as Governor, a law enacted in 1829 authorizing a system of state banks under a Safety Fund. He was always an efficient promoter of New York's economic interests. He did not openly oppose the Bank of the United States till late, or even then conspicuously, and Nicholas Biddle long refused to believe he was not the friend he had seemed to be. Mr. Van Buren's tact was extraordinary; he had superlative skill in political manipulation and the advancement of his own interest without friction or apparent effort. Though self-made, like most of the men on whom General Jackson relied, Mr. Van Buren differed from the others in performing his task with modesty and grace; he was without rancor, without assertiveness, and without psychotic sense of insecurity and inferiority that seemed to torment many of his Jacksonian associates.

Francis Preston Blair replaced Duff Green as journalist spokesman of the Jacksonians. The new journal set up for him was the *Globe*. Amos Kendall said the *Globe* was originated by "those friends of General Jackson who regarded measures more than men and desired his re-election for another four years, not so much for his own sake, as to effect reforms in the government which no other man was capable of bringing about." Chief of these reforms, Mr. Kendall said, was an end to the Bank. Blair, the *Globe*'s proprietor, had been president of the Commonwealth Bank of Kentucky and co-editor with Amos Kendall of the *Argus of Western America*. He was "heavily indebted" to the Bank of the United States— the amount exceeded $20,000—but the difficulty was got around by a settlement at about ten cents on the dollar, and he was fetched to Washington, where he began publication of the *Globe* in December 1830.[5] The paper was very profitable and with the government printing made Blair a rich man.*

Amos Kendall was a native of New England, the son of a typically poor but independent Massachusetts farmer of a typically puritan background. He was educated at Dartmouth. In 1814 he emigrated to Kentucky, where in time he became proprietor and editor in Frankfort of the *Argus of Western America*. Although scarcely a personal acquaintance before they came to Washington, Mr. Kendall became invaluable to President Jackson directly thereafter. He was foremost in the Kitchen Cabinet. He held the

---

[4] Shephard, 30; Baring Papers OC, 16 March 1837.

[5] Catterall, 171; Biddle Papers 28, Folio 5730; 4 PLB, 220; Mackenzie, *Butler and Hoyt,* 87–88; Kendall, *Autobiography,* 372, 374.

* Blair's indebtedness was to one of the Kentucky offices of the federal Bank. As already said, branches of the Bank, though legally offensive because of their subordination to Philadelphia, seem generally to have been well regarded as local or regional institutions in spirit. In 1836 Mr. Blair occupied the handsome Washington residence since known as the Blair House, which remained in his family a century or more till acquired by the government to be maintained as an adjunct to the White House for the lodging of visitors of state.

office of Fourth Auditor of the Treasury but was far beyond his official superiors in influence. It was said that "whatever Kendall went for he fetched." He was known to the generality in Washington as an invincible, sallow, white-haired, unhealthy creature, but seldom seen. Harriet Martineau was fortunate enough to catch a glimpse of him once, and a Congressman who saw him at the same time told her that "he had watched through four sessions for a sight of Kendall and had never obtained it till now." The "invisible Amos Kendall," she reported, was "one of the most remarkable men in America, . . . supposed to be the moving spring of the whole administration; the thinker, planner, and doer; but it is all in the dark." His were the terse and commanding words repeated daily in the Jacksonian press: "The world is governed too much." Being made Postmaster General in 1835, he showed signal administrative ability in reforming the postal service. In 1845 he became associated with Samuel F. B. Morse in the commercial development of the telegraph. He had found Mr. Morse "endeavoring, with little prospect of success, to get an appropriation from Congress to extend a line of his telegraph from Baltimore to New York; it being already in operation between Washington and Baltimore." He asked Mr. Morse "whether he had no project to render his telegraph profitable as a private enterprise." Out of his enquiry an agreement arose which "vested Mr. Kendall with full power to manage and dispose of Morse's interest in his patent-right, according to his discretion." And from this in turn came the erection of telegraph lines everywhere in the country, determined suits in defense of patents, the formation of numerous separate companies, and their eventual consolidation into a nation-wide system. One could not imagine a more explicit example of entrepreneurial behavior. Mr. Kendall fought his way to such wealth and success that in time he had to defend himself from the charge, echoing one he had so often made against the Bank of the United States, that he and his business associates were "autocrats of the telegraph" and that "a more infamous monopoly than the American Telegraph Company" never existed. With Mr. Van Buren, whose talents were of a different order, he was the ablest of the Jacksonians and an outstanding figure in American business enterprise.[6]

Mr. Kendall's progress was a consistent one. As early as 1820 he was denying that labor was a source of value. He had always taken a harsh, puritanical view of things and scorned governmental relief in the days of western distress. He had favored "some degree of relief" but condemned Kentucky's interference with foreclosures. "Things will take their course in the moral as well as in the natural world," he had written. Legislatures could not relieve man of his responsibilities. "The people must pay their own debts at last." He had considered the Bank of the

---

[6] Martineau, I, 257–59; Kendall, *Autobiography*, 372, 527; Kendall, *Circular*.

United States an artificial monopoly poisonous to individualism and its annihilation the paramount aim of "the Democracy." Speaking years later of "reforms in the government" in which he had participated, he said that "chief of these was its severance from the banking power organized and exercised under the charter of the Bank of the United States." It was his belief that Congress should "be content to let currency and private business alone." He never abandoned this view. He was an apostle and exemplar of *laisser faire*. Government, he said, "cannot make the people rich but may make them poor." Americans, in his opinion, were demanding "that their governments shall content themselves with protecting their persons and property, leaving them to direct their labor and capital as they please, within the moral law; getting rich or remaining poor as may result from their own management or fortune." [7] Mr. Kendall turned to religion and philanthropy in his later years; he was a founder and benefactor of what is now Gallaudet College, for the deaf, Kendall Green, Washington, D. C. It was the only such college in the world, and he was its first president.[*]

Churchill C. Cambreleng, member of Congress from New York City, was a close associate of Martin Van Buren and an administration leader in the lower house, where he was known as New York's "commercial representative." He was a self-made man of modest North Carolina origins who had become a confidential agent and friend of John Jacob Astor. He had been friendly to the Bank of the United Staes before Jackson's election. About 1825 he had visited western New York at the request of the Bank, and for a fee, to study the relative advantages of Rochester, Utica, and Buffalo for a new branch office to be established in that region. He understood the operations of the Bank fully; Nicholas Biddle said it would be "difficult to describe more accurately the plan of circulation of the Bank" than he had done. Like Martin Van Buren, Mr. Cambreleng was an efficient promoter of New York's interests, both political and economic. He was tireless and highly capable in his congressional leadership against the Bank.[8]

Roger B. Taney (pronounced Tawney) was President Jackson's second Attorney General and his fourth Treasury Secretary. He shared first place with Kendall and Cambreleng among the President's advisers in relentless, aggressive, resourceful enmity for the Bank of the United States. He was a

---

[7] Kendall, *Autobiography,* 228, 229, 246, 374, 504–05, 510–13, 559.

[*] In 1813, while still at Dartmouth, Amos Kendall had submitted some poetry he had written to the *Port Folio* in Philadelphia, whose editors had offered a prize. He failed even of mention. He was naturally peevish about it; he thought the winning pieces were miserable. So do I, but they were not worse than his. If he later recognized in the president of the Bank of the United States the editor who had rejected his work, I can imagine if spurred the politician to avenge the poet; and in the end the smiling, insufferable aristocrat in Philadelphia who lorded it over borrowers and lenders got punished also for lording it over poor versifiers. Kendall, *Autobiography,* 82.

[8] 22nd Congress, 1st Session, HR 460, p. 357–58; Mackenzie, *Van Buren,* 101 n; *Butler and Hoyt,* 104–06.

Baltimore attorney and member of a family belonging to the landed aristocracy of southern Maryland, where he was reared. He was a shareholder in the Union Bank of Baltimore, its counsel, and an intimate friend of its president, Thomas Ellicott. This bank was one to which federal funds were transferred when he and President Jackson removed them from the federal Bank. Mr. Taney had been interested previously in three other banks and a director of two. In an influential letter to President Jackson, 27 June 1832, he denied the constitutionality and expediency of the Bank on the ground that it bestowed privileges on some and refused them to others. He ignored the regulatory duties of the government and of the Bank, except as an "absolute dominance over the circulating medium of the country," and confined the Bank's usefulness to its safekeeping and transport of federal funds. As he disingenuously put it, "the simple question of selecting the most appropriate agent for conveying the public revenues from place to place has excited as much heat and passion as even the great question of the tariff." The question was not the simple one he said it was, and the regulation of banking and money is no less important than the tariff. He dwelt on the unfairness to the state banks of chartering a federal Bank, exempt from state taxation, on "the burthens now borne by the state banks," and on the "heavy impositions" invidiously put on "the property of individuals in the state banks." For, he said, "the stockholders in the state banks, who are generally men in moderate circumstances, are subject to the weight of unlimited war taxation whenever the public exigency may require it—why should the stock in the Bank of the United States, which is generally held by the most opulent monied men, many of them wealthy foreigners, be entirely free from the additional taxation which war or any other calamity may bring upon the rest of the community? . . . The money of the citizens employed in the state banks is to be diminished in value by new burthens whenever the wants of the country require it, while the money of the opulent citizen and of the wealthy foreigner . . . is not to be allowed to feel the pressure. . . ." This was false. No such line could be drawn between the wealth of the federal Bank's stockholders and that of state bank stockholders, nor had the federal Bank any immunity from taxation, save by the states.[9]

Mr. Taney was eventually appointed Chief Justice of the Supreme Court by President Jackson, where his decisions regularly favored free enterprise and competition—and typically so in the Charles River Bridge case, 1837. In this major decision he denied that rights had been vested in one toll-bridge corporation which must be allowed to obstruct the erection of other bridges needed by the community. The rights of the first, the Charles River Bridge, ran back by succession almost two centuries to a legislative grant to Harvard College for a ferry between Cambridge and Boston.

---

[9] Swisher, 190–93; Jackson Papers 81, Folio 15985, 16008, 16011.

The income from tolls on the bridge that replaced the ferry made it a very profitable investment. But one bridge in time proved not to be enough; and the new bridge that was built being eventually passable without toll, to the loss of income and investment by the Charles River Bridge's proprietors, the latter sued in the Supreme Court for redress. Their suit was rejected. The State, according to Taney's opinion, could not be supposed to have surrendered "its power of improvement and public accommodation in a great and important line of travel along which a vast number of its citizens must daily pass." For though the rights of property are to be "sacredly guarded, we must not forget that the community also have rights and that the happiness and well being of every citizen depends on their faithful preservation." Especially "in a country like ours," declared Chief Justice Taney, "free, active, and enterprising, continually advancing in numbers and wealth, new channels of communication are daily found necessary, both for travel and trade, and are essential to the comfort, convenience, and prosperity of the people." [10]

It does not derogate from the propriety of this opinion to point out that though it is compatible with agrarian doctrine its real affinity is with *laisser faire*. It favored free enterprise, and at the same time it contributed to a new concept of the corporation. Though it seemed at the moment a blow at corporate rights in the sense that it refused to preserve a monopoly of bridge traffic anciently conferred, its beneficiary was not an individual or several individuals but a new and rival corporation competing with the old. It therefore further familiarized people with corporate competition as well as corporate monopoly and definitely helped the corporation replace the individual as an agent of free enterprise in the economy. Mr. Taney, I am sure, intended no such eventuality. Nor, I am sure, did Justice Story and Daniel Webster, by insisting on the preservation of the rights long vested in the original bridge company, intended that future material progress be shackled to 17th century grants appropriate to 17th century life. But Taney just as surely was on the side of *laisser faire* and rampant business individualism as Story and Webster were on the side of economic and technical conservatism. He was not attacking vested rights *per se*, or corporate rights, or property rights, or wealth, or capitalism, but propounding a new democratic concept that within his own lifetime was to be more typical of capitalism than was the clumsy, antediluvian monopoly that he refused to sanction.

And so of his interposition in banking—to say that it was agrarian and anticapitalistic is absurd. By siding with the state banks against the federal Bank, he simply contributed to a new and democratic concept then current, which in New York in 1838 achieved what at the time seemed one of the notable glories of the age of Jackson—the authorization of "free banking."

---

[10] *Charles River Bridge* v. *Warren Bridge*, 11 Peters 419, 546.

Yet even if *laisser faire* be deemed beneficent on the whole, it does not follow that it was properly applicable to the monetary function or warranted Taney's advocacy, in Horace Binney's words, of "an unregulated, uncontrolled, state bank paper currency." The monetary function is within the province of governmental responsibility, and though Mr. Taney and the other Jacksonians did not deny it, they did deny, to their own stultification, that banking was a monetary function. Instead they were interested in banking for the good, earthy reason that it was a fine way to make money. As Secretary of the Treasury in the Cabinet of a President who believed banks to be unconstitutional as well as morally evil, Mr. Taney said publicly and officially that "there is perhaps no business which yields a profit so certain and liberal as the business of banking and exchange; and it is proper that it should be open as far as practicable to the most free competition and its advantages shared by all classes of society." Mr. Taney made little money himself but both in administrative office and on the bench he propounded the philosophy of competitive enterprise with remarkable success. And such was his command of the arts of sycophancy and misrepresentation—always, however, in furtherance of democratic rights—that he readily got the old hero he served to face the opposite way from his real convictions and knife his own agrarian cause.[11]

David Henshaw, one of the most important business men who helped in the assault on the federal Bank, was a poor farmer boy who became a banker, a railway-builder, newspaper-publisher, business-promoter generally, Collector of the Port of Boston, and Jacksonian political boss of Massachusetts. "Though a wealthy man," Professor Arthur M. Schlesinger, Jr., observes, "Henshaw had many of the prejudices of his humble origin. His personal rancor toward the aristocracy which had snubbed him was not unlike that of his good friend, Isaac Hill." Professor Arthur B. Darling says of Henshaw and his associates that "in order to develop political influence over the poorer classes, they themselves made capital of their hostility toward the wealthy." Henshaw's *Remarks upon the Bank of the United States*, 1831, and his proposal in 1832 for a new bank with $50,000,000 of Jacksonian capital which should replace the aristocratic monster in Philadelphia that had a capital of only $35,000,000, were echoed in the message President Jackson sent to Congress when he vetoed the federal Bank's charter in 1832. His arguments were echoed again in the reasons given to Congress by Secretary Taney in 1833 for having ceased to deposit the public funds in the public Bank. "Even if it be expedient to grant a Bank upon the same plan," Henshaw said, "it ought not to be exclusively to the present stockholders. . . . The whole community should be offered the opportunity to have an interest in the institution on equal

---

[11] Congress, *Register of Debates* x, Part 2, 2322; Treasury Department, Secretary, *Reports on Finances, 1789–1849* III, 457.

terms." This argument, though false in its implication, impressed the President. Henshaw in 1830 had deposited in his own bank the public funds he took in as Collector of the Port of Boston, thus pioneering in the action that Jackson and Taney took three years later in removing the federal funds from the federal depository and putting them in pet state banks.[12]

David Henshaw's views on vested rights received still more formidable confirmation. Having had land to sell in South Boston to which free access must be provided, he and his associates had built a bridge, given it to the state, and sold the land profitably. Later Henshaw championed the new Warren Bridge against the old Charles River Bridge in the controversy to which I have just referred in speaking of Roger B. Taney. He was scorned by the more intellectual and idealistic Jacksonians, but the irrefragable arguments he offered in the Boston press against the sanctity of charter grants and in favor of free bridges and free enterprise can be found again in the learned opinion which Chief Justice Taney rendered in the Charles River Bridge case.*

From among the foregoing Jacksonians, Major William B. Lewis is missing. He was one of Andrew Jackson's oldest and closest friends, a neighbor in Tennessee, Second Auditor of the Treasury, and a resident with the General at the White House. He was an expert politician, adept in the manipulation and creation of "public opinion," but seems to have had no economic interest other than that of southern planter. He was the only cultivator of the soil, the only real agrarian, the President kept close to him in Washington, and he was of the well-to-do sort, not the horny-handed. He was also the only one of the President's closest associates to befriend the Bank of the United States. He seems to have thought it more sensible to make the Bank Jacksonian than to destroy it. His was the sole agrarian element in the administration's relations with the Bank, and it was not hostile.

III

. . . With the business interests and objectives of the Jacksonians I have no quarrel save for the cant which made the conflict over the Bank of the United States appear to be one of idealism against lucre and of human rights against property rights. The Jacksonians were no less drawn by lucre than the so-called conservatives, but rather more. They had no

---

[12] Schlesinger, 147; Darling, 7; Henshaw, 36; New England Historical and Genealogical Society, *Memorial Biographies*, I, 491.

* Since writing this, I find that Professor Darling has also compared Jackson's veto with Henshaw's compositions and noticed "that Jackson was familiar with Henshaw's arguments." More than familiar, I should say; and so was Taney. It was sensible of Jackson and Taney to heed Henshaw's advice, which for their purposes was invaluable, and Henshaw deserves credit that he has never got for his help in achieving Jacksonian aims. Darling, 136, note 13.

greater concern for human rights than the people who had what they were trying to get. The millionaires created by the so-called Jacksonian revolution of "agrarians" against "capitalists"—of the democracy against the money-power—were richer than those they dispossessed, they were more numerous, they were quite as ruthless; and *laisser faire,* after destroying the monopolies and vested rights the Jacksonians decried, produced far greater ones. There was nothing sacred about the federal Bank. The defense of it is simply that it was very useful and if not perfect it could have been improved, had its enemies felt any interest in improving it. The Jacksonians paid no heed to its merits but canted virtuously about the rich and the poor, hydras, and other irrelevancies. This was good politics. But it cannot conceal the envy and acquisitiveness that were their real motives. What the Jacksonians decided on, they directed their propaganda toward, and got. What they went for, they fetched, like Amos Kendall. An unusual number of them were not only business men but journalists, and gained both profit and influence through the press—notably Duff Green, Amos Kendall, Francis Preston Blair, Isaac Hill, and David Henshaw. They told the world it was governed too much. They vied with their great contemporary James Gordon Bennett in a glib and vigorous style. The Washington *Globe,* the organ of the administration, was attractively printed on good paper, every active Jacksonian had to take it, and, its contents aside, even the best people could feel satisfied to have it lying on the parlor table. It relied otherwise on unashamed, repetitious adulation of Andrew Jackson and defamation of his enemies. It presented matters in black and white, Bank and President, hydra and hero. "Many a time," Amos Kendall is made to say in John Pendleton Kennedy's satire, *Quodlibet,* "have I riveted by diligent hammering, a politic and necessary fabrication upon the credulity of the people—so fast that no art of my adversary could tear it away to make room for the truth. Therefore, I say to you and our democratic friends—hammer without ceasing." [13]

IV

Andrew Jackson himself had been lawyer, legislator, jurist, merchant, and land speculator, but principally planter and soldier. His origin was humble and agrarian. He was a self-made man. He belonged to an aristocracy of a frontier sort peculiar to the Southwest of his day—landed, proud, individualistic, slave-owning, and more bound by the cruder conventions than the politer ones. Cock-fighting, betting, horse-racing, and the punctilio of the duel seem to have satisfied its cultural needs. It was without the education and discipline of the older aristocracies of the sea-board. It possessed more of the aristocrat's assertive and obnoxious vices than his

[13] Kennedy, 178.

gentler, liberal virtues and stood on property and pretension rather than birth and breeding. In a quarrel General Jackson would resort to the field of honor if his enemy were a "gentleman" but merely beat him with a stick on sight if he were not. Such distinctions seem to have been lost on Albert Gallatin, an aristocrat of a different water, in whose fastidious judgment President Jackson was "a pugnacious animal."[14]

Yet the distinction and courtesy of the General's manners took by surprise those who knew him first as President; he was by then unwell, grieving over the death of his wife, and softened besides by what age will sometimes do to men. He was not now the brawler in taverns and at racetracks. "I was agreeably disappointed and pleased," wrote William Lyon Mackenzie of Upper Canada in 1829—a man of considerable violence himself in word and deed—"to find in General Jackson great gentleness and benevolence of manner, accompanied by that good natured affability of address which will enable persons who wait upon him to feel at ease in his presence. . . ." When he chose, however, the General still could storm outrageously enough. He could simulate bursts of passion that terrified strangers, who shrank from having the President of the United States burst a blood vessel on their account, even though they were not fond of him. But his tongue seldom slipped. No one profited from blunders of his. What mistakes he made arose from a child-like trust in his friends and not from carelessness with his adversaries.[15]

He was exceptionally susceptible to the flattery and suggestion of his friends. This did not impair his maintaining a forceful, determined leadership. He listened to his advisers individually and chose his plan of action hmself. His native views were agrarian and Jeffersonian, though of Jefferson himself he could entertain very low opinions, and no one—not Alexander Hamilton himself—ever went further from the constitutional principles of Jefferson than Jackson did in his nullification proclamation of December 1832. With him, moreover, as with other self-made men of his time, agrarian and Jeffersonian views faded into *laisser faire*. He was a rugged individualist in all directions. He was no friend to the shiftless and indigent who got into debt and then could not get out. He paid his own debts, no matter how hard he found it to do so, and he expected others to pay theirs.

"Andrew Jackson was on the side of the capitalists," writes Mr. Marquis James of his earlier career. "His first case in Nashville in 1788 had landed him as champion of the creditors against the debtors. Jackson desired wealth." He had been opposed to western relief measures taken on behalf of debtors in the ten years preceding his election to the Presidency. They were wicked, pernicious, profligate, and unconstitutional. Opinions like this put him logically on the side of the Bank of the United States, which

---

[14] Marquis James, 109; Henry Adams, *Gallatin,* 651.   [15] Mackenzie, *Sketches,* 46–47.

was the pivotal creditor, and opposed him to the banks made of paper, such as the Bank of the Commonwealth of Kentucky, over which his kitchen adviser, Francis Preston Blair, had presided. But solecisms embarrassed the General very little. On the frontier more than elsewhere, the modification of an agrarian economy into an industrial and financial one was such, in William Lyon Mackenzie's words, as to "make speculation as extensive as life, and transform a Jeffersonian democracy into a nation of gamesters and our land into one great gaming house where all are forced to play, while but few can understand the game." General Jackson's prejudices were stronger than his convictions, and he was himself among the least consistent and stable of the Jacksonians. "Not only was Jackson not a consistent politician," says Professor Thomas P. Abernethy, "he was not even a real leader of democracy. He had no part whatever in the promotion of the liberal movement which was progressing in his own state. . . . He was a self-made man . . . he always believed in making the public serve the ends of the politician. Democracy was good talk with which to win the favor of the people and thereby accomplish ulterior objectives. Jackson never really championed the cause of the people; he only invited them to champion his. He was not consciously hypocritical in this. It was merely the usual way of doing business in these primitive and ingenuous times." Of his election to the Presidency Professor Richard Hofstadter writes that it was not "a mandate for economic reform; no financial changes, no crusades against the national Bank, were promised. . . . Up to the time of his inauguration Jackson had contributed neither a thought nor a deed to the democratic movement, and he was elected without a platform." [16]

What counts is that Jackson was popular. He was a picturesque folk character, and it does his memory an injustice to make him out a statesman. "All the remodelling and recoloring of Andrew Jackson," says Professor Abernethy, "has not created a character half so fascinating as he was in reality." To the dissatisfied, whether through distress or ambition, Andrew Jackson offered a distinct and attractive change from the old school of leaders the country had had—and not the least by his want of real ideas. He became the champion of the common man, even though the latter might be no longer either frontiersman or farmer but speculator, capitalist, or entrepreneur of a new, democratic sort, who in every village and township was beginning to profit by the Industrial Revolution, the growth of population, and the expanding supply of bank credit. This new common man was manufacturer, banker, builder, carrier, and promoter. He belonged to the "active and enterprising," in the luminous contrast put by Churchill C. Cambreleng, as against the "wealthier classes." And his conflict was not the traditionary one between the static rich and the

---

[16] Marquis James, 89; Mackenzie, *Butler and Hoyt*, 105 n; Abernethy, 248–49; Hofstadter, 54.

static poor but a dynamic, revolutionary one between those who were already rich and those who sought to become rich.[17]

General Jackson was an excellent leader in the revolt of enterprise against the regulation of credit by the federal Bank. Though the inferior of his associates in knowledge, he was extraordinarily effective in combat. And as a popular leader he combined the simple agrarian principles of political economy absorbed at his mother's knee with the most up-to-date doctrine of *laisser faire*. Along with several of the best constitutional authorities of his day—but not Mr. Taney—General Jackson believed that the notes issued by state banks were unconstitutional. In 1820 he wrote to his friend Major Lewis: "You know my opinion as to the banks, that is, that the constitution of our state as well as the Constitution of the United States prohibited the establishment of banks in any state. Sir, the tenth section of the first article of the federal Constitution is positive and explicit, and when you read the debates in the convention you will find it was introduced to prevent a state legislature from passing such bills." Seventeen years later, in 1837, he wrote to Senator Benton: "My position now is and has ever been since I have been able to form an opinion on this subject that Congress has no power to charter a Bank and that the states are prohibited from issuing bills of credit or granting a charter by which such bills can be issued by any corporation or order." Yet in effect he did as much as could be done to augment the issue of state bank notes and was proud of what he did. Most statesmen would feel some embarrassment in such a performance.[18]

The Jacksonians were anything but rash. Once decided that they should fight the Bank rather than wed with it, they developed their attack patiently, experimentally, shrewdly, probing the aristocratic victim and teasing public interest into action. The President himself took no unnecessary chances, but those he had to take he took without fear. He was a man of "sagacious temerity," in the words of one of his contemporaries. His attack on the Bank was like his careful slaying of Charles Dickinson in a duel thirty years before. His opponent had been formidable—much younger than he and an expert marksman, which he himself was not. Each was to have one shot. Jackson and his second had gone over the prospects carefully and decided it would be best to wait for Dickinson to fire first. For though Jackson would probably be hit, "he counted on the resource of his will to sustain him until he could aim deliberately and shoot to kill, if it were the last act of his life." So he awaited his adversary's fire and, as he had expected, he was hit. But his coat, buttoned loosely over his breast, as was his wont, had presented a deceptive silhouette, and the ball had missed his heart. He concealed his hurt and concentrated on his helpless

---

[17] Abernethy, 124; 22nd Congress, 1st Session, HR 460, p. 333.
[18] New York Public Library, *Bulletin* IV (1900), 190; Jackson, *Correspondence* IV, 446; Bassett II, 590.

enemy, whose life he now could take. "He stood glowering at him for an instant, and then his long pistol arm came slowly to a horizontal position." He aimed carefully and pulled the trigger. But the hammer stopped at half-cock. The seconds consulted while the principals stood, and Jackson was allowed to try again. Once more he took deliberate aim, his victim waiting in evident horror, and fired. Dickinson fell, mortally hurt. "I should have hit him," Jackson asserted later, "if he had shot me through the brain." The same mystical will power, the same canny and studious appraisal of probabilities and of relative advantages and disadvantages, weighed in the conflict with the Bank. The President tantalized the frank and impatient Mr. Biddle, he waited for him to make the appropriate mistakes, and then with care and effectiveness he struck. His adversaries' weaknesses were no less at his command than his own skill.[19]

❖   ❖   ❖

VI

Despite the fact of a strong and determined rebellion within the business world against the Bank of the United States, the fiction that the attack on the Bank was on behalf of agrarians against capitalists, of humanity against property, of the poor against the rich, and of "the people" against "the money power," has persisted. There was, to be sure, an extremely respectable minority comprising the more conservative and thoughtful men of business, Mr. Gallatin, for example, and Nathan Appleton, who defended the Bank till near the end, but it will scarcely do to say that they represented the business world while C. C. Cambreleng, David Henshaw, and Reuben Whitney did not.

It is obvious that New York, besides gaining most from a successful attack on the Bank, risked the least; for it did not need, as the South and West did, the capital brought in by the Bank's branches. The West's aversion for the federal Bank was like the nationalistic resentment in a 20th century underdeveloped economy which wants and needs imported capital but growls at the "imperialism" of the country that is expected to provide it. The western enemies of the Bank were moved by complex psychological and political considerations—including past distress and present dependence—while its New York enemies were moved, much more simply, by covetousness and rivalry. This was the decisive new ingredient provided in the Jacksonian attack. The agrarian prejudice had been alive since 1791 and most dangerous to the Bank a few years past during its critical days and the distress in the Ohio valley. The state bank opposition was almost as old as the agrarian. And the relative importance of the two varied with the decline of agrarianism and the growth of enterprise. New

---

[19] Ingersoll, 264; Marquis James, 116–18; Bassett, 63–64.

York, now the center of enterprise, added to the long-lived antagonism a hearty and acute self-interest. That Andrew Jackson proved to be the instrument of her interest was the happy result of Mr. Van Buren's skill and devotion.

It goes without saying that Andrew Jackson himself did not understand what was happening. He had started with a vague, agrarian prejudice against banking which on occasion cropped up throughout his life but never led him to deny himself the service of banks or the friendship and support of bankers.* It was no great task for his advisers to arouse this dormant distrust, nourished on what he had read about the South Sea Bubble, and focus it upon the Bank in Philadelphia, a city whence he had suffered years before, at the hands of a bankrupt merchant and speculator, a harsh financial misfortune. Nor was an elaborate plot required to be agreed upon among conspirators. The first harassment of the Bank from the administration group was evidently spontaneous and simply aimed at making the Bank Jacksonian. Some time elapsed before it got under directed control. Even then there is no reason to suppose that the program was not mainly opportunistic. In the early stages the object need have been only to make sure that the charter be not renewed. To this end the General's mind must be fixed against the Bank, and the proper improvement of opportunities could be left to the discretion of those in whose path the opportunities appeared. The adviser who influenced the General most directly or who perhaps left the best record of what he did was Roger B. Taney, though he joined the Jacksonian circle late. He succeeded in filling the General's mind with a vindictiveness that Martin Van Buren or Amos Kendall would probably not have produced. They too would have killed the Bank but with less emotion and less cant. "When a great monied institution," Mr. Taney told the General, "attempts to overawe the President in the discharge of his high constitutional duties, it is conclusive evidence that it is conscious of possessing vast political power which it supposes the President can be made to feel." The Taney reasoning is sound, but the premises are misrepresented, and the effect was to fill the President with bitter suspicion of the Bank; though the alleged "attempts to overawe the President"—this was written in June 1832—were the reasonable attempts of Mr. Biddle to gain support for the Bank, find out what the scowls and rumblings from Washington signified, and remove the doubts that he thought were troubling the President.[20]

But thanks to the sort of thing Mr. Taney kept telling him, the President by now had few doubts such as Mr. Biddle imagined. He was merely

---

* He did not cease transacting personal and family business with the Nashville office of the Bank of the United States, which he presumably dissociated from the main office in Philadelphia. The view was reasonable. Gravitation of the branches toward independence was a perennial source of weakness to the Bank; and eventually they became local banks in fact.

[20] Jackson Papers 81, Folio 16006.

considering how best to proceed against the Bank. Replacement, he realized, was necessary, and for a long time he was fumbling over unintelligible projects to that end. One of these projects, which may be intelligible to those whose understanding has not been corrupted by some knowledge and experience of the subject, was described to James A. Hamilton, 3 June 1830. The President had in mind "a national bank chartered upon the principles of the checks and balances of our federal government, with a branch in each state, the capital apportioned agreeably to representation and to be attached to and be made subject to supervision of the Secretary of the Treasury." He recalls having shown Mr. Hamilton "my ideas on a bank project, both of deposit (which I think the only national bank that the government ought to be connected with) and one of discount and deposit, which from the success of the State Bank of South Carolina I have no doubt could be wielded profitably to our government with less demoralizing effects upon our citizens than the Bank that now exists. But a *national* Bank, entirely *national* Bank of deposit is all we ought to have: but I repeat a national Bank of discount and deposit may be established upon our revenue and national faith pledged and carried on by salaried officers, as our revenue is now collected, with less injury to the morals of our citizens and to the destruction of our liberty than the present hydra of corruption and all the emoluments accrue to the nation as part of the revenue." But these ruminations belonged merely to a period of waiting. As soon as a promising arrangement offered, the President acted. He ordered the federal funds removed from the Bank and put in the banks of his friends.[21]

Besides contributing mainly, by this course, to a shift of the money market from Chestnut Street to Wall Street, the General contributed to the inflation, the speculation, and the various monetary evils which, with a persistent agrarian bias, he blamed on banks and paper money. There were plenty of men in his own party, among them better agrarians than himself, who would have cleared his vision and tried to, but the old gentleman preferred the sycophantic advisers who stimulated his suspicions and prejudices, blinded him to facts, confused him about the nature of the federal Bank's usefulness, diverted his attention from the possibility that it be amended and corrected instead of being destroyed, and allowed him to declaim the most ignorant but popular clap-trap.[22]

VII

Although the Bank was by no means the only thing that occupied the Jacksonians, its destruction was apparently esteemed by many of them their finest accomplishment. It rumpled and demoralized the aristocrats

---

[21] J. A. Hamilton, *Reminiscences*, 167–68.
[22] [J. R. McCulloch], *Edinburgh Review* LXV (1837), 227–28.

they envied. It redistributed vested rights. It established *laisser faire*. It freed banks from federal credit regulation. It reduced the government's monetary powers by more than half. It stimulated business. It furthered the interests of New York City, Boston, and Baltimore at the expense of Philadelphia. In all this there was abundant satisfaction for Van Buren, Kendall, Henshaw, Cambreleng, Taney, and others who were like-minded.

There were many dissidents among the Jacksonians, however, who deplored the materialism of the Democracy. To the intellectuals prominent in the party, and especially to George Bancroft, David Henshaw was an abomination. The *Pennsylvanian* of Philadelphia, itself Jacksonian, felt the presence in the party of too many "Wall Street gamblers." Erastus Root, the up-state New York agrarian in Congress, defended the federal Bank from Martin Van Buren's Albany Regency and the New York banks and got purged for it. When the New York *Evening Post* protested in 1835 at Amos Kendall's order forbidding the use of the mails for abolitionist literature, it was excommunicated by the administration's mouthpiece in Washington: "The *Evening Post* has on various occasions shown a disposition to fly off from the Democratick Party by running into extremes. . . . The spirit of agrarianism was perceivable in all the political views of the editor, and it seemed as if he was inclined to legislate altogether upon abstraction and allow the business of the world and the state of society to have nothing to do with it." A writer in the *Democratic Review* in December 1838 distinguished Democrats by trade from Democrats in principle, ironically disparaging the latter in favor of the more sensible Democrat by trade, who "got a snug slice of the public deposits" for his bank.[23]

From a very different viewpoint, the Canadian patriot, William Lyon Mackenzie, whose great-grandson a century later was Canada's premier, had much to say of the Jacksonians. He had contrasted the economic and political backwardness of the Provinces under British rule with the progress and prosperity of the States and had tried to make both the British government and his fellow subjects learn something from American experience. But in his own province of Upper Canada, and in the others, authority had remained unyielding, with Family Compact, Church, and Seigneury. So, like George Washington and his compatriots sixty years before, Mr. Mackenzie had been driven to conclude that armed rebellion was necessary. With the sentiments of the American Declaration of Independence in mind, he had "engaged at last," he said, "in a desperate though for the time an unsuccessful attempt to transplant the same institutions" into Canada. He had failed and fled to the States, where, expecting to remain, for there was a price on his head in the Provinces and some of his associates had been hanged, he supported the Jacksonians. He was a

---

[23] Niles XLV (1833), 39; Congress, *Register of Debates* VIII, Part 2, 2036 ff; 2069 ff; New York *Evening Post*, 24 September 1835; *Democratic Review* III (1838), 368.

journalist. In singular circumstances he came in possession of the private correspondence of prominent New York Jacksonians—Van Buren, Cambreleng, and others.[24] Reading it, he asked himself, "Is this, can it be, free, enlightened, democratic America? The America of my early dreams it surely is not." No idea, he thought, "can be more erroneous than that men of humble origin are more friendly to the class among whom they were reared than the dwellers in palaces and among the opulent of the land." *

Popular propaganda has acquired more general and familiar use since the age of Jackson, but none more skillful. With the exception of a few persons who, with John Pendleton Kennedy, could appreciate the art of Amos Kendall and his associates, Americans were hypnotized by the Jacksonian propaganda, and Andrew Jackson himself—its main object—got guidance and inspiration from it. That many historians still follow the Jacksonian formula points to its effectiveness. In the words of one, for example, "The poor men of the East and of the West were asserting the power of their mass strength and, putting Andrew Jackson in the presidency, were smashing that symbol of financial autocracy, the great Bank of the United States." I take this quotation not as the isolated judgment of one historian but as typical of the view that seems in recent years to have gained in conventional favor, despite the record of the conspicuous business interests of the leading Jacksonians, of the accomplishments of the federal Bank, and of the disposition of the state banking interests toward it, especially in New York and Boston.[25]

The words of another historian are equally typical. "By doing away with paper money," he says, Jacksonian policy "proposed to restrict the steady transfer of wealth from the farmer and laborer to the business community. By limiting banks to commercial credit and denying them control over the currency, it proposed to lessen their influence and power. By reducing the proporton of paper money, it proposed to moderate the business cycle, and order the economy to the advantage of the worker rather than the speculator." [26]

These statements seem to me fallacious, individually and collectively. For one thing I do not believe that Van Buren, Kendall, Cambreleng, Henshaw, and Taney ever proposed restricting the transfer of wealth from the farmer and laborer to the business community, or lessening the influence and power of banks, or moderating the business cycle, or ordering

---

[24] Mackenzie, *Van Buren*, 16, 90 n; *Butler and Hoyt*, 140 n.

* He published the correspondence he had found, and it was never repudiated. To Mr. Van Buren, however, he was "that somewhat notorious person" who found an old trunk, rifled it of its contents, and published them—a "pitiful enterprise." Upon the grant of amnesty in 1849, Mr. Mackenzie, his mind completely changed about America, returned to Canada, where the efforts in which he had risked hanging had already borne fruit in Lord Durham's brilliant report and in the achievement of responsible government for the Provinces through the further efforts of Robert Baldwin and Louis H. La Fontaine. Van Buren, *Autobiography*, 536–69; Lindsey, 458, 470 ff.

[25] Gabriel, *American Democratic Thought*, 44.   [26] Schlesinger, 125.

the economy to the advantage of the worker. The passage reflects the Jacksonians' views neither of men nor of money. The two latter aims they never thought of, in modern terms, and the two former were nearer the opposite of what they sought. And if Van Buren, Kendall, Cambreleng, Henshaw, and Taney ever supposed that any of these aims could be achieved by getting rid of paper money and limiting banks to commercial credit, then I shall have to acknowledge that they were less bright than I supposed. They probably understood the equivalence of note and deposit liabilities as well as Albert Gallatin did, and they certainly knew that a greater volume of business payments could be made by check more conveniently than by bank notes, if not already so made. Their attack on banking powers, except as exercised by the federal Bank, was pretense. But it was pretense conveniently obscured by the current confusion as to what comprised banking powers. So long as most people identified banking with note issue, an attack on note issue seemed deadly to bankers and the money power. Instead, it would be bad for bankers in the backwoods, for whom note issue was still important, but the bankers in Wall Street it would never touch.

But, of course, the notion that even the note issue function of banks was seriously threatened was not entertained by any sophisticated Jacksonian. Senator Thomas Hart Benton, it is true, seems to have entertained it, for when in 1837 he saw banks and bank issues increasing, he showed signs of real surprise. "I did not join in putting down the Bank of the United States," he said, "to put up a wilderness of local banks. I did not join in putting down the paper currency of a national bank to put up a national paper currency of a thousand local banks." It is doubtful if many Jacksonian leaders shared his *naïveté*. They may rather have been amused at Old Bullion's primitive ideas.[27]

That the party should have been so largely a party of business enterprise and that its leaders should have been men so devoted to the principle of *laisser faire* is not in itself to be reprehended, of course. Even the critics of that principle can excuse the Jacksonians for being impressed by it. In a sense *laisser faire* was idealistic in that it assumed human nature to be good and governments, save at their simplest, evil. But the preoccupations of *laisser faire* were in fact materialistic. It was the device of men who wished to make money. They clothed their new aspirations in the familiar, idealistic language of the religious and agrarian traditions in which they had been reared. There was no other period in American history, one would hope, when language was more idealistic, endeavor more materialistic, and the tone of public life more hypocritical than during the Jacksonian revolution.

On the Bank itself, of course, the party was divided, though the close

---

[27] Congress, *Register of Debates* XIII (1837), Part 1, 610.

associates of the President who befriended it, William B. Lewis, Louis McLane, and Edward Livingston, were exceptional. On the tariff, which rivaled the Bank in importance, the division was far more confusing; though the party was professedly for low tariffs, it was responsible for schedules that provoked the doctrine of nullification. Logically, free trade should have been deduced as directly from Amos Kendall's dictum, "the world is governed too much," as was the quashing of currency and credit regulation, and a substantial number of Jacksonians contended consistently for both, as Cambreleng did. But others, including Jackson himself, and the country as a whole, chose governmental interposition in the form of protective tariffs and rejected it in the form of credit restriction. These were choices that followed the higher logic of what was most profitable: government should boost business but should not bother it—becoming at its best Hamiltonian in one direction and Jeffersonian in the other. Party-wise, and reduced to the simplest terms, the Jacksonian aims—that is, Mr. Van Buren's—were to end Philadelphia's rivalry of New York as financial center and Mr. Calhoun's rivalry of Mr. Van Buren himself as successor to Andrew Jackson in the presidency. Both aims were achieved, at the sacrifice of monetary regulation on the one hand and of low tariffs on the other.*

VIII

Nicholas Biddle, who seems to have been a Jacksonian himself to the extent of having voted for the General in place of his old friend John Quincy Adams, had no such band of helpers to defend the Bank of the United States as General Jackson had to attack it. The older, more conservative, non-political part of the business world supported the Bank with enough decorum but too little energy. Those who defended it the loudest did so because they disliked Andrew Jackson. Henry Clay and Daniel Webster, though they were committed to the Bank on principle, were far more committed to anything that would thwart the General.[28]

Henry Clay was himself a very popular westerner, skillful in politics, ambitious, and able. He too had been a poor boy but singularly fortunate in winning important friends to ease his rise. Except for farming and cattle-breeding, statecraft absorbed him. His policy of fostering American industry with protective tariffs was much approved in the North, though it conflicted in principle and even in practice with *laisser faire*. Clay's policy ultimately prevailed and was of immense consequence to business enterprise, but he was not himself a successful money-maker.

---

* My analysis is the same in substance as Mr. Wiltse's in his biography of Calhoun: "Opposition to internal improvements and opposition to the Bank were the basic economic interests of New York and were therefore the corner stones of Van Buren's policy." Charles M. Wiltse, *John C. Calhoun, Nullifier*, 40; also chap. 10.

[28] Biddle, *Correspondence*, 55–56.

Neither was Daniel Webster. The impracticality and improvidence in business matters of these two brilliant men contrast interestingly with the shrewd acquisitiveness of their Jacksonian opponents, who knew how to make money and hold on to it. For Henry Clay and Daniel Webster, champions of the "money power," of "monopoly," and of "privilege," were always going beyond their means, floundering in debt, and dependent on their friends to keep them on their feet. Thomas Wren Ward, of Boston, a business man of the foremost ability and character, reported to his principals, the Barings, that he considered Mr. Webster "by far the greatest man we have," and "in bringing power on a given point . . . probably greater than any man now living." Yet, he also said, "great as Mr. Webster unquestionably is, and sound as are his views generally, and able as he is on great occasions in defending the true principles of the Constitution and upholding the rights of property, still I do not give him my esteem and confidence." This was because, in Mr. Ward's opinion, he showed "a disregard to his moral obligations and a recklessness in pecuniary matters." Mr. Ward depicts Mr. Webster as living largely by passing the hat among wealthy men, who lent him money because of his public importance and scarcely expected him to repay it; in England he would try to do the same. "It will be easy to have him in your books if you desire it, but whatever he may owe you, I think you will be very safe in writing off to profit and loss." [29]

The two best aides Mr. Biddle had were Horace Binney and John Sergeant, Philadelphia lawyers of great competence. The latter was a personal friend of Nicholas Biddle from the literary days of the *Port Folio.* Neither Binney nor Sergeant had had so golden a social and economic background as Nicholas Biddle, but neither could they be called poor farm boys and self-made men. They were the best of Mr. Biddle's aides in the inadequate sense that they were highly intelligent, judicious, and reputable gentlemen; which, of course, made them no match whatever for President Jackson's array of experts. Unlike Henry Clay and Daniel Webster, they had something of the sincere, understanding loyalty to the Bank that Nicholas Biddle had. They knew its purpose and value as he did. Mr. Webster knew its purpose and value long enough to make a speech; I doubt if Mr. Clay ever bothered to go beyond the simple generalization that the Bank was an important institution which Andrew Jackson did not like.

Politics also kept John C. Calhoun from helping the Bank as he might have done. More than anyone else, he could claim the chartering of the Bank in 1816 as his work, and he understood the Bank's operation bettter than anyone else in Washington. But just at the time when the assault on the Bank was most critical—in 1832 and 1833—Mr. Calhoun was wholly

---

[29] Baring Papers, T. W. Ward to Baring Brothers, 29 April 1839.

absorbed in resistance to the tariff. In January 1834, however, he passed a scathing and accurate judgment on removal of the public deposits from the government Bank and on the reasons offered to Congress by Secretary Taney for this removal. In this address and in another in March, no less brilliant, he discussed the functions of the Bank clearly and objectively. His thorough understanding of its functions in the economy was based, as Nicholas Biddle's had originally been, on intelligent study and not at all on experience. Yet even more forcefully than the Bank had ever done he rested his argument where it belonged—on the constitutional responsibility of the government for the currency. He was distinguished among American statesmen in his realization that banking is a monetary function, that regulation of all the circulating medium is the duty of the federal government, and that the duty is to be exercised through a central bank; not for more than a century was such understanding of the subject to be expressed again in Congress. Daniel Webster in particular had never asserted the positive and proper defense of the Bank of the United States as Mr. Calhoun had. His arguments were merely legal, not economic. According to Webster, the Bank was authorized by the Constitution if necessary to the government's operations. This fell far short of seeing in the Bank the one effective means of meeting the federal government's responsibility, under the Constitution, for the circulating medium. Further, Daniel Webster leaned on the jejune defense of vested rights, an obsolescent contention which weakened the Bank's case by the antagonisms it raised and failed entirely to take it off the ground prepared for it by its selfish enemies. Mr. Calhoun's argument, practically alone, put the case on the high, affirmative, responsible ground of monetary powers, where it belonged. But politically it had no effect. The idea that the federal Bank regulated the monetary supply in accordance with the Constitution's assignment of powers made no appeal to people who did not see that bank credit was part of the monetary supply, or, if they did see, were unwilling to have it regulated.

Jacksonian Democracy—Concept or Fiction?

—————*Lee Benson*

History never repeats itself, historians do. Commenting upon this phenomenon, Thomas C. Cochran estimates that "history probably suffers more
than any other discipline from the tyranny of persuasive rhetoric." To
illustrate his point, he observes that "A. M. Schlesinger, Jr. and Joseph
Dorfman . . . may argue about the interpretation of 'Jacksonian Democracy,' but they both accept the traditional concept as central to the synthesis of the period." [1] Following his lead, I have focused upon two questions: What empirical phenomena can logically be designated by the
concept Jacksonian Democracy? Does the traditional concept help us to
understand the course of American history after 1815?

A. The Concept of Jacksonian Democracy

Although all concepts are logical abstractions, they refer to some empirical phenomena. By definition, they refer "either to a class of phenomena
or to certain aspects or characteristics that a range of phenomena have in
common. . . . [Concepts] are abstractions from reality, designating types
of movements, persons, behavior, or other classes of phenomena." [2]

Analysis of the concept of Jacksonian Democracy reveals that every version contains these elements: 1) Andrew Jackson and his successors led
(really or symbolically) a particular political party; 2) the party drew its
leaders from certain socioeconomic classes or groups; 3) the party received
strong mass support from certain socioeconomic classes or groups; 4) the
party formulated and fought for an egalitarian ideology that envisioned
not only political but social and economic democracy; 5) the party implemented a program derived from or consonant with its egalitarian ideology;
6) the opposing party drew its leaders and mass support from different
socioeconomic classes and social groups, and opposed egalitarian ideas
and policies.

"Jacksonian Democracy—Concept or Fiction" in Lee Benson, *The Concept of Jacksonian
Democracy* (copyright © 1961 by Princeton University Press; Princeton Paperback, 1970),
pp. 329–338. Reprinted by permission of Princeton University Press.

[1] Thomas C. Cochran, "The Social Sciences and The Problem of Historical Synthesis,"
Bulletin 64, The Social Sciences in Historical Study (Social Science Research Council,
New York, 1954), 158–160.

[2] *Ibid.*, 91–93. See also Robert K. Merton, *Social Theory and Social Structure*, 89–93,
114–117.

Having identified the kinds of phenomena and relationships that are designated by the concept, we can go on to ask: did those phenomena and relationships exist in reality during the "middle period" of American history? For example, did the Jackson Party advocate and implement a program of economic democracy and social reform? Or is it more accurate to say that, in general, the Jackson Party denounced and fought against such programs?

1. CHANGING DEFINITIONS OF THE CONCEPT

To my knowledge, no one has shown that contemporaries used the term Jacksonian Democracy to designate the ideology, values, attitudes, principles, and policies of Jackson Men, the contemporary term for men who supported the Republican Party. At present, we cannot be sure who *invented* the Jacksonian Democracy concept or when historians generally began to accept it. But the concept seems to derive from the frontier thesis associated with Frederick Jackson Turner and to have won general acceptance soon after 1900. We can be sure, however, that it has meant and now means very different things to different historians, and that attempts to clarify its meaning constitute a major field of work in American historiography.[3] If at this late date the concept remains unclarified, it seems reasonable to doubt that it is solidly based in reality.

When we examine the literature over time, we find that historians, in trying to abstract from reality a set of phenomena and relationships that could be subsumed under the Jacksonian Democracy concept, had to make assumptions that later proved untenable. In other words, when they systematically collected data that discredited earlier assumptions, they retained the concept by redefining it on the basis of still other erroneous assumptions.

No matter how the concept has been defined, it has assumed that a strong causal relationship existed between Andrew Jackson's real or symbolic role in politics and the progress of movements dedicated to egalitarian and humanitarian ideals or objectives. It has also assumed that during the period from 1825 to 1850, both on leadership and mass levels, party battles represented reasonably clear-cut ideological and political conflicts between two types of men. In different versions of the concept, the types of men are identified by different criteria, for example, "frontier democrats" and supporters of "the old established order," "liberals and conservatives," "the business community and the other sections of society,"

---

[3] See Frederick Jackson Turner, "Contributions of the West to American Democracy," in *The Frontier in American History* (New York, 1950 printing), 243–268, and *passim*. For an illuminating review of the literature on Jacksonian Democracy, see Charles G. Sellers, Jr., "Andrew Jackson Versus the Historians," *MVHR*, 44: 615–634 (March 1958). A less comprehensive, but provocative, analysis is presented in Marvin Meyers, *The Jacksonian Persuasion: Politics and Belief*, 1–10.

"enterprisers and capitalists." No matter how the concept is defined, as I read the source materials and analyze the data, its underlying assumptions are, at least for New York, untenable.

2. CONCEPT VERSUS REALITY

Taking New York as a test case, this book has tried to show the existence of an unbridgeable gap between historical reality and the concept's assumptions about the leadership, mass support, ideology, and program of the Jackson Party. "Old Hero," it is true, served as the party's rallying symbol. But the other assumptions of the concept conflict with the available evidence.

The leadership of the New York Democratic Party does not appear to have been recruited from "the other sections of society" that allegedly struggled "to restrain the power of the business community"—to cite Arthur M. Schlesinger, Jr.'s, version of the concept.[4] Neither Schlesinger's version, nor any other version that assumes there were significant differences in the class nature of party leadership, appears credible. Instead, the evidence indicates that the same socioeconomic groups provided leadership for both parties.

We have also seen that in New York the concept makes erroneous assumptions about the class nature of mass support for the major parties. In one form or another historians have tended to accept Martin Van Buren's analysis, but the evidence discredits his claims that the Jackson Party championed the "producers" against the "special interests." According to his persuasive rhetoric, the Jacksonians took the side of the producers in the conflict between "those who live by the sweat of their brow and those who live by their wits." When we penetrated the rhetorical surface and struck hard data, however, we found that farmers, mechanics, and "working classes" did not form the "main-stay of the Democratic party."[5] Instead of low-status socioeconomic groups, the Jacksonians' strongest support came from relatively high-status socioeconomic groups in the eastern counties, and relatively low-status *ethnocultural and religious groups* in all sections of New York.

Politically hard-pressed by the People's Party, the Antimasonic Party, the Working Men's Party, and finally the Whig Party, the Van Buren faction and then the Jackson party eventually capitulated and adopted the egalitarian ideology advocated by their opponents. But, contrary to the assumptions of the concept, the Jackson Party attacked rather than sponsored the Whig idea of the positive liberal state functioning to "equalize the condition of men" by enabling "the people to act in a joint and vigor-

[4] Arthur M. Schlesinger, Jr., *The Age of Jackson*, 505–523.
[5] Martin Van Buren, *Inquiry into the Origin and Course of Political Parties in the United States*, 175–232. The "sweats" and "wits" division is found on pp. 226–227.

ous concert for the common good . . . [or, as the Founding Fathers phrased it] the general welfare." [6]

Moreover, if action is the real test of doctrine, the Jackson Party in New York stood firmly by its ideology. Instead of vigorously implementing, it uncompromisingly opposed political programs that required the state to act positively to foster democratic egalitarianism, economic democracy, social and humanitarian reform. How then can we reconcile the actual ideology and program with any version of the concept?

The evidence suggests that in New York Jacksonian Democracy can designate men who shared only one general characteristic: after 1828 they voted for candidates nominated by the Republican Party. That part expressed a particular ideology and implemented a program consonant with it, but its ideology and program derived from the old doctrines of state rights, strong executive, freedom of conscience, and the new doctrine of negative government. But why equate those doctrines with *democracy?* Why make the party that advocated them either the champion or the instrument of the democratic, egalitarian, humanitarian movements that emerged during the second quarter of the nineteenth century? Both on logical and empirical grounds, it seems a more credible hypothesis that in New York those movements progressed in spite of rather than because of the "Jackson Men" and the "Jackson Party."

3. IS THE CONCEPT USEFUL?

In addition to asking what empirical phenomena can logically be designated by the Jacksonian Democracy concept, I have raised the question whether the concept helps us to understand the course of American history after 1815. Since the present book has focused upon a single state, I cannot pretend to have answered that question convincingly. But two conclusions do appear to be warranted: 1) The concept of Jacksonian Democracy has obscured rather than illuminated the course of *New York* history after 1815, has distracted historians from the significance of their own work, and has led them to offer interpretations that are contradicted by their own findings. 2) Since events in New York are invariably cited by historians who accept some version of the concept, systematic research may find that in other states the concept also does not conform to reality. These two conclusions receive additional support when we examine one of the most recent, and in many respects most penetrating, studies of the period.

In what may well come to be regarded as a classic study of banking in America, Bray Hammond argues that the Jacksonian "cause was a sophisticated one of enterpriser against capitalist, of banker against regulation,

---

[6] See pp. 243–244 above.

and of Wall Street against Chestnut." The last phrase refers to the New York City bankers who, Hammond claims, played leading roles in the campaign to defeat recharter of the Bank of the United States, operating out of Philadelphia headquarters. Writing in a characteristically ironic vein, he asserts that the "Jacksonian revolution" democratized business "under a great show of agrarian idealism" by humbly-born, rugged individualists who "made the age of Jackson a festival of *laisser faire* prelusive to the Age of Grant and the robber barons." And he stresses heavily the idea that Jacksonians came up from the farm to do battle with "the established urban capitalists, mercantile and financial": "In their attack on the Bank of the United States, the Jacksonians still employed the vocabulary of their agrarian backgrounds. The phraseology of idealism was adapted to money-making, the creed of an earlier generation becoming the cant of its successor. Their terms of abuse were 'oppression,' 'tyranny,' 'monied power,' 'aristocracy,' 'wealth,' 'privilege,' 'monopoly,' their terms of praise were 'the humble,' 'the poor,' 'the simple,' 'the honest and the industrious.'. . . Neither the President, nor his advisers, nor their followers saw any discrepancy between the concept of freedom in an age of agrarianism and the concept of freedom in one of enterprise. . . . Notwithstanding their language, therefore, the Jacksonians' destruction of the Bank of the United States was in no sense a blow at capitalism or property or the 'money power.' It was a blow at an older set of capitalists by a newer, more numerous set. It was incident to the democratization of business, the diffusion of enterprise among the mass of people, and the transfer of economic primacy from an old and conservative merchant class to a newer, more aggressive, and more numerous body of business men and speculators of all sorts." [7]

In my opinion, Hammond's treatment of the democratization of business after 1825 represents a major contribution to American historiography and lights the way to further progress. But, as I have tried to show while tracing the movement for free banking, his own researches help to refute the assumption that business democratization in New York must primarily be attributed to farm-born Jacksonians of humble background, *or to any other kind of Jacksonians*. Attention is directed here toward showing how, in the passages quoted above, the Jacksonian Democracy concept imposes severe strains upon logical consistency.

Were not many of the Wall Street and other New York bankers who worked to destroy the Bank of the United States the very archetypes of the "established urban capitalists" against whom the alleged Jacksonian revolution was allegedly directed? Did not many of those bankers hold high rank in the Republican Party of Andrew Jackson? In New York State, did they not hold either high rank or considerable influence in Tammany

---

[7] Bray Hammond, *Banks and Politics in America*, 326–329.

Hall and the Albany Regency, which contributed so much to Jackson's election? Indeed, didn't many of those bankers owe their position as "established urban capitalists" to the "monopoly charters" granted them for long and loyal service to the Republican Party? Didn't the great majority of the Jackson Party in the New York legislature oppose the movement led and supported by the Whigs to "democratize" banking? But if those and similar questions require affirmative answers—Hammond, I believe, would agree that they do[8]—it becomes logically impossible to attribute the democratization of business in New York State to farm-born Jacksonians revolting against established urban capitalists.

Another logical inconsistency fostered by the Jacksonian Democracy concept is illustrated by Hammond's emphasis upon the "agrarian" vocabulary Jacksonians employed to attack the Bank. Were abusive terms, such as oppression, tyranny, monied power, and aristocracy, exclusively or primarily agrarian? Had they not been used by nonagrarians, too, long before Andrew Jackson became a national political figure and long before business began to be democratized? *Didn't the men who passionately opposed "King Andrew" and his party use essentially the same terms of praise and abuse as the men who passionately supported him?* Had not the Antimasons adapted to politics the vocabulary of sectarian abuse, referred to Van Buren's Safety-Fund "scheme" as a "monster" institution, and denounced the "moneyed aristocracy, existing in the city of Albany, which owns the Mechanics' and Farmers' bank"? Why assign Jacksonians a monopoly on terms commonly used during the Age of Egalitarianism by large numbers of men in all parties? Similarly, if most Jacksonians were farm-born, were not most anti-Jacksonians also farm-born? If some established urban capitalists opposed the party of Jackson, were not others counted among his most ardent supporters? In short, before we draw conclusions about the class composition of the Democratic and Whig parties, we must systematically analyze the opponents of the "Jackson Party," as well as its adherents.

Since Hammond accepts the traditional concept as central to the synthesis of the period, he, like other commentators beginning with Tocqueville, attributes characteristics and ideas and policies to Jacksonians that, at least in New York, are either more accurately associated with their opponents or best described as common to members of both major parties. Thus he emphasizes the importance of the New York Free Banking Act; but instead of attributing its passage to the long campaign waged by the opponents of the Jackson Party (Working Men, Antimasons, Whigs), he attributes it to the groups that actually fought against the Act, the urban

---

[8] Most of these points are implicit, at least, in the political history of New York that Bray Hammond relied upon heavily. See Jabez D. Hammond, *History of Political Parties in the State of New York*, 2: 297–302, 327–333, 349–352, 419–420, 447–449, 478–479, 484, 489–499.

Locofocos and the rural Radical Democrats.[9] Perhaps we could find no better illustration to support the conclusion that the Jackson Democracy concept has distracted historians from the significance of their own work and has forced them to operate within an inadequate framework of ideas.

B. An Alternative Concept and Hypothesis

Since I do not believe that the concept helps us to understand New York history after 1815, the question arises of whether we can replace it with a more adequate and realistic concept. In a sense, of course, that question is premature; systematic studies of other states may show that the traditional concept is well-founded and that New York is, at most, a special case. But suppose it turns out that New York is a representative state and that the findings reported in this book are credible. What then?

Let us go far beyond the evidence now available and assume that we must reject the concept of Jacksonian Democracy. Since its rejection forces us to break out of the traditional framework of ideas, we undoubtedly will stumble and fumble around for some time to come. We can tentatively begin, however, by discarding the old caption for the period and substitute the Age of Egalitarianism for the Age of Jackson. Marvin Meyers has recently observed that historians agree "that the second quarter of the nineteenth century is properly remembered as the age of Jackson." [10] I, for one, disagree. If my assumptions are sound, that caption drastically distorts reality by exaggerating the significance and role of Andrew Jackson, the Age of Egalitarianism expresses the central tendency of the period and does not associate that tendency with a particular party. In Karl Mannheim's phrase, the caption expresses "the ideology of an age." [11]

No doubt any caption for a period distorts reality; for example, an increasingly sophisticated defense of slavery developed simultaneously with the victory of egalitarian ideas. But when we substitute the Age of Egalitarianism for the Age of Jackson, we substitute a general phenomenon for a particular individual, and can go on to substitute the concept of egalitarian revolution for that of Jacksonian revolution (or Jacksonian Democracy). Tocqueville's celebrated dictum to the contrary, Americans were not "born equal" and did have "to endure a democratic revolution." After 1815, not only in politics but in all spheres of American life, egalitarianism challenged elitism and, in most spheres and places, egalitarianism won. Thus, if we accept the egalitarian revolution concept, we are in a better position to see that during the 1830's and 1840's political battles were less over ends than means. The major parties in New York developed the conflicting doctrines of the negative liberal state and the positive liberal state,

---

[9] B. Hammond, op. cit., 572–604.   [10] Meyers, The Jacksonian Persuasion, p. 2.
[11] Karl Mannheim, Ideology and Utopia (New York, n.d., Harvest Books ed.), 55–56.

but in time, both parties accepted egalitarianism as the ideology of the Good Society.

We can push this reasoning further: once we develop the concept of the "egalitarian revolution," we may be in a better position to account for the transformation from the aristocratic liberal republic of the early nineteenth century to the populistic egalitarian democracy of the mid-nineteenth century. One possible answer, or hypothesis, is that the egalitarian revolution after 1815 was largely, although by no means exclusively, the product of the Transportation Revolution which occurred after 1815 and fostered, stimulated, and accelerated tendencies already present in American society and culture.[12] I do not pretend that the present study has "proved" that hypothesis; at the moment, the hypothesis is impressionistic and crude, and it cannot even be stated precisely, let alone verified.

Before we can test the hypothesis that the Transportation Revolution was the "main cause" of the egalitarian revolution, we must state it differently. As stated, the hypothesis probably does suggest some relationships between the two revolutions. But it is too ambiguous to be tested, and it seems to assume that "impersonal forces" determine human behavior—a metaphysical assumption that retards historiographic progress by obscuring the fact that history is made by men.

When we focus upon men or groups of men, rather than upon "forces" or "factors"—terms mechanically borrowed from physical scientists who deal with different kinds of causal problems—we are in a better position to assess the relative importance of determinants. In explaining a sequence of events, we can then claim that certain men played more important roles than other men. Such claims are more precise, more meaningful, more consonant with every-day "common sense" explanations of every-day experience and behavior than are those that purport to assess the relative importance of "economic forces," "cultural forces," and the like. Moreover, when we focus upon human beings, we can support our judgments of relative importance by using criteria such as the number of men, their different power to control the apparatus of opinion-making and decision-making, their persistence over time in translating ideas into action and objectives into reality. In contrast, it is extraordinarily difficult to find and use criteria to measure the relative importance of "impersonal forces." [13] Thus I believe that causal explanations of human behavior might better take the form "Who Caused the Egalitarian Revolution?", than "What Were the Causes of the Egalitarian Revolution?" (Civil War, American Revolution, English Revolution, French Revolution).

If this line of reasoning is valid, my hypothesis should specify who

---

[12] Support for this hypothesis is found in George R. Taylor's illuminating new preface to John R. Commons, et al., eds., *A Documentary History of American Industrial Society* (Russell & Russell: New York, 1958), Vols. V and VI.

[13] See my discussion of the problem in "Causation And The American Civil War," *History and Theory*, Vol. I, No. 2 (1961).

(members of what groups) played greater and lesser roles in the egalitarian revolution after 1815. It also should specify why the Transportation Revolution both impelled and permitted them to speed the transition from an aristocratic to an egalitarian society. At present, I cannot state the hypothesis in those terms. Nevertheless, it does identify some causal relationships that seem consistent with the relevant data for New York, and the relevant data now available for American history between 1815 and 1860. It seems reasonable to assert, therefore, that if further research and analysis shows that we must reject the Jacksonian Democracy concept and hypotheses derived from it, the concept and hypothesis sketched here warrant consideration as alternatives toward a more satisfactory synthesis of the period.

XIII John C. Calhoun: Philosopher of Liberty or Marx of the Master Class?

Introduction Calhoun has been called the "darling of students of American political thought, the thinker who is almost invariably advanced when someone of European stature is asked for in the American tradition." [1] The contemporary of Clay and Webster, he was undoubtedly their intellectual superior, and he was, as Richard Hofstadter says, "probably the last American statesman to do any primary political thinking."

It has been generally conceived that the fundamental contribution of Calhoun to the art and science of politics lay in his exposition and resolution of the problem of the minority under the democratic form of government. De Tocqueville, a friendly French critic of American democracy in Calhoun's own generation, and Lord Acton, an English-Catholic historian in the succeeding generation, were to emphasize the dangers to human liberty inherent in majoritarian democracy. Neither of these, however, created a political device by which the minority might be protected. Calhoun's fertile and inventive mind created two such devices: the doctrines of nullification and concurrent majorities.

R. H. Gabriel, represented in the first selection below, says of Calhoun, "Political scientists have charted his theories, have pronounced them brilliant, and then have tossed them into the scrap-heap of discarded ideas. Perhaps the scholars have been too pre-occupied with his political devices to consider fully the ideas lying behind them. When his philosophy is analysed in terms of the American democratic faith, some new insights are achieved both concerning that faith and in the understanding of his thought." Gabriel, however, points out clearly that all Calhoun's statements regarding the fundamental law and human liberty must be premised and modified by Calhoun's acceptance and approval of the institution of chattel slavery. To Calhoun slavery, rather than being an evil, was a good—a positive good.

Richard Hofstadter, in the second selection below, like Gabriel regards the doctrines of nullification and concurrent majorities as possessing "only antiquarian interest for the twentieth-century mind." He admits that Calhoun's theoretical formulation of the problems of a minority under the democratic form of government may have some "permanent significance," but his practical solutions were designed to protect only a very special kind of minority right, that is, a propertied minority right. "Not in the slightest," Hofstadter writes, "was he concerned with minority rights as they are chiefly of interest to the modern liberal mind—the rights of dissenters to express unorthodox opinions, of the individual against the State, least of all of ethnic minorities." Hofstadter sees the chief interest of Calhoun's thought for the mid-

---

[1] Louis Hartz, "The Reactionary Enlightenment: Southern Political Thought Before the Civil War," *Western Political Quarterly*, V (March 1952), 39.

twentieth century to lie in his consciousness of social structure and class forces. Before Marx published the *Communist Manifesto*, "he placed the central ideas of 'scientific' socialism in an inverted framework of moral values and produced an arresting defense of reaction, a sort of intellectual Black Mass."

A Footnote on John C. Calhoun
—Ralph Henry Gabriel

Calhoun died in 1850 as Melville was rising to his greatest heights. As a brilliant youngster in the arena of Washington politics, Calhoun, like Clay, was a nationalist, ardent in the defense of American honor against British insults. After the War of 1812, his wide-ranging imagination visioned a union of far-separated sovereign states through a system of military roads constructed by the central government. Long before his death, however, he became to both North and South the principal leader of a section. As an old man he seemed to his enemies to personify sectional intransigence. He forged in the busy smithy of his mind the intellectual weapons with which the champions of the Cotton Kingdom sought to defeat the democratic principle of majority rule. Before Robert E. Lee rose to fame, Calhoun was the greatest of the sectionalists, the most brilliant among the champions of a cause which was ultimately lost. In Washington a few weeks after Appomattox, Walt Whitman overheard a conversation of two Union soldiers discussing a monument to Calhoun in the South. One man remarked that the true monuments to the South Carolinian were to be found scattered over the Confederacy in wasted farms, in broken railroads, in destroyed shops, and in the gaunt chimneys which marked the places where families once had made their homes. This soldier expressed a harsh judgment. But his generation in the victorious North was in a mood to agree with him.

Since 1865 Calhoun's thought almost always has been studied by Americans only against the background of sectional conflict. Among the conventions in the teaching of American history in the schools is one which assigns Calhoun and his theory of nullification irrevocably to the past. Washington, Hamilton, and Jefferson, through their beliefs and admonitions, still speak to the present. The issues which they debated still live. The same is not true of Calhoun. Unlike his contemporaries Webster and Marshall, his words are seldom used by moderns to point an argument. Political scientists have charted his theories, have pronounced them brilliant, and then have tossed them into the scrap-heap of discarded ideas. Perhaps the scholars have been too preoccupied with his political devices to consider fully the ideas lying behind them. When his philosophy is analyzed in terms of the American democratic faith, some new insights are achieved both concerning that faith and in the understanding of his

From Ralph Henry Gabriel, *The Course of American Democratic Thought*. Second Edition Copyright © 1956. The Ronald Press Company, New York.

thought. The simplest approach is to interrogate the dead Calhoun with respect to the ruling ideas of those decades when he was the champion of the South.

What was his stand on the tenet of the fundamental law? This concept included both the natural law of the Enlightenment and the moral law of the Christians. Emerson in his transcendentalism had united the two in his theory that the moral sense pervaded nature from the center of the cosmos to its crcumference. Calhoun, unlike Melville, did not reject such absolutism. The opening sentences of his *Disquisition on Government*, published in the year after his death, state his position. "In order to have a clear and just conception of the nature and object of government, it is indispensable to understand correctly what the constitution or law of our nature is, in which government originates; or, to express it more fully and accurately,—that law, without which government would not, and with which, it must necessarily exist. Without this, it is as impossible to lay any solid foundation for the science of government as it would be to lay one for that of astronomy, without a like understanding of that constitution or law of the material world, according to which several bodies composing the solar system mutually act on each other, and by which they are kept in their respective spheres."

In these somewhat ponderous phrases Calhoun repeated the doctrine of the fundamental law. Whence comes this unwritten constitution or law ultimately governing human life? Calhoun answered simply that the fundamental law of human nature compels men to live in society, and that existence in society requires a government. But of the two, thought Calhoun, society is the more important. "Both are, however," he added, "necessary to the existence and well-being of our race, and equally of Divine ordination." [1] The fundamental law comes of God. Calhoun accepted also the concept of the moral law. In the Senate on February 13, 1840, in discussing the right of petition, he elaborated an argument that if they are to be protected at all, rights must be defended at the first challenge. The individual or group that gives way when a moral issue is raised is, therefore, irreparably weakened in its efforts to maintain the justice of its cause. "The moral is like the physical world," he said, employing an unusual metaphor, "Nature has incrusted the exterior of all organic life, for its safety. Let that be broken through, and it is all weakness within. So in the moral and political world. It is at the extreme limits of right that all wrong and encroachments are the most sensibly felt and easily resisted." [2]

One must understand the application of these generalizations in the affairs of everyday life to comprehend their meaning for the man who dur-

---

[1] John C. Calhoun, *A Disquisition on Government, and a Discourse on the Constitution of the United States*, 1852 ed., 5.

[2] R. K. Crallé, ed., *The Works of Calhoun*, 1867, III, 445.

ing Jackson's administration became the acknowledged and militant leader of a section. Calhoun concurred in the general assumption of Southerners concerning the relation between chattel slavery and the fundamental law. "Negroes are not free," said Calhoun's contemporary George Fitzhugh, "because God and nature, and the general good, and their own good, intended them for slaves." [3] Nature, thought Fitzhugh, had created the races unequal and slavery was the institution through which civilized man gave to the African that share in civilization of which he was capable of making use. Slave owners, moreover, found in Holy Writ divine sanction for the institution. This premise must be read into all Calhoun's statements concerning the fundamental law and concerning liberty.

What was his stand on the doctrine of the free individual? Calhoun felt himself to be more sensitive than his age to the problems of liberty. "We have had so many years of prosperity," he said in 1848 as the Mexican War was closing, "we have passed through so many difficulties and dangers without loss of liberty—that we begin to think that we hold it by divine right from heaven itself." "It is harder to preserve than to obtain liberty," he added. "After years of prosperity, the tenure by which it is held is but too often forgotten; and, I fear, Senators, that such is the case with us. There is no solicitude now about liberty. It was not so in the early days of the Republic." [4]

The threat of tyranny which Calhoun saw close at hand was that of a numerical majority within the nation seeking to use the power of the central government to build up an agricultural, commercial, and industrial economy based on free labor to the disadvantage of an agrarian economy resting on the institution of slavery. After 1831, the year of the Nat Turner uprising in Virginia and the first issue of William Lloyd Garrison's *Emancipator* in Massachusetts, Southerners became a "conscious minority" within the nation. Until his death in 1850 Calhoun remained the chief spokesman in Washington for that minority. For him liberty meant freedom for the Southern people to carry on their lives and to develop their institutions in ways that seemed best to them. He saw in the rising antislavery movement in the North a threat that must be faced and countered. He embodied his proposals in the theories of nullification and of the concurrent majority.

Calhoun proclaimed and insisted upon the rights of the states, thirteen of which were older as independent sovereignties than the Constitution. He described this instrument as a compact among sovereign states to set up a central government to perform certain general functions as an agent of the states. In the midst of Jackson's administration, when the protective tariff became an issue, Calhoun developed the theory of nullification. This theory stated, in brief, that when one of the principals (one of the states)

---

[3] George Fitzhugh, *Cannibals All*, 1857, 116.   [4] Crallé, *Works*, IV, 417–418.

believed that the agent had exceeded the authority given it by the compact, the state might nullify the act. South Carolina took such action in 1832 in the matter of a protective tariff. Only South Carolina, however, actively supported so drastic a measure as nullification. This device in Calhoun's mind was merely an aspect of a larger theory, namely, that of the "concurrent majority." Phrased simply, the idea of the concurrent majority meant that each of the major interests—agriculture, commerce, manufacturing—and each of the great sections—North, South, West—should have the power to prevent or halt national actions deemed adverse to its vital interests. On the questions of high policy unanimous consent among major interests must replace decisions by mere majorities. Calhoun devoted the two final decades of his life to the building up of a set of principles which, if accepted throughout the nation, would protect the Southern minority and permit it to carry on without external coercion its chosen way of life. Calhoun supported his theory with an analysis of the doctrine of the free individual and of the sentiment of nationalism unrivaled in his generation.

Calhoun, in his assumptions concerning human nature, was under an unconscious, but nonetheless heavy, debt to Calvin. Man, thought the South Carolinian, was created to live in society but, paradoxically, his egoistic tendencies outweigh the altruism in his nature. Because of this fact government is necessary to prevent self-seeking individuals from overreaching and exploiting their fellows. The purpose of the State is to enable society to function. Government is the policeman of society. "But government," Calhoun went on, "although intended to protect and preserve society, has a strong tendency to disorder and abuse of its powers, as all experience and almost every page of history testify. The cause is to be found in the same constitution of our nature which makes government indispensable. The powers which it is necessary for goverment to possess, in order to repress violence and preserve order, cannot execute themselves. They must be administered by men in whom, like others, the individual are stronger than the social feelings. And hence, the powers vested in them to prevent injustice and oppression on the part of others, will, if left unguarded, be by them converted into instruments to oppress the rest of the community. That, by which this is prevented, is what is meant by CONSTITUTION, in its most comprehensive sense, when applied to GOVERNMENT." [5]

Calhoun had Calvin's low opinion of human nature. The lawyers expressed the same attitude in the maxim *caveat emptor*. Upon such assumptions of human fallibility American politics had been founded. It was this skepticism which held in check, in the politics of the United States, the tendencies toward doctrinaire extremism found in the constitutions written

---

[5] *Disquisition*, 7.

during the French Revolution. Calhoun's words were those of the scholar and the theorist, but his thought was that of the run-of-the-mill American democrat. A realism harvested from a life spent in the practice of the political art prevented Calhoun from putting faith in the power of words, even if written on parchment, to restrain the activities of government officials. For him, in spite of the Constitution, the federal Republic was governed by men. The Constitution could not enforce itself. What power it had to restrain public officials must come from its use as an instrument of protection by free citizens. "Power can only be resisted by power,—and tendency by tendency," said Calhoun. "Those who exercise power and those subject to its exercise,—the rulers and the ruled,—stand in antagonistic relations to each other. The same constitution of our nature which leads rulers to oppress the ruled,—regardless of the object for which government is ordained, —will, with equal strength, lead the ruled to resist, when possessed of the means of making peaceable and effective resistance." [6]

Calhoun's was not exactly the doctrine of the malevolent State. It was rather the doctrine that no public official can be trusted unless he knows that he is being watched by citizens who have the power to check usurpations. But, for all his realism, the South Carolinian was an idealist. He believed that he had discovered a political device which, by making constitutional democracy work, would guarantee liberty. Human liberty, the dream of the free individual, was the vision that beckoned him and urged him on. "With me," he said in 1848, two years before his death, "the liberty of the country is all in all. If this be preserved, every thing will be preserved; but if lost, all will be lost." [7]

It is difficult to picture Calhoun outside that small semicircular Senate chamber in the old Capitol which the Supreme Court later occupied for more than half a century. In this almost intimate room he presided in the prime of life as Vice-President. Here, as Senator, he grew old. In this chamber one day, when his failing strength was proclaimed by his pinched features and his sunken cheeks, he spoke of the destiny of America. He had never been more impressive. "It has been lately urged in a very respectable quarter," he said, "that it is the mission of this country to spread civil and religious liberty over all the globe, and especially over this continent—even by force, if necessary. It is a sad delusion. . . . To preserve . . . liberty it is indispensable to adopt a course of moderation and justice toward all nations; to avoid war whenever it can be avoided; to let those great causes which are now at work, and by which the mere operation of time will raise our country to an elevation and influence which no country has ever heretofore attained, continue to work. By pursuing such a course, we may succeed in combining greatness and liberty—the highest possible greatness with the largest measure of liberty—and do more to extend liberty by our example over this continent and the world

---

[6] *Ibid.,* 12.   [7] Crallé, *Works,* IV, 420.

generally, than would be done by a thousand victories." [8] In such a mood the author of the theory of nullification approached that last doctrine of the democratic faith, that doctrine of destiny which was the essence of the spirit of American nationalism.

Nationalism is a sentiment. It is a thing which is less of the mind than of the emotions. It is a consciousness of the group, a feeling in the heart of the individual that his fate is inextricably bound up with those of his people. It is enhanced by external danger. It deteriorates when the population spreads over an area so wide that communication across the nation becomes difficult. During the decades in which Calhoun urged the adoption of his device of nullification, the American people, with the exception of a brief threat of war with England in 1837, felt secure from attack by foreigners. They did not fear the Mexicans. The civil liberty enjoyed by American citizens was founded upon this sense of security. This liberty, greater than that possessed by any other people in the mid-nineteenth-century world, became the boast of American nationalism. It was the trait which was pointed out to distinguish the civilization of the United States from that of other nations.

Calhoun looked deeper than the superficialities of Independence Day orations. As he felt that liberty was a boon easily lost, so also he was convinced that the sentiment of nationalism might under certain circumstances disappear and leave the citizens of the Republic confounded. Almost alone among his contemporaries, Calhoun saw that nationalism in the United States also depends upon security. The loyalty of the individual or of the local community to the national group is primarily the product of the conviction, often unrecognized, that safety lies in merging the life of the locality with that of the nation. As the middle of the century approached, the growing anti-slavery movement in the North threatened the civilization of the South with disruption. The people of the Cotton Kingdom believed that they had accomplished a practicable solution of that most difficult of all social puzzles, the problem of getting two unlike races to live and work together with a minimum of disorder and a reasonable amount of mutual profit. The solution was the ancient institution of slavery. In communities where Negroes outnumbered the white population by two or three to one, it was impossible in the middle decades of the century for the dominant race to see how civilization could be preserved, if the discipline of slavery were relaxed. The appearance in the North of a vociferous and determined movement to bring African servitude to an end filled the South with apprehension. Calhoun foresaw, what ultimately turned out to be the fact, that this sense of insecurity would erode the sentiment of nationalism until, if measures were not taken to protect the South, the old group loyalty would disappear and the nation would fall apart.

---

[8] *Ibid.,* 416, 420.

Calhoun saw that the numerical majority offered no security to endangered Southern civilization. A majority is made up of men; and, according to the Calhoun theory of human nature, men in the mass can be as selfish and as tyrannical as they are as individuals. He proposed, therefore, the political doctrine of the concurrent majority. Calhoun thought that the sentiment of nationalism can live only so long as the vital interests of all groups within the nation are equally protected. Guarantee such security to all men, to all interests, and to all sections, argued the South Carolinian, and the sentiment of nationalism will flourish as a garden in the warmth of the summer sun. "The concurrent majority . . . ," he said, "tends to unite the most opposite and conflicting interests, and to blend the whole into one common attachment to the country. By giving to each interest, or portion, the power of self-protection, all strife and struggle between them for ascendency is prevented. . . . Under the combined influence of these causes, the interests of each would be merged in the common interests of the whole; and thus, the community would become a unit, by becoming a common centre of attachment of all its parts. And hence, instead of faction, strife, and struggle for party ascendency, there would be pariotism, nationality, harmony, and a struggle only for supremacy in promoting the common good of the whole." [9] Calhoun defined nationalism in terms of a satisfied and happy minority. He was a nationalist in the sense that he preferred that the Union be preserved. But he made the principle of the concurrent majority the condition of union. Give the South autonomy in matters it deemed vital and "patriotism, nationality, and harmony" would follow.

John C. Calhoun:
The Marx of the Master Class
—*Richard Hofstadter*

It would be well for those interested to reflect whether there now exists, or ever has existed, a wealthy and civilized community in which one portion did not live on the labor of another; and whether the form in which slavery exists in the South is not but one modification of this universal condition. . . . Let those who are interested remember that

---

[9] *Disquisition*, 48–49.

Reprinted by permission of the publisher from *The American Political Tradition*, Vintage Edition, by Richard Hofstadter. Copyright, 1948 by Alfred A. Knopf, Inc. Pp. 68–92.

labor is the only source of wealth, and how small a portion of it, in all old and civilized countries, even the best governed, is left to those by whose labor wealth is created.   *John C. Calhoun*

I

Jackson led through force of personality, not intellect; his successors in the White House were remarkable for neither, and yielded pre-eminence to Congressional politicians. Of the three greatest, Clay, Webster, and Calhoun, the last showed the most striking mind. His problem, that of defending a minority interest in a democracy, offered the toughest challenge to fresh thinking.

As nationalists closely allied with capitalistic interests, Clay and Webster could both use the ideas of the Founding Fathers as they were transmitted through the Federalist tradition. Clay, content to leave theoretical elaboration of his "American system" to economists like Mathew Carey and Hezekiah Niles, never presumed to be a thinker, and his greatest contribution to the political art was to demonstrate how a Hamiltonian program could gain strength by an admixture of the Jeffersonian spirit. Webster, who was satisfied, on the whole, to follow the conservative republicanism of the Fathers, is rightly remembered best as the quasi-official rhapsodist of American nationalism. He felt no need to attempt a new synthesis for his own time.

Calhoun, representing a conscious minority with special problems, brought new variations into American political thinking. Although his concepts of nullification and the concurrent voice have little more than antiquarian interest for the twentieth-century mind, he also set forth a system of social analysis that is worthy of considerable respect. Calhoun was one of a few Americans of his age—Richard Hildreth and Orestes Brownson were others—who had a keen sense for social structure and class forces. Before Karl Marx published the *Communist Manifesto*, Calhoun laid down an analysis of American politics and the sectional struggle which foreshadowed some of the seminal ideas of Marx's system. A brilliant if narrow dialectician, probably the last American statesman to do any primary political thinking, he placed the central ideas of "scientific" socialism in an inverted framework of moral values and produced an arresting defense of reaction, a sort of intellectual Black Mass.

Calhoun was born in 1782 into a Scotch-Irish family that had entered the colonies in Pennsylvania and migrated to the Southern back country in the middle of the century. His paternal grandmother had been killed by Indians on the frontier in 1760 and his mother's brother, John Caldwell, after whom he was named, had been murdered by Tories during the Revolution. Patrick Calhoun, his father, acquired over thirty slaves in an area where slaves were rare, became a prominent citizen of the South

Carolina hinterland and a member of the state legislature, and opposed the federal Constitution. When John was fourteen, Patrick died. The boy was tutored for a time by his brother-in-law, Moses Waddel, soon to become one of the South's outstanding educators; he graduated from Yale in 1804, studied law at Tapping Reeve's famous school in Litchfield, and joined the Carolina bar.

Calhoun's warmest attachment during these years, and perhaps all his life, was to an older woman, Floride Bonneau Calhoun, his father's cousin by marriage. After years of close friendship and constant correspondence, he married her eighteen-year-old daughter, whose name was also Floride. It was customary for a bride to keep control of her own fortune, but the young planter indelicately insisted that she place her property in his hands. It was so arranged. Besides these extensive landholdings, the connection brought Calhoun an assured position among gentlefolk of the seaboard.

In 1808, three years before his marriage and shortly after his admission to the bar, Calhoun was elected to the South Carolina legislature. In 1810 he was elected to Congress, where he promptly became a leader among the young "war hawks." When the war with Britain began, he became the foremost advocate of war appropriations, and for fifteen years he remained the most ardent worker for national unity and national power. He was for more troops, more funds, for manufactures, federal roads, a higher tariff, and a new national bank. Impatient with "refined arguments on the Constitution," he waved all constitutional objections aside. In 1817 he became Secretary of War in James Monroe's Cabinet and put through an ambitious program of fortifications and administrative improvement. John Quincy Adams, his colleague in the Cabinet, wrote in his diary that Calhoun was

> a man of fair and candid mind, of honorable principles, of clear and quick understanding, of cool self-possession, of enlarged philosophic views, and of ardent patriotism. He is above all sectional and factional prejudices more than any other statesman of this Union with whom I have ever acted.

Calhoun took a conciliatory view of sectional isues. When the question of slavery first appeared in the controversy over Missouri, he stood for moderation. "We to the South ought not to assent easily to the belief that there is a conspiracy cither against our property or just weight in the Union," he wrote to a friend, adding that he favored supporting such measures and men "without a regard to sections, as are best calculated to advance the general interest." One must agree with William E. Dodd: Calhoun's whole early life as a public man had been built upon nationalism, and at heart he remained a Unionist as well as a Southerner. What he wanted was not for the South to leave the Union, but to dominate it. Even as late as 1838 he cautioned his daughter against the disunionist school of thought. "Those who make it up, do not think of the difficulty involved in the word; how many bleeding [pores] must be taken up on passing the knife of separation through a body politic. . . . *We must remember, it is the most difficult process in the world to make two people of one.*"

Changes at home converted the reluctant Calhoun from a nationalist to a sectionalist. As the cotton economy spread, South Carolina became entirely a staple-growing state. Her planters, working exhausted land, and hard pressed to compete with the fresh soil of the interior, found it impossible to submit quietly any longer to the exactions of the protective tariff. Before long a fiery local group of statesmen made it impossible for any politician to stay in business who did not take a strong stand for sectional interests.

Calhoun, who aspired to be much more than a regional leader, managed for some years to soft-pedal his swing to a sectional position. His initial strategy was to make an alliance with the Jackson supporters in the hope that Jackson, himself a Southern planter and an old Republican, would pursue policies favorable to the South and eventually pass the presidency on to Calhoun. Then Calhoun would cement an alliance between the agrarian South and West against the capitalistic East. Both in 1824, when Jackson was defeated by the Clay-Adams bargain, and in 1828, when he was elected, Calhoun was his vice-presidential running mate.[1]

During the campaign of 1828 the exorbitant Tariff of Abominations became law, and Calhoun wrote his first great document on the sectional question, the *Exposition and Protest,* the authorship of which remained secret for some time for political reasons.[2] Denouncing the tariff bitterly, Calhoun declared: "We are the serfs of the system." After giving an impressive analysis of the costs of the tariff to the plantation economy, he came to political remedies. "No government based on the naked principle that the majority ought to govern, however true the maxim in its proper sense, and under proper restrictions, can preserve its liberty even for a single generation." Only those governments which provide checks on power, "which limit and restrain within proper bounds the power of the majority," have had a prolonged and happy existence. Seeking for some constitutional means, short of secession, of resisting the majority, Calhoun seized upon the idea of state nullification. The powers of sovereignty, he contended, belonged of right entirely to the several states and were only delegated, in part, to the federal government. Therefore the right of judging whether measures of policy were infractions of their rights under the Constitution belonged to the states. When a state convention, called for the purpose, decided that constitutional rights were violated by any

---

[1] Because of the unusual circumstances of the election of 1824, Calhoun became Vice President although Jackson was defeated.

[2] Calhoun's report was not officially adopted, but because the lower house of the Carolina legislature ordered a printing of five thousand copies, it was generally taken as an official statement.

statute, the state had a right to declare the law null and void within its boundaries and refuse to permit its enforcement there. Nullification would be binding on both the citizens of the state and the federal government. The *exposition* closed with the hope that Jackson would be elected and would make a practical test of nullification unnecessary.

Calhoun and the South were soon disappointed with Old Hickory. Personal grievances—among them Jackson's discovery that Calhoun as Secretary of War had wanted to repudiate his free and easy conduct in the Seminole campaign—caused the general to break with the Carolinian. The final breach came during the nullification crisis of 1832, when Jackson turned all his wrath upon South Carolina and incontinently threatened to hang Calhoun. At its close Calhoun, having resigned from the vice-presidency, sat in the Senate for his state, planning to join the anti-Jackson coalition, and militant Southerners were thinking about new ways of stemming Northern capital. Calhoun's trajectory toward the presidency had been forcibly deflected. Henceforth his life became a long polemical exercise, his career a series of maneuvers to defend the South and propel himself into the White House. Nourished on ambition and antagonism, he grew harder, more resolute, and more ingenious.

II

Charleston was the great cultural center of the Old South, a city with a flavor of its own and an air of cosmopolitan taste and breeding, and Charleston was the one part of South Carolina for which Calhoun had no use. He hated the life of ease and relaxation enjoyed by the absentee planters who were the mainstay of its social and cultural distinction. In 1807, when malaria was ravaging the city, he wrote to Floride Bonneau Calhoun with ill-disguised relish that every newspaper brought a long list of deaths. This, he thought, was due far less to the climate of the place than to "the misconduct of the inhabitants; and may be considered as a curse for their intemperance and debaucheries."

Debaucheries of any kind Calhoun was never accused of. There is no record that he ever read or tried to write poetry, although there is a traditional gibe to the effect that he once began a poem with "Whereas," and stopped. Once in his life he read a novel—this at the request of a lady who asked for his judgment on it. A friend, Mary Bates, observed that she "never heard him utter a jest," and Daniel Webster in his eulogy said he had never known a man "who wasted less of life in what is called recreation, or employed less of it in any pursuits not immediately connected with the discharge of his duty." Duty is the word, for duty was the demonic force in Calhoun. "I hold the duties of life to be greater than life itself," he once wrote. ". . . I regard this life very much as a struggle against evil, and that to him who acts on proper principle, the reward is in the struggle more

than in victory itself, although that greatly enhances it." In adult life to relax and play are in a certain sense to return to the unrestrained spirits of
childhood. There is reason to believe that Calhoun was one of those people
who have had no childhood to return to. This, perhaps, was what Harriet
Martineau sensed when she said that he seemed never to have been born.
His political lieutenant, James H. Hammond, remarked after his death:
"Mr. Calhoun had no youth, to our knowledge. He sprang into the arena
like Minerva from the head of Jove, fully grown and clothed in armor: a
man every inch himself, and able to contend with any other man."

For men whom he took seriously, this white-hot intensity was difficult to
bear. Senator Dixon Lewis of Alabama, who weighed four hundred and
thirty pounds and found relaxation a natural necessity, once wrote to
Calhoun's friend Richard K. Crallé during an election year:

> Calhoun is now my principal associate, and he is too intelligent, too
> industrious, too intent on the struggle of politics to suit me except as
> an occasional companion. There is no *relaxation* with him. On the con-
> trary, when I seek relaxation with him, he screws me only the higher in
> some sort of excitement.

Judge Prioleau, when he first met Calhoun, told an inquirer he hoped
never to see him again. For three hours he had been trying to follow
Calhoun's dialectic "through heaven and earth," and he was exhausted
with the effort. "I hate a man who makes me think so much . . . and I
hate a man who makes me feel my own inferiority." Calhoun seldom
made himself congenial. He once admitted that he was almost a stranger
five miles from his home, and we can be sure that his political popularity
was not personal, but abstract. Nor is there any reason to believe that he
often felt lonesome, except for his family. He loved an audience, but did
not especially care for company. He enjoyed spending long hours in
solitary thought.

Colleagues in the Senate who were used to harangues of this tall, gaunt,
sickly man with his traplike mouth and harsh voice, suited, as someone
said, to a professor of mathematics, respected him deeply for his extraordinary mind and his unquestionable integrity, but found him on occasion
just a bit ludicrous. Clay has left a memorable caricature of him—"tall,
careworn, with furrowed brow, haggard and intensely gazing, looking as
if he were dissecting the last abstraction which sprung from metaphysi-
cian's brain, and muttering to himself, in half-uttered tones, 'This is
indeed a real crisis.'"

There is testimony to Calhoun's gentleness and charm, to the winning
quality of his very seriousness at times. "He talked," reports one admirer,
"on the most abstruse subjects with the guileless simplicity of a prattling
child." Benjamin F. Perry, a bitter political opponent, testified to his
kindness, but observed: "He liked very much to talk of himself." He saved

his charm and indulgence particularly for women and children, whose world, one imagines, he considered to be a world entirely apart from the serious things of life. There is a brief and touching picture of him at his daughter's wedding removing the ornaments of a cake to save them for a little child. It is easy enough to believe that he never spoke impatiently to any member of his family, for he could always discharge his aggressions upon a senator. And two of the most effective characterizations have been left by women: it was Harriet Martineau who called him "the cast iron man who looks as if he had never been born, and could never be extinguished," and Varina Howell Davis who described him as "a mental and moral abstraction."

It would be interesting to know what Mrs. John C. Calhoun thought of him. That he was devoted to her one can readily imagine, but devotion in a man like Calhoun is not an ordinary man's devotion. When he was thinking of marrying her, he wrote to her mother: "After a careful examination, I find none but those qualities in her character which are suited to me." In the course of their exemplary married life she bore him nine children, whom he treated with paternal tenderness. But there survives a curious letter written to his cherished mother-in-law on the death of his first-born daughter in her second year of life, which reads in part:

> So fixed in sorrow is her distressed mother that every topick of consolation which I attempt to offer but seems to grieve her the more. It is in vain I tell her it is the lot of humanity; that almost all parents have suffered equal calamity; that Providence may have intended it in kindness to her and ourselves, as no one can say what, had she lived, would have been her condition, whether it would have been happy or miserable; and above all we have the consolation to know that she is far more happy than she could be here with us. She thinks only of her dear child; and recalls to her mind every thing that made her interesting, thus furnishing additional food for her grief.

Here surely is a man who lived by abstractions; it is amazing, and a little pathetic, that he sought to make his business the management of human affairs.

Calhoun had a touching faith in his ability to catch life in logic. His political reasoning, like so many phases of his personal life, was a series of syllogisms. Given a premise, he could do wonders, but at times he showed a fantastic lack of judgment in choosing his premises, and he was often guilty of terrible logic-chopping.[3] His trust in logic led to an almost insane

---

[3] Typical of Calhoun at his worst was his assault on the philosophy of the Declaration of Independence, which he read as "all men are born free and equal": "Taking the proposition literally . . . there is not a word of truth in it. It begins with 'all men are born,' which is utterly untrue. Men are not born. 'Infants are born. They grow to be men. They are not born free. While infants they are incapable of freedom. . . .'" Anyone whose introduction to Calhoun came through such portions of his work would find it hard to believe that he had sound and trenchant criticisms of the natural-rights philosophy, and yet he did.

self-confidence. "Whether it be too great confidence in my own opinion I cannot say," he once wrote, "but what I think I see, I see with so much apparent clearness as not to leave me a choice to pursue any other course, which has always given me the impression that I acted with the force of destiny." "In looking back," he wrote to Duff Green six years before his death, "I see nothing to regret and little to correct."

That all Calhoun's ability and intensity were focused on making himself president was the accepted view of his contemporaries, friend and foe, and has not been denied by his friendliest biographers. But he himself never acknowledged or understood it. "I am no aspirant—never have been," he declared fervently to the Senate in 1847. "I would not turn on my heel for the Presidency." On this score he thought himself "the most misunderstood man in the world." A certain relative purity of motive, however, must be credited to him. He was not primarily an opportunist. He generally sought to advance himself on the basis of some coherent and well-stated body of principles in which he actually believed. It was quite in keeping that he could on occasion be devious with individual men—as he was with Jackson for years—but not with ideas. His scruples about money were matched only by those of Adams, and might have been held up as an example to Webster. He supported a large family—seven of the nine children survived to adulthood—on his declining plantation enterprises, and sincerely professed his indifference to money-making. In 1845 he applied to Webster's rich Boston patron, Abbott Lawrence, for a loan of thirty thousand dollars, and when Lawrence replied in language suggesting that for a man of Calhoun's personal eminence he might be generous beyond the call of commercial duty, Calhoun withdrew his request in a letter of supreme dignity.

Calhoun's failure to understand that politics works through people and requires sustained personal loyalty as well as fidelity to ideas was resented by his followers and partisans. James H. Hammond once complained that the leader was "always buying over enemies and never looks after friends." Again: "He marches and countermarches all who follow him until after having broken from the bulk of his followers he breaks from his friends one by one and expends them in breaking down his late associates—so all ends in ruin." Rhett and Hammond both agreed that he was too unyielding and impersonal to be a great party leader. As Rhett put it, "he understood principles . . . but he did not understand how best to control and use . . . man."

Calhoun, of course, was a slavemaster, and his view of himself in this capacity was what might be expected: "My character as a master is, I trust, unimpeachable, as I hope it is in all the other relations of life." He looked upon his relation to his slaves, he asserted, "in the double capacity of master and guardian." His neighbors testified that he was kind to them, and by the lights of his section and class there is little reason to doubt it.

But the only record of his relation to a slave suggests that kindness to slaves was a mixed quality in the South. In 1831 a house servant, Aleck, committed some offense to Mrs. Calhoun for which she promised a severe whipping, and he ran away. When he was caught in Abbeville a few days later, Calhoun left instructions with a friend:

> I wish you would have him lodged in jail for one week, to be fed on bread and water, and to employ some one for me to give him 30 lashes well laid on at the end of the time. . . . I deem it necessary to our proper security to prevent the formation of the habit of running away, and I think it better to punish him before his return home than afterwards.

The case of Aleck and the "thirty lashes well laid on" does more for our understanding of the problem of majorities and minorities than all Calhoun's dialectics on nullification and the concurrent majority.

III

In 1788 Patrick Henry, arguing against the federal Constitution, asked: "How can the Southern members prevent the adoption of the most oppressive mode of taxation in the Southern States, as there is a majority of the Northern States?" This anxiety about the North's majority ripened like the flora of the Southern swamplands. As the years went by, the South grew, but the North grew faster. In 1790, when Calhoun was eight years old, populations North and South were practically equal. By 1850, the year of his death, the North's was 13,527,000, the South's only 9,612,000. This preponderance was reflected in Congress. Although Southern politicians held a disproportionate number of executive offices, federal policy continued to favor Northern capital, and Southern wealth funneled into the pockets of Northern shippers, bankers, and manufacturers. Of course, the greater part of the drain of Southern resources was the inevitable result of a relationship between a capitalistic community and an agrarian one that did little of its own shipping, banking, or manufacturing. But a considerable portion too came from what Southerns considered an "artificial" governmental intrusion—the protective tariff. It was tariffs, not slavery, that first made the South militant. Planters were understandably resentful as the wealth of the Southern fields, created by the hard labor of the men, women, and children they owned, seemed to be slipping away from them. "All we want to be rich is to let us have what we make," said Calhoun.

Southern leaders began to wonder where all this was going to stop. Given its initial advantage, what was to prevent the North from using the federal government to increase the span between the political power of the sections still further, and then, presuming upon the South's growing weakness, from pushing exploitation to outrageous and unbearable extremes? Humiliated by their comparative economic backwardness, frightened at its political implications, made uneasy by the world's condemnation of their "peculiar institution," Southern leaders reacted with the most intense and exaggerated anxiety to every fluctuation in the balance of sectional power. How to maintain this balance was Calhoun's central problem, and for twenty-two years his terrible and unrelenting intensity hung upon it. "The South," he lamented as early as 1831, ". . . is a fixed and hopeless minority," and five years later he declared in significant hyperbole on the floor of the Senate: "We are here but a handful in the midst of an overwhelming majority." In 1833, speaking on the Force Bill, he saw the South confronted with "a system of hostile legislation . . . an oppressive and unequal imposition of taxes . . . unequal and profuse appropriations . . . rendering the entire labor and capital of the weaker interest subordinate to the stronger."

After 1830, when abolitionism began to be heard, the South's revolt was directed increasingly against this alleged menace. There is little point in debating whether fear of abolition or fear of further economic exploitation was more important in stimulating Southern militancy and turning the Southern mind toward secession. The North, if the balance of power turned completely in its favor, could both reduce the planter class to economic bondage and emancipate its slaves. Southern leaders therefore concentrated on fighting for the sectional equilibrium without making any artificial distinctions about their reasons. As Calhoun put it in 1844, "plunder and agitation" were "kindred and hostile measures." While the tariff takes from us the proceeds of our labor, abolition strikes at the labor itself."

Of course, voluntary emancipation was out of the question. To understand the mind of the Old South it is necessary to realize that emancipation meant not merely the replacement of slave labor by hired labor, but the loss of white supremacy, the overthrow of the caste system—in brief, the end of a civilization. Although Calhoun once condemned the slave trade as an "odious traffic," there is no evidence that he ever shared the Jeffersonian view of slavery, widespread in the South during his youth, that slavery was a necessary but temporary evil. During a conversation with John Quincy Adams in 1820 he revealed how implicitly he accepted the caste premises of slavery. Adams spoke of equality, of the dignity and worth of human life. Calhoun granted that Adams's beliefs were "just and noble," but added in a matter-of-fact way that in the South they were applied only to white men. Slavery, he said, was "the best guarantee to equality among the whites. It produced an unvarying level among them . . . did not even admit of inequalities, by which one white man could domineer over another."

Calhoun was the first Southern statesman of primary eminence to say openly in Congress what almost all the white South had come to feel.

Slavery, he affirmed in the Senate in 1837, "is, instead of an evil, a good—a positive good." By this he did not mean to imply that slavery was always better than free labor relations, but simply that it was the best relation between blacks and whites. Slavery had done much for the Negro, he argued. "In few countries so much is left to the share of the laborer, and so little exacted from him, or . . . more kind attention paid to him in sickness or infirmities of age." His condition is greatly superior to that of the poorhouse inmates in the more civilized portions of Europe. As for the political aspect of slavery, "I fearlessly assert that the existing relation between the two races in the South . . . forms the most solid and durable foundation on which to rear free and stable political institutions."

The South thought of emancipation as an apocalyptic catastrophe. In a manifesto prepared in 1849 Calhoun portrayed a series of devices by which he thought abolitionists would gradually undermine slavery until at last the North could "monopolize all the territories," add a sufficient number of states to give her three fourths of the whole, and then pass an emancipation amendment. The disaster would not stop with this. Since the two races "cannot live together in peace, or harmony, or to their mutual advantage, except in their present relation," one or the other must dominate. After emanicipation the ex-slaves would be raised "to a political and social equality with their former owners, by giving them the right of voting and holding public offices under the Federal Government." They would become political associates of their Northern friends, acting with them uniformly, "holding the white race at the South in complete subjection." The blacks and the profligate whites that might unite them would become the principal recipients of federal offices and patronage and would be "raised above the whites of the South in the political and social scale." The only resort of the former master race would be to abandon the homes of its ancestors and leave the country to the Negroes.[4]

Faced with such peril, the South should be content with nothing less than the most extreme militancy, stand firm, meet the enemy on the frontier, rather than wait till she grew weaker. Anything less than decisive victory was unthinkable. "What! acknowledged inferiority! The surrender of life is nothing to sinking down into acknowledged inferiority!"

It was one of Calhoun's merits that in spite of his saturation in the lore of constitutional argument he was not satisfied with a purely formal or constitutional interpretation of the sectional controversy, but went beyond it to translate the balance of sections into a balance of classes. Although he did not have a complete theory of history, he saw class struggle and exploitation in every epoch of human development. He was sure that

---

[4] Setting aside its valuations and demagogic language, Calhoun's forecast bears a strong resemblance to the plans actually adopted by the Radical Republicans during Reconstruction.

"there never has yet existed a wealthy and civilized society in which one portion of the community did not, in point of fact, live on the labor of the other." It would not be too difficult "to trace out the various devices by which the wealth of all civilized communities has been so unequally divided, and to show by what means so small a share has been allotted to those by whose labor it was produced, and so large a share to the non-producing classes." Concerning one such device he had no doubts; the tariff was a certain means of making "the poor poorer and the rich richer." As early as 1828 he wrote of the tariff system in his *Exposition and Protest:*

> After we [the planters] are exhausted, the contest will be between the capitalists and operatives [workers]; for into these two classes it must, ultimately, divide society. The issue of the struggle here must be the same as it has been in Europe. Under the operation of the system, wages must sink more rapidly than the prices of the necessaries of life, till the operatives will be reduced to the lowest point,—when the portion of the products of their labor left to them, will be barely sufficient to preserve existence.

In his *Disquisition on Government* Calhoun predicted that as the community develops in wealth and population, "the difference between the rich and poor will become more strongly marked," and the proportion of "ignorant and dependent" people will increase. Then "the tendency to conflict between them will become stronger; and, as the poor and dependent become more numerous in proportion there will be, in governments of the numerical majority, no want of leaders among the wealthy and ambitious, to excite and direct them in their efforts to obtain the control."

Such arguments were not merely for public consumption. In 1831 a friend recorded a conversation in which Calhoun "spoke of the tendency of Capital to destroy and absorb the property of society and produce a collision between itself and operatives." "The capitalist owns the instruments of labor," Calhoun once told Albert Brisbane, "and he seeks to draw out of labor all the profits, leaving the laborer to shift for himself in age and disease." In 1837 he wrote to Hammond that he had had "no conception that the lower class had made such great progress to equality and independence" as Hammond had reported. "Modern society seems to me to be rushing to some new and untried condition." "What I dread," he confessed to his daughter Anna in 1846, "is that progress in political science falls far short of progress in that which relates to matter, and which may lead to convulsions and revolutions, that may retard, or even arrest the former." During the peak of the Jacksonian bank war he wrote to his son James that the views of many people in the North were inclining toward Southern conceptions. They feared not only Jackson's power, but "the needy and corrupt in their own section. They begin to feel what I have long foreseen, that they have more to fear from their own people than we from our slaves."

In such characteristic utterances there is discernible a rough parallel to several ideas that were later elaborated and refined by Marx: the idea of pervasive exploitation and class struggle in history; a labor theory of value and of a surplus appropriated by the capitalists; the concentration of capital under capitalistic production; the fall of working-class conditions to the level of subsistence; the growing revolt of the laboring class against the capitalists; the prediction of social revolution. The difference was that Calhoun proposed that no revolution should be allowed to take place. To forestall it he suggested consistently—over a period of years—what Richard Current has called "planter-capitalist collaboration against the class enemy." In such a collaboration the South, with its superior social stability, had much to offer as a conservative force. In return, the conservative elements in the North should be willing to hold down abolitionist agitation; and they would do well to realize that an overthrow of slavery in the South would prepare the ground for social revolution in the North.

> There is and always has been [he said in the Senate] in an advanced stage of wealth and civilization, a conflict between labor and capital. The condition of society in the South exempts us from the disorders and dangers resulting from this conflict; and which explains why it is that the political condition of the slave-holdng states has been so much more stable and quiet than that of the North. . . . The experience of the next generation will fully test how vastly more favorable our condition of society is to that of other sections for free and stable institutions, provided we are not disturbed by the interference of others, or shall . . . resist promptly and successfully such interference.

On January 9, 1838 Calhoun explained further why it was impossible in the South for the conflict "between labor and capital" to take place, "which makes it so difficult to establish and maintain free institutions in all wealthy and highly civilized nations where such instituitons as ours do not exist." It was because the Southern states were an aggregate of communities, not of individuals. "Every plantation is a little community, with the master at its head, who concentrates in himself the united interests of capital and labor, of which he is the common representative." In the Southern states labor and capital are "equally represented and perfectly harmonized." In the Union as a whole, the South, accordingly, becomes

> the balance of the system; the great conservative power, which prevents other portions, less fortunately constituted, from rushing into conflict. In this tendency to conflict in the North, between labor and capital, which is constantly on the increase, the weight of the South has been

and ever will be found on the conservative side; against the aggression of one or the other side, whichever may tend to disturb the equilibrium of our political system.

In 1836 Calhoun had pointed out to "the sober and considerate" Northerners

> who have a deep stake in the existing institutions of the country that the assaults which are now directed against the institutions of the Southern States may be very easily directed against those which uphold their own property and security. A very slight modification of the arguments used against the institutions [of the South] would make them equally effectual against the institutions of the North, including banking, in which so vast an amount of its property and capital is invested.

In 1847 he again reminded Northern conservatives how much interest they had "in upholding and preserving the equilibrium of the slaveholding states." "Let gentlemen then be warned that while warring on us, they are warring on themselves." Two years later he added that the North, without the South, would have no central point of union, to bind its various and conflicting interests together; and would . . . be subject to all the agitations and conflicts growing out of the divisions of wealth and poverty." All these warnings were merely the consequence of a long-standing conviction which Calhoun had expressed to Josiah Quincy that "the interests of the *gentlemen* of the North and of the South are identical." The Carolinian had no serious expectation that his appeals and predictions would change Northern public opinion, but he hoped that events might. Growing discontent among the masses might drive Northern conservatives into the arms of the planters, but as he confessed to Duff Green in 1835, whether the intelligence of the North would see the situation "in time to save themselves and the institutions of the Country God only knows."

Calhoun had an ingenious solution for the sectional problem: in return for the South's services as a balance wheel against labor agitation, the solid elements in the North should join her in a common front against all agitation of the slavery issue. His program for the tariff problem was best expressed in a letter to Abbott Lawrence in 1845: Northern manufacturers should join the planters in producing for the export market. At best it would be impossible for manufacturers to attain prosperity in the home market alone; "the great point is to get possession of the foreign market," and for that the high-duty tariff is nothing but an obstruction. The North should emulate English manufacturers by lowering duties, importing cheap raw materials, and competing aggressively for foreign trade. "When that is accomplished all conflict between the planter and the manufacturer would cease."

IV

During the last seven years of Calhoun's life the sectional conflict centered more and more on the acquisition of new territory and its division between slave and free society. Nullification had failed for lack of unity within the South. The alliance with the West was unstable and uncertain. The proposed alliance with Northern capital Calhoun could not bring about. Hence the problem of defense turned increasingly upon the attempt to acquire new slave territory in Texas, Mexico, and the vast area wrested from Mexico by war, and keeping the North from taking the West for free labor.

Calhoun's interest in Texas was defensive in intent, but exorbitantly aggressive in form. Great Britain, eager for a new market and an independent source of cotton, was encouraging Texas to remain independent by offering financial aid and protection. During 1843, when Lord Brougham and Lord Aberdeen both openly confessed Britain's intent to foster abolition along with national independence in Texas, Calhoun, then Secretary of State, stepped forward in alarm to link the annexation issue with a thoroughgoing defense of slavery. Southerners feared that another refuge for fugitive slaves and the example of an independent, free-labor cotton-producing country on their border would be a grave menace to their social structure. Britain, Calhoun frankly told the British Minister, was trying to destroy in Texas an institution "essential to the peace, safety, and prosperity of the United States"! In 1844 he published an interpretation of Britain's motives. Having freed the slaves in her own colonial empire, he charged, she had lost ground in world production of tropical products, including cotton, had endangered the investment in her empire, and had reduced it to far poorer condition than such areas as the Southern United States and Brazil, where slavery survived. Britain, in her effort "to regain and keep a superiority in tropical cultivation, commerce, and influence," was desperately trying to "cripple or destroy the productions of her successful rivals" by undermining their superior labor system.

Ardent as he had been for annexation of Texas, Calhoun was frightened during the war with Mexico by sentiment in the South for conquest and annexation of all Mexico. If Mexico were taken, he feared that the necessity of controlling her would give the executive tremendous powers and vast patronage, bring about precisely the centralization of federal power that he so feared, and finally destroy the constitutional system. He predicted that conflict between North and South over disposition of the acquired territory might easily disrupt the Union. "Mexico is for us the forbidden fruit; the penalty of eating it would be to subject our institutions to political death."

In 1846 the introduction of the Wilmot Proviso, which banned slavery from all territory to be taken from Mexico, excited the South as nothing had before. Calhoun felt that it involved a matter of abstract right upon which no compromise should be considered, even though it was unlikely that slavery would go into the territories in question. In December he told President Polk that he "did not desire to extend slavery," that it would "probably never exist" in California and New Mexico. Still he would vote against any treaty that included the Wilmot Proviso, because "it would involve a principle." [5]

Calhoun became obsessed with the North's tendency to "monopolize" the territories for free labor. In 1847, when Iowa had entered the Union and Wisconsin was ready for statehood, he expressed his fear that the territories would yield twelve or fifteen more free states. The South was fast losing that parity in the Senate which was its final stronghold of equality in the federal government. In March of that year he called for a united Southern party to force a showdown on Southern rights. In his last great speech, which was read to the Senate for him because he was dying, he declared with finality that the balance of power had already been lost. The South no longer had "any adequate means of protecting itself against . . . encroachment and oppression." Reviewing the growth of Northern preponderance, the exploitation of the South, and the progressive disintegration of the moral bonds of Union, Calhoun warned that the nation could be saved only by conceding to the South an equal right in the newly acquired Western territory [6] and amending the Constitution to restore to her the power of self-protection that she had had before the sectional balance was destroyed.

An amendment to the Constitution would be a guarantee of equality to the South. Calhoun demanded that this guarantee should take the form of the concurrent majority, which was the king pin in his political system. All through his sectional phase Calhoun had been preaching for the concurrent majority. He expressed it as early as 1833 in his speech on the Force Bill and last formulated it in the *Disquisition on Government*, published after his death. Government by numerical majorities, he always insisted, was inherently unstable; he proposed to replace it with what he called government by the whole community—that is, a government that would organically represent both majority and minority. Society should not be governed by counting heads but by considering the great economic interests, the geographical and functional units, of the nation. In order to prevent the plunder of a minority interest by a majority interest, each must be given an appropriate organ in the constitutional structure which would provide it with "either a concurrent voice in making and executing

---

[5] This was not his view alone. "It cannot be a slave country," wrote Robert Toombs to J. J. Crittenden, January 22, 1849. "We have only the point of honor to save . . . and [to] rescue the country from all danger.of agitation."

[6] It is not certain whether Calhoun had changed his mind about not expecting slavery to go into the territory, as he had admitted to Polk, or whether he still considered that the mere victory on principle was of that much importance.

the laws or a veto on their execution." Only by such a device can the "different interests, orders, classes, or portions" of the community be protected, "and all conflict and struggle between them prevented." [7]

Time had persuaded Calhoun that a dual executive would be the best means of employing the concurrent majority in the United States. The nation should have two presidents, each representing one of the two great sections, each having a veto power over acts of Congress. No measure could pass that did not win the approval of the political agents of both sections. The equality between sections that had existed at the beginning of the government would thus be restored.

Calhoun's analysis of American political tensions certainly ranks among the most impressive intellectual achievements of American statesmen. Far in advance of the event, he forecast an alliance between Northern conservatives and Southern reactionaries, which has become one of the most formidable aspects of American politics. The South, its caste system essentially intact, has proved to be for an entire century more resistant to change than the North, its influence steadily exerted to retard serious reform and to curb the power of Northern labor. Caste prejudice and political conservatism have made the South a major stronghold of American capitalism.

But prescient and ingenious as Calhoun was, he made critical miscalculations for the sectional struggle of his own time. He had a remarkable sense for the direction of social evolution, but failed to measure its velocity. His fatal mistake was to conclude that the conflict between labor and capital would come to a head before the conflict between capital and the Southern planter. Marx out of optimism and Calhoun out of pessimism both overestimated the revolutionary capacities of the working class. It was far easier to reconcile the Northern masses to the profit system than Calhoun would ever admit. He failed to see that the expanding Northern free society, by offering broad opportunities to the lower and middle classes, provided itself with a precious safety valve for popular discontents. He also failed to see that the very restlessness which he considered the North's weakness was also a secret of its strength. "The main spring to progress," he realized, "is the desire of individuals to better their

---

[7] The concurrent majority was actually operative in South Carolina from the time of Calhoun's entrance into politics, when apportionment of the state legislature was so arranged as to give one house to the seaboard plantation area and the other to the upcountry farmers. William A. Schaper has pointed out, however, that the concurrent-majority principle could work there because the minority, the planters, kept possession of power "until it had won over the majority to its interests and its institutions."
Some Southerners hoped that since the South had a faction in both major parties, she could exercise an informal equivalent of the concurrent majority within the bisectional party system rather than the Constitution itself. This plan worked for some time, but Calhoun had no faith in it for the long run. He argued that parties must ultimately partake "more or less of a sectional character," a tendency that would grow stronger with the passage of time. And if parties became sectional, the concurrent voice could be found only in a formal constitutional amendment.

condition," but he could not admit how much more intensely free society stimulated that essential desire in its working population than his cherished slave system with its "thirty lashes well laid on."

Calhoun, in brief, failed to appreciate the staying power of capitalism. At the very time when it was swinging into its period of most hectic growth he spoke as though it had already gone into decline. The stirrings of the Jackson era particularly misled him; mass discontent, which gained further opportunities for the common man in business and politics, and thus did so much in the long run to strengthen capitalism, he misread as the beginning of a revolutionary upsurge. Calhoun was, after all, an intense reactionary, and to the reactionary ear every whispered criticism of the elite classes has always sounded like the opening shot of an uprising.

Calhoun's social analysis lacked the rough pragmatic resemblance to immediate reality that any analysis must have if it is to be translated into successful political strategy. He never did find a large capitalist group in the North that would see the situation as he did. Although he joined the Whig Party for a few years after his disappointment with Jackson, a long-term alliance with such firm spokesmen of capitalist tariff economics as Clay and Webster was unthinkable. Under the Van Buren administration he returned to the Democratic fold on the subtreasury issue, and there he remained. During the late thirties, while he was still appealing to Northern conservatives to join hands with the planters, he admitted that the Whig Party, the party most attractive to Northern capital, was more difficult than the Democrats on both the tariff and abolition.

Ironically, for a long time Northern labor was ideologically closer than Northern capital to the planters. The workers had little sympathy for abolitionism, but responded with interest when Southern politicians unleashed periodic assaults on Northern wage slavery. When Francis W. Pickens, one of Calhoun's own lieutenants, rose in the House in the fall of 1837 to point out that the planters stood in relation to Northern capital "precisely in the same situation as the laborer of the North" and that they were "the only class of capitalists . . . which, as a class, are identified with the laborers of the country," Ely Moore, a labor spokesman, endorsed his position. And eight years after Calhoun's death, when James H. Hammond lashed out in a famous speech against "wage slavery," he received many letters of thanks from Northern workers for exposing their condition. Calhoun himself, organizing his presidential drive between 1842 and 1844, found strong support among many members of the former left wing of Northern democracy. Fitzwilliam Byrdsall, ardent democrat and historian of the Locofocos, wrote to him from New York City that "the radical portion of the Democratic party here, to whom free suffrage is dear and sacred, is the very portion most favorable to you." Calhoun had not long before expected this sort of man to frighten the capitalists into the arms of the planters!

The essence of Calhoun's mistake as a practical statesman was that he tried to achieve a static solution for a dynamic situation. The North, stimulated by invention and industry and strengthend by a tide of immigration, was growing in population and wealth, filling the West, and building railroads that bound East and West together. No concurrent majority, nor any other principle embodied in a parchment, could stem the tide that was measured every ten years in the census returns. William H. Seward touched upon the South's central weakness in his speech of March 11, 1850, when he observed that what the Southerners wanted was "a *political* equilibrium. Every political equilibrium requires a physical equilibrium to rest upon, and is valueless without it." In the face of all realities, the Southerners kept demanding that equality of territory and approximate equality of populations be maintained. "And this," taunted Seward, "must be perpetual!"

Moreover, the Calhoun dialectic was so starkly reactionary in its implications that it became self-defeating. There was disaster even for the South in the premise that every civilized society must be built upon a submerged and exploited labor force—what Hammond called a "mud-sill" class. *If* there must always be a submerged and exploited class at the base of society, and *if* the Southern slaves, as such a class, were better off than Northern free workers, and *if* slavery was the safest and most durable base on which to found political institutions, then there seemed to be no reason why *all* workers, white or black, industrial or agrarian, should not be slave rather than free. Calhoun shrank from this conclusion, but some Southerners did not. George Fitzhugh won himself quite a reputation in the fifties arguing along these lines. The fact that some Southerners, however few, followed Fitzhugh was an excellent one for Northern politicians to use to rouse freemen, especially those who were indifferent to the moral aspects of slavery, to take a stand against the spread of the institution.

Calhoun could see and expound very plausibly every weakness of Northern society, but his position forced him to close his eyes to the vulnerability of the South. Strong as he was on logical coherence, he had not the most elementary moral consistency. Here it is hard to follow those who, like Professor Wiltse, find in him "the supreme champion of minority rights and interests everywhere." It is true that Calhoun superbly formulated the problem of the relation between majorities and minorities, and his work at this point may have the permanent significance for political theory that is ofen ascribd to it. But how can the same value be assigned to his practical solutions? Not in the slightest was he concerned with minority rights as they are chiefly of interest to the modern liberal mind —the rights of dissenters to express unorthodox opinions, of the individual conscience against the State, least of all of ethnic minorities. At bottom he was not interested in any minority that was not a propertied minority. The concurrent majority itself was a device without relevance to the protection of dissent, but designed specifically to protect a vested interest of considerable power. Even within the South Calhoun had not the slightest desire to protect intellectual minorities, critics, and dissenters. Professor Clement Eaton, in his *Freedom of Thought in the Old South,* places him first among those politicians who "created stereotypes in the minds of the Southern people that produced intolerance." Finally, it was minority privileges rather than rights that he really proposed to protect. He wanted to give to the minority not merely a proportionate but an *equal* voice with the majority in determining public policy. He would have found incomprehensible the statement of William H. Roane, of Virginia, that he had "never thought that [minorities] had any other *Right* than that of freely, peaceably, & *legally* converting themselves into a *majority* whenever they can." This elementary right Calhoun was prompt to deny to any minority, North or South, that disagreed with him on any vital question. In fact, his first great speeches on the slavery question were prompted by his attempt to deny the right of petition to a minority.

Calhoun was a minority spokesman in a democracy, a particularist in an age of nationalism, a slaveholder in an age of advancing liberties, and an agrarian in a furiously capitalistic country. Quite understandably he developed a certain perversity of mind. It became his peculiar faculty, the faculty of a brilliant but highly abstract and isolated intellect, to see things that other men never dreamt of and to deny what was under his nose, to forecast with uncanny insight several major trends of the future and remain all but oblivious of the actualities of the present. His weakness was to be inhumanly schematic and logical, which is only to say that he thought as he lived. His mind, in a sense, was *too* masterful—it imposed itself upon realities. The great human, emotional, moral complexities of the world escaped him because he had no private training for them, had not even the talent for friendship, in which he might have been schooled. It was easier for him to imagine, for example, that the South had produced upon its slave base a better culture than the North because he had no culture himself, only a quick and muscular mode of thought. It may stand as a token of Calhoun's place in the South's history that when he did find culture there, at Charleston, he wished a plague on it.

XIV *Manifest Destiny: A Mystique or an Extension of the Area of Freedom?*

Introduction "Let me live where I will, on this side is the city, on that the wilderness, and ever I am leaving the city more and more and withdrawing into the wilderness. I should not lay so much stress on this fact if I did not believe that something like this is the prevailing tendency of my countrymen. I must walk toward Oregon and not toward Europe." So Henry David Thoreau (1817–1862) wrote of himself and his generation.

The decade of the 1840's (the Roaring, the Fabulous Forties) is preeminently the decade of the achievement in a continental territorial sense of the "Manifest Destiny" of the United States of America. The "reannexation" of Texas, the "reoccupation" of Oregon, the acquisition by war with Mexico of the provinces of New Mexico and California (comprehending the present states of California, Nevada, Utah, Arizona, New Mexico, and parts of Wyoming and Colorado)—these supply the gross material image of the accomplishment of American Manifest Destiny. But Manifest Destiny in this decade meant something else as well, something that lay deep in the ethos of the American people. Viewed as an essential part of the history of ideas in America, the motivation and ideology of Manifest Destiny, when subjected to acute analysis, throw strong light upon the spiritual, emotional, ethical, and romantic life of that day, as well as setting in a new perspective the more conventional political and economic life of the times.

As acute analysis, as perceptive interpretation, and as poetic appreciation, the works of Bernard DeVoto and of Albert K. Weinberg on this theme have surely never been equaled, if, indeed, they have been approached. DeVoto and Weinberg are not oppositional in their views of the inner meaning of "Manifest Destiny." Rather, they complement each other. Yet read together, they are quite different, quite separate, quite distinct. Through DeVoto's work—he wrote three large volumes on the westward movement during the first half of the nineteenth century—there runs a quality of warmth, of romance, of poetical conception that seems to catch the very mystique of Manifest Destiny. Weinberg's work is distinguished by the qualities of the intellect and of the mind. His analysis, clear and sensitive, applies "the methods of ideological analysis to political attitudes" and leads on to generalizations that illuminate and give new meaning to this whole period.

Build Thee More Stately Mansions
——*Bernard DeVoto*

The first Missouri Mounted Volunteers played an honorable part in the year of decision, and looking back, a private of Company C determined to write his regiment's history. He was John T. Hughes, an A.B. and a schoolmaster. Familiarity with the classics had taught him that great events are heralded by portents. So when he sat down to write his history he recalled a story which, he cautions us, was "doubtless more beautiful than true." Early in that spring of 1846, the story ran, a prairie thunderstorm overtook a party of traders who were returning to Independence, Missouri, from Santa Fe. When it passed over, the red sun had sunk to the prairie's edge, and the traders cried out with one voice. For the image of an eagle was spread across the sun. They knew then that "in less than twelve months the eagle of liberty would spread his broad pinions over the plains of the west, and that the flag of our country would wave over the cities of New Mexico and Chihuahua."

Thus neatly John T. Hughes joined Manifest Destiny and the fires that flamed in the midnight sky when Caesar was assassinated. But he missed a sterner omen.

The period of Biela's comet was seven years. When it came back in 1832 many people were terrified for it was calculated to pass within twenty thousand miles of the earth's orbit. The earth rolled by that rendezvous a month before the comet reached it, however, and the dread passed. In 1839 when the visitor returned again it was too near the sun to be seen, but its next perihelion passage was calculated for February 11, 1846. True to the assignment, it traveled earthward toward the end of 1845. Rome identified it on November 28 and Berlin saw it two days later. By mid-December all watchers of the skies had reported it. The new year began, the year of decision, and on January 13 at Washington, our foremost scientist, Matthew Maury, found matter for a new report.

Maury was a universal genius but his deepest passion was the movement of tides. In that January of '46 he was continuing his labor to perfect the basis for the scientific study of winds and current. Out of that labor came the science of oceanography, and methods of reporting the tides not only of the sea but of the air also that have been permanent, and a revolution in the art of navigation. But he had further duties as Superintendent of the Naval Observatory, and so by night he turned his telescope on Biela's

From Bernard DeVoto, *The Year of Decision: 1846* (Boston: Houghton Mifflin Company, 1950), pp. 3–10; 30–50. Reprinted by permission.

comet. That night of January 13, 1846, he beheld the ominous and inconceivable. On its way toward perihelion, Biela's comet had split in two.

This book tells the story of some people who went west in 1846. Its purpose is to tell that story in such a way that the reader may realize the far western frontier experience, which is part of our cultural inheritance, as personal experience. But 1846 is chosen rather than other years because 1846 best dramatizes personal experience as national experience. Most of our characters are ordinary people, the unremarkable commoners of the young democracy. Their story, however, is a decisive part of a decisive turn in the history of the United States.

Sometimes there are exceedingly brief periods which determine a long future. A moment of time holds in solution ingredients which might combine in any of several or many ways, and then another moment precipitates out of the possible the at last determined thing. The limb of a tree grows to a foreordained shape in response to forces determined by nature's equilibriums, but the affairs of nations are shaped by the actions of men, and sometimes, looking back, we can understand which actions were decisive. The narrative of this book covers a period when the manifold possibilities of chance were shaped to converge into the inevitable, when the future of the American nation was precipitated out of the possible by the actions of the people we deal with. All the actions it narrates were initiated, and most of them were completed, within the compass of a single calendar year. The origins of some of them, it is true, can be traced back as far as one may care to go, and a point of the book is that the effects of some are with us still, operating in the arc determined by 1846. Nevertheless, the book may properly be regarded as the chronicle of a turning point in American destiny within the limits of one year.

This is the story of some people who went west in 1846: our focus is the lives of certain men, women, and children moving west. They will be on the scene in different groupings: some emigrants, some soldiers, some refugees, some adventurers, and various heroes, villains, bystanders, and supernumeraries. It is required of you only to bear in mind that while one group is spotlighted the others are not isolated from it in significance.

Our narrative will get them into motion in the month of January, 1846. But the lines of force they traveled along were not laid down on New Year's Day, and though our stories are clear and simple, they are affected by the most complex energies of their society. They had background, they had relationships, and in order to understand how an inevitability was precipitated out of the possible, we must first understand some of the possibilities. We must look not only at our characters but at their nation, in January, 1846.

The nation began the year in crisis. It was a crisis in foreign relations. The United States was facing the possibility of two wars—with Great Britain and with Mexico. But those foreign dangers had arisen out of purely domestic energies. They involved our history, our geography, our social institutions, and something that must be called both a tradition and a dream.

Think of the map of the United States as any newspaper might have printed it on January 1, 1846. The area which we now know as the state of Texas had been formally a part of that map for just three days, though the joint resolution for its annexation, or in a delicate euphemism its "re-annexation," had passed Congress in February, 1845. Texas was an immediate leverage on the possible war with Mexico. Texas had declared itself a republic in 1836 and ever since then had successfully defended its independence. But Mexico had never recognized that sovereignty, regarded Texas as a Mexican province, had frequently warned the United States that annexation would mean war, and had withdrawn her minister immediately on the passage of the joint resolution which assured it.

In the far northwestern corner our map would tint or crosshatch a large area to signify that it was jointly occupied by the United States and Great Britain. This area would include the present states of Oregon, Washington, and Idaho, and small parts of Montana and Wyoming lying west of the continental divide. It would also include a portion of Canada, extending northward to agree with the political sentiments of the map maker, perhaps as far north as a line drawn east from the southern tip of Alaska. The whole area was known simply as "Oregon" and it was an immediate leverage on the possible war with Great Britain. For the President of the United States had been elected on a platform which required him to assert and maintain the American claim to sole possession of all "Oregon," clear up to 54° 40′, that line drawn eastward from southern Alaska,* and on January 1 the British press was belligerently resenting his preparations to do so.

West of Texas and south of Oregon, from the Pacific Ocean to the continental divide and the Arkansas River, was a still larger area which our map would show as Mexican territory. This area included the present states of California, Nevada, Utah, Arizona, New Mexico, and parts of Wyoming and Colorado. It was composed of two provinces, "California," and "New Mexico," but no American map maker could have approximated the theoretical boundary between them. It too was a powerful leverage, though not often a publicly acknowledged one, on the possible war with Mexico.

It is of absolute importance that no map maker of any nationality, even if he had been able to bound these vast areas correctly, could have filled

---

* Really from the southern tip of Prince of Wales Island.

them in. Certain trails, certain rivers, long stretches of certain mountain ranges, the compass bearings of certain peaks and watersheds, the areas inhabited by certain Indian tribes—these could have been correctly indicated by the most knowledgeful, say Thomas Hart Benton and the aged Albert Gallatin. But there were exceedingly few of these and the pure white paper which the best of them would have had to leave between the known marks of orientation would have extended, in the maps drawn by anyone else, from the Missouri River and central Texas, with only the slightest breaks, all the way to the Pacific. That blank paper would almost certainly have been lettered: "Great American Desert."

The Great American Desert is our objective—"Oregon," "New Mexico," and "California"—the lands lying west of the Louisiana Purchase. Like the Americans who occupied them, however, we must also deal with Texas, the newly annexed republic. The sum of these four geographical expressions composed, on January 1, 1846, the most acute crisis in foreign relations since the Treaty of Ghent had ended the second war with Great Britain in December, 1814, and they were bound together in what can now be understood as a system of social energies. Just how they were bound together will (the hope is) be clear by the end of this book, and we must begin by examining some of the far from simple reasons why they had produced the crisis. It will be best to lead into them by way of the man who in part expressed and in part precipitated the crisis, the President, hopefully called by some of his supporters "Young Hickory," James K. Polk.

Two years before, in the summer of 1844, the first telegraph line brought word to Washington that the Democratic convention, meeting in Baltimore, had determined to require a two-thirds vote for nomination. The rule was adopted to stop the comeback of ex-President Martin Van Buren, who had a majority. That it was adopted was extremely significant—it revealed that Van Buren had defeated himself when he refused to support the annexation of Texas. The convention was betting that the spirit of expansionism was now fully reawakened, that the annexation of Texas was an unbeatable issue, that the Democrats would sweep the country if factionalism could be quelled. Smoke-filled rooms in boarding houses scorned President Tyler (whose renomination would have split the party in two), and would not take General Cass, John C. Calhoun, or Silas Wright, all of whom were identified with factions that were badly straining the party. Factionalism, it became clear, was going to be quelled by the elimination of every prominent Democrat who had ever taken a firm stand about anything. So presently the telegraph announced that George Bancroft, with the assistance of Gideon Pillow and Cave Johnson and the indorsement of Old Hickory in the Hermitage, had brought the delegates to agree on the first dark horse ever nominated for the Presidency, Mr. Pillow's former law partner, James K. Polk.

"Who is James K. Polk?" The Whigs promptly began campaigning on that derision, and there were Democrats who repeated it with a sick concern. The question eventually got an unequivocal answer. Polk had come up the ladder, he was an orthodox party Democrat. He had been Jackson's mouthpiece and floor leader in the House of Representatives, had managed the anti-Bank legislation, had risen to the Speakership, had been governor of Tennessee. But sometimes the belt line shapes an instrument of use and precision. Polk's mind was rigid, narrow, obstinate, far from first-rate. He sincerely believed that only Democrats were truly American, Whigs being either the dupes or the pensioners of England—more, that not only wisdom and patriotism were Democratic monopolies but honor and breeding as well. "Although a Whig he seems a gentleman" is a not uncommon characterization in his diary. He was pompous, suspicious, and secretive; he had no humor; he could be vindictive; and he saw spooks and villains. He was a representative Southern politician of the second or intermediate period (which expired with his Presidency), when the decline but not the disintegration had begun.

But if his mind was narrow it was also powerful and he had guts. If he was orthodox, his integrity was absolute and he could not be scared, manipulated, or brought to heel. No one bluffed him, no one moved him with direct or oblique pressure. Furthermore, he knew how to get things done, which is the first necessity of government, and he knew what he wanted done, which is the second. He came into office with clear ideas and a fixed determination and he was to stand by them through as strenuous an administration as any before Lincoln's. Congress had governed the United States for eight years before him and, after a fashion, was to govern it for the next twelve years after him. But Polk was to govern the United States from 1845 to 1849. He was to be the only "strong" President between Jackson and Lincoln. He was to fix the mold of the future in America down to 1860, and therefore for a long time afterward. That is who James K. Polk was.

The Whigs nominated their great man, Henry Clay. When Van Buren opposed the annexation of Texas, he did so from conviction. It was only at the end of his life, some years later, that Clay developed a conviction not subject to readjustment by an opportunity. This time he guessed wrong— he faced obliquely away from annexation. He soon saw that he had made a mistake and found too clever a way out of the ropes which he had voluntarily knotted round his wrists. Smart politics have always been admired in America but they must not be too smart. The Democrats swept the nation, as the prophets had foretold. It was clear that the Americans wanted Texas and Oregon, which the platform had promised them. Polk, who read the popular mind better than his advisers did, believed that the Americans also wanted the vast and almost unknown area called New Mexico and California.

They did. Polk's election was proof that the energy and desire known as expansionism were indeed at white heat again, after a period of quiescence. This reawakening, which was to give historians a pleasant phrase, "the Roaring Forties," contained some exceedingly material ingredients. Historians now elderly made a career by analyzing it to three components: the need of certain Southern interests and Southern statesmen to seize the empty lands and so regain the power which the increasing population of the North was taking from them, the need of both Northern and Southern interests to dominate the Middle West or at least maintain a working alliance with it, and the blind drive of industrialism to free itself to a better functioning.

Now all those elements were certainly a part of the sudden acceleration of social energies signified by the election of 1844. But society is never simple or neat, and our elder historians who thus analyzed it forgot what their elders had known, that expansionism contained such other and unanalyzable elements as romance, Utopianism, and the dream that men might yet be free. It also contained another category of ingredients—such as the logic of geography, which the map of January 1, 1846, made quite as clear to the Americans then as it is to anyone today. You yourself, looking at a map in which Oregon was jointly occupied by a foreign power and all the rest of the continent west of Texas and the continental divide was foreign territory, would experience a feeling made up of incompletion and insecurity. Both incompletion and insecurity were a good deal more alive to the 1840's than anything short of invasion could make them now. And finally, expansionism had acquired an emotion that was new— or at least signified a new combination. The Americans had always devoutly believed that the superiority of their institutions, government, and mode of life would eventually spread, by inspiration and imitation, to less fortunate, less happy peoples. That devout belief now took a new phase: It was perhaps the American destiny to spread our free and admirable institutions by action as well as by example, by occupying territory as well as by practising virtue. . . . For the sum of these feelings, a Democratic editor found, in the summer of '45, one of the most dynamic phrases ever minted, Manifest Destiny.

In that phrase Americans found both recognition and revelation. Quite certainly, it made soldiers and emigrants of many men (some of them among our characters) who, without it, would have been neither, but its importance was that it expressed the very core of American faith. Also, it expressed and embodied the peculiar will, optimism, disregard, and even blindness that characterized the 1840's in America. As we shall see, the nation which believed in Manifest Destiny came only by means of severe shock and after instinctive denial to realize that Manifest Destiny involved facing and eventually solving the political paradox, the central evasion, of the Constitution—slavery. But it is even more indicative of the 1840's that those who rejected the innumerable statements of Manifest Destiny, repudiated its agencies, and denied its ends, believed in Manifest Destiny. Let Brook Farm speak for them—Brook Farm, the association of literary communists who had withdrawn from the world to establish Utopia a few miles from Boston.

For the Brook Farmers, certainly, did not speculate in Western lands and so cannot come under the economic interpretation of expansionism. Neither were they the spirit of industrialism: they had organized with the declared purpose of nullifying industrialism. Nor were they political adventurers, conspirators, or opportunists: they had formally announced their refusal to adhere to the American political system. But Manifest Destiny had no clearer or more devout statement, and the 1840's had no more characteristic expression, than the editorial which the Brook Farmers published in optimism's house organ, *The Harbinger*, when the curve of the year 1846 began to be clear:—

> There can be no doubt of the design being entertained by the leaders and instigators of this infamous business, to extend the "area of freedom" to the shores of California, by robbing Mexico of another large mass of her territory; and the people are prepared to execute it to the letter. In many and most aspects in which this plundering aggression is to be viewed it is monstrously iniquitous, but after all it seems to be completing a more universal design of Providence, of extending the power and intelligence of advanced civilized nations over the whole face of the earth, by penetrating into those regions which seemed fated to immobility and breaking down the barriers to the future progress of knowledge, of the sciences and arts: and arms seem to be the only means by which this great subversive movement towards unity among nations can be accomplished. . . . In this way Providence is operating on a grand scale to accomplish its designs, making use of instrumentalities ignorant of its purposes, and incited to act by motives the very antipodes of those which the real end in view might be supposed to be connected with or grow out of.

Thus the literary amateurs: it violates our principles but is part of a providential plan. As Providence's instrumentality Polk was much less woozy. Shortly after he was inaugurated, he explained his objectives to George Bancroft, the scholar, historian, and man of letters who had been a Democratic Brain-Truster since Jackson's time, and whom Polk would make acting Secretary of War, Secretary of the Navy, and finally Minister to Great Britain. His objectives were: the revision of the protective tariff of 1842, the re-establishment of the independent treasury, the settlement of the Oregon question, and the acquisition of California. He was to achieve them all.

. . . There were sixteen inches of ice on Walden Pond, and it undulated under a slight wind like water. Mornings, Henry Thoreau woke with a feeling that he had not answered some question asked him during sleep, but there was no question on Nature's lips. He took an axe and chopped through snow and ice but, before drinking, gazed at the sandy bottom where "waveless serenity reigns as in the amber twilight sky." Heaven, he decided, is under our feet as well as over our heads. He watched men fish through the ice for pickerel and went about a job he had set himself, to plumb the bottom of Walden, which was locally believed to have no bottom. He found it at one hundred and two feet, then, after plotting a chart, discovered that the line of greatest length intersected the line of greatest width exactly at the point of greatest depth. Might this not correspond to the law of average? Might not the two diameters of a man's thought similarly be used to determine exactly how and where his depth went down? Henry thought so, and he went on to see whether White's Pond would show the same regularity. It did.

He had cleared his plot above the lake front the preceding spring, while Polk pushed his foreign policy in the direction of war. He had planted his beans and raised the walls of his shack while Frémont and Kearny headed west, had mortared his chimney while Buchanan prepared Gillespie's instructions, and had plastered the walls while Pakenham fished through the President's ice to determine how much he must concede. These things had no present notice in Henry Thoreau's mind. He was conducting an experiment in economy. He had looked at the twin wonders of the age, the developing industrial system and the certainty of universal moral reform, and had seen no need to pay tribute to either. The first chapter of *Walden* accurately analyzes the bank failures, bond repudiations, mortgages, farmsteads, and factories of the thirties and forties, but Thoreau's experiment dealt with a preliminary, or antecedent, problem, the survival of the mind's integrity in such a system. In Arcadia he had seen no one pounding stone, and he wanted to free himself from subjection to horses, plowing, and the day's waste—as the system would have to do if it were to inclose his loyalty. His house cost him twenty-eight dollars and a shilling; at the end of a year he had needed $25.21¾ to live on. (He appears not to have discussed capitalization with the Provident Institution.) Meanwhile he had written *A Week on the Concord and Merrimac Rivers,* beginning it, very likely, during the January of Mr. Buchanan's insubordination, and had begun the notes that were to acquire form in *Walden.* He had also acted as inspector of snowstorms and rainstorms, and had proved conclusively that "it is not necessary that a man should earn his living by the sweat of his brow, unless he sweats easier than I do." . . . What else he had proved we shall see.

There was a further element in Thoreau's expatriation from Concord. The village had reached a tension of conversational reform. Emerson had observed that "Mr. Alcott and Mr. Wright cannot chat or so much as open the mouth on aught less than a new solar system and the prospective education in the nebulae." Thoreau, though he inexplicably thought Alcott so great a man that nature could not let him die, began to repudiate his conversation as soon as the Walden pines shut off the rhythms of that noble drool. Henry had stayed too long among the pure and garrulous; he felt that his manners had "been corrupted by communication with the saints." Concord had suggested to him that the reforms and liberations it exhaled in sitting rooms might not be a cure of the world's ills but only for dyspepsia. "What so saddens the reformer," he had come to think, "is not his sympathy with his fellows in distress but though he be the holiest son of God, is his private ail." Truly, wailing did come up from Southern plains, but was it the wailing alone of blacks, and just how shall we begin to act on it? Just what intemperance and brutality would best serve for the beginning of redemption? "If anything ail a man, so that he does not perform his functions, if he have a pain in the bowels even, for that is the seat of sympathy, he forthwith sets about reforming—the world."

Here Henry was glancing at Harvard Village, ten miles northwest of Walden, where at Fruitlands the pain in Mr. Alcott's bowels had not succeeded in bringing in the rule of right reason, though it had reformed the world for some months. More particularly, toward West Roxbury, where the far happier Brook Farmers, in smocks, ignorant of the catastrophe preparing for them, hated Polk but praised Providence for using him as an instrument, and spent the January evenings chatting and munching apples before log fires, reading *Consuelo* for beautiful sentiments and, as preparation for the more stately mansion they were building, Fourier's *Theory of the Human Passions.*

The smock wearers also were making an experiment in economy, and they were very happy. The newest Newness made amazing progress, they loved one another and humanity, the children did so marvelously well in the progressive school. Everything was so clear, so easily hand-tinted with pretty words, though it was among the benefits of Association that they came less and less to need words, the twitch of an eyebrow conveying a philosophy and the intuitions so sharpening that they could read letters by simply pressing the envelope against the forehead. This showed how their "right development" refined the passions. Wrong development, which the world's people suffered, produced selfishness, injustice, duplicity; but right development produced harmony, justice, unity. Charles Fourier told them so, who was part Alcott and part Marx. Under Association, which was Fourier's principle of economy, right development would go farther still. It would soften and regulate the temperature (a desirable achievement in January at West Roxbury) and increase the warmth at the poles, correct the heat of the equator, bring on eternal springtime, fertilize the desert, and prevent the drying up of streams. Moreover, it would domesticate the beaver and zebra to man's uses and increase the fish in lakes and rivers some twenty-fold. (Thus Mr. Albert Brisbane, translating Fourier. He omitted Fourier's further promise that lions would turn into anti-lions, a soothed, humanitarian species, other savage carnivores into playful anti-beasts, and the great sea itself into soda pop.) Association would also put an end to larceny, there would be no theft, no sharp business practices; nine tenths or more of the diseases that afflict man under incoherence or Civilization would disappear, and men would live three times as long. Moreover, Zachary Taylor's profession would be obsolete and fleets and armies would wither away. So much for Polk.

(Right development had not yet, however, produced the anti-cow. Nathaniel Hawthorne, who had bought two $500 shares in Brook Farm and would later sue to get his money back, had had to flee Association because he could no longer bring himself to fork the bright, symbolic gold out of the stalls.)

Two months short of final extinction, there burned here more appealingly than anywhere else a hope that had built more than two score communities in the last two decades, most of them already dead. It was the design of Brook Farm: "1. To indoctrinate the whole people of the United States with the principles of associative unity. 2. To prepare for the time when the nation, like one man, shall reorganize its townships on the basis of perfect justice." Thus American millennialism had changed its phase: it had given up Christ in favor of Refined Passions and Virtuous Labor. In the earlier phase, the expectation of perfect sainthood in the immediate (or the oncoming) Kingdom of God had begotten such associations as the Shakers, the Latter-day Saints, the Rappites, and the Disciples of Christ. In the new phase a different perfection was expected, perfect justice as an outgrowth of perfect co-operation—the co-operation, that is, of literary people.

Industrialism had spread its first great wave across the countryside, and a misunderstood abhorrence of its bleak factories oppressed sensitive spirits. The sensitive found only two courses: they could flee from industrialism or they could master it with virtue. The first era of Brook Farm, now over, had attempted flight: the literary raking hay in yellow pantaloons, a small but elevated company baking their bread from their own handmade flour to Plato's dream, presumably as an inspiration to greasy mechanics and stunted factory girls. There were many similar companies of the sensitive, and they had reached perihelion at Fruitlands, where the Great Inane voiced thoughts while Mrs. Alcott and the children gathered in the barley, a poor wench was excommunicated for eating a shred of vile flesh, and in the end Alcott turned his face to the wall and hoped to die because virtue had failed. Of forty such congregations, John Humphrey Noyes, who may be granted authority, said that they failed because right reason was not a working substitute for the grace of God, and because you could not defeat industrialism with plow and scythe.

For the others, those who would master industrialism with virtue,

Charles Fourier was the way and the light, and the second era of Brook Farm was dedicated to him. Fourier promised the sensitive that the hideous factories could be transformed into beauty. You refined the passions. You dignified and ennobled labor. You made industry the more attractive as its operations were the more laborious and unpleasant. You put Corinthian columns round the prison house of labor and built it in "fields beautifully laid out and diversified by clusters of fruit and forest trees, flower beds, and fountains." You supplied band concerts and bright uniforms and a series of Eagle Scout badges for the ennobled mechanics. You beguiled the children by inducing them to play in little workshops with little tools. And again and always you refined the passions, inviting mankind to change its heart, to enter into the womb and be born again a second time, to sink the brute and bring the angel in.

Yet mortgages had to be paid, the brute lingered and the angel delayed, and the literary ended in despair. Between Charles A. Dana of Brook Farm, going out to sound Association's trumpet call by lecturing on "Reform Movements Originating among the Producing Classes," and Charles A. Dana of the *Sun*, the century's ablest public disbeliever in mankind, is just the paradox that in all ages overcomes the literary dream. The literary will accept no hybrid of brute and angel; they desire Utopia and will not settle for the human race. They love the people but they hate the mob. On George Ripley's word, and he was the founder of Brook Farm, mankind is dwarfed and brutish. In that common despair ended all that Association had to say.

We are to see several answers to George Ripley worked out to the westward. And at Walden another answer was worked out, to Ripley and to all the decade's reforms as Henry Thoreau saw them. Might not the pain in a reformer's bowels, Thoreau wondered, be just an egoism that debauched his cause? It was necessary to rescue the drowning but also you must tie your shoestrings. Most men lived lives of quiet desperation, and Thoreau could not see that they grew more desperate in factories than on farms, in colleges, or at reason's feast in Mr. Alcott's house. He went down to talk to the Irishmen who were building the Fitchburg railroad, whose whistle he welcomed without a shudder. The railroad was industrialism but also it was making toward Oregon. He anticipated Mr. MacLeish in perceiving that "the rails are laid on them and they are covered with sand, and the cars run smoothly over them." But he would waste no sorrow on them so long as farmers must be subject to their cattle or any man whatsoever was involved in "bankruptcy and repudiation, the springboards from which much of our civilization vaults and turns its somersets."

In short, Thoreau believed that the factory could not be fled from and that it could not be beautified by refining the passions. Labor was dignified only as the laborer was not thought dwarfed and bruitish but granted membership in the human race. And with the race, he told his listeners, you must go much farther back than you have ever dreamed. He who wants help wants everything. Nothing can be effected but by one man. You may begin by sawing the little sticks, or you may saw the great sticks first, but sooner or later you must saw them all. So on the banks of Walden he sat him down, "in the Presidency of Polk, five years before the passage of Webster's Fugitive Slave Bill," to grow his beans and write his book. It was not by chance that when Henry Thoreau went out to walk his needle settled west.

American literature gained a flowerier Brook Farm, this spring of '46. The minister in London who was interpreting the Peel government and the jingo press to Buchanan was Louis McLane. A Tammany technician who had assisted the campaign was sent with him as secretary of legation. In May Buchanan was to receive a letter from McLane earnestly desiring the removal of his secretary of legation, "for the sake of the honor as well as the interest of the country." Mr. Gansevoort Melville, the secretary in question, had taken to London with him the manuscript of a younger brother's book about the Marquesas Islands. Gansevoort had sold it and now *Typee* was being printed in both England and America. Sweet, artless, prismatic with an aspiration that was not Concord Village nor the United States Senate nor the Oregon emigration but partook of all three, it described a poet's stay among some gentle cannibals. Chatting with his Mehevis and Kory-Kory's, Melville feels a splendid scorn for Alcott's orphic platitudes and the colonists sweating with hayforks at West Roxbury. Better in coral bays to swim with islanders uncorrupted by reason, to sleep beside them under thatched palm leaves unregardful of factories, to dine on pork in the pi-pi where the gorged chiefs smoke their coconut-shell pipes. The city of Lowell is obliterated altogether and nothing need be considered but sunrise and violet lagoons and the surf coming in. Moreover Fayaway's shoulders wear epaulettes of tattoo, her tappa skirt ends at the knees, and her tunic makes no effort to conceal her young breasts. . . . This mansion opening to the westward, though built of dream, is also part of expansionism, and though Melville might despise Alanno of Hio-Hio, he breathed the same air.

(But Fayaway's breasts were too sweetly displayed, her olive-tinted thighs were bare when Melville swam with her, and many readers exercised their privilege of conjecture. Moreover, Melville had denounced the missionaries, who were too much debauching paradise with a sense of shame and the city of Lowell's cotton cloth. The nation would hear no criticism of righteousness, and his publishers hurriedly altered such sheets as were not yet bound and rushed another printing which omitted comment on the godly. Meanwhile, in early '46, he sat down to write *Typee's* successor, in Lansingburg, New York, and began to court the daughter of

Lemuel Shaw. In the end he married her and found no tattooing on her shoulders; if she had breasts, no one crushed flowers between them. She is implacable in our literature. Her husband's work turned aside, after *Omoo*, into phantasies of incest and at last an orphic impotence that has too much in common with Bronson Alcott's noblest thoughts.)

Mr. Hawthorne was back in Salem, where a happy marriage had freed him of the old phobia that had kept him from coming outdoors by day. He was writing to his friend George Bancroft, Secretary of the Navy, in hope of the Salem post office, and was due, by summer, to get the custom-house where he was to meet certain ghosts and in old papers was to find a scarlet initial embroidered with threads of gold. Mr. Emerson was finishing his lectures on Representative Men in Boston and making notes quite as acute as Thoreau's about Fourier, reform, politicians, and slavery. Though he was whiggish, he was no Whig. "These rabble at Washington are really better than the snivelling opposition. They have a sort of genius of a bold and manly cast, though Satanic. They see, against the unanimous expression of the people [the seer was wrong, here, and would amend that judgment before the spring was out], how much a little well-directed effrontery can achieve, how much crime the people will bear, and they proceed from step to step. . . ."

Longfellow heard Emerson lecture and worked on *Evangeline*, the second canto, where the lovers' marriage contract is signed in Acadia just when the English ships "ride in the Gaspereau's mouth with their cannon pointed against us." The menace of those guns or something graver oppressed him through January and he could not shake off a heaviness of spirit. Perhaps his gloom was just the Cambridge winter: "This dull dismal cold crushes me down, as if the sky were falling; or as if I were one of the four dwarfs of the northern mythology, who uphold the dome of heaven upon their shoulders." Or maybe it was a poet's premonition as, foreboding but helpless, he saw his country moving inexorably toward war. And, seeing, could remember what he had written four years before:—

> *There is a poor, blind Samson in this land,*
> *Shorn of his strength and bound in bonds of steel,*
> *Who may, in some grim revel, raise his hand,*
> *And shake the pillars of this Commonweal,*
> *Till the vast Temple of our liberties*
> *A shapeless mass of wreck and rubbish lies.*

Walking to Boston with Longfellow, hoping to lighten his dull mood, James Russell Lowell felt the pillars of the commonweal begin to shake. It was a literary achievement of Polk's election that it had stiffened a dilettante into a serious writer. Lowell had written when the Democrats triumphed:—

Careless seems the great Avenger; history's pages but record
  One death-grapple in the darkness 'twixt old systems and the Word;
Truth forever on the scaffold, Wrong forever on the throne,
  Yet that scaffold sways the future and, behind the dim Unknown,
Standeth God within the shadow, keeping watch above his own.

Thereafter he could not be satisfied with the sweet-lavender asininity of Brook Farm; he had found steel and an edge. Since writing it he had married his beloved bluestocking, Maria White, had honeymooned in Philadelphia, had done some prentice work writing tracts for the Abolitionists, and now had come home to Elmwood. On the last day of '45 his daughter Blanche was born and James is seen briefly in January dreaming of a time when she will be "a great, strong, vulgar, mud-pudding-baking, tree-climbing little wench" . . . and beginning some articles for a London paper that will be Lowell taking up arms and going forth to war.

But do not suppose that Mr. Polk lacked literary support. The Democratic Party had an organ in Brooklyn and now there began to resound from it the barbaric if adolescent yawp of Mr. Walter, as he still signed it, Whitman.

Whitman could discern no danger to the eastward: "As for the vaunted ocean-sway of Great Britain, we laugh it to scorn! It can never compete with us, either in time of peace or war. Our Yankee ingenuity has built better ships and manned them with hardier crews than any other nation on earth." A flag goes up on the *Eagle* building, and "Ah! its broad folds are destined to float yet—and we, haply, shall see them—over many a good square mile which now owns a far different emblem." Where? "The more we reflect on the matter of annexation as involving a part of Mexico, or even the main bulk of that Republic, the more do doubts and obstacles resolve themselves away, the more plausible appears that at first glance most difficult consummation. . . . Then there is California, in the way to which lovely tract lies Santa Fe; how long a time will elapse before *they* shine as two new stars in our mighty firmament?" Expansion finds its incident: "Mexico, though contemptible in many respects, is an enemy deserving a vigorous 'lesson.' We have coaxed, excused, listened with deaf ears to the insolent gasconade of her government, submitted thus far to a most offensive rejection of an ambassador personifying the American nation, and waited for years without payment of the claims of our injured merchants." And Manifest Destiny its broadest sentiment: "It is from such materials—from the Democracy, with its manly heart and its lion strength spurning the ligatures wherewith drivellers would bind it—that we are to expect the great FUTURE of this Western World! a scope involving such unparalleled human happiness and rational freedom, to such unnumbered myriads, that the heart of a true *man* leaps with a mighty joy only to think of it!"

Adolescent but perfectly expressive of Walter Whitman's countrymen, in January, 1846.

California, January 24, 1846.
"Many weeks of hardships, close trials, and anxieties have tried me severely, and my hair is turning gray before its time. But all this passes, *et le bon temps viendra.*" Thus Childe Harold's American heir, writing to his wife from Yerba Buena, on the Bay of San Francisco. And, receiving that letter of January 24 in Washington and learning that a Mr. James Magoffin (who will be an actor in our drama) can take an answer to Bent's Fort on the Arkansas, whence it will be forwarded to California, Jessie Benton Frémont grieves: "Poor papa, it made tears come to find that you had begun to turn gray. [He was thirty-three.] You must have suffered much and been very anxious 'but all that must pass. . . . I had not had so much pleasure in a very great while as today. The thought that you may hear from me and know that all are well and that I can tell you again how dearly I love you makes me as happy as I can be while you are away."

Young Francis Parkman found it natural to prefix quotations from *Childe Harold* to the chapters of *The Oregon Trail.* But it was in the person of John Charles Frémont that the nation's enthusiasm for the poetry of Lord Byron found a career. We are to follow him through knotty and hardly soluble controversies. They will be less obscure if it is kept in mind that Frémont was primarily a literary man . . . who had a literary wife.

Greatness was a burden on Childe Harold's soul but nature kept the lines a little out of drawing. Born in high romance outside the law, he had grown up a young Rousseau. He had found a profession plotting the wilderness for the Topographical Corps. His native poetry responded to the solitudes and he had mastered the skilled crafts of living there. If his father's romance was out of Alexandre Dumas, his own was out of Italian opera. It rose in a fine cadenza when, secretly married to Jessie, the beautiful, bluestocking daughter of Thomas Hart Benton, he stood before the Senator to announce defiance of his will. Benton's rage had been know continentally ever since he had shot it out with Andrew Jackson in a community brawl. It now turned on Frémont but to violins Jessie stepped forward and sang her aria, "Whither thou goest I will go, and where thou lodgest I will lodge." Benton, who was one of the best-educated men in Congress, surrendered to a literary allusion.

An obscure lieutenant of topographical engineers had become the son-in-law of the most powerful Senator, of the Senator, furthermore, who was the greatest expansionist, whose lifelong vision it had been to make all the West American. Also, greatness had secured the assistance of a national spotlight. Benton and his colleague Linn had Frémont put in command of two explorations of the West whose sole purpose was to advertise the Oregon country. The first took him to South Pass and a little beyond; the second to Oregon and, looping back, to California by a spectacular if injudicious winter crossing of the Sierra. He proved himself a first-rate wilderness commander, learning his new trade from two of its masters, Kit Carson and Tom Fitzpatrick. He traveled little country that his instructors had not had by heart for twenty years, blazed no trails, though the Republicans were to run him for the Presidency as the Pathfinder, and did little of importance beyond determining the latitude and longitude of many sites which the mountain men knew only by experience and habit. But he learned mountain and desert skills well, was tireless in survey and analysis, and enormously enjoyed himself.

Also he was a literary man and the Thunderer was his father-in-law. Benton roared in the Senate, the other expansionists chimed in, and Frémont had given the West to the American people. With Jessie's eager help he wrote his two reports, which were far more important than his travels. The government printed them, first separately, then together, and sowed them broadcast. The westering nation read them hungrily. Frémont chasing buffalo, Galahad Carson reclaiming the orphaned boy's horses from the Indians, Odysseus Godey riding charge against hordes of the red butchers —there was here a spectacle that fed the nation's deepest need. They were adventure books, they were charters of Manifest Destiny, they were texts of navigation for the uncharted sea so many dreamed of crossing, they were a pageant of daring, endurance, and high endeavor in the country of peaks and unknown rivers. With Benton's advertising, they made Frémont a popular image of our Western wayfaring. Now he could come downstage center with the light on him and begin his role as a hero of romantic drama.

We have noted the start of his third expedition, from St. Louis, in June, 1845. Carson was his adjutant again. Fitzpatrick was with him for a while but was detached to accompany Lieutenant Abert on that other subtly motivated "exploration" to the Southwest. He had such other mountain men as Dick Owens, Lucien Maxwell, Basil Lajeunesse, Alexis Godey, and Joe Walker. The usefulness to Polk of this third expedition, its part in the great game, is clear. While the crises with Mexico and Great Britain were intensifying, on the frontier of Oregon and California there would be an army officer and sixty armed men, most of them thirty-third-degree mountain men. . . . Now there was making toward him a lieutenant of marines vastly impressed by anti-American demonstrations in Mexico City. The lieutenant had been ordered to show him instructions directing the consul at Monterey to procure a peaceful revolution in California, and also carried private letters from Benton and Benton's daughter. In January, Lieutenant Gillespie was crossing Mexico with exceeding slowness, to sail for Honolulu on February 22.

In January greatness burgeoned in Frémont's soul. He had reached his stage and time was on the march. It might be that some great deed could be done. And from then on to the end of his life he was to go, always subtly, astray. Nothing came out quite the way it should have done. Lord Byron, who had imagined him, could not make him rhyme.

He had reached Sutter's Fort (the site of Sacramento) on December 9 of '45, after the outstanding exploration of his career which broke a trail across the Salt Desert west of Great Salt Lake to Ogden's or Mary's River, which Frémont renamed the Humboldt. . . . Well, not quite the first passage of that white waste, though Frémont sincerely believed that it was. Jedediah Smith, the great mountain man, had crossed it from the west, east, south of Frémont's trail, in 1827. Carson seems not to have known of Smith's crossing, though both he and Joe Walker should have known, and it was indicated on at least two well-known maps with which it was Frémont's business to be wholly familiar. No matter, that crossing (under Walker's guidance) was notable enough, and so was the earlier stretch (under Carson's guidance) which had brought the party from the Grand River to the White River and on to the Green.

At the Humboldt Frémont sent the larger part of his force into California under Joe Walker. Then, after another valuable survey, he divided his force again and led a picked party in a forced winter crossing of the high Sierra. The venture was foolhardy, was disapproved by Carson, served only Frémont's consciousness of brave deeds—and beat the snows by just a little while. He and his gaunt companions came down into the great green valley. Sutter fed them and they waited for Walker's party to join them.

Walker delayed, having mistaken the rendezvous appointed. Frémont had now reached his theater and he was restless. He marched his little group vaguely toward Oregon, whither he had been ordered, turned back to Sutter's again (past a site on the American River where Sutter had considered building a sawmill), and on January 14 started south to find his larger party. He met some of the California Indians who lived on horses stolen from their decayed relatives, the mission peons. So he redressed an injury they had done him on his last visit, two years before. Owens, Carson and the Delaware scouts got fresh scalps for their leggins in three sharp, unnecessary skirmishes. It was at least a theatrical deed but it was not judicious. There had arrived in California, from a Mexican government that feared war, orders to warn out of the province all foreigners who were not licensed to hold land. The warning had not been issued but the orders directing it had begot suspicion and unrest. And now a foreigner, accompanied by the mountain men whom the Californians knew from years of forays against their horse herds, was marching through their province killing Indians. To what end? If he meant nothing worse, did he mean to stir up an Indian war?

Frémont went back to Sutter's Fort. He got a passport from Sutter and went to Yerba Buena, where he wrote the letter quoted above. Then he moved down the coast to Monterey, the seagirt town where Richard Henry Dana had first sent down a royal yard and heard the mate's "Well done" with as much satisfaction as ever he had felt in Cambridge on seeing a "*bene*" at the foot of a Latin exercise. Here he called formally on the consul, Larkin, to whom Gillespie was bringing secret instructions.

Sea and sky are pleasant at Monterey, and Frémont stayed on drinking the excellent native wines and talking with the shrewd, hard-bitten consul. On January 29 the prefect, Don Manuel Castro, inquired through Larkin what errand had brought an American army officer to the golden shore. Frémont answered that though he was an army officer his errand was not military but peaceful, to determine the best trade route to the Pacific, and that his company were not soldiers but civilians. That was true. He was a touch diplomatic, however, when he added that he had left his party on the frontier—he did not know where they were but did know that they were moving through the interior—and that he had come to Monterey for supplies. Then another Castro, Don José, the military commander of California (who was bickering with the governor, Don Pío Pico, and whom Larkin had cozened a good way toward revolution), gave Frémont permission to winter in the valley of the San Joaquin. Frémont told Don José that, eventually, he would want to go home along the southern route, up the Gila River.

But he did not go to the San Joaquin Valley, which was east of the coastal mountains and distant from the settlements. He stayed on where he was. Later he was to explain that he had lingered here like any tourist, in the hope of finding a place to build a house for his mother. Maybe. But he was hearing stories from resident Americans. And destiny was stirrring in his soul.

On January 14 James Clyman, encamped in the mountain chaos of northern California, wrote in his journal:—

Heard that Mr. Fremont had arived at suitors Fort and still more recently that Mr. Hastings and Party had likewise arived Both from the U. States. But no information has yet arived of the Politicks in the states in fact information of all Kinds Travels slow and is very uncertain when it has arived you know nothing certain unless you see it yourself.

Jim Clyman, a master mountain man, thus notes the coming of two California authors. Clyman's own role in our story will unfold presently; his immediate convenience here is that he also had literary moments. He had written into his journal a treatise on the hunting of grizzly bears and, just before it, a more extended one on California and the Californians. He found the latter "a proud Lazy indolent people doing nothing but ride after herds from place to place without any appearent object," whose labor and drudgery were done by Indians "kept in a state of Slavery haveing or Receiving no compensation for their labour except a scanty allowance of subsistence . . . and perhaps a cotton Shirt and wool sufficient to make a coarse Blanket." Their government was a series of revolutions, "every change for the worse," and the change meaning merely that "the revenue has fallen into other hands." And "in fact the Military and all parts of the Government are weak imbecile and poorly organized and still less respected."

Jim Clyman, however, liked the California scenery. And he was quite clear about such countrymen of his as he met there. "The Foreigners which have found their way to this country are mostly a poor discontented set of inhabitants and but little education hunting for a place as they [want] to live easy only a few of them have obtained land and commenced farming and I do not hear of but one man that has gone to the trouble and Expence to get his title confirmed and fixed beyond altiration and dispute."

Clyman lingered along the Putah and other mountain creeks during January, chronicling the rains and watching the lush spring come on. And, doubtless, remembering his past. It was his private past, but to saturation it was the American past also.

January in California was already spring. The rains had wrought their resurrection and Jim Clyman "noticed the manseneto trees in full Bloom . . . an evergreen shrub growing in a thick gnarled clump . . . and would make a beautiful shade for a door yard." The season was "fine growing weather verry much resembling a Missouri April or an Eastern May."

But in Missouri and the East January was still winter, an uncommon hard winter. The prairies were deep under snow, frost sank deep in the ground, the wind whistled by from the north and the boughs of trees fired pistol shots when they moved in it. It was a season suspended, a time to finish jobs while the stock stamped in the barn all day long, a time for talking.

They talked in country stores, at the post offices, in the kitchens of farmhouses—along the Sangamon, in the Western Reserve, in the bluegrass country, under the shadow of Mount Equinox. The little weeklies—*Journal, Sentinel, Freedom's Herald*—reprinted what the Washington *Union* said about Texas, the *National Intelligencer's* appraisal of the British fleet, a summary of the impending crisis based on *Niles' Register*. Gittin' on to war, I guess. Polk's bound to take no sass from Johnny Bull, no, nor the Greasers, neither. Or Polk's set to make us fight a war if he can't get slave territory noways else. ("They just want this Californy So's to lug new slave states in, to abuse ye an' to scorn ye', An' to plunder ye like sin.") They talked very much like Benton, Buchanan, Webster, Lincoln, Whitman, Emerson, Dana, Thoreau. Fist on the table, Pa brought the verdict in. Dave listened and had his say but would not mention a young dream of Her Majesty's frigate striking her colors in humiliation or dark-skinned lancers dying in the Halls of Montezuma while a Hoosier farm boy waved an unfamiliar sword. And Ma looked at Dave, a firstborn son whom President Polk might send to war.

But to a long-peacful nation war was an unreal haze on the far horizon. Whereas here at hand, in the Sangamon country or in the Green Mountains, next to Perkins' store or half a mile up the crick, someone who might be named, say, Bill Bowen had sold his place. Bill and Mother, the girls, and three of the boys were going west.

Strange paraphernalia gathered in the Bowen barn and the Bowens were preparing a granary that would have seen the family through a famine year. At least two hundred pounds of flour or meal per person, the *Guide* said, *The Emigrants' Guide to Oregon and California* by Lansford W. Hastings, whose arrival in California Jim Clyman had recorded. All the Bowens thumbed that small volume, arguing, checking, refuting. Twenty pounds of sugar, ten pounds of salt . . . everyone will require at least twice as much as he would need at home, since there will be no vegetables . . . some buffalo can be counted on—and along the icebound Sangamon Bill Bowen sees himself riding down a shaggy beast straight out of fable . . . such goods for the Indian trade as beads, tobacco, handker-chiefs, cheap pantaloons, butcher knives, fish hooks—so young Bill and Nancy and Henry Clay and Joe will truly trade fish hooks for moccasins with a feathered topknot beside streams that are also straight out of fable. That topknot looks just like Tecumseh or Pontiac, and the streams of fable, the Platte, the Snake, the Green, are just such known rivers as the Sangamon, the Connecticut, the Maumee. While the north wind howls over the rooftree, it seems impossible that, come summer, Bill and Nancy Bowen will be unyoking the oxen while the "caral" forms on the banks of the Sweetwater, but they will be, for on page 147 Mr. Hastings says so.

This Hastings was a Frémont in miniature. He is an elusive soul, not much can be said about him with certainty. A young man on the make, he was at this moment engaged in a grandiose and still wholly theoretical real-estate enterprise on the golden shore, and he was the local agent of a bigger one managed from Washington which was a kind of gaudy bet on an insider's guess that there would be war. But he also had specula-tions—or visions—more gaudily ambitious. He may have meditated another overlordship on the frontier of empire, like the one which Sutter had actually established at New Helvetia. He may have seen himself—he would only have been one of a good many—as a kind of Sam Houston, president of another Lone Star Republic. He may have intended to utilize the opportunities provided for a smart man with nerve—precisely as Frémont did. Rumors connected him—loosely—with the Mormons and, on grounds that are apparently more substantial, with one of the current revolutionary intrigues. Whatever was in his mind, he did not have quite enough stuff.

Put him down as a smart young man who wrote a book—it is not a unique phenomenon in literature—without knowing what he was talking about. As the first head of the California Chamber of Commerce, the first Booster on the golden shore. He went from his home town, Mount Vernon, Ohio, to Oregon in 1842 with Elijah White's famous caravan. He found no opening for his talents in that sober commonwealth and moved on to California. He liked what he saw, he perceived there were opportunities for smart men, so he wrote a prospectus and took it east in 1844. It was published at Cincinnati in 1845 and Hastings went back to California. Jim Clyman heard of him just when the Bowens and the Smiths and the Does were reading it. And while they were reading it Mr. Hastings formed a new design, one which shifted him from merely mischievous advertising to really dangerous activity. As, farther along, we shall see.

"Here perpetual summer is in the midst of unceasing winter; perennial spring and never failing autumn stand side by side, and towering snow clad mountains forever look down upon eternal verdure." That strain was not as familiar in '46 as the years have made it now. Bill Bowen, who has to plunge between frozen walls of snow to lug in endless armfuls of hickory lengths, reads with an understandable fascination that no fires are needed in California except to cook by, and those usually outdoors. Mother's knuckles are gnarled and stiff with rheumatism begotten by prairie winters —but by that violet sea it is warmer in winter than in summer, and even in December vegetation is in full bloom. (My sakes! hollyhocks, sweet william, carnation pinks at Christmas time in your own dooryard!) Aunt Esther is racked by chills and fever every autumn, her thin shoulders wrapped with a shawl even in August. But "there being no low, marshy regions, the noxious miasmatic effluvia . . . is here nowhere found" and "while all this region . . . is entirely exempt from all febrific causes, it is also entirely free from all sudden changes and extreme variableness of climate or other causes of catarrhal or consumptive affections." So Aunt Esther can ease her tired old bones in California, and Nancy will not sniffle all winter long, and pink will come back to little Bob's cheeks, they will not have to watch him die of lung fever, after all.

And such farms! Young Bill, chipping at the frozen droppings of the cows, may meditate on the information that California stock require neither feeding nor housing, nor other care, nor any expense. Moreover, Mr. Hastings has seen oats half an inch thick through the stalk and eight feet high, thousands of acres at a stretch. Clover grows to five feet, covering the hills with natural hay. A single stalk of wheat forms seven heads and the grain runs four pounds to the bushel heavier than any the Bowens know. Seventy bushels to the acre, often up to a hundred and twenty bushels—and next year sixty-one bushels spontaneously, with no sowing at all. Also two crops in one twelvemonth, and up to sixty bushels of corn per acre, and wild flax waves as far as the eye can see, and the soil grows everything, tobacco, rice, cotton, crabapples, plums, strawberries the largest and most delicious in the world, peaches blossoming in January, such grapes as you cannot believe in.

Bill Bowen had no reason to know that there were optimisms in Hastings' book. The advertiser told him too candidly that there was no scarcity of fuel east of the Platte River, that all the streams he would cross were easily fordable, that buffalo would be plentiful for hundreds of miles beyond the Rockies, that they could be herded like cattle, that the California Indians were inoffensive, and so on. Publicity is an art of omission— and Hastings' need was to trump Oregon, which drew most of the emigration. There were few difficulties, he said, till you reached the place where the road forked. On the fork that led to Oregon the travel became dreadful and hazardous at once—and even if you survived it you would have only unfruitful Oregon for all your labors. Some remarks here about five months of rain and sleet, whereas rain in California was California rain. They read this in the Sangamon country. They also read the barker's light suggestion that a fine way to shorten the trip would be to try a route which Mr. Hastings had so far not bothered to try (and no one had yet broken), a possible cutoff from Fort Bridger (which Hastings had barely seen) to the southern end of Great Salt Lake and thence due west to Ogden's river (country about which Hastings knew nothing whatever). The saving of several hundred miles seemed promising on a winter evening in the kitchen.

Much more widely read, Frémont's was a much better book. It knew what it was talking about, and when Bill Bowen read that there was wood or water in a given place, or good soil, or difficult travel, he could count on it. The myth of the Great American Desert went down before this literary man's examination—and before his vision (like his father-in-law's) of cities rising in wasteland and the emptiness filling with fat farms. It was filled with solid facts that solid minds could use: it told about the winds, the water, the timber, the soil, the weather. It was extraordinarily seeing and intuitive, remarkably accurate. In the book he wrote, Frémont deserves well of the Republic.

But the book had a much greater importance than this: it fed desire. The wilderness which was so close to Frémont's heart that he has dignity only when he is traveling it was the core of the nation's oldest stream. Kit Carson, Tom Fitzpatrick, Alexis Godey, Basil Lajeunesse, his mountain men, were this generation's embodiment of a wish that ran back beyond Daniel Boone, beyond Jonathan Carver, beyond Christopher Gist, innumerable men in buckskins, forest runners, long hunters, rivermen, *gens du nord*, the company of gentlemen and adventurers of the far side of the hill. Something older than Myles Standish or Captain John Smith fluttered a reader's pulse when the mountain men worked their prodigies before Frémont's admiring eyes. It responded to his exaltation when, pounding his rifle on the saddle to seat a fresh load, he charged through dust clouds at the snorting buffalo. It quickened when he reached the highest peak of the Wind River divide and there pressed between leaves of his notebook a honey bee that was making westward. He went on—across deserts, through untrodden gulches, up slopes of aspen, over the saddle, along the ridge, down the far side. He smelled sagebrush at dawn, he smelled rivers in the evening—alkalai in sun-hardened earth when a shower had passed, pines when the pollen fell, roses and sweet peas and larkspur, carrion, sulphur, the coming storm, greasewood, buffalo dung in the smoke of campfires. He saw the Western country with eager eyes—saw it under sun, bent and swollen by mirage, stark, terrible, beautiful to the heart's longing, snow on the peaks, infinite green and the night stars.

That was what the pulse answered in Frémont's book. And, looking at Bill Bowen, asking why this settled citizen of Sangamon County or Brattleboro or the Mohawk Valley was selling out and heading west, one finds no dependable answer except in that answering pulse. Now it is true that Bill Bowen, reading Frémont by candlelight beside the Cumberland or the Delaware, could jot down a well-considered memorandum that there was first-rate farm land along the Willamette. It is true that the dispossessed Mormons, scrutinizing in their beleaguered city every page he wrote and every similar page they could find, could plot an itinerary toward a destination unknown but known to offer their only chance of surviving. But that is of the slightest importance, and it is not what a young man named Francis Parkman read painfully, with eyes beginning to be diseased, that winter in Boston. Or a boy named Lewis Garrard, reading him in Cincinnati and tossing away his schoolbooks because "the glowing pages of Frémont's tour to the Rocky Mountains . . . were so alluring to my fancy that my parents were persuaded to let me go west-ward." Or a thousand men named Bill Bowen, from Missouri eastward to the state of Maine.

It was certainly an important, an irrevocable climax when Bill Bowen sold his place, and certainly there went into it the hardest, most reasoned motives. Bodies bent by the labor of New England farms would find a longing crystallized in the tidings that the Oregon soil was deep and with-out stones, in gentle weather, beside broad waters, below the brows of timbered hills. Bodies sapped by malarial autumns and prairie winters would feel the tug of a California where there was neither cold nor hard work nor any distempers of the flesh. Furthermore, the prairie crops had slackened for the past several seasons and over a wide area had failed—and, on Mr. Hastings' promise, crops never slackened or failed where rolled the Sacramento. Also, neither the tariff of '42 nor all the rhetoric of Congress had succeeded in fully restoring the farmers' market which had been shattered in '37—and there was a belief that in Oregon the trade with China and the Sandwich Islands would absorb all crops that could be grown, a knowledge that there was a great grazing industry in California, a promise that the same herds could be developed in Oregon. We may also make the conventional genuflection to the texts which tell us that the victims of industrialism's earliest American failures were going westward in new hope—though, after due search, exceedingly few of them have been found in any of the events we deal with and none at all along the Western trails. Finally, those Congressmen who talked so gloriously about stretching the eagle's wing across the setting sun were talking about a fundamental reality, a belief that plumbed deep in Bill Bowen's heart. Bill Bowen had long believed and now believed more passionately than ever before that the Americans must occupy their continent, and if others won't do it while there is yet time, maybe I'd better start right now.

Nevertheless, when all these reasons are totaled up they make a sum far from large enough to explain why, suddenly, the Americans were marching on their last frontier—to explain the evening talk in farm kitchens in January, 1846. One comes much closer to the truth with Boone and Carver and Gist, with the venturers crossing the fixed frontier of Sudbury toward the new land in the Connecticut bottoms—with all those who in two and a quarter centuries had moved up to the Fall Line and beyond it, across to the Mississippi, and, a few years since, beyond that. . . . When Bill Bowen sold his house a national emotion welled in the secret places of his heart and he joined himself to a national myth. He believed with Henry Thoreau in the forest and in the meadow and in the night in which the corn grows. Eastward Thoreau went only by force, but westward, ever since Columbus dared the Ocean Sea, westward he had gone free. The lodestone of the West tugged deep in the blood, as deep as desire. When the body dies, the Book of the Dead relates, the soul is borne along the pathway of the setting sun. Toward that Western horizon all heroes of all peoples known to history have always traveled. Beyond it have lain all the Fortunate Isles that literature knows. Beyond the Gates of Hercules, beyond the Western Ocean, beyond the peaks where the sun sinks, the Lapps and the Irish and the Winnebago and all others have known that they would find the happy Hyperboreans—the open country, freedom, the unknown. Westward lies the goal of effort. And, if either Freud or the Navajo speak true, westward we shall find the hole in the earth through which the soul may plunge to peace.

These people waiting for spring to come are inclosed by our myth. But think of them as hard-handed, hard-minded Americans seeking a new home in the West. Think of them also as so certain in their desire that James K. Polk's war seems trivial and wasted. . . . If the dream filled the desert with a thousand brooks like the one that tinkled in the north pasture, built in the Rocky Mountains a thousand white cottages like those that line a New Hampshire common, sowed alkali plains with such crops as the oak openings knew in Michigan, and sketched on the unknown a familiar countryside of rich green slopes, farm cattle lying in noon shade beside familiar pools, and the jeweled miniature of neighbors striking whetstone to scythe within a shout's reach of one another—why, they would learn about the West soon enough.

Extension of the Area of Freedom
—Albert K. Weinberg

In the "roaring 'forties," a decade thus designated because the spirit of American life rose into high and turbulent flame, there was welded an association of two ideals which gave a new integration to the American's consciousness of national destiny. One of the two ideals was territorial expansion. After several decades of relative quiescence, expansionism was rekindled by the issues of Texas and Oregon and was fanned to white heat by the oratory of Democrats in the presidential election of 1844. For the first time the wish of numerous Americans fathered the thought that their eventual possession of no less a domain than the entire North American continent was "manifest destiny"—a phrase which now passed into the national vocabulary.

The central implication of "manifest destiny" in the 'forties, however, was less a matter of the scope of expansion than of its purpose. The conception of expansion as a destiny meant primarily that it was a means to the fulfilment of a certain social ideal the preservation and perfection of which was America's providential mission or destiny. This ideal, conceived as "the last best revelation of human thought," was democracy— a theory of mass sovereignty but in a more important aspect a complex of individualistic values which, despite Fisher Ames's observation that America was too democratic for liberty,[1] Americans most frequently summarized by the inspiring word "freedom." It was because of the association of expansion and freedom in a means-end relationship that expansion now came to seem most manifestly a destiny.

While the championship of the rights of man appeared from the beginning of national life to be America's special destiny, expansion had not seemed in general to be a necessary element in this preeminent national purpose. It is true that expansionists of the Revolution and the War of 1812 tendered "liberty"[2] to the "oppressed" Canadians, and that Jefferson

---

From Albert K. Weinberg, *Manifest Destiny: A Study of Nationalist Expansionism in American History* (Baltimore: The Johns Hopkins Press, 1935), pp. 100–129. Reprinted by permission. Copyright 1935 by The Johns Hopkins University Press.

[1] *Works of Fisher Ames*, I, 328.

[2] Representative Johnson, *Annals of Cong.*, 12th Cong., 1st sess., col. 458.

once included not only Canada but Cuba and Florida as well in America's "empire for liberty." [3] Yet in all these instances, as foregoing evidence has suggested, the extension of democracy was probably neither a primary motive of any expansionists nor even a secondary motive of many of them. It was not until the 'forties that the popular ideology of expansionism centered in democracy. The new importance of this ideal to the expansionist was shown by the words which rang through the land as his slogan, "extension of the area of freedom."

It was because of its infusion with this ideal that American expansionism of the middle 'forties became possessed, as Professor Adams says in his valuable essay on "Manifest Destiny," of a "spiritual exaltation" in contemplation of the assumed superiority of American institutions. A recognition of the rôle played by idealistic American nationalism in this expansion movement has led to an explanation which is very different from that of most early American historians. Writers close to the passions of the Civil War attributed expansionism to "the glut of our slaveholders," [4] the desire of the Southern States to extend the system of slavery. More objective contemporary historians believe that the intensity and extensity of expansionism, while due partly to sectional interests, were caused primarily by nationalistic attitudes resting not merely upon practical interests but also upon the "emotion" of "manifest destiny" [5] and its correlate, the "idealism" [6] of the spirit of democracy.

However, it is as yet more common to refer to democracy as an explanation of American expansionism than to attempt an explanation of expansionist democratic idealism itself. The zeal for extending the area of freedom raises several interesting and important problems. Why is it that, despite the fact that neither expansionism nor the attachment to democracy was new, the two did not come into fusion before? What were the historical circumstances which overcame the previous estrangement of these pieties? Most important of all, what was the true meaning of the ideal described vaguely as extension of the area of freedom?

The point of the last question is made sharper by the fact that the most usual connotation of such words as "extension of the area of freedom" does not make sense in the light of the historical context. The phrase was used primarily by those who urged the annexation of Texas. But Texas already had a republican government, as was pionted out by anti-expansionists attacking the slogan. Thus Representative McIlvain asked "how, if freedom mean republican liberty, can its area be extended by the union of the two governments?" [7] Perplexed by the same question, Repre-

[3] The Writings of Thomas Jefferson, ed. H. A. Washington (Philadelphia, 1854), V, 444.
[4] James Schouler, History of the United States of America (Washington, 1889), IV, 519.
[5] Ephraim Douglass Adams, The Power of Ideals in American History (New Haven, 1926), p. 93.
[6] William Archibald Dunning, The British Empire and the United States (New York, 1914), p. 138.
[7] Cong. Globe, 28th Cong., 2d sess., App., p. 373.

sentative Marsh characterized "extension of the area of freedom" as "an argument addressed to the ear and not the understanding—a mere jingle of words without meaning, or, if significant, false in the only sense which the words will fairly bear." [8]

Unfortunately the matter cannot be so quickly dismissed. The popular slogan is often vapid, but in this case it did have a meaningful content. Only, it was very different from the significance which contemporary anti-expansionists and even later historians attached to the shibboleth. To understand its rather surprising implication, it will be necessary to turn first to the historical background of the expansionist ideal in order to survey briefly the previous development of the relationship between the ideas of democracy and expansion.

When Representative Severance urged in the 'forties that Americans "rather extend the 'area of freedom' by . . . our bright and shining example as a pattern republic," [9] he was reverting to the conception which had been held by the founders of the nation. Originally "the extension of the area of freedom" signified extension of freedom regardless of political connection. Moreover the chief method chosen for extending freedom was the purely passive one of radiating democratic influence through impressive example. Thus Joel Barlow said in 1787 that "the example of political wisdom and felicity, here to be displayed, will excite emulation throughout the kingdoms of the earth, and meliorate the condition of the human race." [10] Thomas Jefferson spoke of America as "a standing monument and example" which would "ameliorate the condition of man over a great portion of the globe." [11] Jefferson also suggested another non-expansionist method of extending freedom. It was the pioneer migration covering even the Western Coast "with free and independent Americans, unconnected with us but by the ties of blood and interest, and employing like us the rights of self-government." [12] It is clear from many such utterances that Americans at first perceived no necessary logical relationship between the extension of democracy and the extension of America's boundaries.

Why did early Americans see no logical nexus between the two ideals which were firmly associated by their descendants? One reason for the original disassociation of democracy and expansion was the internationlist orientation of many of the founders of the Republic. Early idealists, as the nationalistic Gouverneur Morris complained, had a *penchant* for referring to themselves as "citizens of the world." [13] Associated with this internationalism was a devotion to democracy for its own sake. If only the offshoots of the American Republic blossomed into freedom, the retention

---

[8] *Ibid.,* p. 316.   [9] *Ibid.,* p. 371.

[10] Joel Barlow, *An Oration, Delivered* . . . *July 4, 1787* (Hartford, 1787), p. 20.

[11] *Writings of Thomas Jefferson,* Memorial ed., X, 217.

[12] *Writings of Thomas Jefferson,* IX, 351.

[13] S. E. Morison, ed., *Sources and Documents Illustrating the American Revolution, 1764–1788, and the Formation of the Federal Constitution* (Oxford, 1923), pp. 281–82.

This objection was offered in the Louisiana discussion, and again in Josiah Quincy's speech opposing the creation of Orleans Territory. Quincy avowed frankly that his first public love was the Commonwealth of Massachusetts, whereas his love of the Union was merely devotion to a safeguard of the prosperity and security of his State. He opposed expansion because it introduced a new power to overbalance the political weight of any one State. He decried as an "effective despotism" that condition of things in which the original States must lose their political control to the new States, which, taking advantage of a conflict of interests, would throw themselves into the scale most conformable to their purposes.[18]

A third type of criticism alleged the danger of expansion to the liberties of individual citizens. Representative Griswold opposed the Louisiana Purchase because of fear that "additional territory might overbalance the existing territory, and thereby the rights of the present citizens of the United States be swallowed up and lost." [19] Certain Americans, like Josiah Quincy, not merely feared to throw their "rights and liberties" into "hotch-pot" with those of an alien race.[20] They even feared, as Senator White declared in the Louisiana debate, that their own citizens who roved so far from the capital would lose their affection for the center and develop antagonistic interests.[21] Both fears motivated John Randolph's words of 1813:

> We are the first people that ever acquired provinces . . . not for us to govern, but that they might *govern us*—that we might be ruled to our ruin by people bound to us by no common tie of interest or sentiment.[22]

Thus the original failure to relate democracy and expansion was due not merely to altruism, but also, and perhaps primarily, to egoistic fear for the liberties of the American nation, States, and individual citizens. A general tendency to associate democracy and expansion could not possibly develop before these fears had disappeared.

The years following America's first territorial acquisition did in fact witness the gradual dissipation of one after another of the anti-expansionist's apprehensions. The first to pass was the morbid notion that the Union itself could be destroyed through plethora of territory. Louisiana was scarcely incorporated before it seemed an increment of natural growth rather than of elephantiasis. In his oration of 1804 on the acquisition, Dr. David Ramsay taunted those who had prophesied that the Constitution would never answer for a large territory.[23] Jefferson's inaugural address of

---

[18] *Ibid.*, col. 536.   [19] *Ibid.*, 8th Cong., 1st sess., col. 433.
[20] *Ibid.*, 11th Cong., 3d sess., col. 538.   [21] *Ibid.*, 8th Cong., 1st sess., col. 34.
[22] Quoted by William Cabell Bruce, *John Randolph of Roanoke 1773–1833* (New York, 1922), I, 402.
[23] David Ramsay, *An Oration on the Cession of Louisiana to the United States, Delivered on the 12th May, 1804* . . . (Charleston, 1804), pp. 20–21.

1805 reminded those once fearful of Louisiana that "the larger our association the less will it be shaken by local passions." [24]

The fear that extended territory would prove injurious to the liberties of the individual States also quickly evaporated. By 1822 President Monroe could say with an expectation of general approbation:

> The expansion of our Union over a vast territory can not operate unfavorably to the States individually. . . . With governments separate, vigorous, and efficient for all local purposes, their distance from each other can have no injurious effect upon their respective interests.[25]

State anti-expansionism was lessened not only by the defeat of the particularists in the War of 1812 but also by the rise of the political theory which Monroe's words intimated. The years following the War of 1812 witnessed the increasing popularity of the view that the United States Government was based upon a distinctive principle of federation dividing power between State and Federal Government in a manner safe and efficacious for both. The encouraging implication of this theory for expansion was stated by Edward Everett in an address of 1824:

> . . . by the wise and happy partition of powers between the national and state governments, in virtue of which the national government is relieved from all the odium of internal administration, and the state governments are spared the conflicts of foreign politics, all bounds seem removed from the possible extension of our country, but the geographical limits of the continent. Instead of growing cumbrous, as it increases in size, there never was a moment, since the first settlement in Virginia, when the political system of America moved with so firm and bold a step, as at the present day.[26]

The fear that the inhabitants of the distant sections would subvert the liberties of their eastern fellow citizens also proved unfounded. The Eastern States learned that their western kinsmen were not only the strongest of Unionists but also the most democratic of the democrats. One may again turn to an address by Everett, who, though of the same State as the particularist Josiah Quincy, spoke in 1829 to citizens of Tennessee with utmost friendliness. After prophesying that the sceptre of political power would depart from Judah, the East, to the multiplying States of the West, he said:

> We look forward to that event without alarm, as in the order of the natural growth of this great Republic. We have a firm faith that our

---

[24] Richardson, *Messages*, I, 379.   [25] *Ibid.*, II, 177.
[26] Edward Everett, *Orations and Speeches on Various Occasions* (2d ed.: Boston, 1850–1868), I, 33.

interests are mutually consistent; that if you prosper, we shall prosper; if you suffer, we shall suffer; . . . and that our children's welfare, honor, and prosperity will not suffer in the preponderance, which, in the next generation, the west must possess in the balance of the country.[27]

Not only did Everett trust the West but he regarded westward migration as the *"principle* of our institutions" going forth to take possession of the land.[28]

By the decade of the 'thirties there had disappeared every apprehension of incompatibility between the principle of democracy and America's existing domain; the course of this decade was to witness the beginnings of the belief in the compatibility of democracy and future increased domain. One factor in this development was a growing confidence in the flexibility of the federative principle. Thus a writer in the *Democratic Review* of 1838 affirmed that "the peculiar characteristic of our system . . . is, that it may, if its theory is maintained pure in practice, be extended, with equal safety and efficiency, over any indefinite number of millions of population and territory."[29] Favorable contemplation of indefinite future expansion was also induced by the fact that the self-consciousness and spirital inflammability of Jacksonian equalitarianism brought to most intense fervor, not only the appreciation of democracy, but also the belief that, as Jackson's Farewell Message asserted, Providence had chosen Americans as "the guardians of freedom to preserve it for the benefit of the human race."[30] So grandiose a status seemed to some to demand as its symbol a grandiosity of territorial extent. Thus an essay in the *Democratic Review* of 1838, depicting America as "the Great Nation of Futurity," not only foreshadowed its editor's later coinage of the phrase "manifest destiny" but also exemplified the incipient transition of the idea of manifest destiny from its non-expansionist to its expansionist form:

> The far-reaching, the boundless future will be the era of American greatness. In its magnificent domain of space and time, the nation of many nations is *destined to manifest* [italics mine] to mankind the excellence of divine principles; to establish on earth the noblest temple ever dedicated to the worship of the Most High—the Sacred and the True. Its floor shall be a hemisphere—its roof the firmament of the star-studded heavens, and its congregation an Union of many Republics, comprising hundreds of happy millions, calling, owning no man master, but governed by God's natural and moral law of equality, the law of brotherhood—of 'peace and good will amongst men'.[31]

[27] *Ibid.,* p. 196. [28] *Ibid.,* p. 210.
[29] *Democratic Review,* "The Canada Question," I (1838), 217.
[30] Richardson, *Messages,* III, 308.
[31] *Democratic Review,* "The Great Nation of Futurity," VI (1839), 427.

While the conception of the United States as embracing an entire hemisphere outdid even the ambition of the 'forties, the very ambitiousness of the vision indicates the relegation of its fulfilment to the distant future. With respect to the present, the 'thirties were not a decade of active expansionism. Like others the *Democratic Review* was cool toward the vague possibility of annexation raised by the Canadian revolts.[32] The definite proffers of annexation by Texas after its successful rebellion were successively rebuffed, despite the recognition by Senator Niles and other Americans that "destiny had established intimate political connexion between the United States and Texas." [33] In some measure the apathy regarding immediate expansion was due to the persistence of the sedentary ideal of radiating freedom by example—an ideal expressed by a writer in the *North American Review* of 1832 when he affirmed that "we can wait the peaceful progress of our own principles." [34] But this attitude is an inadequate explanation of the fact that Americans rejected an opportunity to render greatly needed assistance in the progress of their democratic principles. Such assistance was refused the Texans when they appealed for annexation after falling into deplorable difficulties. The reserve of Americans toward their former compatriots was caused not only by the fear of difficulty over annexation with both Mexico and American abolitionists, but also by the absence of any belief in the urgent need for expansion. The speeches of Jackson as president exude the complacency and sense of self-sufficiency of this decade. Especially noteworthy is his confident observation concerning an issue always highly determinative of the attitude toward expansion: "You have no longer any cause to fear danger from abroad. . . ." [35]

One finally comes to the task of explaining the sudden rise in the 'forties of the ideal of extending the area of freedom by expansion. Is it conceivable that, after having been cold to the sufferings of the Texans for seven years, Americans quite spontaneously developed an overwhelming desire to enfold them with their protective democracy? Such a conception is the more difficult because the expansionists themselves made no pretension to undiluted altruism. On the other hand, only a priori cynicism would suppose that the democratic ideology was merely a hypocritical grace whereby the American appeased conscience before indulging the land-hunger of this decade. An examination of the circumstances and ideas attending the inception of the expansionist movement reveals that a definite international development, suddenly placing new problems in the center of the American's political horizon, was the factor which brought into play the spirit of democracy as well as other motives of expansionism.

The development was the emergence of that "danger from abroad"

[32] *Ibid.*, I (1838), 216–17.   [33] *Reg. of Debates*, 24th Cong., 1st sess., col. 1918.
[34] *North American Review*, "North-Eastern Boundary," XXXIV (1832), 563.
[35] Richardson, *Messages*, III, 307.

which Jackson had declared to be absent in the 'thirties. "In Texas, in California, and in Oregon," as Professor Perkins writes with reference to the years following 1841, "the ambition or the intrigue of European nations seemed to the dominant political generation of Americans to threaten fundamental American interests." [36] British and French attempts to establish sovereignty or political influence in adjacent countries appeared to threaten not merely economic and strategic interests but also the security of democracy. The expansionism of the 'forties arose as a defensive effort to forestall the encroachment of Europe in North America. So too, as one can see in the most numerous utterances, the conception of an "extension of the area of freedom" became general as an ideal of preventing absolutistic Europe from lessening the area open to American democracy; extension of the area of "freedom" was the defiant answer to extension of the area of "absolutism."

The European scare started with Texas and at least as early as 1843. In the early months of that year President Tyler was brought by information about British influence in Texas to the fear which was reflected in the reference of his annual message to "interference on the part of stronger and more powerful nations." [37] In 1843, also, Andrew Jackson wrote his famous letter on Texas to Aaron V. Brown, in which, amid warnings of British intrigue, he coined a famous phrase by advocacy of "extending the area of freedom." [38] The year 1844, which witnessed the negotiation of Tyler's unratified treaty of annexation, saw also the publication of Jackson's letter, and the popularization of his felicitous phrase. Although many Southerners wished for annexation primarily to forestall British abolitionist efforts, they also used, without sense of inconsistency, the democratic argument of Andrew Jackson. Texas, Senator Lewis of Alabama wrote to his constituents, was the "great Heritage of Freedom," to be held in defiance of that power which has well-nigh enslaved the world." [39] The New Orleans *Jeffersonian Republican* represented press economico-ethical sentiment in arguing that unless American supremacy were extended to the Rio Del Norte a few years would suffice for the establishment of an influence near us "highly dangerous to our prosperity, and inimical to the spread of Republican institutions." [40] The discussions of annexation in the congressional debates gave rise to numerous similar observations, and the passage by the Senate of the resolution for annexation of Texas was acclaimed by the New Orleans *Picayune* as "the triumph of republican energy over royal finesse; as the triumph of free minds over

[36] Dexter Perkins, The Monroe Doctrine 1826–1867 (Baltimore, 1933), p. 64.
[37] Richardson, Messages, IV, 261.
[38] James Parton, Life of Andrew Jackson (New York, 1860), III, 658.
[39] A Letter of the Hon. Dixon H. Lewis, to His Constituents of the Third Congressional District of Alabama (n.p., 1844) p. 8.
[40] New Orleans Jeffersonian Republican, reprinted in Richmond Enquirer, January 7, 1845.

the diplomacy of foreign task-master." [41] President Polk's message announcing the acceptance of annexation by Texas gave prominent place to an attack upon the attempted application of the European doctrine of the balance of power to America—an application which he attributed to hostility to "the expansion of free principles." [42]

No less frequently did the ideal of defending democracy figure in the Oregon issue, in which the claims of the United States were again pitted against those of Great Britain. This question seemed to Senator Dickinson to be "a question between two great systems; between monarchy and republicanism." [43] The annexation of Oregon, Representative Sawyer declared, would rid the continent of British power and thereby "hand down to posterity, pure and unadulterated, that freedom we received from the fathers of the Revolution." [44] For it seemed, as Representative Levin said, that the spirit of republicanism "permits not the contaminating proximity of monarchies upon the soil that we have consecrated to the rights of man." [45] Such an attitude toward the Oregon issue also occasioned Senator Allen's resolution affirming that European political interference or colonization upon this hemisphere would be "dangerous to the liberties of the people of America." [46]

With justification Americans also feared the British lion in the wilderness of California. The Whig *American Review* spoke typically in accusing Great Britain of seeking sovereignty over California in order to interpose a barrier to the general growth of the American Union and thereby to "the progress of republican liberty, by which she believes her own institutions and the position of the family of European sovereigns, to be seriously menaced." [47] Such interposition, it declared, was dangerous to the self-preservation of the United States and therefore unallowable. Secretary of State Buchanan's despatch of 1845 to Consul Larkin, indicating the favorable view which a petition of the colonists for annexation would receive, spoke of Great Britain's designs as conflicting with the desire of the colonists for republican institutions.[48] The *New York Herald*, calling likewise for protection of free institutions, wished to annex the whole of Mexico instead of merely California.[49] Stephen Douglas hoped to check absolutism by annexing Canada. Representative Cary stated his constituents' broader doctrine:

Their doctrine was, that this continent was intended by Providence as a vast theatre on which to work out the grand experiment of Republican government, under the auspices of the Anglo-Saxon race. If the

[41] New Orleans *Daily Picayune*, reprinted in *Nashville Union*, March 25, 1845.
[42] Richardson, *Messages*, IV, 398.   [43] *Cong. Globe*, 29th Cong., 1st sess., p. 424.
[44] *Ibid.*, App., p. 229.   [45] *Ibid.*, 95.   [46] *Ibid.*, 29th Cong., 1st sess., p. 197.
[47] *American Review*, "California," III (1846), 98.
[48] *The Works of James Buchanan*, ed. J. B. Moore (Philadelphia, 1908–1911), VI, 276.
[49] *New York Herald*, January 6, 1846.

worn-out and corrupt monarchies of the Old World had colonies here; let them be kept within the narrowest limits, consistent with justice and the faith of treaties. Let all which remains be preserved for the growh and spread of the free principles of American democracy.[50]

However, the toleration of existent European colonies seemed to still bolder spirits to be contrary to the true purpose of Providence. In the July number of the *Democratic Review* of 1845 an article on the Texas question affirmed nothing less than continental dominion to be America's "manifest destiny." The historic phrase, as the researchers of Professor Pratt indicate, seems to have been used for the first time in this article. The article is attributed by Professor Pratt [51] on the ground of internal evidence to John L. O'Sullivan, editor of the *Democratic Review* and the *New York Morning News*, later Minister to Portugal, who was called by John St. Tammany rather fulsomely "one of the ablest writers and most accomplished scholars and gentlemen of the times." [52] The passage using the later famous phrase is as follows:

> Why, were other reasons wanting, in favor of now elevating this question of the reception of Texas into the Union, out of the lower region of our past party dissensions, up to its proper level of a high and broad nationality, it surely is to be found, found abundantly, in the manner in which other nations have undertaken to intrude themselves into it, between us and the proper parties to the case, in a spirit of hostile interference against us, for the avowed object of thwarting our policy and hampering our power, limiting our greatness and checking the fulfilment of our manifest destiny to overspread the continent allotted by Providence for the free development of our yearly multiplying millions.[53]

European encroachment must thus be thanked for making manifest the destiny of continental dominion. With truth Professor Rippy remarks that "manifest destiny never pointed to the acquisition of a region so unmistakably as when undemocratic, conservative Europe revealed an inclination to interfere or to absorb." [54] What was not manifest to Americans was the vicious circle which their defensive expansion created; for Europe's inclination to interfere in North America was caused chiefly by fear of the growing economic and political ambition of the United States.

The view that European interference in America menaced American democracy apparently rested on three principal grounds. The first was the

[50] *Cong. Globe,* 28th Cong., 2d sess., App., pp. 161–62.
[51] Julius W. Pratt, "The Origin of 'Manifest Destiny,'" *American Historical Review,* XXXII (1927), 795–98.
[52] *Tri-Weekly Nashville Union,* January 28, 1845.
[53] *Democratic Review,* "Annexation," XVII (1845), 5.
[54] Rippy, *The United States and Mexico,* p. 29.

belief that whatever threatened American security was a danger to the political principle which the nation embodied. The second was the supposition that, irrespective of strategic menace, European absolutism would "pollute" American democracy by its very contiguity. The third and perhaps most influential of all was the recognition that adjacent European power threatened the extension of American democracy—an ideal which was made more precious by this very menace.

European adjacency doubtless entailed commercial and political disadvantages, but the foregoing assumptions may seem great exaggerations in respect to danger to the life of the Republic or its democratic institutions. Though the fear expressed was doubtless sincere—for the fears of nations seldom develop in strict accord with logic—there was much more to the question than the fear of the European menace. Considerations which were logically independent—however much the European menace acted as a catalytic agent in their generation—also caused Americans of the 'forties to believe that expansion was essential to the life or healthful development of American democracy.

Whereas it had once been feared that the existence of the Union was jeopardized by expansion, it was now apprehended that the Union might be imperilled by failure to expand through annexing Texas. The Southern States held Texas to be necessary to their economic prosperity, the security of their "peculiar institution," and their maintenance of a balance of political power with the North. It therefore seemed to many that, as Robert J. Walker wrote in his widely read letter on Texas, the defeat of annexation by the North might lead to a union of the South and Southwest with Texas.[55] Ground for this fear was given by certain statements of some Southerners, such as the observation by Senator Lewis of Alabama that if the treaty were rejected he would consider the Union at an end.[56] The fact that the Union seemed synonymous with republicanism created a logical link between solicitude for the Union and zeal for the extension of freedom. Thus Senator Merrick, who warned his colleagues that the failure of annexation would endanger sectional tranquillity, affirmed that the success of annexation would mean the formation of a more perfect union and the securing of the blessings of liberty to ourselves and our posterity.[57] It seemed similarly to Tomas W. Gilmer that "our union has no danger to apprehend from those who believe that its genius is expansive and progressive, but from those who think that the limits of the United States are already too large and the principles of 1776 too old-fashioned for this fastidious age."[58] In fact it is difficult to know which side endangered the Union more. For the threats of Northern abolitionists to dissolve the

---

[55] Walker, *Letter . . . Relative to the Reannexation of Texas*, p. 15.
[56] Dixon H. Lewis to John Calhoun, March 6, 1844, *Correspondence of John C. Calhoun*, ed. J. F. Jameson, *Fourth Annual Report of the Historical Manuscripts Commission, American Historical Association* (Washington, 1900), p. 936.
[57] *Cong. Globe*, 28th Cong., 2d sess., App., p. 233.   [58] *Niles' Register*, LXIV (1843), 285.

Union in the event of annexation were just as numerous as those of the Southern expansionists with reference to its failure.

A second line of argument gives the impression that to many the chief consideration was not the Union but the individual State. For, just as the traditional argument regarding the effect of expansion on the Union was inverted, so was also the traditional argument regarding the State. It was the original fear of New England particularists that expansion would be prejudicial to States' rights. After the War of 1812, as already stated, this fear was destroyed by a theory of the distribution of powers according to which the needful powers of the State need not be prejudiced by expansion. In the 'forties this theory was developed by circumstances into the view that expansion was not only not injurious to the individual States but was in fact essential to the preservation of their liberties.

The general logic of this view was stated briefly by Representative Belser of Alabama, during the Texas debate, in the words: "Extension . . . was the antagonistical principle of centralization." [59] In amplification of this view one may quote from Representative Duncan's speech on the Oregon bill:

> There is a strong and constant tendency towards consolidation of power toward the centre of federal government; and that tendency has been favored by a party in this country, who desired at first that our federal government should possess unlimited powers.
>
> To oppose that constant tendency to federal consolidation, I know no better plan than to multiply States; and the farther from the centre of federal influence and attraction, the greater is our security. [60]

From this point of view, extension of the area of freedom meant increase of the security of American States against a curious enemy, their own federal government.

Whereas Representative Duncan was an Ohioan, the theory which he expressed was espoused more frequently by Americans of the Southern slave-holding States. The theory came to the fore at this time principally because of the bearing of the annexation of Texas upon the economic and political interests of the South. Opposition to the annexation desired by these interests was attributed by Southerners both to inimical abolitionists and to advocates of a federal authority overriding States' rights. Thus an advocate of the annexation of Texas in the *Southern Quarterly Review* of 1844 attributed such wicked opposition to those using the epithets "general," "national," and "American" to derogate from rights guaranteed to the States by the Constitution. [61] Representative Rhett of South Carolina called for annexation as a means of defeating those antagonistic to the

---

[59] *Cong. Globe,* 28th Cong., 2d sess., App., p. 43.   [60] *Ibid.,* p. 178.
[61] *Southern Quarterly Review,* "The Annexation of Texas," VI (1844), 498.

rights of Southern States. Having declared that the South must be permitted to participate in the nation's expansion, he added:

> Every census has added to the power of the non-slaveholding States, and diminished that of the South. We are growing weaker, and they stronger, every day. I ask you, is it the spirit of the constitution to strengthen the strong against the weak? What are all its checks and balances of power, but to protect the weak and restrain the strong? The very object of a constitution, in all free governments, is to restrain power. . . . If this measure, therefore, will tend to strengthen the weaker interest in the Union it will be moving in strict accordance with the whole spirit of the constitution.[62]

It was thus true that, as anti-expansionists charged, "we were to extend the area of freedom by enlarging the boundary of slavery."[63] But it was not true that, as anti-expansionists also charged, the phrase about extending freedom was used merely to cover up the design of extending slavery. The strange truth of the matter is that the extension of slavery, which virtually no Southern expansionist denied to be one of his motives, did not seem to the slaveholder incompatible with the ideal of diffusing democracy. The harmonization of the two purposes is explained in part by the Southerner's belief that religious and natural law made the negro a necessary exception to the principle of political equality. But it is also explained by the fact that the extension of slavery appeared essential to States' liberties. In this view the Southerner overlooked the consideration that slavery seemed to abolitionist sections an equal infringement of their right to a union based on universal individual liberty.

North and South saw with one eye, however, on one topic—the liberty of the American (white) individual. Here again, as though some Hegelian metaphysical dialectic of antitheses were at work, one meets the inversion of a traditional argument. Anti-expansionists had maintained originally that the political untrustworthiness of a remote pioneer population made extended territory dangerous to individual liberties. Now, with particular view to the very pioneers who were once feared, expansionists declared that territorial extension was essential to the fullest liberty of the individual.

The idea of individualism perhaps did more than anything else to cement the association between democracy and expansion. For the sturdiest element in democracy was its valuation of individualism—the thesis of the individual's right not only to exemption from undue interference by government but also to the most abundant opportunity for self-development. Those entirely misread its spirit who believe that the enthusiasm for democracy was merely enthusiasm over a form of government as such.

---

[62] *Cong. Globe,* 28th Cong., 2d sess., App., p. 146.
[63] Representative Sample, *ibid.,* p. 73.

Fundamentally, indeed, the Jeffersonian American rather disliked government; though recognizing the necessity of giving some power to the State, he at least verged on anarchism in his belief that "the best government is that which governs least." Whereas individualism in its negative phase meant restraint from undue interference with individual rights, in its positive phase it signified that "care of human life and happiness" which Jefferson called the only legitimate object of government.[64]

Although both individualism and the pioneer spirit had prevailed from the beginning, it was not until the 'forties that the enterprise of the pioneer seemed the most perfect expression of American individualism. The coming of the pioneer movement to self-consciousness in this decade was due to various factors: the popular interest aroused by the accelerating trek to Oregon and the Southwest; the fact that the pioneeer movement now became involved with territorial issues of national concern; and above all, perhaps, the general land-hunger which caused the pioneer to seem now not a deviation from but the very expression of Americanism. It was in the fervent appreciation of the pioneer movement that there were forged all the links uniting individualism and expansionism.

Among such links was the conception of the economic value of expansion to the individual. Expansion, later to be depicted by anti-imperialists as a means to economic exploitation and slavery, was seen in this period as a mean to economic liberty. Economic freedom had become as important as political freedom to the philosophy of democracy, which, giving full recognition to the Platonic truth that before one can live well one must live, was unhesitant about attaching an almost moral valuation to even the material values of land-ownership. Land, as Professor Fish has pointed out, seemed to the American of the 'forties the very key to happiness.[65] The demand for abundant territory in the name of economic liberty is exemplified by the words of Representative Duncan in support of the Oregon Bill:

> First, to extend our population we require the possession of Oregon. I have before remarked that personal liberty is incompatible with a crowded population. . . .
> By whatever means the lands and wealth of a country fall into the hands of a few individuals, it establishes a feudal system as oppressive and destructive of the liberties of the people as if it were established by conquest, and equally enslaves the people. . . . The inability of the weak, the humble, and the non-assuming, to contend with the overbearing, the cunning, and the grasping monopolist makes it necessary, to the equality of circumstances and personal liberty, that the advantages of territory should constantly be kept open to all who wish to embrace it.[66]

---

[64] *Writings of Thomas Jefferson*, ed. Washington, VIII, 165.
[65] Carl Russell Fish, *The Rise of the Common Man 1830–1850* (New York, 1929), p. 125.
[66] *Cong. Globe*, 28th Cong., 2d sess., App., p. 178.

The foregoing is unimpeachable in logic so far as concerns the privileges of homestead. It is not clear, however, that the enlargement of individual agrarian opportunities required further national expansion. The anti-expansionist maintained correctly that the Republic already "had an ample area for hundred millions of human beings," [67] with vast regions as yet scarcely explored. Indeed the boast of the average American was like that of Mr. Bovan in *Martin Chuzzlewit:* "We have a vast territory, and not—as yet—too many people on it."

The rub lay precisely in the "as yet." Just as in the issue of Indian lands, the expansionist took his main position on the ground of need of territory for posterity. In calculating the territorial needs of posterity Americans used the rate of population growth which had been maintained as late as the census of 1840—approximately a doubling of population every twenty-five years. According to the typical estimate of John L. O'Sullivan, a century from 1845 would see an American population of approximately three hundred millions. [68] These calculations were a favorite occupation of American nationalists, who agreed with the biblical writer that in the multitude of the people is the king's honor—or more correctly the honor of democracy, to which they actually attributed American fecundity. It seemed, then, a duty to the hasty American to provide territory for a future population even before the need arose. Referring to reproductive capacity as the American multiplication table, Representative Kennedy asked how room would be found for posterity without the acquisition of Oregon. [69] Representative Belser, prophesying the three hundred millions of a century thence, declared confinement of the area of freedom an impossibility. [70] Presentiment of this "stupendous" growth of population seemed to John L. O'Sullivan the fundamental cause of the popular movement toward territorial extension. [71]

But today, nine decades after O'Sullivan's prophecy of three hundred million in a century, America's population is still not much more than a third of that estimate. The gross miscalculation arose from an erroneous statistical method. As an anti-expansionist writer pointed out in 1849, expansionists overlooked the consideration that as a people become denser they multiply more slowly. [72] The unusual growth-rate of American population was ascribed in Alison's work of 1840 on *Principles of Population* to the continual influx of immigrants to better their fortunes on the unappropriated lands of the West. [73] With the settlement of surplus land immigration and likewise the rapid growth of population would subside. The true cure for the overgrowth of population was thus to cease expanding. But instead of adopting this disagreeable cure, the American nationalist pro-

---

[67] Senator Rives, *ibid.*, p. 382.   [68] *New York Morning News*, January 5, 1846.
[69] *Cong. Globe*, 29th Cong., 1st sess., p. 180.   [70] *Ibid.*, 28th Cong., 2d sess., App., p. 43.
[71] *New York Morning News*, January 5, 1846.
[72] Charles T. Porter, *Review of the Mexican War* (Auburn, 1849), pp. 165–66.
[73] Archibald Alison, *The Principles of Population* (Edinburgh, 1840), I, 548.

posed to continue expanding. Thus he was laying the basis for the very superfluity of population which he cited as the justification of expansion.

But reasoning in regard to needs of population was not responsible fundamentally for the association of expansion and individual liberty. The pioneer was not rational as he rushed from the abundant fertile land at hand to stake his claim on land more distant. He was impelled onward, if the contemporary interpretation does not over-romanticize him, by some fever in the blood, some spirit of adventure. So, too, the philosopher of the pioneer movement was thinking of liberty in a sense broader than the freedom to satisfy economic needs. He was envisaging a liberty for the pioneer impulse as such, an impulse of adventure and self-expression. This impulse seemed good in and of itself as an essential element in the energetic spirit produced by free institutions. It was the fact that it gave scope for the satisfaction of such an impulse which primarily caused expansion to be related to individual liberty.

Observations illustrative of this association received at times a naïvely naturalistic expression, as in the words of Major Daveznac at the New Jersey Democratic State Convention of 1844:

> Land enough—land enough! Make way, I say, for the young American Buffalo—he has not yet got land enough; he wants more land as his cool shelter in summer—he wants more land for his beautiful pasture grounds. I tell you, we will give him Oregon for his summer shade, and the region of Texas as his winter pasture. (Applause.) Like all of his race, he wants salt, too. Well, he shall have the use of two oceans— the mighty Pacific and turbulent Atlantic shall be his . . . He shall not stop his career until he slakes his thirst in the frozen ocean. (Cheers.) [74]

So far was Representative McClernand from shame of such cravings that he called the American impulse of expansion "glorious" and "divine." He thought it "a new impulse called into action by free institutions operating upon the restless and daring spirit of the Anglo-Saxon blood." [75] Similarly, Representative Ficklin apotheosized the unmercenary, exploratory spirit which sent Americans to distant Oregon:

> This wild spirit of adventure gives nerve and energy to the mental and physical man, and prompts its possessor to deeds of peril and of danger, from which the tame and timorous would shrink with horror; it expands the heart, and unfetters its joys, its hopes, its aspirations; it lends a new charm to life, a new spring to human energies and desires, and wakens in the breast a kindred feeling with that which animated our first parents in the garden of Eden. [76]

---

[74] *Young Hickory Banner,* October 15, 1845.
[75] *Cong. Globe,* 29th Cong., 1st sess., App., p. 277.   [76] *Ibid.,* p. 175.

"Wide shall our own free race increase," [77] wrote an American poet who was quoted by a congressional expansionist. But what limits would this free race, irresistible to others, set for itself? Even the least grandiose conceptions assumed that under "the influence of free institutions" the pioneer movement would cover "everything in the shape of land not already occupied by comparatively large numbers from some foreign nation." [78] This embraced at least Texas, California, and Oregon. But there was a much broader vision which was confessed by many expansionists and was in the subliminal expectation of nearly all. It was identical with that which De Tocqueville, his dazzled imagination following the course of the deluge of pioneers, expressed in the 'thirties:

> At a period which may be said to be near,—for we are speaking of the life of a nation,—the Anglo-Americans alone will cover the immense space contained between the polar regions and the tropics, extending from the coasts of the Atlantic to those of the Pacific Ocean.[79]

If the detached foreigner could believe that "the continent which they inhabit is their dominion," [80] would not the same belief suggest itself the more readily to self-confident Americans? The literature of the time is replete with the expression of that belief. The toast at a political banquet urged the march of the "Spirit of Democratic progression" until "*the whole unbounded continent is ours.*" [81] In an article of 1844 on "The Texas Question" a writer in the *Democratic Review* declared that the increase and diffusiveness of America's population, occupying all territory until checked by great natural barriers, would at no distant day cover "every habitable square inch of the continent." [82] Continental dominion was predicted by John L. O'Sullivan in the light of both natural law and providential design:

> Texas has been absorbed into the Union in the inevitable fulfilment of the general law which is rolling our population westward; the connexion of which with that ratio of growth in population which is destined within a hundred years to swell our numbers to the enormous population of *two hundred and fifty millions* (if not more), is too evident to leave us in doubt of the manifest design of Providence in regard to the occupation of this continent.[83]

Jefferson and other imaginative early Americans also foresaw a time when "our rapid multiplication will . . . cover the whole northern, if not the southern continent." [84] But whereas Jefferson did not care about the

---

[77] Representative Hamlin, *ibid.*, 29th Cong., 1st sess., p. 187.
[78] John M. Galt, *The Annexation of Texas*, reprinted in *Political Essays* (n.p., 1852?), p. 5.
[79] Alexis de Tocqueville, *Democracy in America*, tr. Henry Reeve (New York, 1898), I, 557.
[80] *Ibid.*, p. 519. [81] *New York Morning News*, January 9, 1846.
[82] *Democratic Review*, "The Texas Question," XIV (1844), 429.
[83] *Ibid.*, XVII (1845), 17. [84] *Writings of Thomas Jefferson*, VIII, 105.

political tie, expansionists of the 'forties insisted upon it as essential to the realization of freedom. They held that seekers for economic and social liberty must be followed by a government solicitous for their political liberty. Thus Representative Bowlin, describing the progress of the pioneer race, declared that the Government should follow them with the laws and instructions which they love and cherish, and thereby also add strength and permanent glory to the Republic.[85] So too, Senator Linn, champion of the Oregon settlers, proclaimed that the irresistible advance of American population should march "with every public right in the lead."[86] The association between the ideal of the free pioneer and that of the extension of the political area of freedom appears in the lines of a contemporary poet who said that the increase of our "free race" would extend widely the elastic chain

That binds in everlasting peace
State after State—a mighty train.[87]

"We are the pioneers of the continent," proclaimed an expansionist editorial in the organ of the author of the phrase "manifest destiny."[88] It is in the light of this pioneer ideal that one must interpret not only the immediate territorial ambitions but even the dream of eventual continental dominion. This future empire, like the immediate annexation of Texas, was not to be achieved through the military conquest which imperialists of 1898 were to conduct in the name of liberty. The continental republic was rather to be the natural consummation of what O'Sullivan called the "destiny to overspread the whole North American continent with an immense democratic population."[89] To paraphrase Walt Whitman, the expansionist proposed to "make the continent indissoluble"[90] by filling it with the spreading but politically cohesive American race.

Freedom for the American nation; freedom for the American State; freedom for the American individual: such, then, were the principal elements in the fundamentally egoistic program of extending the area of freedom. One sees finally why the anti-expansionists talked beside the mark when they pointed out that Texas was already republican. The freedom sought by expansionists was a distinctively American freedom which went far beyond nominal republicanism. The area in question was the domain in which American pioneers might freely spread themselves and all their institutions. The extension of the area of freedom could thus be only the expansion of the United States. Freedom, in sum, had become nationalized.

It is an exaggeration, indeed, to suppose that international philanthropy was entirely absent from the expansionist ideal. However, even its ele-

---

[85] *Cong. Globe,* 28th Cong., 2d sess., App., p. 93.
[86] *Ibid.,* 27th Cong., 3d sess., App., p. 79.   [87] *Ibid.,* 29th Cong., 1st sess., p. 187.
[88] *New York Morning News,* November 15, 1845.   [89] *Ibid.,* January 5, 1846.
[90] Walt Whitman, *Leaves of Grass,* ed. Emory Holloway (New York, 1928), p. 98.

ments of altruism, as analysis will show, were restricted in a manner which can be explained only by the nationalistic orientation of the ideal.

Thus the altruistic phase of democratic expansionism had as one presupposition an egoistic disparagement of the capacity of other peoples to help themselves. This disparagement reflected in some measure, to be sure, the disillusionment which experience had brought to the original hope of extending freedom by mere example. Most of the New World peoples who had followed the example of the American Revolution fell shortly into ways of political disorder which seemed to an American of 1838 to "depress the hopes of those who desire to see civil liberty established throughout the world." [91] Most depression came from those of whom most had been hoped, the Texans. As though they had lost the talent for democracy in losing contact with their native soil, these former Americans exhibited a political and social confusion prompting one American editor's description of Texas as a "Quasi Republic." [92] Despite previous belief in the triumph of democracy through man's "eternal principle of progress," [93] Americans now saw reason to believe that not every Tom, Dick and Harry among nations had the genius for democracy. The disappointment to undue impatience caused the pendulum to swing to a pessimism as extreme as the former optimism.

Abandonment of the hope of teaching democracy by remote example led to acceptance of the alternative pedagogical method, that of taking other peoples into "the district school of democracy." Of course, the Texans strongly resented any patronizing attitude; a prominent Texan diplomat believed that the annexation of Texas was "coupled with the paramount security of Republican institutions in the United States." [94] But Representative Dean and other expansionists regarded it as "philanthropy" to extend to Texans America's blessing of civil, political, and religious liberty.[95] America's expansion seemed even more essential to the liberation of peoples non-American in blood; and Dean saw annexation as a means of releasing from their "shackles" every nation on the continent.[96] While only Canada was subjected to a monarchy, all these republican nations were in shackles in so far as they had not attained American or true freedom.

Above all, the oppressed of Europe, a section of the world in which the American had almost lost hope, were supposed to see in the United States their only refuge. Still far removed from the "one-hundred-per-cent Americanism" of the twentieth-century immigration policy, Americans of the 'forties felt toward their gracious country as did Bryant:

---

91 *Democratic Review*, "Retrospective View of the South-American States," II (1838), 99.
92 *Newark Daily Advertiser*, November 14, 1836, quoted by Justin H. Smith, *The Annexation of Texas* (New York, 1911), p. 66.
93 *Democratic Review* "Democracy," VII (1840), 228.
94 Memucan Hunt to John C. Calhoun, October 2, 1844, *Correspondence of John C. Calhoun*, p. 975.
95 *Cong. Globe*, 28th Cong., 2d sess., App., p. 105.   96 *Ibid.*

There's freedom at thy gates and rest
For Earth's down-trodden and opprest,
A shelter for the hunted head,
For the starved laborer toil and bread.[97]

Benjamin Franklin's still vital conception of America as "an asylum for those who love liberty" [98] easily became an argument for expansion. Thus Representative Duncan proclaimed: "If ours is to be the home of the oppressed, we must extend our territory in latitude and longitude to the demand of the millions who are to follow us, as well of our own posterity as those who are invited to our peaceful shores to partake in our republican institutions." [99] There were those who, disregarding De Tocqueville's observation that the movement toward equality was world-wide, believed as did Governor Brown that "in the order of Providence, America might become the last asylum of liberty to the human family," [100] and must therefore lay its foundations deep and wide for the innumerable refugees of later ages. Similarly Representative Stone, advocating the annexation of Texas and an ocean-bound republic, affirmed that "Providence intended this western hemisphere to be an asylum for the oppressed." [101] Representative Belser related the salvation in freedom to biblical conceptions:

> Long may our country prove itself the asylum of the oppressed. Let its institutions and its people be extended far and wide, and when the waters of despotism shall have inundated other portions of the globe, and the votary of liberty be compelled to betake himself to his ark, let this government be the Ararat on which it shall rest.[102]

Thus the American expansionist's nationalism was so little exclusive that it offered refuge to all the devotees of freedom in a world elsewhere threatened with a rising deluge of despotism.

None the less the typical expansionist's altruism was not only conditioned by but distinctly secondary to his interest in his own people. That expansionist altruism was influenced by nationalism is clear from the fact that the expansionist became concerned about other peoples only as he conceived of them as in some sense American. There was never a period (reference is made to the years of the 'forties preceding the European revolutionary movements of 1848) when the average American was less interested in world developments not bearing directly upon his own hemisphere. But even in viewing his own hemisphere the American was inter-

---

[97] *The Poetical Works of William Cullen Bryant*, Roslyn ed. (New York, 1908), p. 215.
[98] Van Tyne, *The American Revolution*, p. 333.
[99] *Cong. Globe*, 28th Cong., 2d sess., App., p. 178.
[100] "Inaugural Address as Governor of Tennessee, October 15, 1845," *Speeches Congressional and Political, and Other Writings of ex-Governor Aaron V. Brown, of Tennessee* (Nashville, 1854), p. 373.
[101] *Cong. Globe*, 28th Cong., 2d sess., App., p. 227.   [102] *Ibid.*, p. 43.

ested primarily in those sections inhabited altogether or largely by pioneers from the United States. The Texan was a kind of *alter ego,* described affectionately as "bone of our bone, and flesh of our flesh." [103] All three of the immediate territorial interests of the United States—Texas, Oregon, and California—were, or promised to be, settled by Americans. The adjacent Latin peoples were recipients of consideration not so much for their own sake as because they inhabited the American continent, which "the God of nature" had designed for "liberty." [104] The fundamental consideration was that no despotism should "pollute" the soil adjacent to that of the pure American democracy.

The secondary character of the expansionist's altruism is evidenced partly by the fact that most of his encomia of freedom stressed liberty for the American himself. It is also indicated by the concentration of the expansionist's interest not upon territories whose inhabitants stood in greatest need of freedom, but upon territories whose inhabitants, being entirely or largely former Americans, could most advantageously be assimilated to the Union. Aside from Texas, Oregon, and California—territories where Americans had already set their stakes—the American expansionist was willing to postpone annexation until the pioneer's Americanization of the continent had succeeded, as one expansionist said, in "irrigating it for the growth and predominance of liberty." [105] Further instances of the American's long-dominant revulsion from amalgamation with supposedly inferior peoples will be given in a subsequent chapter concerned with the ideal of regenerative expansionism.

Thus, those entirely miss the spirit of the ideal of extending the area of freedom who see it as altogether or primarily an attachment to international philanthropy. Very shortly, indeed, the altruistic form of the democratic ideal was to be developed by the issue of amalgamation raised in the Mexican War. But before the Mexican War democratic expansionism was primarily a concern for the freedom of Americans themselves; the concern for others was such as overflows even from a Nietzschean's euphoria. Precisely because the idealism of the expansionist of this period was rooted in egoism, it had a sincerity and an intensity which later expansionists probably never fully attained in their somewhat forced altruism.

An interesting problem is raised by the contrast between the American's version of extending freedom and the altruistic form which prevailed among French Revolutionists, absolutistic Pan-Slavs, and most other peoples in the history of nationalism. Why did extension of freedom mean to the American of the middle 'forties less the liberation of other peoples than the aggrandizement of his own freedom—and territory?

The reasons are interesting even if not in all cases edifying. Undoubtedly one explanation was the American's healthy-minded egoism, a matter

---

[103] Representative Stephens, *ibid.,* p. 313.   [104] Representative Haralson, *ibid.,* p. 194.
[105] Representative McClernand, *ibid.,* 29th Cong., 1st sess., p. 984.

of instinct rather than of logic. Another was the fact that the American philosophy of individualism blessed egoism in its affirmation of a natural right to the pursuit of happiness. Still another factor lay in the circumstance that the annexation of the willing Texans involved no obvious transgression (Mexico to the contrary notwithstanding) upon alien rights, and thus did not cause the uneasy conscience for which professions of international altruism are so often a compensation. But none of these reasons touches on what is probably the basic ideological explanation—the influence exerted upon the American's democratic thought by his philosophy of manifest destiny.

To understand this influence one must begin by recognizing that the egoism of the American's philosophy of the destiny of democracy did not exclude a love of democracy for its own sake. When the American spoke of extending the area of freedom he had in mind not only greater freedom for Americans but also greater freedom by means of Americans. This impersonal element in the American's attachment to the cause of freedom is abundantly illustrated in the expansionist literature. The *New York Morning News,* affirming that the great experiment of democracy required nothing less than the continent, saw the end of this experiment as "the free development of humanity to the best and highest results it may be capable of working out for itself." [106] The vision which caused the American expansionist's heart to leap was described by Representative Cathcart as that of "State after State coming into this great temple of freedom, and burning their incense upon an altar consecrated to the enjoyment of civil and religious liberty." [107] The migrations which would extend American territory would also, Representative Tibbats declared, "extend the principles of civil liberty, for they march *pari passu* with the migrations of the Anglo-Saxon race." [108]

This very attachment to freedom was one element underlying the American expansionist's self-engrossment. For in his devotion to the ideal he cast about for the best instrument to realize it and found—himself. The philosophy of American nationalism developed a belief incongruous with the equalitarianism of democracy—the belief that, however equal men might be at birth, Americans had become subsequently a super-people.

The American had never been a sufferer from self-depreciation. But the 'forties witnessed the full flowering of national self-esteem in consequence of the undeniable promise in American life, of intensified democratic self-consciousness, of heightened nationalism, and of the partial stupidity of national adolescence. It was in this period that an Iowa newspaper urged ironically that America repudiate its debts to Europe on the ground that Europe was sufficiently recompensed by having assisted the spread of

---

[106] *New York Morning News,* February 7, 1845.
[107] *Cong. Globe,* 29th Cong., 1st sess., p. 324.
[108] *Ibid.,* 28th Cong., 1st sess., App., p. 450.

American civilization! [109] National boasting was reconciled with civilization by one America orator's explanation: "It is not good taste in individuals to indulge in boasting; but a nation is allowed to assume an elevated tone." In an editorial of the *United States Journal* of 1845 one finds an observation in a very elevated tone:

> It is a truth, which every man may see, if he will but look,—that all the channels of communication,—public and private, through the school-room, the pulpit, and the press,—are engrossed and occupied with *this one idea*, which all these forces are combined to disseminate:—that we the American people, are the most independent, intelligent, moral and happy people on the face of the earth.[110]

The foregoing words are not those of a satirist but of one who admitted the truth of the proposition. It was no matter that the very same page of his editorial reported the failure of Pittsburg female operatives in their strike for a ten-hour working day!

But in the national self-complacency of the "fabulous 'forties" there was the redeeming quality of moral ambition. The *United States Journal* entitled its editorial "Forward Forward" and called from drowsy satisfaction to meliorative effort. Walt Whitman, who wrote that "we are the most beautiful to ourselves and in ourselves," also exclaimed: "I will make the most splendid race the sun ever shone upon." [111] While these words are from a later decade, in the 'forties he gave prose expression to the same ideal:

> And it is from such materials—from the democracy with its manly heart and its lion strength, spurning the ligatures wherewith drivellers would bind it—that we are to expect the great FUTURE of this western world! a scope involving such unparalleled human happiness and rational freedom, to such unnumbered myriads, that the heart of a true *man* leaps with a mighty joy only to think of it! God works out his greatest results by such means; and while each popinjay priest of the mummery of the past is babbling his alarm, the youthful Genius of the people passes swiftly over era after era of change and improvement, and races of human beings erewhile down in gloom or bondage rise gradually toward that majestic development which the good God doubtless loves to witness.[112]

These swelling periods exemplify the modern version of the chosen people, which Whitman's compatriots, on six days of the week even if not the seventh, made the chief tenet of their religious philosophy as well as

[109] Adams, *op. cit.*, p. 90.
[110] *United States Journal*, October 18, 1845.   [111] Whitman, *op. cit.*, pp. 286, 98.
[112] *The Uncollected Prose and Poetry of Walt Whitman*, ed. Emory Holloway (New York, 1931), I, 159.

of their nationalism. This thesis differed from the Hebraic in that "a kingdom of priests and a holy nation" was ordained to preserve, not the law of man's duty to God, but the law of man's duty to man—democracy. In his anthropocentric theology, in which God himself served chiefly as a Providence watchful for mankind and human values, the American approached perilously close to changing the traditional dogma, that man exists *ad majorem gloriam Dei*, into the heresy that God exists *ad majorem gloriam hominis*. And Providence had entrusted the fullest achievement of the moral glory of man to the best of human material, the mighty American democracy. It is small wonder that the American like the ancient Hebrew was self-engrossed. The "chosen people" is indifferent to the heathen because it believes that the best material for the creation of its ideal is itself.

Enshrined in expansionism, then, was this dogma of the special mission. Moral idealism divested of all intent of sacrilege the half-belief that God, who walked with Noah, rode with the American pioneer in his journeys over the continent. Even theological literature was scarcely more abundant in references to Providence than was the literature of expansionism. For it seemed that especially in expanding our territory, as a poet wrote upon the prospect of annexing Texas, "we do but follow out our destiny, as did the ancient Israelite." [113] The expansionist conception of destiny was essentially ethical in its assumption that "Providence had given to the American people a great and important mission . . . to spread the blessings of Christian liberty." [114] It was ambitiously ethical in its further assumption that "Providence" had a "design in extending our free institutions as far and as wide as the American continent." [115] But the primary providential end was no more the elevation of the Latin-American heathen than was the elevation of the adjacent Philistines the end of the Israelite's journey to the Promised Land. The end in view was, as stated by John L. O'Sullivan in his first passage on manifest destiny, "the free development of our yearly multiplying millions." But in a second reference to manifest destiny he implied the moral significance of this free development of Americans. Americans were destined to develop themselves as subjects in "the great experiment of liberty and federated self-government entrusted to us." [116]

Such was the credo which encouraged American expansionists to conceive that the free rather than the meek would inherit the earth. Its logic harmonized Calvinistic pride and equalitarianism. Still greater was its service in permitting the harmonization of the American's two deepest impulses—the expansionism oriented toward the good earth, and the democratic idealism oriented toward "Fair freedom's star." Believing like the

---

[113] *Democratic Review*, "Progress in America," XVIII (1846), 92.
[114] Senator Buchanan, *Cong. Globe*, 28th Cong., 1st sess., p. 380.
[115] Representative Duncan, *ibid.*, 2d sess., App., p. 178.
[116] *New York Morning News*, December 27, 1845.

Crusader that "God wills it," the expansionist had the joyful illusion of hitching his pioneer wagon to a star.

There is, of course, the quite different question whether territorial expansion was objectively essential to freedom—the American's or any one else's. The expansionist's cosmology, refreshing as it was, perhaps seemed to offer little convincing evidence that the star of democracy would not have shone as brightly in the world's firmament even with less nationalist heat in man for the addition of stars to the flag.

XV The Thrust of Abraham Lincoln: Toward the American Nation or Toward the American Dream?

Introduction The major thrusts of Abraham Lincoln's thought and idealism have been difficult to fix in the context of either America or the world. His modes of expression—varied and moving, earthy and lofty, plain and subtle—have added to the difficulties of fixing him in a generalized category that would command widespread acceptance. He has been variously the Great Emancipator, the Savior of the Union, the Leader of the Second American Revolution that made business and property rights paramount in the nation, the Dreamer of the American Dream, and much else. Among the various thrusts of Lincoln, probably the one that has come most to the fore in the last generation has been Lincoln as the Savior of the Union.

James A. Rawley [1] in the essay presented here has given clear and concise expression to this view in a compact analysis of the elements of Lincoln's American Nationalism. His view of Lincoln's real thrust is unequivocal: "Abraham Lincoln is the supreme nationalist in the history of the United States. His greatest service to the nation was not freeing the slaves but preserving the body politic . . . he placed the nation uppermost—above peace, above abolition, above property rights, and even above the Constitution." Before Lincoln became president, his nationalism had taken form in a firm conviction, which for all its strength was not noisy and was notable for ". . . its avoidance of spread eagle expansionism, of strident Americanism, of cultural chauvinism, and of excessive legalism." He had defined it on the political side as a system of free government based on the Declaration of Independence and the Constitution; on the cultural side as an emphasis on people and not the state, and on the people's loyalty to the state; and on the economic side as a system based on Henry Clay's American system. In 1862, now president, he declared that the nation had three major components: the territory—"the national homestead"; the people—"this great tribunal"; and the laws—fundamental, organic, and statutory. The saving of the union would give "a new birth of freedom" for all mankind and "for man's vast future."

Gabor Boritt, in a forthcoming book, defines the major thrust of Lincoln's meaning for Americans and for all people as the accomplishment of the American Dream.[2] Boritt states his position clearly: "Historians generally resolve the seeming ambivalence with good instinct but poor logic, by ignoring some of the evidence. The majority of them take his expressions about the union as his fundamental war aim. Allan Nevins, for example, gave his great history of the Civil War the title *The War for the Union*. If we would see it as Lincoln did, how-

---

[1] James A. Rawley, "The Nationalism of Abraham Lincoln," *Civil War History*, IX (1963), 283–298.

[2] "Lincoln and the Economics of the American Dream," from a forthcoming book. Chapter XIX, "Watchman, What of the Night?", is the selection given here.

ever, it would be more accurate, even if more awkward, to call it the War for the American Dream." However, Boritt is not dogmatic and does not exclude all other aspects of Lincoln's thought and feeling. Lincoln was a complex and many faceted man; he spoke feelingly of union, democracy, the free constitutional government of the people, but to Lincoln: "They were all identical to or indispensable means to the American Dream." Professor Boritt has written to me: "As for my book on him: it clearly recognizes the existence of various elements in Lincoln's thought, yet it also attempts to demonstrate that he had one, all-important, *central idea*. I feel that his devotion to this idea dominated and gave a higher meaning to his political career. This was a devotion to *man's right to rise in life*." This was the American Dream.

In contrasting Lincoln the great American nationalist with Lincoln the dreamer of the American dream, Boritt rises to a lofty idealism: "One prizes the Civil War, to quote Francis Lieber, as a 'war for nationality.' It makes Lincoln into 'The Great Nationalist' of the modern historians, a man who had a religious faith in the union. The other cherishes him as an American Moses or Christ, one who spoke to mankind." If Lincoln was the Great Nationalist, he stands with Bismarck and Cavour, and Boritt draws this striking conclusion: "Without gainsaying the achievements of the Europeans, we must note that their degenerate twentieth-century descendants in the worship of the nation as an end in itself were Hitler and Mussolini. In contrast, Lincoln's Dream helped lead America to the nationalism of Theodore Roosevelt, Woodrow Wilson, and Franklin Delano Roosevelt."

The Nationalism of Abraham Lincoln
——*James A. Rawley*

Abraham Lincoln is the supreme nationalist in the history of the United States. His greatest service to the nation was not freeing its slaves but preserving its body politic. When Lincoln became President in 1861 four score and five years had passed since his nation had been "conceived and dedicated"—years marked by phenomenal growth and an attendant theorizing over the exact nature of the Federal Union.

Lincoln's concept of American nationalism differed not only from the Southern interpretations he waged war to refute, but also from Northern interpretations in the formative years preceding his election as the nation's chief executive. His nationalism was a mid-century bridge between the earlier thought of the Founding Fathers, Henry Clay, and Daniel Webster, and the later thought of Francis Lieber and John W. Burgess. In his hierarchy of values he placed the nation uppermost— above peace, above abolition, above property rights, and even above the Constitution. Surprisingly, though it is well-known that Lincoln was a nationalist, historians have not subjected the nature of his concepts to extended, systematic analysis.

Before he took the oath of office in 1861 Lincoln had developed a nationalism notable for its quiet fervor, its avoidance of spread-eagle expansionism, of strident Americanism, of cultural chauvinism, and of excessive legalism—differing markedly from the fervid sentiments of many mid-century nationalists. His pre-Presidential thought is best separated into its political, cultural, and economic components.

Lincoln's political nationalism stemmed from a belief in the uniqueness of the United States. Its government and society were an unexampled experiment—a successful experiment, indeed, but one which had yet to demonstrate its success to skeptical and less happy nations. What was the root of this distinctive national character? It was nothing less than a system of free government. Here was the source of American

From James A. Rawley, "The Nationalism of Abraham Lincoln," *Civil War History*, IX (1963), 283–298. Reprinted by permission.

political prosperity; without this living principle the state was worth nothing.

The incarnation of the spirit of American nationalism was for him the Declaration of Independence. "I have often inquired of myself," he reflected at Philadelphia in 1861,

> what great principle or idea it was that kept this confederacy so long together. It was not the mere matter of the separation of the colonies from the mother land; but something in that Declaration giving liberty, not alone to the people of this country, but hope to the world for all time.

In this statement Lincoln put to one side many conventional explanations of nationalism—language, common descent, cultural tradition, foreign perils, and historical territory—in favor of an idea.[1]

This central concept found legal embodiment in the Constitution— "the only safeguard of our liberties," as he put it. The American government, held in restraint by the Constitution, offered liberty and equality for all. "Free speech and discussion and immunity from whip and tar and feathers, seem implied by the guarantee to each state of a republican form of government," he deliberated. Through the public press our republican institutions "can be best sustained by the diffusion of knowledge and the due encouragement of a universal, national spirit of inquiry and discussion of public events. . . ." He deemed religious and civil liberty "the noblest of causes," and found American political institutions more conducive to their maintenance than any in human history.[2]

Lincoln would not proscribe immigrants, would not make them less eligible for the freedom of the Declaration than those descended by blood from the Revolutionary fathers. ". . . They have a right to claim it as though they were blood of the blood, and flesh of the flesh of the men who wrote that Declaration . . . ," he insisted.

His conception of the place of the Negro in American society flowed from his faith in the Declaration. Unlike Stephen A. Douglas, he believed the Declaration embraced Negroes as well as white persons, but that the commitment was to be realized in the future. Just as the Declaration did not decree immediate abolition of slavery, neither did its embodiment in the Constitution convert that document into an antislavery instrument, as Salmon P. Chase and Charles Sumner contended. The assertion that all men are created equal did not mean they were equal

---

[1] Hans Kohn, *American Nationalism* (New York, 1957), p. 8, finds the root of American nationalism in a more remote idea—"the English tradition of liberty."

[2] Roy P. Basler *et al.* (eds.), *The Collected Works of Abraham Lincoln* (New Brunswick, N.J., 1953–1955), II, 366; Gilbert A. Tracy (ed.), *Uncollected Letters of Abraham Lincoln* (Boston, 1917), p. 121; Archer H. Shaw (ed.), *The Lincoln Encyclopedia* (New York, 1950), pp. 187, 274.

morally, intellectually, or physically, but that they were equal in certain inalienable rights. Lincoln neither credited Negroes with physical equality, nor favored extending citizenship, suffrage, or the rights of jury service or officeholding to Negroes. At the same time, under Douglas' taunts of inconsistency, he stood firm on the ground that "in the right to eat the bread without leave of anybody else which his own hand earns, he is my equal. . . ."

If Lincoln did not favor immediate suffrage for Negroes, neither did he advocate universal manhood suffrage for whites. In 1836, even though Illinois had enjoyed total manhood suffrage since 1818, he announced, "I go for all sharing the privileges of the government, who assist in bearing its burthens. Consequently I go for admitting all whites to the right of suffrage, who pay taxes or bear arms (by no means excluding females)." European liberal nationalists could concur with this conservative approach to suffrage.

Lincoln's world-view was founded upon his belief in the impregnability, isolation, and pacific purposes of the United States. The world mission of America was to be an example, and little more. It was not to foment or assist revolutions abroad; it was not to liberate or to engage in missionary diplomacy. Rather, the United States would discharge its moral obligation by maintaining its example, by inspiring the hopes of man, by welcoming immigrants, and by sympathizing with those struggling to be free. The spirit animating the nation, he maintained, would eventually "grow and expand into the universal liberty of mankind." [3]

A final element of his political nationalism was his espousal of the theoretical right of revolution. In a speech on the Mexican War, Congressman Lincoln had defended the right of the Mexicans and Texans in turn to revolt, recognizing the territorial authority of Texas, however, "just so far as she carried her revolution [geographically], by obtaining the *actual,* willing or unwilling, submission of the people. . . ." His "Resolutions in Behalf of Hungarian Freedom" had asserted "the right of any people, sufficiently numerous for national independence, to throw off, to revolutionize, their existing form of government. . . ." But he qualified his manifesto by a preamble emphasizing "our continued devotion to the principles of free institutions." The right of revolution he had been favoring was on behalf of human freedom, against Spain, Mexico, and Austria. Therefore it is not surprising to find Lincoln writing A. H. Stephens in January, 1859, that "The right of peaceable assembly and of petition, and by Article Fifth of the Constitution, the right of amendment, is the constitutional substitute [in this country] for revolution." [4] The position he was to take as President he had declared well over two years before he assumed office.

---

3 Basler, *Collected Works,* I, 48, 278, II, 499–500, III, 145–146, 249.
4 *Ibid.,* I, 439, II, 115–116; Tracy, *Uncollected Letters,* p. 127.

The cultural aspects of Lincoln's pre-Presidential nationalism clustered about his emphasis upon the people rather than the state. Underlying this was his understanding of human nature. A persisting concept was his rejection of John Locke's famous notion of the malleability of human nature. ". . . Human nature cannot be changed," it is "God's decree," held Lincoln. Man was a blend of good and evil, and some men were better than others. Man was not good enough to live under a system of extreme individualism or anarchy; "if all men were just, there would still be *some*, though not so *much*, need of government." Men were moved by both high principle and self-interest. Part of Lincoln's case against slavery was that "it forces so many really good men amongst ourselves into open war with the very fundamental principles of civil liberty. . . ." Yet the good in man might be expected to prevail. Repeal the Missouri Compromise, repeal all past history, "you still cannot repeal human nature. It still will be the abundance of man's heart, that slavery extension is wrong. . . ."

The laboring element in the population elicited Lincoln's special sympathies. His famous statement that labor is prior to and independent of capital has often been quoted, sometimes to suggest a Marxian outlook, sometimes to suggest a defense of trade unionism. Actually, of course, it was neither; rather, it was a celebration of the virtues of an open society wherein a free laborer could rise to become a capitalist. His conception of labor looked to social harmony in place of strife, and herein he was more sanguine than his contemporary John Calhoun and possibly even Daniel Webster. Moreover, free labor insisted upon education; each head is the natural guardian, director, and protector of the hands and mouth inseparably connected with it. . . ." Lincoln's outlook was still essentially agrarian—the Jeffersonian conception of the yeoman farmer as the base of free government: "No community whose every member possesses this art ['of deriving a comfortable subsistence from the smallest area of soil'] can ever be a victim of oppression in any of its forms. Such community will be alike independent of crowned-kings, money-kings, and land-kings."

It was the people who sustained the government and not the government the people. ". . . The strongest bulwark of any government . . . is the attachment of the people," he wrote. They would suffer much for its sake, but at some point danger might always be expected. "How shall we fortify against it?" he asked in an address in 1838. With an uncharacteristic outburst of chauvinism he urged indoctrination of loyalty. "Let reverence for the laws be breathed by every American mother, to the lisping babe, that prattles on her lap; let it be taught in schools, in seminaries, and in colleges. . . . in short, let it become the *political religion* of the nation. . . ." This exhortation might sound like a recipe for twentieth century totalitarianism were it not checked by counsel for proper repeal of bad laws. The people's loyalty was a staple of nationalism. In the crisis of the 1850's it was helping prevent dissolution of the Union. "You ought rather to appreciate how much the great body of the Northern people do crucify their feelings," he wrote his friend Joshua F. Speed in 1855, "in order to maintain their loyalty to the constitution and the Union."

Lincoln deemed territorial acquisition to be constitutional, and, while not advocating it, he did not oppose "honest acquisition." But he strenuously resisted grabs for territory that would aggravate the slavery question—"the one great disturbing element in our national politics." [5] Finally, he showed little or no interest in the literary nationalism that colored American letters in his day, and indeed once admitted he had never finished reading a novel.[6]

Lincoln's economic nationalism was an inheritance from Henry Clay, a general view of the capacity of the national government to promote the general welfare. In his first reputed public speech he admitted simply that "I am in favor of a national bank." On other occasions he defended the bank's constitutionality and advantages and criticized the Democrats' substitute—the subtreasury system. In his early years he aligned himself with Clay's nationalist policy on the protective tariff as "indispensably necessary to the prosperity of the American people," but by 1860–1861 was confessing that he had no "thoroughly matured judgment" on protectionism. His stand on internal improvements favored government support, though he did not countenance borrowing money or overexpansion of local projects. He sided with the nationalist principle of opening the public lands to free settlement, "so that every poor man may have a home." [7]

Such measures implied a philosophy of broad construction of the Constitution looking to government intervention in the economy to increase national wealth and promote human welfare. Beset by other issues during the war, however, Lincoln as President did not much concern himself about economic legislation.

When Abraham Lincoln became President of the United States on March 4, 1861, he stood at a different stage in the development of nationalism than did his European statesman contemporaries Cavour and Bismarck. It was Lincoln's task not to create a nation but to maintain one. His effort did not hinge, fundamentally, on power rivalries of foreign nations but on perplexing internal dissensions among states with a long history of political cooperation. His task was eased by an American consensus on certain fundamentals, but complicated by a fierce conflict over constitutional interpretation and the place of slavery in the

---

[5] Basler, *Collected Works*, II, 221, 255, 271, 320, III, 235–236, 477–482.
[6] Reinhard H. Luthin, *The Real Abraham Lincoln* (Englewood Cliffs, N.J., 1960), p. 719.
[7] Shaw, *Lincoln Encyclopedia*, p. 220; Basler, *Collected Works*, IV, 214.

national polity. The contours of his task were rounded out by three generations of discord over these issues and by the secession of seven states even before he was clothed with power.

Lincoln gave his own definition of a nation in 1862: "A nation may be said to consist of its territory, its people, and its laws." The element of territory was commonly stressed by European theorists of nationalism, who found in the concept of a historical homeland and agrarianism, powerful springs of national sentiment. Though Lincoln had paid little notice to territory as an element of American nationalism before 1861, in the First Inaugural he stressed the unity imposed upon the American people by their common territory. "Physically speaking, we cannot separate," he maintained. War would not settle questions of intercourse, and separation would only aggravate disputes over fugitive slaves and the foreign slave trade. He spoke of "this favored land," and in closing referred movingly to "The mystic chords of memory, stretching from every battlefield, and patriot grave, to every living heart and hearthstone, all over this broad land. . . ."

The enduring unity given Americans by the "national homestead" occupied a good deal of his State of the Union message in 1862. The territory of the United States was well adapted for "one national family" and not two or more. "Its vast extent, and its variety of climate and productions, are of advantage, in this age, for one people. . . . Steam, telegraphs, and intelligence, have brought these, to be an advantageous combination for one people."

He turned next to a close analysis of American topography. There was no suitable line for separation. The boundary between free and slaves states consisted for one-third its length of rivers easily crossed; the remaining segment was nothing more than a surveyor's line across which people might walk. Separation could not be achieved by scratching demarcations on parchment.

The great interior region between the Alleghenies and the Rockies, and north of the line where corn and cotton cultures met, posed special difficulties. In Lincoln's estimate, this was the great elongated nucleus of the republic; the other parts were but marginal to it. It was destined to have an immense population, and in the production of material subsistence it was one of the most important regions of the world. But it had no seacoast. Separation of the Union would cut it off from its trade outlets to Europe, South America, Africa, and Asia. Divide the nation between North and South however one might, there could be no commerce between separated sections "except on terms dictated by" a foreign government. Lincoln did not argue the advantages of territorial unity to Northern merchants or to the Northern people, but characteristically urged the South to recognize the folly of breaking a natural customs union advantageous to all Americans.

The national homestead, Lincoln concluded, was a permanent mandate for unity. Sectional contention, therefore, did not spring from territorial differences, but from only transient causes. "Our strife pertains to ourselves," he argued, ". . . and it can, without convulsion, be hushed forever with the passing of one generation." On this foundation he recommended to Congress three constitutional amendments which provided for the gradual emancipation of slaves, compensation to loyal slaveowners, and federal financing for voluntary African colonization of free Negroes.[8]

The second element in Lincoln's wartime definition of a nation was people. "This country, with its institutions, belongs to the people who inhabit it." They were the same people North and South; the nation belonged to all.

The war seems to have reinforced his faith in the public—"this great tribunal." Free institutions had developed the powers and improved the condition of "our whole people, beyond any example in the world." From almost every military regiment could be chosen "a president, a cabinet, a congress, and perhaps a court, abundantly competent to administer the government itself." The plenteous outpouring of loyalty in April, 1861, had shown him that "the people will save their government, if the government itself, will do its part, only indifferently well." The war was not a conflict of militarists, politicians, or classes; it was essentially a people's contest, "a war upon the first principles of popular government—the rights of the people." The people's stake in the war —maintaining a nation whose leading object was to elevate the condition of men—was well understood by the public, he felt.

Uppermost was his faith that "workingmen are the basis of all governments." In a letter of 1864 he made clear his conception of free labor in an open society. Laboring men of the world should unite by a bond of sympathy only less strong than the family tie. They should beware of the divisive force of prejudice and hostility. But labor solidarity should not lead to a war on property. "Property is the fruit of labor— property is desirable—is a positive good in the world. That some should be rich, shows that others may become rich, and hence is just encouragement to industry and enterprise." He therefore advocated social harmony and defined opportunity for social mobility in terms of the individual rather than the class. He once used himself as an example. To the assembled 166th Ohio Regiment he declared, "I happen temporarily to occupy this big White House. I am a living witness that any one of your children may look to come here as my father's child has."

Under popular government, Lincoln observed, "The chief magistrate derives all his authority from the people. . . ." This fiduciary relationship

8 *Ibid.*, V, 527–530; N. W. Stephenson, "Lincoln and the Progress of Nationality in the North," *Annual Report of the American Historical Association for the Year 1919* (Washington, 1923), I, 351–366.

between President and people, he believed, warranted his exercise of extra-Constitutional authority in the national emergency. Presidential actions not explicitly authorized by the people might be made in their interest. If the President "uses the power justly, the . . . people will probably justify him; if he abuses it, he is in their hands to be dealt with by all the modes they have reserved to themselves in the Constitution."

One of these modes was the Presidential election, which occurred in normal course once during the war. It added not a little to the strain, admitted Lincoln, for "It has long been a grave question whether any government not *too* strong for the liberties of its people, can be strong enough to maintain its own existence, in great emergencies." So viewed, the outcome of the 1864 election was a success; moreover, it demonstrated the people's determination to preserve the Union. "The most reliable indication of public purpose in this country," he remarked approvingly, "is derived through our popular elections." [9]

Popular sovereignty went hand in hand with majority rule. In his first Inaugural, Lincoln referred to the questions about slavery as having arisen from the failure of the Constitution to give express answers to them. His approach is reminiscent of Locke's famous query and answer:

> Who shall be the judge whether the prince or legislative act contrary to their trust? . . . To this I reply, The people shall be judge. . . . If a controversy arise betwixt a prince and some of the people in a matter where the law is silent or doubtful and the thing be of great consequence, I should think the proper umpire in such case should be the body of the people.[10]

Lincoln observed that over slavery the American people divided into a majority and minority. "If the minority will not acquiesce, the majority must, or the government must cease." He applied this doctrine of popular sovereignty not merely to mooted questions where the Constitution was silent, but also to certain kinds of decisions already made by the Supreme Court, having in mind the proslavery Dred Scott case: ". . . If the whole policy of the government, upon vital questions affecting the whole people, is to be irrevocably fixed by decisions of the Supreme Court, the instant they are made, in ordinary litigation between parties, in personal actions, the people will have ceased, to be their own rulers. . . ."

The people's loyalty to the nation was Lincoln's reliance. Skillfully he appealed to it, even exploited it, through his wartime messages to Congress and letters (often ostensibly private but intended for the public). In these documents he put his case, the national case, with glowing words and persuasive logic; among the best examples of his

---

9 Basler, *Collected Works*, IV, 270, 432, 437–438, VI, 303, VII, 259–260, 512, VIII, 100, 149.
10 John Locke, *Two Treatises of Government* (New York, 1947), pp. 245–246.

letters are those to Horace Greeley, Erastus Corning, J. C. Conkling, and Mrs. Bixby. The two Inaugurals and the Gettysburg Address are classics, in part because of the national vision limned in them and the inspiring faith in "government of the people, by the people, for the people. . . ." A good portion of the First Inaugural is addressed to those "who really love the Union. . . ."

His conception of loyalty embraced the use of oaths, but the oaths were to be liberal—for insuring future allegiance only—and no man was to be forced to take one. His amnesty proclamation of December, 1863, embodied an oath that he looked upon as a means of waging war, hastening peace, and effecting reunion. It would encourage desertion from the Confederacy, assure certain rights to the oath taker, and form a nucleus of loyal citizens who, he thought, would give an affirmative answer to the question he put in his last public address: "Can Louisiana be brought into proper practical relation with the Union *sooner* by *sustaining* . . . her new state government?" And what would be true of Louisiana would be true of other seceded states.

Finally, Lincoln believed that the people and he all dwelt under the ultimate authority of the Divinity. The people were God's instrument; His way was inscrutable and He might exact heavy payment for wrongdoing, as by civil war. But He was a just God, and "in His own good time, will give us the rightful result." The President, he insisted, had an oath registered in Heaven to "preserve, protect, and defend" the Constitution. "The will of God prevails"; and if God willed that this mighty scourge of war continue,

> until all the wealth piled by the bondman's two hundred and fifty years of unrequited toil shall be sunk, and until every drop of blood drawn with the lash, shall be paid by another drawn with the sword, as was said three thousand years ago, so still it must be said "the judgments of the Lord, are true and righteous altogether."

The third essential point of Lincoln's final concept of a nation was its laws: fundamental or higher law, organic or constitutional law, and statutory or legislative law. The American nation was founded upon law; it emanated from the fundamental law, and proceeded through organic law to statutory law.

This orderly progression lay at the heart of his conception of the origin of the nation. For nearly three generations the philosophical nature of the Union had been hotly contested. Among the most influential views was John C. Calhoun's theory that the Union was merely a compact among sovereign states, which had created it by writing and ratifying the Constitution. Each state might nullify an act of the national legislature by following a formula patterned on the mode of ratification. Indeed, each state might withdraw unilaterally from the Union by following a prescribed plan.

Various challenges to national sovereignty had previously been repudiated by John Marshall, Andrew Jackson, and Daniel Webster. Not until 1860, however, had any state exercised an asserted right of secession. To the question of the origin of the nation Lincoln addressed himself in his First Inaugural and elsewhere. He contended that the nation was *not* the creation of the Constitutional Convention and the state ratifying conventions, was *not* born in 1787–1788, and was *not* a compact among the states. He argued that the nation was older than the Constitution, and even older than the states. It was born in 1774, founded by the Articles of Association (or perhaps in 1776, as he suggested in the Gettysburg Address). The birth of the nation before the colonies became states gave the nation precedence over the states; "The original ones passed into the Union even *before* they cast off their British colonial dependence. . . ." Formed by the Articles of Association, the American nation

was matured and continued by the Declaration of Independence in 1776. It was further matured and the faith of all the then thirteen states expressedly plighted and engaged that it should be perpetual by the Articles of Confederation in 1778. And finally, in 1787, one of the declared objects for ordaining and establishing the Constitution was *"to form a more perfect union."*

Calhoun's starting point, therefore, was actually the outcome of an organic progress.

In his conception of the nation as a living organism, capable of evolutionary growth, Lincoln differed not merely from Calhoun but also from those nationalist stalwarts Marshall, Jackson, and Webster. Marshall in *McCulloch* v. *Maryland,* for example, like Calhoun saw the origin of the nation in the Constitution. He read its history differently, however, insisting that the Constitution derived its whole authority not from the states but from the people. Jackson, in his "Proclamation to the People of South Carolina," shared Calhoun's assumptions that the nation originated with the Constitution and that the nation was a compact. But it was a compact to form a government that "operates directly on the people individually, not upon the States"; and "it is precisely because it is a compact that" the states could not breach it. Webster, too, as in his Second Reply to Hayne, agreed that the nation began with the constitutional contract. However, it was "an executed contract" and he roundly denied that the national government was the creature or agent of the states. "It is, Sir, the people's Constitution, the people's government, made for the people, and answerable to the people."

Lincoln, then, departed from the consensus that the American nation was born with the Constitution and that it was a contract. He was perhaps the first President to emphasize strongly the ideas that the Union was more than a government and that the American political organization was a nation-state. He reached beyond the Constitution to the mystique of "its territory, its people, and its laws." The compact theory he dismissed summarily: "If the United States be not a government proper, but an association of states in the nature of contract merely . . . does it not require all to lawfully rescind it?"

Fundamental law and organic law alike combined to disprove the theory of secession. "I hold, that in contemplation of universal law, and of the Constitution, the Union of these states is perpetual. Perpetuity is implied, if not expressed, in the fundamental law of all national governments," and the Constitution could not be destroyed "except by some action not provided for in the instrument itself." Secession, he was saying to strict constructionists and states rights men, was not justified by a literal interpretation of the Constitution or by the history of the formation of the nation. It followed, therefore, that the secession ordinances were legally void. Moreover, the disunionist doctrine once applied could be indefinitely multiplied; if one portion of the nation might secede might not another part secede from *it?* "Plainly, the central idea of secession is the essence of anarchy," he concluded.

But what of the right of revolution that he had upheld in the antebellum years? In the First Inaugural he reiterated his defense of the right, acknowledging that whenever people weary of a government "they can exercise their *constitutional* right of amending it, or their *revolutionary* right to dismember, or overthrow it." He then pursued the line of thought he suggested in 1859 to A. H. Stephens, that the right of amendment is a constitutional substitute for revolution. An amendment had been proposed to forbid federal interference with slavery in the states; believing this already implied, he would not oppose it.[11]

Lincoln had, after all, favored revolution against oppression; he argued now that no vital right of a minority or an individual had been abridged. It was better to remain in the Union, relying on elections, amendments, the ultimate justice of the people, and Divine guidance:

The right of revolution is never a legal right. The very term implies the breaking, and not the abiding by, organic law. At most, it is but a moral right, when exercised for a morally justifiable cause. When exercised without such a cause revolution is no right, but simply a wicked exercise of physical power.[12]

---

[11] Basler, *Collected Works*, IV, 264–265, 267–271, 433–435, VI, 410, VIII, 333.
[12] Thomas J. Pressly, "Bullets and Ballots: Lincoln and the 'Right of Revolution,'" *American Historical Review*, LXVII (1962), 647–662 (quotation from p. 659).

Secession, then, was justified neither by the theoretical right of revolution nor by the notion of state sovereignty—"the assumption, that there is some omnipotent, and sacred supremacy, pertaining to a *state*. . . ." It was basic to his theory of federalism that the Union was older than the states; from this followed Lincoln's unconventional and rather dubious historical argument that the Union created the states. "Originally, some dependent colonies made the Union; and, in turn, the Union threw off their old dependence, for them, and made them states. . . ." The states had never been and were not now sovereign; they in fact derived their power from the Union. "The states have their status in the Union, and they have no other *legal status*." [13]

State sovereignty was one thing, state rights another. It is not true, as one historian has suggested, that Lincoln would sink the states to the level of counties. He was not a "consolidationist," to use Calhoun's term. "Unquestionably, the states have the powers, and rights, reserved to them in, and by the national Constitution," Lincoln asserted. The control of slavery within their boundaries was one of these, and in the First Inaugural he repeated a section of the Republican party platform: "*Resolved*, That the maintenance inviolate of the rights of the states . . . is essential to that balance of power on which the perfection and endurance of our political fabric depend. . . ." [14]

Lincoln took issue, too, with Calhoun's contention that "the character of the Government has been changed . . . from a federal republic . . . into a great national consolidated democracy." [15] "Such of you as are now dissatisfied, still have the old Constitution unimpaired," Lincoln maintained. He revered the Constitution, and recurringly had opposed amendment before 1861. In the original draft of the First Inaugural he had repelled rather than approved any changes of the great document, but on this point deferred to William H. Seward's advice. True, he later proposed three amendments to the Constitution, but not until the war had dragged on for a year and a half and then only to hasten peace. For Lincoln the Constitution remained a source of national strength and unity. His words of 1848 were applicable: "Better not take the first step, which may lead to a habit of altering it. Better, rather, habituate ourselves to think of it as unalterable."

If the Federal Constitution was a part of the laws and the laws part of the nation, what of the Confederate constitution and Southern nationalism? He found the temporary Confederate constitution objectionable in principle because its preamble substituted for "We the people" the phrase "We, the deputies of the sovereign and independent states."

---

[13] Basler, *Collected Works*, IV, 433–435.
[14] Dwight Lowell Dumond, *Antislavery Origins of the Civil War in the United States* (Ann Arbor, 1959), p. 109; Basler, *Collected Works*, IV, 263, 435.
[15] Richard K. Crallé (ed.), *The Works of John C. Calhoun* (New York, 1861), IV, 551.

"Why this deliberate pressing out of view, the rights of men, and the authority of the people?" asked Lincoln.

Nor could he square the new Southern state constitutions with his liberal nationalism. "In those documents we find the abridgement of the existing right of suffrage," he insisted (having moved beyond his 1838 position on manhood suffrage), "and the denial to the people of all right to participate in the selection of public officers, except the legislative[,] boldy advocated, with labored arguments to prove that large control of the people in government, is the source of all political evil." In this he saw the approach of returning despotism.

He refused to recognize the existence of Southern nationalism. The long history of the development of separate consciousness, with its geographical, social, cultural, political, and constitutional aspects, he relegated to one erroneous notion held by some Americans—the inequality of man. This was inadmissible in a nation dedicated to the philosophy of the Declaration of Independence. Beyond this it was inadmissible in the family of nations. As Lincoln stated in a resolution he prepared for the English liberal John Bright:

> . . . For the first [time] in the world, an attempt has been made to construct a new Nation, upon the basis of, and with the primary, and fundamental object to maintain, enlarge, and perpetuate human slavery, therefore,
> Resolved, That no such embryo State should ever be recognized by, or admitted into, the family of christian and civilized nations. . . .

A nation may be said to consist of its laws, and according to its laws the American nation was permanent. The Confederacy had come into being unlawfully, repudiating law in its organic structure and thus having no claim to recognition in the society of nations.

In the extraordinary crisis of war Lincoln discovered a perfectly new source of national authority—the warmaking power belonging to the executive. He not only asserted his right in an emergency to wield powers of doubtful legality, but further, the right of the President to wield powers assigned to the legislature. When he did consult Congress on July 4, 1861, after eleven weeks of "dictatorship," he cooly said that he believed he had done nothing "beyond the constitutional competency of Congress." "It was with the deepest regret," he said, "that the Executive found the duty of employing the war-power, in defense of the government, forced upon him. He could but perform this duty, or surrender the existence of the government." As the war continued, he found in late 1863 "that the war power is still our main reliance."

His nationalistic purpose wholly governed his war leadership—his relations with Union generals, his attitude toward civil liberties, his

policy of emancipation, his plan of reconstruction. He abridged civil
liberties by suspension of the writ of *habeas corpus* in sections where
the civil courts were open; he subjected over sixteen thousand persons
to military arrests; he suppressed liberty of speech and press; he proclaimed a blockade of the Confederate ports without a declaration of
war; he spent money and raised troops without authorization by Congress. All this he justified: "I felt that measures, otherwise unconstitutional, might become lawful, by becoming indispensable to the preservation of the constitution, through the preservation of the nation."

His emancipation policy requires but brief treatment here. He reversed General John C. Frémont's liberating proclamation, he told
Orville H. Browning, in order to save the government. His famous letter
to Horace Greeley, written one month before he issued his preliminary
Emancipation Proclamation, succinctly declared that "What I do about
slavery, and the colored race, I do because I believe it helps to save
the Union; and what I forbear, I forbear because I do *not* believe it
would help to save the Union." The following year he said, "I issued the
proclamation on purpose to aid . . . in saving the Union."

The issuance itself of the liberation manifesto was the most nationalistic
act he performed during the war. He had repeatedly said earlier that
he and the national government had no power to touch slavery in the
states. Now, in 1862, he drew on John Quincy Adams' theory of a wartime
right to emancipate slaves. In the exigency of conflict Lincoln invaded
the rights of the states, dealt a staggering blow to the structure of
federalism, and confiscated two billion dollars worth of property.

His reconstruction policy, standing on the premise that no right to
secede existed, looked to speedy resumption of normal political relations.
Believing in an unbroken Union, he rejected the views of Charles
Sumner and Thaddeus Stevens, who held respectively that the rebelling
states had committed suicide or were conquered provinces. One of his
objections to the Congressional plan of reconstruction lay in its "fatal
admission" of secession. Wanting to avoid social revolution or revenge,
he spoke of merely reinaugurating the national authority or of again
getting the states into their proper practical relation with the Union.
He early expressed his belief that the Union after the war would be no
different from what it was before. In his proclamation on amnesty and
reconstruction he suggested that the reconstructed states be maintained
"as before the rebellion," with small exception; the loyalty oath incorporated in it affirmed support of "the union of the states" under the
Constitution.[16]

Moreover, his vision was broader than that of almost all his con-

---

[16] John G. Nicolay and John Hay, *Abraham Lincoln: A History* (New York, 1909), III,
322–323; Basler, *Collected Works*, I, 488, IV, 429, 438, 440, V, 51, VI, 176, VII, 56, 281.

temporaries; unceasingly he saw the American war in world perspective and tried to foresee its meaning to posterity. Lincoln was fully as conscious as the Founding Fathers that the American experience concerned all mankind. His Fourth of July, 1861, message to Congress recognized far-reaching significance in the conflict:

> . . . This issue embraces more than the fate of these United States. It presents to the whole family of man, the question, whether a constitutional republic, or a democracy—a government of the people, by the same people—can, or cannot, maintain its territorial integrity against its own foes. It presents the question, whether discontented individuals, too few in numbers to control administration, according to organic law, in any case, can always, upon the pretense, break up their government, and thus practically put an end to free government upon the earth.

And moving on to even higher ground, "It forces us to ask: 'Is there, in all republics, this inherent, and fatal weakness?' 'Most a government, of necessity, be too *strong* for the liberties of its own people, or too *weak* to maintain its own existence?' "

Few, if any, American Presidents have been as acutely conscious of the meaning of the unique American experiment to the future of man as Abraham Lincoln. The struggle of today "is for a vast future also," he told the Congress in December, 1861. He concluded his next annual message with his memorable remark, "We cannot escape history." His letter to James C. Conkling contained a magnificent outburst of eloquence: "Thanks to all. For the great republic—for the principle it lives by, and keeps alive—for man's vast future—thanks to all." The nation would not be merely preserved, he foresaw in the Second Inaugural, but would have "a new birth of freedom."

The Civil War (to paraphrase Carlton Hayes on the French Revolution) [17] created a truly national state, in which distinctions of section and caste were blurred, states were subordinated, and political and economic institutions were placed on a national basis and made to serve national ends. It repudiated the doctrine of secession, formerly considered lawful in the South. It inculcated the doctrine that all citizens owe their first and paramount loyalty to the nation, and it adopted various measures to give effect to this doctrine: conscription of manpower, the income tax, a national banking system, the legal tender acts, national subsidies to education and railroads, a protective tariff, and a new national immigration policy. Not surprisingly, perhaps, the faction and leader identified with nationalism went overfar in discrediting the

---

[17] Carlton J. H. Hayes, "Nationalism: Historical Development," *Encyclopaedia of the Social Sciences*, ed. E. R. A. Seligman (New York, 1930–1934), XI, 240–249.

loyalty of their opponents, were often intolerant of criticism, and often overrode liberalism in the drive for nationalism. Nor could liberal nationalism in the United States, as in Europe, be fulfilled without sacrifice of the liberal ideal of peace.

Lincoln had played the crucial role in the maintenance of American nationalism. He had made possible the new concept of an organic nation, a people's government not bound to the letter of the Constitution nor fettered by state rights. In his administration the center of gravity shifted to the national government; what emerged from the derangement was a nation-state. Four years after his death the Supreme Court in *Texas* v. *White* wrote into American constitutional law his theory of the origin of the Federal Union, stating that it began among the colonies, grew out of kindred principles, was ordained as "a more perfect Union" by the Constitution, and was perpetual and indissoluble.[18]

True, the hegemony of the national state in the generation after the Civil War was shadowed by a laissez-faire political economy, but the conception endured, to be drawn on by twentieth-century nationalists like Theodore Roosevelt, Herbert Croly, and Woodrow Wilson. Nor should Lincoln be censured for failing to see that nationalism has its limitations, or for believing that the world might be inspired to make itself over in the American image. His task had been to save the nation, and in this he signally succeeded, making it possible for America to wield its strength in the twentieth-century family of nations.

---

[18] The court, however, departed from Lincolnian constitutionalism in flatly asserting that the rights of the seceded states were suspended by civil war and leaving to Congress the power to restore them to proper constitutional relations. For an acute analysis of *Texas* v. *White* see Eric L. McKitrick, *Andrew Johnson and Reconstruction* (Chicago, 1960), pp. 115–117.

Watchman, What of the Night?
—*G. S. Boritt*

"This is a People's contest." Thus Abraham Lincoln defined in 1861 the war he was to lead for four ever more painful years.

On the side of the Union, it is a struggle for maintaining in the world, that form, and substance of government, whose leading object is, to elevate the condition of men—to lift artificial weights from all shoulders

---

From "Lincoln and the Economics of the American Dream" from a forthcoming book. Reprinted by permission of the author.

—to clear the path of laudable pursuit for all—to afford all, an un-
fettered start, and a fair chance, in the race of life.[1]

The President repeated that definition many times thereafter without
substantial variation. Yet he also spoke of the war in terms more political
than economic, as a war for the Union, or democracy, and—less frequently—as a war for free constitutional government, or justice, or the
rights of the people. Indeed, elsewhere in the very address quoted above,
his first to Congress as Chief Magistrate, he spoke of the conflict as a test
of the idea that "a government of the people, by the same people" was
practical.[2]

Historians generally resolve the seeming ambivalence, or at least
duality in Lincoln's thought, with good instinct but poor logic, by
ignoring some of the evidence. The majority of them take his expressions
about the Union as his fundamental war aim. Allan Nevins, for example,
gave his great history of the Civil War the title *The War for the Union*.
If we would see it as Lincoln did, however, it would be more accurate,
even if more awkward, to call it the War for the American Dream.

An earlier chapter has explained that Lincoln placed his central idea
of the Republic even above the Union, but, being a politican rather than
a philosopher, he treated the two concepts as identical. The difference
between the two was the kind he liked to dismiss as "a merely metaphysical question and one unnecessary to be forced into discussion." [2a]
What has been said of the Union may also be said of democracy and of
the less frequent formulations of the President's war aims. The American
Dream, Union, democracy, liberty, all became interchangeable in his
utterances.

Lincoln made many attempts to define democracy, and some of these
appear curious to the political scientist. "As I would not be a *slave*, so I
would not be a *master*," his most often quoted version begins. "This
expresses my idea of democracy. Whatever differs from this, to the extent
of the difference, is no democracy." Lincoln knew, of course, that the
absence of slavery was no foolproof criterion of free government. Neither
England nor continental Europe practiced slavery, yet he knew they were
not the best hope of democracy; quite the contrary. When Czar Alexander
II abolished serfdom in Russia, that country still remained, as Lincoln said
earlier, a land "where they make no pretence of loving liberty . . .
where despotism can be taken pure and without the base alloy of
hypocrisy." He also knew, as he declared from the White House, that "we

---

[1] *C.W.*, IV, 438.   [2] *Ibid.*, 426.   [2a] Hay, *Diaries*, 205.

cannot have free government without elections," and he thus mentioned what even in his troubled days was a more generally recognized attribute of democracy than the mere absence of slavery.[3]

And yet Lincoln's definition of democracy in terms of slavery, however questionable as political science, cut to the heart of his thinking. It was certainly more than a mere political device; indeed he never appears to have used it in public. It becomes fully meaningful only if one recognizes that after 1854 slavery became the most direct antithesis of the American Dream in his thought. No longer was the peculiar institution a mere remnant of barbarism for him, but the diametrical opposite of the central idea of the Republic. If his definition of democracy is restated as follows, it still remains questionable political theory, but it will express his meaning in more accurate terms: As I would not want my *chance to rise in life* obstructed, so I would not want to obstruct the chance of others to rise. This expresses my idea of democracy. Whatever differs from this, to the extent of the difference, is no democracy.

For Lincoln, unobstructed upward mobility was the most important ideal America strove for. Although there had to be "yielding to partial, and temporary departures, from necessity," he explained repeatedly during the war that this ideal was "the leading object of the government for whose existence we contend." Mobility was the ideal and slavery its antipode. But as the Dream was not perfectly attainable, thus perhaps was almost a symbol, so slavery, and its dangers, had degrees, and thus it, too, grew to be a symbol in Lincoln's thought.

When he raised the threat of enslavement before the white laborers of the North, a contention historians reject, he was using slavery as the symbol of a loss of mobility. He did not wish to argue, as students and presumably many of his contemporaries understood him, that free labor faced an immediate and total loss of mobility, that is literal enslavement; but that the degree of its freedom might be diminished by the expansive tendency which was totally antithetical to mobility. For slavery was the principle that "You work and toil and earn bread, and I'll eat it." [4]

Attempting to define liberty in 1864—not democracy this time—Lincoln spoke of the same fundamental idea, of the opportunity "for each man to do as he pleases with himself, and the product of his labor." About half a year later he wrote on a piece of cardboard a few sentences, which he humorously labeled "The President's Last, Shortest, and Best Speech," but which he valued sufficiently to procure its publication. The cardboard essay criticized a religion which set men to "fight against their government, because, as they think, that government does not sufficiently

---

[3] C.W., II, 532, 323; VIII, 101.   [4] *Ibid.*, IV, 438; III, 315.

help *some* men to eat their bread in the sweat of *other* men's faces. . . ."

Ten years earlier he had already indicated that he saw the Dream, most fundamentally the right to the fruit of one's labor, almost as a law of nature, and had said triumphantly, "you still cannot repeal human nature." About the same time he wrote:

> The ant, who has toiled and dragged a crumb to his nest, will furiously defend the fruit of his labor, against whatever robber assails him. So plain, that the most dumb and stupid slave that ever toiled for a master, does constantly *know* that he is wronged. So plain that no one, high or low, ever does mistake it. . . .

This in turn harks back to his definition of 1847, or earlier, that a "most worthy" object of good government was the securing "to each labourer the whole product of his labour, or as nearly as possible. . . ." Indeed, if we accept Lincoln's own 1861 recollection, his faith was as old as his ability to think seriously, and probably older. Whatever ideal he held to, whatever stood for America in his eyes, in the most basic sense, it meant to him this faith.[5]

If the shock of the great rebellion against the "best hope of earth" made the President brood much more than before about the political aspects of democracy, about majority rule, about the appeal to arms and other matters, his central concern remained unchanged. This explains why in its defense he was more willing to make temporary sacrifices of certain *political* liberties—the right of *habeas corpus* for example—than were others who did not share his primarily *economic* definition of democracy. Thus he defended the Union, expatiated on the futility of appealing "from the ballot to the bullet," but also explained with clear pragmatism why he spoke thus, why such a doctrine was essential, why the "laboring many" had an immeasurable stake in America. Union, democracy, the free constitutional government of the people—in the final analysis all meant the same thing in his usage. They were all identical to, or indispensable means to, the American Dream.

These concepts had always been interchangable to an extent in Lincoln's mind. During the war they became that ever more so. Once, in 1861, he even used his distinctive expression, "the central idea," to describe American political democracy—if Hay's diary recorded his words accurately. Scholars are therefore correct when they see no contradiction in Lincoln's various explanations of the Civil War. In the most fundamental sense, even when he was not explicit, he was speaking always about the same thing. As he told the soldiers of an Ohio regiment in

---

[5] *Ibid.*, VII, 301 (cf. II, 493); VIII, 155 (cf. VII, 368); II, 271, 222; I, 412; and *infra*, p. 415–7.

1864, the war was a quest for "an open field and a fair chance for your industry, enterprise and intelligence; that you may all have equal privileges in the race of life. . . ."[6]

To recognize Lincoln's variations on his great theme helps to clarify his thinking. Reviewing his life, nearly at its end, he stated that he was "naturally anti-slavery" and that he could "not remember" when he "did not so think and feel." Scholars question the truthfulness of his reflection, rather unjustly even if his words are taken literally. But some of the doubts can certainly be dispelled if Lincoln's words are interpreted in the light of what has been said. Looking back from the vantage point of the Civil War, his lifelong struggle for the American Dream appeared to him as the same as a lifelong struggle against the bondage of labor. In a very basic sense his view was correct, although it is fair to note that not until 1854 was he fully conscious of the supreme significance of the anti-thesis of the Dream and slavery.

Lincoln avowed similarly that "I have never had a feeling politically that did not spring from the sentiments embodied in the Declaration of Independence." Once more his affirmation becomes meaningful only if we recall from an earlier chapter that to Lincoln the essence of Jefferson's Declaration was its preamble, which in turn meant, as he explained repeatedly, "that *all* should have an equal chance."[7]

The President's emphasis on the Union was fully compatible with the supremacy of his "central idea." Paul C. Nagel's interpretation that the war leader saw the Union as "absolute," or, as Lincoln preferred to say, "perpetual," is appropriate. For practical purposes this was the logical consequence of his outlook. Yet in Lincoln's theory, if so cold a term can be applied to his feeling, the Union was not an end but a means. It was to be upheld so long as it upheld "that thing for which the Union itself was made." The Union was the ship, he explained in 1861, and the American Dream its cargo: "the prosperity and the liberties of the people." And "so long as the ship can be saved, with the cargo," he added, "it should never be abandoned." There is no evidence to show that he ever changed his mind.

Without the ship the cargo would go down and therefore it was senseless to emphasize a distinction between the two. Yet this imagery implied that had there been another equally seaworthy ship available, Lincoln might have been satisfied with transferring the cargo. But there was no other ship, the idea itself was beyond the realm of his practical thought. And so there had to be a war, to save the ship, yes, but to save the ship so that the cargo could be saved.

---

[6] *C.W.*, V., 537; VI, 410; VII, 512 (cf. 528–9); Hay, *Diaries*, 19.
[7] *C.W.*, VII, 281; IV, 240; and see ch. XIII.

A plausible case can be made that in his obsession with the Dream Lincoln approached what in others he at times called monomania. The religious mysticism that Edmund Wilson and others perceived in him was there, above and beyond a strong rationalism. But it is not enough to say, indeed to a degree it is inaccurate to say, that it centered on the entity of the Union—the ship. The *right to rise,* for black and white, was Lincoln's central idea, as his entire life's work demonstrates. It was for this idea that the war had to be fought. It was this idea that made the "right result . . . worth more to the world, than ten times the men, and ten times the money," which he asked from the nation.[8]

This distinction, however unimportant it may have appeared to most Americans at the time, held fateful meaning. The idea of the Union is essentially national, that of the Dream is universal. One prizes the Civil War, to quote Francis Lieber, as "a war for nationality." It makes Lincoln into "the Great Nationalist" of the modern historians, a man who had a religious faith in the Union. The other cherishes him as an American Moses or Christ, one who spoke to mankind.[8a]

In the same time, paradoxically, the first view denies the uniqueness of the United States. It values Lincoln as a New World counterpart of Cavour and Bismarck whose highest goal, to use the German's expression, was "*staatsbildung.*" Without gainsaying the achievements of the Europeans, we must note that their degenerate twentieth-century descendants in the worship of the nation as an end in itself were Hitler and Mussolini. In contrast, Lincoln's Dream helped lead America to the nationalism of Theodore Roosevelt, Woodrow Wilson, and Franklin Delano Roosevelt.

If for Lincoln the most "central idea" of the Union war effort was the preservation of man's right to rise, the "central idea of secession" was a monstrous hybrid of anarchy and despotism. In using such a description he appealed to the deep American attachment to law and order that he himself shared. Indeed, enlarging on this, he pointed to the Rebels' subversion of political democracy. But that there was something more behind his renewed use of the words "central idea" grew clear when he later spelled out that by Southern "despotism" he meant that the ultimate Confederate aim was closing down "the door of advancement" before the common people. Or as he explained still later, "at the bottom" of the rebellion was the desire to overthrow the central principle of the Declaration of Independence.[9]

---

[8] C.W., IV, 264, 232, 432; Nagel, One Nation Indivisible, 13 et passim (Nagel also surveys the popular use of the ship as a symbol of the Union, pp. 215–19); Wilson, Patriotic Gore, Studies in the Literature of the American Civil War (New York, 1962), 99–130; Lamon, Recollections, 275. Lincoln made the same point via a less clear metaphor from Proverbs, 25:11, in C.W., IV, 169.

[8a] Lieber to Charles Sumner, Aug. 31, 1864, Lieber Papers, Huntington Library; Williams, "Lincoln: Pragmatic Democrat" in Graebner, ed., The Enduring Lincoln, 37.

[9] C.W., IV, 268; V, 51–3; VI, 320.

It bears repeating that although we are justified in considering Lincoln's Dream as economic in substance, it was always much more to him. With the war it grew in his mind to purely moral dimensions. It is revealing that his second annual message, which developed his economic argument for the Union, did not, in so many words, refer to the Dream at all.

It was his perception of the moral truth that the President made his most incessant efforts to communicate. In nearly all of his important speeches he made allusions or direct references to it. He built the Gettysburg Address on "the proposition" he believed the United States had been founded on, "that all men are created equal." It was this, Jefferson's Declaration, which Lincoln saw as the first enunciation of the American Dream, for which his soldiers "gave the last full measure of devotion." They had died, he also said, so that the "nation might live," and they had died so that the "government of the people, by the people, for the people shall not perish from the earth." The Dream, the Union, democracy —these three Lincoln held up before his people through the darkness of war. They, not unlike the Trinity, were one and the same and also different. But of the three, for him and in a fundamental sense for his people, the greatest was the Dream.[10]

Lincoln was "happy to believe" that the "plain people" understood his message. He professed to be certain that they saw, as he did, the all-important stakes of the war, that none were "so deeply interested to resist the present rebellion as the working people." He found myriad proofs of the people's clear perception. In his first message to Congress he contrasted the military aristocracy, the large number of officers who had resigned their commissions, with the common people in uniform, of whom "not one common soldier, or common sailor is known to have deserted his flag." (Presumably he did not realize that enlisted men were rarely given the privilege of resigning.) Later, too, he emphasized that "no classes of people" were so devoted to the cause as the common "soldiers in the field and the seamen afloat." In numerous ways he emphasized the common people's loyalty, using the term "common" with great pride. He pointed to the national debt that financed the war, much of which, he said in 1861 had been taken by "citizens of the industrial classes." [11]

The President was deeply imbued with the belief that the American Dream had a worldwide significance, and so it must have been heartening for him to receive the congratulatory message of the workingmen of Manchester, England, in 1863. This spoke of America as "a singular, happy abode for the working millions" and of Lincoln as the leader who decisively upheld the great belief that all men are created free and

---

[10] *Ibid.*, VII, 23.   [11] *Ibid.*, V, 53; VII, 259; VIII, 53; V, 39.

equal. Here was evidence for Lincoln that the laboring folk not only of his nation but also of the entire world understood the meaning of the Civil War. He sent a long reply, commending the Manchester cotton-mill workers for their "sublime Christian heroism" in accepting unemployment and privation for the great cause of all workingmen.[12]

Although Lincoln consistently maintained that the plain people "understand, without an argument" what the conflict is about, he could not but have some questions which he did not entirely keep to himself. Certainly elections were hotly contested in the North; there were even riots against the "government of the people." Rather lamely he explained such matters as the fruit of "prejudice, working division and hostility" among the "laboring many," and he also spoke of "ambitious and designing men." Later he added to his store of explanations the inexplicable workings of the divine will.[13]

More important than Northern divisions was the near unanimity of Southern support of the rebellion, at least among whites. This Lincoln was slow to admit and, indeed, never managed to admit fully. Such an admission would have challenged his basic faith in the good sense of the common people. After more than two years of war he could still declare that force, the Confederate Army, was Jefferson Davis's only hope, "not only against us, but against his own people. If that were crushed the people would be ready to swing back to their old bearings." [14]

In the North, he argued, there was no real "diversity among the people" concerning the necessity of maintaining the Union. Still he wished that "it might be more generally and universally understood what the country is now engaged in," and he labored valiantly in this cause. To what extent his message about the Dream did get across to his people must yet be studied. Not surprisingly, among leading intellectuals, who also happened to be mostly upper class, his success appears to have been minimal. Whatever the actual consensus (if any) of the North's people during the conflict, the post-war rise of Lincoln's central idea as that of the nation testifies that over the long run he was heard.[15]

It had all begun long before, with a poor boy's conviction that man should receive the whole fruit of his labor so that he might get ahead in life. The boy became a man and a politician, and worked through the better part of his life to the end that government might always be dedicated to that proposition. Both politics and political economy were moral enterprises for him, and so his goal, which we call the American Dream, was a moral goal. When he, and the majority of the nation, took a stand against slavery, the moral ingredient of his faith assumed exalted propor-

---

[12] *Ibid.*, VI, 53–5; Abel Haywood to Lincoln, Jan. 1, 1863; *Sen. Ex. Doc.*, 49, 37:3 (1863).
[13] *C.W.*, IV, 439; VII, 259, 529. [14] Hay, *Diaries,* 77. [15] *C.W.*, VIII, 150.

tions. Then the war came and he accepted it to save the nation of the Dream—this "light to the world," in Isaiah's words. Lincoln felt that as the Founding Fathers did "*fight*, and *endure*" for the central idea, the great hope, of America, so must their descendents. And they did as he bade them—for four long, bloody years.[16]

Early in 1861, on his way to Washington, Lincoln spoke in Trenton, New Jersey, about the Revolutionary War and the battle there in which Washington defeated the Hessians. His thoughts went back to his first childhood readings in history:

> you all know . . . how these early impressions last longer than any others. I recollect thinking then, boy even though I was, that there must have been *something more* than common that those men struggled for. I am exceedingly anxious that *that thing* which they struggled for; *that something* even more than National Independence; *that something* that held out a promise to all the people of the world to all time to come; I am exceedingly anxious that this Union, the Constitution and the liberties of the people shall be perpetuated in accordance with *the original idea* for which that struggle was made, and I shall be most happy indeed if I shall be an humble instrument in the hands of the Almighty, and of this, his almost chosen people, for perpetuating *the object* of that great struggle.

It was perhaps the emotions born out of the remembrance of the Fathers, and also of his own beginnings, that so possessed Lincoln's mind that he did not then explicitly define "*that something*," "*the original idea*" of America, which he believed the nation's founders had already struggled for. Or perhaps it was the fault of the *New York Tribune* reporter that the President-elect's reflections in Trenton remained incomplete.

A day later, however, speaking in Independence Hall, at Philadelphia, Lincoln continued his Revolutionary theme. He still spoke "with deep emotion," and now the press reported his completed thought: "It was that which gave promise that in due time the weights should be lifted from the shoulders of all man, and that *all* should have an equal chance." [17]

One suspects that remembering "way back," Lincoln exaggerated the clarity of his youthful ideas. Nevertheless the seeds of his ideals must have been there early, in the "earliest days of my being able to read," as he recalled. They matured slowly, over decades. They were not learned from Parson Mason Weems's *Life of Washington*, as Lincoln appears to

---

16 *Ibid.*, IV, 169.
17 *Ibid.*, 235–6, 240. The italics in the Trenton speech are the author's.

have thought, not from the other histories he reputedly had read as a boy, not from the general literature of those times. None of those writers saw his Dream as the "central idea of the Republic." The role Lincoln gave to man's right to rise through the reward of labor was of his own making more than of the age. And as he reminisced on the threshold of the presidency, his faith in that central role had become unshakable. The United States had to be saved *with* that Dream. "If this country cannot be saved without giving up that principle," he declared, "I would rather be assassinated. . . ." [18]

Lincoln had the fortune, so very rare, to live his dream from childhood to the last full measure of his days. Preaching the right to rise, he preached also by example. In a sense, he preached himself to the nation. If this contained an element of inherent egotism, as does perhaps all great work, it was so far below the surface as to make one hardly dare label it as such. In his first annual message he told the country: "No men living are more worthy to be trusted than those who toil up from poverty. . . ." Humble man that Abe Lincoln was, he could speak thus in praise of his own triumph because of an unawareness of the all-important self-generated aspect of his thought.[19] He believed that he was preaching America to America, not Lincoln to America. When he had accomplished his life's work, the two indeed were the same thing. If the world came at last to identify the man from Illinois with his nation, it is wonderful and wondrous that the first to have done so was the child Lincoln himself.

As the Civil War reached its climax and end, the President's concept of the American Dream also reached its ultimate heights. In the spring of 1865 he summed up for a final time the Rebel cause, as he saw it: "It may seem strange that any men should dare to ask a just God's assistance in wringing their bread from the sweat of other men's faces." But he added now: "let us judge not that we be not judged." Even for one of his legendary fortitude the "nation's wounds," and those of the men who had "borne the battle, and . . . his widow, and his orphan," proved too much to endure by reason alone. As his years of trial were about to end, he turned for support from a central idea that was the law of man, perhaps the law of nature, to that same idea as the law of God. Not surprisingly, for such is the way of man, Lincoln had found that the purposes of his Maker were like his own purposes.

---

18 *Ibid.,* 240. Indeed Weems explained at the beginning of his book that he would concentrate on Washington's private life because his public life may be "instructive to future generals and presidents, yet it but *little* concern our *children.*" The ordinary man's son, he declared, could never rise so high. Marcus Cunliffe, ed., *The Life of Washington by Mason L. Weems* (Cambridge, Mass., 1962), 4–5.

19 *C.W.,* V, 52–3; yet see for ex.: VII, 512.

"Fondly do we hope—fervently do we pray," he called his countrymen to worship, "that this mighty scourge of war may speedily pass away."

Yet, if God wills that it continue, until all the wealth piled by the bondman's two hundred and fifty years of unrequited toil shall be sunk, and until every drop of blood drawn with the lash, shall be paid by another drawn with the sword, as was said three thousand years ago, so still it must be said "the judgments of the Lord, are true and righteous altogether."

Unrequited toil, bloodstained wealth, war as judgment. The extorted labor of two and a half centuries had to be paid for. Lincoln's American Dream had become the will of God.[20]

---

[20] *Ibid.*, VIII, 332–3; cf. V, 478; VII, 282, 535, etc.

XVI *The American Civil War: The Last Capitalist Revolution Versus the Slave South*

Introduction   The real, wide, and inner meaning of America's great Civil War has been much written about. There is an extensive revisionist literature: that the Civil War resulted from a moral repugnance against slavery; that it was a conflict between northern industrialism and the agrarian, plantation economy of the South, a second American Revolution; that it was "a blundering generation" of politicians that turned a "repressible" conflict into an "irrepressible" one; and that the Civil War came on because of the temporary failure of "consensus" in American life. These themes appear to have been about worked out, and, developed as they were largely in the 1930's, 1940's, and 1950's, new approaches have been coming forward in the middle 1960's.

Two recent pieces of historical writing break new ground. In the first of these presented below, Barrington Moore attempts, from a comparative historical point of view, to place the Civil War in a vast panoramic view of the process by which six different traditional societies have evolved into modern industrial societies. He studies three western societies—Great Britain, France, and the United States—showing how, through the Puritan Revolution in Britain, the French Revolution in France, and the Civil War—the real American Revolution—in the United States, these countries have come to the modern world as parliamentary democracies. He then considers three Asian societies —China, Japan, and India—and shows how in the process of modernization China took the communist road, Japan took the fascist road, and India the democratic road. J. H. Plumb, in his review of this book in the *New York Times Book Review* (October 9, 1966), declared flatly, "Moore's topic is vast, the most important historical topic with which a scholar can deal—the routes by which various countries have come to the modern industrial world."

The work is of the essence of controversy in a controversial world. By necessity it is not based upon primary sources—this would be entirely beyond the wit and industry of man—but it is fresh, stimulating, provocative, witty, and profound. Michael Rogin (*Book Week*, January 1, 1967) wrote of Moore's work: "How do traditional societies become modern? According to Marxism bourgeois revolutions provide the impetus [rather than] peasants. . . . Liberal historians have attacked this conception of modernization. . . . In this brilliant new book [the author] rescues bourgeois revolution from Marxist orthodoxy and liberal skepticism alike. . . ." Moore contends that in America in the middle decades of the nineteenth century, instead of the marriage of "rye and iron"—conservative agrarian and industrial interests—there was the union of northern industry with the free farmers of the West. This prevented the "classic reactionary" solution of the union of northern industrialists and southern planters against slaves, smaller farmers, and industrial workers. It was the linkage of northern industrialism with the free farmers of the West that precipitated the war and ended slavery. Moore writes, "German experience suggests that if the conflict between North and South had been compromised, the compromise would have been at the expense of the subsequent democratic development in the United States, a possibility that, so far as I am aware, no revisionist historian has explored."

Eugene D. Genovese, a sophisticated modern Marxist critical of dogmatic Marxism and of the writings of Marx and Engels themselves upon the American Civil War, both approves and disapproves of Moore's study. He is particularly critical of Moore's handling of the prebourgeois, aristocratic planter leadership of the South. Genovese writes: "He (Moore) does not consider the possibility of a social system and ethos at war with itself, much less one in which the old was prevailing over the new—the prebourgeois over the bourgeois—because nowhere does he analyse the plantation as community and way of life. Despite a framework that places social classes at the center, he never analyses the slaveholders as a class; he merely describes certain of their features and interests in a tangential way. Finally he settles for the extraordinary formulation: 'the South had a capitalist civilization, then, but not a bourgeois one. Certainly it was not based on town life.' " [1]

It was precisely to this task, the analysis of the slave owners as a social class, that Genovese, in an earlier work, addressed himself. Part One of that work is reproduced below. Of the conflict between North and South leading up to the Civil War Genovese writes: "I begin with the hypothesis that so intense a struggle of moral values implies a struggle of world views and that so intense a struggle of world views implies a struggle of worlds—of rival social classes or of societies dominated by rival social classes." In defense of this hypothesis Genovese gives us a brilliant analysis of the ante-bellum slave holders as a distinctive and dominating social class whose world view and ethos made them entirely antipathetic to the North. As a class they were precapitalist, quasi aristocratic, feudal in their values and attitudes, yet living in a republic in the nineteenth century whose life style was not only completely out of phase with the planter-dominated slave society but totally antagonistic to it. The dilemma was complete: "When we understand that the slave South developed neither a strange form of capitalism nor an undefinable agrarianism but a special civilization built on the relationship of master to slave, we expose the root of its conflict with the North. The internal contradictions in the South and the external conflict with the North placed the slaveholders hopelessly on the defensive with little to look forward to except slave strangulation. Their only hope lay in a bold stroke to complete their political independence and to use it to provide an expansionist solution for their economic and social problems. The ideology and psychology of the proud slaveholding class made sur-

---

[1] Barton J. Bernstein (ed.), *Towards a New Past: Dissenting Essays in American History* (Pantheon Books: A Division of Random House, N.Y., 1968), p. 119.

render or resignation to gradual defeat unthinkable, for its fate, in its own eyes at least, was the fate of everything worth while in Western Civilization."

For a review of Genovese's work, see Stanley Elkins in *Commentary*, XLII (July, 1966), 73–75.

The American Civil War:
The Last Capitalist Revolution
—*Barrington Moore, Jr.*

1. Plantation and Factory: An Inevitable Conflict?

The main differences between the American route to modern capitalist democracy and those followed by England and France stem from America's later start. The United States did not face the problem of dismounting a complex and well-established agrarian society of either the feudal or the bureaucratic forms. From the very beginning commercial agriculture was important, as in the Virginian tobacco plantations, and rapidly became dominant as the country was settled. The political struggles between a precommercial landed aristocracy and a monarch were not part of American history. Nor has American society ever had a massive class of peasants comparable to those in Europe and Asia.[1] For these reasons one may argue that American history contains no revolution comparable to the Puritan and French Revolutions nor, of course, the Russian and Chinese twentieth-century revolutions. Still there have been two great armed upheavals in our history, the American Revolution and the Civil War, the latter one of the bloodiest conflicts in modern history up to that time. Quite obviously, both have been significant elements in the way the United States became the world's leading industrial capitalist democracy by the middle of the twentieth century. The Civil War is commonly taken to mark a violent dividing point between the agrarian and industrial epochs in American history. Hence in this chapter I shall discuss its causes and consequences from the standpoint of whether or not it was a violent breakthrough against an older social structure, leading to the establishment of political democracy, and on this score comparable to the Puritan and French Revolutions. More generally I hope to show where it belongs in the genetic

[1] Like many such terms it is impossible to define the word peasantry with absolute precision because distinctions are blurred at the edges in social reality itself. A previous history of subordination to a landed upper class recognized and enforced in the laws, which, however, need not always prohibit movement out of this class, sharp cultural distinctions, and a considerable degree of *de facto* possession of the land, constitute the main distinguishing features of a peasantry. Hence Negro sharecroppers in the present-day South could be legitimately regarded as a class of peasants in American society.

sequence of major historical upheavals that we can begin arbitrarily with the sixteenth-century peasant wars in Germany, that continues through the Puritan, French, and Russian Revolutions, to culminate in the Chinese Revolution and the struggles of our own time.

The conclusion, reached after much uncertainty, amounts to the statement that the American Civil War was the last revolutionary offensive on the part of what one may legitimately call urban or bourgeois capitalist democracy. Plantation slavery in the South, it is well to add right away, was not an economic fetter upon industrial capitalism. If anything, the reverse may have been true; it helped to promote American industrial growth in the early stages. But slavery was an obstacle to a political and social democracy. There are ambiguities in this interpretation. Those that stem from the character of the evidence are best discussed as the analysis proceeds. Others lie deeper and, as I shall try to show at the end of the chapter, would not disappear no matter what evidence came to light.

Aside from questions of space and time at the reader's disposal as well as the author's, there are objective reasons for passing over the American Revolution with but a few brief comments. Since it did not result in any fundamental changes in the structure of society, there are grounds for asking whether it deserves to be called a revolution at all. At bottom it was a fight between commercial interests in England and America, though certainly more elevated issues played a part as well. The claim that America has had an anticolonial revolution may be good propaganda, but it is bad history and bad sociology. The distinguishing characteristic of twentieth-century anticolonial revolutions is the effort to establish a new form of society with substantial socialist elements. Throwing off the foreign yoke is a means to achieve this end. What radical currents there were in the American Revolution were for the most part unable to break through to the surface. Its main effect was to promote unification of the colonies into a single political unit and the separation of this unit from England.

The American Revolution can be trotted out from time to time as a good example of the American (or sometimes Anglo-Saxon) genius for compromise and conciliation. For this, the Civil War will not do; it cuts a bloody gash across the whole record. Why did it happen? Why did our vaunted capacity for settling our differences fail us at this point? Like the problem of human evil and the fall of Rome for Saint Augustine, the question has long possessed a deep fascination for American historians. An anxious if understandable concern seems to underlie much of the discussion. For some time, it often took the form of whether or not the war was avoidable. The present generation of historians has begun to show impatience with this way of putting the problem. To many the question seems merely a semantic one, since if either side had been willing to submit without fighting there would have been no war.[2] To call it a semantic problem dodges the real issue: why was there an unwillingness to submit on either side or both?

It may be helpful to put the question in less psychological terms. Was there in some objective sense a mortal conflict between the societies of the North and the South? The full meaning of this question will emerge more clearly from trying to answer it on the basis of specific facts than through theoretical discussion at this point. Essentially we are asking whether the institutional requirements for operating a plantation economy based on slavery clashed seriously at any point with the corresponding requirements for operating a capitalist industrial system. I assume that, in principle at any rate, it is possible to discover what these requirements really were in the same objective sense that a biologist can discover for any living organism the conditions necessary for reproduction and survival, such as specific kinds of nourishment, amounts of moisture, and the like. It should also be clear that the requirements or structural imperatives for plantation slavery and early industrial capitalism extend far beyond economic arrangements as such and certainly into the area of political institutions. Slave societies do not have the same political forms as those based on free labor. But, to return to our central question, is that any reason why they have to fight?

One might start with a general notion to the effect that there is an inherent conflict between slavery and the capitalist system of formally free wage labor. Though this turns out to be a crucial part of the story, it will not do as a general proposition from which the Civil War can be derived as an instance. As will appear shortly, cotton produced by slave labor played a decisive role in the growth not only of American capitalism but of English capitalism too. Capitalists had no objection to obtaining goods produced by slavery as long as a profit could be made by working them up and reselling them. From a strictly economic standpoint, wage labor and plantation slavery contain as much of a potential for trading and complementary political relationships as for conflict. We can answer our question with a provisional negative: there is no abstract general reason why the North and South had to fight. Special historical circumstances, in other words, had to be present in order to prevent agreement between an agrarian society based on unfree labor and a rising industrial capitalism.

---

[2] Donald in the preface to Randall and Donald, *Civil War,* vi. Fully documented and with an excellent bibliography, this general survey provides a most helpful guide to the present state of historical opinion. An enlightening general survey of past discussions may be found in Beale, "Causes of the Civil War" (1946). Stampp, *Causes of the Civil War* (1959), provides an illuminating collection of contemporary and modern historical writings about the reasons for the war. In his editorial preface (p. vi) Stampp repeats Beale's observation, made more than a dozen years before, that the debate remains inconclusive while modern historians often merely repeat partisan themes set out at the time.

For clues as to what these circumstances might have been, it is helpful to glance at a case where there was an agreement between these two types of subsocieties within a larger political unit. If we know what makes an agreement possible, we also know something about circumstances that might make it impossible. Once again the German record is helpful and suggestive. Nineteenth-century German history demonstrates quite clearly that advanced industry can get along very well with a form of agriculture that has a highly repressive system of labor. To be sure, the German Junker was not quite a slave owner. And Germany was not the United States. But where precisely did the decisive differences lie? The Junkers managed to draw the independent peasants under their wing and to form an alliance with sections of big industry that were happy to receive their assistance in order to keep the industrial workers in their place with a combination of repression and paternalism. The consequence in the long run was fatal to democracy in Germany.

German experience suggests that, if the conflict between North and South had been compromised, the compromise would have been at the expense of subsequent democratic development in the United States, a possibility that, so far as I am aware, no revisionist historian has explored. It also tells us where we might look with profit. Why did Northern capitalists have no need of Southern "Junkers" in order to establish and strengthen industrial capitalism in the United States? Were political and economic links missing in the United States that existed in Germany? Were there other and different groups in American society, such as independent farmers, in the place of peasants? Where and how were the main groups aligned in the American situation? It is time now to examine the American scene more closely.

2. Three Forms of American Capitalist Growth

By 1860 the United States had developed three quite different forms of society in different parts of the country: the cotton-growing South; the West, a land of free farmers; and the rapidly industrializing Northeast.

The lines of cleavage and cooperation had by no means always run in these directions. To be sure, from the days of Hamilton and Jefferson there had been a tug-of-war between agrarians and urban commercial and financial interests. The expansion of the country westward made it seem for a moment, under President Jackson in the 1830s, that the principles of agrarian democracy, in practice an absolute minimum of central authority and a tendency to favor debtors over creditors, had won a permanent victory over those of Alexander Hamilton. Even in Jackson's own time, however, agrarian democracy had severe difficulties. Two closely related developments were to destroy it: the further growth of industrial capitalism in the Northeast and the establishment of an export market for Southern cotton.

Though the importance of cotton for the South is familiar, its significance for capitalist development as a whole is less well known. Between 1815 and 1860 the cotton trade exercised a decisive influence upon the rate of growth in the American economy. Up until about 1830 it was the most important cause of the growth of manufacturing in this country.[3] While the domestic aspect remained significant, cotton exports became an outstanding feature at about this time.[4] By 1849, sixty-four percent of the cotton crop went abroad, mainly to England.[5] From 1840 to the time of the Civil War, Great Britain drew from the Southern states four-fifths of all her cotton imports.[6] Hence it is clear that the plantation operated by slavery was no anachronistic excrescence on industrial capitalism. It was an integral part of this system and one of its prime motors in the world at large.

In Southern society, the plantation and slave owners were a very small minority. By 1850 there may have been less than 350,000 slave owners in a total white population of about six million in the slaveholding areas.[7] With their families, the slaveholders numbered perhaps a quarter of the white population at the most. Even within this group, only a small minority owned most of the slaves: a computation for 1860 asserts that only seven percent of the whites owned nearly three-quarters of the black slaves.[8] The best land tended to gravitate into their hands as well as the substance of political control.[9]

This plantation-owning élite shaded off gradually into farmers who worked the land with a few slaves, through large numbers of small property owners without slaves, on down to the poor whites of the back country, whose agriculture was confined to a little lackadaisical digging in forlorn cornpatches. The poor whites were outside of the market economy; many of the smaller farmers were no more than on its periphery.[10] The more well-to-do farmers aspired to owning a few more Negroes and becoming plantation owners on a larger scale. The influence of this middling group may have declined after the Jacksonian era, though there is a whole school of Southern historians that tries to romanticize the yeomen and "plain folk" of the old South as the basis of a democratic social order.[11] That, I believe to be utter rubbish. In all ages and countries, reactionaries, liberals, and radicals have painted their own portraits of small rural folk

[3] North, Economic Growth, 67, 167, 189.   [4] North, Economic Growth, 194.
[5] Gates, Farmer's Age, 152.   [6] Randall and Donald, Civil War, 36.
[7] Randall and Donald, Civil War, 67.
[8] Cited by Hacker, Triumph of American Capitalism, 288. Randall and Donald's figures are close to these.
[9] Gates, Farmer's Age, 151, 152.   [10] North, Economic Growth, 130.
[11] Owsley, Plain Folk, 138–142. This study impresses me as folklorish sociology that misses nearly all the relevant political and economic issues.

to suit their own theories. The element of important truth behind this particular notion is that the smaller farmers in the South by and large accepted the political leadership of the big planters. Writers tinged with Marxism claim that this unity within the white caste ran counter to the real economic interests of the smaller farmers and came about only because fear of the Negro solidified the whites. This is possible but dubious. Small property owners in many situations follow the lead of big ones when there is no obvious alternative and when there is some chance of becoming a big property holder.

Since plantation slavery was the dominant fact of Southern life, it becomes necessary to examine the workings of the system to discover if it generated serious frictions with the North. One consideration we can dispose of rapidly. Slavery was almost certainly not on the point of dying out for internal reasons. The thesis is scarcely tenable that the war was "unnecessary" in the sense that its results would have come about sooner or later anyway by peaceful means and that therefore there was no real conflict. If slavery were to disappear from American society, armed force would be necessary to make it disappear.

On this question the best evidence actually comes from the North, where peaceful emancipation during the Civil War faced nearly insuperable difficulties. Union states that had slavery dragged their feet and expressed all sorts of apprehension when Lincoln tried to introduce a moderate scheme of emancipation with compensation for the former owners. Lincoln had to drop the plan.[12] The Emancipation Proclamation (January 1, 1863), as is well known, excluded slave states in the Union and those areas of the South within Union lines; that is, it emancipated slaves, in the words of a contemporary English observer (Earl Russell, ancestor of Bertrand Russell) only "where the United States authorities cannot exercise any jurisdiction." [13] If peaceful emancipation faced these difficulties in the North, those in the South scarcely require comment.

These considerations point strongly toward the conclusion that slavery was economically profitable. The author of a recent monograph argues cogently that slavery persisted in the South primarily because it was economically profitable. Southern claims that they were losing money on the operation he dismisses as part of the rationalizations through which Southern spokesmen tried to find a higher moral ground for slavery, an early version of the white man's civilizing burden. Ashamed to justify slavery on crude economic grounds, which would have made them resemble money-grubbing Yankees, Southerners preferred to claim that slavery was the natural form of human society, beneficial both to the slave and the master.[14] More recently still, two economists dissatisfied with the evidence upon which previous studies rested, mainly fragmentary and

---

[12] Randall and Donald, *Civil War*, 374, 375.   [13] Randall and Donald, *Civil War*, 380–381.
[14] Stampp, *Peculiar Institution*, esp. chap. IX.

incomplete accounting records from early plantation activities, have tried to find the answer by examining more general statistical information. In order to find out whether slavery was more or less profitable than other enterprises, they have collected statistics about average slave prices, interest rates on prime commercial paper, costs of maintaining slaves, yields per prime field hand, cotton marketing costs, cotton prices, and other relevant facts. Though I am moderately skeptical about the reliability and representative value of the original statistics, their conclusions are in line with other considerations and about as close to reality as we are likely to get in this fashion. They, too, conclude that plantation slavery paid, moreover that it was an efficient system which developed in those regions best suited to the production of cotton and other specialized staples. Meanwhile, less productive areas in the South continued to produce slaves and export the increase to the main regions producing staple crops.[15]

To know that plantation slavery as a whole was a money-making proposition is important but insufficient. There were differences of time and place among the plantation owners that had significant political consequences. By the time the war broke out, plantation slavery had become a feature of the lower South. It had disappeared from the tobacco plantation before 1850 mainly because there were no great advantages to large-scale operations. In Maryland, Kentucky, and Missouri even the term "plantation" had become almost obsolete before the Civil War.[16] Around 1850 really fat pickings were to be had, chiefly in virgin areas; at first such places as Alabama and Mississippi provided such opportunities; after 1840, Texas. Even in virgin lands, the best way to make money was to sell out and move on before the soil gave out.[17]

To the extent that plantation slavery migrated from the South toward the West, it did create a serious political problem. Large parts of the West were still unsettled or sparsely settled. Though cotton growing had obvious limitations of climate and soil, no one could be certain just what the limitations were. If slavery spread, the balance between slave and free states might be upset—something that mattered of course only if the difference between a society with slavery and one without mattered. By 1820 the problem was already acute, though a settlement was reached in the Missouri Compromise, balancing the entry of Missouri as a slave state by that of Maine as a free state. From then on the problem erupted intermittently. Solemn and statesmanlike political bargains hopefully settled the question for good, only to become unstuck after a short while. The issue of slavery in the territories, as partly settled areas that had

[15] Conrad and Meyer, "Economics of Slavery," 95–130; see esp. 97 for the general thesis.
[16] Nevins, Ordeal, I, 423.
[17] Gates, Farmer's Age, 143; Gray, Agriculture in Southern United States, II, chaps. XXXVII, XXXVIII for more detail.

not yet become states were called, played a major part in bringing on the war. The inherent uncertainty of the situation very likely magnified economic conflicts out of all proportion.

The migratory tendency of the plantation economy was important in other ways as well. As cotton planting declined in the old South, there was some inclination to adapt to the situation by breeding slaves. The extent to which this took place is difficult to determine. But there are at least moderately clear indications that it was not enough to meet the demand. The costs of slaves rose rather steadily from the early 1840s until the outbreak of the war. The price of cotton also tended to rise, but with much more marked fluctuations. After the financial panic of 1857, the price of cotton fell off, while the price of slaves continued to climb steeply.[18] Slaves could not be legally imported, and the blockade seems to have been moderately effective. Together with Southern talk about re-opening the slave trade, talk that became fairly vigorous just before the final outbreak of hostilities, such evidence points in the direction of a serious labor shortage facing the plantation system. How serious? That is much harder to tell. Since capitalists are nearly always concerned about the prospect that labor may be short, it will be wise to treat Southern laments on this count with a touch of skepticism. It is very doubtful that the plantation system was about to expire from Northern economic strangulation.

So far the argument that the requirements of the plantation economy were a source of economic conflict with the industrial North does not turn out to be very persuasive. After all, was not the plantation owner just another capitalist? Nevins observes correctly: "A great plantation was as difficult to operate as a complicated modern factory, which in important respects it resembled. Hit-or-miss methods could not be tolerated; endless planning and anxious care were demanded." [19] Might it not therefore have been perfectly possible for the plantation owner to get along with his equally calculating capitalist brethren in the North? In my estimation it would have been quite possible had strictly rational economic calculations been the only issue. But, *pace* Max Weber, the rational and calculating outlook, the viewing of the world in terms of accounts and balances, can exist in a wide variety of societies, some of which may fight one another over other issues.[20] As we have already noticed in examining the

---

[18] See table in Phillips, *Life and Labor*, 177, and the discussion of alleged overcapitalization of the labor force in Conrad and Meyer, "Economics of Slavery," 115–118. Even if the plantation owner was not caught in a net of his own making—Phillips's thesis that Conrad and Meyer combat—it seems clear enough, and not denied by these two authors, that many planters did face increasing labor costs. See further, Nevins, *Ordeal*, I, 480, for some contemporary views.

[19] *Ordeal*, I, 438.

[20] Nevins' description of the plantation is strikingly similar to the rational methods of calculation that prevailed, even without the use of writing, on the medieval English manor. See the vivid description in Bennett, *Life on the English Manor*, 186–192, espc. 191.

French nobility, this type of outlook is not by itself enough to generate an industrial revolution. Certainly it did not in the South, where urban growth, outside of a few major entrepôts such as New Orleans and Charleston, remained far behind that in the rest of the country. The South had a capitalist civilization, then, but hardly a bourgeois one. Certainly it was not based on town life. And, instead of challenging the notion of status based on birth, as did the European bourgeoisie when they challenged the right of aristocracies to rule, Southern planters took over the defense of hereditary privilege. Here was a real difference and a real issue.

The notion that all men were created equal contradicted the facts of daily experience for most Southerners, facts that they had themselves created for good and sufficient reasons. Under the pressure of Northern criticism and in the face of worldwide trends away from slavery, Southerners generated a whole series of doctrinal defenses for the system. Bourgeois conceptions of freedom, those of the American and the French Revolutions, became dangerously subversive doctrines to the South, because they struck at the key nerve of the Southern system, property in slaves. To grasp how a Southern planter must have felt, a twentieth-century Northerner has to make an effort. He would do well to ask how a solid American businessman of the 1960s might feel if the Soviet Union existed where Canada does on the map and were obviously growing stronger day by day. Let him further imagine that the communist giant spouted self-righteousness at the seams (while the government denied that these statements reflected true policy) and continually sent insults and agents across the border. Southern bitterness and anxiety were not just the expressions of a fire-eating minority. In his appeal for compromise among the sections Henry Clay, the most famous of Southern moderates, made this revealing and much quoted statement: "You Northerners are looking on in safety and security while the conflagration I have described is raging in the slave States. . . . In the one scale, then, we behold sentiment, sentiment, sentiment alone; in the other, property, the social fabric, life, and all that makes life desirable and happy." [21]

As industrial capitalism took more and more hold in the North, articulate Southerners looked about themselves to discover and emphasize whatever aristocratic and preindustrial traits they could find in their own society: courtesy, grace, cultivation, the broad outlook versus the alleged money-grubbing outlook of the North. Shortly before the Civil War, the notion took hold that the South produced in cotton the main source of American wealth upon which the North levied tribute. As Nevins points out, these ideas parallel physiocratic doctrines to the effect that the profits of manufacture and trade come out of the land.[22] Such notions crop up everywhere as industrialization takes hold, even to some extent without

[21] Quoted after the version in Nevins, *Ordeal*, I, 267.
[22] Nevins, *Emergence of Lincoln*, I, 218.

industrialization. The spread of commercial agriculture in a precommercial society generates various forms of romantic nostalgia, such as Athenian admiration of Sparta or that of late Republican Rome for the supposed virtues of early days.

Southern rationalizations contained a substantial portion of truth. Otherwise they would have been too hard to believe. There were differences between Northern and Southern civilizations of the type suggested. And Northerners did make profits, big ones too, in marketing cotton. There was no doubt a much larger proportion of sheer fake in the Southern rationalizations. The supposed aristocratic and precommercial or anti-commercial virtues of the plantation aristocracy rested on the strictly commercial profits of slavery. To try to draw the line between what was true and what was fake is extremely difficult, probably impossible. For our purposes it is not necessary. Indeed to do so may darken counsel by obliterating important relationships. It is impossible to speak of purely economic factors as the main causes behind the war, just as it is impossible to speak of the war as mainly a consequence of moral differences over slavery. The moral issues arose from economic differences. Slavery was the moral issue that aroused much of the passion on both sides. Without the direct conflict of ideals over slavery, the events leading up to the war and the war itself are totally incomprehensible. At the same time, it is as plain as the light of the sun that economic factors created a slave economy in the South just as economic factors created different social structures with contrasting ideals in other parts of the country.

To argue thus is not to hold that the mere fact of difference somehow inevitably caused the war. A great many people in the South and the North either did not care about slavery or acted as if they did not care. Nevins goes so far as to assert that the election of 1859 showed that at least three-quarters of the nation still opposed radical proslavery and antislavery ideas at what was almost the last moment.[23] Even if his estimate exaggerates the strength of neutral sentiment, one of the most sobering and thought-provoking aspects of the Civil War is the failure of this mass of indifferent opinion to prevent it. It is also this substantial body of opinion that has led intelligent historians such as Beard to doubt the importance of slavery as an issue. That I hold to be an error, and a very serious one. Nevertheless the failure and collapse of moderation constitute a key part of the story, one on which those with Southern sympathies have shed valuable light. For a situation to arise in which war was likely to occur, changes had to take place in other parts of the country besides the South.

The main impetus behind the growth of Northern capitalism itself through the 1830s came, as we have seen, from cotton. During the next decade the pace of industrial growth accelerated to the point where

---

[23] *Emergence of Lincoln,* II, 68.

the Northeast became a manufacturing region. This expansion ended the dependence of the American economy on a single agricultural staple. The Northeast and the West, which had in the past supplied the South with much of its food and continued to do so, became less dependent on the South and more on each other. Cotton remained important to the Northern economy, but ceased to dominate it.[24] Measured by the value of its product, cotton still ranked second among Northern manufactures in 1860. On the other hand, the North by this time produced a wide variety of manufactured goods, generally, to be sure, in small factories. A high proportion of the output was to meet the needs of an agricultural community: flour milling, lumber, boots and shoes, men's clothing, iron, leather, woolen goods, liquor, and machinery.[25] As we shall see in a moment, Northern manufacturing output came to be exchanged very heavily with the rapidly growing Western areas of the country.

Though the diminution of Northern dependence on Southern cotton and the development of some economic antagonisms were the dominant trends, there are others that deserve our attention. It will not do to over-emphasize the divisive tendencies. In its relation to the plantation economy, the Northeast provided the services of financing, transportation, insurance, and marketing.[26] The bulk of the cotton exported left from Northern ports, of which New York was the most important. Thus—and this was a source of friction—Southern incomes were spent very largely in the North to purchase services for the marketing of cotton, to buy what was needed on the plantation that could not be produced on the spot, and, no small item, for holidays from the heat by rich planters. Furthermore both the North and the West still sold manufactured goods and food to the South. The 1850s were the heyday of the Mississippi steamboat trade.[27] Most important of all, the relative efficiency of New England cotton textile mills in relation to foreign competition improved between 1820 and the outbreak of the war. From 1830 onward, they enabled the United States to enter the export market.[28] Had this push been stronger, Northern and Southern interests might have come closer, and conceivably the war might not have taken place. In any event Northern business interests were very far from bellicose advocates of a war of liberation or even war for the sake of the Union. An adequate study of the political attitudes and activities of Northern industrialists remains to be written.[29] It seems wide of the mark, however, to entertain any notion

---

[24] North, *Economic Growth*, 204–206.   [25] North, *Economic Growth*, 159–160.
[26] North, *Economic Growth*, 68.   [27] North, *Economic Growth*, 103.
[28] North, *Economic Growth*, 161.
[29] As in the case of the French bourgeoisie prior to the bourgeois revolution, I have not found a good monograph that deals with the decisive political and economic questions. Foner, *Business and Slavery*, is very helpful as far as it goes but cannot be depended on for a general analysis because it concentrates on New York business interests closely connected with the South. The author is a well-known Marxist but in this study seems quite undogmatic. Industrial interests in Pennsylvania and Massachusetts need to be considered, but no adequate studies exist here either.

to the effect that Northern industrialists were itching to work the levers of the federal government on behalf of their purely economic interests.

What Northern capitalism needed from any government was the protection and legitimation of private property. It took some very special circumstances, however, to make the owners of Southern plantations and slaves appear as a threat to this institution. What Northern capialists also wanted was a moderate amount of government assistance in the process of accumulating capital and operating a market economy: more specifically, some tariff protection, aid in setting up a transportation network (not all of which need be strictly ethical—though many of the big railway scandals came later), sound money, and a central banking system. Above all, the ablest Northern leaders wanted to be able to do business without bothering about state and regional frontiers. They were proud of being citizens of a large country, as of course others were too, and in the final crisis of secession reacted against the prospect of a balkanized America.[30]

The economic issue that aroused the most excitement was the tariff. Since American industry made remarkable progress under relatively low tariffs after 1846, the Northern demand for a higher tariff and Southern opposition to it look at first like a false issue, one that people quarrel about when they are really mad about something else. If Northern industry was booming, what earthly need did it have for political protection? The whole thesis that the South was trying to exercise some sort of veto on Northern industrial progress begins to look very dubious as soon as one asks this question. A closer look at the time sequence dispels much of the mystery, though it will be necessary to discuss the point again after other relevant facts have appeared. There was a very rapid industrial growth after 1850. But trouble became acute in certain areas, iron and textiles, during the middle of the last decade before the war. By the end of 1854 stocks of iron were accumulating in every market of the world, and the majority of American mills had shut down. In textiles Lancashire had learned to produce low-priced goods more cheaply than New England mills; between 1846 and 1856 imports of printed dyed cotton leaped from 13 million yards to 114 million, those of plain calico from 10 million to 90 million. In 1857 came a serious financial crash. A tariff passed in that year, reflecting Southern pressures, gave no relief and actually reduced duties in these two areas.[31] Partly *because* they followed a period of prosperity and rapid growth, it seems, these events aroused sullen indignation in Northern industrial circles.

---

[30] On sentiment about the Union see Nevins, *Ordeal,* II, 242, and on contemporary editorial opinion Stampp, *Causes of Civil War,* 49–54. The selection from the Buffalo *Courier,* April 27, 1861 (pp. 52–53), is interesting for its protofascist language.

[31] Nevins, *Emergence of Lincoln,* I, 225–226. In his final assessment of the causes of the war, Nevins deprecates the role of the tariff and economic factors generally. See *Emergence of Lincoln,* II, 465–466. More on this later, but at least on the tariff his argument seems to me contradictory.

Northern capitalists also needed a reasonably abundant force of laborers, to work at wages they could afford to pay. Here was a serious sticking point. Free land to the west tended to draw off laborers, or at least many people thought so. And a major thrust behind the Jacksonian system had been a working coalition of planters, "mechanics" or workers, and free farmers on the one hand against finance and industry in the Northeast. Where then was the labor to come from? And how was Northern capital to break out of its economic and political encirclement? Northern political and economic leaders found a solution that enabled them to detach the Western farmers from the South and attach them to their own cause. Significant alterations in the economy and social structure of the West made these changes possible. It will be necessary to examine them more closely in a moment. But we may perceive their significance at once: by making use of these trends, the Northern capitalists freed themselves from any need to rely on Southern "Junkers" in order to keep labor in its place. Perhaps more than any other factor, these trends set the stage for armed conflict and aligned the combatants in such a way as to make possible a partial victory for human freedom.

Between the end of the Napoleonic Wars and the outbreak of the Civil War what is now known as the Midwest, but was then simply the West, grew from the land of pioneers to that of commercial farming. Indeed many of those who lived through the rugged age of the pioneer seem to have left it rapidly behind for others to praise. Marketable surpluses of food with which to buy a few necessities and still fewer amenities appeared quite early. Up until the 1830s the bulk of this surplus made its way South to feed the more specialized economy of that area, a trend that was to continue but lose its significance when the Eastern market became more important.[32] Thrown heavily still on their own resources, the small independent farmers in the first third of the nineteenth century were keen to wrest control over the public lands from politicians in Washington who either speculated in land on a large scale or were otherwise indifferent to the claims and needs of the West. They sought local autonomy sometimes at the expense of slim ties that connected them to the Union.[33] They were sympathetic to Andrew Jackson's attacks on the Eastern citadels of wealth and formed one wing of the superficially plebeian coalition that then ruled the country.

The growth of manufacturing in the East and the consequent rise in an effective demand for Western grain and meat changed this situation. Waves of expansion into the West in 1816–1818, 1832–1836, 1846–1847, and 1850–1856 reflect the increasing profitability of wheat, corn, and their derivatives.[34] From the 1830s onward, there was a gradual redirection of

[32] North, *Economic Growth*, 143, 67–68, 102.
[33] Beard and Beard, *American Civilization*, I, 535–536.
[34] North, *Economic Growth*, 136, and chart on 137.

Western produce toward the Eastern seaboard. The "transportation revolution," the rise of canals and railroads, solved the problem of cross-mountain haulage, making possible a new outlet for Western farm products. The West's trade with the South did not decline absolutely, but actually increased. It was the proportions that shifted and helped to draw the West closer to the North.[35]

The demand for farm products gradually transformed the social structure and psychological attitudes of the West in such a way as to make a new alignment possible. The outlook of the early individualist and small-scale capitalist, characteristic of the Northeast, spread to the dominant upper stratum of the Western farmers. Under the technological conditions of the day, the family farm was an efficient social mechanism for the production of wheat, corn, hogs, and other marketable products.[36] "As quick transportation carried farm produce to eastern markets and brought ready cash in return," says Beard in one of the many passages that capture the essence of a basic social change in a few rolling sentences, "as railways, increasing population, and good roads lifted land values, brick and frame houses began to supplant log cabins; with deep political significance did prosperity tend to stifle the passion for 'easy money' and allay the ancient hatred for banks. At last beyond the mountains the chants of successful farmers were heard above the laments of poor whites. . . . . ."[37] A further consequence was the spread and deepening of antislavery sentiment, probably traceable to the rooting of the family farm as a successful commercial venture in Western soil.[38] There are puzzles here, since the family farm run without slaves was very common in the South as well, though it seems to have been less of a commercial affair and more of a subsistence undertaking. In any case it is clear that growing up outside the shadow of the plantation, and depending mainly on family members for labor, the Western system of farming generated considerable fear of competition from slavery.[39]

Before the middle of the nineteenth century, Southern planters who had once welcomed Western farmers as allies against the plutocracy of the North came to see the spread of independent farming as a threat to slavery and their own system. Earlier proposals to divide up Western lands on easy terms for the small farmer had antagonized Eastern seaboard areas that feared emigration and loss of labor, including even some in the South, such as North Carolina. Initiatives in support of free land had come

[35] North, *Economic Growth*, 103, 140–141.   [36] North, *Economic Growth*, 154.

[37] Beard and Beard, *American Civilization*, I, 638. Nevins, *Ordeal*, II, chaps. V, VI, tells essentially the same story.

[38] A map of the distribution of Abolition Societies in 1847 (Nevins, *Ordeal*, I, 141) shows them to be nearly as thick in Ohio, Indiana, Illinois as in Massachusetts.

[39] See Nevins, *Ordeal*, II, 123. As support for Seward was strong in rural New York (Nevins, *Ordeal*, I, 347), there is reason to suspect that the same sentiment was strong among Eastern farmers.

from the Southwest. With the establishment of commercial farming in Western areas, these alignments altered. Many Southerners dug in their heels against "radical" notions of giving land away to farmers that would "abolitionize" the area.[40] Plantation interests in the Senate killed the Homestead Bill of 1852. Eight years later President Buchanan vetoed a similar measure, to the delight of nearly all Southern congressmen who had been unable to prevent its passage.[41]

The response in the North to the changes in Western agrarian society was more complex. Northern mill owners were not automatically ready to give away land to anyone who asked for it, since doing so might merely diminish the number of willing hands likely to appear at the factory gates. Southern hostility to the West gave the North an opportunity for alliance with the farmer but one that Northerners were slow to grasp. The coalition did not become a political force until very late in the day, in the Republican platform of 1860 that helped to carry Lincoln to the White House, even though a majority of the country's voters opposed him. The rapprochement appears to have been the work of politicians and journalists rather than businessmen. The proposal to open up Western lands for the smaller settlers provided a way that a party attached to the interests of those with property and education could use to attract a mass following, especially among urban workers.[42]

The essence of the bargain was simple and direct: business was to support the farmers' demand for land, popular also in industrial working-class circles, in return for support for a higher tariff. "Vote yourself a farm— vote yourself a tariff" became Republican rallying cries in 1860.[43] In this fashion there came to be constituted a "marriage of iron and rye"—to glance once more at the German combination of industry and Junkers— but with Western family farmers, not landed aristocrats, and hence with diametrically opposite political consequences. On into the Civil War itself, there were objections to the wedding and calls for a divorce. In 1861 C. J. Vallandigham, an advocate of the small farmers, could still argue that "the planting South was the natural ally of the Democracy of the North and especially of the West," because the people of the South were an agricultural people.[44]

But these were voices from the past. What made the realignment possible, in addition to the changes in the character of Western rural society, were the specific circumstances of industrial growth in the Northeast. The

---

[40] Zahler, *Eastern Workingmen*, 178–179, 188, esp. note 1, p. 179.

[41] Beard and Beard, *American Civilization*, I, 691–692; more details on the attitudes in Congress in Zahler, *Eastern Workingmen*, chap. IX.

[42] Zahler, *Eastern Workingmen*, 178.

[43] Beard and Beard, *American Civilization*, I, 692. For further information on the background of this rapprochement, which represented a significant reversal of earlier notions prevalent in the East, see Zahler, *Eastern Workingmen*, 185; Nevins, *Emergence of Lincoln*, I, 445.

[44] Beard and Beard, *American Civilization*, I, 677.

existence of free land gave a unique twist to the relations between capitalists and workmen in the beginning stages of American capitalism, stages which in Europe were marked by the growth of violent radical movements. Here energies that in Europe would have gone into building trade unions and framing revolutionary programs went into schemes providing a free farm for every workman whether he wanted it or not. Such proposals sounded subversive to some contemporaries.[45] The actual effect of the Westward trek, nevertheless, was to strengthen the forces of early competitive and individualist capitalism by spreading the interest in property. Beard is too colorful when he speaks of the Republicans' flinging the national domain to the hungry proletariat "as a free gift more significant than bread and circuses," after which the socialist movement sank into the background.[46] There was hardly time for all that to happen. The Civil War itself, as he remarks a few sentences later, cut short the drift to radicalism. And just how much help Western land may have been to the Eastern workingman before the Civil War remains a very open question. Already speculators were getting their hands on big chunks of it. Nor is it likely that the really poor in Eastern cities could leave the mine shaft and the factory bench to buy a small farm, equip it even with simple tools, and run it profitably, even if they benefited from the prospect that others might be able to do so.

Despite all these qualifications, there is a vital remnant of truth in the famous Turner thesis about the importance of the frontier for American democracy. It lies in the realignment of social classes and geographical sections that the open West produced at least temporarily. The link between Northern industry and the free farmers ruled out for the time being the classic reactionary solution to the problems of growing industrialism. Such an alignment would have been one of Northern industrialists and Southern planters against slaves, smaller farmers, and industrial workers. This is no abstract phantasy. Quite a few forces pushed in this direction before the Civil War, and it has been a prominent feature in the American political landscape ever since the end of Reconstruction. In the circumstance of midnineteenth-century American society, any peaceful solution, any victory of moderation, good sense, and democratic process, would have had to be a reactionary solution.[47] It would have had to be at the expense of the Negro, as it was to be eventually anyway, unless one is ready to take seriously the notion that more than a hundred years ago both Northerners and Southerners were ready to abandon slavery and incorpo-

---

[45] Beard and Beard, *American Civilization*, I, 648–649.
[46] Beard and Beard, *American Civilization*, I, 751.
[47] Drawing on Latin-American experience, Elkins, *Slavery*, 194–197, presents a "catalogue of preliminaries" that might have helped to eliminate slavery without bloodshed: to bring the slaves under Christianity, safeguard the sanctity of the slave family, allow the slave use of free time to accumulate his purchase price. These measures still seem to me highly reactionary, a form of tokenism within the framework of slavery.

rate the Negro into American society. The link between Northern industry and Western farmers, long in preparation if sudden in its arrival, for the time being did much to eliminate the prospect of a straightforward reactionary solution of the country's economic and political problems on behalf of the dominant economic strata. For the very same reason, it brought the country to the edge of Civil War.

3. Toward an Explanation of the Causes of the War

The alignment of the main social groupings in American society in 1860 goes a long way toward explaining the character of the war, or the issues that could and could not come to the surface—more bluntly what the war could be about. It tells us what was likely *if* there was to be a fight; by itself the alignment does not account very well for *why* there actually was a fight. Now that some of the relevant facts are before us it is possible to discuss with greater profit the question of whether or not there was an inherent mortal conflict between North and South.

Let us take up the economic requirements of the two systems one by one in order of 1) capital requirements, 2) requirements for labor, and 3) those connected with marketing the final product.

Though the point is open to some dispute, it is possible to detect definite expansionist pressures in the plantation economy. Fresh virgin lands were necessary for the best profits. Thus there was some pressure on the side of capital requirements. There are corresponding indications that the labor supply was tight. More slaves would have been very helpful. Finally, to make the whole system work, cotton, and to a lesser extent other staples, had to fetch a good price in the international market.

Northern industry required a certain amount of assistance from the government in what might be called overhead costs of capital construction and the creation of a favorable institutional environment: a transportation system, a tariff, and a sufficiently tight currency so that debtors and small men generally did not have undue advantages. (Some inflation, on the other hand, that would keep prices moving up would probably be rather welcome, then as now.) On the side of labor, industry needed formally free wage laborers, though it is not easy to prove that free labor is necessarily superior to slavery in a factory system, except for the fact that someone has to have money in order to buy what industry produces. But perhaps that is a sufficient consideration. Finally, of course, growing industry did need an expanding market, provided still in those days quite largely by the agricultural sector. The West furnished much of this market and may be regarded as part of the North for the sake of this crude model.

It is difficult to perceive any really serious structural or "mortal" conflict in this analysis of the basic economic requirements, even though I have deliberately tried to bias the model in that direction. Here it is indispensable to remember, as revisionist historians of the Civil War correctly point out, that any large state is full of conflicts of interest. Tugging and hauling and quarreling and grabbing, along with much injustice and repression, have been the ordinary lot of human societies throughout recorded history. To put a searchlight on these facts just before a violent upheaval like the Civil War and call them the decisive causes of the war is patently misleading. To repeat, it would be necessary to show that compromise was impossible in the nature of the situation. From the analysis so far this does not seem to be the case. The most one can say along this line is that an increase in the area of slavery would have hurt the free farmers of the West badly. Although the areas where each kind of farming would pay were determined by climate and geography, no one could be sure where they were without trying. Still this factor alone does not seem sufficient to account for the war. Northern industry would have been as happy with a plantation market in the West as with any other, if such considerations were all that mattered, and the conflict could very likely have been ironed out. The other points of potential and actual conflict seem less serious. Northern requirements in the area of capital construction, the demand for internal improvements, a tariff, etc., cannot be regarded as threatening a crushing burden for the Southern economy. To be sure quite a number of marginal planters would have suffered, a factor of some importance. But if Southern society was run by the more successful planters, or if this influence was no more than very important, the smaller fry could have been sacrificed for the sake of a deal. In the question of slave labor versus free there was no real economic conflict because the areas were geographically distinct. Every account that I have come upon indicates that Northern labor was either lukewarm or hostile to the antislavery issue.

In addition to the conflict between free farmers in the West and the plantation system, about the strongest case one can make in strictly economic terms is that for the South secession was not an altogether unreasonable proposal mainly because the South did not need much that the North really had to offer. In the short run the North could not buy much more cotton than it did already. The most that the North could have offered would have been to reopen the slave trade. There was talk about taking over Cuba for slavery, and even some desultory action. As quite recent events have shown, under other circumstances such a move might be an extremely popular one in all parts of the country. At that time it seems to have been both impractical and impolitic.

To sum up, the strictly economic issues were very probably negotiable. Why, then, did the war happen? What was it about? The apparent inadequacy of a strictly economic explanation—I shall argue in a moment that the fundamental causes were still economic ones—has led historians to search for others. Three main answers are distinguishable in the literature. One is that the Civil War was fundamentally a moral conflict over slavery.

Since large and influential sections of the public in both the North and the South refused to take a radical position either for or against slavery, this explanation runs into difficulties, in effect the ones that Beard and others tried to circumvent in their search for economic causes. The second answer tries to get around both sets of difficulties by the proposition that *all* the issues were really negotiable and that the blunderings of politicians brought on a war that the mass of the population in the North and in the South did not want. The third answer amounts to an attempt to push this line of thought somewhat further by analyzing how the political machinery for achieving consensus in American society broke down and allowed the war to erupt. In this effort, however, historians tend to be driven back toward an explanation in terms of moral causes.[48]

Each of the explanations, including that stressing economic factors, can marshal a substantial body of facts in its support. Each has hit at a portion of the truth. To stop at this observation is to be satisfied with intellectual chaos. The task is to relate these portions of the truth to each other, to perceive the whole in order to understand the relationship and significance of partial truths. That such a search is endless, that the discovered relations are themselves only partial truths, does not mean that the search ought to be abandoned.

To return to the economic factors, it is misleading, if at times necessary, to take them separately from others with the traditional labels political, moral, social, etc. Similarly, it is a necessity for the sake of comprehensible exposition to break the issues down one by one in some other series—such as slavery as such, slavery in the territories, tariff, currency, railroads and other internal improvements, the alleged Southern tribute to the North. At the same time, the breakdown into separate categories partially falsifies what it describes because individual people were living through all these things at once, and persons who were apathetic about one issue could become excited about another. As the connection among issues became apparent, the concern spread among articulate people. Even if each individual issue had been negotiable, a debatable point, collectively and as a unit they were almost impossible to negotiate. And they were a unit, and so perceived by more than a few contemporaries, because they were manifestations of whole societies.

Let us begin the analysis afresh with this viewpoint in mind. Primarily

---

[48] Nevins stresses moral causes at the same time that he reports most people were unconcerned about them, a paradox that, as far as I can see, he does not directly confront. See *Emergence of Lincoln*, II, 462–471, for his general explanation; on the widespread desire for peace, *ibid.*, 63, 68. But Nevins does give much factual material helpful in trying to resolve the paradox. For a succinct statement of the thesis that the politicians were responsible, see the extract from Randall's *Lincoln the Liberal Statesman*, reprinted in Stampp, *Causes of the Civil War*, 83–87. Nichols, *Disruption of American Democracy*, and Craven, *Growth of Southern Nationalism*, present versions of the third thesis. No one author, it should be noted, presents a pure version or a lawyer's brief for a specific explanation. It is a matter of emphasis, but very strong emphasis.

for economic and geographical reasons, American social structure developed in different directions during the nineteenth century. An agrarian society based on plantation slavery grew up in the South. Industrial capitalism established itself in the Northeast and formed links with a society based on farming with family labor in the West. With the West, the North created a society and culture whose values increasingly conflicted with those of the South. The focal point of the difference was slavery. Thus we may agree with Nevins that moral issues were decisive. But these issues are incomprehensible without the economic structures that created and supported them. Only if abolitionist sentiment had flourished in the South, would there be grounds for regarding moral sentiments as an independent factor in their own right.

The fundamental issue became more and more whether the machinery of the federal government should be used to support one society or the other. That was the meaning behind such apparently unexciting matters as the tariff and what put passion behind the Southern claim that it was paying tribute to the North. The question of power at the center was also what made the issue of slavery in the territories a crucial one. Political leaders knew that the admission of a slave state or a free one would tip the balance one way or another. The fact that uncertainty was an inherent part of the situation due to unsettled and partly settled lands to the West greatly magnified the difficulties of reaching a compromise. It was more and more necessary for political leaders on both sides to be alert to any move or measure that might increase the advantages of the other. In this larger context, the thesis of an attempted Southern veto on Northern progress makes good sense as an important cause of the war.

This perspective also does justice, I hope, to the revisionist thesis that it was primarily a politician's war, perhaps even an agitator's war, if the terms are not taken to be merely abusive epithets. In a complex society with an advanced division of labor, and especially in a parliamentary democracy, it is the special and necessary task of politicians, journalists, and only to a somewhat lesser extent clergymen to be alive and sensitive to events that influence the distribution of power in society. They are also the ones who provide the arguments, good and bad alike, both for changing the structure of society and for maintaining things as they are. Since it is their job to be alert to potential changes, while others keep on with the all-absorbing task of making a living, it is characteristic of a democratic system that politicians should often be clamorous and intensify division. The modern democratic politician's role is an especially paradoxical one, at least superficially. He does what he does so that most people do not have to worry about politics. For that same reason he often feels it necessary to arouse public opinion to dangers real and unreal.

From this standpoint too, the failure of modern opinion to halt the drift to war becomes comprehensible. Men of substance in both North and South furnished the core of moderate opinion. They were the ones who in ordinary times are leaders in their own community—"opinion makers," a modern student of public opinion would be likely to call them. As beneficiaries of the prevailing order, and mainly interested in making money, they wanted to suppress the issue of slavery rather than seek structural reforms, a very difficult task in any case. The Clay-Webster Compromise of 1850 was a victory for this group. It provided for stricter laws in the North about the return of fugitive slaves and for the admission of several new states to the union: California as a free state, New Mexico and Utah at some future date with or without slavery as their constitutions might provide at the time of admission.[49] Any attempt to drag the slavery issue out into the open and seek a new solution made large numbers of these groups cease being moderates. That is what happened when Senator Stephen A. Douglas put an end to the Compromise of 1850 only four years later by reopening the question of slavery in the territories. Through proposing in the Kansas-Nebraska Act that the settlers decide the issue for themselves one way or the other, he converted, at least for the time being, wide sections of Northern opinion from moderation to views close to abolitionism. In the South, his support was not much more than lukewarm.[50]

By and large the moderates had the usual virtues that many people hold are necessary to make democracy work: willingness to compromise and see the opponent's viewpoint, a pragmatic outlook. They were the opposite of doctrinaires. What all this really amounted to was a refusal to look facts in the face. Trying mainly to push the slavery issue aside, the moderates were unable to influence or control the series of events generated by the

---

[49] On social groupings that supported the Compromise in the South, see Nevins, *Ordeal*, I, 315, 357, 366, 375. On 357 he remarks, "the . . . largest element was a body of moderates . . . who believed both in Southern Rights and the Union, but hoped they could be reconciled." In other words, they wanted to have their cake and eat it too. On general reactions and those in the North, see Nevins, *Ordeal*, I, 346, 293–294, 348; more detail on selected Northern business reaction in Foner, *Business and Slavery*, chaps. 2–4. Excitement about fugitive slaves in both the North and the South seems to have been greatest in states where the problem was least likely to occur. But it was Clay and Webster who provided the evidence for this thesis. See Nevins, *Ordeal*, I, 384.

[50] On reactions to Douglas's proposal in the North and the South see Nevins, *Ordeal*, II, 121, 126–127, 133–135, 152–154, 156–157. A sympathetic treatment of Douglas may be found in Craven, *Coming of the Civil War*, esp. 325–331, 392–393. On the Kansas-Nebraska affair Craven makes a plausible case for the thesis that dishonest Northern politicians stirred up slavery as a false issue. On the Lincoln-Douglas debates he argues that Lincoln's own high-sounding moral ambiguities had the effect of making Douglas appear thoroughly indifferent to moral issues. This treatment is diametrically opposite to that in Nevins. Commenting on Douglas's action in reopening the issue of slavery by the Kansas-Nebraska bill, Nevins remarks (*Ordeal*, II, 108), "When indignation welled up like the ocean lashed by a hurricane, he [Douglas] was amazed. The fact that the irresistible tidal forces in history are moral forces always escapes a man of dim moral perceptions." This is commencement oratory, not history. Successful political leaders have to be morally ambiguous in their efforts to cope with conflicting moral forces. Subsequent historians make the politicians that win into moral heroes. Generally Nevins does not succumb to such nonsense.

underlying situation.[51] Crises such as the struggles over "bleeding Kansas," the financial panic of 1857, John Brown's melodramatic attempt to put himself at the head of a slave insurrection, and many others eroded the moderate position, leaving its members increasingly disorganized and confused. The practicality that tries to solve issues by patiently ignoring them, an attitude often complacently regarded as the core of Anglo-Saxon moderation, revealed itself as totally inadequate. An attitude, a frame of mind, without a realistic analysis and program is not enough to make democracy work even if a majority share this outlook. Consensus by itself means little; it depends what the consensus is about.

Finally, as one tries to perceive American society as a whole in order to grasp the causes and meaning of the war, it is useful to recall that searching for the sources of dissension necessarily obscures a major part of the problem. In any political unity that exists for a long time, there must be causes to produce the unity. There have to be reasons why men seek accommodation for their inevitable differences. It is difficult to find a case in history where two different regions have developed economic systems based on diametrically opposite principles and yet remained under a central government that retained real authority in both areas. I cannot think of any.[52] In such a situation there would have to be very strong cohesive forces to counteract the divisive tendencies. Cohesive forces appear to have been weak in the midnineteenth century in the United States, though there is always the risk of exaggerating their weakness because the Civil War did happen.

Trade is an obvious factor that can generate links among various sections of a country. The fact that Southern cotton went mainly to England is almost certainly a very important one. It meant that the link with the

[51] During the winter of 1858–1859 plans were afoot in the South to create a new party, characterized by Nevins, *Emergence of Lincoln*, II, 59, as "a conservative, national, Union-exalting party which should thrust aside the slavery issue, denounce all secessionists, push a broad program of internal improvements, and on constructive grounds overthrow the Democrats." It drew on men of substance, political leaders, journalists, tried to appeal to small farmers versus big slaveholders, but made hardly any dent. During the last phase, when secessionists were in charge of events, the main opposition seems to have come from those who had direct trade connections with the North, i.e., merchants and professional men in some Southern ports, and the smaller farmers. See Nevins, *Emergence of Lincoln*, II, 322, 323, 324, 326. New York business circles blew hot and cold. After being vigorous defenders of the Compromise of 1850, they turned nearly abolitionist over Douglas's Kansas-Nebraska action, reversing themselves again shortly afterward. As Foner remarks (*Business and Slavery*, 138), "Ever since 1850, the great majority of New York merchants had operated under the illusion that the sectional struggle would right itself in time if 'politicians and fanatics' would only leave the controversial incidents alone." This desire to dodge the issues seems to be the one constant theme in their outlook. Excitement was bad for business. On October 10, 1857, the *Herald* predicted (Foner, *Business and Slavery*, 140–141): "The nigger question must give way to the superior issues of a safe currency, sound credits, and solid and permanent basis of security upon which all the varied commercial and business interests of the country may repose." On this platform, at least, moderates North and South could agree. In time it became the one upon which the Civil War and its aftermath were liquidated.

[52] The British Commonwealth may be the most obvious candidate. Its breakup into independent units in the last fifty years supports the above generalization.

North was so much the weaker. English partiality to the Southern cause during the war itself is well known. But it will not do to put too much weight on the direction of trade as an aspect of disunity. As pointed out earlier, Northern mills were beginning to use more cotton. When the Western market fell off sharply after the crash of 1857, New York merchants relied for a time more heavily on their Southern connections.[53] In a word, the situation in trade was changing; had the war been averted, historians who look first for economic causes would have had no difficulty in finding an explanation.

Though the fact that cotton still linked the South with England more than with the North was significant, two other aspects of the situation may have been more important. One has already been mentioned: the absence of any strong radical working-class threat to industrial capitalist property in the North. Secondly, the United States had no powerful foreign enemies. In this respect, the situation was entirely different from that facing Germany and Japan, who both experienced their own versions of political modernization crises somewhat later, 1871 in Germany, 1868 in Japan. For this combination of reasons, there was not much force behind the characteristic conservative compromise of agrarian and industrial élites. There was little to make the owners of Northern mills and Southern slaves rally under the banner of the sacredness of property.

To sum up with desperate brevity, the ultimate causes of the war are to be found in the growth of different economic systems leading to different (but still capitalist) civilizations with incompatible stands on slavery. The connection between Northern capitalism and Western farming helped to make unnecessary for a time the characteristic reactionary coalition between urban and landed élites and hence the one compromise that could have avoided the war. (It was also the compromise that eventually liquidated the war.) Two further factors made compromise extremely difficult. The future of the West appeared uncertain in such a way as to make the distribution of power at the center uncertain, thus intensifying and magnifying all causes of distrust and contention. Secondly, as just noted, the main forces of cohesion in American society, though growing stronger, were still very weak.

4. The Revolutionary Impulse and its Failure

About the Civil War itself, it is unnecessary to say more than a few words, especially since the most important political event, the Emancipation Proclamation, has already been mentioned. The war reflected the fact that the dominant classes in American society had split cleanly in two, much more cleanly than did the ruling strata in England at the time of the

---

[53] Foner, *Business and Slavery*, 143.

Puritan Revolution or those in France at the time of the French Revolution. In those two great convulsions, divisions within the dominant classes enabled radical tendencies to boil up from the lower strata, much more so in the case of the French Revolution than in England. In the American Civil War there was no really comparable radical upsurge.

At least in major outline the reasons are easy to see: American cities were not teeming with depressed artisans and potential *sansculottes*. Even if only indirectly, the existence of Western lands reduced the explosive potential. In the second place, the materials for a peasant conflagration were lacking. Instead of peasants at the bottom of the heap, the South had mainly black slaves. Either they could not or they would not revolt. For our purpose it does not matter which. Though there were sporadic slave outbreaks, they had no political consequences. No revolutionary impulse came from that quarter.[54]

What there was in the way of a revolutionary impulse, that is, an attempt to alter by force the established order of society, came out of Northern capitalism. In the group known as the Radical Republicans, abolitionist ideals fused with manufacturing interests to ignite a brief revolutionary flash that sputtered and went out in a mire of corruption. Though the Radicals were a thorn in Lincoln's side during the war, he was able to fight the war to a successful military conclusion mainly on the basis of preserving the Union, that is, without any serious offensive against Southern property rights. For a brief time, about three years after the end of the fighting, 1865–1868, the Radical Republicans held power in the victorious North and mounted an offensive against the plantation system and the remnants of slavery.

Leading members of this group perceived the war as a revolutionary struggle between a progressive capitalism and a reactionary agrarian society based on slavery. To the extent that the conflict between the North and the South really had such a character, a conflict some of whose most important struggles came after the actual fighting stopped, this was due to the Radical Republicans. From the perspective of a hundred years later, they appear as the last revolutionary flicker that is strictly bourgeois and strictly capitalist, the last successors to medieval townsmen beginning the revolt against their feudal overlords. Revolutionary movements since the Civil War have been either anticapitalist, or fascist and counterrevolutionary if in support of capitalism.

From abolitionist ideologues and Free Soil radicals, a small band of Republican politicians took over the conception of slavery as an anachronistic "remnant of a dying world of 'baron and serf—noble and slave.'" The Civil War itself they perceived as an opportunity to root out and destroy this oppressive anachronism in order to rebuild the South in the

---

[54] The well-known Marxist scholar Aptheker collects these instances in his *American Negro Slave Revolts*, chap. XV.

image of the democratic and progressive North, based on "free speech, free toil, schoolhouses, and ballot boxes." Though his public statements were somewhat milder, the leader of the Radical Republicans in the House of Representatives, Thaddeus Stevens, wrote privately to his law partner during the year that what the country needed was someone in power (i.e., *not* Lincoln) "with sufficient grasp of mind, and sufficient moral courage, to treat this as a radical revolution, and remodel our institutions. . . . It would involve the desolation of the South as well as emancipation, and a repeopling of half the Continent. . . ." What put steam behind this movement and lifted it out of the realm of noisy talk was the fact that it coincided with the interests of crucial segments of Northern society.[55] One was the infant iron and steel industry of Pennsylvania. Another was a set of railroad interests. Stevens acted as a Congressional go-between for both of these interests, from each of whom he received cash favors in accord with prevailing political morals.[56] The Radical Republicans also received substantial support from Northern labor. Even though Northern workers were very cool to abolitionist propaganda, fearing Negro competition and regarding New England abolitionists as hypocritical representatives of the mill owners, they were enthusiastic about Radical conceptions of tariff protection and going slow on the contraction of inflated Northern currency.[57] Financial and commercial interests, on the other hand, were unenthusiastic about the Radicals. After the war, principled Radicals turned against the "plutocracy of the North." [58]

Thus the Radical offensive did not represent a united capitalist offensive on the plantation system. It was a combination of workers, industrialists, and some railroad interests at the time of its greatest power. Still it would not be amiss to label it entrepreneurial and even progressive capitalism; it attracted the main creative (and philistine) forces that Veblen later liked in American society and repelled those that he disliked: snobbish financiers who made their money by selling instead of doing. In Thaddeus Stevens and his associates, this combination had skilled political leadership and sufficient minor intellectual talent to provide a general strategy. Radicals had an explanation of where society was heading and how they could take advantage of this fact. For them the Civil War was at least potentially a revolution. Military victory and Lincoln's assassination, which they welcomed with scarcely disguised joy, gave them a brief opportunity to try to make it a real one.

Thaddeus Stevens again provided the analysis as well as the day-to-day political leadership. Essentially his strategy amounted to capturing the machinery of the federal government for the benefit of the groups for

[55] See the excellent study by Shortreed, "The Antislavery Radicals," 65–87, esp. 68–69, 77, from which the remarks in quotations·are taken.
[56] Current, *Old Thad Stevens*, 226–227, 312, 315–316.
[57] See Rayback, "American Workingman and Antislavery Crusade," 152–163.
[58] Sharkey, *Money, Class and Party*, 281–282, 287–289.

which he was spokesman. To do so it was necessary to change Southern society lest the old type of plantation leadership return to Congress and frustrate the move. Out of this necessity came what little revolutionary impulse there was to the whole struggle. Stevens had enough sociological insight to see what the problem was and to cast about for a possible remedy, as well as enough nerve to make a try.

In his speeches of 1865 Stevens presented to the general public and to Congress a surprisingly coherent analysis and program of action. The South had to be treated as a conquered people, not as a series of states that had somehow left the Union and were now to be welcomed back. "The foundation of their institutions both political, municipal, and social *must* be broken up and *relaid*, or all our blood and treasure have been spent in vain. This can only be done by treating and holding them as a conquered people." [59] They should not be allowed to return, he asserted, "until the Constitution shall have been so amended as to make it what its framers intended; and so as to secure perpetual ascendency to the party of the Union," that is, the Republicans.[60]

If the Southern states were not "reconstructed"—the revealing euphemism for revolution from above has passed from contemporary usage into all subsequent histories—they might easily overwhelm the North, Stevens calculated carefully and openly, and thus enable the South to win the peace after losing the war.[61]

Out of these considerations, came the program to rebuild Southern society from top to bottom. Stevens wanted to break the power of the plantation owners by confiscating estates over two hundred acres, "even though it drive (the Southern) nobility into exile." In this way, he argued, citing statistics, the federal government would obtain enough land to give each Negro household some forty acres.[62] "Forty acres and a mule" became in time the catchword slogan to discredit the supposedly utopian hopes of the newly freed Negroes. But the Radical Republicans were no utopians, not even Stevens. The demand for sweeping land reform reflected realistic awareness that nothing else would break the power of the planters. These had already set about to recover the substance of their old power by other means, something they were able to do because the Negroes were economically helpless. All this, at least a few Radicals saw quite clearly. And there are indications that dividing up the old plantations to give the Negroes small farms was feasible. In 1864 and 1865, Northern military authorities made two experiments along these lines in order to take care of the troublesome problem of thousands of destitute Negroes. They turned over confiscated and abandoned lands to more than 40,000 Negroes

---

[59] Speech of September 6, 1865, in Lancaster, Pennsylvania, as given in Current, *Old Thad Stevens*, 215.

[60] *Reconstruction, Speech, December 18, 1865*, p. 5.

[61] *Reconstruction, Speech, December 18, 1865*, p. 5.

[62] Speech of September 6, 1865, in Current, *Old Thad Stevens*, 215.

who are said to have been successful in working the land as small farmers until President Johnson returned the estates to their former white owners.[63] Still the experience of slavery was scarcely one to prepare Negroes to manage their own affairs as small rural capitalists. Stevens was aware of this and felt that the Negroes would need supervision by his friends in Congress for a long time to come. At the same time he saw that, without minimal economic security and minimal political rights, including the right to vote, they could do little for themselves or for Northern interests.[64]

In a nutshell, the Radical version of reconstruction came down to using the North's military power to destroy the plantation aristocracy and create a facsimile of capitalist democracy by ensuring property and voting rights for the Negroes. In the light of Southern conditions at the time, it was indeed revolutionary. A century later, the movement for civil rights for the Negroes seeks no more than this, indeed not quite all that, since the economic emphasis remains muted. If being ahead of the times is revolutionary, Stevens was that. Even sympathetic Northerners professed shock. Horace Greeley, editor of the *New York Tribune*, long sympathetic to the abolitionist cause, wrote in response to Stevens's speech of September 6, 1865, ". . . we protest against any warfare on Southern property . . . because the wealthier class of Southerners, being more enlightened and humane than the ignorant and vulgar, are less inimicable to the blacks." [65] Greeley's misgivings give a hint of what was to come when men of substance North and South were to bury their differences and, by another famous compromise, leave the Negroes to make what they could of their freedom.

It is not surprising therefore that defeat came soon to the Radicals, or more precisely to what was radical in their program, as soon as it encountered Northern property interests. The Radicals were unable to force confiscation into the reconstruction acts of 1867 against the wishes of more moderate Republicans. In the House, Stevens's "40 acres" measure received only 37 votes.[66] Influential Northern sentiment was in no mood to tolerate an outright attack on property, not even Rebel property and not even in the name of capitalist democracy. The *Nation* warned that "A division of rich men's lands amongst the landless . . . would give a shock to our whole social and political system from which it would hardly recover without the loss of liberty." The failure of land reform was a decisive

---

[63] Stampp, *Reconstruction*, 123, 125–126.

[64] "Without the right of suffrage in the late slave States, (I do not speak of the free States,) I believe the slaves had far better been left in bondage."—*Reconstruction, Speech, December 8, 1865,* pp. 6, 8.

[65] Quoted from the issue of September 12, 1865, by Current, *Old Thad Stevens,* 216–217. Greeley also criticized Stevens for failing to include a suffrage plank in this speech, which he did in the later one, mainly it seems in response to pressure from Senator Charles Sumner of Massachusetts. I have not tried to present differences of opinion within Radical ranks, but have concentrated on Stevens as its most revolutionary figure, as well as its most influential day-to-day strategist when the movement was at its height.

[66] Current, *Old Thad Stevens,* 233.

defeat and removed the heart of the Radical program. Without land reform the rest of the program could be no more than palliatives or irritants, depending on one's viewpoint. To say that this failure cleared the way for the eventual supremacy of Southern white landholders and other propertied interests may nevertheless be an exaggeration.[67] The Radicals had never even really managed to bar the way. Their failure at this moment revealed the limits American society imposed upon the revolutionary impulse.

In the absence of confiscation and redistribution of land, the plantation system recovered by means of a new system of labor. At first there were attempts with wage labor. These failed, at least partly because Negroes were inclined to draw their wages in slack months and abscond when the cotton had to be picked. Hence there was a widespread turn toward sharecropping which gave the planters superior control of their labor force. The change was significant. As we shall see in due course, sharecropping in many parts of Asia has constituted one way of extracting a surplus from the peasant through economic rather than political methods, though the latter are often necessary to buttress the former. Hence it is instructive to see fundamentally similar forms appear in America without the prior existence of a peasantry.

The country merchant gave a local twist to the American situation, though similar devices occurred also in China and elsewhere. The country merchant was often the large planter. By making advances of groceries to tenant and sharecropper, charging much higher rates for them than ordinary retail prices, he kept control of the work force. Tenants and sharecroppers could trade at no other store, since they had credit at no other and were usually short of cash.[68] In this fashion economic bonds replaced those of slavery for many Negroes. How much real improvement, if any, the change meant is very difficult to say. But it would be a mistake to hold that plantation owners prospered greatly under the new system. The main effect appears to have been to make the South even more of a one-crop economy than before, as banker pressed planter, and planter pressed cropper to grow crops that could be quickly turned to cash.[69]

Political recovery proceeded along with economic recovery, reenforcing each other rather than in any simple relationship of cause and effect. There is no need to recount here the political twistings and turnings of the successors to the antebellum ruling groups in the South as they sought for political leverage, though it is worth noticing that "scalawags"—white collaborationists they might be called today—included numerous planters, merchants, and even industrial leaders.[70] A good deal of violence, perhaps

---

[67] See the excellent account in Stampp, *Reconstruction*, 128–130; the quotation from the *Nation* occurs on 130.
[68] See Shannon, *American Farmers' Movements*, 53 for a succinct description.
[69] Randall and Donald, *Civil War*, 549–551.
[70] Randall and Donald, *Civil War*, 627–629, sketches these maneuvers.

deprecated by the better elements, though skepticism is in order here, helped to put the Negroes "in their place" and reestablish overall white supremacy.[71] Meanwhile industrialists and railroad men were becoming increasingly influential in Southern affairs.[72] In a word, moderate men of substance were returning to power, authority, and influence in the South, as they were in the North as well. The stage was being set for an alliance of these across the former battle lines. It was consummated formally in 1876 when the disputed Hayes-Tilden election was settled by allowing the Republican Hayes to take office in return for removing the remnants of the Northern occupational regime. Under attack from radical agrarians in the West and radical labor in the East, the party of wealth, property, and privilege in the North was ready to abandon the last pretense of upholding the rights of the propertyless and oppressed Negro laboring class.[73] When Southern "Junkers" were no longer slaveholders and had acquired a larger tincture of urban business and when Northern capitalists faced radical rumblings, the classic conservative coalition was possible. So came Thermidor to liquidate the "Second American Revolution."

5. The Meaning of the War

Was it a revolution? Certainly not in the sense of a popular uprising against oppressors. To assess the meaning of the Civil War, to place it in a history that is still being made, is just as difficult as to account for its cause and course. One sense of revolution is a violent destruction of political institutions that permits a society to take a new course. After the Civil War, industrial capitalism advanced by leaps and bounds. Clearly that was what Charles Beard had in mind when he coined the famous phrase, the "Second American Revolution." But was the burst of industrial capitalist growth a consequence of the Civil War? And how about the contribution to human freedom that all but the most conservative associate with the word revolution? The history of the Fourteenth Amendment, prohibiting the states from depriving any person of life, liberty, or property, epitomizes the ambiguity on this score. As every educated person knows, the Fourteenth Amendment has done precious little to protect Negroes and a tremendous amount to protect corporations. Beard's thesis that such was the original intent of those who drafted the amendment has been rejected by some.[74] That in itself is trivial. About the consequence, there is no doubt. Ultimately the way one assesses the Civil War depends on the assessment of freedom in modern American society and the connection between the institutions of advanced industrial capitalism and the Civil

---

[71] Randall and Donald, *Civil War*, 680–685.
[72] Woodward, *Reunion and Reaction*, 42–43. Chapter II provides a first-rate analysis of the whole process of moderate recovery.
[73] Woodward, *Reunion and Reaction*, 36–37.
[74] Randall and Donald, *Civil War*, 583; see also 783–784 for a review of the literature.

War. Another whole book would scarcely serve to argue these issues. I shall do no more than try to sketch a few of the more important considerations.

Certain very important political changes did accompany and follow the Northern victory. They may be summed up in the remark that the federal government became a series of ramparts around property, mainly big property, and an agency to execute the biblical pronouncement, "To him that hath shall be given." First among the ramparts was the preservation of the Union itself, which meant, as the West filled up after the war, one of the largest domestic markets of the world. It was also a market protected by the highest tariff to date in the nation's history.[75] Property received protection from state governments with unsound inclinations through the Fourteenth Amendment. Likewise the currency was put on a sound footing through the national banking system and the resumption of specie payments. Whether such measures hurt the Western farmers as much as was once supposed is dubious; there are indications that they were doing quite well during the war and for some time afterward.[76] At any rate they received some compensation through the opening of the public domain in the West (Homestead Act of 1862), though it is on this score that the federal government became an agency of the biblical statement just quoted. Railroads received huge grants, and disposal of public domains also formed the basis of great fortunes in timber and mining. Finally, as a compensation to industry that might lose laborers in this fashion the federal government continued to hold open the doors to immigration (Immigration Acts of 1864). As Beard puts it, "All that two generations of Federalists and Whigs had tried to get was won within four short years, and more besides." [77] "Four short years" is a rhetorical exaggeration; some of these measures were also part of Reconstruction (1865–1876), and the resumption of specie payment did not take place until 1879. But that is a small matter, since Reconstruction was definitely a part of the whole struggle. If one looks back and compares what happened with the planter program of 1860: federal enforcement of slavery, no high protective tariffs, no subsidies nor expensive tax-creating internal improvements, no national banking and currency system,[78] the case for a victory of industrial capitalism over the fetters of the plantation economy, a victory

---

[75] The Morrill Tariff of 1861 was the beginning of a sharp upward climb in tariffs. It raised average tariff rates from 20 percent of value to 47 percent, more than double the rates prevailing in 1860. Designed at first to raise revenues for the wartime Union treasury, it established protectionism deeply in American economic policies. The acts of 1883, 1890, 1894, and 1897 granted even more protection. See Davis and others, *American Economic History*, 322–323.

[76] Sharkey, *Money, Class, and Party*, 284–285, 303.

[77] Beard and Beard, *American Civilization*, II, 105; see pages 105–115 for a survey of the measures summarized here; also Hacker, *Triumph of American Capitalism*, 385–397, for a similar and in some ways more concise analysis.

[78] Beard and Beard, *American Civilization*, II, 29.

that required blood and iron to occur at all, becomes very persuasive indeed.

Reflection may make much of this conviction evaporate. It is worth noticing that Beard's own position is quite ambiguous. After recounting the victories of Northern capitalism just summarized above he remarks, "The main economic results of the Second American Revolution thus far noted would have been attained had there been no armed conflict. . . ." [79] But Beard's views are not in question except insofar as the provocative writings of a first-rate historian shed light on the issues. Three related arguments may be brought to bear against the thesis that the Civil War was a revolutionary victory for industrial capitalist democracy and necessary to this victory. First, one might hold that there is no real connection between the Civil War and the subsequent victory of industrial capitalism; to argue in favor of this connection is to fall victim to the fallacy of *post hoc, ergo propter hoc*. Second, one might hold that these changes were coming about of their own accord through the ordinary processes of economic growth and needed no Civil War to bring them about. [80] Finally, one could argue on the basis of evidence discussed at some length earlier in this chapter that the economics of North and South were not really in serious competition with one another: at best they were complementary; at worst, they failed to link up with each other due to fortuitous circumstances, such as the fact that the South sold much of its cotton to England.

All such arguments would receive an effective answer only if it were possible to demonstrate that Southern society, dominated by the plantation, constituted a formidable obstacle to the establishment of industrial capitalist democracy. The evidence indicates very clearly that plantation slavery was an obstacle to democracy, at least any conception of democracy that includes the goals of human equality, even the limited form of equality of opportunity, and human freedom. It does not establish at all clearly that plantation slavery was an obstacle to industrial capitalism as such. And comparative perspectives show clearly that industrial capitalism can establish itself in societies that do not profess these democratic goals or, to be a little more cautious, where these goals are no more than a secondary current. Germany and Japan prior to 1945 are the main illustrations for this thesis.

Once again the inquiry leads back toward political questions and incompatibilities between two different kinds of civilizations: in the South

---

[79] Beard and Beard, *American Civilization*, II, 115.

[80] Cochran, "Did the Civil War Retard Industrialization?" 148–160 seems to me a version of this and the preceding argument. I do not find it persuasive because it merely shows on the basis of statistics that the Civil War temporarily interrupted industrial growth. It touches only briefly and tangentially on the problem of institutional changes, which I hold to be the center of the question.

and in the North and West. Labor-repressive agricultural systems, and plantation slavery in particular, are political obstacles to a *particular kind* of capitalism, at a specific historical stage: competitive democratic capitalism we must call it for lack of a more precise term. Slavery was a threat and an obstacle to a society that was indeed the heir of the Puritan, American, and French Revolutions. Southern society was based firmly on hereditary status as the basis of human worth. With the West, the North, though in the process of change, was still committted to notions of equal opportunity. In both, the ideals were reflections of economic arrangements that gave them much of their appeal and force. Within the same political unit it was, I think, inherently impossible to establish political and social institutions that would satisfy both. If the geographical separation had been much greater, if the South had been a colony for example, the problem would in all probability have been relatively simple to solve at that time —at the expense of the Negro.

That the Northern victory, even with all its ambiguous consequences, was a political victory for freedom compared with what a Southern victory would have been seems obvious enough to require no extended discussion. One need only consider what would have happened had the Southern plantation system been able to establish itself in the West by the middle of the nineteenth century and surrounded the Northeast. Then the United States would have been in the position of some modernizing countries today, with a latifundia economy, a dominant antidemocratic aristocracy, and a weak and dependent commercial and industrial class, unable and unwilling to push forward toward political democracy. In rough outline, such was the Russian situation, though with less of a commercial emphasis in its agriculture in the second half of the nineteenth century. A radical explosion of some kind or a prolonged period of semi-reactionary dictatorship would have been far more probable than a firmly rooted political democracy with all its shortcomings and deficiencies.

Striking down slavery was a decisive step, an act at least as important as the striking down of absolute monarchy in the English Civil War and the French Revolution, an essential preliminary for further advances. Like these violent upheavals, the main achievements in our Civil War were political in the broad sense of the term. Later generations in America were to attempt to put economic content into the political framework, to raise the level of the people toward some conception of human dignity by putting in their hands the material means to determine their own fate. Subsequent revolutions in Russia and China have had the same purpose even if the means have in large measure so far swallowed up and distorted the ends. It is in this context, I believe, that the American Civil War has to be placed for its proper assessment.

That the federal government was out of the business of enforcing slavery was no small matter. It is easy to imagine the difficulties that organized labor would have faced, for example, in its effort to achieve legal and political acceptance in later years, had not this barrier been swept away. To the extent that subsequent movements toward extending the boundaries and meanings of freedom have faced obstacles since the end of the Civil War, they have done so in large measure because of the incomplete character of the victory won in 1865 and subsequent tendencies toward a conservative coalition between propertied interests in the North and the South. This incompleteness was built into the structure of industrial capitalism. Much of the old repression returned to the South in new and more purely economic guises, while new forms appeared there and in the rest of the United States as industrial capitalism grew and spread. If the federal government no longer concerned itself with enforcing the fugitive slave laws, it either acquiesced or served as an instrument for new forms of oppression.

As far as the Negro is concerned, only in quite recent times has the federal government begun to move in the opposite direction. As these lines are being written, the United States finds itself in the midst of a bitter struggle over the Negroes' civil rights, a struggle likely to ebb and flow for years to come. It involves a great deal more than the Negroes. Due to the peculiarities of American history, the central core of America's lowest class are people with dark skins. As the one major segment of American society with active discontents, the Negroes are at present almost the only potential recruiting ground for efforts to change the character of the world's most powerful capitalist democracy. Whether this potential will amount to anything, whether it will splinter and evaporate or coalesce with other discontents to achieve significant results, is quite another story.

At bottom, the struggle of the Negroes and their white allies concerns contemporary capitalist democracy's capacity to live up to its noble professions, something no society has ever done. Here we approach the ultimate ambiguity in the assessment and interpretation of the Civil War. It recurs throughout history. There is more than coincidence in the fact that two famous political leaders of free societies chose to express their ideals in speeches for their fallen dead given more than two thousand years apart. To the critical historian both Pericles and Lincoln become ambiguous figures as he sets what they did and what happened alongside what they said and in all likelihood hoped for. The fight for what they expressed is not over and may not end until mankind ceases to inhabit the earth. As one peers ever deeper to resolve the ambiguities of history, the seeker eventually finds them in himself and his fellow men as well as in the supposedly dead facts of history. We are inevitably in the midst of the ebb and flow of these events and play a part, no matter how small and insignificant as individuals, in what the past will come to mean for the future.

The Slave South: An Interpretation
—*Eugene D. Genovese*

The Problem

The uniqueness of the antebellum South continues to challenge the imagination of Americans, who, despite persistent attempts, cannot divert their attention from slavery. Nor should they, for slavery provided the foundation on which the South rose and grew. The master-slave relationship permeated Southern life and influenced relationships among free men. A full history would have to treat the impact of the Negro slave and of slaveless as well as slaveholding whites, but a first approximation, necessarily concerned with essentials, must focus on the slaveholders, who most directly exercised power over men and events. The hegemony of the slaveholders, presupposing the social and economic preponderance of great slave plantations, determined the character of the South. These men rose to power in a region embedded in a capitalist country, and their social system emerged as part of a capitalist world. Yet, a nonslaveholding European past and a shared experience in a new republic notwithstanding, they imparted to Southern life a special social, economic, political, ideological, and psychological content.

To dissolve that special content into an ill-defined agrarianism or an elusive planter capitalism would mean to sacrifice concern with the essential for concern with the transitional and peripheral. Neither of the two leading interpretations, which for many years have contended in a hazy and unreal battle, offers consistent and plausible answers to recurring questions, especially those bearing on the origins of the War for Southern Independence. The first of these interpretations considers the antebellum South an agrarian society fighting against the encroachments of industrial capitalism; the second considers the slave plantation merely a form of capitalist enterprise and suggests that the material differences between Northern and Southern capitalism were more apparent than real. These two views, which one would think contradictory, sometimes combine in the thesis that the agrarian nature of planter capitalism, for some reason, made coexistence with industrial capitalism difficult.[1]

[1] For a succinct statement of the first view see Frank L. Owsley, "The Irrepressible Conflict," in Twelve Southerners, *I'll Take My Stand* (New York, 1930), p. 74. One of the clearest statements of the second view is that of Thomas P. Govan, "Was the Old South Different?" *JSH*, XXI (Nov. 1955), 448.

The first view cannot explain why some agrarian societies give rise to industrialization and some do not. A prosperous agricultural hinterland has generally served as a basis for industrial development by providing a home market for manufactures and a source of capital accumulation, and the prosperity of farmers has largely depended on the growth of industrial centers as markets for foodstuffs. In a capitalist society agriculture is one industry, or one set of industries, among many, and its conflict with manufacturing is one of many competitive rivalries. There must have been something unusual about an agriculture that generated violent opposition to the agrarian West as well as the industrial Northeast.

The second view, which is the more widely held, emphasizes that the plantation system produced for a distant market, responded to supply and demand, invested capital in land and slaves, and operated with funds borrowed from banks and factors. This, the more sophisticated of the two interpretations, cannot begin to explain the origins of the conflict with the North and does violence to elementary facts of antebellum Southern history.

Slavery and the Expansion of Capitalism

The proponents of the idea of planter capitalism draw heavily, wittingly or not, on Lewis C. Gray's theory of the genesis of the plantation system. Gray defines the plantation as a "capitalistic type of agricultural organization in which a considerable number of unfree laborers were employed under a unified direction and control in the production of a staple crop." [2] Gray considers the plantation system inseparably linked with the international development of capitalism. He notes the plantation's need for large outlays of capital, its strong tendency toward specialization in a single crop, and its commercialism and argues that these appeared with the industrial revolution.

In modern times the plantation often rose under bourgeois auspices to provide industry with cheap raw materials, but the consequences were not always harmonious with bourgeois society. Colonial expansion produced three sometimes overlapping patterns: (1) the capitalists of the advanced country simply invested in colonial land—as illustrated even today by the practice of the United Fruit Company in the Caribbean; (2) the colonial planters were largely subservient to the advanced countries—as illustrated by the British West Indies before the abolition of slavery; and (3) the planters were able to win independence and build a society under their own direction—as illustrated by the Southern United States.

In alliance with the North, the planter-dominated South broke away from England, and political conditions in the new republic allowed it

[2] *History of Agriculture in the Southern United States to 1860* (2 vols.; Gloucester, Mass., 1958), I, 302.

considerable freedom for self-development. The plantation society that had begun as an appendage of British capitalism ended as a powerful, largely autonomous civilization with aristocratic pretensions and possibilities, although it remained tied to the capitalist world by bonds of commodity production. The essential element in this distinct civilization was the slaveholders' domination, made possible by their command of labor. Slavery provided the basis for a special Southern economic and social life, special problems and tensions, and special laws of development.

The Rationality and Irrationality of Slave Society

Slave economies normally manifest irrational tendencies that inhibit economic development and endanger social stability. Max Weber, among the many scholars who have discussed the problem, has noted four important irrational features.[3] First, the master cannot adjust the size of his labor force in accordance with business fluctuations. In particular, efficiency cannot readily be attained through the manipulation of the labor force if sentiment, custom, or community pressure makes separation of families difficult. Second, the capital outlay is much greater and riskier for slave labor than for free.[4] Third, the domination of society by a planter class increases the risk of political influence in the market. Fourth, the sources of cheap labor usually dry up rather quickly, and beyond a certain point costs become excessively burdensome. Weber's remarks could be extended. Planters, for example, have little opportunity to select specifically trained workers for special tasks as they arise.

There are other telling features of this irrationality. Under capitalism the pressure of the competitive struggle and the bourgeois spirit of accumulation direct the greater part of profits back into production. The competitive side of Southern slavery produced a similar result, but one that was modified by the pronounced tendency to heavy consumption. Economic historians and sociologists have long noted the high propensity to consume among landed aristocracies. No doubt this difference has been one of degree. The greater part of slavery's profits also find their way back into production, but the method of reinvestment in the two systems is substantially different. Capitalism largely directs its profits into an expansion of plant and equipment, not labor; that is, economic progress is qualitative. Slavery, for economic reasons as well as for those of social

---

[3] *The Theory of Social and Economic Organization* (New York, 1947), pp. 276 ff. The term "rational" is used in its strictly economic sense to indicate that production is proceeding in accordance with the most advanced methods to maximize profits.

[4] This simple observation has come under curious attack. Kenneth M. Stampp insists that the cost of purchasing a slave forms the equivalent of the free worker's wage bill. See *The Peculiar Institution* (New York, 1956), pp. 403 ff. The initial outlay is the equivalent of part of the capitalist's investment in fixed capital and constitutes what Ulrich B. Phillips called the "overcapitalization of labor" under slavery. The cost of maintaining a slave is only a small part of the free worker's wage bill, but the difference in their productivity is probably greater than the difference in their cost under most conditions.

prestige, directs its reinvestments along the same lines as the original investment in slaves and land; that is, economic progress is quantitative.

In the South this weakness proved fatal for the slaveholders. They found themselves engaged in a growing conflict with Northern farmers and businessmen over such issues as tariffs, homesteads, internal improvements, and the decisive question of the balance of political power in the Union. The slow pace of their economic progress, in contrast to the long strides of their rivals to the north, threatened to undermine their political parity and result in a Southern defeat on all major issues of the day. The qualitative leaps in the Northern economy manifested themselves in a rapidly increasing population, an expanding productive plant, and growing political, ideological, and social boldness. The slaveholders' voice grew shriller and harsher as they contemplated impending disaster and sought solace in complaints of Northern aggression and exploitation.

Just as Southern slavery directed reinvestment along a path that led to economic stagnation, so too did it limit the volume of capital accumulated for investment of any kind. We need not reopen the tedious argument about the chronology of the plantation, the one-crop system, and slavery. While slavery existed, the South had to be bound to a plantation system and an agricultural economy based on a few crops. As a result, the South depended on Northern facilities, with inevitably mounting middlemen's charges. Less obvious was the capital drain occasioned by the importation of industrial goods. While the home market remained backward, Southern manufacturers had difficulty producing in sufficient quantities to keep costs and prices at levels competitive with Northerners. The attendant dependence on Northern and British imports intensified the outward flow of badly needed funds.

Most of the elements of irrationality were irrational only from a capitalist standpoint. The high propensity to consume luxuries, for example, has always been functional (socially if not economically rational) in aristocratic societies, for it has provided the ruling class with the façade necessary to control the middle and lower classes. Thomas R. Dew knew what he was doing when he defended the high personal expenditures of Southerners as proof of the superiority of the slave system.[5] Few Southerners, even few slaveholders, could afford to spend lavishly and effect an aristocratic standard of living, but those few set the social tone for society. One wealthy planter with a great house and a reputation for living and entertaining on a grand scale could impress a whole community and keep before its humbler men the shining ideal of plantation magnificence. Consider Pascal's observation that the habit of seeing the king accompanied by guards, pomp, and all the paraphernalia designed to command respect and inspire awe will produce those reactions even when he appears alone and informally. In the popular mind he is assumed to be naturally

[5] *The Pro-Slavery Argument* (Charleston, S. C., 1852), p. 488.

an awe-inspiring being.[6] In this manner, every dollar spent by the planters for elegant clothes, a college education for their children, or a lavish barbecue contributed to the political and social domination of their class. We may speak of the slave system's irrationality only in a strictly economic sense and then only to indicate the inability of the South to compete with Northern capitalism on the latter's grounds. The slaveholders, fighting for political power in an essentially capitalist Union, had to do just that.

Capitalist and Pseudo-Capitalist Features of the Slave Economy

The slave economy developed within, and was in a sense exploited by, the capitalist world market; consequently, slavery developed many ostensibly capitalist features, such as banking, commerce, and credit. These played a fundamentally different role in the South than in the North. Capitalism has absorbed and even encouraged many kinds of precapitalist social systems: serfdom, slavery, Oriental state enterprises, and others. It has introduced credit, finance, banking, and similar institutions where they did not previously exist. It is pointless to suggest that therefore nineteenth-century India and twentieth-century Saudi Arabia should be classified as capitalist countries. We need to analyze a few of the more important capitalist and pseudo-capitalist features of Southern slavery and especially to review the barriers to industrialization in order to appreciate the peculiar qualities of this remarkable and anachronistic society.[7]

The defenders of the "planter-capitalism" thesis have noted the extensive commercial links between the plantation and the world market and the modest commercial bourgeoisie in the South and have concluded that there is no reason to predicate an antagonism between cotton producers and cotton merchants. However valid as a reply to the naive arguments of the proponents of the agrarianism-versus-industrialism thesis, this criticism has unjustifiably been twisted to suggest that the presence of commercial activity proves the predominance of capitalism in the South.[8] Many precapitalist economic systems have had well-developed commercial relations, but if every commercial society is to be considered capitalist, the word loses all meaning. In general, commercial classes have supported the existing system of production. As Maurice Dobb observes,[9] their fortunes

---

[6] Blaise Pascal, *Pensées* (Modern Library ed.; New York, 1941), p. 105.
[7] This colonial dependence on the British and Northern markets did not end when slavery ended. Sharecropping and tenantry produced similar results. Since abolition occurred under Northern guns and under the program of a victorious, predatory outside bourgeoisie, instead of under internal bourgeois auspices, the colonial bondage of the economy was preserved, but the South's political independence was lost.
[8] Govan, *JSH*, XXI (Nov. 1955), 448.
[9] *Studies in the Development of Capitalism* (New York, 1947), pp. 17 f. In the words of Gunnar Myrdal: "Trade by itself . . . rather tends to have backwash effects and to strengthen the forces maintaining stagnation or regression." *Rich Lands and Poor* (New York, 1957), p. 53.

are bound up with those of the dominant producers, and merchants are more likely to seek an extension of their middlemen's profits than to try to reshape the economic order.

We must concern ourselves primarily with capitalism as a social system, not merely with evidence of typically capitalistic economic practices. In the South extensive and complicated commercial relations with the world market permitted the growth of a small commercial bourgeoisie. The resultant fortunes flowed into slaveholding, which offered prestige and economic and social security in a planter-dominated society. Independent merchants found their businesses dependent on the patronage of the slaveholders. The merchants either became planters themselves or assumed a servile attitude toward the planters. The commercial bourgeoisie, such as it was, remained tied to the slaveholding interest, had little desire or opportunity to invest capital in industrial expansion, and adopted the prevailing aristocratic attitudes.

The Southern industrialists were in an analogous position, although one that was potentially subversive of the political power and ideological unity of the planters. The preponderance of planters and slaves on the country-side retarded the home market. The Southern yeomanry, unlike the Western, lacked the purchasing power to sustain rapid industrial development.[10] The planters spent much of their money abroad for luxuries. The plantation market consisted primarily of the demand for cheap slave clothing and cheap agricultural implements for use or misuse by the slaves. Southern industrialism needed a sweeping agrarian revolution to provide it with cheap labor and a substantial rural market, but the Southern industrialists depended on the existing, limited, plantation market. Leading industrialists like William Gregg and Daniel Pratt were plantation-oriented and proslavery. They could hardly have been other.

The banking system of the South serves as an excellent illustration of an ostensibly capitalist institution that worked to augment the power of the planters and retard the development of the bourgeoisie. Southern banks functioned much as did those which the British introduced into Latin America, India, and Egypt during the nineteenth century. Although the British banks fostered dependence on British capital, they did not directly and willingly generate internal capitalist development. They were not sources of industrial capital but "large-scale clearing houses of mercantile finance vying in their interest charges with the local usurers." [11]

The difference between the banking practices of the South and those of the West reflects the difference between slavery and agrarian capitalism.

---

[10] An attempt was made by Frank L. Owsley and his students to prove that the Southern yeomanry was strong and prosperous. For a summary treatment see *Plain Folk of the Old South* (Baton Rouge, La., 1949). This view was convincingly refuted by Fabian Linden, "Economic Democracy in the Slave South: An Appraisal of Some Recent Views," *JNH*, XXXI (April 1946), 140–89.

[11] Paul A. Baran, *The Political Economy of Growth* (New York, 1957), p. 194.

In the West, as in the Northeast, banks and credit facilities promoted a vigorous economic expansion. During the period of loose Western banking (1830–1844) credit flowed liberally into industrial development as well as into land purchases and internal improvements. Manufacturers and merchants dominated the boards of directors of Western banks, and landowners played a minor role. Undoubtedly, many urban businessmen speculated in land and had special interests in underwriting agricultural exports, but they gave attention to building up agricultural processing industries and urban enterprises, which guaranteed the region a many-sided economy.[12]

The slave states paid considerable attention to the development of a conservative, stable banking system, which could guarantee the movement of staple crops and the extension of credit to the planters. Southern banks were primarily designed to lend the planters money for outlays that were economically feasible and socially acceptable in a slave society: the movement of crops, the purchase of land and slaves, and little else.

Whenever Southerners pursued easy-credit policies, the damage done outweighed the advantages of increased production. This imbalance probably did not occur in the West, for easy credit made possible agricultural and industrial expansion of a diverse nature and, despite acute crises, established a firm basis for long-range prosperity. Easy credit in the South led to expansion of cotton production with concomitant overproduction and low prices; simultaneously, it increased the price of slaves.

Planters wanted their banks only to facilitate cotton shipments and maintain sound money. They purchased large quantities of foodstuffs from the West and, since they shipped little in return, had to pay in bank notes. For five years following the bank failures of 1837 the bank notes of New Orleans moved at a discount of from 10 to 25 per cent. This disaster could not be allowed to recur. Sound money and sound banking became the cries of the slaveholders as a class.

Southern banking tied the planters to the banks, but more important, tied the bankers to the plantations. The banks often found it necessary to add prominent planters to their boards of directors and were closely supervised by the planter-dominated state legislatures. In this relationship the bankers could not emerge as a middle-class counterweight to the planters but could merely serve as their auxiliaries.

The bankers of the free states also allied themselves closely with the dominant producers, but society and economy took on a bourgeois quality

---

[12] The best introduction to this period of Western banking is the unpublished doctoral dissertation of Carter H. Golembe, "State Banks and the Economic Development of the West, 1830–1844," Columbia University, 1952, esp. pp. 10, 82–91. Cf. Bray Hammond, "Long and Short Term Credit in Early American Banking," *QJE*, XLIX (Nov. 1934), esp. p. 87.

provided by the rising industrialists, the urban middle classes, and the farmers who increasingly depended on urban markets. The expansion of credit, which in the West financed manufacturing, mining, transportation, agricultural diversification, and the numerous branches of a capitalist economy, in the South bolstered the economic position of the planters, inhibited the rise of alternative industries, and guaranteed the extension and consolidation of the plantation system.

If for a moment we accept the designation of the planters as capitalists and the slave system as a form of capitalism, we are then confronted by a capitalist society that impeded the development of every normal feature of capitalism. The planters were not mere capitalists; they were pre-capitalist, quasi-aristocratic landowners who had to adjust their economy and ways of thinking to a capitalist world market. Their society, in its spirit and fundamental direction, represented the antithesis of capitalism, however many compromises it had to make. The fact of slave ownership is central to our problem. This seemingly formal question of whether the owners of the means of production command labor or purchase the labor power of free workers contains in itself the content of Southern life. The essential features of Southern particularity, as well as of Southern backwardness, can be traced to the relationship of master to slave.

The Barriers to Industrialization

If the planters were losing their economic and political cold war with Northern capitalism, the failure of the South to develop sufficient industry provided the most striking immediate cause. Its inability to develop adequate manufactures is usually attributed to the inefficiency of its labor force. No doubt slaves did not easily adjust to industrial employment, and the indirect effects of the slave system impeded the employment of whites.[13] Slaves did work effectively in hemp, tobacco, iron, and cotton factories but only under socially dangerous conditions. They received a wide variety of privileges and approached an elite status. Planters generally appreciated the potentially subversive quality of these arrangements and looked askance at their extension.

Slavery concentrated economic and political power in the hands of a slaveholding class hostile to industrialism. The slaveholders feared a strong urban bourgeoisie, which might make common cause with its Northern counterpart. They feared a white urban working class of unpredictable

---

[13] Slavery impeded white immigration by presenting Europeans with an aristocratic, caste-ridden society that scarcely disguised its contempt for the working classes. The economic opportunities in the North were, in most respects, far greater. When white labor was used in Southern factories, it was not always superior to slave labor. The incentives offered by the Northern economic and social system were largely missing; opportunities for acquiring skills were fewer; in general, productivity was much lower than in the North.

social tendencies. In general, they distrusted the city and saw in it some-thing incongruous with their local power and status arrangements.[14] The small slaveholders, as well as the planters, resisted the assumption of a heavy tax burden to assist manufacturers, and as the South fell further behind the North in industrial development more state aid was required to help industry offset the Northern advantages of scale, efficiency, credit relations, and business reputation.

Slavery led to the rapid concentration of land and wealth and prevented the expansion of a Southern home market. Instead of providing a basis for industrial growth, the Southern countryside, economically dominated by a few large estates, provided only a limited market for industry. Data on the cotton textile factories almost always reveal that Southern producers aimed at supplying slaves with the cheapest and coarsest kind of cotton goods. Even so, local industry had to compete with Northern firms, which sometimes shipped direct and sometimes established Southern branches.

William Gregg, the South's foremost industrialist, understood the modest proportions of the Southern market and warned manufacturers against trying to produce exclusively for their local areas. His own company at Graniteville, South Carolina, produced fine cotton goods that sold much better in the North than in the South. Gregg was an unusually able man, and his success in selling to the North was a personal triumph. When he had to evaluate the general position of Southern manufacturers, he asserted that he was willing to stake his reputation on their ability to compete with Northerners in the production of *"coarse cotton fabrics."* [15]

Some Southern businessmen, especially those in the border states, did good business in the North. Louisville tobacco and hemp manufacturers sold much of their output in Ohio. Some producers of iron and agricultural implements sold in nearby Northern cities. This kind of market was pre-carious. As Northern competitors rose and the market shrank, Southern producers had to rely on the narrow and undependable Southern market.[16] Well before 1840 iron-manufacturing establishments in the Northwest provided local farmers with excellent markets for grain, vegetables, mo-lasses, and work animals. During the antebellum period and after, the grain growers of America found their market at home. America's rapid industrial development offered farmers a magnificently expanding urban market, and not until much later did they come to depend to any important extent on exports.

[14] Richard C. Wade's recent *Slavery in the Cities* (New York, 1964) provides new support for these conclusions.

[15] William Gregg, *Essays on Domestic Industry* (first published in 1845; Graniteville, S.C.; 1941), p. 4. Original emphasis.

[16] Consider the experience of the locomotive, paper, and cotton manufacturers as reported in: Carrol H. Quenzel, "The Manufacture of Locomotives and Cars in Alexandria in the 1850's," *VMHB*, LXII (April 1954), 182 ff; Ernest M. Lander, Jr., "Paper Manufacturing in South Carolina before the Civil War," *NCHR*, XXIX (April 1952), 225 ff; Adelaide L. Fries, "One Hundred Years of Textiles in Salem," *NCHR*, XXVII (Jan. 1950), 13.

To a small degree the South benefited in this way. By 1840 the tobacco-manufacturing industry began to absorb more tobacco than was being exported, and the South's few industrial centers provided markets for local grain and vegetable growers. Since the South could not undertake a general industrialization, few urban centers rose to provide substantial markets for farmers and planters. Southern grain growers, except for those close to the cities of the free states, had to be content with the market offered by planters who preferred to specialize in cotton or sugar and buy foodstuffs. The restricted rations of the slaves limited this market, which inadequate transportation further narrowed. It did not pay the planters to appropriate state funds to build a transportation system into the back country, and any measure to increase the economic strength of the back-country farmers seemed politically dangerous to the aristocracy of the Black Belt. The farmers of the back country remained isolated, self-sufficent, and politically, economically, and socially backward. Those grain-growing farmers who could compete with producers in the Upper South and the Northwest for the plantation market lived within the Black Belt. Since the planters did not have to buy from these local producers, the economic relationship greatly strengthened the political hand of the planters.

The General Features of Southern Agriculture

The South's greatest economic weakness was the low productivity of its labor force. The slaves worked indifferently. They could be made to work reasonably well under close supervison in the cotton fields, but the cost of supervising them in more than one or two operations at a time was prohibitive. Slavery prevented the significant technological progress that could have raised productivity substantially. Of greatest relevance, the impediments to technological progress damaged Southern agriculture, for improved implements and machines largely accounted for the big increases in crop yields per acre in the Northern states during the nineteenth century.

Slavery and the plantation system led to agricultural methods that depleted the soil. The frontier methods of the free states yielded similar results, but slavery forced the South into continued dependence upon exploitative methods after the frontier had passed further west. It prevented reclamation of worn-out lands. The plantations were much too large to fertilize easily. Lack of markets and poor care of animals by slaves made it impossible to accumulate sufficient manure. The low level of capital accumulation made the purchase of adequate quantities of commercial fertilizer unthinkable. Planters could not practice proper crop rotation, for the pressure of the credit system kept most available land in cotton, and the labor force could not easily be assigned to the required tasks without excessive costs of supervision. The general inefficiency of labor thwarted most attempts at improvement of agricultural methods.

The South, unable to feed itself, faced a series of dilemmas in its attempts to increase production of nonstaple crops and to improve its livestock. An inefficient labor force and the backward business practices of the dominant planters hurt. When planters did succeed in raising their own food, they also succeeded in depriving local livestock raisers and grain growers of their only markets. The planters had little capital with which to buy improved breeds and could not guarantee the care necessary to make such investments worth while. Livestock raisers also lacked the capital, and without adequate urban markets they could not make good use of the capital they had.

Thoughtful Southerners, deeply distressed by the condition of their agriculture, made a determined effort to remedy it. In Maryland and Virginia significant progress occurred in crop diversification and livestock improvement, but this progress was contingent on the sale of surplus slaves to the Lower South. These sales provided the income that offset agricultural losses and made possible investment in fertilizers, equipment, and livestock. The concomitant reduction in the size of the slave force facilitated supervision and increased labor productivity and versatility. Even so, the income from slave sales remained an important part of the gross income of the planters of the Upper South. The reform remained incomplete and could not free agriculture from the destructive effects of the continued reliance on slave labor.

The reform process had several contradictions, the most important of which was the dependence on slave sales. Surplus slaves could be sold only while gang-labor methods continued to be used in other areas. By the 1850s the deficiencies of slavery that had forced innovations in the Upper South were making themselves felt in the Lower South. Increasingly, planters in the Lower South explored the possibilities of reform. If the deterioration of agriculture in the Cotton Belt had proceeded much further, the planters would have had to stop buying slaves from Maryland and Virginia and look for markets for their own surplus slaves. Without the acquisition of fresh lands there could be no general reform of Southern agriculture. The Southern economy was moving steadily into an insoluble crisis.

The Ideology of the Master Class

The planters commanded Southern politics and set the tone of social life. Theirs was an aristocratic, antibourgeois spirit with values and mores emphasizing family and status, a strong code of honor, and aspirations to luxury, ease, and accomplishment. In the planters' community, paternalism provided the standard of human relaitonships, and politics and state-craft were the duties and responsibilities of gentlemen. The gentleman lived for politics, not, like the bourgeois politician, off politics.

The planter typically recoiled at the notions that profit should be the goal of life; that the approach to production and exchange should be internally rational and uncomplicated by social values; that thrift and hard work should be the great virtues; and that the test of the wholesomeness of a community should be the vigor with which its citizens expand the economy. The planter was no less acquisitive than the bourgeois, but an acquisitive spirit is compatible with values antithetical to capitalism. The aristocratic spirit of the planters absorbed acquisitiveness and directed it into channels that were socially desirable to a slave society: the accumulation of slaves and land and the achievement of military and political honors. Whereas in the North people followed the lure of business and money for their own sake, in the South specific forms of property carried the badges of honor, prestige, and power. Even the rough parvenu planters of the Southwestern frontier—the "Southern Yankees"—strove to accumulate wealth in the modes acceptable to plantation society. Only in their crudeness and naked avarice did they differ from the Virginia gentlemen. They were a generation removed from the refinement that follows accumulation.

Slavery established the basis of the planter's position and power. It measured his affluence, marked his status, and supplied leisure for social graces and aristocratic duties. The older bourgeoisie of New England in its own way struck an aristocratic pose, but its wealth was rooted in commercial and industrial enterprises that were being pushed into the background by the newer heavy industries arising in the West, where upstarts took advantage of the more lucrative ventures like the iron industry. In the South few such opportunities were opening. The parvenu differed from the established planter only in being cruder and perhaps sharper in his business dealings. The road to power lay through the plantation. The older aristocracy kept its leadership or made room for men following the same road. An aristocratic stance was no mere compensation for a decline in power; it was the soul and content of a rising power.

Many travelers commented on the difference in material conditions from one side of the Ohio River to the other, but the difference in sentiment was seen most clearly by Tocqueville. Writing before the slavery issue had inflamed the nation, he remarked that slavery was attacking the Union "indirectly in its manners." The Ohioan "was tormented by wealth," and would turn to any kind of enterprise or endeavor to make a fortune. The Kentuckian coveted wealth "much less than pleasure or excitement," and money had "lost a portion of its value in his eyes." [17]

Achille Murat joined Tocqueville in admiration for Southern ways.

[17] Alexis de Tocqueville, *Democracy in America* (2 vols.; New York, 1945), I, 364.

Compared with Northerners, Southerners were frank, clever, charming, generous, and liberal.[18] They paid a price for these advantages. As one Southerner put it, the North led the South in almost everything because the Yankees had quiet perseverance over the long haul, whereas the Southerners had talent and brilliance but no taste for sustained labor. Southern projects came with a flash and died just as suddenly.[19] Despite such criticisms from within the ranks, the leaders of the South clung to their ideals, their faults, and their conviction of superiority. Farmers, said Edmund Ruffin, could not expect to achieve a cultural level above that of the "boors who reap rich harvests from the fat soil of Belgium." In the Northern states, he added with some justification, a farmer could rarely achieve the ease, culture, intellect, and refinement that slavery made possible.[20] The prevailing attitude of the aristocratic South toward itself and its Northern rival was ably summed up by Wililam Henry Holcombe of Natchez: "The Northerner loves to make money, the Southerner to spend it." [21]

At their best, Southern ideals constituted a rejection of the crass, vulgar, inhumane elements of capitalist society. The slaveholders simply could not accept the idea that the cash nexus offered a permissible basis for human relations. Even the vulgar parvenu of the Southwest embraced the plantation myth and refused to make a virtue of necessity by glorifying the competitive side of slavery as civilization's highest achievement. The slaveholders generally, and the planters in particular, did identify their own ideals with the essence of civilization and, given their sense of honor, were prepared to defend them at any cost.

This civilization and its ideals were antinational in a double sense. The plantation offered virtually the only market for the small nonstaple-producing farmers and provided the center of necessary services for the small cotton growers. Thus, the paternalism of the planters toward their slaves was reinforced by the semipaternal relationship between the planters and their neighbors. The planters, in truth, grew into the closest thing to feudal lords imaginable in a nineteenth-century bourgeois republic. The planters' protestations of love for the Union were not so much a desire to use the Union to protect slavery as a strong commitment to localism as the highest form of liberty. They genuinely loved the Union so long as it alone among the great states of the world recognized that localism had a wide variety of rights. The Southerners' source of pride was not the Union, nor the nonexistent Southern nation; it was the plantation, which they raised to a political principle.

---

[18] Achille Murat, *America and the Americans* (Buffalo, 1851), pp. 19, 75.
[19] J. W. D. in the *Southern Eclectic*, II (Sept. 1853), 63–66.
[20] *Address to the Virginia State Agricultural Society* (Richmond, Va., 1853), p. 9.
[21] Diary dated Aug. 25, 1855, but clearly written later. Ms. in the University of North Carolina.

The Inner Reality of Slaveholding

The Southern slaveholder had "extraordinary force." In the eyes of an admirer his independence was "not as at the North, the effect of a conflict with the too stern pressure of society, but the legitimate outgrowth of a sturdy love of liberty." [22] This independence, so distinctive in the slaveholders' psychology, divided them politically from agrarian Westerners as well as from urban Easterners. Commonly, both friendly and hostile contemporaries agreed that the Southerner appeared rash, unstable, often irrational, and that he turned away from bourgeois habits toward an aristocratic pose.

Americans, with a pronounced Jeffersonian bias, often attribute this spirit to agrarians of all types, although their judgment seems almost bizarre. A farmer may be called "independent" because he works for himself and owns property; like any grocer or tailor he functions as a petty bourgeois. In Jefferson's time, when agriculture had not yet been wholly subjected to the commanding influences of the market, the American farmer perhaps had a considerable amount of independence, if we choose to call self-sufficient isolation by that name, but in subsequent days he has had to depend on the market like any manufacturer, if not more so. Whereas manufacturers combine to protect their economic interests, such arrangements have proved much more difficult, and until recently almost impossible, to effect among farmers. In general, if we contrast farmers with urban capitalists, the latter emerge as relatively the more independent. The farmer yields constantly to the primacy of nature, to a direct, external force acting on him regardless of his personal worth; his independence is therefore rigorously circumscribed. The capitalist is limited by the force of the market, which operates indirectly and selectively. Many capitalists go under in a crisis, but some emerge stronger and surer of their own excellence. Those who survive the catastrophe do so (or so it seems) because of superior ability, strength, and management, not because of an Act of God.

The slaveholder, as distinct from the farmer, had a private source of character making and mythmaking—his slave. Most obviously, he had the habit of command, but there was more than despotic authority in this master-slave relationship. The slave stood interposed between his master and the object his master desired (that which was produced); thus, the master related to the object only mediately, through the slave. The slaveholder commanded the products of another's labor, but by the same process was forced into dependence upon this other.[23]

---

[22] William M. Sanford (?), *Southern Dial*, I (Nov. 1857), 9.
[23] Cf. G. W. F. Hegel, *The Phenomenology of Mind* (2 vols.; London, 1910), I, 183 ff.

Thoughtful Southerners such as Ruffin, Fitzhugh, and Hammond understood this dependence and saw it as arising from the general relationship of labor to capital, rather than from the specific relationship of master to slave. They did not grasp that the capitalist's dependence upon his laborers remains obscured by the process of exchange in the capitalist market. Although all commodities are products of social relationships and contain human labor, they face each other in the market not as the embodiment of human qualities but as things with a seemingly independent existence. Similarly, the laborer sells his labor-power in the way in which the capitalists sells his goods—by bringing it to market, where it is subject to the fluctuations of supply and demand. A "commodity fetishism" clouds the social relationship of labor to capital, and the worker and capitalist appear as mere observers of a process over which they have little control.[24] Southerners correctly viewed the relationship as a general one of labor to capital but failed to realize that the capitalist's dependence on his laborers is hidden, whereas that of master on slave is naked. As a Mississippi planter noted:

> I intend to be henceforth stingy as far as unnecessary expenditure—as a man should not squander what another accumulates with the exposure of health and the wearing out of the physical powers, and is not that the case with the man who needlessly parts with that which the negro by the hardest labor and often undergoing what we in like situation would call the greatest deprivation . . .[25]

This simultaneous dependence and independence contributed to that peculiar combination of the admirable and the frightening in the slaveholder's nature: his strength, graciousness, and gentility; his impulsiveness, violence, and unsteadiness. The sense of independence and the habit of command developed his poise, grace, and dignity, but the less obvious sense of dependence on a despised other made him violently intolerant of anyone and anything threatening to expose the full nature of his relationship to his slave. Thus, he had a far deeper conservatism than that usually attributed to agrarians. His independence stood out as his most prized possession, but the instability of its base produced personal rashness and directed that rashness against any alteration in the status quo. Any attempt, no matter how well meaning, indirect, or harmless, to question the slave system appeared not only as an attack on his material interests but as an attack on his self-esteem at its most vulnerable point. To question either the morality or the practicality of slavery meant to expose the root of the slaveholder's dependence in independence.

---

[24] Cf. Karl Marx, *Capital* (3 vols.; New York, 1947), I, 41–55.
[25] Everard Green Baker Diary, Feb. 13, 1849, in the University of North Carolina. The entry was unfinished.

The General Crisis of the Slave South

The South's slave civilization could not forever coexist with an increasingly hostile, powerful, and aggressive Northern capitalism. On the one hand, the special economic conditions arising from the dependence on slave labor bound the South, in a colonial manner, to the world market. The concentration of landholding and slaveholding prevented the rise of a prosperous yeomanry and of urban centers. The inability to build urban centers retricted the market for agricultural produce, weakened the rural producers, and dimmed hopes for agricultural diversification. On the other hand, the same concentration of wealth, the isolated, rural nature of the plantation system, the special psychology engendered by slave ownership, and the political opportunity presented by the separation from England, converged to give the South considerable political and social independence. This independence was primarily the contribution of the slaveholding class, and especially of the planters. Slavery, while it bound the South economically, granted it the privilege of developing an aristocratic tradition, a disciplined and cohesive ruling class, and a mythology of its own.

Aristocratic tradition and ideology intensified the South's attachment to economic backwardness. Paternalism and the habit of command made the slaveholders tough stock, determined to defend their Southern heritage. The more economically debilitating their way of life, the more they clung to it. It was this side of things—the political hegemony and aristocratic ideology of the ruling class—rather than economic factors that prevented the South from relinquishing slavery voluntarily.

As the free states stepped up their industrialization and as the westward movement assumed its remarkable momentum, the South's economic and political allies in the North were steadily isolated. Years of abolitionist and free-soil agitation bore fruit as the South's opposition to homesteads, tariffs, and internal improvements clashed more and more dangerously with the North's economic needs. To protect their institutions and to try to lessen their economic bondage, the slaveholders slid into violent collision with Northern interests and sentiments. The economic deficiencies of slavery threatened to undermine the planters' wealth and power. Such relief measures as cheap labor and more land for slave states (reopening the slave trade and territorial expansion) conflicted with Northern material needs, aspirations, and morality.[26] The planters faced a steady deterioration of their political and social power. Even if the relative prosperity of the 1850s had continued indefinitely, the slave states would have

---

[26] These measures met opposition from powerful sections of the slaveholding class for reasons that cannot be discussed here. The independence of the South would only have brought the latent intraclass antagonisms to the surface.

been at the mercy of the free, which steadily forged ahead in population growth, capital accumulation, and economic development. Any economic slump threatened to bring with it an internal political disaster, for the slaveholders could not rely on their middle and lower classes to remain permanently loyal.[27]

When we understand that the slave South developed neither a strange form of capitalism nor an undefinable agrarianism but a special civilization built on the relationship of master to slave, we expose the root of its conflict with the North. The internal contradictions in the South and the external conflict with the North placed the slaveholders hopelessly on the defensive with little to look forward to except slow strangulation. Their only hope lay in a bold stroke to complete their political independence and to use it to provide an expansionist solution for their economic and social problems. The ideology and psychology of the proud slaveholding class made surrender or resignation to gradual defeat unthinkable, for its fate, in its own eyes at least, was the fate of everything worth while in Western civilization.

---

[27] The loyalty of these classes was real but unstable. For our present purposes let us merely note that Lincoln's election and federal patronage would, if Southern fears were justified, have led to the formation of an antiplanter party in the South.